The Daily Telegraph

CENTURY
of
SPORT

First published 1998 by Macmillan

This revised edition published 1999 by Macmillan
an imprint of Macmillan Publishers Ltd
25 Eccleston Place, London SW1W 9NF
Basingstoke and Oxford

Associated companies throughout the world

www.macmillan.co.uk

ISBN 0 333 74328 8

BCS Publishing
Editorial Director: Penelope Isaac
Art Director: Steve McCurdy
Editing and research: Penelope Isaac, Jenny Roberts, Marion Paull, Iain Zaczek, Ray Driscoll, Hal Norman
Design: Nigel Partridge
Picture research: Matt Homes and Rob Harborne of Allsport UK Ltd, London; additional research by David Pratt
Index: Dorothy Frame

Reprographics by Speedscan Ltd

Printed and bound by New Interlitho

Special thanks to Gordon Wise of Macmillan Publishers Ltd, to Susannah Charlton and the staff and journalists of *The Daily Telegraph* sports desk, and to the staff of the *Telegraph* library, who could not have been more helpful or accommodating.

The Daily Telegraph

CENTURY

of

SPORT

GREAT SPORTING EVENTS AND PERSONALITIES
OF THE TWENTIETH CENTURY

EDITED BY DAVID WELCH

MACMILLAN

CONTENTS

Foreword *by David Welch* 7

Foreword

by

David Welch

As the eyewitness accounts by contributors to this book bear out, it has been a century of much sporting excellence. Who can forget, for instance, the ruthless but brilliant way in which Australia won the cricket World Cup in June 1999? They proved beyond doubt that they were the best cricket team around, and individual performances by players like Shane Warne and Lance Klusener of South Africa were inspirational.

Nothing, though, lifts spirits as much as a 'home' win, and as far as sport in this country is concerned there have been precious few successes in recent years. As a century of sport closes, there seems no end to the sense of prevailing disappointment. Is there any hope for the long-suffering follower of British sport?

True, in the last year of the 20th century, Scottish rugby union fans watched as their team took the Five Nations championship against all predictions, while Wales savoured a revival in fortunes, culminating in an historic first win over South Africa.

However, for England fans the final year of the millennium was often a frustrating one. They had suffered English cricket's nervous breakdown, as the team had gone out of the World Cup competition at the same stage as Bangladesh, Scotland and Kenya; they had endured watching England's pampered footballers struggling to qualify for the European championship after their spectacular failure in the 1998 World Cup.

Tennis players Tim Henman and Greg Rusedski appeared to offer the best chance of allowing fans to go into the next millennium in a mood of hope and expectation. Then, out came, and out went, Rusedski in the fourth round of Wimbledon 1999. Henman ran the gauntlet a little longer, but succumbed in the end to the eventual champion, Pete Sampras, in the semi-finals.

So British players will not be defending the football World Cup, the cricket World Cup, the European championship or any Wimbledon title at the dawn of the 21st century. No need to follow Manchester United's example of withdrawing from a major competition as a result of being too successful.

Followers of British sport are well accustomed to such vicissitudes, though, and not all is lost. Sport in this country at all levels, and in all fields of activity, enjoys enormous opportunities. If they are not squandered, it should be a matter of time before we start to emulate the performances we have admired regularly from afar.

Television and radio stations are engaged in cut-throat battles over expensive broadcasting rights, and newspapers are offering far more coverage of sporting matters...all of which are much more widely read than ever before. Recent surveys for *The Daily Telegraph* show that 70 per cent of male readers and a hugely significant 41 per cent of women regularly read our sports pages.

Sport is awash with money. We now *have* our role models. Crowds are high, queues are long. Hospitality packages are booming. Never has interest been greater. Nor, as a result, have the commercial possibilities. If those responsible for our sporting reputation – organisers and players alike – waste these unparalleled opportunities, who will sympathise with them? There can be no further excuses.

Some changes are happening. A few unsuccessful national team managers and captains (with occasional help from the tabloid press) have gone. And there is a clear and admirable attempt by some sports to use their share of the Lottery bonanza to bring in the best overseas coaches and performance directors to redefine and focus their business. For that is what it is.

In 2000 the Sydney Olympics should provide the biggest and most memorable sporting occasion any of us will experience. British success should not be impossible to achieve. Neither should it prove so elusive in the years ahead in other sporting arenas around the world. Not if we get our act together.

This book is a fascinating voyage through a sporting century of unprecedented variety and change. Few of the sports journalists who have written for *The Daily Telegraph* over the past 100 years could have accurately predicted what the end of the millennium would bring, though the 'Old Player' writing in 1900 clearly had some inkling of the way things might go when he worried about 'sport being ruined by commercial speculation'.

It is my privilege to work with many award-winning sportswriters. Whatever the fate of sport in the next century, *The Daily Telegraph* writers will continue to record and reflect upon it with the same skill and flair shown in these pages by their predecessors.

David Welch, Summer 1999

1900

Magnificent innings by Stoddart

PUBLISHED WEDNESDAY 6 JUNE

At Lord's yesterday A. E. Stoddart put together the highest innings of his great career. Against the Somerset bowlers he scored 221, and thus beat by six runs his famous display at Old Trafford nine years ago, when he went in first and carried out his bat for 215. It is no disparagement of his splendid display yesterday to say that it did not equal his earlier innings of over 200, for on that occasion the bowling was of a far higher quality than the Somerset attack yesterday. Stoddart's achievement yesterday was one of which he might well be proud. From the first he played with a combination of skill and vigour worthy of his best days, timing his drives splendidly and making several of his masterly strokes on the leg side. He gave two or three sharp chances, it is true, and batted rather recklessly for a time after completing his first 100. In other respects his batting was of the highest order, for even in the midst of administering severe punishment he could always ready himself to play a good ball, and play it well. Quite a number of times he sent the ball among the pavilion seats, and once he lifted it higher than the players' room.

It is hardly necessary to state that Stoddart's powerful hitting delighted the crowd of about 10,000 people who had assembled at Lord's: indeed the crowd were in a state of great exhilaration all the afternoon. Perhaps the most remarkable point in connection with Stoddart's batting was the fact that he should have put together his record score, after having been practically out of first-class cricket for a season and a half. Indeed, his participation in the game now in progress was only a personal compliment to J. T. Hearne. For his kindly action in assisting at the famous Middlesex bowler's benefit Stoddart has certainly received his reward. The pity is that a man who can play such an innings should, while still almost in the prime of a batsman's life, have practically abandoned first-class cricket.

DID YOU KNOW?

One of the events featured for the first, and only, time in the 1900 Olympic Games was live pigeon shooting. The winner, Belgian Léon de Lunden, killed 21 birds, Maurice Faure of France got 20, while Australian Donald Macintosh and Briton Crittenden Robinson tied for third with 19 each.

Prince of Wales's horse wins Grand National

From our special correspondent
PUBLISHED SATURDAY 31 MARCH

Another Grand National is over, and the foremost sportsman in the land has now established a unique record. To the Blue Riband of the Turf he has added the Blue Riband of the Chase, giving a distinction to the great Liverpool event which will live in horse-racing history.

Slowly but surely the Prince is making his mark upon the pages of Weatherby. A St Leger, a 1,000, an Eclipse, an Ascot Cup, a Goodwood Cup, a Manchester Cup – these are trifles not to be despised.

Ireland will rejoice at the victory of a horse which celebrated St Patrick's Day by a complimentary triumph in a contest intrinsically magnificent. Inspiriting weather made the multitude glad, and a huge attendance was a foregone conclusion. The mass of holiday-makers gathered together when the numbers were hoisted for the opening race showed us that, war or no war, people are disinclined to be deprived of their accustomed measure

of enjoyment. Stands and rings exhibited a multitude of familiar faces, and Liverpool's 'great day' fully maintained its greatness. I fancy that numbers of Liverpudlians together with the strangers within their gates must have had sore throats last night. Never was there a more 'cheering' day.

It was necessary to forgo the paddock inspection if one wanted a good place for watching the struggle, and the appearance of the horses on the course came as a pleasant relief to the tension. What with the people on the rails and the scattering throngs on other parts of the course – either massed around the big jumps or scurrying from point to point to see the horses pass and repass – there was plenty of animation during the contest. Emphatically it was a battle to be seen and remembered. That Hidden Mystery should have fallen a victim to the chances of the game was a matter of general regret; and, while the victory of Ambush II proved far more popular than any other could possibly have been, the splendid fight of grand old Manifesto **(below left)** caused us a sigh of regret that success had not, for the third time, attended his gallant efforts. At the last fence the veteran was up alongside the Prince's representative, and it was only in the run-home that his welter burden made him bite the dust.

No sooner did the populace perceive that Ambush II had the verdict safe than a long roar of cheering broke forth. Up went hats, away went sticks, while vociferations from thousands of throats exultantly rent the air. Cheers for horse, cheers for rider, cheers for owner were given again and again, for Ambush II was decidedly the people's horse, and the Prince, as he stepped down to meet the winner, must have felt that the triumph was not to himself alone.

J. H. Taylor is winner of Open golf championship

From our own correspondent
ST ANDREWS, THURSDAY 7 JUNE

Play at the Open championship was brought to a close today, when J. H. Taylor, of Richmond, achieved his third success in the great event.

No doubt the conditions were favourable enough for low scoring, but from the spectators' point of view they were very unpleasant. The wind was again easterly, and it was chilly for the season of the year. A thick mist, too, hung over the links during the day, and there was no sunshine to light up the scene.

As compared with the opening day, the attendance of spectators showed a considerable increase, despite the unpropitious surroundings. A number of the members of the club lent valuable aid in controlling the crowd, who, with an eager desire to witness every stroke in the play of

the leading men in the field, pressed at times uncomfortably close upon them.

With his score of 156 yesterday Taylor stood in a very hopeful position, having a clear lead of four strokes from Harry Vardon, and the opinion was generally held that, assuming he maintained his form, the cup was again well in his grasp.

From start to finish Taylor played almost perfect golf. In fact he excelled himself, and not only did he do so, but he excelled all other records over the St Andrews Medal Round. It is unnecessary to go into minute particulars regarding his grand score. It had but one feature, and that was its extraordinary brilliancy. Right well did the Richmond professional deserve the ovation which he received from a crowd of several thousand people at the completion of the round. His average for the four rounds was $77\frac{1}{4}$.

Sport being ruined by commercial speculation

By an old player

PUBLISHED FRIDAY 7 SEPTEMBER

The first week of another season's football has come and gone. Throughout the warm evenings of August various players have been getting into training, and now, before cricket is well over, the First and Second Divisions of the League, the Southern League, and all the ramifications which attract the modern lover of football are in full swing.

But what cricket has escaped, football has apparently been unable to avoid. The guardians (or shall we say the promoters?) of our modern English football have determined to run the thing on business lines, to play for big gate-money, to lay out capital in order to make a good percentage, and to turn what was once a national sport into a huge machine organised by limited liability companies.

Out of the 36 clubs which form the two divisions of the League, it would probably be over the mark to say that one-sixth are beginning this season with a balance on the right side of their accounts. One result is that committees are anxious to offer lower wages to their players. In spite of that some players are keeping up the prices merrily, and Booth (captain of the Rovers) was only to be bought (by Everton) at the stiff figure of £350. West Bromwich Albion, too, have been able to spend no less than £4,000 on a new ground. But Stoke have had to sell all their expensive players, and secure a cheaper lot. Sheffield Wednesday have imported some half-dozen Scotchmen to make up for the loss of their captain. Having lost M'Aulay to Aston Villa, the Walsall authorities have only been able to begin the season by dividing the gate-money among their players.

My point is that Association Football is being ruined by being made a commercial speculation. Local *esprit de corps* is being shattered by purchases of players from outside the district of the club, and is being replaced by merely mercenary ambitions on the part of the players and by betting operations on the part of those who are looking on.

This consequence was inevitable as soon as the players were bought and sold like so many horses, and the best purse naturally commanded the best 'stable'. Fortunately, the system reacts as much upon the limited liability companies as upon individuals. A large proportion of the Second Division of the League clubs are so hard up that they can never hope to buy good enough players to rise to the First Division, with its big gates and large resources.

Any reader who is still sceptical may go to the next big football match in his vicinity and see for himself. He will find that far from being the 'athletic country' he has always boasted about, we have developed, on the one hand, into a ring of financiers, who have captured sport for its value in the market, and, on the other hand, into a raucous, grasping multitude, who are good enough at pushing through the turnstiles, or bellowing at a player, or even battering a referee, but who have no notion of taking any decent exercise for themselves at any time.

SPORT IN BRIEF

OLYMPICS

The second modern Olympics are held in Paris **(left)**, birthplace of Pierre de Coubertin, the pioneer of the modern Olympic movement. The Games are held in conjunction with the Universal Exposition in the city, and quickly descend into a shambles. Reigning discus champion Robert Garrett (US) scatters the 'too close' crowd by hurling all his throws into their midst; swimmers have to struggle against currents in the River Seine, and there are allegations that foreign marathon runners are impeded by partisan French spectators (Frenchman Michel Théato wins the race).

GOLF

A new method of joining the clubhead to the shaft, which allows mass production of golf clubs, signals the end of the traditional clubmakers' craft in Britain. By 1903 100,000 clubs a year will be imported from America.

LAWN TENNIS

Reggie Doherty **(below)** wins the Wimbledon singles title for the fourth consecutive year. He and his younger brother, Laurie, also take the Olympic doubles gold in Paris, and win the Wimbledon doubles title for the fourth year in succession.

1901

C.B. FRY (1872–1956)

CHARLES BURGESS FRY WAS BORN IN CROYDON on 25 April 1872, the son of a civil servant. The greatest all-round athlete of his generation, his prodigious versatility was evident from an early age. While still a schoolboy he played in the FA Cup and, at Oxford, gained blues in football, cricket and athletics. In 1893 he set a new world record in the long jump.

After graduating, Fry worked for some time as a schoolmaster before dividing his time between football and cricket. Fry played soccer for England in 1901 and for Southampton in the FA Cup final of 1902, but his greatest achievements came as a batsman.

He scored more than 30,000 runs at an average of 50.21, and made 94 first-class centuries. Six of these were notched up in successive innings, a record which has never been surpassed. Fry also took part in 26 Test matches, gaining his captaincy in 1912. Here his record was impressive (won two, drawn two), and would doubtless have been better still, but for the outbreak of war.

Fry also made his mark in public life. He stood for Parliament as a Liberal, joined the Indian delegation at the League of Nations, and was even – supposedly – offered the throne of Albania. He was also the longest serving director of the Mercury, *a training ship for young seaman, holding the post from 1908 to 1950.*

Extraordinary scenes at FA Cup final

PUBLISHED MONDAY 22 APRIL

Never in the history of football has a game attracted anything approaching the number of people who made their way to the Crystal Palace on Saturday to see Tottenham Hotspur and Sheffield United contend for possession of the Football Association Challenge Cup.

Beyond all question, the fact of a London club having qualified for participation in the final tie had aroused an enormous amount of interest in the struggle not only amongst regular followers of the game in the metropolis, but in circles where football enthusiasm was previously unknown.

That a huge body of Londoners would assemble on the Sydenham slopes was generally expected, but with only one provincial team taking part, a falling off in the number of visitors from the country would have occasioned no surprise. The match, however, proved a tremendous attraction; the total number of visitors was up to the unprecedented figure of 114,815.

Two years ago, when Sheffield United beat Derby County, a record crowd of nearly 74,000 excited widespread comment about the extraordinary popularity of the game, but, after a slight falling off last season, these figures have been surpassed by more than 40,000 – a number which less than ten years ago would have been regarded as highly satisfactory for the total attendance at the final tie.

The huge mass of spectators took up their places on the extensive banks surrounding one side and one end of the field of play. Denser and denser grew the pack, until it became in truth a sea of faces. At times the mass surged dangerously, and there was one rush stated to have resulted in a breaking through, but the people steadied themselves almost as soon as the game began, and generally speaking their behaviour was admirable.

Hooting of the referee – and there was a deplorable amount of this – is not to be commended, but fortunately it did not take the form of personal violence, and if that official did blunder, a feeling of irritation was scarcely to be wondered at, seeing that the large majority of those present were anxious to see Tottenham win.

Only one thing detracted from the complete success of the afternoon and that was the unsatisfactory termination of the contest. No doubt the teams were well matched, but drawn games in final ties are so unusual that no one comes prepared to see the struggle left undecided, and the level scoring on Saturday unquestionably occasioned a lot of disappointment.

Spectators spill on to the pitch at Crystal Palace; a record number of people attended the Cup final. It was the first match to be filmed.

C. B. Fry scores sixth successive century

PUBLISHED FRIDAY 13 SEPTEMBER

The Yorkshiremen had an experience at Lord's yesterday that they will not readily forget. They were bowling and fielding for five hours, and in that time the England team – very strong in some respects, but by no means representative – scored 460 runs against them for the loss of five wickets.

Nothing more startling has been seen on a London ground this season. Though successful from start to finish, however, the England batting was not at all uniform in character. Everyone who went in did more or less well, but if it had not been for Gilbert Jessop, the Yorkshire bowlers might have got through the day without discredit or the slightest wound to their pride. A. O. Jones opened the innings with some brilliant hitting, but so normal was the rate of run-getting for three hours that when, at half-past three, the third wicket went down, the total only stood at 201. England, of course, had made a very flattering start, but the runs had been fought for, and the loss of another wicket or two would have been sufficient to put the Yorkshiremen on excellent terms with themselves.

Jessop, however, upset everything, and treated the 4,000 spectators to a display of hitting that even he has never surpassed. He took much longer than usual to play himself in, and for about half an hour did nothing out of the common, scoring at little more than the same pace as C. B. Fry **(below left)**. As soon as he felt set, however, he let himself go, and gave the Yorkshire bowlers a rougher time than, with one exception, they have had all the year.

When Jessop went in at 201, Fry had already made 48, and, with such a start, naturally wanted some catching. After a time, however, he became nothing more than an interested spectator of his partner's hitting, and was passed at 79 to 78. Two or three runs later he drew level again, but then Jessop went right ahead, and there was no further competition in the matter of scoring. To cut a long story short, the two batsmen were together for an hour and a half, and added 204 runs to the score. The total was 300 at twenty minutes past four, and 400 at five o'clock. Then at last the batsmen were separated, Fry, at 405, being out to a catch at extra-cover-point. He was naturally overshadowed by Jessop's amazing brilliancy, but his innings of 106 was by no means the least remarkable of the many fine displays he has given this season. This 106, by the way, is his sixth successive 100 in first-class matches, the feat thus performed being altogether without precedent.

America retains the trophy

From our own correspondent

PUBLISHED SATURDAY 5 OCTOBER

Yesterday *Shamrock* again met *Columbia* over a 30-mile course off Sandy Hook, and as a result the America Cup remains, for another year, at least, in the country to which it was carried half a century ago.

The race, a 15-mile run to leeward and beat back, was by far the most exciting and interesting of the series. The yachts started practically on even terms, and after a thrilling contest and a marvellous display of seamanship, *Shamrock* crossed the finishing line a couple of seconds ahead of her rival. She lost the race, however, on her time allowance, and with it the cup.

Britannia may rule many waves, but in these waters *Columbia* remains the 'gem of the ocean' tonight, and the famous America Cup now rests more securely than ever upon its pedestal, while Sir Thomas Lipton confesses that *Shamrock II*, like *Shamrock I*, is not the equal of the peerless *Columbia*. Yet there is some consolation for Sir Thomas Lipton and Mr G. L. Watson in the knowledge that no other owner or designer came so near 'lifting the cup' as they, and that no other boats, previous to the two Shamrocks, met such a racer as *Columbia*.

It was a glorious struggle today, from the moment Captain Sycamore of *Shamrock II* out-generalled Captain Barr of *Columbia* at the start, forcing him over the line first, and then blanketing him, until the two crossed the finish, only a few seconds apart, *Shamrock* leading the way but doomed to lose both race and cup owing to the 43-second allowance she gave her rival.

The great crowds on the excursion boats shouted themselves hoarse all over the course as the two yachts fought out the battle that would decide if the challenger was to be given another chance to lift the cup. When the yachts crossed the finish line, and it was seen that *Columbia* would win, making it 'three straight', every steam-whistle, siren, foghorn and watch-bell was turned loose in celebration of the victory.

It was just 1.12 pm when it was seen that *Columbia* had turned the odd trick in windward work, and was ahead. The Yankee skipper had turned what looked like a

The battle for the America (later the America's) Cup: *Shamrock II* and *Columbia* are pictured minutes before crossing the line in the first race on 26 September.

defeat into what seemed a victory. After almost as hard a fight as a man would make for his life, Sycamore found himself outsailed and out-generalled.

1902

Herd gains title of champion

PUBLISHED FRIDAY 6 JUNE

Seldom, if ever, in the Open golf championship has there been a more sensational finish than that witnessed in the concluding stage of the 43rd competition, at Hoylake, yesterday afternoon. Victory ultimately rested with the Huddersfield professional, Alexander Herd (below), who time and again has shown form to justify the belief that championship honours, sooner or later, must fall to him.

The close character of yesterday's play may be gathered from the fact that it was only by a single stroke that Herd succeeded in gaining the title of champion. He had finished the first day's play four strokes to the bad, with a score of 153 for the 36 holes, James Braid of Romford (the then champion) coming next with 154. The ex-champion, Harry Vardon of Ganton, on the other hand, thanks largely to his magnificent record score of 72 in the morning, was able, with an afternoon round of 77, to head the first day's list with 149. By the time the third round was completed yesterday, however, Herd, with a splendid 73 (making his score 226 for 54 holes), had assumed the lead, and although in his fourth round, which cost him 81 strokes, he fell off somewhat, he just kept clear of Vardon and Braid with a grand total of 307 strokes for the 72 holes.

Braid, last year's champion, was playing a splendid round, and gradually but surely wiping off stroke after stroke from his arrears. Coming home in a magnificent 34 for the last nine holes, the best nine holes of the competition, Braid only lost his title by a stroke with 308 for the 72 holes, and he and Vardon thus tied for second place.

MILESTONES

Hungary played their first international football match on 12 October this year. Held in Vienna, the match, against Austria, was also the first international game involving European sides other than British. Hungary's debut was not a successful one; they lost the match 5–0.

Australians suffer batting collapse at new cricket venue

PUBLISHED SATURDAY 31 MAY

People had to wait for four hours for cricket at Birmingham yesterday, but patience was abundantly rewarded, the second stage of the big match being so sensational that nobody who had the good fortune to be at the Edgbaston ground will ever forget the experience. The Australians made history to the extent of being out for the smallest total ever obtained in a Test game, either in this country or the Colonies. They were batting for 85 minutes, and were got rid of by Wilfred Rhodes and George Hirst for 38 runs.

A lot of rain fell in Birmingham on Thursday night, and the weather yesterday morning was of the most unpromising kind. The sky looked heavy with clouds, and the downpour of the night was followed by drizzle.

When it was seen that play was practicable Archie MacLaren came to the wise decision not to close the England innings at once, as some people fancied he might do with the score of 351 for nine wickets. His side stood in a position of absolute security, but fortune having played into his hands by ruining the pitch, he, of course, wanted to take every possible means to win the match. No one could tell exactly how the wicket would play and a score of 202 would have enabled the Australians to escape the follow-on.

No one could help sympathising with them when, on a wicket which was bound sooner or later to become treacherous, they went in against a total of 376. They were in the unhappy position of having a chance of being beaten and no possibility of winning. They are not wont to lose heart, but very likely these discouraging conditions in a match of such importance told a little on their nerves. For the way they collapsed, however, no one was prepared. The wicket was still wet and when Hirst and Rhodes were seen to be using sawdust it was expected that there would be some hitting.

The first wicket fell at nine, and Clement Hill joined Victor Trumper. Hill made a single from Rhodes, but directly he faced Hirst he was out, Len Braund bringing off a marvellous right-handed catch at slip. The ball was turned so near the wicket as to be just out of Lilley's reach, and Braund caught it in brilliant fashion as it was flying past him on its way to the boundary. Nothing in the match so far has been finer than this. In such lightning catches there must be an element of luck, but only very gifted fieldsmen can make them.

After this, misfortune for the Australians followed thick and fast. Trumper alone upheld the reputation of Australian batting. He scored 18 runs out of 31, and was at the wicket for 70 minutes. With his downfall the last hope of a decent score disappeared.

Victor Trumper and the 1902 Australian team (below). In the fourth Test at Old Trafford, Trumper scored a century in 108 minutes before lunch.

Gordon Bennett Cup goes to Englishman

From our own correspondent
PARIS, SUNDAY 29 JUNE

According to the dispatches received this afternoon in Paris, the great motor race to Vienna, over a distance of 1,402 km (870.6 miles), concluded exactly at two minutes and 26 seconds past two o'clock today. The first man in was Marcel Renault, who has not been much heard of. He drove a light autocar of the firm of Renault Brothers.

The events on the road between Bregenz and Innsbruck, and Innsbruck and Salzburg were exciting. The Chevalier de Knyff was first in at Bregenz on Friday. On Saturday morning he was the first to start, followed by Henry and Maurice Farman. Then came Selwyn Edge, the Englishman, who was destined to win the Gordon Bennett Cup, although there is some talk of disqualification in his case as he employed peasants to help him out of trouble on the road.

The run to Innsbruck was of importance owing to the prize which it was confidently asserted would fall to M. de Knyff. That motorist met with a mishap about 30 kilometres from Innsbruck. Edge, therefore, had the race to himself, and got in on his Napier car after the Farmans and others who were not registered for the run for the cup to Innsbruck. Thus, an Englishman obtained the international prize, which has hitherto been in French hands.

Grandstand calamity at Ibrox Park

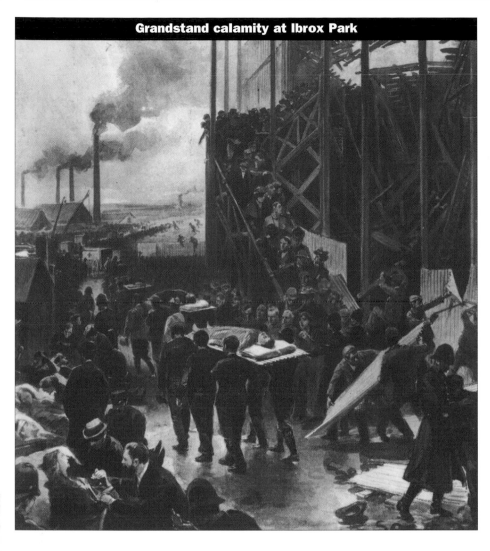

Casualties are carried from the collapsed Ibrox stand.

PUBLISHED MONDAY 7 APRIL

Ibrox Park, Glasgow, was on Saturday afternoon the scene of a shocking accident, involving the loss of many lives and injuries to over 100 people. To witness the annual Association football match between England and Scotland fully 70,000 people had assembled there, but as the ground is arranged to accommodate 80,000, the presence even of so vast a gathering as that of Saturday occasioned no anxiety.

Before the start of the game the pressure became so great that the spectators began to clamber over the iron railing in front of the huge uncovered stand. In this rush several people were hurt and received medical attention. The injuries so far were few and not very severe. The invading spectators, however, spread out in all directions, crowding up to the goal-line and the touchline on one side of the ground. It seemed as if no play would be possible, but the efforts of police eventually resulted in the people being driven back to the cinder path.

The game was accordingly commenced, and had been in progress some seven or eight minutes, when from the uncovered stand people swarmed on to the field in thousands, the rush being so tremendous that it stopped play between the forcing of a corner kick and the taking of it. Within a few moments the scene was one of wild disorder, the police being quite overpowered in their endeavours to keep people off the playing arena. Spectators dashed madly across the field and, almost before it could be realised, there must have been 10,000 people in the middle of the ground. The white shirts of the English players could still be distinguished, but, clad in dark blue, the Scotchmen were at once swallowed up, and very soon the players on both sides made their way to the pavilion. For fully 20 minutes the field remained in possession of the crowd.

Comparatively few people, apart from those on the stand, knew what had happened to cause such an uncontrollable rush. What had occurred was this. On the highest part of the stand a portion of the planking had proved unequal to the strain to which it was subjected, and, giving way, had precipitated the spectators standing there to the earth. One or two people were killed outright; others received such terrible injuries that they succumbed during the evening; and a number had their limbs fractured or sustained serious internal damage.

SPORT IN BRIEF

FOOTBALL
In the FA Cup final on 26 April, a record crowd sees Sheffield United and Southampton draw. C. B. Fry is on the Southampton team. A replay is fixed for the following week, which Sheffield win 2–1.

CRICKET
On 28 April, two days after his appearance in the FA Cup final (see above), C. B. Fry opens the batting for London County against Surrey. He scores 82 in the first innings and 49 not out in the second, helping London County to a nine-wicket victory.

GOLF
Sandy Herd's victory at Hoylake is achieved with the aid of a new type of golf ball, named after its inventor, Coburn Haskell. The 'Haskell' has a rubber centre and a balata cover. Herd's fellow competitors prefer to stick to the more familiar 'gutty', a ball made from the latex of the gutta-percha tree.

CRICKET
The 1903–4 tour of Australia is the first to be sponsored by the Marylebone Cricket Club (MCC). The national team will continue to play under the MCC name until 1977–8, after which the team will play under the name of England.

MOTOR RACING
The Gordon Bennett Cup is raced in conjunction with the Paris–Vienna race for the first time, and is to be awarded to the winner of the 350-mile stage to Innsbruck (see main text). Inaugurated in 1900, the trophy is donated by James Gordon Bennett, an American newspaper tycoon living in Paris, who wishes to encourage other countries to challenge French dominance in motor racing.

1903

Cup race held in Ireland

From our special correspondent
DUBLIN, FRIDAY 27 JUNE

All day long the International Commission of the Automobile Club has been sitting in solemn conclave; at a quarter to eight tonight the official figures respecting yesterday's Gordon Bennett Cup race were announced. Camille Jenatzy of Germany was first; René de Knyff of France second, Henri Farman third.

By those who have not been engaged in statistical study, the day has chiefly been spent in getting ready for the motor speed trials tomorrow, and in the interchange of congratulations upon the brilliantly successful contest from which Jenatzy emerged so triumphantly. Seeing that the race was a huge experiment, it was carried to an issue in a fashion that was alike creditable and fortunate. It would be possible, of course, to find flaws in the arrangements, but as a whole things went smoothly and satisfactorily. Jenatzy's victory is highly popular, for a more daring driver probably never gripped a lever.

H. L. Doherty wins All-England championships

PUBLISHED THURSDAY 2 JULY

Although there was only one match to be played to bring this highly successful meeting to a conclusion, the courts at the All-England Club's ground at Wimbledon were crowded with spectators. The weather was again delightful, and the courts, in spite of the wear and tear they have received during the last eight days, were in superb condition.

The match which had to be decided was one of the most important of the whole meeting. Last year, it will be remembered, F. L. Riseley and S. H. Smith wrested the title of doubles champions of England from the brothers R. F. and H. L. Doherty (**right**). By all-round superiority over all their opponents this season the Dohertys had once more won their way into the championship round, and the two Gloucestershire players were called upon to meet the opponents whom they so narrowly defeated here last year.

This time, however, the Dohertys were strong favourites. As it turned out, one player on each side was not at his best, Smith not showing his real form for the champions, and R. F. Doherty for the challengers was much inferior to the player he used to be in his singles championship days. So it turned out that H. L. Doherty was able to devote his attention mainly to his opponent in the challenge round of the singles and outplayed him.

Sir Thomas Lipton fails again in challenge for America Cup

PUBLISHED FRIDAY 4 SEPTEMBER

After waiting three hours for a breeze of fair strength, *Reliance* and *Shamrock III*, at one o'clock this afternoon, started on the third Cup race. The course was the same as that set for last Thursday and Monday, 15 miles to windward and return.

The starting-gun was fired at one o'clock, the expiration of the limit fixed for the beginning of the race. The wind was blowing seven knots an hour from a little east of south, and the troublesome fog had cleared away from the land early in the day, but still hung over the sea until noon, and even when the yachts started there was a heavy haze.

Not much excitement was manifested about the start, although the big boats manoeuvred lazily about the lightship, from the preparatory gun at 12.45 until the final gun. *Reliance* seemed to have the advantage in going over the line. The official times were: *Reliance* 1 hr 1 min 56 sec; *Shamrock* 1 hr 2 min.

Both boats were on the starboard tack, and carried the same sails, mainsails, staysails, No. 2 jib-topsails, and the largest club-topsails. They held on that tack for the Jersey shore for some time after the start. *Reliance*

seemed to be making her usual gain, and a few minutes after the start, with a mile of the course covered, she appeared to be well to windward and in the lead.

Sir Thomas Lipton's guests arrived on board the *Erin* by the steamboat *Fletcher*. Only one steamboat, the *Grand Republic*, left the city for the race, and when she departed, her broad decks seemed to be almost deserted.

After half an hour's sailing the wind increased and the boats picked up speed. The sea was so smooth that both boats seemed to glide through it without making a ripple. That the conditions were to the defender's liking was manifest from the beginning, for she kept steadily eating to windward and fore-reaching her rival.

After 35 minutes *Reliance* took in her jib-topsail and set a smaller one. The change was made to enable her to point higher, and the new sail was in place inside of two minutes. Reliance continued to gain, eating out to windward of *Shamrock*, although the latter seemed, under the brisker wind, to foot almost as fast.

At 1.32 pm both yachts were four miles off the Jersey shore, and it was evident that both skippers were expecting a shift of wind to the south and west.

Both boats made smart sailing in the fresher breeze, travelling well and looking high to windward. The port

tack, taken soon after the yachts started, was held until they reached a point a mile northeast of Long Branch, and about the same distance offshore. *Reliance* had outsailed her adversary on this board, so that when *Shamrock* went about on the starboard tack, at 2.08 pm, a move which *Reliance* duplicated five seconds later, the latter was more than half a mile in the lead, and almost as far to windward.

After the turn for home the race was a procession, with *Reliance* well in the lead. The wind softened a little, but she maintained her advantage. A dense fog rolled up when *Reliance* was about two miles from the finish, but she crossed over the line triumphantly at 5.29 pm, unofficial time.

DID YOU KNOW?

The Tour de France was inaugurated this year by Henri Desgrange, editor of the sports newspaper *L'Auto*, in an effort to boost circulation above that of rival paper *Le Vélo*. The Tour began at Montgeron on 1 July and was won by Frenchman Maurice Garin 19 days and 2,428 km later.

A great Welsh rugby union victory

PUBLISHED MONDAY 12 JANUARY

To the satisfaction of some 30,000 spectators, the Welsh XV at Swansea on Saturday gained a notable triumph, beating England by 3 goals and 2 tries to 1 goal. The decisive nature of the result came as a surprise, a close game having been anticipated by both sides. However, it may at once be said that the victory was a thoroughly genuine one, and was rendered all the more meritorious from the fact that after the first quarter of an hour Wales played one man short.

The forwards held the pack, and the halves and three-quarters had full scope for the execution of those clever movements for which Welsh backs have made themselves famous.

Though their backs did all the scoring, the chief honours of the victory rested with the forwards. When after Tom Pearson's accident Jehoida Hodges was withdrawn from the front rank to go on the left wing, the seven scrummagers were left with an enormous task. Had they failed, and no blame could have attached to them if such had been the case, the match might easily have had another ending. As it happened the seven proved quite equal to the occasion, fairly and squarely beating the English eight, in the first half at all events.

After the interval the handicap began to tell, but that mattered little. They had done all that was required of them, having afforded their backs a sufficient number of opportunities to enable them to place the result beyond all reasonable doubt. The Welsh forwards began at a great pace, packing rapidly and well, and doing good footwork in the open. As soon as they had the measure of the Englishmen, they scarcely made any attempt to go through with the ball, but after carrying the scrummage cleverly left it behind them for the halves to deal with. In the first half, at least, they were much the more often in possession of the ball and were quite clearly the masters of the situation.

The play of the English forwards was as surprising as it was disappointing. The form that had been shown in the international trial games rightly induced the belief that England's forwards would turn out well.

The English scrummagers failed and failed badly. They had nothing like the life and dash of their opponents, and were seemingly all sixes and sevens. They packed in a ragged manner, and they rarely got their heads down properly. They appeared unable to move at any pace, being slow in following up, while their tackling left much to be desired. They hesitated to go for their man in the open, a Welsh back frequently getting in his kick when he might have been collared. The English forwards clearly needed a strong leader, who by his personal example would be able to arouse them to the proper pitch.

Harry Vardon sets record in Open golf championship

From our own correspondent
PRESTWICK, THURSDAY 11 JUNE

Conditions similar to those of the opening day prevailed today at Prestwick, where the competition for the Open golf championship was brought to a conclusion. It was a day of burning sunshine, with a light wind from the northeast to temper the heat. In the early morning a thick haze and cloudy sky bore a possibility of rain, but at the starting hour clouds and haze had disappeared. With the sun's ascent the effect of the dew on the turf was quickly lost, and the greens were as keen as ever. Though the wind was less troublesome, the difficulties of the putting were a little obviated in some cases by shifting the position of the holes.

Public interest, as indicated by the number of spectators on the course, increased as the final stages were entered upon. In the forenoon a general view of the links showed groups of spectators moving about with the respective couple of players, as if in accordance with some strategic scheme of which the key was concealed. The excellent performance of Harry Vardon on the first day secured him a specially large following. He again lowered the record of the previous day by doing the first round in 72, and when he started on his fourth journey over the course this afternoon he was followed by a crowd of several thousands, the general feeling being that with ordinary steadiness in his final round he had the championship well in hand. This presumption proved correct, Vardon winning the honour with an aggregate of 300. The condition which excludes all competitors more than 20 above the total of the leader for the first day from further play reduced the number left in the competition yesterday by more than a half, only 59 starting.

Harry Vardon's victory is remarkable in several respects. It is the first time since the days of Willie Park, old Tom Morris and young Tom Morris that any golfer has won the championship on four occasions. It is, further, the first occasion in the history of the competition on which the four rounds have been done in just 300.

Vardon (left) won the Open twice more to gain a record total of six titles.

SPORT IN BRIEF

RUGBY UNION
The first rugby union match between Australia and New Zealand takes place in Sydney in front of a 30,000-strong crowd. Fullback Billy Wallace kicks 12 points to take the All Blacks to a 22–3 win over Australia.

CRICKET
In his debut match against Australia in Sydney, R. E. 'Tip' Foster scores a record 287 runs for England, who win the Test by five wickets. A talented footballer as well, he plays inside forward in five matches for England. Foster suffers from diabetes; ill-health and business commitments prevent him playing more than one full first-class cricket season, but in that he scores 2,128 runs at an average of 50.66. He dies aged just 36 in 1914.

BOXING
In August J. J. Jeffries **(below)**, reigning heavyweight champion, retains his title against J. J. (Gentleman Jim) Corbett in San Francisco. Corbett has not fought in three years, and Jeffries wins by a knock-out in the tenth round.

1904

FA ponders question of football players' wages

PUBLISHED FRIDAY 2 SEPTEMBER

A question greatly agitating association football circles at the present moment is that of players' wages. Under the rules of the Football Association, a professional must not be paid more than £4 a week, cannot receive a bonus of more than £10, and before he leaves a club which is willing to give him the maximum wage, he has to satisfy the council of the Association that there are special grounds for allowing him to accept employment with another club. All these regulations are obviously conceived in the interests of organisations with limited resources. It is now urged that these rules bear hardly both upon the individual player of pronounced excellence, who is certainly worth more to the club which employs him, and upon the wealthy organisations that in the endeavour to build up an especially powerful team are prepared to give their professionals a higher remuneration. These regulations certainly inflict some hardship upon the players of exceptional skill.

Bosanquet's bowling effective in fourth Test match

SYDNEY, THURSDAY 3 MARCH

England beat Australia here this afternoon by 157 runs, and thereby won the rubber in the Test matches. The Australians made a very plucky effort at the finish, but it came far too late, and the result was never in doubt.

A feeling that the Englishmen had the game in their hands affected the attendance, which at the start was only very moderate. The weather was pleasant, and the wicket, considering the rainfall since Saturday, was in good condition.

England entered upon today's task with a big advantage, leading by 273 runs, and having still a wicket to fall. Exercising the power conferred upon him by Law Nine, Pelham Warner did not allow the wicket to be rolled before play began.

Wanting 329 to win, Australia sent in R. A. Duff and P. McAlister, the bowling being started by George Hirst and Len Braund. At lunchtime six runs had been scored without loss. On resuming the same bowlers were put on, and with the last ball of his first over, Hirst beat McAlister, the wicket falling at seven.

Clem Hill joined Duff, and some very steady cricket followed. When the total had reached 35, E. G. Arnold displaced Braund, and bowled Duff with his third ball. Two wickets for 35. Victor Trumper came in next, and Braund bowled at Hirst's end. The pace quickened, but at 59 Trumper was out lbw to Arnold, who at this point had taken two wickets for 13 runs. From the commencement of the innings the fielding had been decidedly smart.

Monty Noble was next in, and the cricket became quieter. Hill had the game stopped once until people had moved from behind the sight-board. W. Rhodes was tried in place of Braund at 65, and off his bowling Hill, when 24, was missed by Braund at slip. With nine runs added B. J. T. Bosanquet (left) relieved Arnold, and this change, as it happened, met with marvellous success. From Bosanquet's sixth ball Hill was stumped at 76, and directly afterwards S. E. Gregory was out lbw. The interval for tea was then taken, the score standing at 76 for five wickets. Hill withstood the bowling for one hour 25 minutes, but was not seen at his best.

The crowd numbered 8,000 when the game was continued. Bosanquet, at once finding his length, bowled in deadly form, and in quick succession took three more wickets. From his second ball on resuming — with the score still at 76 — A. J. Y. Hopkins was stumped, ten runs later C. E. McLeod was caught at the wicket, and at 90 H. Trumble was stumped.

J. J. Kelly joined Noble, and the crowd cheered wildly at every stroke that was scored. A section of them began, without the slightest reason, to jeer at the umpire, but others cheered when the players waited for the disturbance to cease.

When Noble had made 19 runs he might have been caught by R. E. Foster at slip off Bosanquet, but the chance was a hard one.

At 109 Rhodes, who had bowled 11 overs for a dozen runs, gave place to Arnold. Then at 114 Kelly was caught at slip. The match seemed over, but A. Cotter gave valuable help to Noble, and the last wicket caused a good deal of trouble. Cotter scored very fast — getting most of his runs from Bosanquet — and quite excited the crowd.

When the total had been raised to 153, Hirst went on for Arnold and Braund for Bosanquet. The first of these changes finished the game, Hirst bowling Cotter at 171. The innings lasted three hours and 26 minutes. Noble played sterling cricket, and Cotter, with five fours as his chief hits, scored 34 in a little over half an hour.

Beyond everything else the feature of the cricket was Bosanquet's bowling. Except when Rhodes and Arnold put Victoria out for 15, nothing more startling has been done with the ball during the tour.

Just before the tea interval Bosanquet to all intents and purposes won the match by getting rid of Hill and Gregory at 76, and he followed up his success in such style that at one point he had taken five wickets for 12 runs. His average afterwards suffered through Cotter's hitting, but that did not matter at all.

That he bowled wonderfully well there cannot be a doubt, Noble's testimony being sufficient. The Australian captain, without urging any reference to the condition of the wicket, said that at one stage he was practically unplayable.

Early in the tour Bosanquet was more than once very expensive, and one could not help thinking that Warner leaned too much on him. However, his captain's faith in his bowling — expressed again and again in letters home — has now been more than justified. In this connection it is only right to add that some of the Australian critics — most of them keen judges — predicted success for Bosanquet as soon as they saw the amount of spin he could get on the ball.

England won the Ashes series 3–2.

B.J.T. BOSANQUET

Lawn tennis championships at Wimbledon

PUBLISHED THURSDAY 30 JUNE

Yesterday the championship meeting of the All-England Lawn Tennis Club, at Wimbledon, came to its close, before a crowd that was even larger than any yet seen in this year of record attendances. The most important and popular game was the challenge round of the doubles championship, in which the two Dohertys defended their title against S. H. Smith and F. L. Riseley.

It would be difficult to pick out four better players in England at this moment; three of them are in the English team which is to defend the Davis International Cup; and when the two brilliant Irishmen are kept hard at work by a pair of plucky and persistent opponents, it would be impossible to see much better tennis anywhere.

The figures of the actual score give little idea of the interest of the game. The Irish players took their three sets straight off; the first to one, the second to two and the third to four. In this last set Riseley fairly surpassed himself, and at one time, during the fifth and sixth games, he was playing finer strokes than anyone on the court, serving with accuracy and severity, volleying with magnificent skill and direction, and repeatedly beating both the brothers off his own racquet.

Smith, roused out of his customary apathy by this meteoric display, suddenly began driving with a bitterness and strength that for a moment enabled his side fairly to dominate their redoubtable opponents, and the score was called 4–3 in favour of the challengers.

This woke up H. L. Doherty to some purpose, and the service that produced 4–4 proved almost untakeable. 'R. F.' made the necessary effort without showing it, and the brothers, running up to the net together with that unanimity of purpose and graceful precision which is their greatest charm, soon took Riseley's service game, and the next game gave them the set and the match, Riseley losing the last return by a frown of fortune which he did not deserve.

Wimbledon-born Reginald Frank Doherty and his brother, Hugh Laurence, formed one of the most powerful tennis doubles partnerships in history. They won eight doubles titles at Wimbledon as well as successfully competing as individuals at Wimbledon, in the US Open championships, the Davis Cup and in the 1900 Olympic Games.

Miss Lottie Dod wins Ladies' Open championship

PUBLISHED SATURDAY 14 MAY

Yesterday, at Troon, the 12th annual tournament for the championship was won by Miss Lottie Dod of the Moreton Club, who, in the final tie, defeated Miss May Hezlet, of the Royal Portrush Club, after a fine match, by one hole. Miss Dod, who has held the ladies' lawn tennis championship on several occasions, and represented England in ladies' international hockey matches, has improved considerably as a golfer during recent years, and has played consistently well in the championships. She had, however, to wait until yesterday to gain the object of her ambition.

In the semi-final Miss Dod beat Miss Dorothy Campbell (North Berwick) by four and two, and Miss Hezlet defeated Miss M. A. Graham (Hoylake) by a like margin. A strong wind severely tested the judgment of the players, and a heavy shower of rain fell just after the start. Nevertheless there was a great gathering, and, owing to the press of spectators, play proceeded slowly.

Lottie Dod's sporting achievements were wide-ranging. As well as her success in tennis, golf and hockey, she also won a silver medal for archery at the 1908 Olympic Games.

SPORT IN BRIEF

OLYMPICS
The Olympic Games are held in St Louis, Missouri, US, to coincide with the world's fair in the city, as in Paris in 1900. Once again the Games fail to excite public attention, and are badly organised. Irish athlete Thomas Kiely wins the 'combined events' (which in later years will become the decathlon); he has to complete all ten events in one day. Fred Lorz claims victory in the marathon, until it is discovered that – after suffering cramp – he hitched a lift in a passing car, and Thomas Hicks is awarded the gold medal instead. In the rowing competition, the course is too short for some of the events, so competitors have to make a turn.

RUGBY UNION
In a tour of Australia and New Zealand, Scotsman Darkie Bevell-Sivright leads a British side dominated by the Welsh three-quarters Percy Bush, Rhys Gabe and Teddy Morgan. The Lions win their three Test matches against Australia, but lose 9–3 to New Zealand.

CYCLING
The Tour de France degenerates into farce as riders tackling extremely long stages are forced to race in the dark. Some competitors are attacked with stones and clubs. The leading riders are suspected of collusion with the culprits, and the first four finishers are disqualified.

FOOTBALL
The Fédération Internationale de Football Association (FIFA) is formed in Paris on 21 May. Members of the world governing body of football are Belgium, Denmark, France, Holland, Spain, Sweden and Switzerland. England will join in 1905.

1905

James Braid recovers well to take championship

PUBLISHED SATURDAY 10 JUNE

Yesterday, at St Andrews, the Open golf championship was won for the second time by James Braid (below), the Scottish professional, who left the amateur ranks some 11 years ago, and after a long stay at Romford, accepted two years back the post of professional to the Walton Heath Club.

His total of 318 did not compare very favourably with Jack White's winning score of 296 at Sandwich last year, or even with J. H. Taylor's 309, accomplished with a gutta-percha ball in 1900, when the championship was last held at St Andrews. It was indeed, the highest successful aggregate since Taylor won with 333 at St Andrews in 1893, but it should be mentioned that the St Andrews course this week was infinitely the most difficult one on which the championship has ever been played.

Every hole was of a testing length, and the new bunkers seemed to fill the links with hazards. They were placed on and off the line, and perfect judgement, with a certain amount of luck in avoiding kicks the wrong way, proved the surest road to success. The greens were also difficult, while the cold wind which prevailed on the first two days helped render the scoring high.

Braid was in a good many difficulties during the competition, but his recoveries were magnificent. Somewhat curiously, he started with 81 and finished with 81. Between these rounds were sandwiched two 78s, so that his scoring was consistent.

MILESTONES

The football world was stunned by the first four-figure transfer fee. It was paid for Alf Common, who moved from Sunderland to Middlesbrough for £1,000. The England forward had also earned the first £500 transfer fee when he joined Sunderland from Sheffield United in 1902.

Bosanquet plays first Test match in England

PUBLISHED THURSDAY 1 JUNE

England beat Australia at Nottingham yesterday by 213 runs, the splendid batting that made the game safe being followed by some truly remarkable bowling on the part of Bernard Bosanquet. Those who said before the match began that England's chance of actually winning on a hard wicket depended to a great extent on Bosanquet proved to be quite correct in their judgement. Of course, nothing is certain at cricket, but, judging from yesterday's play, it seems highly improbable that the match would have been finished if Bosanquet had not been in the England team. The Australians were set such an impossible task that they had only a draw to hope for, but the wicket was so good that in the ordinary way they might easily have stayed in for the four hours and a half that remained for cricket when England's second innings was declared closed.

The match ended in a shockingly bad light at ten minutes past five, and a quarter of an hour later rain set in, and continued with little intermission till after the time for the drawing of stumps. The magnitude of what Bosanquet did cannot well be overestimated. His record, as it stands – eight wickets for 107 runs – is remarkable enough, but there is the additional fact that he got rid very cheaply indeed of the three batsmen, who, with Victor Trumper away, were most to be feared – Clem Hill, Monty Noble and Warwick Armstrong. It was impossible to see from the press-box how much leg-break he was able to put on, but we were told that the ball often turned the width of the wicket. To all appearances it was his reverse break that beat Joe Darling – a leg-break to the left-handed batsman – but on this point we would speak with some reserve. That he was very difficult to deal with was clear from the way in which, under conditions perfectly favourable to run-getting, he demoralised a very strong side.

It was his first Test match in this country, but as everyone knows he won the game at Sydney which last year gave the MCC's XI the rubber in Australia. For the remaining matches this season, if the wickets be hard, he will be the one indispensable bowler.

Doherty gets better of brilliant Brookes

PUBLISHED MONDAY 10 JULY

It is hardly possible that Saturday's lawn tennis can be beaten as an event in the history of the game. Before the championship began the gates of the All-England Club had to be closed; not another person could be packed into the centre court at Wimbledon; every inch had two inches of humanity crammed inside. In the space within the stands not a breath of breeze arrived, yet spectators forgot the heat in the play.

In one sense the play in the ladies' final was disappointing, for Miss Douglas was never on her game. How far the injured wrist was responsible it is impossible to say. In practice the holder of 1903 and 1904 has been playing magnificently; on the other hand, the wrist is needed as an explanation, because Miss Douglas is the most consistent of players.

It was a surprise that Miss Sutton won in two straight sets, but not a surprise on the play. Miss Douglas never looked like winning. She could not find her length or her accuracy. Her drives had only the ghost of their proper force, and the pace told on her more than it ought. Nothing of this detracts from the sincere congratulations which everyone offers to the American lady champion – now the English lady champion also. She has lost not one set in the championships or the Northerns, and has played with pluck, judgement and tremendous energy throughout.

In the championship England took a vicarious revenge. Norman Brookes was at the top of his grand game. Until the last few games he was everything he has been. Following up each shot to the net he was brilliant. H. L. Doherty was better still. The perfect ease of his accuracy and pace was never more noticeable. He passed Brookes – over, to right, to left – dealt beautifully with the puzzling service, and played off the ground in wonderful style. Those low volleys were all in order; everything was in order, part of a scheme of play which could understand and execute at once.

Brookes has done well, and shown that Australian tennis is everything but the very best. Doherty has done everything we have learned to expect from him, and goes on unbeaten for another year. His patience is one of the pillars of his game. Able to kill, he is content to wait to give rope time after time with every encouragement to suicide. Sooner or later Doherty's opponents grow tired and hang. The mistake is made convenient to a degree that makes it inevitable.

Norman Brookes (above left) was nicknamed 'Wizard' because of his uncanny ability to disguise his service.

Startling New Zealand triumph against Devon

PUBLISHED MONDAY 18 SEPTEMBER
New Zealand 54 pts; Devon 4

Astartling triumph was achieved by the New Zealand team in the opening match of their tour at Exeter on Saturday, and the prestige of Devon football sustained a severe blow.

That our visitors would probably win was quite expected. It was only reasonable to assume that a combination with any real pretensions to engage in international encounters with each of the four unions would be more than a match for any county XV.

No one, however, would have been prepared for the utter rout of the Devon men, who were practically beaten in the first five minutes, and never made the semblance of a fight of it. Instead of the hard struggle which they naturally expected from a team of repute, the Colonials had matters simply all their own way. At all points they were clearly the superior, and were in no way flattered by the score, heavy as it was.

The New Zealand rugby team posing (above), and in action against Midland Counties at Leicester (top).

Starting in a brilliant and determined manner, they speedily gained a substantial lead, and after the first quarter of an hour the only question was the number of points by which they would win. At half-time they had obtained 27 points, and they more than doubled their score afterwards, the Devon line being crossed 12 times and a penalty goal being kicked in the first few minutes.

Rubber balls lead to golf victory

PUBLISHED FRIDAY 9 JUNE

Early in 1901 rumours were in the air of an American golf ball that possessed prodigious powers of flight, but the matter was not taken seriously until in the autumn of 1901. Mr W. J. Travis used these new balls, and won the American Amateur championship with consummate ease.

From that time until the following spring the battle of the rubber balls was hotly waged. The leading amateurs were averse from their introduction. The professionals to a man were strongly opposed to them, and even went so far as to address to the governing committee a request that the rubber balls might be barred in the Open championship. When Mr Balfour was asked for an expression of his opinion, he said that he would 'view with great apprehension … the standardisation of the implements to be used by the player'. In the event the Royal and Ancient Club declined to interfere, and the rubber-cored balls are now firmly established in golfing favour.

The influence they have exercised in the scoring at the Open championship is very marked. Since they were first used at Hoylake in 1902 the winning figures have been as follows: 307, 300, 296. With the gutta it is certain that no such reduction would have been witnessed.

SPORT IN BRIEF

RUGBY UNION
In a change to the points system, a try is now worth three points rather than two and a conversion two points rather than three. Field goals (where the ball is kicked from the ground over the posts in open play) are abolished.

FOOTBALL
Gus Mears and his brother take over the London Athletic Club site at Stamford Bridge and begin building a stadium, and Chelsea Football Club's bid for League status begins. John Tait Robertson is brought down from Glasgow Rangers as player/manager; impressive signings include William 'Fatty' Foulke, who at over 6 ft and 22 stone is a formidable sight in the Chelsea goal. Chelsea are admitted to the Second Division, finishing the season in third place. By 1907 they have earned promotion to Division One.

RUGBY UNION
Following their demolishing of Devon on 16 September (see main text), Dave Gallaher's 'Originals', from New Zealand, go on to win all but one of their matches in their tour of Britain. Gallaher is highly effective as a wing forward or 'rover', a position not known to his British opponents.

BOXING
On 20 December, defending light-heavyweight champion Bob Fitzsimmons suffers a technical knock-out at the hands of 'Philadelphia' Jack O'Brien after collapsing in his corner at the end of the 13th round. O'Brien immediately moves up to the heavyweight division, and the fight becomes the last light-heavyweight title contest for nearly nine years.

Michael Parkinson

The greats

GREAT PLAYERS JUST DON'T TURN UP. THEY HOLD COURT. I was a kid when I first knew the difference. I was watching Don Bradman's 1948 Australian team when a tall, broad-shouldered, sun-tanned man with black hair and blue eyes came down the pavilion steps. I was standing by the gate and as he passed me he winked. When I told them at school the next day they said he must have had something in his eye. But they couldn't put me off. From that day to this Keith Miller has been my hero, and if I ever needed to call a witness to define my love of sport he would be that man.

Miller attracted a large female following, including my mother, who once confessed she wouldn't mind washing his kit.

Miller played every game as if it might be his last day on earth. He lived his life that way too. He bowled like the wind, batted like he had a train to catch, and in the slips discussed current racing form with his neighbours only breaking off to swoop on a half-chance, making the impossible look like an afterthought. He was as glamorous as he was chivalrous and attracted a large female following, including my mother, who once confessed she wouldn't mind washing his kit.

I was fortunate to know Miller well in later years. I once played in the same cricket team. At the time we were both employed by the *Daily Express,* and there was an annual game between Lord Beaverbook's men and the *Daily Mail*. Which explains how I came to be standing next to Mr Miller who, from his position at first slip, was well placed to see a colleague whose job was to stand by the sightscreen and tic-tac the results of race meetings in which the great man had an interest. In the second over the *Daily Mail*'s opening bat snicked the ball in my direction. I hadn't even thought about moving before Miller dived across me and took a wonderful catch at full stretch. He rolled over, handed me the ball and said: 'I wonder what won the three o'clock at Wincanton?'

Fred Trueman might have lacked Miller's charm, but he lost nothing by comparison as someone who held centre stage and commanded attention no matter what else might be happening on the field of play. My earliest memory of Fred is black and white. Barnsley playing Leeds at Headingley, Parkinson and H. D. Bird batting, Trueman bowling. He was quick. How quick? It's unlikely that Dickie saw the ball that hit him. He went down like a sack of turnips. I attended my stricken partner who was having a good moan, having been struck in the ribs.

Having revived him I walked back to my end, passing on the way the bowler, who had observed events as he squatted on his haunches. 'How's thi' mate?' he asked. 'Very well, thank you,' I said. 'That's all right, then. But think on, lad, you're next,' he said. I didn't hang about. I slogged at the other opening bowler and made a cowardly exit. Watching Trueman bowl after that I was convinced I had made the right decision.

When I think of the glories of watching cricket I think of Fred Trueman. Nowadays his reputation depends as much upon what he said and how he behaved as anything he did on the field of play. Anyone who saw him in full flight would have no problem remembering the glorious rhythm of his action.

I keep a photograph of Fred Trueman in my study. It captures him at the moment of delivery. He is side on, head still and pointed over his left shoulder. The forward arm is high, the left leg poised to drive down in the delivery stride. It is an action full of menace and yet relaxed. Trueman's gift was that possessed by only the very best athletes, the capacity to achieve maximum effect with minimum strain. Of all the fast bowlers I have seen, he was the one who pleased me most.

Trueman's gift was that possessed by only the very best athletes: the capacity to achieve maximum effect with minimum strain.

Nowadays I sit next to Fred at the rugby league final, where he fills a pipe the size of a plant pot with what smells like innersoles of shoes and puffs away contentedly while commenting on this and that. He has always been convinced of his place on the planet. Norman O'Neil, the Australian cricketer was once with Fred in India when he turned to him and observed, 'Fred, I think the people at the next table are talking about you.' Fred said: 'Ay, they talk about me all over t'world, Norm lad.'

If Frederick Sewards Trueman defined the joys of bowling fast, then Shane Warne performed the same function on behalf of those who bowled at a gentler pace. It is difficult to believe there has ever been a slow bowler to equal him. It is also unlikely there has ever been a more satisfying and fulfilling spectacle than Warne bowling and Ian Healy keeping wicket. In my idea of cricket heaven Fred would be at one end and Warne the other.

Who would the batsmen be? First choice is easy: David Gower. I admire style and grace in sport more than most qualities, and Gower possessed them in abundance. He was the loveliest of stroke-players, with an artist's imagination and respect for line and form. Who would partner him in my fantasy game? Viv Richards was easily the most awesome batsman I ever saw. If Gower used a rapier, Richards' chosen weapon was broadsword. When Gower walked to the crease it was a promise; when Viv Richards strode out it constituted a threat.

Of the footballers I have seen in my lifetime three stand out: Tom Finney, John Charles and George Best. But the one who made the most lasting impression on me was Danny Blanchflower. He was a good footballer, but not a great one, not like the other three were great. Yet from the very first moment I saw him he changed the way I thought about football. He came to Barnsley from Glentoran and immediately expanded the boundaries of my imagination. He played football with the precision and calculation of a Grand Master at chess.

Up until his arrival we had been fed a diet of raw meat at Barnsley. What he placed before us was altogether different. Later on he masterminded a great team at Spurs and I came to know him well when he was a writer and commentator on the game. He used to talk about the 'glory' of football and was one of the few who could do so without sounding sentimental. He warned of the problems ahead if football became the plaything of financiers. He clearly saw the pitfalls in giving large salaries to largely unschooled and naive young men, and he never forgot that that which he loved most of all was, when all is said and done, only a pastime. His message has largely gone unheeded, but that tells you more about the way football is run than it does about Danny Blanchflower. He would have taken a perverse pleasure in being proved right, having believed throughout his career in what might most politely be termed the fallibility of football's decision-makers.

Best was the one I enjoyed most. For four or five years before his lifestyle took its toll he played in such a creative and joyful manner it was difficult to imagine a better footballer. David Sadler, his teammate at

Manchester United, said that such was Best's mastery of the game, he could play in any position on the field and be better than the specialist United player of the time. When you consider he was talking about the likes of Bobby Charlton and Nobby Stiles it gives some idea of the range of his artistry.

The sportsmen I have written about moved me in different ways but had one thing in common: they all left me with imperishable memories. It says everything about my final choice that not many people would argue if I made the case for him being the most remarkable athlete of the 20th century. Muhammad Ali entwined us all in his dreams and fantasies, and if at times he was baying at the moon, the only person who suffered, in the end, was himself. It doesn't do him justice to judge him merely as a prizefighter. It's a bit like saying Fred Astaire was simply a hoofer. What was he? The only way I can convey what it was like to meet him is to say that he had the most powerful 'presence' of any human being I have ever met. The sadness of Ali is that he should finally be brought down by the sport that gave him the chance to display his unique personality. Boxing will continue into the next millennium and beyond, but future participants would do well to consider the fate of the greatest of them all when calculating their chances of getting out unscathed.

Muhammad Ali entwined us all in his dreams and fantasies.... The sadness is that he should finally be brought down by the sport that gave him the chance to display his unique personality.

One last observation. The most significant change in sport in my lifetime has been the transition of the game into a product. The commercialisation of sport has changed everything. Phrases like 'it isn't cricket' or 'he's a good sport' are redundant. Maybe they were meaningless in any case, but they did denote a philosophy which at least anticipated a moral base for games.

It is also significant that sport has become the property of the young and super-fit. Mature men, both mentally and spiritually, are no longer to be found in the football, rugby and cricket teams of today. They are missed because it takes a while to understand the eternal truth: a game is a diversion from real life, and not a substitute.

1906

First Grand Prix is staged

From our own correspondent
PARIS, WEDNESDAY 27 JUNE

François Szisz on his Renault I, is the winner of the Grand Prix of the Automobile Club de France. He headed the list yesterday, and his performance today was equally remarkable. On both days he had the advantage of starting first, and he firmly maintained it. This Sarthe circuit race has, from all accounts, been a terrible ordeal. The heat has been overpowering and, after the wear and tear of yesterday, the roads were in a shocking state today. Rugged stones in many places meant serious danger to tyres, with consequent pauses for repairs.

It is argued that the fact of a competitor having been able to come up to time today is in itself a success for him, as only 17 responded to the call this morning. The automobiles were removed from the resting-places, each drawn by one horse. Each was handed over to its particular driver, who had then to take in his supply of petrol and to make whatever repairs were requisite. Some lost about half an hour while so engaged.

According to the records now to hand Szisz's total time was 12 hr 14 min 7 sec. The exact amount of ground covered in the two days is 1,238.16 km (773.8 miles). So this means a speed of 101.2 km (63¼ miles) per hour.

François Szisz winning the first Grand Prix, on the Sarthe circuit west of Le Mans.

Dogged style of Bachelor's Button wins the day

PUBLISHED FRIDAY 22 JUNE

A great deal of interesting matter could be written round the Gold Cup, which is said to have been originated by the Duke of Cumberland, the hero of Culloden, who so far back as 1772 instituted a cup to be raced for by five-year-olds here over a four-mile course. In 1807 it was raised to the dignity of the Gold Cup, and for a very long period it has been highly esteemed by owners, not only on account of its intrinsic value, but because it is one of the unwritten laws of the Turf that no horse has indubitably set the seal on his fame until he has secured this race.

The victories of mares have been singularly few and far between, and in a period of half a century only three members of the gentler sex have won it, viz, Brigantine, Apology, and La Flèche. That Pretty Polly would have secured the coveted prize 12 months ago had she been able to run has always been accepted as certain, though doubtless the view may be modified after today's sensational race, when the cup furnished one of those remarkable surprises which have from time to time distinguished it.

When Throwaway won two years ago people were incredulous, and it was considered on all hands that the victory of Mr Alexander's horse was a fluke. What will be thought after the downfall of Major Leder's redoubtable mare this afternoon it is impossible to say. Everybody seemed to be too stupefied to realise that a catastrophe had somehow occurred. This expression is permissible where Pretty Polly is concerned, for she had never previously been beaten in this country, having achieved a triumphant and unbroken series of successes extending over three seasons. Almost universal regret was expressed that she should at last have received a check in the zenith of her career. Odds were, of course, freely laid on her, though many supported Bachelor's Button on account of the extended prices.

As they cantered down to the post, Pretty Polly's splendid and almost inimitable action was intensely admired. The race was run at a tremendous pace, St Denis settling down well clear of Cicero and Achilles, with Bachelor's Button waiting behind Pretty Polly. As they entered the Swinley Bottom, St Denis was five or six lengths in front of Cicero and Achilles, of whom Lord Rosebery's horse became whipper-in immediately they had turned on to the old course.

After passing the brick-kilns, Achilles deprived St Denis of the lead, and was followed into the straight by Bachelor's Button and Pretty Polly. A quarter of a mile from home Achilles was done with, and excitement reached a high point as the favourite made her effort to overhaul Bachelor's Button.

For a few strides it looked as though she would win easily, and then Dillon had suddenly to take up his whip. It was at once seen that the mare was in difficulties, and with Bachelor's Button struggling on in the most dogged style, he won by a length.

New Zealand take honours in close struggle

PUBLISHED MONDAY 1 JANUARY
Swansea 3 pts; New Zealand 4

The New Zealanders brought their remarkable tour to a close at Swansea on Saturday, when, after a memorable struggle, they just defeated the local XV by the narrowest possible margin.

In a hard-fought match, Swansea scored a try during the first half, and for a long time it seemed as though the Colonials would, after all, be once more beaten. With characteristic energy, however, they strove their hardest, when, subsequent to change of ends they had the wind in their favour.

Amidst a scene of tremendous excitement, Billy Wallace dropped a goal, and thus by four points to three the New Zealanders triumphed. The Swansea XV are to be congratulated upon making such a splendid fight of it.

On all hands they were regarded as the weakest of the three most important Welsh clubs, and it was generally expected that the New Zealanders would wind up with a comfortable win. Placing their strongest available team in the field, Swansea, as a matter of fact, scarcely ever looked like being beaten, and in the first half only the resolute tackling and fine kicking of Wallace at fullback saved the situation for the Colonials.

At the same time, the New Zealanders were by no means at full strength. Once again Wallace was the hero of the match. Over and above the fact that by dropping a goal he turned what looked like defeat into victory, his methods all through were thoroughly sound, and he hardly made a mistake.

Like all their other matches in Wales the fixture proved a tremendous attraction, the crowd on the St Helen's ground being estimated at 30,000.

Olympic Games held in Athens

From our special correspondent
ATHENS, TUESDAY 26 MAY

Glorious weather prevailed today, and the whole of Hellas seemed concentrated at Athens to see the result of the great marathon race in the stadium. The day began well with Patrick Leahy winning the high jump for England, but our flag did not rise again in the final of the half-mile.

The Americans made the pace, as usual, for both the Englishmen, Lieut. Wyndham Halswelle and Crabbe, had drawn outside places at the start. Before halfway had been reached, Halswelle went up, and then Crabbe led, but at the last corner both the Americans spurted, shutting out the Englishmen, and won with Pilgrim, James Lightbody, Halswelle, Crabbe, in that order. The time was very fast indeed, being 2 min 1 sec for the 800 m. Expectancy rose high

as the time approached for the finish of the marathon race, and the enormous amphitheatre of marble seats was fairly humming with voices in every language. Every inch of the hill above the marble arena was packed with Greeks from every district south of Turkey, and there was a solid line of soldiers right round the top against the blue sky.

At ten minutes to six a sudden roar began gathering in the distance, and finally swelled up to the stadium gates, where a cavalry officer was seen riding ahead of a solitary runner. This was Sherring of Canada, a small, light man, running happily with a smile on his face. He finished his long and dusty journey in front of the King and Queen of Greece, who handed him a bouquet of flowers. Some time after, a Swedish runner came in second. The winner's time was 2 hr 51 min 28 sec.

Nothing remains now but tomorrow's prize-giving and the memory of the entire Greek nation, which is wildly enthusiastic over the greatest athletic meeting ever seen here.

The 100-m sprint (left), won by American Archie Hahn in the Olympic Stadium in Athens (above). Athens was to have hosted every alternate Games; following the decision to hold the Games once every four years, in different cities, Athens was awarded these 'Intermediate' or 'Intercalated' Games as compensation.

SPORT IN BRIEF

BOXING
Canadian Tommy Burns makes three successful defences of his heavyweight title during the year.

RUGBY UNION
France face England at the Parc des Princes in Paris in their first official international rugby union match. England win 35–8.

FOOTBALL
Merseyside celebrates as the League title goes to Liverpool and Everton win the FA Cup against Newcastle United by one goal to nil.

CRICKET
Frank Woolley begins his first-class career with his home county of Kent, helping them to a win in the county championship. A stylish and exciting left-handed all-rounder, he will break numerous records in his 33 years at this level.

1907

Wimbledon title goes overseas

From our special correspondent
PUBLISHED FRIDAY 5 JULY

In yesterday's two singles an English crowd experienced the pleasure of hope without expectation, and the blessing of those who expect little. Miss Sutton was altogether too good for Miss Wilson. She was at her best, and at her best her pace and variety of stroke can hardly be beaten. Yet for a long time Miss C. M. Wilson held her. From 2–5 she caught up to 4–5, after being within a point of losing, and though the score was less even in the second set, hardly a game was not closely fought, hardly a point was won without a struggle. Miss Sutton took the match at 6–4, 6–2.

The final of the All-Comers singles, bearing with it the championship, has now gone out of England for the first time since its inception by the All-England Club in 1877. It has never been in better hands than it is today. At the close of his match Mr Norman Brookes was heartily cheered for a victory well deserved. A strong favourite from the first, he has won his seven rounds by hard and, above all, clever play.

No one who has ever seen Mr Gore play will imagine that he was not game from beginning to end. But it is idle to pretend that he was not completely outplayed. After 3–3 in the first set he never got level with his opponent. And though the match was all over in 38 minutes, it was plain that the pace told. The match should have been weight for age, save that it is difficult as one watches to remember that Mr Gore needs any such allowance. In the first set Mr Gore was all over the court, and he gained the net constantly and smashed with fine judgment. But afterwards he was kept back. The second and third sets went in just the same way. Usually no kind of break in the service upsets Mr Gore, but yesterday he failed several times to get his racquet fairly on to the ball. In all the match he won one only of Mr Brookes's services – the sixth game of the last set.

DID YOU KNOW?

Basil Maclear, a rugby union player who won 11 caps for Ireland between 1905 and 1907, was in the great tradition of eccentric Irish players. Following in the footsteps of D. B. Walkington, who always wore a monocle during games, Maclear sported white gloves when playing.

PUBLISHED MONDAY 14 JANUARY
Wales 22 pts; England 0

Severely damaged in the match with the South Africans at the beginning of December, the reputation of Welsh rugby football was completely rehabilitated at Swansea on Saturday, when the 24th encounter between Wales and England ended in a brilliant victory for the representatives of the principality by two goals and six tries to nothing.

At all points of the game the Welshmen showed a marked superiority, and their triumph was as well deserved as it was complete.

They ran a considerable risk in playing an extra back and trusting to seven forwards to hold the English pack of eight, but the course adopted proved astonishingly successful, the Welsh scrummagers not only holding their opponents, but securing possession of the ball five times out of six.

With the forwards thus accomplishing much more than the most hopeful follower of Wales could possibly have expected, the halves found themselves most happily situated, and the latter broke away time after time with a skill and celerity that quite nonplussed the Englishmen. The ball, indeed, was nearly always with the Welsh backs, and although somewhat difficult to handle owing to a drizzling rain, the players, after a few mistakes from this cause at starting, subsequently brought off bout after bout of passing in a manner which could scarcely have been surpassed under the most favourable conditions.

In each half the visitors' defence held out fairly well for about 20 minutes, but that was all, and three tries before the interval were followed

by an equal number after change of ends. Only about three or four times all through the match did the Welshmen find their powers of defence seriously taxed, and upon two of these occasions they cleared in such masterly style that within another minute or so some rare combination had resulted in their crossing the English line, the sudden transformation in the game being worthy of the New Zealanders at their best.

For England the occasion was one of grievous disappointment. From the series of matches – North v South, England v The Rest, and England v South Africa – the selection committee of the Rugby Union had this season enjoyed exceptional opportunities of building up a really fine side, and there can be little doubt the material existed. All the experience of the South African matches tended to show that forward play stood at a higher level in the West than in any other part of the country, yet of the pack which took the field on Saturday three belonged to the North, two to Kent, one to the Midlands, and only two to the West. The result was what many people feared – a stalwart band, it is true, but one which packed indifferently, pushed only moderately, generally failed to secure the ball and, except in one or two instances, lacked pace in the open. Undoubtedly a fine opportunity was thrown away by the authorities, and, with English football full of promise, the struggle for the international championship has opened with a crushing defeat.

The game took place under rather dismal conditions, the drizzling rain, which had been falling hard all the morning, continuing practically all through the match, but although this made the ball a little awkward to hold and rendered the turf somewhat slippery, there was no reason to complain of the state of the ground. The attendance, although amounting to between 15,000 and 20,000, fell far short of expectations, the match, no doubt, suffering in point of interest through following so soon upon the visit of the South Africans to Wales.

The Welsh rugby team posing for the cameras (left), and engaging in their 22–0 rout of England (below) at Swansea.

SPORT IN BRIEF

MOTOR RACING
Brooklands, the first purpose-built motor-racing track in the world, is opened **(left)**. As well as staging motor races, the circuit will also be used for record attempts. British drivers Henry Segrave and Malcolm Campbell will be among the record-breakers to use the track.

FOOTBALL
Middlesbrough player Steve Bloomer makes his last appearance for England. His record total of 28 goals for his country in 23 matches will remain unbeaten for 50 years.

RUGBY LEAGUE
Another major rules change comes into effect following last year's reduction of a rugby league team from 15 to 13 players. Any player who is tackled while in possession will now restart the game by dropping the ball and trying to tap it back to a teammate.

BOXING
German-born American Frank Mantell scores a surprise victory over Honey Mellody of the United States to claim the welterweight title. Mantell has formerly worked as Mellody's sparring partner, earning $5 a day for the privilege. He knocks out his old employer in the 15th round.

FOOTBALL
Celtic are the first club to achieve the Scottish Double, winning the League and the Scottish Cup. They beat Hearts 3–0 in the Cup final, and win the League by seven points.

GOLF
Arnaud Massy becomes the first non-British player to win the British Open. Massy names his newly born child Hoylake after the scene of his triumph.

Burns in successful defence of heavyweight title

PUBLISHED TUESDAY 3 DECEMBER

Matches with the gloves between heavyweights of any note have been so few and far between in England for some time past, that it was not surprising to find a very large amount of interest centred in the contest decided at the National Sporting Club last night, between Gunner Moir, of England, and Tommy Burns, of America. Such a demand for seats has never previously been made at headquarters, not even excepting the greatest bout of all times – that fought out in the same building 15 years ago by the late Peter Jackson and the Australian, Frank Slavin. On that memorable occasion the National gave a purse of £2,000, while, yesterday, Moir and Burns boxed for £1,300 in addition to a stake of £500 aside.

The match being for the heavyweight championship was, of course, at catch weights. These conditions favoured Moir to some extent, seeing that although at 29 he is nearly two years older than the other, he stood 5 ft 9½ in to the 5 ft 7 in of the American, and scaled 13 st to the 12 st 3 lb of the stranger.

At a quarter-past ten the men entered the ring. Burns took the middle and worked his man round, and the American landed a light one first. Both sparred lightly. Moir was cautioned three times for holding with his left

hand, and was nearly disqualified before the end of the first round. Burns seemed to hit him fairly easily when he wished, but nothing much was done. By the seventh round, Burns went for his man, which roused Moir, but the visitor led his left when he liked, and landed easily, but rather too lightly for effect. Moir was clearly out-generalled, and Burns's tactics of leaning his head forward evidently bothered Moir.

In the eighth round, the American was all over him, and Moir was bleeding freely from repeated blows in the face. For the ninth round, Mr Corri took off his coat and walked into the ring, standing by the ropes. Burns came up very fresh, and Moir's punches at close quarters seemed to have no sting. They had repeatedly to be separated by the referee. Burns landed the best hits and Moir remained puzzled by the American's tactics. The Englishman was the more tired of the two men when the bell rang.

In the tenth round, Burns again hit Gunner with both right and left whenever he liked. Twice Moir went down from heavy blows, and twice he tottered up again. Then came the finish, and Moir was counted out.

It was a poor contest for a heavyweight championship. The American was too clever in his defence especially; too tricky and too fast for the Britisher. He always looked a winner after the third round.

1908

W. G. Grace braves Easter snow

By Major Philip Trevor
PUBLISHED TUESDAY 21 APRIL

There was snow on the ground at Kennington Oval when the sun rose on Easter Monday, and there was more snow afterwards. One had to be thankful for small mercies and lucky it was that the sun shone. Had it been otherwise, we might have added to an already long list yet another cricket curiosity. There is no lack of weird stories about English games played in difficulties created by English weather, and not the least weird of them would have been one which recorded the sweeping of the snow from the pitch prior to the start of a first-class cricket match.

Still the Easter Monday match at Kennington Oval is a pleasant testimonial to the keenness of many of the leading cricketers, and, if the veteran champion is ever ready to brave the weather at such a time, young men, who might well be his grandsons, should not complain of it. Frankly, the public interest in this particular match is largely, if not exclusively, caused by the presence on the cricket field of the greatest of all cricketers.

Next July, W. G. Grace **(above)** will be 60 years old. The inexorable laws of Anno Domini deprive the London public nowadays of what used to be to them a frequent treat, and, in consequence of that deprivation, it takes more than an east wind or a fall of snow to dissuade the enthusiasts from seizing the one chance they now get of watching on the field of play the man who has done more than anyone else to make first-class cricket a national institution.

MILESTONES

The first black heavyweight champion of the world was Jack Johnson, who defeated reigning champion Tommy Burns of Canada in 1908. American promoters had effectively operated a colour bar to prevent challenges to white boxers, and the fight was staged in Sydney, Australia.

A heroic marathon finish by Dorando Pietri

PUBLISHED SATURDAY 25 JULY

Yesterday the marathon race, run from Windsor Castle to the stadium, a distance of some 26 miles, produced as dramatic and unexpected a finish as any lover of sensation might desire. The British representatives were strongly in front for half the course; then the running was taken up by Charles Hefferon, the South African. Longboat, the much-fancied Canadian athlete, retired at the 20th mile, and Appleby, one of the best of the English contingent, gradually disappeared from the contest. Just before the stadium, Hefferon was passed by Dorando Pietri. The Italian entered the enclosure amid a scene of wild excitement, followed by Joseph Hayes, a representative of the United States, the latter having succeeded in passing the South African, after a gallant struggle.

Then ensued the most remarkable, and also the most painful, scene of the day which had obviously tried the strength of the competitors to the uttermost. Pietri, in going round the stadium enclosure, fell through sheer exhaustion, more than once. Helped by the officials, who immediately came to his rescue, he managed to breast the tape somehow. But as it was due to the assistance of others that he finished first, the race was very properly given to the American representative, Hayes, and Pietri was disqualified.

Hundreds of thousands of people witnessed the gallant efforts of the 55 runners of 16 countries who were started by the Princess of Wales on the East terrace of Windsor Castle. In the stadium there were between 50,000 and 60,000 persons awaiting the arrival of the first man. At about 20 minutes past five a rocket denoting that the first runner had passed the 26 miles mark was fired. It was known that the Italian, Dorando Pietri, was leading.

An opening in the stand through which the runners had to pass, was cleared. No runner was seen in the archway. Presently some ambulance men ran across the cycle track with a stretcher. The multitude was all excitement. Could it be that, like the Greek runner in whose honour the race was initiated, the plucky little Italian had fallen when within an ace of grasping his wreath of olive? There were tense, drawn faces in the stands, and the silence was unnerving. In a moment or two the diminutive figure in a wet, white vest and crimson drawers came into view. A deafening roar greeted him. The noise seemed to make no impression on the champion. He walked slowly, painfully, and was obviously only half-conscious of what was going on around him.

Twenty yards and Pietri faltered and fell. In half a minute Pietri was on his feet again and a trot, or a roll, carried him to the bend near the competitors' stand. Great cheering, full of wholehearted sympathy, greeted him, but he was again to falter. He again went his weary way, and before entering the straight once more fell. Everyone felt the tragic situation. A roar from the crowd outside the stadium indicated the approach of a second runner. The Italian's time was short. Coaxed, entreated by attendants who had watched every inch of the way, he was once more lifted to his feet. He was set going. Facing him, 100 yards away, was the tape. The spectators were sighing for him to break it when a shout from the American stand proclaimed that Hayes, a United States representative, had reached the path.

Hayes was running. Pietri led him by 200 yards. But he only moved by inches. Twenty yards from the worsted, Pietri fell a fifth time. Two friends lifted him up and almost pushed him on the tape, where he was received by friends and placed upon a stretcher. His was a moral victory. Nature robbed him of his triumph, and though the Olympic Council very properly under the rules adjudged him disqualified from taking the prize, there were 60,000 persons ready to proclaim him the marathon champion.

Dorando Pietri is helped across the finishing line in 2 hr 54 min 46.6 sec. The officially declared winner, Joseph Hayes, finished in 2 hr 55 min 18.4 sec.

Prize-giving in the Olympic stadium

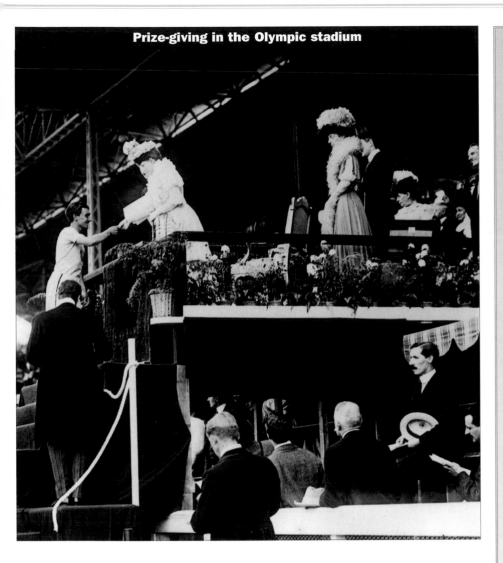

Queen Alexandra presents the marathon prize to the American, Joseph Hayes.

PUBLISHED MONDAY 27 JULY

Saturday brought to a splendid conclusion the long series of contests in the Olympic Games. In the middle of the prize-giving by Her Majesty the Queen, the magnified voice of the red-coated gentleman with the megaphone was silenced by a mighty shout which went up from the southern arc of the stadium. All eyes sought to discover the cause. The figure of a man in cycling dress moved over the cycle track, below the competitors' stand. It reached the cinder path, and then came one long, deep, welcoming shout of 'Dorando'. The man who in the popular belief is the real winner of the marathon of 1908 had arrived. 'Nature's soft nurse' had brought back power to his strong limbs, and he paced with soldierly stride around the track full of pride that, though an unkind Fate had denied him the prize he had coveted for his nationality, he was to receive a special trophy from the gracious lady who had witnessed his helplessness on the previous day – the Queen.

Dorando Pietri, the hero of the Games, was the unwitting cause of the complete cessation of the prize-distribution proceedings. Tax his voice as he would, the megaphonist, from his exalted platform, could not make

himself heard. He called for prize-winners to come up for their medals. His voice was lost in the sea of plaudits which rolled from one end of the stadium to the other, and then rolled back again. The megaphone gentleman gave it up. The prize-winners were watching Pietri.

Presently his name was called through the megaphone, and, doffing his cap, he marched to the platform. Her Majesty bent over the balustrade to say a word or two in congratulation, and then handed to Pietri, as her personal gift, a gold cup of exquisite design. Pressing the cup to his left breast, Pietri bowed and retired, and, after receiving his sprig of oak leaves, he completed his circuit of the cinder path.

There could be no doubting the fact that the popular mind will always associate Pietri with the English marathon race. The torrent of cheering which marked the Italian's triumphant procession to the dressing room of his compatriots was unmistakable evidence of this. As Dorando Pietri passed through the competitors' gate he was lifted shoulder high, and he left the arena to the accompaniment of three tremendous cheers.

SPORT IN BRIEF

RUGBY UNION
In their first Test match against New Zealand in Dunedin on 6 June, a British Isles side are defeated 32–5. The British Isles draw 3–3 in the second Test against the All Blacks, and lose the final Test 29–0.

FOOTBALL
Manchester United, back in the First Division for only two seasons, run away with the League title by a margin of nine points. Earlier in the season they scored a 6–1 victory over champions Newcastle, who once more fail to take the FA Cup, losing – to Wolves on this occasion – for the third time in four years.

MOTOR RACING
Germany triumphs in the Grand Prix, held at Dieppe. Christian Lautenschlager, in a 13.5-litre Mercedes, finishes ahead of Benz cars in second and third. Alarmed at soaring costs and their lack of success, French car manufacturers withdraw from grand-prix racing, and the Automobile Club de France are forced to cancel the 1909 race. The Grand Prix is finally reinstated in 1912.

CRICKET
The retirement of W. G. Grace from first-class cricket brings to an end an extraordinary career spanning more than 40 years. 'W. G.' has scored 54,896 runs in first-class cricket, including 126 100s, and taken 2,876 wickets. He has set numerous records, including scoring the first ever first-class triple century (344 for the MCC against Kent), and being the first player ever to score 100 first-class centuries. His huge frame, bushy beard and strong personality have made him one of the most famous figures in Britain.

1909

Gore fights back in tennis final

From our special correspondent
PUBLISHED MONDAY 5 JULY

When M. J. G. Ritchie, challenging A. W. Gore for the championship at Wimbledon on Saturday, led by two sets to love and two games to love, there could not have been a man in the crowd, over 3,000 strong, who did not consider the match fought and won.

Ritchie was undoubtedly the favoured candidate before the match began. The well-known tonic effect which the environment of the centre court has on Gore's game was certainly a point in his favour, but his exhibition in the first two sets rather gave a fallacious aspect to this advantage. Probably the explanation for his erratic display in the first half of the match was due to a preconcerted notion that to win at all he must win quickly. For a championship round the standard was admittedly much below the average.

The one-sided character of the contest at the beginning of the second set may be judged from the fact that in it Ritchie won his 12th successive ace, and Gore only secured a solitary game. Then came Ritchie's tragic miscalculation. Lulled into a sense of security, with the prize seemingly within his immediate grasp, he began to rest on his oars. The aggressive note in his game was modulated, and gradually died away.

Gore took on a new lease of life, hit with greater freedom and a lower trajectory, and assumed the aggressive for the first time. Could Gore last out and achieve a memorable triumph? The holder won the first two games, the second after deuce; the challenger, his last desperate spurt, as it proved, replied by taking the next two. Then there was only one man left to fight. Conscious of approaching triumph, the holder played in these last four games, two of which he won to love, in his best and breeziest style. For the second successive year the man whose heart was said to be weak had won the championship after a five-set struggle.

DID YOU KNOW?

King Edward VII became the first reigning monarch to own a Derby winner when 2,000 Guineas winner Minoru stormed home at Epsom to a rapturous reception. 'Wonderhorse' Minoru tried to complete the Triple Crown in the St Leger but was well beaten by Bayardo.

Australia inflict decisive defeat on England

By Major Philip Trevor
PUBLISHED MONDAY 11 JANUARY
England 3; Australia 9

The Australians beat England on Saturday last at Blackheath in decisive manner, and they very thoroughly deserved the victory which rewarded their efforts. For the greater part of the match the beaten side were obviously outplayed, and the winners are to be most heartily congratulated, not only on what they did, but more particularly on the way in which they did it. It would have surprised no one who took the trouble to watch Saturday's game intelligently and without prejudice if the Australians had won it by more than half a dozen points. They could easily have gained more than three tries, and, had Carmichael been in his usual form as a place-kicker, the defeat of England must have been more severe than was actually the case.

The keen disappointment felt by the English spectators at the exhibition given by the home team was the greater, seeing that the men who disappointed them began playing smartly enough, and were early encouraged to do better still. The game had not lasted a couple of minutes when an ill judged cross-kick by an Australian back allowed Edgar Mobbs on the left wing to get up speed before any of his opponents could realise that danger threatened them. Mobbs sprinted along the touchline, and, without a foot of it, he gave Tarr a neat in-pass, which was very neatly taken. Tarr swerved inwards, ran straight for about 20 yards, and then repassed the ball to Mobbs, who scored a clever try. The whole movement was admirably planned and admirably executed. It began about 30 yards from the English goal.

Of course, the cheering that ensued was long and loud, and the subsequent disappointment of the cheerers was the greater in consequence. That disappointment, however, was not immediate. The English attack was renewed again and again, and for 20 minutes, almost without a break, the Australians were put on their defence. At the end of that time they drew level, but the try which enabled them to do so was rather unexpected in the getting.

That a rugby football bounces queerly every player knows, and for that reason it should not be allowed to bounce when there is a possibility of catching it. The ball bounced wrong for one of the English backs. The Australian forwards invariably follow up finely, and England had to pay the penalty for an error of judgement. The ball was kicked over the English goal line, and Rowe, always the readiest of ready players, smartly seized his opportunity. The try he gained was in an easy position, but Carmichael failed to kick a goal. However, the Englishmen at once renewed their attack, and the Australians were compelled to touch down in self-defence. It looked, just then as if the scoring of Australia's try could be regarded as a mere episode.

Play, in fact, had lasted only three minutes short of half an hour before the Australians made anything which could be called a really systematic attack. But, having once begun to attack, they never ceased doing so. At half-time the score was three points all, but for the last ten minutes of the first half of the game the Englishmen had been called upon to tackle continuously. In that respect they did well, but very soon after change of ends it was obvious that some of them had become very tired. Yet their hardest work was still to come.

For 18 minutes assault after assault was made by the Australians, and then for the first time since change of ends a subdued cheer announced that the Englishmen had succeeded in forcing the ball over the halfway line. But it did not remain there long, and by this time it was quite plain to everyone that the English XV would indeed be lucky if they escaped defeat. The only matter for surprise was that the decisive blow took so long in coming.

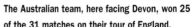

The Australian team, here facing Devon, won 25 of the 31 matches on their tour of England.

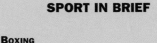

Well-deserved championship win for J. H. Taylor

PUBLISHED SATURDAY 12 JUNE

A splendid wind-up has to be recorded of the Open championship meeting at Deal. The weather was perfect, and the day's play strenuous in the extreme. The result was a well-deserved win for J. H. Taylor, who now shares with Harry Vardon and James Braid the honour of having won the title four times.

At the close of the previous day Taylor led the field with an aggregate of 147, C. Johns coming next with 148, and Tom Ball with 149.

Throughout yesterday Taylor played wonderfully steady golf, and made two fine rounds of 74 each, his grand total thus being 296 – a record only once before bettered in the championship, viz, by James Braid, at Prestwick, last year. Beyond being occasionally weak with his approach putts, Taylor made few mistakes.

James Braid and Tom Ball tied for second place with aggregates of 302. The feature of Ball's game was its straightness but Braid was scarcely at his best.

Young Johns, who finished fourth, was the surprise of the tournament, and although a little lucky in some of his recoveries, he deserved his position for the attractive and enterprising character of his play

J. H. Taylor was one of the greatest golfers of his decade. He was in the top six of the British Open a record 18 times, and represented England nine times against Scotland.

Disgraceful scenes at football match in Glasgow

From our own correspondent
GLASGOW, SUNDAY 18 APRIL

Glasgow, which holds the record for football disasters, was on Saturday afternoon and evening the scene of a riot which will take rank as one of the most disgraceful blots disfiguring the annals of the game. The finalists in the competition for the Scottish Cup are the Celtic and Rangers, two Glasgow clubs, which on the 10th of this month drew with two goals each. The replay took place on Saturday on the ground of the Queen's Park, at Hampden, Mount Florida, and again the teams drew, on this occasion with one goal each. At the close of the game the spectators, incensed at the decision not to play an extra half-hour and thus resolve the destiny of the cup, broke all bounds, and a riot ensued, in which the police and the mob came into prolonged conflict, with the most serious consequences.

The scene resembled that of a battlefield, and when, after the long-drawn mêlée, the horrors of which were heightened by the action of the crowd in setting fire to all the combustible material on which they could lay their hands, it was found that no fewer than 60 people were on the official list of casualties suffering from injuries, in some cases of a dangerous nature. Altogether over 100 persons were treated for wounds.

Between 60,000 and 70,000 people witnessed the match. It seemed to have been generally understood that in the event of a draw on this occasion the contest would be fought to a finish with an extra half-hour's play. After the referee had blown his whistle announcing the finish,

the members of the Celtic team remained on the field, but the Rangers left, and their example was followed shortly afterwards by their opponents. The majority of the spectators retained their positions, believing that further play would take place, but in the meantime the Football Association had decided that the game would not be renewed. When this became known the playing pitch was invaded by a number of the dissatisfied onlookers.

Soon the mob vented its rage on the constables who were subjected to a fusillade of stones, bottles, and brickbats. Overwhelmed and swept aside by superior numbers, the police were forced to use their batons, and shortly they were engaged in a hand to hand fight. Many members of the force were rendered prostrate, and had to be carried off the field. Whilst lying on the ground many of the constables were beaten and injured.

Maddened by excitement and relying on their overwhelming numbers, the rioters now proceeded to the extremest limits. The goal-posts were uprooted, the net torn to pieces, and the woodwork around the enclosure broken down to be used as weapons. A number of mounted constables were found to be of great assistance, but the mob took a malicious delight in surrounding the horsemen, and endeavouring to force them to dismount. They beat man and horse most unmercifully.

The riot lasted until 7.30 pm, nearly two hours and a half, and the enclosure at the end of this time was completely wrecked. When the mob were ultimately ejected from the field they remained in great crowds outside, and continued the fusillade of brickbats on the persons of the police and firemen.

SPORT IN BRIEF

BOXING
Following his defeat of Tommy Burns last December, in May Jack Johnson makes the first of four successful defences of his world heavyweight title this year.

FOOTBALL
Vivian Woodward moves to Chelsea from Tottenham Hotspur. One of the greatest centre forwards of all time, Woodward will win 23 caps and score 29 goals for his country between 1903–11. In an amateur international against Holland this year he scores a double hat trick.

LAWN TENNIS
Wentworth Gore is the only player aged over 40 to have won a Wimbledon singles title – first in 1908, and then again this year (see main text). He will appear again in the final in 1912 aged 44, but will lose to Tony Wilding.

CRICKET
Left-hander Warren Bardsley enjoys a hugely successful tour as he makes his Test debut for Australia. In the fifth Test at the Oval he scores 136 and 130, becoming the first player ever to make centuries in both innings of a Test match. Australia lose the first Test at Edgbaston **(below)**, but follow this with two wins and two draws to retain the Ashes.

29

1910

James Braid gains fifth Open success

PUBLISHED SATURDAY 25 JUNE

James Braid, the Walton Heath professional (**below with Harry Vardon**), made two records at St Andrews yesterday. He won the championship for the fifth time, a feat accomplished by no other player, although it may be yet achieved by either Vardon or J. H. Taylor, each of whom has already four victories to his credit. The other record made by the lengthy Scot was in returning a score of less than 300. All along Braid had been first favourite for the championship, but he had some dangerous opponents, whilst Alexander Herd was always in the running.

Fully 5,000 people saw the favourite finish. The disappointment of the spectators was manifest when Braid missed his putt of less than a yard, but when he holed his next for a round of 76 and an aggregate of 299 he was loudly cheered and carried shoulder-high from the green. He played magnificent golf.

Jeffries knocked out in 15th round

From our own correspondent

RENO (NEVADA), MONDAY 5 JULY

No fight in modern times has created more universal interest than the contest between Jim Jeffries and Jack Johnson, which took place at Reno, Nevada, yesterday.

Jeffries and Johnson, amid a tornado of cheers, flag-waving, and wild shrieks of delight, entered the ring at 2.30 pm, Nevada time, to do battle for the world's championship. At this time the huge arena was densely crowded. Probably 18,000 persons were present, while outside 15,000 more clamoured vainly for admission. Johnson had a black-and-white bathrobe round his broad shoulders; he seemed well pleased, and the smile, showing his six golden teeth, extended almost from ear to ear. Jeffries, as he stepped into the ring, stamped heavily, testing the platform. He seemed satisfied, and then found time to gaze curiously and unmoved on the big audience ranged in ascending tiers on four sides. The white champion wore a grey business suit and grey golf cap, of which he divested himself in the presence of the spectators, revealing a natty pair of purple tights.

The first three rounds favoured Jeffries, who sent three big punches into Johnson's ribs, and the crowd went wildly enthusiastic. In the fourth round Jeffries rushed Johnson to the ropes and punched him on the nose, securing first blood.

In the fifth round Jeffries was cut under the mouth and eye. Both men gave and received heavy punishment.

Johnson, in the sixth round, sent a terrific left to Jeffries' right eye, almost completely closing it. Johnson taunted and laughed at Jeffries, and seemed increasingly confident. It was Johnson's round entirely, and in the interval Jeffries' seconds tried to patch the injured eye.

In the seventh round Jeffries' eye seemed to worry him a great deal, and the round ended with Johnson laughing merrily. Jeffries in the seventh round sent a heavy left to Johnson's chin, who still smiled, and retorted by sending two strong lefts to the face, making Jeffries' bad eye still worse. It was again Johnson's round.

Johnson showed beautiful defensive work in the eighth round. The eighth round was Johnson's by a slight margin.

In the ninth round Johnson seemed exceptionally cool. During a clinch he nodded to a friend in the crowd and laughed outright. Jeffries' eye bled freely, and caused his friends much anxiety. Johnson sent a left to the mouth, and received a hard right on the body, both men clinching at the bell. It was Jeffries' round by a considerable margin.

The tenth round found Johnson boxing hard, but

England play first game at new stadium

By Major Philip Trevor at Twickenham
PUBLISHED MONDAY 11 JANUARY
England 11 pts; Wales 6

The thing has been done at last. An English XV have beaten the Welshmen, and beaten them fairly and squarely by play that was not merely worthy and respectable, but really dashing and clever.

On Saturday last I ventured to predict the success of England if only Adrian Stoop's bold finesse was in evidence; and the international match was only two seconds old when a most reassuring instance of it was forthcoming. Stoop caught the ball at kick-off, and very characteristically omitted to do the stereotyped thing. The orthodox person would have had him run a few yards and then with a neat punt find touch.

Stoop did the proper thing on this occasion – namely, the unexpected. Stoop is a great player and a great captain, and to him do we primarily owe the gaining of a victory which was badly needed. A dash, a swerve, and he was off, with the result that the Welshmen were subjected to a sudden attack. There was a scrummage, and then in a flash Stoop made an opening for J. G. G. Birkett, who showed his appreciation of it by running with fine strength and resolution. He gave his wingman, F. E. Chapman, a beautiful pass. Chapman dashed over the line and so, one minute after the start, England were three points ahead.

It was in the first 20 minutes that the Englishmen won the game, and well did they deserve that the bold and clever tactics of their captain should receive the best of all practical rewards. It is not, therefore, out of place to call attention to the very real value of early impressions and moral effect. There is no doubt that the Welsh backs were dazed by the suddenness and the fearlessness as well as by the strength and neatness of the Englishmen's attack. The Welsh pack as a whole was excellent, and its short rushes were only prevented from being long ones by their lucky opponents.

A crowd estimated at nearly 30,000 persons witnessed the match, and practically every one of them, as far as one could tell, had a good view of the game.

---

most of the blows seemed to lack steam. The tenth was Johnson's round, and ended with him smiling all over his face and winking at friends at the ringside.

In the 11th round Johnson's famous right upper-cut sent Jeffries' head back three times in rapid succession.

Jeffries now bled badly from nose and mouth. It was Johnson's round by a shade.

Jeffries' right eye in the 12th was almost closed, and the round ended largely in Johnson's favour. The 13th round found Jeffries wobbly, almost blind, and with his face covered with blood.

Johnson pursued his advantage to the uttermost in the 14th, and early in the 15th knocked out Jeffries, greatly to the consternation and disappointment of the vast majority of the spectators.

In anticipation of witnessing the greatest boxing match between heavyweights of the present generation, thousands of people left Reno before midday to find seats in the great wooden amphitheatre. The road leading thereto was thronged by all manner of vehicles and pedestrians of every nationality.

In view of the threats to shoot Johnson if he won, all suspicious characters – and we have a varied selection of crooks here from all parts – were searched before entering the arena, and any firearms found were impounded. Flasks for whisky or other spirit, blackjacks and knuckledusters were also detained.

Jeffries, who was attended by doctors as he sat in his corner, was led to his dressing room. The ring was then completely dismantled by souvenir hunters.

Jim Jeffries (inset above left) was 'the great white hope' in the quest to dethrone black heavyweight Jack Johnson, seen here training with his opponent and Jeffries' manager, Sam Berger (left of car).

SPORT IN BRIEF

FOOTBALL
A football ground at Warwick Road, Old Trafford, is opened on 19 February. Manchester United's new home, complete with billiard room, gymnasium and tip-up seats, has a capacity of 80,000.

GOLF
Large crowds gather to see woman golfer Cecil Leitch play former Open champion Harold Hilton over two rounds at Walton Heath, followed by a further two rounds at Sunningdale. Hilton has to give half a stroke per hole, and Leitch wins at the 71st. She has played the last 17 holes in 77 strokes, Hilton in 75.

CRICKET
The England tour of South Africa ends with a 3–2 victory for the South Africans, despite a series batting average of 67.37 by English batsman Jack Hobbs. For South Africa, Bert Vogler takes 36 wickets and Aubrey Faulkner 29, while the English underarm bowler George Simpson-Hayward takes 23 wickets.

FOOTBALL
Dundee win the Scottish Cup for the first time. Facing Clyde in the final, they are 2–0 down seven minutes from the whistle, but John Hunter and Johnny Langland score to force a replay. The first replay ends goalless; in a further replay Dundee beat Clyde 2–1.

RUGBY UNION
Following their first win against Wales since 1898 (see main text), England draw 0–0 with Ireland, defeat France and Scotland 11–3 and 14–5, and clinch the newly enlarged Five Nations championship. It is England's first title since 1892.

1911

Wales take rugby championship

By Major Philip Trevor
PUBLISHED MONDAY 13 MARCH
Wales 16 pts; Ireland 0

In the presence of a huge crowd at Cardiff, Wales beat Ireland on Saturday last by 3 goals, one a penalty goal, and a try to nothing. To say that the actual crowd was a record one is to understate the case. Play was advertised to begin at half-past three, and at a quarter to three the order was given to close the gates. This very necessary proceeding led to much wall climbing, and many hundreds obtained admittance to the ground in this way, though they did not all get a sight of the game as a reward for their enterprise. Surrounding trees were also well patronised, while the sloping roof of the cricket pavilion had no perils for a number of enthusiasts.

At three o'clock the Irish team, ready dressed for play, in vain clamoured for admittance, first at one and then at another entrance. The police were unable to assist them or to advise; nor could they, of course, answer the rather pertinent inquiry of one of Erin's most stalwart forwards, 'What sort of a game will ye have, if ye don't let us in?' The team finally found salvation via the back door of the County Club – thanks to the timely intervention of the Welsh honorary secretary, Mr Rees.

It was not an especially attractive game from the spectacular point of view which this huge concourse of people witnessed, nor was the issue ever in any real doubt. Only in one particular did the Irishmen excel. The rushes of their forwards when they did come were quite up to the best Irish standard, but these were only seen at the rarest intervals, and they were unsupported by any combined attack on the part of the Irish backs. In tackling and in kicking there was little or nothing to choose between the two teams, but in all other respects the Welshmen were clearly superior.

Wales thus regain the championship, which they lost last year to England, and our English team alone in the season have given the champions a fright.

MILESTONES

The overlapping grip that is now used by most leading golfers was invented by a Scotsman, Johnny Laidlaw. It was demonstrated to a wider public by Harry Vardon; it is still often known as the 'Vardon grip'.

Superb display of batting by Fry

PUBLISHED SATURDAY 12 AUGUST

Yesterday's cricket at Southampton was rendered noteworthy by a superb display of batting on the part of C. B. Fry, who followed up his two hundreds earlier in the week against Kent by putting together a score of 258 not out. This is his highest score in first-class cricket. Thanks almost entirely to him, Hampshire increased their overnight score of 57 for one wicket to 594 for six, and then, on the drawing of stumps, they declared the inning closed. Gloucestershire therefore will go in again today no fewer than 277 runs behind.

Fry began his wonderful innings when the third wicket went down at 96, and altogether he was batting five hours and a quarter. He scored his first 100 in two hours and a half, reached 200 in another hour and fifty minutes, and obtained the odd 58 in 55 minutes, thus increasing his pace as he progressed. All this time he maintained such mastery over the attack that he gave only two chances, the first not until he had made 220.

Fry's cricket, therefore, was practically faultless, and from the outset he played with an ease and confidence that was delightful. As usual with him, powerful and well-timed driving brought him the majority of his runs, but his leg-side strokes were beautifully executed, and at times he cut well. Among his hits were 34 fours.

Vardon and Massy play off for Open title

PUBLISHED SATURDAY 1 JULY

The tie for the Open championship between Harry Vardon and Arnaud Massy was played off at Sandwich yesterday, when the Totteridge man gained a brilliant victory, completing the 36 holes in ten strokes fewer than his opponent.

Vardon established a very useful advantage of five strokes on the morning round, and if only he could have putted more consistently he would probably have been even further ahead. His long game was nearly perfect, for he almost invariably kept the true line, and in this department it is hardly too much to say that he outclassed his opponent. There was, however, a different story to tell when it came to the short game, for on the greens Vardon was strangely inconsistent. Over and over again the approach shots left him with an advantage, but he was frequently short with his run-up putts, and Massy more than once was enabled to retrieve the position owing to Vardon's deficiencies in putting. As an instance, it may be mentioned that Massy

was bunkered off his drive at the 12th hole, and had to play a difficult shot on to the green, yet he secured a five, the same score as Vardon's, owing to the latter missing a putt of less than a yard. That was one phase of Vardon's putting; but in proof of the inconsistency referred to above, he sank a putt of two yards at the 11th hole, one of ten feet at the 13th, and a beauty of fully five yards at the long 14th, this last giving him a perfect four at a hole which measured 505 yards in length.

Both Massy and Vardon went out in an average of fours, but the Channel Islander had established a lead of two strokes when the 14th hole was played, and this advantage he increased to five at the 17th, where Massy was bunkered and otherwise in trouble. Striking a stone in playing out, Massy sent his ball into the long grass. He was then short with his approach, and, missing a holeable putt, registered a seven. Vardon now had a five-stroke lead, which he held at the end of the round.

On restarting Massy pulled his second to the first hole, and Vardon added a stroke to his advantage. Weak putting caused Vardon to lose a stroke at each of the next two holes, but a splendid shot enabled him to get a fine three at the fourth, and Massy, who was short with his second and erratic in his putting, lost the two strokes he had regained. Massy now began to hook his long shots badly, and at the turn was seven strokes behind; whilst at the 14th Vardon had the commanding lead of it.

The Frenchman was not yet done with, however, for sinking a five yards' putt, he reclaimed a stroke at the 15th, but he lost it at the 16th where Vardon put his tee shot a couple of yards from the pin and holed his for two. Massy again found trouble at the 17th and, realising the hopelessness of his task, picked up his ball and shook hands with Vardon, who thus became champion. This was Vardon's fifth victory, and he and James Braid are the only men who have won it more than four times.

Vardon demonstrating his fine, relaxed swing en route to a fifth British Open title.

De Rosier sets new records at Brooklands

PUBLISHED MONDAY 10 JULY

Jake de Rosier, the American motor cyclist, riding a seven-hp twin Indian at Brooklands on Saturday, successfully attacked the world's records for the flying kilometre, mile, and five miles.

Favoured by almost ideal conditions, he went off at a very fast pace, and covered the distances in $26\frac{1}{5}$ sec for the kilometre, $41\frac{1}{5}$ sec for the mile and 3 min 43 sec for the five miles.

The meeting concluded with the gymkhana events. In one, motor bicycles were placed on a line, with the driving belts removed. At the pistol, competitors 100 yards away ran with the belts, fitted them to the machines, and drove to the finishing line. The first machine across was that of Cooper ($3\frac{1}{2}$-hp Bradbury), with Brittain ($3\frac{1}{2}$-hp Rudge) second.

The shortest distance of any race of the day was that of the 'organ-grinding' race, and necessarily so, for drivers had to propel their cars by means of the starting handle, the engine not being allowed to fire. This was won by Bray, who also carried off the engine-starting race, in which drivers had to run 100 yards to their cars, start the engine, and drive to the finishing line.

During the afternoon several of the Brooklands airmen were out on aeroplanes.

1912

Barry is sculling champion

By an old Blue
PUBLISHED WEDNESDAY 30 JULY

After yesterday's most sensational race, in which Ernest Barry gained a victory over Frank Arnst, the latter not completing the course, England can once more boast the possession of a sculling champion of the world after the lapse of 36 years.

The race was a supreme test of style versus strength, and style came out of the ordeal with flying colours. Barry's strong point is his superb watermanship, and this gave him his victory, for everything else was against him.

Giving away 28 lb in weight, he yet proved himself to possess the better pace, even with a strong wind dead against him, whilst his opponent was able to seek a certain amount of shelter under the Surrey shore, for he had won the toss and had chosen, on the advice of his trainer, 'Bossy' Phelps, that side, which always must be the better one, except on the very rare occasions when there is a strong wind from the northeast.

After Barry's victory, the most sensational thing in the race was the magnificent final spurt of the old champion, which was so great an effort as to make defeat honourable, but which so completely used up all his remaining strength that he ceased rowing 100 yards or so from the finish. In this spurt he must have made up nearly three lengths, getting up to within two lengths of Barry, although he had the outside station and the rougher water. He would have had to be more than human to have kept up his spurt right to the finish.

Arnst's records of victories held everyone in awe, and after it had become known that Arnst had won the toss and taken the Surrey shore, most of the critics held that the Englishman's chance had gone. That we were all wrong the race of a lifetime proved.

Ernest Barry won the world professional title a total of five times: in 1912–15 and again in 1920.

MILESTONES

A change in the laws of football in 1912 meant that goalkeepers could no longer handle the ball outside the penalty area. Previously they had been allowed to pick the ball up anywhere in their own half.

Two hat tricks in triangular Test series

PUBLISHED WEDNESDAY 29 MAY

A most peculiar record was set up yesterday at Manchester when T. J. Matthews twice did the 'hat trick' in the Test match. Probably such a performance will never be seen again. Matthews is one of the change bowlers of the Australian team. He is a slow medium leg-breaker who has effective command of a fast ball, and he is also a very useful batsman. He will certainly have good reason to remember his first Test match. Put on for the second time when G. A. Faulkner looked extremely like saving the follow-on, he got rid of R. Beaumont, S. J. Pegler and T. A. Ward with successive deliveries, and so brought the innings to a dramatic end.

Later, in the South African second innings, Matthews did his hat trick a second time, his victims on this occasion being H. W. Taylor, R. O. Schwarz and T. A. Ward. It was largely due to Matthews that the Australians gained so easy a victory. From start to finish they were the better side. For the cricket played by the South Africans it would be idle to make excuses.

Australia won by an innings and 88 runs.

Kelleway scores a century for Australia against South Africa at Old Trafford in the triangular Test series. England won the series, but rain marred the experiment, and it has not been repeated.

Victory for Boillot in Grand Prix

From our motoring correspondent
DIEPPE, WEDNESDAY 27 JUNE

'A marvellous triumph of endurance' was the universal verdict of all those who saw Georges Boillot, on the 200-hp Peugeot, win the Grand Prix motor race at Dieppe today. There were, however, many expressions of sympathy with Bruce-Brown and Wagner, driving Fiat cars, whom misfortune robbed of the laurels of victory. The former, when leading, was disqualified for taking in petrol away from the control, and the latter finished second, 13 minutes six seconds behind the winner. The race proved the brilliant qualities of the British motor cars, small in size as compared with the big racing machines, yet only a little slower.

At six o'clock this morning 22 cars out of the 27 left in the race from the preceding day came to the starting-line. Of these, nine were British cars – three Sunbeams, three Arrol-Johnstons, two Vauxhalls and one Calthorpe. One German car, the Mathis, one Belgian, the six-cylinder Excelsior, and the two Italian Fiats were left with the nine English cars to battle for the spoils with the nine remaining French vehicles. The cars had to fill up with oil and petrol and make any adjustments or tyre changes that might be necessary before proceeding on their 450-miles journey, for all these duties were counted as part of the running time.

Great excitement was shown by the spectators when Boillot took the lead. Their spirits were damped when Wagner began slowly but surely to creep up nearer to the then leader. Still Boillot drove excellently, and the Peugeot kept him ahead to the last. On the running times the little British cars were beating all the big ones, besides the competitors in their own class.

For the 906 miles Boillot's average speed was $68\frac{1}{2}$ miles per hour.

World's greatest athlete competes at Games

From our special correspondent
STOCKHOLM, SATURDAY 6 JULY

Again today the Games were greatly favoured by the weather. The opening hour found the competitors for the decathlon ready for action.

This last competition is an all-round proficiency test. It is of a more exacting character than the single-handed pentathlon, which was decided in favour of the American-Indian, Jim Thorpe. He figures here again. The Americans are enthusiastic about him, as the greatest athlete the world over. High- and long-jumping, javelin- and discus-throwing, a run of 100 yards or one mile, all come alike to him. We saw the tenacity of his temperament most practically the other day when he plodded on and on, though in a half-fainting condition long before the end, to take second place to the world-beating Hannes Kolehmainen in the 10,000-m run.

Gold stars: South African Rudolph Lewis, winner of the 200-mile cycling road-race (above), and the phenomenal all-rounder, the Native-American star Jim Thorpe (below and right).

From our special correspondent
STOCKHOLM, MONDAY 8 JULY

Today the story of the fifth Olympic Games revived comes to a full stop. Its opening chapters were enticing enough to compel one to go through the whole. Never, surely, have the Olympiads, ancient or modern, been enacted under more glowing skies. Stockholm has indeed been well favoured.

Though the morning programme is but a scanty one, with only the decathlon rivals undertaking their pole-jump test, the public attendance is quite good. It is as nothing, however, compared with the mass of humanity which flooded the arena and the amphitheatre last night. After the flush of excitement induced by the marathon race, with its establishment of a principle that the South Africans possess lasting powers second to none, the evening was devoted to a sort of anticlimax.

The observed of all observers was the marathon winner, K. McArthur, happy and smiling, with a ready reply to any question addressed to him about the nature of the task he had so well come through. 'It is no kind of course for a big man,' said the hero of the day. He was making reference to his own physical conformation.

Standing nearly 6 ft in height and weighing nearly 12 st in running attire, he is indeed a big man among the distance runners of the day.

The closing scenes in the stadium today call for the decision of the decathlon. There was left but the 1,500-m race among the ardent all-rounders who have been at the decathlon these past two days.

Three poor mile heats of the decathlon, each serving to attract the sympathies of the crowd to the two successful Swedish athletes figuring in them, witness the due completion of the Games within the stadium. They leave America head of the poll, with Sweden second and England third. The concluding scenes mark the triumph of the American-Indian Thorpe, who, by winning the decathlon, in addition to the pentathlon, stamps himself as a proficient, all-round athlete.

SPORT IN BRIEF

HORSE RACING
Tagalie is the first horse ever to win the 1,000 Guineas and the Derby. Two days after the Derby she runs again, in the Oaks, but is beaten.

FOOTBALL
England retain their Olympic title in Stockholm when they beat Denmark 4–2 in the final.

OLYMPICS
Six months after his triumph in the Olympic Games (see main text), Jim Thorpe is stripped of his medals. His crime was to receive payment for playing in a minor league baseball game three years ago, which is in contravention of the amateur code. Thorpe is finally pardoned, and his medals returned to his family in 1983, 30 years after his death.

RUGBY UNION
Billy Millar captains South Africa on a tour of the British Isles. The team includes three brothers: Freddie, Dick and John Luyt. The Springboks beat Scotland 16–0, Ireland by a record 38–0 and Wales 3–0 before meeting England in January 1913.

CRICKET
The MCC, captained by Lord Hawke, tour Argentina and play three games against a representative Argentinian XI. These are the first first-class matches to be played in Argentina. When they return in April the MCC players report that the tour has been a sporting and social success, and that the quality of cricket was much higher than they had expected.

YACHTING
The huge gilded eagle from the stern of the famous yacht *America* is returned to the New York Yacht Club. It was removed from the boat when it was being repaired in Hampshire in 1854, and has hung for many years in front of the Eagle Hotel on the Isle of Wight.

1912

1913

Golf championship of the United States

From our special correspondent
BROOKLINE, SUNDAY 21 SEPTEMBER

After one of the most exciting contests recorded in the history of golf, Mr Francis Ouimet, the young Boston amateur, won the Open championship of the United States from the English professionals, Harry Vardon and Ted Ray, on Saturday.

At the close of the four 18-hole rounds played on Thursday and Friday, the three men reached a tie with 304 strokes each. A play-off was therefore necessary, and this took place over 18 holes in the morning on Saturday.

Halfway through there was nothing in it, each man at the ninth hole having a card of 38.

At the tenth hole Ouimet was one stroke to the good over Vardon, and at the 12th was two to the good, but at the 13th Vardon regained one.

By wonderful putting, the American increased his lead, and won with five strokes to spare over Vardon and six over Ray.

Mr Ouimet **(above left)** establishes a record for the American Open championship, as he is the first amateur to win it.

Mr Francis Ouimet's victory over two of the greatest living professional golfers, at Brookline yesterday, is the talk of the whole country today. As Ray, in a generous speech at the subsequent presentation proceedings, observed, Mr Ouimet played better golf than anybody else, and earned his victory. Vardon's comment was, 'We were fairly and squarely beaten.'

It was no fluke. The boy – he is not yet 21 – is the golfing miracle of the New World and, I believe, is quite capable of winning the British Open championship or defeating any group of players that either hemisphere could array against him. He seems to have every shot in his locker. He is without exception the straightest driver and most accurate putter I have ever seen, and he rejoices in a brave, stout heart and nerves of steel. The boy's fame and fortune are now assured.

Boillot wins the motor Grand Prix

From our motoring correspondent
AMIENS, SATURDAY 12 JULY

After a most exciting race Georges Boillot won the motor Grand Prix over the Picardy circuit, near Amiens, on a Peugeot car, thus repeating his success twelve months ago. Boillot thus shares with another famous French driver, Léon Théry, of Gordon Bennett Cup fame, the honour and glory of being the holder twice in succession, on the same make of car, of the Blue Riband of the motor-racing world.

This year the Grand Prix was a remarkable run in many ways. The circuit was shorter than usual and so had to be covered 29 times to make the full distance of 569 miles. Another remarkable point was the low consumption of tyres. Boillot and the other Peugeot drivers used Pirelli tyres, and the winner only changed twice in the race. Jules Goux, the second in the race, another Peugeot driver, only changed one tyre throughout.

The shortage of practice on their racing cars led many to expect accidents to the drivers. Fortunately no serious ones did occur, but unfortunately a spectator was killed. Shortly before two pm Boillot finished amid the cheers of the crowd, who shouldered him to the pavilion.

Boillot drives to a second successive grand prix victory at Moreuil near Amiens, at an average speed of 72.29 miles per hour.

South Africa rugby union team remain unbeaten on tour

By Major Philip Trevor
PUBLISHED MONDAY 6 JANUARY
England 3 pts; South Africa 9

The fine place kicking of Douglas Morkel, who captained the winning side, enabled South Africa to beat England at Twickenham on Saturday by nine points to three. Each side got an unconverted try, and it was left to Morkel to win the match for the South Africans by scoring a couple of penalty goals. In each case the kick was a very fine one, the first being rather the better.

The match, in spite of its intense excitement, was rather disappointing as an exhibition of the game in its most modern form. The turf was firm, the ball dry. It was a day for cleverness in combination. But in neither attack was exact combination in evidence. It was hard, clean football that was played.

The tackling of both teams was unerring, indeed, magnificent; there was effective spoiling, splendid footwork by the English forwards; long kicking and fast running by individual members of the South African team. It was a strong, straightforward game that we saw – but it was without guile.

By defeating England on Saturday they broke two records. They are the first Colonial side to beat all four countries of the Union, and they are also the first side to bring disaster at Twickenham to an England XV in an international match.

The huge crowd had plenty of time to discuss what they had seen, for they had to crawl (with many halts) to the railway station. It took, on the average, some 45 minutes to cover half a mile or so. The popularity of rugby football will be seriously endangered if no drastic step is taken to deal with the congestion of traffic in the single approach to the headquarter ground. One can only hope there will not be a bad accident – caused, say, by a restive horse or a careless chauffeur – that will force definite action to be taken.

DID YOU KNOW?

In the 1912–13 League season, every player who turned out for Morton, the Scottish League club, scored a goal, including the goalkeeper, who scored from the penalty spot.

SPORT IN BRIEF

FOOTBALL

Having lost to Aston Villa in the FA Cup final, Sunderland beat Bolton 3–1 to win the League. The prospects for Sunderland at the beginning of the season had not looked promising; they lost five of their first seven matches and drew two.

HORSE RACING

Emily Davison, the suffragette who threw herself under the king's horse on Derby day (see main text), dies on 8 June from her injuries.

RUGBY UNION

W. J. A. 'Dave' Davies makes his debut for England against South Africa in their 9–3 defeat by the Springboks (see main text). It is the only time Davies is on the losing side in his 22 international appearances,

CRICKET

Sydney Barnes, one of the greatest bowlers of his or any other era, takes an unsurpassed record 49 wickets in four Test matches in South Africa, 1913–14, at an average of 10.93. In the second Test in Johannesburg he takes eight for 56 and nine for 103 (17 for 159), which is only bettered by Jim Laker in 1956.

HORSE RACING

In September Tetrarch wins his sixth race, the Champion Breeders' Foal Stakes. Descended from the Byerley Turk, a 17th-century horse that was ridden in the Battle of the Boyne, Tetrarch is known as the 'Spotted Wonder'. Although the horse only runs this year, he wins all seven of his races, and is believed to be one of the fastest horses of all time.

FOOTBALL

Falkirk and Raith Rovers both appear in their first Scottish FA Cup final. Falkirk win the match 2–0.

Suffragette brings down King's horse in the Derby

By 'Hotspur'

PUBLISHED THURSDAY 5 JUNE

The most unsatisfactory, sensational, and lamentable Derby in the history of the race was added to the records at Epsom yesterday. The horse to finish first was the favourite, Mr C. Bower Ismay's Craganour. He passed the judge a head in front of the extreme outsider Aboyeur.

Half a mile from the finish a dreadful thing had happened. As the horses were swinging at a tremendous pace round Tattenham Corner, a woman by deliberate design flung herself at Anmer, the horse carrying the colours of His Majesty the King, who, with Her Majesty, was looking on. Horse and rider were brought down heavily, the jockey, Herbert Jones, being flung clear, but striking the hard ground with his head. He lay prostrate. So, too, did the wretched creature who had caused the terrible fall, while the horse rose again and galloped after the receding horses.

Emily Davison lies fatally injured, left of Anmer and jockey Herbert Jones.

Let me return to the finish of the race. As Craganour's number was hoisted in the frame there was plenty of cheering, and Mr Ismay went out to meet his horse. Suddenly there occurred a distinct lull in the buzz of conversation. At the end of half an hour of intolerable suspense, a statement was issued by the Stewards. They found that Craganour did not keep a straight course, having bumped and bored the second horse; they disqualified Craganour and awarded the race to Aboyeur. The greatest sensation was caused. A raging hot favourite, a popular horse with the people, had won the Derby at 6 to 4 against; here he was deprived of honour and, instead, the one enthroned in his place was an animal whose starting price was 100 to 1. What a Derby to go into history!

1914

Brookes victorious at Wimbledon

By A. Wallis Myers
WIMBLEDON, WEDNESDAY 2 JULY

Norman Brookes won King George's Cup on the centre court today, but the Australian did not achieve his victory until he had fought one of the most exciting five-set finals ever witnessed at Wimbledon. Two sets down and 5–4 against him in the third set, Otto Froitzheim, by dint of his stamina and strategic genius, made so gallant a rally that, an hour later, he was leading in the fifth set, apparently the fresher of the two.

The final set was begun amid universal excitement – every stroke in it was felt to be critical. Brookes quickly showed that he was going to last by reassuming his close-in position. Brookes went ahead at 4–3, some of the fastest and keenest play in the whole match being seen in this game. A marvellous drop volley by Brookes closed it. In front at 5–4 and 6–5, Brookes failed to win Froitzheim's service game. Admirably judged cross-drives characterised the German's play. In the 14th game, when 30–15, Froitzheim experienced a bit of grievously bad luck – a winner of his, down the far sideline, was given out. He battled on bravely. Brookes won three fine aces by forehand forcing shots, and after four deuces he went out at 8–6 to the accompaniment of much applause.

The King attends his first FA Cup final

By our football correspondent
PUBLISHED MONDAY 27 APRIL
Burnley 1; Liverpool 0

We who take our football seriously will best remember this year's final tie of the Football Association Cup competition, which was played on Saturday at Crystal Palace between Burnley and Liverpool, because of the presence of the King. In the matter of play the match was not a great one; there was not that sharp distinctiveness about it that we had hoped for; the players were obviously affected by the occasion; the majority of them were unable to be their usual, clever, everyday selves; their football was more of a helter-skelter than a brilliant exposition of a great game. What appealed to the average mind most was the wonderful setting given to the match. For life and colour it was unexampled; and in this respect it was the most remarkable football final I have ever seen.

Only the Burnley man could have squeezed out of the match real joy. For Burnley won. A goal by Freeman, their centre forward, scored when the second half was some 12 minutes old, decided the match. It was a great shot, typical of Freeman, for it came in a way altogether unexpected and like lightning. It told of the opportunist, for when Freeman had the ball sent over to him from the right wing he did not seek to make it dead. It was all life when he got his right foot to it, and with a flick he sent it into the corner of the net with such rapidity that I am sure that even Kenneth Campbell, keenly alert though he always is and gifted with a rare power of anticipation,

was totally unprepared. Freeman is not an uncommonly clever and designing centre, but, unlike the majority of modern forwards, who are much given to over-elaboration, he is an eminently practical footballer in that he is not afraid to shoot from any position.

The halfback of the match was Tommy Boyle, the Burnley captain. He was here, there, and everywhere; he did the work of three men. He never lost heart, and was much admired for his great pluck in returning to the field in the second half after being rather badly hurt. Boyle was the pivot of the Burnley side in a strictly literal sense, and had his forwards responded to his efforts with greater readiness they must have won more distinctly than they did. He was a proud man indeed when the King handed him the cup.

Never has there been such a display of unbounded enthusiasm at the close of a final tie before as when the King gave to Boyle the Cup which had brought people from everywhere. And then when the massed bands played the National Anthem, the crowd, as one mighty choir, sang 'God Save the King', we were made certain that there is nothing in the realm of sport like a Cup final day at the Crystal Palace.

The King arrives at the pavilion (right) before the last Cup final match to be staged at the Crystal Palace ground (below). More than 72,000 people attended the game.

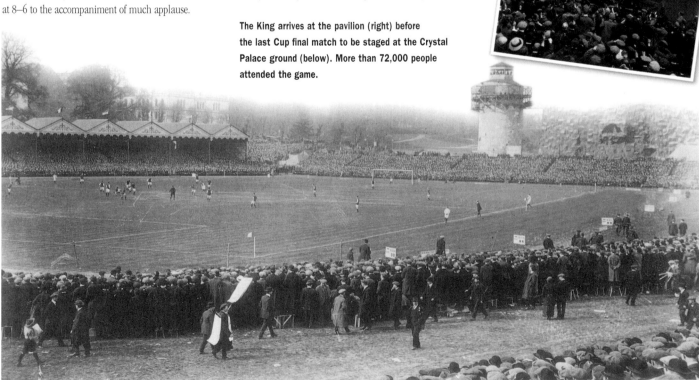

Miss Cecil Leitch is Ladies' Golf champion

PUBLISHED SATURDAY 16 MAY

Miss Cecil Leitch **(right)** won the Ladies' Golf championship at Hunstanton yesterday. She beat Miss Gladys Ravenscroft by two and one. It was a great, a stirring and exciting, final, not because of the brilliancy or the exceptional standard of play, but because temperament entered so largely into it. It has long been agreed that Miss Cecil Leitch, one of five golfing sisters, had all the qualifications to beat everybody. She is a natural golfer; her skill is undoubted, her strength obvious. At some time or other she has sailed triumphantly through many events in which our greatest lady golfers have competed, but not until yesterday has she so disciplined herself as to come near her normal game. And even yesterday, when in the final round, which, for the first time, was over 36 holes, she came perilously near making a complete surrender to her highly strung nature. It was indeed touch and go.

However, she won, and so hearty congratulations to our new champion lady golfer.

Vardon's great golf at Prestwick

By Henry Leach

PRESTWICK, FRIDAY 19 JUNE

It was not until nearly seven o'clock tonight that everybody was certain as to who was to be Open champion of the year. Arnaud Massy, of France, was the last possible danger to Harry Vardon, and when he failed it was established that the man who is recognised as the greatest golfer of modern times, and the most perfect stylist, became the champion of the game for the sixth time. The fact that Vardon and Taylor were drawn together today added greatly to the popular interest of the proceedings. That it was good for the players themselves is a very open question. Vardon began today with a lead of a couple of strokes over the great Devonian. It might well be that they would kill each other in their efforts to win, and once or twice in the course of the game it looked as though this would be the case.

Going out in the morning, Vardon appeared to have the victory safe. Taylor was getting into all kinds of

trouble. Vardon, on the other hand, played delightful golf. His brassie shot at the ninth, for instance, was one of the finest strokes played in the championship. The hole is over 400 yards in length. Vardon played a 'peach' of a brassie to within three yards of the pin. He only just missed his putt for a three. He was out in 37 to Taylor's 38. After this there was a great change. Vardon developed a tendency to pull his shots through the green. Taylor appeared to have run into his best form, and finished with an excellent 74. Vardon was four strokes worse, so that at this stage his two strokes' lead was converted into a two-stroke deficit. No wonder that excitement was in the air when the afternoon round began. From tee to green the spectators were densely packed. The excitement seemed to affect the players, too, judging by their form.

Clearly it was a case of who would crack first. As it happened it was Taylor. He struggled gallantly, as Taylor always does when he is in a tight corner, but the fates and his golf were against him. He took 44 to reach the turn; Vardon, in spite of his initial six, was out in 39. At this point, therefore, the Channel Islander had not only drawn level, but actually led by two strokes, with nine to play. It was all over now. Try as he might Taylor could not get on terms with his opponent. Except that he missed a holeable putt, Vardon cannot be said to have made a serious mistake on the homeward journey. He finished in 78, which left him a winner with 306. Taylor took 83. This gave him second place with 309. Thus Vardon gained his sixth victory. It was a great victory, and one that was worthy of a great golfer.

DID YOU KNOW?

In 1914, on the outbreak of war, the Footballers' Battalion was formed with its headquarters at the Richmond Athletic Ground. The Battalion was designated as the 17th Service Battalion of the Middlesex Regiment.

SPORT IN BRIEF

RUGBY LEAGUE
Huddersfield's 'prince of centres', Harold Wagstaff, leads Great Britain in a tour of Australia. In the third Test on 4 July the British team are reduced through injuries to ten men for the final half-hour, but they still win the match 14–6. The list of casualties leads the game to be dubbed the 'Rorke's Drift' Test, after the battle in which 120 British soldiers faced thousands of Zulu warriors.

RUGBY UNION
England beat France 39–13 at the Parc des Princes on 13 April. They have already beaten Ireland 17–12, Scotland 16–15 and Wales 10–9, and they take the Grand Slam title for the second year in succession.

LAWN TENNIS
Dorothea Lambert Chambers (née Douglass) wins her seventh Wimbledon singles title. She has won the Wimbledon women's doubles title twice (in 1903 and 1907), and the mixed doubles three times (in 1906, 1908 and 1910). She has also won the All-England women's doubles and mixed doubles badminton titles, and has played hockey for Middlesex.

MOTOR RACING
In the French Grand Prix held in Lyons on 4 July, six days after the assassination of Archduke Ferdinand, German driver Christian Lautenschlager wins his sixth title, his second in a Mercedes. In a thrilling race, Lautenschlager takes the lead from Georges Boillot on the 18th of 20 laps. Germans Louis Wagner and Otto Salzer take second and third places, also in Mercedes; Jules Goux is fourth in a Peugeot. The French crowd do not applaud the German winners; the two countries will be at war within a month.

1914–1918

By Iain Zaczek

The terrible carnage of the Great War cast a long shadow over the sporting world. In most participating countries, professional sport was suspended for the duration of hostilities, as athletes went to try their mettle in the most dangerous arena of all.

International fixtures were the first to go. The 'intercalated' Olympic Games, which should have been held in Athens in 1914, were soon called off and the next full Olympics, scheduled for Berlin in 1916, never took place. Similarly, at the Wimbledon All-England Croquet and Lawn Tennis Club, the committee wasted no time in severing its ties with the enemy, symbolically removing German nationals from their list of honorary members.

Developments in domestic sport occurred more slowly. In Britain, as elsewhere, the true horror of the war was slow to sink in. Players and fans alike, it seemed, were convinced that the conflict would be a minor affair, and that it would do no harm to wait until the end of the season before volunteering their services. As the casualty lists began to mount, however, there was a growing public outcry against such an attitude. This mood was epitomised by a letter from W. G. Grace, which appeared in the *Sportsman* on 27 August 1914: 'The fighting on the Continent is very severe, and will probably be prolonged. I think the time has come when the county cricket season should be closed, for it is not fitting at a time like the present that able-bodied men should play and pleasure-seekers look on. I should like to see all cricketers set a good example and come to the aid of their country without delay.'

Grace's call was swiftly heeded. The cricket season was wound up speedily and the championship was awarded to Surrey, even though they still had two matches to play. The sorry circumstances of this victory overshadowed the brilliant contribution of Jack Hobbs, who had managed to amass 2,499 runs in just 42 innings. No more first-class games were held until May 1919, although a certain amount of league cricket continued in the North and the Midlands.

The traditional Eton–Harrow fixture was also retained, but instead of a full-length match at Lord's, a series of one-day matches was played at the schools themselves. In Australia, the winding-down process took a little longer, and the Sheffield Shield season was not finally abandoned until July 1915.

The football authorities were presented with a slightly different dilemma, as their season had only just begun. After consulting with the War Office, though, the FA decided to allow the League and Cup competitions to go ahead. In return, special efforts were made to boost recruitment to the armed services. On non-match days, football grounds were laid open to the War Office, for use as drill grounds or venues for recruiting rallies. At the rallies fans were urged to join one of the so-called 'Football Battalions' – the 17th, 23rd and 27th Middlesex Regiments. 'Do you want to be a Chelsea diehard?' enquired one of the posters. 'Then join the 17th Battalion of the Middlesex Regiment and follow the lead given by your favourite football players.'

Despite these measures, criticism mounted as the season wore on; the final fixtures were completed in a distinctly half-hearted fashion. Everton won the First Division title, while Sheffield United carried off the FA Cup after beating Chelsea 3–0. This match, which was staged at Old

(continued on page 42)

Below left: Jockey Steve Donoghue (in stripes) poses with his son Pat. Donoghue was one of the most popular figures of the age. He rode the 'wonder horse' Tetrarch in 1913, and in 1914 was champion jockey for the first time. He would go on to take the title a further five times in succession.
Below: The captains of Sheffield United and Chelsea shake hands before the 1915 'khaki' Cup final, won 3–0 by Sheffield.
Right: The 1914 Surrey side. Inspired by the magnificent Jack Hobbs, they won the county championship for the first time since 1899.

M.C.Bird.

Goarly

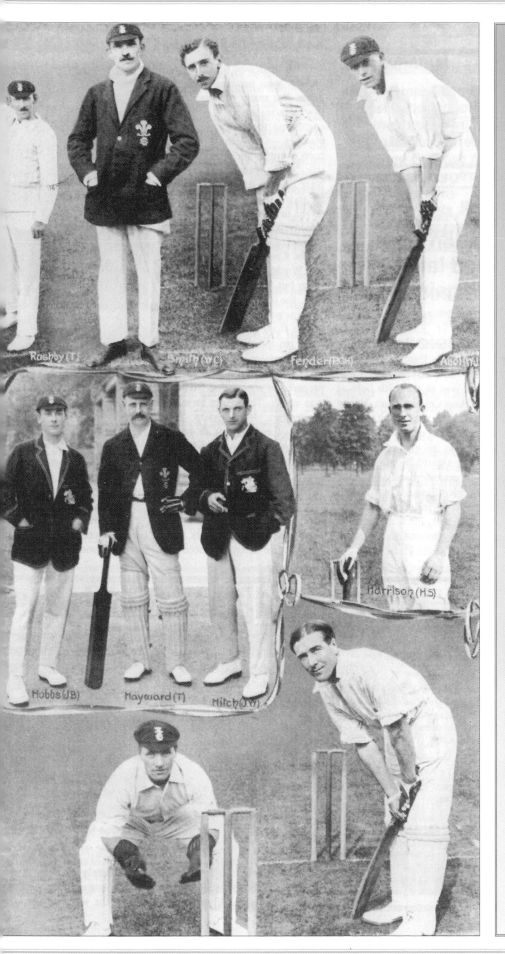

Rashby (T) Smith (WC) Fender (PGH) Abel (W)

Hobbs (JB) Hayward (T) Hitch (JW)

Harrison (HS)

SPORT IN BRIEF

RUGBY UNION

Ronald Poulton-Palmer (né Poulton) is killed in Belgium on 5 May 1915 while serving with the Berkshire regiment. An outstanding winger and centre, he scored a record four tries for England against France in last year's Five Nations championship.

FOOTBALL

The 'khaki' Cup final is held at Old Trafford in 1915. Many of the 50,000-strong crowd are in uniform. Sheffield United enjoy a 3–0 victory over Chelsea. Lord Derby, presenting the Cup, urges spectators to 'join with each other and play a sterner game for England'.

BOXING

In February 1916 Welshman Jimmy Wilde knocks out Joe Symonds to win the British flyweight title, then defeats Johnny Rosner to claim the world title. Weighing about 108 lb, and standing less than 5 ft 3 in tall, Wilde is one of the great British fighters. Between 1910 and 1923 he is involved in 145 contests, 141 of which he wins, retaining his world championship title until 1923. During the war, Wilde works as a physical education instructor at the military college at Sandhurst.

MOTOR RACING

Peugeot and Mercedes dominate racing in the United States, which continues until the US enters the war in April 1917. Dario Resta wins the 1915 Vanderbilt Cup and the American Grand Prize in a Peugeot; Howard Wilcox wins the 1916 Vanderbilt Cup, also in a Peugeot. The 1915 and 1916 Indianapolis 500 races go to Ralph de Palma in a Mercedes and Dario Resta in a Peugeot respectively.

1914–18

1914–1918

(continued from page 40)

Trafford on a murky April afternoon, soon became known as the 'khaki' Cup final, because of the number of servicemen watching from the terraces. Many of these troops already carried injuries from fighting in the front line; these reminders of war added to the subdued atmosphere of the occasion.

At the end of the season, professional football was dramatically scaled down. Leagues and clubs were still allowed to function, but they were barred from offering cups, medals or prizes. Players could no longer receive payment and matches had to be held on Saturday afternoons or public holidays, so that they did not interfere with war work.

The possibility that key matches might distract munitions workers was taken very seriously, especially after the production standards in some factories manufacturing explosive shells dropped alarmingly. In the wake of this scandal, some games were held behind locked doors.

In Scotland, the League continued as before, while in England it was broken down into three sections: the Lancashire Regional Tournament, the Midland Regional Tournament, and the London Combination. Players in these leagues were obliged to carry out war work during the week and, as they were also allowed to move freely between different clubs, the teams situated closest to munitions factories held a certain advantage. Many Arsenal players, for example, obtained work at the nearby Woolwich Arsenal, while Celtic's dominance of the Scottish League may have owed something to its proximity to the shipyards.

Shortages of manpower were not the only problem at this time. Many sporting facilities were requisitioned for use by the military. Surrey had to secure their county championship at Lord's, since the Oval had been commandeered at the outbreak of war, while Old Trafford's cricket ground was transformed into a military hospital. Dozens of golf courses were given over to farming, though efforts were made to preserve the greens, while the FA headquarters in London became a storehouse for one of the Football Battalions, packed to the gills with army kits and thousands of packets of cigarettes. Even the motor-roller at Wimbledon's tennis courts was removed for a time, until the Ministry of Munitions decided that its condition was unsatisfactory.

Racing was badly hit by the policy of requisitioning, which resulted in several of the Classics being run on substitute courses. When Epsom was taken over by the

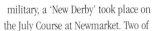

Above: the Royal Garrison Artillery Signalling Training School cricket team, based in Yorkshire, who played and won 14 games in the 1917 season.
Below left: Competitors from the No. 2 Officer Cadet Battalion run over the golf links at Coton in the inter-company cross-country race; and left: Cadet Guess crosses the finishing line, an easy winner for 'A' Company.

military, a 'New Derby' took place on the July Course at Newmarket. Two of these wartime Derbys were won by Steve Donoghue, the leading jockey of the day, who eventually clocked up a total of 14 Classic victories. Donoghue rode Pommern to a Derby victory in 1915, and Gay Crusader in 1917, both on the Newmarket course. Renamed versions of the Oaks (the 'New Oaks') and the St Leger (the 'September Stakes') were also run at Newmarket, although this was not the only available course. The 1915 Grand National was held at Aintree, where Lady Nelson became the first female owner to capture the coveted prize, but the next

FOOTBALL

In Scotland midweek football matches are cancelled during the war. On 21 April 1917, in a Saturday fixture, Glasgow Celtic finally lose – after an undefeated run of 62 matches – to Kilmarnock, 2–0 at home.

GOLF

In the United States Bobby Jones and Alexa Stirling (winner of the Women's Amateur title in 1916) team up with Perry Adair and Elaine Rosenthal (runner-up in the 1914 US Women's Amateur championship) to play charity events during the war. The foursome raise thousands of dollars for the Red Cross in their travelling displays.

FOOTBALL

The Lancashire and Midland regional winners compete for the wartime English League championship; ticket receipts are donated to the National Footballers' War Fund. Leeds City beat Stoke 2–0 and 0–1 for the 1918 title, while, after a goalless first leg, Nottingham Forest beat Everton 1–0 at Goodison to take the 1919 championship. Winners of the London Combination league are Chelsea in 1918 and Brentford in 1919.

HORSE RACING

Gainsborough, by winning the 1918 2,000 Guineas, Derby, and St Leger, takes the racing Triple Crown.

FOOTBALL

On the last day of the 1918 season, Rangers win the League title by one point from Celtic. Rangers are accused of making unfair use of well-known players who are stationed in Scotland during the war, and for whom they obtain 'temporary transfers'.

three races were staged at Gatwick. This preserved the Grand National's unbroken run of races since 1839, though the new venue was scarcely a success, largely because of its lack of proper training facilities.

As with other sports, racing became a target for public criticism. This reached a peak in 1917, when questions were raised in Parliament about the wisdom of producing high-grade oats for racehorses. Shortly afterwards, politicians imposed a ban on the sport, although this was soon lifted when the Jockey Club and the Bloodstock Breeders' Association complained that their very livelihoods were under threat.

These protests highlighted a problem that was common to much of the sporting world. With the loss of subscriptions, fewer games and dwindling gate receipts, a wide range of clubs and other organizations came close to bankruptcy. The FA's pre-war assets of £15,000 plummeted to less than £1,000 by 1918; the All-England Club at Wimbledon was rescued by the generosity of its president, Henry Wilson Fox; while Arsenal Football Club ended the war £60,000 in debt. The plight of overseas' bodies was equally bad. Melbourne Cricket Club was £3,000 in the red, while the Tasmanian Association was so poor that it could not afford to print its annual report.

On the front line

Within the armed forces, sport was used to maintain fitness and morale, whether on the front lines or in prison camps. Accordingly, Lancashire Cricket Club sent out a supply of kit to the notorious camp at Ruhleben. In return, they were delighted to receive a scorecard showing that the inmates had staged a Roses match (Lancashire v Yorkshire) to keep up their spirits.

Commonwealth troops also pursued sporting activities. In most New Zealand units, whether they were stationed in Egypt, France or Palestine, there was generally a core of young recruits who spent all their leisure time playing rugby. This enthusiasm paid dividends when they came to challenge for the King's Cup, an inter-services contest held at the end of the war. Competing against Britain, the Royal Air Force, the Australian Imperial Forces, the Canadian Expeditionary Force and the South African Forces, the New Zealand Services' team swept aside the opposition with ease, winning all but one of their matches.

The hostilities did not cause the same problems for all the Allies. Because of its huge resources and its late entry into the war (in March 1917), the United States suffered comparatively few disruptions to its sporting programme. On the contrary, it was able to make up ground in those fields where the Europeans had traditionally been predominant. Before the war, no American had ever won the men's singles or doubles title at Wimbledon, but in 1920 Bill Tilden would end the European and Commonwealth domination of the competition.

Paul Hayward

The changing face of sport

IN 1989 MANCHESTER UNITED CAME CLOSE TO BEING SOLD to a certain Michael Knighton for £10 million. Ten years later the same sum would have bought him half of Alan Shearer. Sport changed more in the Nineties than the previous nine decades of the century put together. The new religion, some called it. With the Millennium close, the Queen spoke glowingly to the Commonwealth about the social and moral value of games. Sport's conquest was complete.

> *Television and sport are really blood brothers, plotting in a perpetual huddle to create wall-to-ceiling action, an endless tape of scores running along the bottom of life's screen.*

Television is the 20th-century's dominant cultural force. But sport is not far behind. The two are really blood brothers, plotting in a perpetual huddle to create wall-to-ceiling action, an endless tape of scores running along the bottom of life's screen. 'There are no age, racial or cultural barriers to participation,' said the Queen, perhaps stretching the idealism a bit too far. 'It demonstrates the value of cooperation, team work and team spirit. It teaches the need to abide by rules and regulations; it emphasises the importance of self-control and how to take victory or defeat with good grace.'

At the start of the century a monarch might have spoken that way only about church-going or military service. But remove religion, ghettoise the arts and marginalise party politics and you create a void into which pop, consumerism and sport have rushed. Assisted by TV, its door-to-door salesman, sport has broken its way into just about every British home. As the century drew to its close, sport ceased to be regarded with suspicion by the intelligentsia ('war minus the shooting,' said Orwell), as well as those left-wing councils who had decreed that competition, even on the field of play, was inherently unhealthy.

It may appear that sport has been hijacked by business and TV executives and agents. One look at contemporary rugby union might encourage the casual observer to conclude that professionalism was the ruination of sport, that Corinthianism and the simple pleasures of playing sport for its own sake are dead. Yet a close look at the history of sport in this last century confirms that it is no more or less riven by avarice or corruption than it was in the supposedly honeyed age of C. B. Fry, the last of the great Corinthians, who played in 26 Tests for England, won an FA Cup winners' medal and held the world long-jump record.

Sport was included in school curriculums in 1906, and many of the structures of our modern sporting industries were constructed in that decade: baseball's World Series, grands prix and the Tour de France. The Professional Football Association and the Professional Golfers' Association were formed. It was the decade in which W. G. Grace hung up his bat and whiskers, and markets for betting on sport began to form. Tragedy and venality are recurring themes of the last 100 years. In 1902, 25 fans were killed when a wooden stand at Ibrox collapsed. In the Eighties the Heysel, Hillsborough and Bradford City disasters almost dispatched English football to the undertakers. Emily Davison threw herself under the King's horse in the 1913 Derby and was killed. The Chicago White Sox threw the 1919 World Series as part of a betting scam. White society was outraged when Jack Johnson became the first black heavyweight champion in 1910. Sport has never been an innocent utopian realm.

> *At no time was sport purer or less complicated than the rest of life. It was a reflection of society, not an escape from it.*

Inter-continental travel and mass communications turned sport from a localised into a global passion. The legend of Babe Ruth and Jack Dempsey travelled down the wires to create worldwide communities of shared passions. But at no time was sport purer or less complicated than the rest of life. It was a reflection of society, not an escape from it. In the 1930s, England's 'Bodyline' tour of Australia provoked widespread political controversy, and confirmed that cricket was not all about cucumber sandwiches on the village green. The sometimes brutal separation of winners from losers is seldom nice.

Politics have always shaded into sport, sometimes triumphantly for the latter. Hitler's attempt to turn the 1936 Olympics into a Nazi rally was confounded by Jesse Owens and the other ten black American athletes who won gold medals. Yet sometimes politics has won. The murder of 11 Israeli athletes by Palestinian gunmen at the 1972 Games in Munich destroyed the cherished notion that sport was sacred and so should be above the violent machinations of state. Twenty-five years later the Grand National was halted by a hoax bomb warning. The IRA had crossed another line. Aintree is a favourite haunt of the Irish and Liverpool a city with a distinctly green hue. Now there were no rules, and the metal grip of security tightened again round sport.

Sport has become so relentlessly dramatic, meticulously staged and accessible (and expensive), that the few who have resisted its charms must feel like non-believers stranded in the midst of a religious cult.

Drug abuse and cheating has increased in proportion to the rewards on offer but, again, are nothing new. Tommy Simpson died of a drug overdose during the Tour de France in 1967. In the Seventies the Soviet satellite countries in Eastern Europe turned steroid abuse into a state-sponsored industry. Those methods are thought by many to have taken up new residence in sections of Chinese sport. Athletics may never escape the legacy of Ben Johnson, whose yellow-eyed charge down the 100-m track in Seoul was the ultimate demonstration of drug-induced depravity in sport. There is evidence for believing that the war on drugs is unwinnable; but most agree that the war must still be fought.

For all the dispiriting evidence of duplicity and iniquity, the primary theme of sport this century has been the throwing up of glories at a rate which perhaps no other field of creative activity can match. Sport has become so relentlessly dramatic, meticulously staged and accessible (and expensive) that the few who have resisted its charms must feel like non-believers stranded in the midst of a religious cult.

All around there are signs of progress. South Africa emerging from apartheid to win the rugby World Cup was progress. All-seater football stadia are progress. The trick in the next century may be to exercise the democratic right not to buy when the spectacle before us is false. Nobody is forced to buy a Don King heavyweight fight. Nobody is forced to buy a Newcastle United shirt for £60. And nobody who doubts the veracity of the Olympic ideal in the age of drugs is compelled to buy into the four-yearly selling of the Games.

Television gave, and television will take away. Cable and satellite broadcasters are winning the struggle for the right to broadcast exclusively events that were previously open to all for the price of a TV licence. Pay-per-view football will surely supplant the current BSkyB deals with the football Premiership and the Football Association. Governing bodies such as the Rugby Football Union will set up their own TV stations to maintain control of their own rights and so maximise the amount of money that can be ratcheted out of their audience. This is one of the biggest changes of our times: the reclassification of sport as commodity, as produce.

Ali, Pelé, Nicklaus and Piggott are among the cultural icons of our age, conduits through which many of the themes of the century have flowed, and we have all stood enviously and admiringly in their glow.

But nobody who loves sport thought of Muhammad Ali or Pelé or Jack Nicklaus or Lester Piggott as commodities, though they all came to prominence in an age when sportsmen and -women became global celebrities trailing advertising and endorsement contracts that brought in more than the simple act of playing sport. These and many others are among the cultural icons of our age, conduits through which many of the themes of the century have flowed, and we have all stood enviously and admiringly in their glow. If this Century of Sport has a figure through which it can define itself, it is surely Ali, who, like sport itself, is both ruined and forever glorious.

1919

Victory for the ladies

By our golfing correspondent
PUBLISHED MONDAY 5 MAY

By the narrow margin of one point the ladies gained a meritorious victory over the gentlemen in the Test match at Worplesdon on Saturday. In the singles the ladies were one match to the good, while the four-ball foursomes were halved. The match was played under novel conditions, viz, the giving of distance as against strokes, and the handicapper was extremely liberal to the ladies. At the two long holes – over 520 yards in length – the forward tees were advanced as much as 100 yards, which enabled the ladies to tee up clear of the rough. Consequently the bunkers placed to catch erratic drives from the ordinary tees had no terrors; in fact, they ceased to exist as hazards. In my opinion, the concession of strokes rather than distance is the more equitable in games of this character.

A big crowd turned up to witness the match between the two champions, Miss Cecil Leitch and Mr Harold Hilton. This was the first time they had met since their famous 72-hole contest in 1910, when, receiving a half, Miss Leitch won by two and one.

Miss Leitch should have beaten Mr Hilton easily on Saturday, but, as it turned out, she had a desperate time to keep the game alive. But Miss Leitch is a born fighter, and she stuck gamely to her task to the very end. To be two down against an opponent like Mr Hilton is enough to crush the hopes of the best of players, but not so Miss Leitch, who played two grand holes to square the match on the last green. It was an exhilarating finish, and a sigh of relief went up from the crowd as she performed a tricky yard putt on the 18th for a four, as against Mr Hilton's five. Frankly Miss Leitch did not deserve to halve, for a sorrier exhibition of putting it is difficult to conceive. Of the other part of her game there is nothing but praise. Her driving was powerful in the extreme; her iron-play was that of the first-class professional.

MILESTONES

After complaints from spectators who could not pick out the leader in the Tour de France, the race's founder, Henri Desgrange, introduced the *'maillot jaune'* this year. Eugene Christophe was the first cyclist to wear the yellow jersey; the overall race winner was Firmin Lambot.

Jess Willard defeated by Jack Dempsey

PUBLISHED SATURDAY 5 JULY

Jess Willard was defeated by Jack Dempsey in the contest for the heavyweight championship, which took place at Toledo, Ohio, yesterday. A Reuter's message states that Willard threw up the sponge in the third round of the contest, which was only scheduled for 12 rounds. Dempsey floored Willard twice in the first round. Willard's second threw the towel into the ring as time was called for the third round to begin.

From our own correspondent
FRIDAY 4 JULY, NEW YORK

A great crowd, estimated at 150,000, sweltered and gasped under the terrific sun to witness the fight for the heavyweight championship of the world at Toledo, Ohio, today. The vast arena, exposed to the sky, resembled a great black-and-white furnace. Hundreds of men and women fainted where they sat.

Despite great congestion, the crowd was good-natured, and, due to the strict enforcement of Prohibition, strictly sober, with the exception of a few isolated cases. At eight o'clock this morning, 10,000 enthusiasts were battling at the gates to see the event timed for seven hours later. One barrier gave way, and some hundreds who went without paying into the reserved ground fought with the guards who tried to evict them. Toledo the night before the fight was the scene of a drunken orgy, in which all sorts of bad characters participated. Despite Prohibition, there was plenty of whisky; in fact, more drink was available than food.

Patterson wins Wimbledon singles title

By our special correspondent
WIMBLEDON, MONDAY 7 JULY

The sands of Wimbledon have almost run out. Today another young champion came into his own at the expense of an old. Gerald Patterson defeated Norman Brookes in the challenge round of the singles championship by three sets to love, and one's conviction that a new generation of players had come in with the war's close was confirmed. Patterson might exchange his ground strokes with several English players and be a sounder model for youth to imitate, but his service, volleying, and lobbing proved enough to win the championship, and these weapons, coolly directed by an unruffled mind, suggest that the qualities of youth and athletic fitness will henceforward dominate the game.

That the holder had shed much of his pace of foot and ball since 1914 could escape no discerning eye. Today he was clearly outpaced and outfooted. His mantle was passed to a fellow townsman of Melbourne.

The challenge round pitched the title-holder against the new winner: Patterson beat Brookes (below) 6–3, 7–5, 6–2.

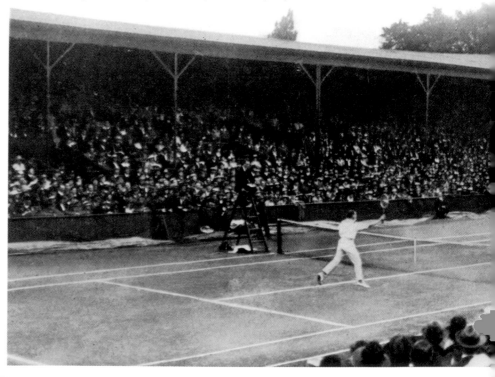

Final of great tension and excitement at Wimbledon

By our special correspondent
WIMBLEDON, SATURDAY 5 JULY

The greatest ladies' challenge round in the history of lawn tennis! After 20 years' experience of the game in many countries and amid many vicissitudes, one may safely declare that the match between Mrs Lambert Chambers and Mlle Lenglen on the centre court today has never been equalled in the high quality of its play, the sustained uncertainty of its issue, and the tense excitement of its finish. On the one hand was a British player who had won the blue riband of the lawn on seven occasions, and had not been beaten at Wimbledon for 11 years – a lady who, if she had retained her title today, would have retired from singles with a record superior to that of Willie Renshaw on the men's side; on the other a young French girl, who had brought her racquet across the Channel for the first time, and who was playing on a surface and before a crowd foreign to her nature, and perhaps inimical to her training.

The technical conditions were about as good as they could be – no wind, the sun veiled by cloud, the temperature normal. Mlle Lenglen **(right)** opened the service and lost the first game to love. If she had expected shorter-length returns, hit with less speed and confidence, she was instantly disillusioned. For this was Mrs Chambers at her very best.

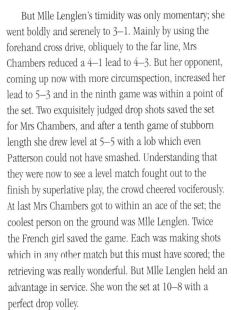

But Mlle Lenglen's timidity was only momentary; she went boldly and serenely to 3–1. Mainly by using the forehand cross drive, obliquely to the far line, Mrs Chambers reduced a 4–1 lead to 4–3. But her opponent, coming up now with more circumspection, increased her lead to 5–3 and in the ninth game was within a point of the set. Two exquisitely judged drop shots saved the set for Mrs Chambers, and after a tenth game of stubborn length she drew level at 5–5 with a lob which even Patterson could not have smashed. Understanding that they were now to see a level match fought out to the finish by superlative play, the crowd cheered vociferously. At last Mrs Chambers got to within an ace of the set; the coolest person on the ground was Mlle Lenglen. Twice the French girl saved the game. Each was making shots which in any other match but this must have scored; the retrieving was really wonderful. But Mlle Lenglen held an advantage in service. She won the set at 10–8 with a perfect drop volley.

Would the fierce pace of the protracted first set find its reflex in the second? Mrs Chambers quickly solved the problem by hitting just as hard and resolutely, her fine aim unimpaired. Mlle Lenglen was hitting as hard, but she made unsound excursions to the net, and when there her volleying was less sure. Mrs Chambers went to 4–1. But Mlle Lenglen was soon volleying again with supreme confidence and reached 4–4. But Mrs Chambers was not to be denied the fruits of her consistently sound baseline campaign. She went out, to great cheering, at 6–4. One set all.

Level in score though the players now were, the odds seemed to favour the English defender. She appeared to be less distressed physically than her opponent – Mlle Lenglen had to send for brandy at the interval, and she asked a linesman to vacate his seat so she might rest.

The crowd were now worked up to a pitch of the tensest excitement, and the umpire had to call for silence during the rallies. You could almost have heard a pin drop; 10,000 pairs of eyes were glued on the players. A long deuce game, and Mlle Lenglen drove out: 6–5 to Mrs Chambers. Mrs Chambers went to 40–15 in the next game – twice within an ace of the match. Another gruelling volley, won by the French girl, brought her to deuce; once more they were level. From that moment she moved forward steadily to victory. The 16th game Mlle Lenglen took to love, and the long tension was over. The scores were 10–8, 4–6, 9–7.

SPORT IN BRIEF

FOOTBALL
Celtic beat Rangers by one point to win the 1919 League title, avenging their defeat by Rangers last year.

GOLF
Walter Hagen wins the US Open at Brae Burn in Massachusetts after a play-off against Mike Brady. Hagen had spent the previous night out on the town, going to the theatre, meeting Al Jolson and snatching around three hours' sleep before taking the title by one shot – 77 to Brady's 78.

FOOTBALL
On 26 April Chelsea play Fulham for the Victory Cup, amid further controversy about the 'borrowing' of players from other clubs. Arsenal's Jock Rutherford is one of those who turns out in Chelsea colours, helping them to a 3–0 win.

RUGBY UNION
More than 100 rugby union internationals have lost their lives in the war. Dave Gallaher, who captained the New Zealand 'Originals' on their triumphant tour of Britain in 1905–6, is among those who have been killed.

MOTOR RACING
The 1919 Indianapolis 500 is the first classic race to be run since the war's end. The race differs from its European counterparts in that the cars start together rather than at timed intervals, and are positioned on the grid according to their qualifying times. Howard 'Howdy' Wilcox wins the event in a 1914 Peugeot at an average speed of 88.050 mph.

FOOTBALL
England beat Scotland after a thrilling match at Hillsborough. Four–two down at half time, Bob Kelly scores two goals and Fred Morris one within seven minutes to give England a 5–4 victory.

1920

By Colonel Philip Trevor, CBE

PUBLISHED MONDAY 19 JANUARY

Once again, on Saturday last, did England lose an international match at Swansea, for Wales won by a goal from a try, two dropped goals, one penalty goal, and a try to a goal from a try – 19 points to 5. Certainly the Welsh victory was well deserved, and it could easily have been greater, seeing that after half-time, although they held a lead of two points, England played like a beaten side. The Welshmen were superior to their opponents all through the match and, even if the weather had been good – it rained steadily most of the afternoon – the chances are that the superiority of the home XV would have been equally noticeable. There was a curious incident just before the match began at a quarter to three. W. N. Lowry was selected as the left-wing three-quarter back, and at half-past two, wearing the England rose on his jersey, I am told that he was photographed with the other members of the English team. However, ten minutes later, it was officially notified that the wet ground was likely to suit H. L. V. Day better than Lowry. It was indeed an 11th-hour alteration, and I content myself with stating the facts in the simplest possible form.

So far as the scoring was concerned, it was more or less a case of 'England versus Jerry Shea'. Shea was responsible for 16 of the 19 points scored by his side, and had he chosen to run a small risk he could have got the try which he elected should be got by W. J. Powell. Magnificently as he played, some of the Welsh experts condemned him for being over-individualistic, for, true to Welsh conviction, they held that he should have done more for his wing men. I cannot myself agree with that criticism. The ball was greasy, the ground was very muddy, and the wing players did not impress one with the idea that they were up to the best Welsh standard. Shea excels as a dropper of goals, and the laws of football still say clearly that a dropped goal is to count more than a try. He played a great game for Wales on Saturday.

DID YOU KNOW?

Percy Fender of Surrey scored the fastest ever century in the history of first-class cricket in 1920. Coming out to bat at Northampton on 26 August, he took 19 minutes to reach 50, and in 35 minutes had scored 100.

By B. Bennison

ANTWERP, SATURDAY 21 AUGUST

We came to Antwerp diffidently, more than half afraid that our little band of athletes, though keen, enthusiastic, and of excellent material, would be overwhelmed.

Today there is much joy in the British camp. For it has to be recorded that not only has Albert Hill, the Polytechnic Harrier, won a second triumph, but Bevil Rudd, the South African Rhodes scholar, has carried off the 400 m, and Percy Hodge (England) the steeplechase pretty well as he pleased. The story of Hill's success in the 1,500 m has already been the subject of a brief telegraphic message, but such a victory was it that it demands enlargement, so that the merit of it may be better appreciated and understood.

It had been a quiet, uninspiring day – the weather had broken down badly – and had it not been for the fact we were to see Hill again, a visit to the stadium would not have been nice to contemplate. Though Hill had captured the hearts of everybody by the brilliant manner in which he had finished first in the 800 m, it was felt that few men could be expected to accomplish a similar feat after so brief an interval. But Hill again did wonders. Joie Ray and Lawrence Shields made the pace, both ran smoothly and strongly. Hill and Philip Baker and Duncan McPhee very wisely were content to allow the Americans to show the way, and as we watched the three Britishers and felt that they were holding fast to a sharply cut and well-considered plan of campaign – they refused to make their effort too soon – we waited for the last lap breathlessly. Would they last; would the Britishers crack? The last lap. Ray fell back, and Hill went to the front, with Baker

Albert Hill, winner of the Olympic 800 m (in a British record time) and the 1,500 m.

immediately behind. Shields, running desperately, caught Baker in the back stretch, but he could not rob Hill of the lead, who broke the tape amid much enthusiasm; Baker, a yard or so behind, was second, and Shields third.

SUZANNE LENGLEN (1899–1938)

SUZANNE RACHEL FLORE LENGLEN was an outstanding French tennis player, who helped to revolutionise her sport. Trained by her father, at the age of 15 she won the clay-court championship at St Cloud and a promising career seemed to beckon. But the First World War intervened and her next chance for glory did not come until the Wimbledon tournament of 1919. There she defeated the defending champion Mrs Lambert Chambers 10–8, 4–6, 9–7, in a gruelling match during which she was fortified with a brandy-soaked sugar lump, handed her by her father.

From this point on, Lenglen dominated women's tennis. She won Wimbledon a further five times between 1920 and 1925, only missing out in 1924 through illness. In addition she secured five

victories in the French championships, a gold medal in the 1920 Olympics at Antwerp, and a whole string of doubles titles. One factor in her success was her choice of clothing. Lenglen opted for garments that gave her complete freedom of movement. In place of long skirts and petticoats she wore shorter, pleated skirts, short-sleeved vests and a bandeau that became her trademark.

Lenglen's amateur career ended abruptly in 1926, when she withdrew midway through the Wimbledon championships. In the same year she went on tour as a professional in the United States, supported by players like Mary Browne (a former US champion) and Vincent Richards (a doubles specialist). After retirement Lenglen managed a tennis school until her premature death at 39.

Ray's great triumph

By George W. Greenwood

ST ANDREWS, SUNDAY 15 AUGUST

It would seem that it was Mr E. Ray's wonderful putting and his extraordinary knack of extricating himself from seemingly impossible places that won him the United States Open championship. There is no more beautiful or consistent putter than Ray. Like most of us, he has his black days, when the hole looks the size of an egg-cup and the ball jumps in and then out again in the most fiendish manner. But unlike many a weaker mortal he does not fling away his putter in a fit of anger and fly to another of a different weight or pattern. Whether the gods smile or whether they frown, he sticks faithfully and manfully to his aluminium putter. He swings and follows through with delightful ease and smoothness.

Where Ray succeeded Mr H. Vardon lamentably failed. How many of those fatal short putts of two feet and a yard he must have missed, goodness only knows. I am afraid Vardon, who still possesses an incomparable lucidity of style when playing the shots up to the green, has arrived at a mental condition when he would infinitely prefer to face a pair of runaway horses than be asked to accomplish a yard putt. However, the great point is that the American Open championship has come to Britain for the second time.

Mlle Lenglen retains lady champion's title

By A. Wallis Myers, OBE

PUBLISHED FRIDAY 2 JULY

Mlle Suzanne Lenglen is still the lady champion. A year ago, when she first entered the lists at Wimbledon, she played Mrs Lambert Chambers, the holder. The champion was then twice within a point of saving her title, and, who shall say, of retiring with it after a great career. This year, to everyone's keen delight, Mrs Chambers re-entered the All-Comers, and showed her undecaying talent by winning it. Thus she exchanged shoes with Mlle Lenglen – hers were those of the challenger, the French girl wore those of the holder. A vast throng gathered in a dun light to see this great return battle. It was a debate, with the whole of the lawn tennis world listening, to settle an issue that, by the score, had been adjourned 12 months ago.

Last year 40 momentous games! This year, only 15, and only the first four waged between equal parties. At 5–2 Mrs Chambers won another game; that was her last; the holder took the second set to love. Was Mrs Chambers herself? She certainly did not give her friends that impression, for her driving had neither its sting nor its length of Wednesday, and she seemed to get worse as the match developed. I can only assume something ailed her.

I do not think the challenger could have won on the form which Mlle Lenglen displayed yesterday. Every stroke included in the lawn tennis repertoire was exploited by the French girl with ease and elegance; when she had put the first set behind her, the variety of her play and her confidence both increased. There remained the impression that the all-court game of Mlle Lenglen, supported by great agility and the cutest sense of anticipation, were proof against the best driving. At the age of 21, Mlle Lenglen is champion for the second year.

Mlle Suzanne Lenglen (below) beat Mrs Lambert Chambers, 6–3, 6–0.

SPORT IN BRIEF

BADMINTON

George Thomas claims the first of four consecutive All-England singles titles. Between 1903 and 1928 he will win a record 21 All-England badminton titles. A man of many talents, Thomas also plays tennis, reaching the doubles semi-finals at Wimbledon in 1907 and 1912. In addition he is a county hockey player, and twice wins the British chess championship.

FOOTBALL

Kilmarnock win the Scottish FA Cup for the first time, beating Albion Rovers 3–2. Although Albion Rovers finish bottom of the League, they have won their place in the Cup final by beating Glasgow Rangers – after two replays – in the semi-finals.

GOLF

George Duncan of Scotland stages a dramatic comeback to take the British Open championship at Deal. Having been 13 strokes behind the leader, Abe Mitchell, Duncan sets a course record of 71 in the third round, and finishes with a round of 72. He wins £100.

FOOTBALL

The new season begins on Saturday 28 August with a reorganised League of 66 clubs divided into three divisions. Grimsby Town are demoted to the new Third Division. There they join most of the clubs from the old Southern League, except Cardiff, who are promoted to Division Two in their place. One club will be automatically relegated or promoted between Divisions One and Two at the end of each season.

1921

Crushing defeat in golf match

By George W. Greenwood
HOYLAKE, SUNDAY 22 MAY

The first international golf match ever played between Great Britain and America has resulted in an overwhelming victory for the representatives of the United States. They won all the foursomes and five matches in the singles – a total of nine points to three. It comes as a staggering blow; a blow so totally unexpected that there is a well-grounded fear that one of these Americans will next month depart with our championship. Quite a large body of British golfers have steadfastly refused to believe that there was anything serious to worry about in this organised American invasion. On the contrary, they treated it with a certain measure of scorn.

After yesterday's debacle they have suddenly awakened to the fact that these businesslike gentlemen from over the water constitute a real menace. Since their arrival in this country I have been to some pains to inform English golfers of the danger that threatened. I have been accused in some quarters of placing these Americans – at least some of them – on pedestals which they had no prescriptive right to occupy. Those who yesterday saw Master Bobby Jones, Mr Francis Ouimet, Mr Chick Evans, and Mr Jesse Guilford hit the ball round the Hoylake links will, I feel sure, now think differently. At the end of a long and fascinating day's golf – fascinating because we were at grips at last with the invaders – a deep and impenetrable gloom settled over a certain section of people who now see nothing but disaster ahead. This of course is a state of morbidity verging on the ludicrous. I will go so far as to concede the possibility of an American and an Englishman fighting out the final.

On 25 June, after a play-off against British amateur Roger Wethered, Jock Hutchison (Scottish-born but now resident in the United States) won the British Open championship at St Andrews.

MILESTONES

The first international meeting for female athletes was held by the International Sporting Club of Monaco in Monte Carlo on 25 May 1921. Competitors from Britain, France, Italy, Norway and Switzerland took part.

From our own correspondent
NEW YORK, SUNDAY 3 JULY

On Friday Jack Dempsey knocked out Georges Carpentier in the fourth round to win the heavyweight championship of the world. Here is Dempsey's own story of how he won. 'I sent mother a telegram,' he said. 'It read, "I have made good my promise to keep the championship in America." I promised to put forth my every effort to win, and I did in beating Carpentier. I did not defeat any mediocre man. I found in him the gamest warrior I ever faced, and, don't forget, he has a punch to be reckoned with. I tried hard to end it in the first round, but Carpentier's gameness and his fine condition saved him. In the second he uncorked a desperate rally, but I took all he had.

'This is how the fight comes back to me today. Carpentier slapped me on the back as I stepped into the ring through his corner. I returned his salute, but barely looked at him. Then I received a floral horseshoe from the good folks of Jersey City. Carpentier came out fast. I bided my time – I had to measure this Frenchman a bit. I started in to batter him down in the in-fighting, and then let him have two rights. They were to the jaw. I then brought blood to his nose with a right hook. There was no mistaking the fact I was up against a game man.

More than 100,000 people – a record crowd for a sporting event – came to watch the Dempsey–Carpentier fight in Jersey City.

'Carpentier weathered the first round, but my corner told me that the French boy was a bit wobbly. I came out in the second round with a crouch. Carpentier clipped me with a right to the jaw. I did not turn a hair, and I had him backing away. Then he shook me up a bit with three right-hand wallops that were certainly stingers. But I stood "the gaff". I learned he had a stiff right, but I had him bleeding at the nose when the round ended. I missed several with my left at the opening of the third, but got in a hook. Carpentier missed with a sizzling right upper-cut. I got him with rights and lefts, but he took them like a man. I began to try for his body, to bring his hands down. In the fourth and final slam I put over the old "one, two" with a snappy left and a hammer blow with "old iron mike", my right hand. I then knocked him flat again with a volley – and then the "knock-out".'

I can express in one sentence the opinion in the editorial columns today. It is as follows: 'The Stars and Stripes have been exalted and the Tricolour lowered, but not trailed in the dust', and the *New York Times* adds, philosophically, 'The agony is over and the world may now regain its equipoise.'

King George meets the Cup-tie teams

By B. Bennison

PUBLISHED MONDAY 25 APRIL

We saw the real heart of the nation on Saturday – a great, loyal heart. It was revealed in circumstances and on an occasion never to be forgotten. In rain that pelted and slashed and drenched, the King, together with the Duke of York and Prince Henry, walked on to the field of the Chelsea Club to be introduced to and to shake hands with the players of Tottenham Hotspur and Wolverhampton Wanderers, who had come to do battle for the Cup, most magical and coveted of all trophies, offered by the Football Association. These footballers had drawn up and stood rigid on a white line that, in a twinkle, was obliterated by a deluge, sudden and rampageous. More than 70,000 people, already on their feet, sang, 'God Save the King' as some wonderful, disciplined choir; then, as with one voice, they broke into deafening cheers. Never in my long experience of sport can I recall a scene so profoundly impressive; the King was with his people, and there was only joy.

The Cup was won by Tottenham Hotspur by one goal to none; their triumph was the just reward of obvious superiority.

Tottenham Hotspur left-winger Bert Bliss makes his way on to the waterlogged pitch at Stamford Bridge. Recently promoted Spurs beat Second Division Wolves 1–0 to win the Cup for the first time in 20 years.

Angry scenes at the Oval

By Colonel Philip Trevor, OBE

PUBLISHED MONDAY 15 AUGUST

Actual cricket in the fifth and last Test match, which began at Kennington Oval on Saturday, was limited to two hours and 40 minutes, and in that time England scored 129 runs for the loss of four wickets. At 20 minutes to three a heavy shower drove the players to shelter. The shower was not a very long one, and the ground looked fit for play when the two captains, Lionel Tennyson and Warwick Armstrong, went out to inspect the wicket some little time after the rain had ceased.

Armstrong is very popular with English cricket crowds, and understandably so. But a very slight indication by pantomime which Armstrong gave was the beginning of an angry scene that could easily have developed into something more serious. Armstrong felt the pitch with his fingers, and then made as if he were wringing the water out of his hands. Probably Armstrong only meant by what he did to tell the public that the wicket was still very wet, and that there was no chance of more cricket for a while. However, as Lionel Tennyson (very rightly) neither concurred nor demurred by gesture, the public jumped to the conclusion that the Australian thought the wicket unfit for play, and that the Englishman thought it fit. They knew it was to England's advantage to go on batting, and they began to murmur.

Had they known the laws and rules of cricket (or remembered them) they would have reassured themselves. When the captains disagree about the condition of a wicket, the umpires are referred to.

Clearly then, Tennyson did not disagree with Armstrong, for the umpires did not come out. Nothing came out; not even information. The crowd were left to wait and guess. They broke bounds, gathered in front of the pavilion, shouted and misbehaved themselves. They 'booed' Armstrong. At last a belated notice informed the public that if no more rain fell there would be play at 5.15. But when will cricket authorities realise their obligations to the public? For years I have pressed the powers-that-be to give cricket crowds information which those crowds have a right to expect. Why ask for trouble?

Frank Woolley catches Australian batsman Warren Bardsley at slip in the third Test at Headingley. Australia went 3–0 up in the series here to take the Ashes, though the last two matches were drawn.

SPORT IN BRIEF

RUGBY UNION
England beat the French 10–6 in Paris to win the Grand Slam. Central to the English team are fly half W. J. A, (Dave) Davies and scrum half Cyril Kershaw, 'Dave and K' play in 14 internationals together over four seasons, and are never on the losing side. Between 1913 and 1923 Davies will captain England in 11 matches, and will hold the record as most capped fly half until it passes to Rob Andrew in 1989.

FOOTBALL
Having staged a record run of 30 matches without defeat, Burnley meet Manchester City at Maine Road and lose 3–0. Despite this setback, they now have a commanding lead at the top of the First Division, and will go on to win the League title by five points.

CRICKET
Glamorgan join the county championship. It is won by Middlesex, aided by prolific scorers Patsy Hendren and Jack Hearne.

HORSE RACING
Steve Donoghue rides Humorist to victory in the Derby in the first of a record three successive Derby wins.

CRICKET
Australian Jack Gregory, playing against South Africa in the second Test in Johannesburg, scores 100 in 70 minutes off only 67 balls to claim the fastest century in Test cricket.

51

1922

England pack routed by Wales

By Colonel Philip Trevor, CBE
PUBLISHED MONDAY 23 JANUARY

The unexpected happened at Cardiff on Saturday, for Wales beat England there – in the mud – by two goals and six tries to two tries – 28 points to 6. The afternoon was fine, but the ground was a quagmire. However, even if it had been a morass that fact would not have excused the display given by the England pack. In such conditions it would not have surprised the careful student of rugby football to see them outplayed. As a matter of fact they were routed, although they were half a stone per man the heavier pack; and if there is a stronger word than routed it could be used here without exaggeration. The Welsh backs supported the pack capitally, but the game was one long, unbroken series of victories for the Welsh forwards.

The English forwards were slow from the start on the heavy ground, and they got slower and slower. They seemed to think slowly too. When they had made mistakes or when they had been outwitted and danger threatened in consequence they were very slow in recovery. The England back division never looked like atoning for the sins of the England forwards. Their defence was uncertain, and they did not turn to advantage the occasional chances of counter-attack which they got.

Those who did not see that match may ask: 'Was this debacle occasioned because of the superb performance given by Wales, or because of a very indifferent performance given by England?' I will try to answer that double question. England began not exactly by playing badly, but by not playing at all. The Welshmen seized their chance. They attacked, and found that success came comparatively easy. They went on

New golf champion

By George W. Greenwood
SANDWICH, FRIDAY 23 JUNE

There is a new golf champion, and again he is an American. The superhuman efforts put forward by the whole army of British golfers, amateur and professional, to win back the cup which Jock Hutchison took to the States last year for the first time in its history have signally failed. Walter Hagen, of Detroit, today won the British championship with a score of 300 for the four rounds. I am not in the least surprised at his triumph,

DID YOU KNOW?

As a professional, Walter Hagen was not allowed into the clubhouse during the British Open. His solution was to park a stretch limousine outside the clubhouse, and use that as his changing and dining room.

attacking, conscious that they had not to fear counter-attack. Certainly it was not two or three members of the English team who had much to do with the loss of the match. It was nearer a dozen. I shall not be surprised if our selectors say of the form shown by the men who they chose to represent England: 'Too bad to be true.'

Filthy business: members of the English rugby union team are washed down during a break in their 28–6 defeat by Wales. Wales went on to win the 1922 Five Nations championship title.

because he has played the most convincing and business-like golf, without being in any way brilliant, of all the world's competitors. Hagen is a sturdy fellow, who gives the impression of a well-trained athlete. Golf is his profession, and in his efforts to climb the Olympian heights he long ago concluded that something more than science and skill in the game were required; preservation of health by careful methods of living was absolutely essential. He is practically an abstainer, and the use of tobacco is reduced to a minimum. When he strode off the last green amid a shower of congratulations he lit a cigar for the first time for a week.

Hagen was born at Rochester, New York, and is 29 years of age. He commenced to play golf on a small, unpretentious inland course at Rochester, and in his early days was a caddie. As a matter of fact, Hagen first hit a golf ball when he was just able to toddle. Here we have an example of the benefits to be derived from swinging a club in infancy. In 1914, at the second time of asking, and when only 21 years of age, he took the American golfing public by storm by winning the national championship.

Hagen is the finest home-bred professional golfer that America has produced, and, as an indication of his skill, I need only say that Harry Vardon, a wise judge, is of the opinion that he is the best golfer he has seen for years.

A flamboyant figure, Walter Hagen's *joie de vivre* and sartorial sense did much to raise the profile of golf among the public. He was the first American-born professional to win the British Open.

The Cup final

By B. Bennison
Published Monday 1 May

When, a minute or so before three o'clock the players of Preston North End and Huddersfield Town, typifying the old and very new in Asssociation football, bounded on to the field, to make the last stand in the 'feight for t'Co-op', enthusiasm, partisanship, knew no bounds. If there be such a thing as inspiration, it was at hand in plenty. But they failed to be inspired; they produced what I shall long remember as a monstrosity.

I have seen every final tie for more than a quarter of a century; that upon which I must write was in almost every particular the worst I have witnessed. The winners were Huddersfield. Through the agency of a penalty kick imposed after some 20 minutes of play in the second half they carried the day. But there was precious little virtue, and there can be only small joy in their victory. Long before the end I had sickened of the football, not because of its sameness or its woodenness, but by reason of its lack of wholesomeness. Ever since I have been of the game I have been an advocate of the full-blooded charge, but I will have none of the ankle-rapping and the nastiness for which Saturday's game was chiefly notable.

If there were a better team, it was Huddersfield, and on the run of play they deserved the Cup. W. Smith who, together with C. Stephenson and J. Richardson was the best forward on the field, was on a dribble and going

splendidly when he was tripped by Hamilton, and he fell all of a heap. As I saw it, the foul was committed outside the penalty area, and loud were the protests of the Preston players when Mr Fowler awarded the kick by which the game was decided. Morally, his decision was justified; strictly and technically, he was wrong – at least in my judgement.

Thereafter Preston made a valiant effort to pull the match out of the fire, but they never looked like capturing the Huddersfield defence; indeed had Islip, the Yorkshire centre, availed himself of oppportunities created by Smith, Preston would have been beaten by two, if not three goals. Smith was the bright particular star among the Huddersfield forwards; he was well served by Stephenson, and in the second half there was much merit in the football of Richardson at outside right. Mutch, in goal, could not have been improved upon. When I left the ground at Stamford Bridge many men of Lancashire and Yorkshire were engaged in a battle of words, by which they hoped to decide whether the referee was justified in giving the penalty kick which decided the match.

A dreadful FA Cup final played at Stamford Bridge was won 1–0 by Huddersfield Town (right).

1922

SPORT IN BRIEF

FOOTBALL
Celtic beat Rangers by one point to win the Scottish League title. Rangers suffer disappointment again when they lose to Morton 1–0 in the Scottish Cup.

BASEBALL
'Babe' Ruth creates a sensation on 26 May when he throws earth in the face of the umpire for calling him out, then chases another critic through the grandstand. The unruly Ruth has only just returned to the New York Yankees' team after suspension for playing exhibition matches during the winter months.

FOOTBALL
In the home international at Villa Park, Birmingham, Scotland beat England 1–0. It is Scotland's first footballing victory away from home in 19 years.

MOTOR RACING
The French Grand Prix, held on 16 July on public roads in Strasbourg, is the first grand prix to have a mass start. Veteran driver Felice Nazzaro, in a Fiat, dominates the race, winning by nearly an hour from Pierre de Vizcaya in a Bugatti. Tragically Biagio Nazzaro, Felice's nephew, is killed during the race.

CYCLING
In July Firmin Lambot of Belgium wins the Tour de France for the second time. Lambot's first win was three years ago.

RUGBY LEAGUE
The Northern Rugby Football Union, made up of the teams that left the Rugby Football Union in 1895, changes its name to the Rugby Football League. From now on the breakaway game is known as rugby league.

1923

Film of Dublin boxing match

PUBLISHED TUESDAY 20 MARCH

Little more than 36 hours after the finish of the much-discussed fight in Dublin between Battling Siki and Mike McTigue, a London audience was able to see yesterday at the West End cinema a filmed record of the event. Though the film runs for barely a quarter of an hour, while the fight was really an exceptionally long one, amateurs of boxing are afforded ample opportunities to judge the capabilities of the two men. The impetuosity of the Senegalese is most marked, as is the calculated defence of the Irish-American. In the 20th round, when the referee adjudges McTigue to be the victor on points, Siki appears to be almost as full of vim as ever. It may be added that this simulacrum of a fight may be viewed from a comfortable fauteuil in the London theatre with far greater equanimity than was felt by the spectators of the real thing in Dublin.

MILESTONES

The first supercharged car to win a grand prix is the Fiat 805-405. It is driven by Carlo Salamano, who wins the Italian Grand Prix from his compatriot Felice Nazzaro, also driving a Fiat 805-405.

Donoghue's triumph in the Derby

By Hotspur

PUBLISHED THURSDAY 7 JUNE

With the Prince of Wales present and the customary vast crowd participating, the race for the Derby was decided at Epsom yesterday and resulted as follows:

Mr B. Irish's Papyrus (S. Donoghue) 1
Lord Derby's Pharos (E. Gardner) 2
Mr M Goculdas's Parth (A. Walker) 3

The favourite, Town Guard, finished nearly last of all.

Such is the outcome of the great race. The all-important residue as set out above, after many weeks of discussion and sifting, is what has now been passed into history. For once the highest honours of the Turf have not been given to the patrician owners and breeders. They find themselves overlooked in favour of the 'small' owner, an owner, moreover, of but a single horse, but that one, Papyrus, now ranking as the Derby winner.

I have written before that an owner must have luck to win a Derby. Has it ever been more exemplified than in the case of Mr Ben Irish, for most of his life a farmer in the Fen Country and only comparatively late in life yielding to the glitter and allurements of ownership on the Turf? He has simply stormed his way to the summit of all owners' ambitions, while others spend their lifetimes in vain endeavour. A very few years ago he gave a matter of 300 guineas for a yearling colt by Radium, which he came to name Periosteum. He sent it to be trained by the young Newmarket trainer, Basil Jarvis. Periosteum prospered, and the owner of a single racehorse found himself suddenly famous as the owner of an Ascot Gold Cup winner. At the Doncaster yearling sales his eye settled on a brown colt by Tracery from a mare named Miss Mattie. Mr Irish became the owner of the colt, which he afterwards named Papyrus, only when he bid 3,500 guineas. It was great good luck to dip once into the lottery of the yearling sales at Doncaster, buy a single yearling for big a price, and with it win the Derby!

The triumph of Papyrus was also the triumph of Stephen Donoghue, who for the third year in succession rode the Derby winner, and so created a record which is not likely to be surpassed in our time. Now read Donoghue's own description of the race as he recounted it to me: 'I had always liked the horse from the time last autumn I beat Town Guard on him. He gave me the right sort of feel when I cantered to the post, and I felt more than ever it would take a pretty good one to beat him. I had the luck to get well away on him.

'As we went on I felt I could go to the front on him at any time. He gave me that wonderful feel. Coming round Tattenham Corner he moved as if he owned it, and I simply had to let him go to the front when once in the line for home.

'Lord Derby's horse came to me and challenged, but I could feel the grit and determination in my horse. It was pure stamina and gameness that won him the race.'

For Lord Derby, who came so near to realising his life's ambition on the Turf, there was some genuine sympathy, but this great good sportsman accepted the result with his customary smile and admirable philosophy. This is the third time in 13 years that he has run second for the Derby.

For Donoghue it was a wonderful achievement. Luck may not always be with him, but it has stuck leechlike to him in the modern history of the Derby. So the jockey's sun is as high in the heavens as ever, and he was made to realise his personal popularity in the splendid reception accorded him.

Mr Ben Irish leads the Derby winner, Papyrus, ridden by Steve Donoghue, into the winners' enclosure.

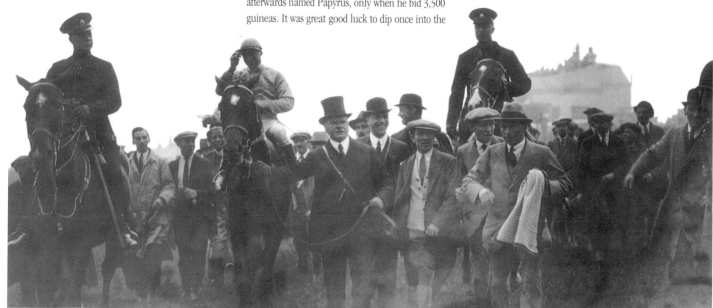

Chaos at the first Wembley Cup final

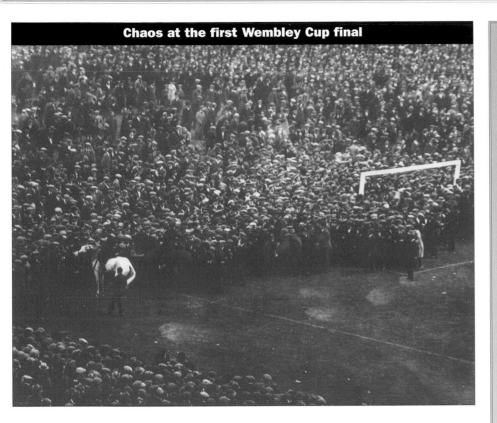

From our special correspondent
PUBLISHED MONDAY 30 APRIL
Bolton Wanderers 2; West Ham 0

At Wembley on Saturday failure unprecedented in the annals of British sport trod hard on the heels of success. The earlier period stands out as a great achievement to all concerned in the marshalling and transporting of so huge a crowd. The trek towards Wembley began quite early in the morning, and it was soon apparent that as a national institution Derby Day was threatened with a serious rival. Everybody was supremely happy, all wore club colours of some description, and nearly all carried a rattle, a bugle, or a bell. What with the coloured hats, rosettes, the minstrels and ice-cream merchants, the scene was reminiscent of Blackpool sands in the height of the season, a comparison strengthened by the broad Lancashire dialect heard at every turn.

By midday the terraces inside the stadium were comfortably packed, and there were many hundreds strolling about outside. An hour later the stream of arrivals was swollen to the dimensions of a torrent, as thousands of Londoners, freed from the week's labours at midday, joined in the already considerable multitude which poured through the turnstiles. It was at this point that the temper of the crowd began to change, and supreme content gave place to a discontent almost amounting to rage as some thousands of these later arrivals, having paid their admission money, found that they could not penetrate beyond the outer walls of the stadium. And each moment they were being joined by

thousands more as hopelessly situated. Instructions were given to close the turnstiles at the main entrances. The effect was as unexpected as it was disastrous.

A few venturesome spirits began to climb the barricades on either side of the turnstiles. In a moment barriers, officials, and police were swept aside, and the crowd surged through and over the broken fences into the grounds. Mounted police were hurried to the scene, and while these held back the crowd, their comrades on foot formed a double cordon across the gap in the barrier.

Inside the grounds those already without accommodation were augmented by the influx of the thousands who had stormed the barriers. To relieve the congestion on the terraces a large section of the crowd had been allowed over the railings on to the running track; faced with the prospect of further crushing from behind, they swept right down on to the goal-line. Thousands more followed, and in a few moments had overrun the entire playing pitch. Only the white crossbar of the goals could be seen above the heads of the people.

It was at this point that the King arrived. The news of his arrival was almost magical in its effect. A way was quickly made for the royal car, and what had been an angry demonstration was turned in an instant into a truly wonderful welcome. Thereafter the situation became easier, and as it became apparent that there was little else to wait for, a steady exodus back to town began and continued throughout the afternoon.

The image of a lone mounted policeman attempting to control the vast crowds at Wembley led to the event being remembered as the 'White Horse' Cup final.

SPORT IN BRIEF

FOOTBALL

Although West Ham are beaten at home by Notts County in the last game of the season, Leicester's defeat at Bury means that West Ham are promoted to the First Division, above Leicester on goal average, It is some consolation for their FA Cup disappointment.

MOTOR RACING

When Sir Henry Segrave crosses the line in the French Grand Prix at Tours, he becomes the first British driver to win a grand prix. His two-litre Sunbeam proves more resilient than the Italian Fiats on the difficult surface.

GOLF

Bobby Jones wins his first 'major' championship when he takes the US Open title at Inwood, Long Island. The 21-year-old from Atlanta is forced into a play-off, but wins that by two strokes from Bobby Cruickshank.

BOXING

Jack Dempsey and Luis Angel Firpo undergo a bruising 3 minute 57 second contest for the world heavyweight championship in New York. Saved by the bell in the first round, Dempsey puts an end to his opponent's challenge in round two.

GOLF

The Americans retain the Walker Cup by one point after a closely fought match at St Andrews. After receiving the trophy **(right)**, the American captain, Robert Gardner, entertains the crowd with a song.

1924

Amazing scenes in the Olympics

By B. Bennison
PARIS, SATURDAY 12 JULY

On a day of blinding light and terrific heat, there was spread before us in the stadium of Colombes a spectacle which I would never wish to see again – magnificent, amazing, terribly cruel: a fight almost to the point of death. And only for honour and glory. Of 39 lion-hearted men, drawn from all parts of the world, who set out on the 10,000-m cross-country race, only 15 reached and passed the finishing post. The other 24 had fallen prostrate by the wayside. Wildest rumours reached the stadium long before Paavo Nurmi, the phenomenal Finn, had won with something like half a mile to spare from his countryman, Ville Ritola. Men and women stood as if transfixed as they saw this and that man come into view, reeling, rocking, their eyes glazed, their wet, grimy faces distorted as they struggled to complete the most gruelling, heart-breaking race I have ever seen.

And now I would tell of the wonder-man, Nurmi. Whether on grass or cinders, or whatever conformation the course took, he was just his giant self. He ran as if heat and sun to him, though a Finn reared in a country of hardiness, meant nothing. He bent his elbows so as to give them the appearance of piston rods and, with head held high, he strode along with a smoothness and an indifference to his awful task that left us spellbound. And when he came through the archway leading to the track, such was his condition, so strong was he within himself, that he might have only run a few hundred yards instead of having raced more than six miles. We shouted a welcome to him; a thunderous roar that grew in volume so as to become deafening when he broke the tape.

Nurmi's time was 32 min 54⅘ sec, which represents an altogether extraordinary performance. I am sure that no other living man could have done that which Nurmi achieved today. He is the wonder of all athletic ages.

Nurmi (right) had already won gold in the 1,500-m and 5,000-m races, breaking world records for both these events in the heats. He added a 10,000-m cross-country team gold to his individual gold, and the following day won another team gold in the 3,000 m.

Victory of H. M. Abrahams

By B. Bennison
PARIS, MONDAY 7 JULY

It was past seven o'clock when the speed team began to prepare. From the inside of the track the positions were C. Paddock, J. Scholz, L. Murchison, H. Abrahams, C. Bouman and A. Porritt. When the leather-lunged announcer gave it out that all was in readiness for the start, the silence was awe-inspiring. Not a whisper could be heard. Holes had been carefully dug and, to a perfect start, off the men went like a shot. This and that man's name was screamed. On they flew, with Abrahams, in the centre, showing just a suspicion of daylight between himself, Scholz and Porritt.

And then at 50 yards Abrahams, amid yells of joy from the British, made his effort. It was herculean in its mightiness, and he took a lead of a quarter of a yard from Scholz, with Porritt only inches behind. The flying American, Bouman, was next, and then the awkward Paddock and Murchison.

Would Abrahams live through? He did. He tugged at his big heart, his jaws seemed to snap, his finely chiselled face was distorted, telling a tale of iron determination.

Harold Abrahams (above) won a silver medal in the sprint relay to add to his gold in the 100 m.

There was no cracking of Abrahams, and on he flashed to break the tape in front of Scholz. It was one of the closest finishes; it was the merest trifle that the Cambridge Blue won by. But it was enough, and there was given off a crack of enthusiasm. No more popular victory could have been. For the first time in the history of the Olympic Games, as they have come to be, an Englishman has won the sprint. Except in 1908, when Reggie Walker, the South African, won at Shepherd's Bush, the 100 m has been captured by America, and we had only come to regard the winning of the blue riband of the track by the United States as a matter of course.

The placings were Abrahams (1), Scholz (2) and Porritt (3). Abrahams did 10⅗ sec, which was precisely the time in which he won his heat yesterday. That Murchison was last came as something like a bombshell in the American camp, but there was no begrudging Abrahams of his triumph. On every hand he was warmly congratulated, and when he stood and saluted the British flag as it was unfurled in token of his victory, there was one long cheer. Then, as the British National Anthem was played, all the thousands of people present stood at attention. It has been a memorable day for England.

A Basque champion at Wimbledon

By A. Wallis Myers, CBE

PUBLISHED MONDAY 7 JULY

Wimbledon closed on Saturday with all five championship crowns resting on new heads. France won the men's singles for the first time in the history of lawn tennis. Public interest did not decline when England was excluded from the main bill. On Saturday there was the unique spectacle of an all-French singles final and an all-American doubles final.

Writing in *The Daily Telegraph* on 23 June, the first day of the meeting, I ventured to say, 'The present French champion has now come to his prime. The denizens of Wimbledon have not yet seen this gay cavalier at his best.' And now Jean Borotra, 26 years of age, first emerging from the Basque provinces three or four years ago to take a course of studies at the Paris Polytechnic and importing to the covered courts of Paris, as to its rugby football fields, a quality of speed and endurance and an exuberance of spirit that made one fearful lest he should burn himself out too quickly, has won the highest prize lawn tennis can offer.

The final on Saturday was not a great match, because neither of the two compatriots, Jean Borotra and René Lacoste, had any surprise in store for his opponent. I have seen these two in conflict in France, and lately, at any rate, Borotra has always carried a slight moral advantage by virtue of his stronger personality. This is not to say that Lacoste has not got the strokes and the temperament to beat him; at present, until he acquires a little more speed of drive, he is inclined to use the lob a little too freely.

Lacoste (in the foreground) and Borotra, on their way to a doubles final victory at Wimbledon in 1925.

In the final set Borotra's ground shots were weakening, and his service was slower. But after Lacoste led 4–3, the younger man faltered. In the ninth game he served a double fault, which was ominous. This was the key game and, having secured it, the Basque entered into his championship kingdom. Modestly, if discerningly, did he say to me after the match: 'Lacoste will forgive me for beating him this year. He knows, and I know, that he will beat me next year.' A boisterous, lovable fellow!

J. Borotra (France) bt R. Lacoste (France), 6–1, 3–6, 6–1, 3–6, 6–4

SPORT IN BRIEF

LAWN TENNIS

The first international women's tennis competition to take place in Britain is staged at Wimbledon, and pitches the home team against the United States. The prize is the Wightman Cup, inaugurated a year ago at Forest Hills. In a reversal of last year's result, the British team takes the trophy.

CRICKET

Herbert Sutcliffe makes his debut for England against South Africa in the first Test at Edgbaston. English bowlers Maurice Tate (with four wickets for 12 runs) and A. E. R Gilligan (with an astounding six for seven) reduce South Africa to 30 all out. In the second Test at Lord's, English batsmen put on 531 for the loss of only two wickets before declaring. Jack Hobbs scores 211, which will be a career-highest score, and a record eighth three-figure innings in a Test. Herbert Sutcliffe makes 122, his first Test century. England go on to win by an innings and 18 runs. England take the series 3–0.

1924

British Bobsleigh team in serious accident

CHAMONIX, THURSDAY 31 JANUARY

A serious accident befell the British bobsleigh team taking part in the Olympic Games here this morning. The British team were the first to undertake a descent upon it, and, on reaching one of the turns, the sleigh ran off the track and completely capsized. Captain F. Browning, an officer of the Brigade of Guards, was picked up unconscious, with both legs broken, and his fellow competitors were badly bruised.

DID YOU KNOW?

Johnny Weissmuller (who went on to star as cinema's Tarzan) was the first man to swim the 100-m freestyle in under a minute. He achieved the feat at the 1924 Olympic Games, where he won three gold medals as well as a bronze in the water-polo competition.

1925

Revolutionary change

By our special correspondent

PUBLISHED MONDAY 21 AUGUST

Association football must of necessity undergo considerable change on the tactical side during the 1925–6 season, which opens in England on Saturday next. The offside law, the cause of much bitterness in recent years, both on the field and amongst the spectators, has been altered so that in future an attacker will be in play if two opponents instead of three are nearer their own goal-line when the ball is last played. This is the most revolutionary change since the English League came into being in 1888, and demands the entire remodelling of defensive plans. The change was forced by the development of what was known as the 'one-back' game, and the consequent numerous irritating stoppages.

Opinion is by no means unanimous that the new law will improve the game as a spectacle. Its opponents declare that speed will be rendered more important than scientific manoeuvre, and that goal-scoring will be made too easy. That remains to be seen. Trial games have certainly produced more goals, but not any great abundance, and compensations claimed by the sponsors of the new law are that stoppages have been fewer and that forwards, with greater freedom, have been the better able to develop their plans. In the opening month the advantage should certainly rest with the attackers, for the various defensive plans formulated by the clubs to meet the conditions need time for development. An upheaval in the form of the past season is a possibility, for brains in the board room and the dressing room as well as on the field will be put to the test.

Another interesting law change gives the player greater freedom in the 'throw-in', for it will no longer be necessary for the thrower to stand with part of both feet on the line. This will enable longer throws to be delivered by the player who cares to practise.

MILESTONES

In Europe riding mechanics were barred from grand prix racing, as they had already been in the United States. In a role involving great danger and little glory, mechanics accompanied the driver, changing tyres and topping up fuel en route. Some graduated to greater things: driver Felice Nazzaro began his career as a mechanic.

By Colonel Philip Trevor, CBE

PUBLISHED TUESDAY 6 JANUARY

A great side have just brought to a close a wonderful tour and established a great record. You can scarcely do more than win every match you play. I have written so much in these columns about the all-conquering New Zealanders that if I now write more I do not see how I can hope to escape being found guilty of the crime of repetition. I must make the excuse that I am only trying to sum up.

I think, after a long experience, when you watch closely for the first time players who are appreciably international form, you can tell what they are in the habit of doing, from what they are obviously trying to do. I was sure then that I had seen a very fine side play, and, as readers of *The Daily Telegraph* may remember, I said so unequivocally at the time. But I also said that from

The 'Invincibles' end their victorious tour by beating England 17–11 at Twickenham, despite having forward Cyril Brownlie sent off.

our point of view they had more than a little to learn about forward play. Their attacking power behind the scrummage has always been clear except to the wilfully blind. Well, they proceeded to learn – that is to say, to teach themselves – the kind of forward play which was necessary for games played in these Isles. But they wisely scrapped nothing as they did so. They just added to what existed. Their improvement forward was very slow, but it was sure, and in the last two matches of their tour – versus London and England – they showed how magnificently it is possible for seven forwards to play against eight. They have now a great pack.

I must content myself with a brief reference to their leading player. George Nepia stands alone among moderns as a full-back, and the personal record he has established is, in the circumstances, marvellous. He has played in every match, yet, when you watch his performance, you think he ought to be 'laid out' twice out of five times. I offer him my hearty congratulations on coming through such an ordeal unscathed. His pluck is equal to his play, and that is saying a good deal. The names of these New Zealanders are before me as I write. I decline the responsibility of leaving out of the honours list any man who played against England, and I would put in about four or five who did not.

What are the lessons which they have taught or ought to have taught us? Chiefly I think the value, the combined value, of pace and inter-understanding, and obviously, as I have already had occasion to write, initial pace is of infinitely more consequence than subsequent pace. 'Do it at once' is the essential motto of the modern rugby football field, and these New Zealanders are very much moderns. I would say that we learn our lessons slowly; that attitude was in evidence 19 years ago when the predecessors of these men swept the board in England. Those 1905 New Zealanders gave us a warning of the extreme value of pace, and also suggested to us that if you were always attacking yourselves you need not bother overmuch about the attack of the other fellows.

Only a minority over here heeded those warnings. After they had left us we still persisted in saying that scrummaging, solid scrummaging was the all-important thing. We seemed to say that there was a right way and a wrong way to attack, thus inferentially committing ourselves to the contention that there was one way only of attacking. The hooker was to get the ball when it was put into a scrummage, the second and third row forwards were to do the heeling, and the scrum half was to pass it back to his partner. Now we have seen back divisions playing against the New Zealanders attempt this sort of thing. It has met with no success in dry weather; it has failed dismally in wet. The big, fast, quick-breaking-up New Zealand forwards have strangled these attacks at birth.

How do they attack themselves? More often than not they do not spring back at all; they pick up the ball and go on with it. They are marvellous in avoiding getting in each other's way. They support without hampering one another. They are off before the scrum has broken up, and very judicious in the use of their three-quarter line. And how seldom do they give a wild pass, hoping that a comrade will be there to take it. This is where their inter-understanding comes in. At the critical moment one or more New Zealander is always there or thereabouts.

This time we must surely sit down and think a bit. It was after a very extensive tour in the Dominions that the Prince of Wales came home and said: 'Wake up, England.'

We must get on or get out.

Hobbs equals W. G.'s record

By Colonel Philip Trevor, CBE

PUBLISHED TUESDAY 18 AUGUST

Yesterday morning, at Taunton, Jack Hobbs got the 100th run of his 126th hundred, and by so doing equalled the record of W. G. Grace. Very early there was a long queue outside the gates of the county ground. Hobbs was 91 not out, and the desire to see a great feat accomplished found expression in a gathering of 10,000 persons.

Not until 11.25 was the game continued. A few singles and a four (off a no-ball) brought the great batsman's total to 99, and then, placing a good-length ball neatly to leg, he got his 100th run. No doubt in the mighty cheering that followed there was relief as well as joy. Hobbs said afterwards that he wished that it could have happened at his Oval home. Yet perhaps it was well that it did not. No one could accuse those 10,000 cheerers of partisanship, and it was acclamation of the right sort that they gave – good, hearty, unrestrained cheers.

The Surrey captain brought Hobbs out a glass of champagne, and he raised it in toast to those who continued to cheer him. Very soon after their applause was over, Hobbs's innings was over too. But his ordeal was not over; he had to face the concentrated frontal attack of a battalion of photographers. To this form of martyrdom he is probably getting used, and no doubt the pain has passed away. One hopes so. He will certainly have to go through it again when he makes his next hundred, and in consequence beats the record of 'W. G.'.

Hobbs scored another century in his second innings, breaking W. G.'s record.

1925

Christopher Martin-Jenkins

Key moments in cricket history

FROM A STATELY PAVILION PACKED WITH PALE, impeccably dressed gentry at Lord's in the closing years of Queen Victoria's long reign, cricket has moved along a path strewn with extraordinary events to the even more tightly packed crowds of sun-tanned, noisy, irreverent spectators in the twilight years of Queen Elizabeth II's. It would have taken a super-human imagination in 1900 to envisage, for example, the scene 98 years later at St John's, Antigua, once an unconsidered backwater of the Empire, as the 6 ft 8 in descendant of a sugar-plantation worker ran in to torment the cream of England's batting, watched in the flesh (the all too pink and solid flesh) by air-conveyed holiday-makers from the old country; or to conceive that exactly the same scene might be witnessed simultaneously by millions sitting at home in England on a cool spring evening.

'The Summer Game' – as Peter Tinniswood's brigadier alone still calls it – is no less a metaphor for life when Curtly Ambrose bowls to Alec Stewart than it was when the demon Fred Spofforth was running in to threaten stumps protected by W. G. Grace in the age of the moralising Victorians. No less, either, a mirror on society.

An institution has to adapt or die, and for a game popularly imagined to be steeped in conservatism it is extraordinary how cricket has adjusted to social trends. By means of coloured clothes, floodlights, widespread professionalism, commercialisation in all its forms, shortened versions of the two-innings game, and in many other ways the game has either been forced, or has voluntarily chosen, to cut its coat according to its cloth.

For all its association with ethics, that – as a matter of fact – is nothing new. William Clarke's 18th-century Old England XI played one-day cricket in coloured clothes for the simple purpose of making money and entertaining crowds. In a way the Golden Age of the Edwardian era was a step back rather than an advance.

Nevertheless the railways had enabled cricket to become an easily accessible game for everyone to play or watch by the time of those sepia-tinted years before 1914. The game, in whichever country of the Empire it was played, was part of the social fabric of life.

The Great War enforced a hiatus in cricket as it did in everything, but especially in the two lands where the roots of cricket went deepest – England and Australia – county and Sheffield Shield cricket resumed immediately afterwards, and so did the great battles for the Ashes. It was a sporting contest, home and away every two years, to which all other cricket was subordinated.

For a time, however, it was unbalanced by one extraordinary batsman. Don Bradman, born at Cootamundra in 1908 and brought up in Bowral in the New South Wales country, was a legend in Australia by the age of 20, and throughout the cricket world soon after. In successive seasons from 1928 he played innings of 340 not out against Victoria and 452 not out against Queensland; on his first visit to England in 1930 he scored 131 at Trent Bridge, 254 at Lord's, 334 in a single day at Headingley, and 232 at the Oval.

Leg-theory to Englishmen – most of them judging from a distance on the basis of inadequate newspaper reports – soon became 'Bodyline' to incandescent Australians.

To beat Australia England had to stop Bradman. During his double hundred at the Oval, one of his opponents noted an apparent discomfort against the relatively small but lithe and muscular Nottinghamshire fast bowler, Harold Larwood. The shrewd observer was England's chosen skipper for the return series in 1932–3, the dour, Winchester-educated, Oxford and Surrey batsman Douglas Jardine. He devised a plan during the first weeks of the tour to unsettle Bradman with short balls aimed at the ribs, in the hope of inducing catches to a semi-circle of leg fielders.

Leg-theory to Englishmen – most of them judging from a distance on the basis of inadequate newspaper reports – soon became 'Bodyline' to incandescent Australians.

The plan actually worked better against lesser batsmen. Bradman, often countering by stepping away to leg and hitting through the offside, still topped Australia's averages with more than 50, but England won the Ashes. So bitter was the reaction, however, that strong cables passed between London and Sydney, in one of which Jardine's strategy, brilliantly exploited by Larwood and his broad-shouldered, left-arm Nottinghamshire partner Bill Voce, was condemned as unsportsmanlike.

That was a terrible accusation to make to an MCC committee who prided themselves on upholding the game's traditions of fair play, but the debate reached Cabinet level in both countries and the prophecy made when Jardine's captaincy was announced – 'We shall win the Ashes but we may lose a Dominion' – almost came true. Jardine never captained against Australia again; Larwood, partly because he had burned himself out, played no more Test cricket. A goodwill tour was arranged, and any lingering resentment ended when Aussies and Poms once again fought shoulder to shoulder against the Germans.

Larwood and Voce had merely confirmed the only generalisation that may safely be made about cricket at almost any level during the century: the side with the best bowlers usually wins. If the best bowlers happen to be wrist spinners, that is a safer statement still – Shane Warne of Australia, Mushtaq Ahmed of Pakistan and Anil Kumble of India have all been regular matchwinners in the 1990s. But it is an almost inalienable truth when it comes to possessing the best fast bowlers.

Larwood and Voce merely confirmed the only generalisation that may safely be made about cricket: the side with the best bowlers usually wins.

The deprivations of war made England weak in fast bowling after both world conflicts, whereas Australia produced Ted McDonald and Jack Gregory after 1919, then Ray Lindwall and Keith Miller after 1945, and dominated accordingly. When in the 1950s England had Frank Tyson, Brian Statham and Fred Trueman to choose from, with Peter Loader, Alec Bedser, Trevor Bailey and others in reserve, the boot was on the other foot.

Dennis Lillee and Jeff Thomson took more than ample revenge 20 years later but, in the aftermath of the 'Packer Revolution', the West Indies produced a stream of high-quality fast bowlers and used them not in pairs but in fours, thereby proving virtually invincible for 20 years, far more so than they had been when Gary Sobers, the greatest all-round cricketer of the century, was at his peak in the 1960s.

The Packer Revolution was spawned by television, the invention that has had more impact on the conduct of human life in the last 100 years than penicillin or computers, cheap air travel or nuclear bombs. Cricket, reluctant though it may have been at first, has been dragged into its mould. Big matches these days start when it suits the television programme-planners. They pay the money that oils the wheels.

In the mid-1970s Kerry Packer, owner of one of Australia's commercial television channels, was keen to cash in on the boom in cricket in his homeland. Lillee and Thomson were in their pomp; England had a young all-rounder called Ian Botham who was showing unusual promise; the old country had turned the rocky finances of its first-class counties by experimenting with a sponsored single-innings one-day competition called the Gillette Cup; and, besides, Packer had envisaged the possibility of playing televised cricket under floodlights at night, as they did with baseball in America.

The son of a wealthy entrepreneur and a man accustomed to having his own way, Packer objected so strongly when, despite being offered far more than before, the Australian Cricket Board refused him television rights to Test cricket, that he resorted to sophisticated blackmail. With willing advisers who included the former Australian captain, Richie Benaud, and the then England captain, Tony Greig, he simply signed up most of the best cricketers in the world for matches to be shown on his own channel.

For the better part of two years the whole international game was disrupted, but the cricket authorities failed in their attempt to defeat Packer in the courts, and the best ideas from two seasons of his so-called World Series cricket were soon officially adopted. One-day international cricket has been so successful in attracting spectators, sponsorship and television coverage that in some countries it has eclipsed Test cricket, the subtler, sterner test of true quality.

The four-yearly World Cup is now the biggest cricketing event; profits from the 1999 World Cup will be, it is anticipated, well over £50 million. Much of this money will be invested in the attempt to develop and promote the game in parts of the world – notably the United States – where hitherto its influence has been peripheral, setting the scene for more momentous changes in the game in the 21st century.

1926

Doubles defeat of Mlle Lenglen

By A. Wallis Myers, CBE
PUBLISHED FRIDAY 25 JUNE

Returning to the centre court yesterday after a day's absence, Mlle Lenglen, partnered by Mlle Vlasto, was defeated in the doubles championship in a great three-set match by the Californian pair, Miss Ryan and Miss Mary Browne. The score in favour of the Americans was 3–6, 9–7, 6–2.

This morning Suzanne may resign possibly her singles championship. The exciting sequence of events of the last two days, reacting on a cold, mercurial temperament, and a physical effort denied the tonic of success, left her in a condition last night that made her retirement from the tournament conceivable. She was down to play a singles match after her doubles – and another large crowd, loyal as ever to their idol, waited for this tie. But the thunderstorm of the afternoon had swamped the outside courts, placing them out of commission. This accident delayed matches which were more important to the programme-builders than Mlle Lenglen's. Word was, therefore, conveyed to the exhausted champion that her appearance in singles was not of pressing importance; she has not yet been scratched; this afternoon we shall know whether she has recovered sufficiently to pick up further challenges.

If she does not play again I hope none will fail to pay their tribute to a great player, who fought every inch of the court with unyielding tenacity yesterday – a match in which, with the volleying formation of the Americans and the tandem formation of her own side, the odds were against her; a match which she so nearly won, and so smilingly lost. Whether it proves to be her last match at Wimbledon this year or not, the standard of her play and the unique character of her record will not be impaired.

On 28 June, after a disagreement with officials, Suzanne Lenglen retired from Wimbledon and turned professional. She did not play there again.

DID YOU KNOW?

Bowler Bill Copson of Derbyshire and England only took up cricket at the age of 17 when he was invited to join in a game near his home. It was during the General Strike; the players were striking miners trying to while away some time.

First British Grand Prix staged at Brooklands

From our motoring correspondent
PUBLISHED MONDAY 9 AUGUST

Last Saturday proved that the English public will not take that keen interest in motor-car racing our friends do across the Channel. Only between 10,000 and 12,000 spectators paid to see the first international motor event run in this country at Brooklands, compared with the hundreds of thousands who flock to the grands prix motor races held on the Continent. Yet excellent arrangements for seeing every portion of the British Grand Prix race had been made by the Royal Automobile Club, no matter in what part of the Brooklands course spectators gathered.

Like many another of these long-distance events, victory does not always go to the swiftest, and in this race the steady running of No. 14 Delage car, driven by R. Senechal and L. Wagner, over the 287 miles, or 110 circuits of the Brooklands course, gained the first prize and victory for France. England, out of five starters, unfortunately did not have a representative that finished the course.

The Delage car won by about four laps, or some ten miles, averaging a speed of 71.61 miles per hour for the race, with Captain Malcolm Campbell second on a French-built Bugatti, and another French Delage third, about a lap behind.

A British car, however, won the Stanley Cup for the fastest lap. Major H. O. D. Segrave on a Talbot, averaging a speed of 85.99 miles per hour, as he circled the course in 1 min 50⁴/₅ sec.

After 83 circuits Senechal left the driving seat of No. 14 Delage and Wagner took his place, his own car having retired on the eighth lap as the exhaust gases had burnt a hole through the metal pipe and made it impossible to drive. Wagner won by about ten miles, with 2¹/₂ miles dividing second and third. All the runners had their 1,500-cc cars fitted with superchargers, and timed over the half-mile unofficially the Delage averaged a speed of 120 miles an hour, which gives some idea of their capabilities. It was a tribute to England that the French cars all used Dunlop tyres, which well withstood the gruelling treatment of constant and severe braking to negotiate the 880 hairpin bends.

In 1926 Britain joined the growing number of European countries – such as Germany, at its Avus circuit in Berlin (below left) – hosting grands prix races. The first British Grand Prix was held at Brooklands (bottom), constructed 20 years earlier as the first purpose-built racing circuit in the world. Racing and record-breaking attempts continued at the 'Ascot of motor racing' until 1939, but the venue was outshone by the new international tracks.

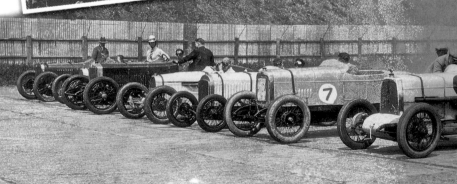

Slow-moving Dempsey loses to Gene Tunney

Gene Tunney outmanoeuvres a sluggish Jack Dempsey for the world heavyweight title. Dempsey (below left) had held the crown since 4 July 1919.

From our own correspondent
PHILADELPHIA, THURSDAY 23 SEPTEMBER
Relayed by wireless from New York

By seven o'clock every seat was taken, and the great arena was a solid mass of humanity. It was undoubtedly the largest audience which ever witnessed a prize fight. For most of those present the brilliantly illuminated ring must have appeared as a tiny spotlight on a darkened stage. How many millions listened in by radio through 32 broadcasting stations, it is impossible to estimate.

Tunney entered the ring first, and received an ovation. Dempsey followed; the crowd cheered wildly. He greeted Gene with a broad smile and a wave of the hand.

When the fight started Dempsey rushed Gene and they sparred. The champion wavered in looking for an opening. Dempsey was not the tigerish fighter the public is accustomed to, and Tunney won the first round easily.

In the second round Dempsey began to fight, but Gene reached the champion's face at will. The challenger's defence was perfect, and Dempsey was slow. Dempsey took numerous punches on the face. He hit Gene often, but without evident damage. Gene led by a long margin at the end of the second round.

In the third round Tunney kept away from Dempsey, and it was chiefly a sparring match. In the fourth the champion became more aggressive, but could not break through Tunney's defence, and took considerable punishment. All the rounds so far were Tunney's.

Dempsey's big punch was missing, the fifth round looking amateurish, with much sparring and few blows. In the sixth Jack got several left hooks to the body, and Tunney showed their effect. It commenced to rain hard at this stage.

In the seventh the fight quickened, and Tunney seemed still to have a slight advantage, his straight arm punches keeping Jack away. The eighth was a tame affair, and the fight became somewhat boresome.

Dempsey took his terrific beating manfully and fought furiously in the last round. He drove Gene frequently to the ropes, but the challenger's defence was perfect.

1926

63

SPORT IN BRIEF

GOLF
Cecil Leitch wins a record fourth British Ladies' Amateur golf title, adding to her victories in 1914, 1920 and 1921. In 1929 Joyce Wethered also wins her fourth British Ladies' title to share the record.

CRICKET
England finally regain the Ashes for the first time since 1912, despite a superb performance by Australia's Charles Macartney, who scores three centuries in successive innings. In the final Test at the Oval, English batsmen Jack Hobbs and Herbert Sutcliffe score 100 and 161 respectively in an extraordinary opening partnership of 172 on a sticky wicket.

HORSE RACING
British Chancellor of the Exchequer Winston Churchill announces that in future betting will be taxed. The proposal meets with some vociferous opposition, but is nevertheless implemented from 1 November.

FOOTBALL
Herbert Chapman, Huddersfield's manager since 1921, has now moved to Arsenal, but has left behind one of his final purchases, the talented Scottish right-winger, Alec Jackson. Jackson helps Huddersfield to their third consecutive League title this year, and to the 1928 and 1930 FA Cup finals.

RUGBY UNION
Australia, New Zealand and South Africa join the International Board, originally formed in 1886.

CRICKET
English fast bowler Harold Larwood, who will later make headlines on the infamous 'Bodyline' tour of Australia in 1932–3, makes his debut for England in the second Test of the Ashes series.

1927

The Ryder Cup

From our own correspondent
WORCESTER (MASS), SATURDAY 4 JUNE

The British Ryder Cup team of professional golfers flattered only to deceive in the singles, where, in the early part of the contest, there were visions of making up ground lost in the foursomes. Player after player was caught, passed, or trounced. Aubrey Boomer was going well enough to warrant the belief that he would make it interesting for Johnny Farrell to the bitter end, but after holding the American magnificently in the first round, fell off in the second.

Ted Ray never had any chance with Leo Diegel, who, in one of his most brilliant moods, scored 70 in the morning for a lead of six, while H. Jolly fell an easy prey to Johnny Golden. Scotch stubbornness helped George Duncan to win Britain's only point against Joe Turnesa. There was also a dash of the old Duncan brilliance as George holed a nice putt for a winning 'birdie'.

The brilliant start of Charles Whitcombe led to expectations of at least one overwhelming British success, but after standing five up at the 15th in the morning, his play began to deteriorate in marked degree, and in the long run it was Gene Sarazen who was unlucky not to win. Archie Compston gave as much as he received with Bill Mehlhorn, but eventually the point went to the American. Fred Robson expressed satisfaction at holding Al Watrous in the morning; in the afternoon Robson won only two holes, a temporary slump on three consecutive holes by the Englishman bringing about his own downfall.

Walter Hagen's golf still was unsatisfactory to himself, but in his own inimitable fashion he staggered Arthur Havers with unexpected blows.

Aggregate on foursomes and singles: the United States, nine matches, Great Britain, two. One match halved.

MILESTONES

The first BBC radio sports commentary was transmitted on 15 January 1927. Captain H. B. T. Wakelam described action from the England v Wales rugby union international being held at Twickenham. He was given one simple instruction by his superiors: 'Don't swear.'

Newcastle are League champions

From our special correspondent
PUBLISHED MONDAY 2 MAY

Any doubt that remained about Newcastle United carrying off the championship was removed by their victory over Sheffield Wednesday on Saturday, and a great crowd at St James' Park gave the team a rousing reception at the close of the match. Huddersfield Town, although badly beaten at Bolton, where Wright, an emergency forward, scored three goals, finish as runners-up, after three times holding first place – a remarkable display of consistently good football.

Centre forward Hughie Gallacher (right) leads Newcastle to the 1927 League title.

How Cardiff won the FA Cup

By B. Bennison
PUBLISHED MONDAY 25 APRIL

To all who were present at Wembley on Saturday, this year's Cup final will remain an imperishable memory. Not on account of the football, which was seldom thrilling; rather was it after long-established fashion: the occasion beat the man. And that is why the highly prized trophy for the first time in history was won by Wales, as represented by Cardiff City, who beat the Arsenal by the only goal scored. Dan Lewis, a Welshman curiously enough, keeper of the citadel of the London club, a quarter of an hour or so before the finish, went down to a shot fired at him by Hughie Ferguson, leader of the Cardiff attack. He was apparently all preparedness: he gathered the ball with both hands, his fullbacks in a position to protect him if needs be. But having apparently reduced the shot to a simple, puny thing, he turned his back to Len Davis and others of the opposition, and while still on the ground he lost possession. And when all tangled up, he sought to throw the ball, so I thought, round the post by way of conceding a corner. Instead he threw the ball into the net. And so he beat himself and his club. There never was such a tragedy. Most of the 100,000 onlookers were left dumbfounded. The Cup can never have been won by such a tremendous fluke.

Goalmouth action at the FA Cup final. Arsenal lost 1–0 to Cardiff City after a disastrous goalkeeping error.

Major Segrave sets new record

From our own correspondent
NEW YORK, TUESDAY 29 MARCH

On the burning sands of the famous Daytona Beach, Florida, Major H. O. D. Segrave, the Englishman, in his four-ton, bright red, high-speed car, today broke the official world's record for a mile by travelling at 203.841 miles an hour.

Major Segrave, the premier of European racing drivers, sent his mystery car at the astounding pace of 207.015 miles per hour down the course, after beating up the track into a quartering headwind that threw his huge racer into skids threatening instant death. His average

time for the mile on the two runs was 203.841 mph.

After his second run Major Segrave stopped for a change of tyres. The wind pressure, he said, was such as to make steering all but impossible. He exhibited wind burns, and complained of aches in his wrists caused by his efforts to fight the wind. Just before the start he had read a cablegram from his wife, wishing him the best of luck. On the second trip the huge four-ton car struck three course-marking flags without the major knowing.

Henry Segrave, the first man to travel at over 200 mph. The official time for his run on 29 March was eventually given as 203.79 mph (327.97 km/h).

SPORT IN BRIEF

RUGBY LEAGUE
The New Zealand rugby league team tour of Britain ends disastrously, with financial losses all round. The touring party is riven with dissent; seven players consistently argue with the manager, who threatens to send them home. The tour is completed but the rebels are given life bans by the New Zealand governing body, while the manager defects to his native Australia.

SNOOKER
Joe Davis wins his first world snooker championship. His superiority to any challengers will ensure that he retains the world title until he decides to retire from competition after winning his 15th championship in 1947. Davis will also win the first of five consecutive world billiards titles in 1928.

RUGBY UNION
Wavell Wakefield wins a record 31st cap for England. He has captained England 13 times, winning three Grand Slams and two Triple Crowns. An astute tactician, Wakefield radically changes the way forwards are organised in rugby union.

BABE RUTH (1895–1948)

BORN IN BALTIMORE, MARYLAND, on 6 February 1895, George Herman (Babe) Ruth began his baseball career in 1914 as a left-handed pitcher with the American league team, the Boston Red Sox. In 1920 he was sold to the New York Yankees for $125,000.

Standing 6 ft 2 in tall, and weighing more than 15 stone, Babe Ruth was a powerful striker of the ball; in 14 years with the New York Yankees he set numerous records.

In each season from 1919–21 he broke the major-league home run record, and in 1927 he scored 60 home runs in one season, a record that stood for 27 years. He played in ten World Series, and his lifetime total of 714 home runs was only bettered 39 years later, in 1974, by Henry Aaron.

Babe Ruth was a flamboyant figure, perfectly suited to a golden age of sport and entertainment in the United States. The big-hitting 'Sultan of Swat' attracted widespread support for the New York Yankees as well as for the game of baseball, which continued to grow in popularity even through the Depression years of the 1930s.

In 1935 Babe Ruth moved to the Boston Braves, and the following year was elected to the Baseball Hall of Fame. Although he became coach to the Brooklyn Dodgers in 1938, he never achieved his aim of becoming manager for a major-league club.

Ruth's exploits gained him worldwide fame. In World War II Japanese soldiers are supposed to have taunted American troops with what they believed to be the ultimate insult: 'To hell with Babe Ruth!'

1928

Dramatic incidents at Sandwich

By George W. Greenwood
SANDWICH, FRIDAY 11 MAY

The Prince of Wales saw Walter Hagen win the British Open championship at Royal St George's, Sandwich, today, this being America's seventh success in the last nine years – a truly amazing sequence.

Hagen's winning score was 292, two strokes in front of Gene Sarazen, another American. This is Hagen's third triumph in the championship. But in view of his wholesale defeat in the recent match with Archie Compston, today's victory must be regarded as the most wonderful in Hagen's remarkable career in golf. The laugh is now with Hagen, more especially when in certain quarters it was prophesied that he was no longer the great personality in international contests, and that his golf had lost its magic touch. We have seen all the old magic come back, even supposing that it had ever been lost, and as regards pluck and courage in fighting through desperate situations, he is the same Hagen, indomitable of spirit and will.

Hagen won the championship by reason of two magnificent rounds of 72 each, which, in view of the severity of the course, the testing wind, and the psychology of the occasion, can be considered as an achievement equal to anything that has been accomplished in an event of this character.

Hagen drives his way to a third victory in the British Open. He went on to win a fourth title in 1929.

MILESTONES

The first numbered football shirts were introduced (to general disapproval) by Herbert Chapman, manager of Arsenal. His efforts to introduce floodlighting had already met with difficulties. A great innovator, Chapman also championed the introduction of 'goal judges', to help the referee in deciding whether a player had scored or not.

Gallant outsider wins after disaster at the Grand National

PUBLISHED SATURDAY 31 MARCH

Something awful was bound to happen. Forty-two horses went to the post for the Grand National steeplechase at Liverpool, and only one stood up to the end. Yesterday morning Mr H. S. Kenyon's Tipperary Tim was practically unheard-of. In the afternoon he became world famous. He came in alone for a steeplechase worth over £11,000. Only one other, the American Billy Barton, was placed by the judge, and that after the horse had been on the ground through falling at the last fence when holding a short lead.

A great massacre had occurred during the race, making it amount to something far worse than a mere debacle. Fiction cannot compete with the cold facts of this latest celebration of burlesque steeplechasing, for the winner of so much money would scarcely be ranked as a humble selling-plater elsewhere. He has a tube in his throat because he was a roarer, and could not possibly have done what he did without this resort to artifice. Need it be added that his starting price was 100–1, which means that no one scarcely had considered him worthy of a passing thought.

Yet it says something for the sportsmanship of our people when, though they had lost their money on others, they rushed to the paddock to meet the horse and give a rousing cheer to horse and rider for what, after all, had been a display of gallantry and endurance, though aided by that all-powerful ally we call luck.

My story begins with the crowding in the paddock of all these 42 competitors. They lined up, and three times the single line of tape was broken because some of the jockeys were even more anxious than the starter to get this detail over. At last they were sent on to the battlefield, which was so soon to become a sort of shambles. Becher's did not seem to gather in its usual toll. The holocaust happened at the Canal Turn, which makes a sharp left-handed move necessary. I have written on previous

Tottenham Hotspur in the Second Division

By B. Bennison
PUBLISHED MONDAY 7 MAY

Tottenham Hotspur, together with Middlesbrough, have been relegated to the Second Division, where they will be joined by Millwall and Bradford. Everton finished champions, with Huddersfield runners-up.

There has never been a more remarkable campaign than that which was brought to a close on Saturday. There was a period when the relegation of Tottenham Hotspur, perhaps the wealthiest club in the country, appeared to be a remote possibility; indeed, there was a time when they had an outside chance of carrying off the championship. No fewer than seven clubs finished level with 39 points, but two marks ahead of the last team of all and only one more than Tottenham Hotspur.

Whether this breakneck competition is all to the good of the League is a debatable question. Maybe it will lead to more frantic bartering for players; if such be the outcome, then it will be bad for the game: that positions may be bought is unthinkable, and yet it will not be denied that Everton, because of the employment of their well-filled purse, have achieved the ambition of all clubs.

Twelve months ago they were in the doldrums; they then set about acquiring players of high renown, and they have carried off the championship.

There has dropped out of the Arsenal ranks Charles Buchan, who, after a long and distinguished career, has retired from the game. A Londoner by birth, Buchan found his great opportunity at Sunderland, with whose side, season after season, he carried himself as one of the most successful – certainly one of the most remarkable – inside rights of this or any other age. He was fast approaching to the end of his football tether when he became linked up with the Arsenal, but he nevertheless had most to do with changing what had hitherto been a team of moderate capacity into one of high quality.

Buchan was one of very few players who struck an individual, a distinctive note. For the better part of 20 years he had it in him to win matches all by himself, and it was fitting that after the Arsenal had made a most creditable draw with Everton, he was presented with a token of the regard and appreciation of his club and his fellows. Buchan was one of the last of his kind, rich in personality and those gifts which only a complete footballer may possess.

occasions how Easter Hero has jumped awkwardly to the right at these National fences. Anyhow, he distinguished himself now by jumping on to the top of the fence, and there he remained until finally he fell back into the ditch. Two or three horses following immediately on his heels stopped for the simple reason that they could not jump, and they, in their turn, stopped others.

We shall be told that it was due to an accident altogether exceptional that so many horses were put out of the race. Personally I shall maintain that when nearly 50 horses go to the post for a Grand National the race is robbed of its sporting character through those enormous risks of interference which would not be present were, say, a score of the best steeplechasers in the world bidding for what should be the blue riband of steeplechasing.

Heading for disaster: horses approach the first fence of the Grand National steeplechase. The race was won by Tipperary Tim – the only horse not to fall in the race – at odds of 100–1. Only two horses finished.

The Wembley Wizards

By B. Bennison

PUBLISHED MONDAY 2 APRIL

The King and Queen of Afghanistan, together with the Duke of York, saw England's Association football match against Scotland on Saturday. Scotland won by five goals to one. This is the most decisive victory gained by either country for 40 years. The game was watched in heavy rain by 80,000 people.

Beaten for speed, bankrupt of ideas, without a definite, common purpose, England's failure was indeed a woeful and incredible one. Only a single member of the team, Ted Hufton, the goalkeeper, justified himself; the rest were slow to move, slow to think, sorry, hapless, helpless. England suffered, and deserved to be routed. Except in the first minute, when Smith, with Harkness sprawling, struck the upright, Scotland had little or no cause for apprehension. The Scotsmen took the lead almost immediately; thereafter they did as they pleased, their football was delightful, at times amazingly clever and precise. So emphatically were England outplayed, the wonder was that Scotland did not win by ever so many more goals. Great gaps in the home defence were discernible in the game's infancy; they widened unbelievably.

Scotland were a team of masters; all the delights of the game did they spread before what for an international in this country was a record crowd. Only at odd moments did the Scots put the ball in the air; passes were given on the ground, and as if to measure. There was no scrambling; every man had the closest regard for positional play. And it came about that Alan Morton centred perfectly, so that Alex Jackson, cutting inwards from the extreme right, got a goal.

The second of Scotland's goals, the best of the match, was scored by Alex James. He was just beyond the halfway line when he was given the ball. Making a pretence at going forward, he stepped back, and with a hard drive found the net. After the change of ends, Scotland romped home. England's solitary score was made by Bob Kelly from a free kick 30 yards out.

English defenders Goodall and Jones look on helplessly as Hughie Gallacher shoots at goal; Hufton is the goalkeeper signalling it wide.

SPORT IN BRIEF

ATHLETICS
Fraulein Lina Radke-Batschauer of Germany wins the final of the women's 800 m in the Olympic Games in a world record time, but due to the 'weary and overwrought' state of the competitors at the end of the race, the event is not staged again until 1960.

CRICKET
On 25 June Nottinghamshire achieve a record for English cricket when they score 656 for three in their match against Warwickshire.

MOTOR RACING
American driver Frank Lockhart poses **(below)** in his 16-cylinder Stutz, in which he attempted to break the speed record held by England. He was killed at Daytona Beach, Florida, on 25 April.

1929

How Wales beat Scotland

By Colonel Philip Trevor, CBE

Published Monday 4 February

It was indeed a well-deserved victory which Wales won over Scotland at Swansea on Saturday, and the method of the scoring may be regarded as a fair indication of the superiority of the winners.

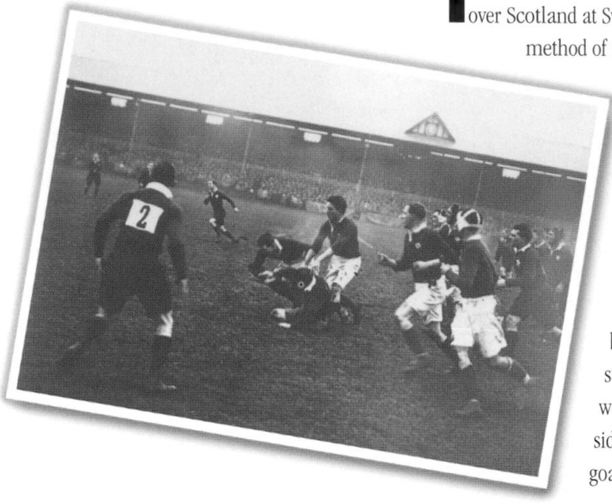

By means of intelligently definite attack the Welshmen crossed the Scottish goal-line four times, while not once could the Scotsmen retaliate in that way. Their seven points were given them by the individual smartness of their stand-off halfback, A. H. Brown (he was quite the best man on the losing side), who kicked quite a good penalty goal and dropped a very good one.

At the outset, I admit the excellence of the Welsh forwards in their tight scrummaging and in the ever important duties of hooking and heeling. They gave their backs the necessary chances. It was the intelligent straight running of the Welsh backs which gave Wales their entirely satisfactory victory.

The game was as disappointing to Scotland as it was encouraging to Wales. The Scots played without inspiration and without a definite objective. When, at rugby football, you wait and see, it's a question of all waiting and no seeing.

I regret to say that arrangements for accommodation of the press were such as ought not to have been made. Some flimsy boards a few inches wide hastily nailed together did duty as writing desks, and even so this structure was put in a bad place.

Scotland struggling in the misty, slippery conditions (left). Wales scored three tries in their 14–7 victory.

DID YOU KNOW?

At the age of 50 the eccentric Nottinghamshire batsman George Gunn was selected to play for the England cricket team for the third time. He was called up to join the touring party travelling to the West Indies – a record 17 years 316 days after his last selection. He acquitted himself honourably in the series, scoring 85 and 47 in his final Test match.

Totalisator at Newmarket

By Hotspur

Newmarket, Tuesday 16 July

If there had been no Tote operating at Newmarket today it would have been said that the wonderful weather was the cause of the big attendance. Certainly the actual racing was singularly lacking in bright features.

It was the Tote, of course. Being a fortnight old, it had added to its powers of magnetism, for how otherwise could one account for the size of the gathering. I noticed that since the last meeting they had introduced facilities for wagering in £10 units. I could not see that they were being rushed for; rather did the public generally continue to lament the absence of a 10-shilling unit.

On the first day the Tote has not advertised itself anything like as sensationally as was the case a fortnight ago; neither have the bookmakers found it necessary to go to extremes to fight their case. This may be because well-backed winners have been scoring and some better-backed ones have been gaining the places. As a matter of fact, there were several instances in which the bookmakers beat the Tote in both respects.

Racegoers consult the first official Totalisator, in use at Newmarket. The machine recorded bets, worked out odds and calculated winnings.

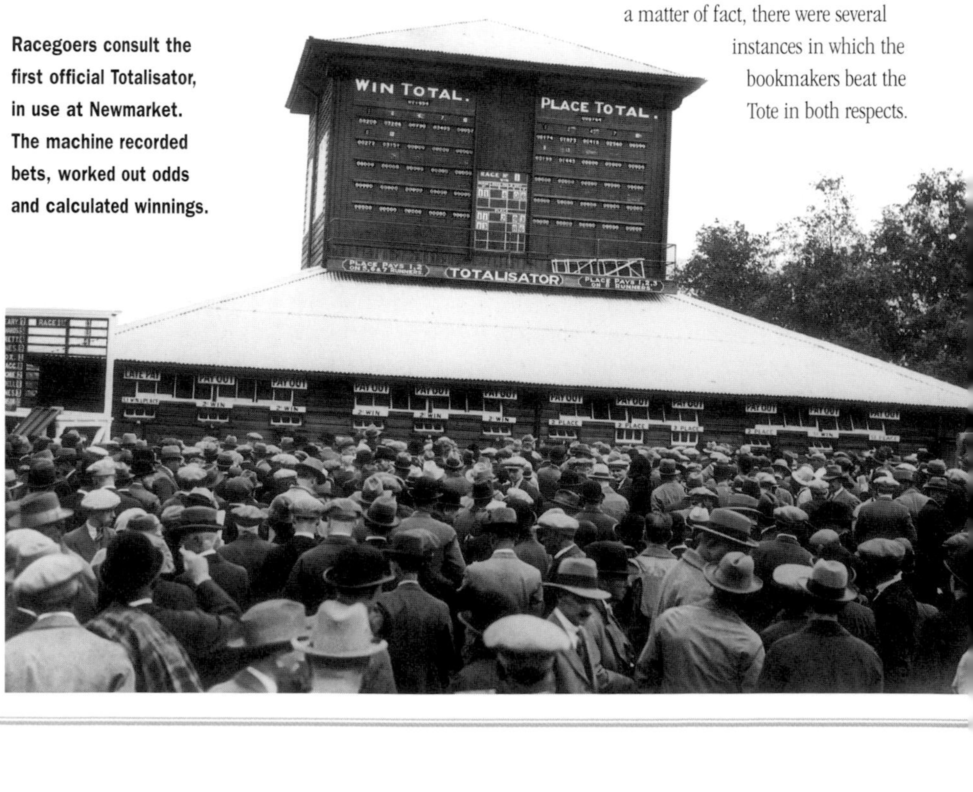

Australia's well-earned win

By Clem Hill

Melbourne, Sunday 17 March

After losing five Tests straight off the reel, Australia have at last won a match, and they deserved their victory yesterday by five wickets. Having to face 519 was a tremendous task, and even to make 287 in the last innings was a good performance.

My sincere congratulations to Percy Chapman and the England team on retaining the Ashes, 4–1. They have played the game right up to the hilt. Both sides can be commended on this fact.

The only thing wrong was the number of unnecessary appeals, but, after all, the umpires are there to be kept awake. There has been some tremendously slow batting right through. There is no doubt that the limitless Tests are causing this calamity. I have always advocated that they should be played out, but am now in favour of five days in Australia and four in England, the latter having longer hours' play, which makes up a difference in time.

Italian car wins Irish Grand Prix

By The Daily Telegraph *motoring correspondent*
PUBLISHED MONDAY 15 JULY

Spectators examine the cars in the pit lanes before the race; more than 100,000 attended the Grand Prix.

By a margin of 14 seconds Boris Ivanovsky, on the two-litre supercharged Alfa Romeo car, completed a double event for Italy in winning the Irish motor Grand Prix race today for high-powered cars. Yesterday he won the light car race in 3 hr 41 min 30 sec.

Ivanovsky by his victories takes the Grand Prix trophy, a replica of the Phoenix Monument, the Irish Cup for the race today, and the Free State Cup he won yesterday. He also was awarded £1,000 for each day's race. Today, on the larger car, he averaged a speed of 76.42 mph.

Brilliant sunshine had somewhat softened the tarred surface of this excellent road course, so fears were expressed that the more powerful cars today might slide and get out of control. The race proved otherwise, as the handicap start given to the Alfa Romeo of four laps from Thistlethwaite's Mercedes, and H. R. S. Birkin's and Bernard Rubins' supercharged Bentleys, made the back-markers astonish the spectators by lapping the circuit at

over 80 mph without a mishap, although there was a certain amount of well-controlled skidding by the pilots.

It was indeed a battle of giants as the Mercedes dashed off with the lead at the fall of the flag, with 'Tim' Birkin on his Bentley close on his tail for one hour and a half. There was only a few lengths between them until the Mercedes blew a gasket and retired hurt. So interested were the public in this duel that they had forgotten Ivanovsky, on the handicap of four laps start, who had been steadily pegging away. Great excitement was aroused when, with 12 laps left to Ivanovsky to finish the race, it was found that Glen Kidston was only two minutes 35 seconds behind the leader. Could he overtake him in the time available?, was the query. Both camps put out signals to tell their champions to drive faster. Kidston gained from 15 to 25 seconds per lap on his opponent, but a skid at one corner marred his chance, and amid great cheering Ivanovsky finished the winner.

SPORT IN BRIEF

RUGBY UNION
Despite losing against Wales (see main text), Scotland beat England on 16 March to win the Calcutta Cup and the Five Nations championship. Johnny Bannerman captains the side; it is his 38th consecutive international match. This will stand as a record until 1962.

FOOTBALL
On 27 April a crowd of more than 92,000 watch Bolton Wanderers beat Portsmouth 2–0. It is Bolton's third win in an FA Cup final at Wembley; they scored a 2–0 win against West Ham in 1923, and a 1–0 victory against Manchester City in 1926.

GOLF
On 27 April, as Bolton are winning at Wembley, Great Britain make a brilliant recovery in the golf match against America, held at Moortown, near Leeds, Yorkshire, to win the Ryder Cup by six matches to four. George Duncan scores a fine victory, by ten and eight, over his rival captain, Walter Hagen.

HOCKEY
In April the women's committee of the German Hockey Association rules that women must henceforth wear dresses and not shorts to play the game. The Berlin Women's Hockey Association is opposed to the ruling.

FOOTBALL
Sheffield Wednesday are winners of the League championship. They have only managed a draw with Burnley in the last match of the season, but so have their nearest rivals, Leicester City, against Huddersfield.

1930

Bradman the record breaker

By F. G. Lavers
LEEDS, FRIDAY 11 JULY

Don Bradman, Australia's 21-year-old batsman, again made cricket history when the third Test match opened at Leeds today. Going in when the first wicket had fallen for two runs, he completed 100 before lunch – an achievement only equalled by V. T. Trumper and C. G. Macartney – and, batting all day, reached the magnificent total of 309 not out. He was at the wicket for five hours and 50 minutes.

With this astonishing performance, following his 254 at Lord's a fortnight ago, he broke the following Test match records:

Highest individual score ever made (287 by R. E. Foster at Sydney in 1903–4);

Highest aggregate made by an Australian in a full series of such matches (574 by V. T. Trumper).

Bradman has made 703 runs in the present series of Test matches. Only one batting record is now left for him to break – Hammond's aggregate of 905 in the 1928–9 series.

Bradman's marvellous innings is no mere numerical record, although it exceeds the previous best by 22 and is still unfinished.

All who saw it account this effort, on the part of a 21-year-old cricketer from the other side of the world, unique by virtue of the ease and masterful efficiency with which he accomplished everything he essayed to do.

A crowd of 20,000 people watched these marvels spellbound. They had paid some £2,929 to witness, as they hoped, something quite different, but they realised they were getting full value for their money.

At 194 Bradman lost W. M. Woodfull for an invaluable 50, and then entered upon a partnership with A. F. Kippax that was destined to put all previous third-wicket partnerships in the shade. Bradman went on to pass his own record score for Australia at Lord's, and then Foster's for all Tests at Sydney.

After Kippax was out, beautifully caught at backward point, Bradman with Stan McCabe as partner imperturbably registered his 300th run. With the last ball of the day he drove M. W. Tate magnificently for four past mid-off. He ended, therefore, on the same brilliant note as that on which he began. There was no sign of physical or mental fatigue; no relaxation of the extraordinary combination of watchfulness and agility.

Bradman still lives to show us fresh marvels. The credit that must go to him, which was expressed in the final ovation of the great crowd before the pavilion steps, cannot be overestimated. Neither the bowling nor the fielding of England was anything but good; sometimes, indeed, it was brilliant. Yet Bradman dominated the play as no man has ever dominated in Test match cricket before. He is without doubt a cricket phenomenon.

Bradman (on left, below) reaches 334 on the second day of the third Test. The score was an Ashes record.

Speed king Segrave is dead

PUBLISHED SATURDAY 14 JUNE

Sir Henry O'Neal Dehane Segrave **(right)**, who died yesterday in an attempt on Windermere to achieve a world record for speed in watercraft, was the most famous and most successful of the comparatively small band of specialists, colloquially known as 'speed kings', evolved by the internal combustion engine. He had since March last year held the world's record for the fastest speed attained on land. He seemed certain to attain the same honour for speed on water when disaster overtook him.

Tall, slenderly built, erect, with piercing deep-set eyes and a hawk-like face, he was all that imagination called for in a speed king. He had nerves, but they were nerves of steel; a vivid imagination, controlled by a cool brain.

By 1924 Segrave's reputation as a racing driver was thoroughly established, and soon afterwards he began his wonderful career as a maker and breaker of records as well as a winner of races.

On March 29 he drove the Sunbeam over the Daytona course in Florida at 203.79 mph, the first man in the world to travel at over 200 mph.

Captain Malcolm Campbell went to Daytona and raised the record to 206.96 mph, and then an American driver, Ray Keech, went a fractional part of a second quicker over the measured mile and captured the honour for his country.

The record had to be regained, and Segrave set out to do it. Captain J. S. Irving, who had been in charge of the construction of his Sunbeam, designed for him a new racer, the famous Golden Arrow. The Golden Arrow was taken to Daytona early in 1929, and on March 11, at its first serious effort, Segrave drove it to and fro over the measured mile at a mean speed for the two runs of 231.55 mph.

Commodore Gar Wood and his boats still held the world's water-speed record and the international trophy. It was with the object of capturing both that Sir Henry Segrave designed and built the ill-fated *Miss England II*, undoubtedly the fastest boat ever put into the water.

MILESTONES

The first goal ever to be scored in the World Cup was by Lucien Laurent of France, who put his team into the lead in their match against Mexico on 13 July. Laurent had only had five days to recover from the team's 15-day voyage from Europe to Montevideo in Uruguay.

Alex James is hero of Cup final

By B. Bennison

PUBLISHED MONDAY 28 APRIL

The Arsenal, for the first time in their history, won the Football Association Cup today, at Wembley, by defeating Huddersfield Town by two goals to nil. They triumphed not because of the superiority of their football but because they were quicker into their stride.

There were of the teams some players who were obviously affrighted by the bigness of the occasion. Others, notably Alex James, a little, waddling Scotsman, of the Arsenal, were as men inspired. But neither side reproduced their normal game. They did infinitely better, however, than many teams I have seen at Wembley in other seasons.

Indeed, there were periods when the football was remarkable for cleverness and unity of purpose. Especially was this so in the first 20 minutes and for half an hour after the interval, when Huddersfield were fighting to rob the Arsenal of the lead established by James after play had been in progress a little more than a quarter of an hour.

The hero and the most successful of all the players was James. A very ordinary line of forwards the Arsenal would have had but for him. Everything he attempted did not come off, but he had most to do with his side's success. His ball control was wonderful; his daring often amounted to impudence. There was little that he did not seem able to do.

The victory of the Arsenal was a popular one, and was met with unbounded enthusiasm.

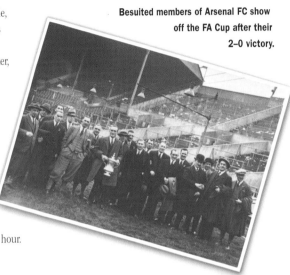

Besuited members of Arsenal FC show off the FA Cup after their 2–0 victory.

Easter Hero shows the way at Cheltenham

By Hotspur

CHELTENHAM, TUESDAY 11 MARCH

For the second year in succession Easter Hero is the winner of the Cheltenham Gold Cup, but as a great match between him and Gib the affair was a profound disappointment. How could it be otherwise when Gib should have done the last thing expected of such a brilliant jumper? He fell two fences from home just as he was drawing alongside his rival to battle out what remained of the distance.

The other two runners had been utterly negligible: indeed Donzelon fell after keeping Grakle company for half the journey. The rivals had been a long way ahead of them, Easter Hero showing the way from the outset. He would vary his lead from three to half a dozen lengths, and all the way he was going temperately, and never making the slightest mistake, after he had landed none too well over the first fence.

Half a mile from home Fred Rees gave Gib a reminder or two with the whip. He was rousing a lazy rather than a tired horse, for there was a response which brought

him up to Easter Hero at the fateful second fence from the finish.

Whether he went unbalanced into the fence, or the effort took the last out of him, I do not know. When, however, it was realised that Easter Hero was alone, and that Gib was down, it was in the nature of an anticlimax. Yet it would be ungenerous not to credit Easter Hero with a beautifully smooth performance. I believe he would have won had Gib stood up, for there were reserves in him still untouched, while Gib had to be put under strong pressure.

Easter Hero, Gold Cup winner for the second time.

SPORT IN BRIEF

GOLF
Bobby Jones retires from serious competition at the age of 28 having achieved the 'Impregnable Quadrilateral': winning the British Amateur, British Open, US Amateur and US Open titles. In 1934 Jones stages the first Augusta Invitational at his new golf course in Georgia; this will become famous as the US Masters tournament.

CRICKET
Jack Hobbs, the 'Master', plays his final Test series for England at the age of 47. He is the first batsman in Test cricket to reach 4,000 runs (in 1926) and 5,000 runs (in 1929). His runs total of 61,237 remains a record in 1998.

FOOTBALL
The first football World Cup is inaugurated by FIFA president Jules Rimet, who gives his name to the trophy. Just 13 nations contest the first competition held in Uruguay. France is among the few European countries represented: British teams have withdrawn from FIFA after a row over payments for amateur players, and so do not take part. Other European nations such as Austria, Italy, Germany and Spain refuse to go, citing expense and the three-week boat trip as their excuse. While the French team only win one game, the home side, Uruguay, get through to the final, fighting back from a 1–2 deficit at half-time to beat Argentina 4–2 for the trophy.

RUGBY LEAGUE
The Australian tour of Britain is marred by a dispute over the third Test result. The Australians demand a final and deciding Test, which they lose.

1931

Famous goalkeeper killed

PUBLISHED MONDAY 7 SEPTEMBER

John Thomson, the Celtic and Scottish international goalkeeper, died in hospital on Saturday night, following an accident in the Celtic v Rangers Scottish League football match at Ibrox Park, Glasgow.

Thomson, in diving at the feet of an attacking forward, received a kick on the head. He was taken to the Victoria Infirmary with a fractured skull.

This is the first time that a death has been immediately attributable to an accident in first-class association football.

MILESTONES

The first television broadcast of a sporting event in Britain was of this year's Derby. The Baird Company sent pictures direct from the racecourse via a BBC transmitter; *The Daily Telegraph* reported that 'all the scenes were easily discernible.'

British hope Berg defeated by Canzoneri

From our boxing correspondent
PUBLISHED MONDAY 27 APRIL

One blow, one devastating short-arm jolt, and the best British 'hope' who has challenged American supremacy for more than ten years was knocked out. The defeat of Kid Berg at the hands of Tony Canzoneri in the third round of their bout, at Chicago on Friday, was very disappointing, and not a little surprising. There was so much on which to build our expectations.

Even the Americans were sufficiently impressed to lay odds against the retention of the title by the champion. Berg had already beaten him, and since then had fought frequently and well.

Berg has always adopted a strong attack as the first line of defence, and a man who does that must inevitably face the risk of a knock-out. The challenger started slowly; he usually does. He was feeling his way. Then he warmed up to his work. He used both hands to Canzoneri and had him guessing.

I am quite sure that Berg was enjoying himself immensely. It was not that he forgot to defend himself, but just that he was obsessed with the task of attacking. His jaw was 'open wide'. Canzoneri, quick as thought, smashed in his right and the fight was over.

It is, we might claim, honours easy. Canzoneri has avenged that heavy defeat which Berg administered to him a year ago, but that does not mean there will be a deciding bout. It is hoped that Berg will be given another chance, but to accord it to him would be generous.

The champion has successfully resisted a challenge. That being so, he would want a strong inducement to risk his title again. If he agrees to another fight, he would appear to be confident of beating Berg again.

Londoner Jackie 'Kid' Berg (left) lost his own world junior welterweight title in his challenge for Canzoneri's world lightweight title. Later in the year he fought Canzoneri again, but was beaten on points.

Rout of British players in Ryder Cup

By George Greenwood
PUBLISHED MONDAY 29 JUNE

America defeated Great Britain in the Ryder Cup contest at Scioto, Columbus, on Saturday, by a total of nine matches to three.

The United States players, who won the foursomes by three games to one, and the singles by six games to two, have thus won the rubber match.

The rout of the British players, following on the loss of the championship at Carnoustie, will come as a great disappointment. While the chances of victory were never substantial, there were good grounds for believing that Britain would make a more determined bid for victory than the results indicate. W. H. Davies, the sturdy little golfer from the north of England, one of the newcomers, and Arthur Havers, who has made a welcome return to form after several years of almost complete eclipse, were the only successful British players in the singles.

Others with more illustrious reputations, Archie Compston and Fred Robson in particular, collapsed badly, though it is only fair to say that Robson, in partnership with his old friend Abe Mitchell, won the one foursome for Britain. Charles Whitcombe, who, I cannot help thinking, committed a tactical error in standing down from the foursomes, thereby endangering the success of the side, was defeated by Walter Hagen.

The American captain has exploded the idea prevalent in the States that he is a past number. Throughout the encounter, which ended on the 33rd green, Hagen was his own brilliantly eccentric self. On four occasions he almost holed out from bunkers into which he gaily sailed, only to sail as gaily out again straight at the flag.

Anywhere on the course, apparently it did not seem to matter where, the pin was his magnet. Hagen, who went into luncheon with the comfortable lead of four holes, having accomplished the round in 70 as against Ernest Whitcombe's 74, held on grimly to his advantage to the end. Though the British captain made a characteristic effort to wipe out the deficit, it was all to no purpose against the conjuring tricks of Hagen, who alternately exploded, hacked and chipped the ball from doubtful places always on to the green.

I shall be surprised if Robson, Mitchell, Whitcombe, and even Compston, unless he recovers the match-winning faculty, are again chosen to represent Britain in international contests. Having had their day, they must make room for younger players, who may reasonably be expected to stand the physical test of an exhausting match.

The gamble on men whose ages are nearer 50 than 40 has failed dismally, and the time has now arrived when our house, if ever we are to regain our golfing prestige, should be put in order. From the comments of the spectators at Scioto, it would seem that the American public has not been favourably impressed either with the attack or the defence of our players, a state of things which does not occasion great surprise.

While excuses for failure are never satisfactory and rarely carry conviction, the point may reasonably be advanced that with the use of the American larger and lighter ball the scales were slightly weighted against Britain. However, we should have lost the match no matter what type of ball had been employed, the plain truth being that the Americans are better players.

Two goals in a minute in Wembley's most thrilling Cup final

By Frank Coles

PUBLISHED MONDAY 27 APRIL

One of West Bromwich Albion's two Billy Richardsons (this is the centre forward, Billy 'G' for Ginger) scoring the decisive goal in their 2–1 win over Birmingham.

West Bromwich Albion, in winning the Cup with the youngest team that have ever appeared in the final, have buried the bogey of Wembley 'atmosphere' for all time.

Their triumph came in the most thrilling and dramatic 60 seconds of football ever witnessed at a big match, a breathless minute which will live in the memory of the 92,406 people who were at Wembley.

In the 13th minute of the second half Birmingham, after half an hour's desperate striving, deprived the Albion of a precious lead gained when the game was 26 minutes old. In doing so they had achieved the almost unbelievable, for no team had scored an equalising goal in a Cup final for 21 years. Joe Bradford, the scorer, overwhelmed with joy, leapt into the air, and the rest of the Birmingham players did their best to overwhelm Bradford.

But it was all too good to be true — or, rather, to last. Before the cheering had ended, and before many of us had made a note of Bradford's goal, the ball was in the Birmingham net again!

As if goal-scoring could be made to order, the Albion's three inside forwards, straight from the restart of play, bored a hole clean through the astonished Birmingham

defence by good, old-fashioned dribbling and short passing. Liddell, the right back, half-stemmed the tide, then sliced his kick so badly that the ball rolled towards his own goalkeeper.

Harry Hibbs dashed out, slipped, and fell. He could do no more than push the ball to the feet of W. 'G'. Richardson, who scored. So was the Cup won and lost.

The lasting impression I shall have of this magnificently fought final is that, though half the Albion team were mere boys and had never played in an important Cup tie until this season, they began like veterans, and in less than a quarter of an hour were playing in a well-ordered, confident way which suggested that they had no fears about the outcome.

Never has the Cup been won with greater assurance and never has a team in a final tie risen so markedly superior to the difficulties created by stormy wind, driving rain, and treacherous turf. Rain fell pitilessly and almost without cessation, but in conditions which should have favoured Birmingham it was the Albion who played the football that mattered and delighted the eye. In ball control and accuracy in passing, short or long, the winners were incomparably the better side.

SPORT IN BRIEF

MOTOR RACING
Luigi Arcangeli, driving a Type A Alfa Romeo, is killed during practice for the Italian Grand Prix. Arcangeli last year won the Rome Grand Prix in a Maserati.

RUGBY UNION
France has long had a reputation for violence and professionalism, but when 12 French clubs begin openly to pay their players, the country's team is expelled from the Five Nations competition. France will not be permitted to rejoin until after the war.

FOOTBALL
Manchester United make the worst ever start to a football season, losing their first 12 matches. United will win just seven and draw eight of their 42 matches, conceding 115 goals. They are relegated to Division Two along with Leeds United.

GREYHOUND RACING
Mick the Miller, the legendary racing greyhound, wins his fifth and last classic race. The St Leger, run over 700 yards, is the furthest distance he has ever raced.

LAWN TENNIS
The American tennis player Bill Tilden **(below)** turns professional. He won the Wimbledon singles title last year for the third time, and will play on the professional circuit for the next 20 years.

1932

Vines wins Wimbledon

By A. Wallis Myers

PUBLISHED MONDAY 4 JULY

Wimbledon is over and America rules the lawn. As conclusively as Mrs Moody won the women's championship the day before, Ellsworth Vines, also of California, won the men's on Saturday. He beat H. W. Austin in the final, 6–4, 6–2, 6–0.

Vines, the third American champion in succession, equalled the record of W. Tilden and G. Patterson by capturing the title on his first visit to England. He beat the record of H. L. Doherty, Tilden, W. Johnston, R. Lacoste, and H. Cochet by winning both the American and British championships under the age of 21. That feat alone makes Vines the greatest young player of all time.

But if Vines played wonderful tennis, it was not a wonderful match. It was a one-sided contest. Austin did not put up the fight which was expected. He was not, as we had hoped, the David for the Goliath.

Vines was strong, menacing and ruthless – but not at first. He was, indeed, palpably nervous at the start, as if his youth and the occasion were not quite compatible. Austin did not take advantage of this unsteady Vines. By failing to use his cooler complex in the first set – to win it, that is, so that he had some reserve of capital – Austin exposed his limitations to the enemy. Vines was evidently saying to himself, 'If he cannot prevail when I am playing badly, my accuracy and confidence, which are coming, must beat him.' And they did - right along the lines, in every department of the game, in every segment of the court.

Vines won the championship – his winning shot, by the way, was an untouchable service stroke – by unadulterated lawn tennis. A wise and prudent general, he reserved his best display for the last two rounds. He did not play as well against Austin as against J. Crawford, but that was because Austin did not tax him as much.

DID YOU KNOW?

Arguably the greatest woman athlete of all time, Mildred 'Babe' Didrikson was relegated to second place after winning the Olympic high-jump title. The judges ruled that her 'Western Roll' style of jumping was illegal because her head went over the bar before her body.

By White Willow

PUBLISHED SATURDAY 31 DECEMBER

Australia's conquerors in the first Test match go marching on. From Sydney to Melbourne they have carried the flag of old England with such magnificent confidence that at yesterday's opening of the second Test the Australian batsmen failed again, and seven wickets were lost before the close of play for only 194 runs.

England are already in an even better position than they were at the beginning of their fiery onslaught three weeks ago. D. Bradman is out, bowled first ball, as well as W. Woodfull, S. McCabe, and V. Y. Richardson, and the only resistance to England's fast bowlers was offered by J. Fingleton, who scored 83, and is now regarded as Woodfull's successor.

The continued failure of Woodfull and Bradman has infused the match with a poignancy that must temper the exultation of even the out-and-out Englander. Unless Woodfull redeems himself in the second innings, the agitation for his retirement from the side, already pronounced, will be intensified. As for Bradman, the position of this one-time wonder batsman has become tragic. It need not be dwelt upon, except in relation to yesterday's disaster. Before the match began he published a protest against the attitude of the Australian Board of Control towards him as a player-writer, and when he came out to bat the wild cheering that greeted him showed that he had the sympathy of the whole crowd.

The manner of Bradman's dismissal appears to have illustrated how utterly his luck has deserted him. W. Bowes sent down a short delivery on the leg side. The batsman shaped for a vigorous hook, mistimed the ball

by a split second, and pulled it down on to his stumps. His carelessness lay in the fact that he had not covered up his wicket. As Bradman returned to the pavilion he was smiling again.

Instead of a reduction of the shock bowlers, they were increased in number. Fingleton and Woodfull batted against H. Larwood and W. Voce. Both bowlers exploited the leg-trap, and murmurs ran round the arena at this typical gesture of defiance on the part of D. Jardine, the England captain.

The annoyance broke out afresh when Fingleton found it necessary to duck four times in one over to Larwood's 'bumpers'. Woodfull was so cautious against them that he took nearly half an hour to score his first run, but when 'Gubby' Allen came on for Larwood at 17, Woodfull was unable to avoid a heavy blow on the heart. No wonder an hour was spent on the first 20 runs of the innings. When nine had been added, Jardine had the satisfaction of seeing Allen bowl Woodfull off his pads.

Fingleton was the only player to be excepted from the sweeping condemnation of a famous ex-captain of Australia,

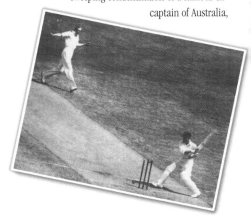

DONALD BRADMAN (1908–)

DONALD GEORGE BRADMAN, Australia's most celebrated cricketer, is regarded by many as the greatest batsman in the history of the game.

He was born at Cootamundra, New South Wales, on 27 August 1908. He was a farmer's son and taught himself the mechanics of his future trade in the outback. As a child, he would spend hours hurling a golf ball at a water tank and then hitting the rebound with the twisted stump of a gum-tree. This helped him develop his lightning-fast reflexes and footwork.

Bradman made his debut for New South Wales in 1927, remaining with the club until his move to South Australia in 1935. Initially, his rural background and natural reserve made him a figure of fun among some of his teammates. This merely stiffened his resolve to succeed.

His technical skill was superb, enabling him to make shots all round the wicket and to acquire runs at an astonishing rate. Trademark shots were off the back foot – the cut, hook and pull. In the 1930 Test series Bradman scored 254 at Lord's and a triple century in a single day at Headingley, going on to make 334 there. In his 20-year, 52-match Test career, Bradman scored 6,996 runs at an incredible average of 99.94 (the next highest average is 60.97). Small wonder that bowlers despaired. As one England captain remarked, bowling at Bradman was like 'casting pebbles at the Rock of Gibraltar'.

Bradman captained Australia from 1938–48, retaining the Ashes and his run rate throughout. In 1949 he was knighted, and 30 years later was made Companion of the Order of Australia.

who declared over the cables that the day's batting was 'the worst I have ever seen in Test cricket! The Englishmen pinned their faith in shock troops, believing that fast bowling was the surest way to defeat the Australians,' says the *Melbourne Argus.* 'The bowlers worked to a plan which succeeded surely beyond their most sanguine expectations. It was a triumph of tactics and generalship.'

Fingleton ducks another 'bumper' from Larwood in the second Test at Melbourne. 'Bodyline' or 'leg-theory' bowling was designed by England to contain Bradman's phenomenal scoring rate. Fast, short-pitched balls were delivered on the line of leg stump; up to six fielders were placed on the leg side to pick up catches. The strategy aroused much controversy during the 1932–3 tour.

Vienna listens to football match

From our own correspondent
VIENNA, WEDNESDAY 7 DECEMBER
England 4; Austria 3

Nothing approaching the excitement over today's match has ever been aroused by football in Vienna. Parliament itself was affected, and the Finance Committee of the Chamber suspended the session to enable deputies to hear the broadcast from Chelsea by Austria's leading sports reporters, Prof. Schmieger and Herr Naumann. Big business was done by Vienna cafés, which broadcast the match within.

In the grounds of the old Imperial Palace thousands of football enthusiasts paid a small sum to the Winter Rescue Fund for the poor of Vienna to hear the broadcast from loudspeakers fixed to the former emperor's balcony.

Many factories closed down, and others installed loudspeakers. Most shops released half their employees.

Prof. Schmieger was enthusiastic in praise of the sporting spirit of the British crowd, and seemed as astonished as his Viennese hearers when the same storm of cheering greeted Austrian as English successes. So good was the transmission that individual shouts in English and even the excited barking of a London dog were clearly audible.

Several times the excitable broadcaster shrieked and seemed on the point of tears at the failure of some Austrian player. At least 2,000,000 thumbs must be aching in Vienna tonight as the result of Schmieger's frenzied appeals to his hearers to 'hold your thumbs tight', which, according to Viennese belief, have guaranteed luck to the hard-pressed Austrians.

At seven pm, the whole game, as described at the time by Prof. Schmieger, was relayed from London again on gramophone records that were made as he was speaking during the match.

1933

Jockey Richards gets his record

PUBLISHED THURSDAY 9 NOVEMBER

By winning the first race, on Golden King, at Liverpool yesterday, Gordon Richards broke Fred Archer's 48-year-old record of 246 winners in a single season. Richards's record-breaking winner was the 1,400th success of his career, and by riding Attwood to victory in the last race of the afternoon he brought up his season's total to 248.

News of the champion jockey's success on Golden King was telephoned to Buckingham Palace, and a few minutes later Richards received a congratulatory telegram from the King's private secretary. Richard's face lit up with joy as he read it. 'Isn't that marvellous?' he said, and there was a thrill in his voice. He looked round at his fellow-jockeys who surrounded him in honest, boisterous enthusiasm. His boyish face beamed.

He must have shaken hundreds of hands. Owners, trainers, jockeys, and unknown admirers all somehow reached him, while outside the weighing room the chorus of cheering continued with unabated enthusiasm.

Later, he made perhaps one of the shortest speeches on record to the 'talkie' camera. It was just this: 'I am delighted to have broken the record and to know that it is all over.'

Richards is escorted to the weighing room after his record-breaking ride; he finished the 1933 season with a total of 259 winners.

FREDERICK PERRY (1909–95)

FREDERICK JOHN PERRY was born in Stockport, Cheshire, on 18 May 1909. His father was a self-made man; a cotton-spinner who had risen to become a Justice of the Peace, a Wesleyan minister and, by 1929, a Labour Member of Parliament. He encouraged his son's ambitions, supporting him until he made his sporting breakthrough.

Initially, this was as a table-tennis player. Perry won the world championship in 1929, and then abandoned the game to concentrate on his tennis. His big chance came in the following year, when he knocked out the fourth seed at Wimbledon. His performance caught the eye of selectors, who picked him for a forthcoming tour in the United States. After this, he became a regular in the Davis Cup side, winning all but seven of his 52 matches between 1931 and 1936. He was the first player to gain all

four of the Grand Slam titles (though not in the same year), winning a total of eight championships in all.

In British circles, it was his three Wimbledon victories (1934–6) for which Perry was chiefly famed. No Englishman had won the title since 1909, and none has won it since. Even so, the achievement was marred by the snobbish attitudes of the All-England Lawn Tennis Club committee members who, in Perry's words, seemed to regard him as 'a determined young cuss from the wrong side of the tracks'.

In 1936 Perry turned professional, terminating his Wimbledon career. Two years later he became an American citizen, serving with the US Air Force during the war. His Fred Perry sportswear business was a great success; he also commentated on tennis matches for the BBC.

Everton convincing Cup winners

By Frank Coles
PUBLISHED MONDAY 1 MAY
Everton 3; Manchester City 0

Everton, on their first visit to Wembley, set up a minor record in defeating Manchester City by 3–0. It is the most emphatic Cup final win since the tie was first played at the famous stadium ten years ago.

For the Everton partisan I am sure it must have been a very thrilling match; but for the spectator with no prejudices it was a game of few thrills and no sparkle. For nearly the whole of the first half, the play was negative.

It took Everton 30 minutes to force their first corner. In the next quarter of an hour five more corner-kicks came their way. The City defence, sound as a bell at the beginning, was losing its grip.

The Everton pressure should have taken effect at the 38th minute, but Dixie Dean – the goal-getting Dean – missed his kick completely when a pass by Stein left him with only the goalkeeper to beat from six yards away.

Not many teams in a final tie have enjoyed the rare fortune, following such a first-class blunder, to be presented with a goal within a couple of minutes. This was Everton's good luck. A long shot from out on the wing by Cliff Britton was misjudged by Langford, who took a step too far forward, got underneath the ball, and pushed it on to Stein. The Everton left-winger scored.

Once more a goalkeeper had erred dramatically in a Cup final, and, at half-time, we all felt sorry for poor Langford. His cup of bitterness was not yet filled, however. Six minutes after the second half had begun he was involved in another tragedy. Again Britton speculated with a long kick from 40 yards, and again Langford's judgement was fatally at fault. The ball, when it left Britton's foot, dropped plumb under the crossbar, and as the goalkeeper shaped to punch it away Dean came charging down on him. It should have been Langford's ball, but Dean's head beat the goalkeeper's fists – the Everton player and the ball were in the net.

Nine minutes from time, with Everton already being heralded as Cup winners, Dunn scored his side's third goal with a fine header from Geldard's corner-kick. Comparing the two sides strictly upon performance in this match, Everton take all the honours.

DID YOU KNOW?

When numbered shirts were worn by players for the first time in the FA Cup final on 29 April. Everton players wore numbers 1 (the goalkeeper) to 11, while opponents Manchester City wore numbers 12 to 22 (their goalkeeper). Numbering was not introduced in the League until 1939.

Wimbledon title returns to Empire after epic match

By A. Wallis Myers

PUBLISHED SATURDAY 8 JULY

Jack Crawford has made history for Australia and Wimbledon, bringing glory to both; and Ellsworth Vines helped to provide the epoch.

The final in which Vines, the American holder, was beaten by the Australian champion after five sets (4–6, 11–9, 6–2, 2–6, 6–4) yielded one of the finest matches in the 53-year story of the championship.

My own experience of Wimbledon finals only goes back 34 years. Mr S. A. E. Hickson, who was referee at the first and who witnessed his 53rd consecutive final yesterday, had no hesitation in affirming that for sustained quality of play, mutual attack on the service and the tense excitement of the last phase, the two-hour contest which Crawford and Vines waged was Wimbledon's greatest match.

The match began, as all long-distance journeys must, on a jog-trot note. The men were winding up their service arms; both machines were slow in starting.

The second set was an epic one of 20 games. The value of its possession was visualised by both men; they strove for it like the heroes both were. For Vines to win it would give him a line on the match; for Crawford to lose it meant an Everest climb.

It was a service-governed set right through until the last game, when Crawford, mid a great shout, turned back two cannonballs and won his two-game break.

The fifth set opened with tension high; the crowd held their breath, while the performers were expending it.

Despite suffering from the virus that caused 63 other players to withdraw from the championship, Jack Crawford (top) beat Ellsworth Vines (above) in the men's singles final at Wimbledon.

Rarely, if ever, have two valiant men given more value to a gallery.

The tenth and last game saw Crawford inspired and Vines his hapless victim. A perfect lob on the baseline prepared the way for the first point; the second was gained by Vines netting on his backhand. For the third, Crawford made an exquisite backhand pass. Love–40 on Vines's service. Could there be any sweeter music in Australian ears? We all strained forward at the first match ball. None other was required. Vines netted for a second time, and the centre court echoed with a hundred cheers.

As the new champion and the old left the court they were saluted by more applause; as they passed under the archway which led to the dressing room, both were still as self-possessed as if the match was about to begin. Australians flocked round their hero; many Americans added their congratulations. The match could have had no more sporting finish; and, of course, Jack Crawford has not an enemy in the world.

SPORT IN BRIEF

CRICKET

In the third Test at Adelaide between England and Australia, wicketkeeper Bert Oldfield and captain Bill Woodfull are casualties of 'Bodyline' bowling. Amid growing criticism of England captain Douglas Jardine's methods, the Australian Board sends a telegram to the MCC calling leg-theory bowling 'unsportsmanlike'; in response the MCC suggest that spectators' acrimony towards England players is also 'unsportsmanlike'. In 1934 Jardine resigns from the England side; Voce and Larwood refuse to apologise for their methods, and are not selected for the 1934 Ashes series.

FOOTBALL

Everton's 3–0 victory over Manchester City in this year's FA Cup final completes a unique achievement; they have now won the Second Division championship, the First Division championship and FA Cup in successive seasons.

CRICKET

In the second Test at Old Trafford in July, West Indian bowlers Manny Martindale and Learie Constantine adopt the 'Bodyline' technique practised by England in their controversial tour to Australia. Despite this, England captain Douglas Jardine scores a century and England win the series 2–0.

BOXING

Primo Carnera defeats Jack Sharkey to win the world heavyweight title. At 18 st 8 lb and nearly 6 ft 6 in tall, Carnera is nicknamed the 'Ambling Alp'. He is not a popular champion; many believe that his fights have been fixed, and next year he will lose his title to Max Baer.

1934

HENRY COTTON (1907–87)

Thomas Henry Cotton was born at Holmes Chapel, Cheshire, on 26 January 1907. He came from a prosperous, middle-class background; both his father and his older brother, Leslie, were keen golfers. Cotton spent many hours hitting practice shots into a net in the family garage before following his brother's example and turning professional.

At 19 Cotton became the club professional at Langley Park, remaining there until 1932, when he moved to a more lucrative post at the Waterloo Club in Brussels. Cotton's sights, however, were firmly set on breaking the American stranglehold on golf. In 1928 he toured the US, sizing up the opposition and improving his swing. He won the PGA Match Play championship in 1932 (and again in 1940 and 1946), and his first British Open in 1934, effectively ensuring his victory with opening rounds of 67 and 65. The victory made him a national hero, with fans hailing him as 'King Cotton'; a special golf ball, the Dunlop 65, was rushed into production to commemorate his remarkable second round.

Cotton won the Open twice more; in 1937 and in 1948. He also played on three Ryder Cup teams. For more than a dozen years he seemed invincible on the course, a result of sheer hard work and his marvellous powers of concentration. He was awarded an MBE in 1946 and, shortly before his death, learnt that he was to receive a knighthood.

DID YOU KNOW?

Australia gained revenge for their Ashes defeat in the Bodyline tour by winning the series in England 2–1. In the fifth Test at the Oval, Don Bradman and Bill Ponsford put on a record stand of 451 for the second wicket in only 316 minutes. The record stood for 57 years until beaten by New Zealanders Andrew Jones and Martin Crowe with 467 against Sri Lanka.

How Cotton won the Open golf title

By George Greenwood
Sandwich, Friday 29 June

Henry Cotton won the British Open championship at Royal St Georges here today with 283, a score equalling the record established by Gene Sarazen at Prince's two years ago. Cotton has thus broken the American monopoly of the championship which has run for 11 years.

He had established so enormous a lead that it seemed impossible anyone could catch him. With the last round to play he had a clear advantage of ten shots over the next man. It should have been something in the nature of a triumphant procession, but as things turned out it was altogether different.

As the strokes began to slip away Cotton became fidgety and restless. Cotton's progress on the downward path was not arrested until the 13th hole was reached where he was even over fours.

It was a critical position, but to his everlasting credit he made a supreme effort to pull himself together. The situation was saved, and playing the next five holes normally he wanted a four at the 18th to beat Sarazen's record. He was bunkered on the right of the green with his second shot, and could do no better than a five. Anyhow, he had equalled Sarazen's total. He was carried from the green by an excited mob of spectators.

Challenging American golfing supremacy, Henry Cotton won the British Open in 1934 (below), 1937 and 1938.

The Battle of Highbury

By Frank Coles
Published Thursday 15 November
England 3; Italy 2

Those people who like their football served up hot and strong saw more thrills in the match yesterday than in any international ever played in this country.

England won at Highbury by 3–2 after holding a half-time lead of three goals. They looked like walking away with the game then, but Italy, though a man short, fought back with great courage and very nearly made what would have been a sensational draw.

I congratulate the Italians on their tremendous rally. It was all highly dramatic. But as a spectacle of how football should be played the match failed almost completely.

I had been warned to expect plenty of vigour from these Italian players. Unfortunately, their vigour too often exceeded the rules of the game as we know. No representative match in this country has produced so many fouls. The referee's whistle was constantly heard, and some of the infringements were flagrantly unfair.

It was not a pleasant sight when an Italian defender so far lost his self-control as to aim a blow at Ted Drake, or when the same player grabbed Wilf Copping round the waist, as if trying to put him down with a rugby tackle.

Maybe one cause of the Italian outbursts was the charging-the-goalkeeper rule which operates in England, but not on the Continent. They resented Drake's rushes at Carlo Ceresoli when he had possession of the ball.

As Italy were compelled to play practically through the game with ten men — Luisito Monti, their centre half and star player was injured at the seventh minute, and took no further part in the match — they are justified in claiming to be unlucky losers.

But England did not go free of casualties. After the match it was revealed that Eddie Hapgood pluckily played on although his nose was broken. Again, Eric Brook had to go to hospital to have a badly injured elbow X-rayed, and Drake received attention for a damaged arm. It is feared that Monti has broken a bone in his foot.

I would like to add a word of congratulation to the referee, Mr Otto Olsson, of Sweden. He handled a most difficult match firmly and with quick decision.

Manchester City win FA Cup final with dramatic late goal

By Frank Coles

Published Monday 30 April

Manchester City 2; Portsmouth 1

Cup finals come and go, and are soon forgotten. One is so much like another. The 1934 match, however, will live in my memory for all time.

Thunder and lightning; the winning goal scored in the dying minutes of a most dramatic game; the Manchester City goalkeeper falling in a swoon at the finish – these are some of the incidents I shall not forget.

I went to Wembley expecting a Manchester triumph, but I was not at all prepared for the manner of it. After being a goal down at the 26th minute, the City fought magnificently to regain the lost ground. They got their reward. Yet it was rather a lucky win.

If ever a team deserved sympathy it was Portsmouth. To the last quarter of an hour they held on to their slender lead, packing their goal so skilfully that every Manchester raid was repulsed. Then stark tragedy.

Jack Allen, who had been doing two men's work with a heart as big as the football he was kicking, was knocked unconscious in a collision with the Manchester City captain, Cowan. They led him to the touchline and worked feverishly to bring him round, but before Allen came back Freddie Tilson scored.

Most of us felt it was a death-blow to Portsmouth. They rallied for a few minutes, but the City were playing like men possessed, and when, five minutes from the end, Tilson scored again, it seemed an inevitable happening.

As the final whistle sounded most of the Manchester players made a rush for Tilson; he thoroughly deserved their gratitude.

Frank Swift, the 19-year-old goalkeeper, started to run to the centre of the field, stumbled – and fell in a faint. The tense excitement had been too much for him. He quickly recovered, however, and, with the rest of the team, received his medal from the King

Team captains Thackeray (Portsmouth) and Cowan (Manchester City) shake hands under the gaze of referee S. Rous before the dramatic 1934 Cup final (below).

FOOTBALL

In January the football world is shocked by news of the death of 55-year-old Herbert Chapman **(on left, above)** from pneumonia. A hugely successful manager, he created a team at Arsenal that – in his eight years in charge – reached the Cup final three times and won the Football League championship twice. Previously he was in charge for four years at Huddersfield Town; under his management the club won one FA Cup and two consecutive League titles, and a third successive League title the year after Chapman left.

MOTOR RACING

A formula limiting the weight of grand prix cars to 750 kg (without driver, fuel or oil) is introduced. German Führer Adolf Hitler offers huge subsidies to those German car companies that can demonstrate the superiority of German engineering.

FOOTBALL

Italy's World Cup win against Czechoslovakia – 2–1 in extra time – is claimed by dictator Benito Mussolini as a triumph for fascism.

LAWN TENNIS

Briton Dorothy Round beats Helen Jacobs to win the Wimbledon women's singles title. She also triumphs in the mixed doubles this year with partner Ryuki Miki, the Japanese Davis Cup captain.

1935

By Frank Coles

PUBLISHED MONDAY 16 DECEMBER

Aston Villa 1; Arsenal 7

'How does it feel suddenly to be the hero of the whole world of football?' I asked Edward Drake **(in training, below)** an hour after he had equalled a 47-year-old record by scoring seven goals in a First League match. But he declined to be drawn.

A very modest young man is Edward Drake, for all his forceful personality on the field. 'It just happened to be my day – and everything came off for me,' was all he had to say.

Certainly the ball ran kindly for Arsenal's leader in an astonishing game at Villa Park. At the same time, I count myself extremely lucky to have been one of the 60,000 witnesses of one of the finest centre-forward displays seen for many years.

Drake was the complete footballer. Apart from deadly shooting, his ability to control the ball and beat an opponent when tackled was quite exceptional. He was also unorthodox. He roamed from wing to wing, waiting for the loose ball, which on this remarkable day seemed to be drawn to him like a magnet.

Some of his goals looked simple, but one of them, the second of the sequence, was the effort of a master. Just when the centre forward appears to be sandwiched he got his right foot to the ball, which was in the net in a flash. A wonderful goal.

So much for Drake and his great feat, which may never be equalled in modern football. He has a permanent reminder of it, for in the dressing room afterwards the ball was presented to him by the Aston Villa directors. It was autographed by the Villa players.

The Villa, on the field and off, took their humiliating defeat with fine sportsmanship. There was not one deliberate foul throughout the match and no sign of ill-feeling. The heavy reverse is bound to have a disturbing effect at Villa Park. This is the third time this season the Villa have conceded seven goals at home.

By Frank Coles

PUBLISHED MONDAY 29 APRIL

Sheffield Wednesday 4; West Bromwich Albion 2

Wembley's 13th Cup final was easily the best of all. For all time it will be remembered as the thrill-a-minute match. I am sure no one in that vast 93,000-crowd had seen a big game so crowded with hot drama and tense excitement.

A goal in two minutes; two goals in the last four minutes; Albion twice equalising the scores: half a dozen easy scoring chances missed and – for the first time in more than 30 years – six goals that counted.

The form of Wednesday and Albion had suggested a dour battle, in which defence would be supreme. One goal, I thought, would settle the issue. Instead we had the refreshing spectacle of both sides throwing their last ounce into attack. None of the 'What-we-have-we-hold' business in this game. Hence the thrills and the six goals.

There were other surprises too. Such as the sparkling form of Walter Boyes, Albion's outside left and the youngest and smallest player of the 22.

I congratulate Sheffield Wednesday on their win. They deserve to hold the Cup because, late in the game with the score 2-2, they accepted their chances. Albion had had similar chances, easier in fact, and missed them.

Yet I shall always regard Albion as the unlucky team. Certainly their courage was magnificent. Remember that they recovered from the hammer-blow of being a goal down after two minutes, that they rallied again when Wednesday regained the lead midway through the second

Edward VIII meets the players before the Cup final. Sheffield Wednesday's Ellis Rimmer scored twice in the final three minutes to clinch victory; he was only the second player ever to score in every round of the Cup.

half and – most vital point – Carter, key man of Albion's forward line, was hurt after ten minutes. Albion's finest defender was Murphy, the right-half. I do not hesitate to describe him as the outstanding man on the field.

MILESTONES

The first indoor athletics meeting was held in Britain. The Amateur Athletic Association Indoor Championships took place on 6 April at Wembley Empire Pool and Sports Arena in northwest London.

By Frank Coles

PUBLISHED MONDAY 8 APRIL

Scotland 2; England 0

England, after all, only share the international soccer championship with Scotland.

A great crowd of 129,693, which included the Duke of York, saw the Scots triumph at Hampden Park, the graveyard of English hopes on many former occasions.

Disappointment at the result was accentuated by the extremely moderate display of the Englishmen. They were never in the game with a winning chance, and if the Scottish forwards had finished reasonably well, the score would have been doubled.

Hampden Park atmosphere is supposed to be worth a goal start to Scotland. Well, we heard precious little of the famous Hampden roar at this colourless match. The play on both sides fell far below the expected standard. It was the old story of defence overwhelming attack. The

English forwards had a dreadfully bad day, so bad that John Jackson, in Scotland's goal, was not called upon to save one difficult shot.

The Scottish attack was much better, more menacing, yet Harry Hibbs, like Jackson, was rarely in trouble with a direct drive. Scotland's two goals were headed through by Duncan from corner kicks.

The obvious lesson of the match is that English forward play has further deteriorated, especially on the wings. Geldard and Eric Brook suffered from the same shortcoming. Neither attempted to use his speed – and England were fatally handicapped.

As the second half advanced England had more of the play, but only because the Scottish wing half-backs thought the moment ripe to relax their grip and move up to support their forwards. Even so, there was only the remotest hope that England would score. Their attacks fizzled out in the goal area.

A sorry day for England.

Golden Miller wins Gold Cup in record time

By Hotspur

CHELTENHAM, THURSDAY 14 MARCH

It was Golden Miller's day here today in the widest sense. Miss Paget's remarkable horse won his fourth Cheltenham Gold Cup, and won it in the record time of 6 min 30 sec by three-parts of a length from Thomond II. And he won it amid scenes the like of which have never been seen on this course since the National Hunt meeting was established at Cheltenham.

Golden Miller is always a draw, even if he has nothing to run against. The presence of a formidable rival like Thomond II made the race doubly attractive. A great crowd was expected. Every foot of space seemed to be occupied.

To reach the parade ring was impossible. The public had taken up their positions there as soon as the horses had left the paddock for the previous race. The only view one had of the five runners was as they paraded past the stands, where the complete nonchalance of Golden Miller, who repeatedly turned his head towards the stands to look at the crowd, could be noted.

One of the secrets of this horse's pre-eminence among chasers is his perfect disposition and the fact that nothing excites him. Thomond II, on the other hand, was on his toes and fretting for the fray.

It was a moot point which horse would go in front, but Fawcus had no doubts on the matter. He sent Southern Hero ahead at once and he settled down in front, followed by Thomond II and Golden Miller. They had not gone more than half a mile when Golden Miller and Thomond II were running almost level. It was at the third fence from home that Southern Hero shot his bolt, and thereafter he was to all intents and purposes out of the race. Golden Miller then took a slight lead of Thomond II, and the crowd, now hushed, prepared themselves for a great finish.

Over the last fence but one they raced, with Golden Miller still holding to his slight lead and under no pressure from Wilson, who was sitting still and leaving it all to his horse. Coming to the last fence, Speck was more active. He drew his whip and pushed Thomond II. The response was the sort that is always expected from this courageous little horse.

Golden Miller had not yet won. Thomond II landed over the last fence less than a length behind Golden Miller and then began a terrific race between them. Thomond II was finding something but it was of no avail. Golden Miller was always holding him and, without having to be put under severe pressure, he won amid a tornado of enthusiasm.

Golden Miller displaying his nonchalant disposition in front of a crowd. But two weeks after his Gold Cup success, and trying for a second successive Grand National win, Golden Miller unseated jockey Gerry Wilson at the first fence, and again at the first fence in the Champion Chase the following day.

Simon Hughes

Sport and the media

H E'S SPORTS MAD, MY FRIEND STEVE: he has six remote controls by his settee. One is for terrestrial television, another for satellite, a third for his stash of football videos, a fourth for laser discs versions and a fifth to activate widescreen, narrowscreen, sensurround or a myriad of other formats. The sixth is a device that can call up all sorts of background sports information via an interconnected computer. With one or two modifications it will enable him to muck about with the match in progress, substituting players or even altering the path of the ball. A real 21st-century interactive gizmo.

The media has penetrated sport to such an extent that it is in danger of coming out the other side. Television ultimately decides the what, the where and the when.

The media has penetrated sport to such an extent approaching the Millennium it is in danger of coming out the other side. Television ultimately decides the what, the where and the when. Four channels show sport exclusively 24 hours a day (with a zillion more imminent in the digital revolution), there are numerous on-screen text sources, a million websites and videos and no less than 343 specialist sports magazines. No wonder newspapers have had to adapt, adding value by offering more colour and in-depth analysis, and Fantasy Leagues. Their main concern will be box-gogglers like Steve ruining their eyesight to the extent that they will eventually lose their ability to read.

Press boxes at sports venues are becoming more and more futuristic – witness the Starship Enterprise erected opposite the pavilion at Lord's, and a budget of £200 million has been allocated for the provision of the media at the Sydney 2000 Olympics.

Compare that with the sports coverage in *The Daily Telegraph* (price 1d) on Monday 1 January 1900. The weekend's football matches were rounded up in one column, with the only comment on the 1–1 draw between Manchester City–Blackburn Rovers being: 'This score fairly indicates the value of the play, for there was little to choose between the two clubs from first to last, the attack and defence on both sides being of

an even character.' How astute. Horse racing occupies another column and the rest of the page is dominated by items headed 'Exciting Police Capture' (the arrest of some jewel thieves, and not a reference to early 20th-century football hooliganism) and 'Chevalier Recitals'. There wasn't a photo or a feature in sight.

This sketch format remained largely unchanged for half a century in the heavyweight papers (though the *People* had four pages of sport and sold over four million copies). Major events like the 'Bodyline' series (1932–3) and the death of W. G. Grace (1915) commanded extra space: in his *Times* obituary of the doctor, Sir Arthur Conan Doyle wrote: 'the fastest bowler in England sent one like a cannon shot through his beard with only a comic shake of his head and a good-humoured growl in reply.' *The Times* covered cricket adequately, but thought the FA Cup Final of 1914 between Liverpool and Burnley 'of comparatively little interest except to the Lancashire working classes'.

At least the New Year sporting weekend of 1950 enjoyed a page to itself in *The Daily Telegraph*. Accompanied by a dingy picture of the horse who won the Queen Elizabeth Chase, there were four-paragraph reports of football matches, a short account of the 'exciting' 3–3 draw between Harlequins and London Scottish, and E. W. Swanton's epistle on South Africa v Australia. 'Something of the ruthless, cold-blooded aggression has left Australian cricket with the departure of Bradman,' he wrote. If only they hadn't rediscovered it.

Live sport had been seen on TV by this time, though believe it or not, Murray Walker hadn't: he was working in radio. The BBC's outside broadcast unit cranked into action at Wimbledon in 1937 to relay fuzzy images of Bunny Austin's first-round match to about 2,000 well-heeled Londoners. The pictures were augmented by radio commentary. Nothing much has changed there, then. To this day, many sports viewers zap the TV sound and turn up the radio coverage. The Wimbledon coverage was such a success, the whole of the England–Scotland match was shown the following year. These were the world's first live pictures of a football game, and the sporting masses' first sight of David Coleman, allegedly in block 108 row 75, perched on his father's shoulders.

'Grandstand' didn't kick in until Coleman had grown up a bit, though, and a few more people had televisions. At last there was an alternative to the five pm 'Sports Report' on the Light (wireless) programme. Football was used to ignite the TV touchpaper, persuasive slogans like 'When they are talking about the big match on TV, will you have to remain silent?' tempting the working class to hire sets. So you see it wasn't BSkyB who invented this tactic. 'Grandstand' was first broadcast in 1958, four years after the launch of 'Sportsview', later to become 'Sportsnight'. Both were relatively cheap programmes to produce since there were no celebrity analysts to pay, and at the time sports rights went for a song: Wimbledon was £100 a day, a Test match £250 a day, and permission to cover the FA Cup final all of £750.

ITV followed the BBC's lead with 'World of Sport', erroneously named as it featured hardly anything except wrestling. London Weekend's 'The Big Match' aped the BBC's 'Match of the Day', culminating in the biggest TV British audience of all time in 1970 when 32.5 million watched the Chelsea v Leeds FA Cup final, broadcast simultaneously on ITV and BBC. Only a military junta would be able to demand that sort of attention now.

The press seized on the TV ball and ran with it, often, in the case of the *News of the World* and the *People*, into murky corners. The *People* financed a year-long investigation into match-fixing in the early Sixties (the basis of the 1995 drama-documentary 'The Fix'), the advent of George Best aroused the gossip columnists, and a rash of nose-to-the-ground sports reporters emerged with tags like 'Alan Hoby – The Man Who Knows' (or 'The Man Who Knows F*** All', as he was dubbed by some readers).

*A rash of nose-to-the-ground sports reporters emerged with tags like 'Alan Hoby – The Man Who Knows' (or 'The Man Who Knows F*** All', as he was dubbed by some readers).*

Someone who did have a bit of authority, Sir Neville Cardus, was still writing in the *Guardian* in 1969, when he confessed to walking out of a Test match before lunch on the second day. He was, he said, 'Bored to limpness because I had seen Geoff Boycott and John Edrich compile, or rather secrete, 100 runs from 56 overs bowled by game, inexperienced New Zealanders.'

The rejuvenation of snooker in the mid-Seventies underlined the power of the sports media. It was the perfect television package –

compact and easy to cover, yet providing hours of riveting entertainment. The interminable time I spent practising pots with deep screw on the table at my local cricket club confirmed I had caught the bug. Whispering Ted Lowe became a household sound, if not name, and neatly embraced the technological advance of television with his definitive remark, 'and for those watching in black and white, the green is behind the brown'.

The developments in this last decade have been almost as dramatic as those in the rest of the century put together. The advent of Sky TV transformed the market, blowing tradition out of the water and offering a veritable cornucopia of choice. Suddenly there were live Monday night football matches, entire England Tests broadcast from the Caribbean, and round-the-clock golf. The newly-formed Premier League jumped into bed with Rupert Murdoch's satellite station in a £673 million deal, and the BBC lost the monopoly they had in sports broadcasting, though Radio Five Live took up the cudgels. Precipitating the mood, newspapers actually started putting sport on the back page, oblivious to the silent choking of the old Fleet Street brethren.

David Welch, sports editor of *The Daily Telegraph* since 1990, was at the forefront of this movement. 'It was only when the big proprietors took over news groups that there was proper analysis of what sold newspapers,' he says. 'It was a struggle at first but eventually the owners and editors had to acknowledge the value of sport, that it wasn't socially unacceptable any more. It also became a vehicle for quality writing; now Conrad Black believes *The Daily Telegraph*'s sports coverage accounts for 50 per cent of our sales.' Consequently, Welch's staff doubled and so did its output. Interactive competitions, self-contained sections and special-event pull-outs keep the presses turning and the lumberjacks in overtime.

Throughout all this upheaval, Test Match Special's radio commentary has remained almost unimpaired, and in 1997 celebrated its 40th anniversary. Love it or hate it, this informed (and sometimes misinformed) burble is a throwback to the way sport was covered early in the century and, for non-technocrats, still offers a bit of light relief from the electronic gimickry of the Nineties.

Which is where we came in. As well as fine-tuning his sixth remote control, my friend Steve is constructing an R2D2-type character to fetch snacks and beer from the fridge so that he will never have to miss a ball kicked, bowled or hit except to go to the toilet. The only sports programme that makes him switch off is 'Topless Darts'.

1936

Perry's third championship win

By A. Wallis Myers
LONDON, 4 JULY

Wimbledon's chief prize, the men's singles championship, remains in British custody, and F. J. Perry is the holder for the third successive year.

But this record for the New Wimbledon was achieved without the customary ovation from a 15,000 gallery, without the customary struggle, and with Baron von Cramm, after the opening set, physically out of action and unable to run. It was a disappointing finish to a final that promised so much. Von Cramm's injury – a torn muscle in the thigh – came in the second game, when he was serving.

Von Cramm then realised, as he told me afterwards, that something had 'gone'. The perfect adversary, anxious to give Perry the full fruits of victory, he concealed his handicap as long as was humanly possible. 'I did not appreciate how serious it was,' he said, 'until movement no doubt aggravating my complaint, I found that I could not run for the wide drive nor turn on my hips in my usual way.'

The huge expectant crowd, gathered for the match of the meeting between two great players, were at first mystified. They saw the keyed-up, rampant Perry serving like a demon and hitting winners on the drive and volley. But the German respondent, though he gave no outward sign to the gallery of any impediment or pain, and though he answered a friendly enquiry by Perry as they crossed over after the first set with a smiling assurance that nothing was wrong, was, for all practical purposes, out of the hunt.

I was reminded when I saw the courtly, chivalrous manner in which the German champion concealed his mortification from the crowd that Perry's demeanour had been the same at Forest Hills last September when, in his match against Allison, he had fallen and sustained a painful internal injury. Not a sign of petulance or dismay to the vast and eager American crowd when, obviously wounded, he continued to the end. These great players are great gentlemen, too.

Fred Perry (left) beat G. Von Cramm of Germany 6–1, 6–1, 6–0.

Jesse Owens smashes more records

Jesse Owens gets into his stride in the Berlin Olympics (right), the poster for which depicted the horse-drawn chariot on the Brandenburg Gate (above). Owens' time of 10.3 sec in the 100 m equalled the world record. His broad jump of 8.06 m was a new Olympic record, as was his 200-m time of 20.7 sec. His final medal came in the 4 x 400-m relay, in which the Americans again set a world record.

By Howard Marshall
BERLIN, 4 AUGUST

This was another day of records in the Olympic Games. More world records have been beaten, subject to ratification, and six Olympic records have gone.

Without a doubt Jesse Owens, the American negro, is the outstanding personality of this Olympiad. Having already equalled the world record for the 100 m with a time of 10.3 sec, he today broke two more records.

His running broad jump of 26 ft 6¼ in (8.06 m) beat the previous Olympic best by 1 ft 1½ in. In two 200-metres heats, running well within himself, he beat the Olympic record of 21.2 sec by 0.1 sec.

Owens – the Alabama Antelope they call him in America – is extremely popular with his fellow competitors, and his remarkable triumph has not in the least affected his modesty. Tall and perfectly built, he is one of the greatest athletes of history, and he may well break yet another world's record in the 200-m final tomorrow.

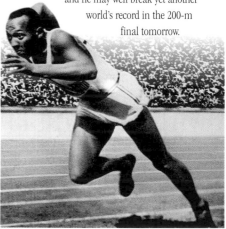

JESSE OWENS (1913–80)

ONE OF THE GREATEST OF AMERICAN ATHLETES, James Cleveland Owens was born in Danville, Alabama, on 12 September 1913. He was one of 11 children, the son of a struggling sharecropper. Their plight worsened when the cotton crops failed, and the family moved north to Cleveland, Ohio. There Jesse attended the secondary school, working as a shoeshine boy in his spare time. Introducing himself to a teacher as J. C. Owens, he was thereafter known as 'Jesse'.

While at school, Owens' talent was spotted by his sports teachers. With their encouragement, he managed to equal the world record for 100 yd at an inter-school athletics tournament. He went on to attend Ohio State University, where he broke a series of records with the college track team. His most impressive feat came at the college championships in Ann Arbor, Michigan. There, on 25 May 1935, Owens succeeded in breaking world records in the 220-yd dash, the 220-yd low hurdles and the running broad jump, and equalling the world record for the 100-yd dash.

The following year Owens competed in the Olympic Games in Berlin, which were being exploited by Adolf Hitler as a showcase for Nazism. The German notion of Aryan supremacy was soon shattered by the outstanding black athlete, who won four gold medals and stole the show.

Owens was opposed to the politicising of the Games, however. 'The road to the Olympics leads to no city, no country…,' he wrote. 'The road to the Olympics leads, in the end, to the best within us.'

Setback for the 'Brown Bomber'

From our own correspondent

NEW YORK, 21 JUNE

Max Schmeling, victor in one of the greatest heavyweight fights of modern times, will return to Germany in the airship *Hindenburg* on Tuesday. In the autumn he will come back to the United States for his match with James Braddock, in which he hopes to recapture the title that he himself held for two years.

That is the situation after 12 amazing rounds in the ring at New York's Yankee Baseball Stadium on Friday night, in the course of which a madly yelling and

Max Schmeling lands a left to the jaw of Joe Louis before his 12th-round knock-out of the 'Brown Bomber' on 19 June. Louis exacted swift revenge on their return meeting: he knocked Schmeling out in the first round.

gesticulating crowd saw the high hopes of the supposedly invincible Joe Louis shattered.

Schmeling was modest about his win when I talked over the big battle with him yesterday. Coloured glasses concealed his badly swollen eyes, but he was as pleased with himself as when he jumped wildly round the ring, waving his arms like a windmill, after knocking out Louis.

'I realised that Louis carried his left too low,' said Schmeling. 'That right was the punch to beat him with. I had got near to him to hit with my right, and was prepared for the black eye you now observe.

'I decided after a few rounds that it was safe to let him hit me. Louis is a good natural fighter. He is young yet and can learn.'

So exciting was the blow-by-blow description of the fight that 12 people died while listening to it.

MILESTONES

The practice of bringing an Olympic flame from Greece to the Games venue was introduced for the first time in 1936. The torch was brought overland from the Temple of Zeus in Greece. It was carried through seven countries, by a relay of 3,000 runners, to the stadium in Berlin.

SPORT IN BRIEF

RUGBY UNION
England's first triumph over the All Blacks comes at Twickenham, by 13 points to nil (three tries and a dropped goal). The hero of the match is Russian-born wing three-quarters Alexander Obolensky, whose second try shows his breathtaking change of pace to full advantage.

WINTER OLYMPICS
The winter Games are held in Garmisch-Partenkirchen, amid Nazi propaganda and censorship. Britain's ice-hockey team is helped to an astonishing triumph by two Canadian-born players, Alec Archer and Jimmy Foster. A 5–0 win over Czechoslovakia earns the team its first European title for 26 years. Norwegian Sonja Henie wins her third successive Olympic gold medal to become the most successful female figure skater of all time.

HORSE RACING
The surprise winner of the Derby is the Aga Khan's Mahmoud, ridden by Charlie Smirke, in a record time of 2 min 33⁴/₅ sec. The Aga Khan's Taj Akbar, ridden by Gordon Richards, takes second place.

OLYMPICS
German Führer Adolf Hitler uses the Berlin Olympic Games as a vehicle for Nazi propaganda. His message about Aryan supremacy is undermined by black American successes, but Germany still win 33 gold medals.

CRICKET
Brilliant stroke play by Mushtaq Ali gives him a century and brings his side back into the game on the second day of the Test between All India and England at Old Trafford on 27 July. A total of 588 runs – 398–6 for England, and 190–0 for India – are scored in one day on an 'absurdly easy' wicket.

1937

Benny Lynch retains world title

By Harold Lewis

GLASGOW, WEDNESDAY 13 OCTOBER

Amid the delirious excitement of 40,000 spectators, Benny Lynch, of Glasgow, knocked out his youthful challenger, Peter Kane, of Golborne, in the 13th round at Shawfield Park, Glasgow, tonight. He thus retains his world and British flyweight championships.

The central figure of the final scene, forlorn and pitiful, was Kane, the brilliant Lancashire prodigy, as he lay across the lower rope, conscious enough to know that he was being counted out, yet unable to move, the last shred of resistance having been battered out of his body.

Over him bent the tall, thin figure of the referee, Mr Barrington Dalby, with his mouth close to Kane's ear, shrieking out the passing of the seconds and hitting the floor with his fist. Mr Dalby continued to watch the timekeeper, for the din was ear-splitting. People were already clambering over the press benches into the ring.

There was a smile on the dour face of Lynch for the first time since he had entered the ring. For 13 rounds Kane had fought with all his usual aggression and dash, sometimes rocking him back with a decisiveness and impudence that Lynch plainly did not relish.

In the last two rounds Kane had taken more punishment than a young boy of 19 ought ever to have to accept, no matter how willing he may be.

Benny Lynch, flyweight champion of the world, pictured before addiction to alcohol destroyed his career and led to his death aged 33.

Steve Donoghue's triumph in Oaks

By Hotspur

PUBLISHED SATURDAY 5 JUNE

The King and Queen saw the race for the Oaks at Epsom yesterday, when Sir Victor Sassoon's filly, Exhibitionnist, ridden by Steve Donoghue, gained an easy victory. The most popular jockey of all time was given a great reception on his return to the enclosure.

It was the first occasion in his long career that he had won this particular Classic at Epson – he was successful in the wartime substitute at Newmarket on My Dear in 1918.

Donoghue, who is in his 53rd year, is riding as well as ever. He won the 1,000 Guineas on Exhibitionnist, and is enjoying a wonderful last season in the saddle. Unless he changes his plans, Donoghue intends to take up training next year. He has been riding for more than 30 years and included in his 14 Classic victories are six Derby winners.

There was never any doubt about Exhibitionnist's victory. As soon as the field settled down, Exhibitionnist was second to Burlington Lass, with Sculpture next. Burlington Lass and Exhibitionnist increased their lead approaching Tattenham Corner, and Donoghue sent his mount to the front as soon as the straight was reached.

From that point there was no danger, and the roar of 'Come on, Steve,' rivalled that of one of the biggest Yorkshire crowds. Steve 'came on' to such good purpose that he had three lengths to spare passing the post.

The cheering that greeted the winner on her return to the unsaddling enclosure was a tribute to a great rider and a game filly.

Sunderland fight back to win Cup

By Frank Coles

PUBLISHED MONDAY 3 MAY

So it was Sunderland's Cup year, after all! How many times the prophecy has been spoken and written in the last four months, goodness knows. Now the great ambition is realised.

Sunderland are worthy Cup-holders. They went to Wembley determined to gain the only football honour that has persistently eluded the club for nearly half a century – and pluck and determination won Wembley's 15th Cup final.

In the history of the Cup few teams have achieved Sunderland's feat against Preston North End. To fight back from a losing position at half-time, equalise, and then dominate the play completely, put Sunderland in the gallery of most gallant Cup winners.

I opposed Sunderland as probable winners of the Cup because I judged Preston to have the sounder defence, and at the halfway stage the viewpoint seemed to be right. The first half was emphatically Preston's; moreover, the men from Durham had revealed the flaws I had feared.

When the teams lined up for the second half, I knew instinctively that the next ten minutes or so would decide. If Preston could have survived the crisis of Sunderland's desperate bid to strike swiftly after the interval, they would have won the Cup.

But they could not hold the challenge. Bobby Gurney's goal that brought the scores level seven minutes after change of ends proved the turning point. It was the match that set alight a Sunderland bonfire that rapidly enveloped poor Preston.

The goal we all knew meant triumph came 18 minutes from the end. Preston's defence was wide open when Gurney let his pass go and Raich Carter saw to it that Burns had no chance to save his shot. Another five minutes, and Sunderland closed the discussion with a third goal, scored by Eddie Burbanks.

Sunderland, 3–1 winners of the FA Cup final, are presented to the King. Scottish international Frank O'Donnell scored Preston's only goal.

Budge's triumph at Wimbledon

By A. Wallis Myers

PUBLISHED SATURDAY 3 JULY

After an hour's beautiful play, watched by Queen Mary and 15,000 spellbound spectators, Donald Budge defeated Baron von Cramm in three sets, winning with the score of 6–3, 6–4, 6–2.

Of Budge's display yesterday it may be asserted that it was worthy to rank with any that has gone before. To come through a field representing the picked talent of 27 countries with the loss of only one set, and with no vantage set among the 21 collected, was a feat Fred Perry never equalled in any of his three years' reign. Since Budge is only 21, seven years Perry's junior, the record needs no extra boosting. The first red-headed champion of Wimbledon has no weakness and nearly every virtue on the court.

The end of the match came with Budge opening his last service game with an ace and then eventually passing to 40–15 to have two match points. These were taken from him by splendid salving strokes from the German, one a low forehand volley that pitched just inside the line.

Von Cramm had vantage point twice, but Budge was in no mood to press unduly. He waited for the backhand volley that gave him the championship.

Budge (on the left, with von Cramm) also won the 1937 men's doubles title with Gene Mako and the mixed doubles with Alice Marble to become Wimbledon's first triple champion.

Both men left the court with fine bearing; there was never the slightest hint of any 'gallery play' and no untoward incident in a thoroughly sporting contest.

Sensational end to big fight

COMISKEY PARK, CHICAGO, TUESDAY 22 JUNE

Joe Louis, the young negro boxer and hero of America's coloured population, tonight won the world heavyweight championship from James Braddock, the 32-year-old holder of the title. He knocked out Braddock in the eighth round of a thrilling 15-round fight.

Louis, who is 23, is the second negro fighter to capture the championship. The first was Jack Johnson, who gained the title in 1907. His hundreds of supporters went wild with enthusiasm.

A crowd estimated at more than 55,000 and including statesmen and film stars, paid £150,000 to see the fight. Braddock was the first to enter the ring. He was accorded a great reception. He looked confident. Louis followed, also warmly applauded.

Round One. Braddock started the fight with a right swing and a jab to the head. Then Louis was doing the attacking. After an exchange of blows Louis went down from a right to the chin, but he was up again in a moment. Braddock backed him against the ropes. Braddock's round.

Round Two. Louis swung three rights at Braddock's face, landing each time. Louis' round. Round Three. Louis opened, jabbing his left. Braddock swung a right to the head and Louis countered with a right to the chin. Louis' round.

Round Four. Braddock scored a left to the head. After an exchange of blows to the head in the middle of the ring, the round ended. Braddock's round.

Round Five. The champion reddened Louis' nose with a left jab. Braddock's eye had been slightly cut since the second round. Braddock landed another nasty right to the nose and a right to the chin. Braddock's round.

Round Six. After another exchange of punches, Louis opened the cut over Braddock's left eye with two well-aimed rights. Louis kept landing punishing rights. Louis' round.

Round Seven. Roused by the punishment he received in the previous round, Braddock attacked fiercely. But his lip was now cut and he was beginning to lose his sense of distance. Louis came in with straight blows to the head, forcing Braddock to protect himself by folding his hands over his face. Louis' round.

Round Eight. Louis was not in a hurry for a kill. A left to the stomach and another left to the head did Braddock no good. Another left, followed by two stinging rights to the head, put Braddock on the floor, where he was counted out. Braddock was carried to his corner unconscious.

SPORT IN BRIEF

CRICKET

The first women's Test match is held in England in June. England, 95 for one at lunch in their second innings, need 199 to win, but within two hours Australia have taken seven more wickets for the addition of only 47 runs, and beat the home team by 31 runs.

BOXING

On 30 August, in an extraordinarily brave performance, Welsh boxer Tommy Farr **(below, on the right)** goes the full 15 rounds against heavyweight champion Joe Louis, but is outpointed. The British heavyweight title-holder is one of only three men to have gone the distance against Louis, who admits afterwards, 'It was the hardest fight I have ever had.' This is one of 25 successful defences Louis will make of his title in an astonishing 12-year reign as heavyweight champion of the world.

CRICKET

Twenty-one-year-old English batsman Len Hutton makes his debut in the first Test against New Zealand, and scores 0 and 1 in his two innings. His second appearance is more of a success: he scores a century in the next Test, the first of 19 hundreds he will record in his Test career.

1938

Derby televised

By our radio correspondent
PUBLISHED THURSDAY 2 JUNE

Pictures of the King and Queen as they walked along the course at Epsom were televised by the BBC yesterday before the Derby transmission. Their Majesties could be seen acknowledging the cheers of the crowds.

It was estimated that at least 10,000 persons saw the scenes at Epsom by television. Reception was reported from places as distant as Cheltenham and Malvern.

MILESTONES

The American tennis player, Donald Budge, became the first player to win all four major singles titles – the Australian, French and US Open and Wimbledon – in one year , thereby completing tennis's Grand Slam.

Huddersfield's unlucky Cup final

By Frank Coles
PUBLISHED MONDAY 2 MAY

Forbidding Wembley has relented again. Preston North End, beaten in last year's Cup final by Sunderland, won the precious prize on their second appearance there by defeating Huddersfield Town, after the most dramatic finish of all time.

Ninety minutes – no goals. An extra half-hour ordered (the first time this has happened in 18 years), and – with less than a minute left – still no goals. Our thoughts were on a replayed final on Aston Villa's ground next Wednesday when, suddenly, George Mutch, Preston's inside right, went darting through.

He reached the penalty area, chasing the ball full tilt. A breathtaking moment, and it ended in stark tragedy for Huddersfield. Their captain, Alf Young, brought the Preston flier to earth with a mistimed and technically unfair tackle. The extreme penalty was inevitable, and Mutch, taking the kick himself, won the cup for Lancashire with 30 seconds to spare.

There you have the plain story of how, 50 years after their first triumph, North End recaptured their glory. They richly deserve the honour because of the high standard they have set this season. However, I cannot go so far as to say that they deserved to beat Huddersfield in the final.

Huddersfield were unlucky losers. To be beaten with practically the last kick of the match after two hours' gallant endeavour — and a penalty kick at that – is as near heartbreak as anything I can think of, and it is a tribute to their players that not one with whom I talked after the match disputed the justice of the referee's decision in awarding the penalty.

That last minute of the 1938 Cup final will remain an indelible memory.

The King and Queen arrived at Wembley ten minutes before the match started. His Majesty presented the Cup to T. Smith, the Preston captain, and medals to the members of both teams.

Last year's defeated finalists, Preston North End, lift the FA Cup after their 1–0 win against Huddersfield Town.

Nuvolari wins at 80 mph

By our motoring correspondent
PUBLISHED MONDAY 24 OCTOBER

Tazio Nuvolari, the Italian leader of the Auto-Union team, won the Donington Grand Prix on Saturday from Hermann Lang and Richard Seaman, driving Mercedes, after a race packed with incident. The crowd was officially reported as 61,000.

The race was started at noon. In the front row on the grille were Lang (Mercedes), Nuvolari (Auto-Union) and Manfred von Brauchitsch, and Seaman (Mercedes). Nuvolari shot off the mark and was ten yards ahead at the first corner with Otto Müller, Seaman and Lang behind. In a few laps the little man, with his red helmet, mustard yellow pullover and blue trousers, had settled down in the lead, with Müller and Seaman fighting furiously for second place.

Auto-Union suffered the first casualty. On the third lap Kautz went off the road at Coppice and clouted the fence. He got going again at once, but as he shot down to the Melbourne turn he found he could not stop and dashed straight on over the grass into the earth bank.

On the 13th lap, Percy Maclure's Riley stopped with a broken half-shaft, leaving Cuddon-Fletcher to take the race promoters' £250 prize if he could finish. Five laps

later his MG was lying alongside Kautz's car, his brakes, too, having failed.

All in turn came in to refuel, and in some cases change tyres. Lang did not need a change and went by into the lead, which was now for the first time held by Mercedes.

But there was still Nuvolari to reckon with. Driving like a demon the little man was gaining on his rivals by two seconds a lap. Müller dropped back, von Brauchitsch was suffering from blistered hands; Seaman was a lap behind; Lang

drove his hardest but he could not stave off Nuvolari, and 13 laps from the end the Auto-Union shot past the Mercedes on the straight down to Melbourne Corner, not to be caught again.

The legendary Tazio Nuvolari drives to another victory in his Auto-Union Type D car at the Donington Grand Prix. He was 46 years old.

Len Hutton smashes all records

By Howard Marshall

PUBLISHED WEDNESDAY 24 AUGUST

Hutton making his record score of 364 in the final Test match at the Oval, Don Bradman being carried off the field with a fractured shinbone, England declaring at the phenomenal total of 903 for seven wickets – these were the outstanding events in one of the most remarkable day's cricket ever played.

That Australia lost three wickets for 117 after tea seemed entirely unimportant. The match is over, to all intents and purposes, and all that remains is to add up the records – eight in total.

Records do not make cricket, however, and we can only hope that these fresh ones will prove to be eight stout nails in the coffin of timeless Tests played on wickets which turn a great game into a farce.

First of all though, let us praise Hutton for his tremendous exhibition of concentration, endurance and skill. He gave point and purpose to the early hours, for the excitement was intense as he slowly and surely approached Bradman's record of 334, the previous highest individual score in Test matches between England and Australia.

We could almost feel the huge crowd willing Hutton to succeed, and when, with a beautiful square-cut, he hit the decisive four off L. O'B. Fleetwood-Smith, a roar went up which must have shaken the Houses of Parliament across the river. Bradman raced up to shake his hand, and while drinks came out and all the Australians toasted him the crowd cheered, and sang 'For he's a jolly good fellow,' and cheered and cheered again. An astonishing

The scoreboard testifies to the last player's 364, an Ashes record score for 22-year-old Englishman Len Hutton (left).

scene, and Hutton richly deserved this wonderful ovation. When at last his concentration wavered and he was caught at cover by Lindsay Hassett off W. J. O'Reilly, he had batted for 13 hours and 20 minutes, and hit 35 fours, 15 threes, 18 twos and 143 singles.

A prodigious effort, and if Hutton's innings was immensely prolonged, it was also logically and strictly in accordance with the conditions imposed by such a wicket and such a match.

JOE LOUIS (1914–81)

KNOWN TO HIS FANS AS THE 'BROWN BOMBER', Joe Louis eclipsed all his rivals in the boxing ring. He was born on 13 May 1914 in Lexington, Alabama, the son of a penniless sharecropper. In 1924 the family moved to Detroit, where Louis learned to box. Ten years later he won the Golden Gloves award for light-heavyweights, turning professional in the same year. This was followed by a string of victories, the principal victims being two former champions, Primo Carnera and Max Baer.

Louis became world heavyweight champion in 1937, after knocking out James Braddock. During the 12 years he held the title he gained an aura of invincibility, disposing of his challengers with such ease and regularity that the Press dubbed his victims 'Bums of the Month'.

Louis' style was deceptive. Critics accused him of being slow and flat-footed, but his awesome punching power compensated for this. 'As soon as I catch them, I put them to sleep', was his claim. In his long career, he was beaten just three times: once in 1936 by German Max Schmeling – a defeat he avenged with a devastating first-round win in 1938 – and twice in the 1950s, during an ill-advised comeback.

Louis earned $4.8 million from his fights, but the money drained away and he was forced to work as a professional wrestler and casino host to pay off his debts. Nevertheless, he inspired a generation of black athletes. Muhammad Ali paid tribute to him after he died: 'Joe Louis was my idol,' Ali said. 'He wrote the book on boxing.'

SPORT IN BRIEF

RUGBY UNION
Scotland clinch a dramatic 21–16 victory against England at Twickenham to lift the Calcutta Cup. They have also beaten Wales and Ireland and so take the Triple Crown and the championship. The international is the first to be televised.

FOOTBALL
German newspapers note 'with approval' that the English football players have given a Nazi salute before their match against Germany in Berlin on 14 May. England win the contest 6–3.

LAWN TENNIS
Helen Wills Moody wins a record eighth Wimbledon singles title when she beats Helen Jacobs 6–4, 6–0 in the final.

FOOTBALL
Italy repeat their 1934 success by winning the World Cup 4–2 against Hungary. Austria, annexed by Hitler's troops, have been forced to withdraw, though many of the best Austrian players have been poached by Germany. No teams are sent from Britain.

BOXING
Californian Henry Armstrong creates an extraordinary record when he wins the lightweight championship from Lou Ambers on 18 August. He now holds the world lightweight, featherweight and welterweight boxing titles.

MOTOR RACING
Talented German driver Rudolf Caracciola wins his third European championship, following his triumphs in 1935 and 1937 and his second world championship last year. Caracciola will win a total of 26 major grands prix.

1939

England's task in first Test today

By D. R. Jardine

PUBLISHED SATURDAY 24 JUNE

England and the West Indies meet in a Test match for the 15th time at Lord's today. Though their matches with the mother-country hardly compare with those of Australia and South Africa, they have done far better than their modern Test contemporaries, India and New Zealand, both of whom have yet to beat an England side.

The West Indies can not only claim three victories against seven defeats, but they actually won the last rubber played in their own islands in 1935.

The present team began their tour badly in cold and cheerless weather, but they have steadily improved, and this month have held their own against all county opposition. In George Headley they possess one of the best batsmen in the world. He has hit six centuries against England in previous Tests.

They also have, in Learie Constantine, a bowler who mixes pace with spin, and a genuine fast attack in Manny Martindale and L. G. Hylton. Walter Hammond's team will have to be on their toes to force a win against these tourists in three days.

It has been suggested that the groundsman at Lord's has had instructions to prepare his pitch for speed. Such suggestions are to be deprecated.

Inaccuracy apart, for there is no secret about the instructions to the groundsman at headquarters, neither the Board of Control nor the Marylebone Club would take the responsibility of giving any such detailed and particular instructions for an important match, if these involved any variation or departure from existing practice.

It is as well to be quite clear on this point. Epitomised, the present instructions are that the wickets at Lord's should aim at being fair to both batsmen and bowlers by avoiding unduly favouring either. The tourists have played sufficiently often at Lord's to have a very adequate idea of what to expect from a Lord's wicket.

Only the weather can rob us of one treat, and that is the certain pleasure of seeing great fielding on both sides worthy of the occasion.

K. H. Weekes (left) on his way to a century for the West Indies. England won the first match at Lord's; the next two were drawn.

Hammond and Hutton save England

By D. R. Jardine

PUBLISHED WEDNESDAY 23 AUGUST

The final day's play in the Oval Test match was something of an anti-climax. For the match to be thoroughly alive it was necessary that the West Indies should either score apace and then cause English wickets to tumble, or themselves get out quickly and for few more runs, leaving England to press for runs and a decision which would go some way towards redeeming a far from convincing or distinguished performance.

The West Indies duly got a good many more runs than are normally associated with their last four wickets, and got these runs, moreover, at the rattling pace of 103 in the first hour's play of the day.

In retrospect, the major part of the day's interest was concentrated in their first hour, with Constantine scoring 11 fours and a six against the two English fast bowlers,

In what would be the last Test series before war broke out – and his last match for the West Indies – Learie Constantine scored 79 runs in 60 minutes and took five for 75 in the first innings. A dynamic player, he was highly popular in the Lancashire league, but was a victim of prejudice off the field.

who bowled all the time unchanged, and were in the end reduced to bowling without a single slip.

With the close of the West Indies innings two minutes before midday the tourists' run of success almost ended. No one will grudge it to them, even if, on reflection, it be considered that some of it was all but handed to them on a platter.

When it was England's turn to bat, despite some fresh life added to the wicket by the application of the Oval's heaviest roller, there never seemed any serious danger of an English batting debacle.

Hutton and Hammond, in the course of a long partnership, first placed any question of defeat beyond the bounds of possibility, and thereafter proceeded to enjoy an extended slice of excellent and entertaining batting practice. Coming together with the score at 77, the pair added 264 runs for the third wicket, Hutton's share being 117 to his captain's 138. Apart from breaking the record

partnership of 262 for the third wicket in Test matches by two runs, a partnership in which, incidentally, Hammond had himself had the major share, the tally of Hammond's Test centuries now stands at 22 to Bradman's 21.

After lunch, when Hutton had skied a no-ball to mid-off, Oldfield was out off Johnson's next delivery, which looked to straighten in the most disconcerting manner; all the others of the left-handers' deliveries had been coming into the batsmen and frequently rapping their legs. Thereafter it was all Hutton and Hammond, with the bowlers nowhere. More than once at the start Hammond snicked the ball through the slips, and throughout the stand the ball was more often in the air than usual, though nothing quite came to hand.

The wicket, which got progressively better the longer the match lasted, though it was never difficult at any time, would probably have precluded a finish in four days. As it was the later stages of the play were somewhat unreal, and the England innings was declared ten minutes before time, when it was too late for the West Indies to go in again.

Hammond got his runs in just over three hours to Hutton's five hours, the latter hitting 17 fours.

Riggs triumphs at Wimbledon

By our special representative
PUBLISHED SATURDAY 8 JULY

Robert L. Riggs **(right)**, of America, yesterday joined the select band of those who have conquered Wimbledon at the first attempt. He beat his compatriot, E. T. Cooke, by 2–6, 8–6, 3–6, 6–3, 6–2, in the final of the men's singles.

G. L. Patterson, W. T. Tilden and Ellsworth Vines are the only other players who have done it. Riggs joins high company – but how vastly different his methods from those of the redoubtable hitters with whom his name is now linked. And what a strange sight to see empty benches and walking-room on the terraces on a Wimbledon finals day! Hundreds of the open stand seats for which the midnight queues once formed were unsold. And after two sets the vast arena half-emptied and the tea marquee filled. Presumably, after a long reign of speed champions, who smote and smashed their way to titles in the grand spectacular manner, the quieter and more studious art of Riggs is poor 'box-office'. Indeed I heard one man who can remember Wimbledon in its pre-war setting describe this final as an anachronism.

Riggs is to be praised for the fact that he won when below his best form. The effort to raise his game to its highest level was at times obvious. The strokes did not flow with the same spontaneity and sparkle as they had against Puncec, for example, but his will and determination were rigid, and even when everything appeared to be going against him he never lost sight of the ultimate goal. There were many rallies that, frankly, were boring, long backhand exchanges that cried out for a stroke of enterprise. But there were many just as enthralling, and the fluctuations of the score should have been enough to keep interest alive.

All Wimbledon titles go to America

By our special representative
PUBLISHED MONDAY 10 JULY

A Wimbledon of lowly beginnings became a Wimbledon of revelations in the end. America, or to be more geographically precise, the state of California, carried every title, yet I doubt after the first week's play if anyone had realised the complete invincibility of Miss Marble or the real strength of Robert Lorimer Riggs, both of whom became triple champions.

The combined feat of these two players was in itself a record, and Miss Marble's achievement in playing through six rounds with the loss of only 21 games, only two of which were dropped in the semi-final and final, ranges her with such great players as the late Mlle Lenglen and Mrs Helen Wills Moody.

On Saturday, in the final of the women's singles, Miss Stammers' best game was worth a mere handful of points against the crushing, withering lawn tennis that Miss Marble produced with an ease and certainty of touch that were simply astonishing. The score was 6–2, 6–0.

So completely was Miss Marble mistress of the match that she could interrupt a barrage of the fiercest driving to interpose a drop-shot, or send an attacking adversary scurrying back in pursuit of a cunningly hoisted lob, to say nothing of the stop-volley that died as soon as it made contact with the ground. I judged the pace to be quite twice as great as that of the men's singles the day before, a truly extraordinary state of affairs.

Miss Stammers won the third and sixth games of the first set. It was a splendidly defiant gesture, but opposition of the kind that could not possibly last, and Miss Marble sailed serenely to victory from that point.

The packed arena were quick to recognise the magnitude of the American performance. As the players ran forward to shake hands, posed before a battery of cameras, thanked the umpire, gathered up their spare racquets, and bowed low in front of the Royal box, cheer upon congratulatory cheer for Miss Marble filled the air.

Alice Marble (left, wearing hat) and Kay Stammers arrive on the centre court. Diagnosed as having TB in 1934, Marble recovered and in 1939 won the Wimbledon singles, mixed and women's doubles titles.

SPORT IN BRIEF

FOOTBALL
Rangers win the Scottish League. Top-scorer is Rangers' Alec Venters, who has notched up 34 goals this season.

BASEBALL
In May Lou Gehrig is forced to retire from the New York Yankees with an incurable wasting disease. He has played in an incredible 2,130 consecutive games for his team since 1 June 1925.

RUGBY LEAGUE
At the end of August a New Zealand side arrives to tour Britain. Within three days of their arriving, Adolf Hitler's German troops have invaded Poland; and a day after their first match (a 19–3 victory over St Helens), Britain declares war on Germany. After another win, this time a 22–10 win against Dewsbury on 7 September, the tourists head home.

1939–1945

By Iain Zaczek

Official attitudes to sport differed considerably in the two World Wars. In 1939, sporting bodies reacted much more quickly to the situation, and many competitions were cancelled within days of the outbreak of hostilities. In part this was due to concerns for public safety, since crowds of spectators might be at risk from air-raids. Once the initial panic had subsided, however, sport was viewed in a more positive light. There were still some critics who condemned it, but greater stress was placed on its advantages – as a means of maintaining fitness and morale, both at home and at the front.

This was certainly the pattern followed in the football world. At first there was a total ban on civilian games, although the FA made a donation of £1,000 for football equipment for the services. Within a couple of months, however, many of the restrictions had been relaxed. Both friendly and competitive matches were revived, although crowd numbers were limited and the ban on games in city centres remained in force. Even here, there was flexibility on the big occasions. West Ham's 1–0 triumph over Blackburn in the 1940 War Cup attracted more than 42,000 spectators, many of them survivors from the recent evacuation of Dunkirk, and Preston's victory over Arsenal in the following year also drew large crowds.

Alongside professional games, the authorities introduced a host of amateur and charity fixtures. In September 1940, munitions workers and civil defence units were given permission to participate in Sunday matches, as a relaxation from the rigours of war work. The arrival of American, Commonwealth and other Allied forces in Britain also gave rise to a number of competitions for servicemen. The most important of these was the Inter-Allied Services Cup, which was launched in 1941 and continued until the invasion of Normandy in 1944. This proved just as popular as League football, and the 1943 final, which pitted the British Army against the

Above: Pictured in 1940, Arsenal's Wilf Copping (on left) and Denis Compton. Compton won 12 wartime soccer caps for England; he was also an outstanding cricketer, playing for Middlesex and England.
Below: Watched by servicemen, Pont L'Eveque wins the 1940 Derby.

RAF, was watched by 31,000 spectators.

In order to combat the arguments of the anti-sport lobby, the proceeds from the forces' matches and other charity games were used to aid soldiers on active duty. Here, the main administrative bodies were the Prisoners of War Department of the Red Cross and the St John War Organisation. From the money raised, they despatched sporting equipment of all kinds to men at the front, as well as those in enemy camps.

Charity matches were also an important feature of wartime cricket. Two sides, the British Empire and the London Counties XI, toured the country and raised money by playing local teams. The British Empire players were amateurs, while the Counties' side was mainly professional, but both included celebrities to draw in the crowds.

A former batsman and Test selector, Sir Pelham 'Plum' Warner, also assembled a side and staged a series of matches against combined counties or army teams. These proved extremely popular. A Bank Holiday meeting between Middlesex and Essex and Kent and Surrey attracted more than 22,000 spectators to Lord's.

The emergency conditions prompted the cricketing authorities to make bold innovations to their sport. Just as the Football Association agreed to Sunday soccer long before this was accepted in the professional game, so the MCC sanctioned the introduction of one-day matches. Several fixtures were arranged between different branches of the services, culminating in the four official contests between the Army and the RAF, which were held at Lord's in 1941.

This varied programme of matches offered some compensation to cricket fans for the loss of the first-class game. For, in contrast to football, the county championship had to be suspended at the start of the war. In part, this was due to difficulties with the pitches. Some were requisitioned by the War Office – Lord's, for example, was used for a time as an intake centre by the RAF – but the destruction caused during air-raids was an even greater hazard. Both the Oval and Old Trafford suffered considerable bomb damage. In the latter part of the war, many of these difficulties were overcome, although spectators at the London grounds in 1944 still had to contend with flying bombs.

Of course, many parts of the Commonwealth were not affected in this way. In Australia, the 1939–40 cricket season went ahead as normal, after the Prime Minister, Robert Menzies, declared that it would boost the morale of the people. Fans were treated to a vintage display, with Don Bradman at the peak of his form. In nine matches he scored 1,475 runs, at an average of 122.9. Among

(continued on page 94)

SPORT IN BRIEF

RUGBY UNION
In a match in aid of the Red Cross in December, a combined England and Wales team beat a combined Scotland and Ireland team 17–3.

BASEBALL
Despite the loss of their star Lou Gehrig, the New York Yankees are helped by a new discovery, Joe Dimaggio, to a fourth consecutive World Series. In the following decade they will take the title four more times: in 1941, 1943, 1947 and 1949.

SNOOKER
In 1940 Joe Davis wins the world championship for the 14th time. After winning it for the 15th time in 1946, Davis retires. His brother Fred will become world champion in 1949, and from 1951–6.

HORSE RACING
Racing continues throughout the war. with the Derby run at Newmarket rather than Epsom, as it was during the First World War. Jockey Bill Nevett – the 'Cock of the North' – rides three Derby winners during the war years: Owen Tudor in 1941, Ocean Swell in 1944 and Dante in 1945.

RUGBY LEAGUE
Leeds are the winners of the 1941 Challenge Cup, beating Halifax 19–2. The same teams contest the 1942 trophy: once more Leeds win, this time by 15 points to ten.

GOLF
In 1941 Craig Wood wins his second major in one year. He takes the US Masters title three shots ahead of Byron Nelson, then the US Open title by three shots from Densmore Shute. Nelson will avenge the Masters defeat next year, however; he dons the green jacket after a play-off against Ben Hogan which he wins by one shot.

1939–1945

(continued from page 93)
these, there were double centuries against Queensland, Victoria and Western Australia. This golden interlude was shattered in the following year, however, when the Japanese assault on Pearl Harbor brought the nation into the front line. After the devastating air attack on Darwin in February 1942, most cricket competitions were cancelled and the grounds handed over to the military.

Even so, servicemen from the southern hemisphere were encouraged to continue playing sport whilst on active duty around the globe. Accordingly, Lindsay Hassett, a talented Australian all-rounder, organised a highly successful series of cricket matches for his compatriots in Egypt and Palestine. At the same time, members of the NZEF (New Zealand Expeditionary Force) spent their leisure hours playing rugby at their base in Maadi, a few miles from Cairo. Different units competed for the Freyberg Cup, a trophy donated by their divisional commander, General Freyberg. A combined team also played against other Allied servicemen. The New Zealand side, which included a number of All Blacks, defeated their British and Australian opponents with comparative ease, but met with stiffer opposition from the South Africans in the 'Rest

of Egypt' squad. Some of these games were played under most unusual conditions. One of the matches against the Springboks took place in the sands of the Western Desert region, right next to an anti-aircraft battery.

Meanwhile, Australians stationed in England formed two cricket teams, representing the RAAF (Royal Australian Air Force) and the AIF (Australian Imperial Forces). These participated in a number of games against British service sides. Then in the summer of 1945, in the months between VE-Day and VJ-Day, they amalgamated to compete in the so-called 'Victory Tests'. These were not recognised as

official Test matches although, with the presence of figures like Walter Hammond, Len Hutton and Keith Miller, they could easily have been classed as such.

The Victory Tests provided some thrilling entertainment, with England just managing to tie the series in the final game. The matches were played out amid an air of celebration, although wartime conditions still prevailed. At some of the bomb-scarred grounds, German prisoners of war were brought in to repair the damaged terraces, to prevent them from collapsing. At others, the pitches were uneven because all the rollers

Above: West Ham beat Blackburn in the 1940 League Cup final.
Top left: The England football team's half-back line of Cliff Britton, Stan Cullis and Joe Mercer were based in Aldershot, and played for the Third Division club there.
Left: The 1941 League Cup final was between Arsenal and Preston North End; Arsenal's Leslie Compton (brother of Denis) missed this penalty, and Preston won.
Right: The boarded-up members' pavilion at Lord's; the Royal Air Force used the ground during the war.

had been shipped out to the Middle East, to help with the creation of new airstrips.

These minor irritants were typical of the difficulties that had bedevilled sporting authorities throughout the war. In most cases, though, the problem was eventually solved with a little ingenuity. During the period of the early air-raids, for example, when the blackout was strictly enforced, the managers of Wembley Arena had its glass roof painted black, so that the venue could remain in use. Similarly ping-pong players experimented with luminous balls, which enabled them to use rooms with subdued lighting.

Shortages of equipment were also a problem, particularly for those men serving overseas or held in prison camps. Here, improvisation was the only solution. In one famous instance, the inmates of Stalag Luft III used a Red Cross crate as a vaulting-horse, while escapers tunnelled their way to freedom beneath it. At another German camp, prisoners at least managed to rig up a makeshift golf course. Between them they had just one club – a lady's wooden mashie – and a strange

variety of home-made balls. The first attempts were carved out of wood and covered with wool or cotton, while later versions were wrapped in scraps of leather or the rubber soles of old plimsolls. The surface of the nine-hole course was composed exclusively of sand or soil, but its par 28 proved an enjoyable test for the 300 soldiers who queued up to try it out.

Problems of this kind must have seemed very remote to American sports fans. Their domestic programme was scarcely affected by the hostilities, although some of the golfing championships were suspended. In other events, it was a vintage era. Baseball was dominated by the New York Yankees and the St Louis Cardinals, both of whom won the World Series twice during the war years. Meanwhile, in the boxing ring, the rising star was Sugar Ray Robinson, who turned professional in 1940 and won his next 40 bouts. In contrast, some of the best-known sporting personalities were swift to enlist. In 1942, Joe Louis became a physical education instructor in the US army, and in the following year, Joe Dimaggio also volunteered his services.

SPORT IN BRIEF

BOXING
Scottish boxer Jackie Paterson becomes world flyweight champion in 1943 when he knocks out Peter Kane in Glasgow in the first round. Kane returns to the bantamweight division, and holds the European title from 1947 to 1948.

GOLF
In November 1943, talented British golfer Pam Barton is killed in a plane crash while serving with the Women's Auxiliary Air Force. She won the British Open Amateur championship in 1936 and 1939, and the American Amateur title in 1936.

CRICKET
In the summer of 1945, with the war in Europe now over, the Australian cricket team arrives in Britain for five three-day Victory matches. In one innings, Australian Keith Miller, who has served in England during the war, scores 185 in 165 minutes for the Dominions.

MOTOR RACING
The first post-war race meeting is held on 9 September 1945 in the Bois de Boulogne in Paris. Drivers compete for the Robert Benoist Trophy, named after the 1927 world champion who fought with the French Resistance during the war and was captured and hanged by the Gestapo. The race is won by Amedée Gordino, in a hybrid Fiat and Simca car.

FOOTBALL
In October 1945 the Moscow Dynamos arrive in Britain to huge acclaim. In their first match against Chelsea the Soviets present each of their bemused opponents with a bunch of flowers. The match ends in a 3–3 draw. They beat Cardiff City 10–1, Arsenal (the team includes Stan Mortensen and Stanley Matthews) 4–3, and draw 2–2 with Rangers. Their skill and artistry thrill the public; nearly 250,000 people see them play.

Andrew Baker

Technology and drugs in 20th-century sport

TECHNOLOGY HAS MARCHED HAND-IN-HAND WITH SPORT throughout the 20th century. In the latter half of those 100 years a technological medium – television – has revolutionised the way that the majority of mankind experiences sport. But we would do well to remember that many of the advances trumpeted by sports goods manufacturers are more about marketing than technological progress: we can run without shoes.

The right shoes, however, can help us run faster, and the right drugs faster still. Doping is a problem that has blighted many sports over the last two decades, but it is not only a recent problem. At the start of this sporting century, in 1904, the winner of the St Louis Olympic marathon, Thomas Hicks, was refuelled with numerous doses of strychnine and brandy, *during the race*. A post-event photograph shows the winner looking not elated, not even drained, merely dazed. We will return to the matter of doping later.

It is perhaps useful to divide the matter of technology and sport into those sports which are technology driven and those in which the human element is paramount. The exemplar of technology-driven sport (if you will forgive the pun) is motor racing, which was in its infancy at the start of the century: the first international races, the Gordon Bennett series, began in 1900, and the first grand prix, the French, was held in 1906.

The first grand prix cars were terrifying leviathans, vast engines perched precariously on primitive wooden chassis, driving solid-tyred wheels through chains that were effective transmission devices, but also, occasionally, equally effective decapitators of unfortunate drivers or their ride-along mechanics.

The sport of motor racing is inseparable from the technology on which it relies, and each significant mechancial breakthrough has conferred great advantages on the drivers of the revolutionary vehicles.

Such advances are too numerous to list in full, but among the most significant were the streamlined Mercedes W196 of the 1950s, the rear-engined Cooper-Climax of 1959, the introduction of the monocoque chassis in the 1960s, the aerodynamic 'ground effect' revolution of the 1970s, and the introduction of carbon-fibre technology in the 1980s. In the late 1990s grand prix motor racing is arguably more a contest between designers and rule-makers than between individual drivers.

This is also true in other technology-driven sports. Compare, for instance, the triumphant four-man bobsled at the 1932 Lake Placid winter Olympics, which resembles a bedstead on skates with a steering wheel that would not be out of place on a London bus, with the sleek, hi-tech, ultra-lightweight machines on view in Nagano in 1998.

Complete sports have arisen solely to exploit recent technological advances: aerobatics, hang-gliding and jet-skiing, to name but a few.

Compare also the yachts competing in the Whitbread Round-the-World Race, with their satellite guidance systems, synthetic sails and carbon-fibre hulls, with the lumbering hulks that raced between Paris and Le Havre in the 10 to 20-ton class at the 1900 Olympics.

Complete sports have arisen solely to exploit recent technological advances: aerobatics, hang-gliding, snowboarding and jet-skiing, to name but a few. Others – perhaps 'virtual' sports, in which competitors in the same event may be in different towns or even countries – will no doubt follow.

In certain sports the relative input of competitor and equipment is difficult to define: alpine skiing is perhaps the best example. Ski technology has advanced a long way since the heavy planks of the early part of the century, but for all the talk of lightweight, flexible blades and fancy waxes, the equipment remains essentially rudimentary and the skill and bravery of the competitor remain paramount.

This is overwhelmingly the case in high-profile sports in which technology plays a subsidiary role, but one which can be turned to lucrative effect by clever, marketing-savvy manufacturers.

In tennis, for instance, commentators often complain that modern racquets have 'killed the game'. But they have not. They have changed it. It is true that recent steps forward in frame and string manufacture have tended to favour the power-server over the touch player. But it is also true – as Björn Borg found in his abortive comeback in 1991, using a wooden racquet – that you cannot disregard progress.

What is significant about technology in tennis, and in other skill-reliant sports such as football and cricket, is that possession of state-of-the-art equipment does not make a mediocre player into a champion. Pete Sampras achieved dominance by playing a particular kind of game particularly well, not because he had a better racquet than any of his competitors.

In cricket and football the century's story has been one of technological refinement of existing equipment rather than revolution. Dennis Lillee's aluminium bat of 1979 made more headlines than runs; the much-hyped Adidas Predator football boot has made millions of pounds, but not careers. Cricket pads and gloves have become lighter, as have football boots and balls; these have been the only significant advances on the field of play.

Off the field, television developments have not only revolutionised the finances of sports, they have also begun to affect results. Here cricket, for all its fuddy-duddy image, has led the way, with the introduction of the third umpire and his television replays. Horse racing, another supposedly traditional pastime, has benefited from replay technology. Surely it cannot be long before football, and perhaps tennis, follow suit.

All four of these sports, like many others, have experienced problems with doping. But drug abuse in sport has more commonly been associated with disciplines that rely more on strength than dexterity, notably cycling, weight-lifting and athletics.

Amphetamine abuse in cycling was the first to achieve widespread notoriety, after the death of the British cyclist Tommy Simpson during a climb in the 1967 Tour de France. But the practice had been common in the sport for years. Tests conducted in Belgium in 1965 revealed that more than half of all professional cyclists were taking amphetamines, and the following year the first five competitors in the World Professional Road Race refused to take a dope test. Other sports were soon following suit, albeit with potions better adapted to their specific requirements. Increased state funds for sports research behind the Iron Curtain were one catalyst for the spread of drug abuse in athletics.

The great Russian sprinter Valery Borzov – Olympic 100 m gold medallist in 1972 – was no drug-taker, but the way in which his campaign was planned was scientific in the extreme. As his coach,

Valentin Petrovsky explained: 'For Borzov to be able to clock ten seconds flat over 100 m, a whole team of scientists conducted research resembling the work of, say, car or aircraft designers…'.

It was a short step from there to modifying the chemical composition of the athletes themselves. The East Germans led the way, particularly in the area of anabolic steroids, preparations related to the male sex hormone testosterone which were effective in building muscle bulk and strength in female athletes.

They were also, as the coaches responsible for their administration must have known, extremely dangerous. Among the side-effects for women taking such steroids were hair loss, deepening of the voice, menstrual irregularities and decreased breast size. Male athletes took steroids too, and they could expect to suffer testicular atrophy, decreased fertility and psychological side-effects such as increased aggressiveness.

The full scale of the damage caused by the mass doping scandals of the East German sporting establishment are only now becoming clear.

The full scale of the damage caused by the mass doping scandals of the East German sporting establishment are only now becoming clear. But it should be emphasised that they were far from alone in such practices, as cases such as that of the shamed Olympic sprint 'champion' Ben Johnson, of Canada, make clear.

Increased testing, and increasingly accurate testing techniques, seem to have reduced the epidemic of doping in sport. But, in much the same manner that those at the forefront of research in technology-driven sport are constantly testing the ingenuity of both law-makers and enforcers, so the rogue chemists seem likely to continue to refine their strategies in the next century.

But we should not be distressed by the notion that doping and cheating are a uniquely modern phenomenon. In the Olympic Games of 300 BC, competitors are known to have sought to improve their performance by consuming certain special fungi. The quest for victory, whether through legitimate technological progress or chemical cheating, has been and will be a factor in every sporting century.

1946

Snead wins golf Open

By Leonard Crawley

ST ANDREWS, FRIDAY 5 JULY

Sam Snead, aged 33, of Virginia, US, won the British Open championship on the Old Course here today with a score of 290 for the 72 holes.

It was a clear-cut victory, for he finished four strokes ahead of his fellow-countryman Johnny Bulla and Bobby Locke, the South African champion, each with 294.

Snead has thus emulated the feat of Densmore Shute, the American, by winning the world's greatest golf event at St Andrews at his first attempt. There may have been more fascinating stylists who have come here from America to win our title, but none more dashing and utterly courageous. His driving throughout was stupendous, and another contributory factor to his victory was his ability to pitch and stop the ball on greens not meant for this type of shot.

As a putter, like all great Americans, he is far above the British standard. He always gives the hole a chance and is never afraid of the putt back. It must never again be said that these Americans cannot play in a wind. Snead delivers the clubhead so square and solidly at the back of the ball that he disregards the wind altogether. His vast experience of tournament play makes an Open championship such as he has won just another day's work.

'Slamming' Sam Snead (above) at St Andrews. Snead went on to win 84 PGA tournaments and every major except the US Open in a career lasting over 40 years.

DID YOU KNOW?

Charlton Athletic became the only club to lose an FA Cup tie and still reach the final. Ties up to the semi-final were played over two legs, with aggregate scores deciding the winner. Although Charlton lost in the first leg at Fulham, they won 4–3 on aggregate to reach the third round.

By Frank Coles

PUBLISHED MONDAY 11 MARCH

Thirty-three spectators have been killed and more than 500 injured following the collapse of barriers at Burnden Park, Bolton, during an FA Cup tie between Bolton Wanderers and Stoke City.

The crowd disaster on the Bolton Wanderers ground on Saturday, the worst in the history of British football, has shocked the country and cast a deep shadow over a world of sport awakening to the biggest boom year it has ever known.

The sad loss of life raises in acute form the responsibility of sports promoters to a public more eager than ever before to be present at major events which have been restored to the sporting calendar after a break of six years.

A victim of the Burnden Park tragedy, 9 March 1946, is carried away. Around 65,000 people had paid to see Stoke play Bolton, but thousands more managed to gatecrash the ground and crush barriers collapsed. In the greatest tragedy the football world had seen, 33 people died and more than 500 were injured.

One certain remedy for football gatecrashing is the all-ticket match. The Wembley Stadium authorities have proved this over a long period in handling Cup final crowds, and it has been equally successful elsewhere.

The time has arrived when the system of selling all the tickets, standing accommodation as well as seating, before a big Cup-tie is played should be applied to all enclosures. I hope the FA Council, who meet today to make the draw for the Cup semi-finals and choose the grounds, will decide upon all-ticket admission.

Thirty-two nations at the reopening of Wimbledon

By John Olliff
PUBLISHED MONDAY 24 JUNE

The reopening of the lawn tennis championships at the All-England Club, Wimbledon, today after six years of war provides the most tangible and poignant symbol of peace for all lawn tennis followers. Thirty-two nations of widely differing colours and creeds are here to contend for the highest honours in the game.

Never before have the players from overseas been so keen to get here and never has their enthusiasm reached such a pitch. Many of them have had to overcome great difficulties in making the journey.

Never before have countries shown themselves to be such ardent lovers of the game as they have now by raising public subscriptions to meet their players' expenses in order that their country might be represented at Wimbledon.

An example of this enthusiasm is the case of Miss Jadwiga Jedzrejowska, who arrived by air from Warsaw via Berlin just in time for the championships. She has had little practice, and on arrival possessed no tennis clothes or shoes. She did not touch a racquet during the whole of the war, and her experiences in Poland do not bear repetition. She is thinner and obviously wearied and worn by her country's sufferings. Her obvious joy at being back once again at Wimbledon is shared by all the competitors from European countries ravaged by the Nazis. If it is in some way an austerity Wimbledon this year, it will not be in the quality of play.

England win Test against India by ten wickets

By Sir Guy Campbell
PUBLISHED WEDNESDAY 26 JUNE

England won the first Test match by ten wickets at Lord's yesterday, Hutton making the deciding stroke just when the luncheon interval would normally have been taken. England won on merit and decisively but, for all that, not as easily as the result would suggest. Twice India had to start the day's batting with the dew – what there was of it – on the ground, and on Monday morning, when J. Hardstaff and P. A. Gibb were faced with a similar task, it appeared to me there was no dew at all.

Then there was the batting of Hardstaff which, giving full credit to the assistance of Gibb and the bowling of A. V. Bedser, D. V. P. Wright and T. F. Smailes, was the decisive factor. It was Hardstaff's second hundred that really did the trick. Deduct it and see how different the picture would have appeared.

And lastly, there was yesterday that inspired ball of Wright's, only possible to a great bowler, that sent the Nawab of Pataudi back to the pavilion just when he looked like settling down to become a thorn in England's flesh. Although L. Armanath batted bravely and well for his 50, and runs came at the habitual Indian pace, Bedser and Smailes did the needful.

The Indian team need have no more than the conventional regret at defeat. Their batting, for all that each potential scorer got out just when he looked like making a lot of runs, was in timing, fluency and power of the stuff that batting dreams are made. Their bowling never grew ragged and their fielding crystallised the highest traditions of the game.

Making his debut for the Indian Test team (below) was Vinoo Mankad, beginning an outstanding 44-match Test career. The final two matches in the series were drawn.

SPORT IN BRIEF

FOOTBALL
After three unsuccessful Cup final attempts, the last in 1903, Derby County finally win the FA Cup when they beat Charlton Athletic 4–1. The match is full of bizarre incident: in the second half Bert Turner turns the ball over his own line to put Derby one ahead, but then takes a free kick, which is deflected into the Derby net for an equaliser. As Derby's Jack Stamps tries a shot, the ball bursts; but he is rewarded with three goals in extra time.

CRICKET
Australia face New Zealand in Wellington in the first Test to be played since the end of the war. Australia win by an innings and 103 runs. Keith Miller makes his debut for Australia.

FOOTBALL
The home international championship is resumed in September after a seven-year break. In the first match, England beat Ireland 7–2.

BOXING
Algerian-born Frenchman Marcel Cerdan, holder of the European middleweight title, raises a weary arm **(right)** after his points victory over the leading US middleweight boxer, Georgie Abrams, at Madison Square Gardens in December. In 1948 Cerdan will knock out American Tony Zale for the world middleweight title.

CRICKET
Ashes cricket resumes after the war, and England travel to Australia. Batting in the first Test, Bradman receives a not-out decision for a catch when on 28. He goes on to score 187.

1948

Mills causes upset to claim light-heavyweight title

By Lainson Wood
PUBLISHED TUESDAY 27 JULY

Freddie Mills is world light-heavyweight champion, the most unpredictable champion we have ever had. In the vast White City (London) Stadium last night, before 46,000 at first ironic and finally yelling fans, he beat Gus Lesnevich of America on points and avenged a bad battering he received at Lesnevich's hands two years ago.

The story of the fight is a simple one to tell. Mills, quite different from his usual exuberant and reckless self, did not come in arms swinging. Instead we saw a contained and cautious boxer quelling all his fighting instincts, tucking his elbows closely into his side, and burying his chin behind his massive left shoulder.

He clearly took Lesnevich by surprise. The American, still a fast, straight and correct puncher, and an easy mover, set out, as we all expected, to seal an early victory.

Australia are worthy Test winners

By E. W. Swanton
THE OVAL, WEDNESDAY 18 AUGUST

The curtain fell quickly on the England innings and the last Test match here this morning. The last three wickets were disposed of in a quarter of an hour (on a pitch not quite to be trusted) to give Australia the victory by an innings and 149 runs. Thus our visitors ended their drastic lesson and so became the first team to win four Tests in a rubber in England.

Several thousand spectators had come to give atmosphere to a scene that one feared might be somewhat cold and hollow. They were rewarded by a pleasing exchange of speeches from the pavilion.

Freddie Mills (on left of picture) became Britain's first world light-heavyweight champion for nearly 50 years. Lesnevich never regained the title.

His very first sally resulted in a cut over his right eye inflicted by Mills's counter-punch. It did not upset him. He went in at Mills again, threw three menacing straight rights and prodded home his left. But neither then nor ever afterwards could he open up the way to Mills's jaw.

Lesnevich, his early essays at a knock-out having failed, changed his tactics entirely. He fenced with Mills, directed his now occasional attacks to the body, and began to forge ahead on points. The contest as a spectacle deteriorated, and soon the crowd was slow-clapping and cat-calling derisively. As a world championship, the fight had developed into a sorry affair.

So the contest ambled on to the tenth round, when it suddenly flared up. Mills scored with a grand left hook, which sent Lesnevich reeling back, and Mills was quick to see his chance. He leapt after his man, lunging out with both fists.

Soon Lesnevich was on his knees, taking a count of nine. He got up, stalled for a moment or two but, still groggy, was caught again by a left hook of great power and down he went for a second time. This time, I am convinced Lesnevich did not beat the count. He was on his knees immediately above me when the count reached nine. There was a perceptible pause before he rose – but no count of ten. I happened at the time to be watching the electric seconds clock and made Lesnevich to be still on one knee when the hand reached ten.

There were no more knock-downs, but much fiercer fighting. Lesnevich now getting slower and slower, his efforts to score became feebler, and an extremely tired Mills easily won the last round.

Lesnevich thought he had won the fight. He must conveniently have forgotten that long tenth-round count.

Mr H. D. G. Leveson-Gower expressed just the sentiments that are felt generally by the cricket world at the retirement of Don Bradman. Bradman himself made a speech which, as always, blended modesty and tact.

His team, he thought, were one of the strongest ever to tour this country. With that no one will be disposed to disagree, and the only regret we should have is that the England XI was not able, in three matches out of the five, to stretch them to the full.

There are a lot of vain 'ifs' about England's performances this summer. The solemn truth is that there are, I think, about six English cricketers of true Test match capacity, and after them follows a longish hiatus.

W. J. Edrich's lack of form in June and D. V. P. Wright's unfitness were especially embarrassing. The Australians had their share of injuries, but their reserve strength was equal to whatever was demanded.

Generally speaking, our bowling was every bit as effective as could have been hoped, and the fielding, though it could never match the athleticism of a considerably younger side, except on the disastrous last day at Leeds, kept a reasonable level. The chief discrepancies lay in the failure of our batting against some fast bowling of very high quality.

I feel that, for all N. W. D. Yardley's many sound qualities as a captain, his mildness should have been replaced, for the final Test, by some stronger medicine supplied by R. W. V. Robins. But that conjures up yet another unprofitable 'if', and the last thing to be said is that Australia won in every way worthily, and that we must hope to have profited by the happenings of this series when the time comes to choose the MCC team for Australia in two years' time.

The greatest: Australian Don Bradman, who made his final Test appearance in this Oval match. Four runs would have ensured a Test batting average of 100; he was out for a duck; his average is 99.94.

Blankers-Koen is female Jesse Owens

From Lainson Wood

WEMBLEY, WEDNESDAY 4 AUGUST

Snatching up the crumbs from the table of the athletically rich, a 70,000 largely British crowd in the stadium here today grabbed one dainty morsel with long and loud cheers. A British athlete broke an Olympic record and then had to take the runner's up position on the Olympic Games' victory rostrum.

The King and Queen arrived in time to hear the Dutch national anthem being played in honour of an inches' victory by Mrs F. Blankers-Koen over Miss Maureen Gardner, a 20-year-old Oxford dancing teacher in the 80-m hurdles.

Mrs Blankers-Koen, a 30-year-old mother of two children, is the woman 'Jesse Owens' of these Games. Her victory completed a brilliant double, for yesterday she won the 100-m flat race. She was expected to win today's race unchallenged.

Three hurdles from home the crowd was yelling 'Maureen' as the black-shorted English girl jumped side by side with her Dutch rival. They leaped the last three flights like Siamese twins. Mrs Blankers-Koen had to exert every ounce of strength to get that little more that

Fanny Blankers-Koen (nearest the camera, above) won an amazing four gold medals at the 1948 Olympics, in the 100 m, 200 m, 80-m hurdles and 4 x 100-m relay. The Games were televised by the BBC (left); 500,000 people watched the opening ceremony on TV.

proclaimed her the winner. The judges' stopwatches could not separate them. Both were returned as having done 11.2 sec — one-tenth of a second faster than Signorina C. Testoni's world record set up in 1939 and equalled by Mrs Blankers-Koen in 1942.

All three US runners qualified for the semi-finals of the 400 m, Whitfield, the 800-m winner on Monday, being most impressive. But for sheer style and beauty of action Arthur Wint, the 6 ft 4 in tall Jamaican, had all the 'quarter-milers' beaten. He returned the best time and yet was running so well within himself that in the second round, when lying second, he looked over his shoulder to find a pursuer. In two strides he had almost doubled his pace and he won the race as he liked.

Arthur Wint went on to win gold in the 400 m and a silver in the 800 m.

SPORT IN BRIEF

WINTER OLYMPICS

The first winter Games are held since 1936. Frenchman Henri Oreiller wins gold in the downhill and the combined skiing, and bronze in the slalom. American Gretchen Fraser is the surprise winner of the women's slalom, earning the United States' first Olympic skiing medal.

FOOTBALL

On 24 April, in one of the best FA Cup finals held at Wembley, Manchester United beat Blackpool. A penalty and a goal from Mortensen give Blackpool a 2–1 lead at half-time, but United come back to win 4–2.

BASEBALL

'Babe' Ruth, one of the greatest players in the game's history, dies aged 53. At one point he earned £16,000 a year – more than the American president.

FOOTBALL

England face Italy in front of 85,000 people in the heat of Turin on 16 May. The Italians waste good chances, captain/keeper Frank Swift makes some incredible saves – including three shots in succession from point-blank range **(below)** – and the Italians have two goals disallowed. The 4–0 scoreline is flattering to England, but it is still a famous victory.

1949

Yeovil in Cup last sixteen

By Frank Coles

PUBLISHED MONDAY 31 JANUARY

Yeovil Town, proudly wearing Colchester Town's mantle of giantkillers, are the team all others still interested in the fifth round are hoping to avoid when today's draw is made. No side in the country can feel safe if called upon to visit the Yeovil ground.

Their 2–1 victory over Sunderland's £60,000-worth of stars equalled Colchester's feat last year. They were the first non-League club to reach the fifth round. If the gallant little Somerset team have the good luck again to be drawn at home they may beat all records by qualifying for the sixth round.

Bradford's 1–1 draw with Manchester United was almost as big a triumph as Yeovil's win. The Cup-holders were the more polished footballers, but were lucky not to be beaten. The teams meet again at Bradford next Saturday and it is no longer certain that the Cup-holders will reach the fifth round.

Manchester United did reach the fifth round, and Yeovil Town were drawn to play against them at Maine Road. Yeovil lost 8–0.

Locke's great golf clinches Open

By Leonard Crawley

PUBLISHED MONDAY 11 JULY

Bobby Locke, of South Africa, won the Open golf championship at Royal St George's, Sandwich, beating the Irish professional, Harry Bradshaw, by 12 strokes. Locke, who is 31 years old, is likely to win this championship again, and if Harry Bradshaw never rises to such heights of brilliance as he did last week, he will for ever be able to look back with pride and pleasure upon the four rounds which earned him the right of replaying for the championship with one of the greatest golfers of this generation.

We have known Locke since he was 17 years old. It was my predecessor, Mr George Greenwood, who first gave prominence in the columns of *The Daily Telegraph* to the tremendous ability of this astounding youth, who already held the Open and Amateur championships of South Africa. As a professional since the war, he has almost dominated American tournaments, but this is the first major championship he has won.

Locke is of the opinion that Henry Cotton is the finest shot-maker in the world today. Cotton is of the opinion that Locke is the best judge of distance he has ever seen, and to their respective views of each other I wholeheartedly subscribe.

American opinion is that Locke is the best putter of all time; Locke does not agree. I would like to say that I have never seen his equal within 30 yards of the pin. It seems to me that the only American part of his game is his uncanny use of the club known as the wedge, with which he plays an astonishing variety of strokes that either buzz, hop, fizz or bumble to the premeditated spot.

He shows no outward sign of emotion when things go wrong and, coupled with his lovely smile when things go right, his golfing manners are as charming as those of Bobby Jones.

On Saturday Locke took 135 strokes for 36 holes, and he looked and played like an emperor. Only one man could have stood up to this sort of treatment – Henry Cotton – and he was watching and admiring the magnificent exhibition.

MILESTONES

The first Badminton Horse Trials were held by the Duke of Beaufort in the grounds of his ancestral home in Gloucestershire. The first winner was Captain John Shedden on Golden Willow. Despite the Duke's concern that nobody would turn up, the event became one of the most important events on the equestrian calendar.

Bobby Locke drives from the 11th in the third round of the Open. Bradshaw and Locke tied with a total of 283 before the play-off, equalling the record for the championship held jointly by Gene Sarazen, Henry Cotton and Alfred Perry.

Photo shows Nimbus won by 12 inches

From Hotspur
PUBLISHED NEWMARKET, WEDNESDAY 27 APRIL

In a desperately exciting finish the favourite, Abernant, was caught and beaten by the ten-to-one chance Nimbus in the last two strides in the 2,000 Guineas today.

For the first time in a Classic race the judge called for the photograph of the finish. Many people expected a dead heat, but the camera showed that Abernant had been beaten by a short head – in actual fact about 12 inches.

Abernant came to the foot of the hill a length clear of Nimbus. But in the last 50 yards he began to weaken and C. Elliott, who had never given up the struggle of Nimbus, began to catch him steadily. Abernant gave of his best. It was just not good enough.

It was Elliott's fifth 2,000 Guineas success and his Guineas record is now superior to that of any living jockey. Only J. Robinson, who rode in the first part of the 19th century, and J. Osborne, who rode in the 1850s and 1860s, have won the Guineas more often. Elliott's five winners have been spread over 26 years, with Lord Rosebery's Ellangowan, in 1923, the first of them.

Gordon Richards could not have had a better run on the favourite, who just failed to stay home up the hill.

On 4 June Nimbus (above) won the Derby in another photo-finish. He was the first horse since Blue Peter in 1939 to follow his success in the 2,000 Guineas with a Derby win.

The race leaves the Derby outlook extremely open. Abernant can be dismissed as a Derby possibility, and Nimbus today looked to be trained to the minute.

Boxer Cerdan among 48 dead in airliner crash

From our own correspondent
PARIS, FRIDAY 28 OCTOBER

An Air France Constellation, bound from Paris to New York, crashed early today near the top of the 3,600 ft Algarvia Peak, on the island of San Miguel, in the Azores. All 48 people on board lost their lives.

The first person to reach the wreckage was a peasant, who later guided a search party through fog and rain to the spot. Messages received here late tonight said that the plane had burst into flames on hitting the ground and all the victims had been badly burned.

Among the 37 passengers were Ginette Neveu, 30, the French violinist, and Marcel Cerdan, 33, the French boxer and former world middleweight champion.

The aircraft left Orly at 9.35 last night and just before three o'clock this morning radioed that it was about to land at the airport at Santa Maria, in the Azores, in clear weather. People at the airport heard the engines fade into the distance and then there was silence.

Nothing more was heard, and rocket signals failed to produce a reply. At four am the search began.

Nine ships and many planes, including four Flying Fortresses, took part in the hunt. The wreckage was sighted this afternoon near the top of the mountain on San Miguel, 60 miles from Santa Maria.

The aircraft which spotted the wreck reported that figures could be seen moving about; this gave rise to the hope that there might be survivors. The figures may have been those of the peasants who reached the crash scene before the official search parties.

The crash occurred in a remote area and the search party had great difficulty in reaching the wreckage, which was completely burned out.

Frenchmen had waited all day for news. Marcel Cerdan, who was regarded as a national hero, was on his way to New York to fight Jake La Motta for the world title which he lost to him last June.

Crowds stood outside newspaper offices waiting for details. Others listened all day for radio news bulletins.

Cerdan was in unusually high spirits when he drove to the airfield last night. He said to friends seeing him off: 'I will do everything in my power to regain the title. I have never trained so much or so hard.'

If original plans had been followed, he would not have been flying in the plane. The fight with La Motta was to have been held last month, but was postponed because La Motta sustained a shoulder injury. Even so, he might have flown to New York earlier but for an exhibition match at Troyes on Wednesday.

Cerdan, married and with three children, had his home in Casablanca.

SPORT IN BRIEF

RUGBY UNION

On 15 January, defying their critics, the 'old men' of Wales beat England at Cardiff Arms Park. Wales score three tries to record a 9–3 victory.

FOOTBALL

The FA Cup final is contested between Wolverhampton Wanderers and Leicester. Wolves win 3–1. Second Division Leicester are without their inside right, Don Revie, who is ill.

HORSE RACING

A split-second decision by Australian jockey W. Johnstone to check his horse and go to the far rails costs them the Derby. Amour Drake loses by a head to Nimbus, involved in his second photo-finish within six weeks (see main text).

FOOTBALL

Italy's champion team, Torino FC, together with their English trainer Leslie Lievesley, are killed when their aircraft crashes on 4 May. The pilot has been attempting to land at Turin airport in bad visibility; the plane hits the Superga hill. Torino have won the Italian championship four times in succession, and are again leading the League at the time of the crash. Many of the Italian national side are among the dead, including Italy's captain, Valentino Mazzola.

CRICKET

Australia tour South Africa as Test play begins there again after the war. In the Test at Durban Australia are dismissed by South Africa for a first-innings total of 75, and are 59 for three in the second innings, needing 277 to win. Australian batsman Neil Harvey puts together an innings of 151 not out to take the tourists to victory by five wickets. Australia win the series 4–0.

1950

Finney scores four goals

LISBON, SUNDAY 14 MAY

Portugal 3; England 5

England had all their work cut out to beat Portugal 5–3 (including two penalties) in the soccer match here today after romping through the first half and getting a 3–0 lead.

Four of England's goals came from the foot of Tom Finney, including both penalties. The Preston winger was in brilliant form and the man of the match, Stan Mortensen, got England's other goal.

The Portuguese centre forward, Ben David, from the Cape Verde Islands, got two of Portugal's goals and Vasques the third.

Some 70,000 people saw Bentley kick off for England, and a shot from Finney in the third minute skimmed the crossbar. Finney was tripped two minutes later. He took the kick himself and calmly placed the ball past the goalkeeper. Only two minutes later Jackie Milburn also skimmed the crossbar with a terrific drive.

The game was 15 minutes old when Mortensen got a beautiful goal. At 23 minutes England got the third goal, Finney netting cleverly following approach work by Milburn and Roy Bentley.

The second half had no sooner started than the Portuguese got a lovely goal. Vasques moved out to the right wing and put acrosss a perfect centre which David nodded past Bert Williams.

The next goal went to England. Finney dribbled through the defence and put in a lovely shot wide of the goalkeeper. Portugal now attacked in earnest and David scored. Then Vasques headed in a beautiful centre, and with the score 4–3 the crowd were standing up and cheering like mad. Here was a chance of a lifetime to beat England. The Englishmen did not wilt. Mortensen had his legs taken from under him. Finney calmly and coolly scored from the spot.

MILESTONES

The inaugural Formula One drivers' championship was won by Giuseppe Farina. In a seven-race series, Farina's victory in the European Grand Prix was followed by wins in Switzerland and Italy. Farina, 44, had been coaxed out of retirement by the Alfa Romeo team.

Clean sweep for Alfa Romeo at Silverstone

Rugby tourists draw in New Zealand

DUNEDIN, NEW ZEALAND, SUNDAY 28 MAY

The British Isles rugby touring team gave an excellent display here yesterday and drew the first Test with New Zealand, each side scoring a penalty goal and two tries. It was only a late New Zealand rally which earned them a draw, for the British team, playing much better than many thought possible, led by nine points to three well into the second half.

The British team took command straight from the kick-off and only twice in the first half did the powerful All Blacks penetrate far enough into their half to become dangerous.

The British side went ahead after ten minutes with a penalty goal by J. Robins, the Birkenhead Park front-row forward. After the interval J. Kyle, Belfast stand-off half, received a fine pass from A. Black of Edinburgh, and eluding all defenders went over for a try near the posts.

New Zealand then came more into the picture and R. A. Roper went over for a try, but Ken Jones, Newport three-quarter, regained the British advantage of six points by another try. In a New Zealand rally, R. W. H. Scott kicked a penalty goal and R. R. Elvidge scored a try.

Ken Jones, Wales and Britain, touches down against New Zealand Combined at Hamilton. Jones scored 16 tries for the British Lions in their four-month tour of Australia and New Zealand, including two in Tests. The tour was characterised by some stylish and inventive rugby from players such as Irish fly-half Jackie Kyle, but while the Lions won both their games in Australia, they lost three out of the four Test matches in New Zealand.

By our special correspondent
SILVERSTONE, SUNDAY 14 MAY

The 120,000 spectators who watched the Italian Alfa Romeo team win the first three places in the Grand Prix of Europe here yesterday were thankful that earlier they had seen the nationally made British BRM Grand Prix car show something of its paces. Raymond Mays, after driving the pale green BRM three laps at varying speeds said: 'I am pleased with the car. I only accelerated spasmodically, but she topped 11,500 rpm in low gear.'

The British Motor Racing Research Trust announced over loudspeakers that one or more BRM cars would compete in the International Trophy race here on 26 August against the best Italian opposition.

The Alfa Romeo chief tuner, Signor Satta, at his pit, said: 'The BRM car looks right. It has a fine engine note and it sits well.'

From the start of the Grand Prix of Europe the four red Alfa Romeos were never headed until number one, driven by the favourite, J. M. Fangio **(above, in car)**, coasted in at the end of the 63rd lap. It had a broken oil pipe. Reginald Parnell, of Derby, drove his Alfa Romeo with tremendous verve, and was only 52 seconds behind the winner, Giuseppe 'Nino' Farina **(above, with Fangio, and above left)**, at the end of 70 laps.

Farina had a brilliant opening lap in 1 min 50 sec, an average of 94.02 mph, but when the race settled down the Italians realised that an average of 90 to 91 mph was sufficient to win and maintained it to the end.

The private British entries in their out-of-date machines strove valiantly against the Italian factory team. Results were:

Grand Prix of Europe: 1. G. Farina (Alfa Romeo); 2. L. Fagioli (Alfa Romeo); 3. R. Parnell (Alfa Romeo).

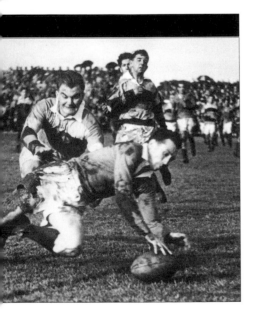

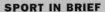
SPORT IN BRIEF

GOLF
Ben Hogan plays in the Los Angeles Open in January. It is less than a year since his car was involved in a head-on collision with a Greyhound bus and Hogan narrowly escaped death. He has made an incredible recovery from terrible injuries, and forces a play-off against 1949 golfer of the year, Sam Snead. Hogan loses by four strokes, but goes on to win the Golden Anniversary Open at Merion.

BOXING
Rocky Marciano comes close to surrendering his unbeaten record on 24 March when he faces Roland LaStarza over ten rounds in New York. In a split decision, Marciano is awarded the bout.

GOLF
Babe Zaharias wins the Women's Open at Rolling Hills, Wichita, by nine strokes from amateur Betsy Rawls. It is her second Open title; she first won the event in 1948. A remarkable athlete, Zaharias, née Didrikson, played in 1930 and 1931 for the American women's basketball team. In the 1932 Olympics she won two gold medals, in hurdles and the javelin. A talented baseball, softball and football player, swimmer and figure-skater, by 1934 she is concentrating on playing golf, winning the Women's Amateur (as Mildred Zaharias) in 1946, and 17 further championships in 1947.

HOCKEY
England, celebrating playing their 150th international, are beaten for the first time in their history by a foreign side. Holland are their conquerors, beating them 3–0 at the Wagener Stadium in Amsterdam.

1950

By Frank Coles

PUBLISHED MONDAY 2 OCTOBER

West Ham 3; Sheffield United 5

Every other week brings a new claim to a football curiosity only for someone with an extra long memory to recall that it has occurred before. But I doubt if the story of what happened on West Ham United's ground on Saturday will be repeated.

Sheffield United defeated West Ham 5–3, and of the eight goals three came from penalties, two were kicked into his own net by Devlin, the West Ham back, and one was scored from an indirect free kick in the penalty area.

The three penalties, converted by Furniss for Sheffield United, and the other by Robinson for West Ham, were all awarded in an eight-minute spell in the second half. This may be a record in referee spotting, and to complete the strange tale Robinson did the hat trick for West Ham only to find himself on the losing side.

A second eight-goal game on Saturday was played at Middlesbrough. This was a clean-cut affair, Middlesbrough 8; Huddersfield 0. Wilf Mannion in the first half and McCrae in the second were hat-trick specialists against a demoralised defence. Huddersfield have conceded 18 goals in the last three matches and 31 to date.

Compare this landslide with the solid defence of Newcastle United, who have only been beaten seven times in 11 games. Newcastle were held to a goalless draw on Sheffield Wednesday's ground, but they still lead Middlesbrough and Arsenal by one point.

Incidentally, Newcastle's request for the release of their centre forward, Jackie Milburn, who has been chosen as a reserve for England, has been refused by the FA. It would have been unfair to other clubs.

DID YOU KNOW?

With British teams entering the World Cup for the first time, FIFA decreed that the home international championship would be a qualifying group for the tournament, with the top two nations to go through. When Scotland finished second to England in the table, they decided in a fit of pique not to take part in the finals.

Locke retains Open with record total of 279

By Leonard Crawley

TROON, FRIDAY 7 JULY

Bobby Locke of South Africa **(right)** won the Open Championship for the second year in succession here tonight, his four rounds being 69, 72, 70 and 68, giving him a total of 279, which beat the previous record by four strokes.

In the course of the 72 holes Locke missed the fairway from the tee only twice and, oddly enough, each time it was at the 12th hole. Locke won on merit as the best player in the field, and because he was, in my judgement, the most intelligent golfer of all those playing.

Old Troon is by modern standards a short course, and Locke drove throughout the championship with a brassie or a spoon. His accuracy was deadly, and even the warm-hearted Scottish crowds who supported him became at times rather bored with the golfing robot.

Usually the most critical round in the championship when titles are won and lost is the third. Yet it was Locke's second round when he played downright badly and still scored a 72 that kept him going. He then showed tremendous courage and a temperament that seems to be a curious mixture of Walter Hagen and Bobby Jones – it is impossible to tell what is going on in his mind.

Without wishing to detract from Locke's wonderful performance, it should be stated that, since the wind refused to puff from any quarter throughout the championship, it has been the fairest of tests. Having played at Troon for more than 29 years I have learned to like and respect this great course. Yet I have never seen it played for five days under easier conditions.

Locke, who was hitting the ball much better than yesterday, had, if such a thing is possible in the third round of a championship, a comfortable 70. It could have been better and could also have been much worse. But I always felt that his master mind was in complete control, and so it proved.

It looked as though the championship rested between the three leaders, Locke, Roberto de Vicenzo and Dai Rees at lunch, and Vicenzo, who had the advantage of going out first, had a great chance of setting up a target for the others to shoot at if they could.

Vicenzo's last round was a bewildering mixture of courage and bad golf. He is one of the finest hitters of the ball in the world, but his driving was awful and his putting wonderful.

Locke was on his trail and knew exactly what he had to do, and there is no golfer more competent of doing what is required on the greatest occasions. He was out in 33, playing quite beautifully. I thought he must have been disappointed when his putt for three at the seventh failed to drop, but he paid no attention.

Locke's second to the 12th finished over the green and he took five, missing a putt of four feet. He put this right with a magnificent two at the 14th.

At the 17th he missed the green with his tee shot and knew perfectly well that if he could get his three the last hole would look twice the size. He chipped up with infinite skill and holed the putt.

The end was therefore easier. He never bothered to watch where his tee shot had gone at the last hole and got the easiest of fours from the centre of the fairway and the centre of the green.

England lose World Cup game to United States

BELO HORIZONTE, THURSDAY 29 JUNE

England were today beaten 1–0 by the United States in the World Cup Soccer tournament now being played in Brazil.

The Americans hung stubbornly on to the lead they gained in the 38th minute when their centre forward, the Argentine-born player Gaetjens, scored with a lovely shot from 20 yards into the corner of the net.

The United States thus brought off the sensation of the world series so far, and they beat a team which gave probably the worst display ever by an England side.

The English forwards were particularly at fault. In the 30th minute Wilf Mannion missed a golden opportunity when Tom Finney put him in possession unmarked close to goal. He shot wildly over. But England had bad luck when Finney hit the upright with the goalkeeper beaten in the 35th minute.

Teamwork gains West Indies win by 326 runs

By E. W. Swanton

LORD'S, THURSDAY 29 JUNE

Soon after lunch today West Indies gained the victory that had seemed theirs from the time on Monday afternoon when England's batting failed against S. Ramadhin and A. Valentine. The difference was 326 runs. Thus West Indies follow South Africa, who not only chose Lord's as the scene of their first and only success in a Test in England 15 years ago, but also won by a handsome and conclusive margin.

There could be no possible question of the justice of today's result. The two young spin-bowlers certainly were chiefly responsible, but A. Rae and C. Walcott, F. Worrell, E. Weekes and G. Gomez have distinguished deeds against their names in the score sheet. Indeed, every member of John Goddard's team contributed, not least the captain himself, who made several shrewd assessments in the field and set an admirable lead by his performance.

The England batting was thrown completely back on unconvincing defence, whereas the West Indies, faced by spin bowlers whose performance certainly could be expected to lose little or nothing by contrast with their own, declined to be dictated to at the wicket.

The delightful innings of Worrell and Weekes on the first day has a significance not properly expressed in the score. When this game is looked back to it may always be used as the model illustration of the ancient axiom that bowlers bowl as well as they are allowed to.

The most significant of all the statistics connected with the game, even making allowance for the fact that England were latterly playing for a draw, is that in the two innings West Indies received only 11 overs more than they bowled themselves, and they scored 326 more runs.

From the English angle it is fair to say that the side was considerably weakened beyond the expected absence through a knee injury of D. Compton, and by the injuries to R. T. Simpson and T. Bailey.

Jubilant spectators rush on to the field at the Oval after the West Indies win the final Test – and the series, 3–1. After their first win, at Lord's, West Indies supporters composed a calypso that ended: 'All through our bowling was super-fine/With Ramadhin and Valentine.'

1950

SPORT IN BRIEF

BOXING
On 27 September, 36-year-old Joe Louis **(above, in training for his comeback)** returns to the ring after two years in retirement. Reigning heavyweight champion Ezzard Charles completely outboxes Louis and wins a unanimous decision over 15 rounds.

FOOTBALL
A surprise 2–1 victory for Uruguay against Brazil in the World Cup in Rio de Janeiro earns them the Jules Rimet Trophy for the second time.

CRICKET
In the first Test between England and Australia at Brisbane, Trevor Bailey and Alec Bedser bowl Australia out for 228. The wicket deteriorates badly. England declare at 68 for seven and Australia at 32 for seven (Bailey has got four wickets for 22 runs). In their second innings England are 30 for six when Len Hutton comes in and scores 62 not out. England still lose by 70 runs.

FOOTBALL
On 13 December Scotland are beaten at home for the first time by a foreign team. Austria win 1–0.

1951

French win on English soil

By J. P. Jordan

PUBLISHED MONDAY 26 FEBRUARY

England 3 pts; France 11

France gained a thoroughly deserved victory over England at Twickenham by a goal, a dropped goal and a try to a try, and so achieved their ambition of winning for the first time on English soil after waiting 44 years.

France now have an excellent chance of tieing for the international championship, but for England it is the wooden spoon again. English rugby, or to be more correct, English back play, is in the doldrums. The Frenchmen made it look ponderous and second-rate.

A day or so of drying winds and a liberal application of sand had enabled the ground to recover extraordinarily well, but it was still on the heavy side and treacherous on top. Yet surprisingly the Frenchmen adapted themselves to the conditions far more readily than England.

Their teamwork was better, and their handling and picking up – especially that of R. Arcalis at fullback – often bordered on the brilliant. But it was the *joie-de-vivre* and initiative of the French backs and their speed in following up that contributed largely to England's defeat.

How much the absence of G. C. Rittson-Thomas with a damaged ankle for over half the game affected the outcome it is difficult to say. Had he been in his position as blindside wing forward he might perhaps have prevented both French tries. Even so it must be admitted that France were the better side.

England's forwards put up a brave fight, and cannot be blamed for the defeat. V. G. Roberts, J. McG. Kendall-Carpenter, R. V. Stirling and the others played like heroes, and it was a remarkable performance on their part to obtain more of the ball from the scrums when reduced to six than when at full strength.

England scored first, 25 minutes after the start. Rittson-Thomas began the movement, I. Preece carried on, and after Stirling and Hardy had handled, B. Boobbyer raced across in the corner for a try that Hewitt narrowly failed to convert.

Five minutes later France went ahead, G. Dufau breaking away from a loose scrum to send G. Basquet crashing over. J. Prat converted.

Midway through the second half Prat ran through for a try, and five minutes before the end he positioned himself to take Dufau's pass and drop a beautiful goal.

Miss Hart is in tradition of modern champions

By Lainson Wood

PUBLISHED MONDAY 9 JULY

Farewell to an all-change Wimbledon. New names have been inscribed on all five championship rolls. On Saturday Miss Hart, from Florida, took on the mantle of Miss Louise Brough, who, labouring under the physical and psychological handicap of 'tennis elbow' which plagued her throughout the fortnight, defended three titles and retained none.

Has it been an auspicious Wimbledon? Not more so than any of its predecessors in which surprises have come in crops to confound the seeding committee. The general view is that in-and-out form is bad form.

Are the new champions likely to make their mark on the game as others have done before them? That question is less easy to answer.

Miss Hart on Saturday showed herself a champion in the true mould of the moderns, such as Miss Brough, Margaret Osborne, Pauline Betz and, before the war, Alice Marble, the great Helen Wills, and

even Suzanne Lenglen, the forerunner of the moderns.

Miss Hart has been in the forefront these past three years, beating Miss Brough and Mrs Osborne du Pont from time to time, but never until now at Wimbledon.

Her 6–1, 6–0 victory over Miss Shirley Fry in Saturday's final, following successes fluent but less imposing over Miss Chaffee and Miss Baker **(on right of picture below, with Miss Hart)**, does suggest that the American Wightman Cup team resources have diminished.

It still does not suggest that the British women's team has better than a 10–1 chance of picking up a few comforting crumbs in next month's Wightman Cup contest at Boston.

Miss Fry, without wishing to be in the least derogatory, was put in her place by Miss Hart. Without an imposing service she can never hope to rise out of the upper ruck. Miss Chaffee is possibly the best of the oncoming American women, but more singleness of purpose is required to make a champion while such as Miss Hart are still playing.

May's remarkable debut

By E. W. Swanton

LEEDS, SUNDAY 29 JULY

The third day of the Test against South Africa here followed the first two in its general characteristics, the bat again holding a stubborn, unexciting sway on an utterly placid wicket, which still gave only the briefest hints of later encouragement for the bowler.

But though a vast deal can happen in 12 hours, even in a modern Test, and this one can certainly not yet be written off as a draw, the clock threatens to run against both sides.

To Peter May, of course, must go the palm, and when in the evening he reached his hundred with a handsome straight drive to the boundary off Rowan, the crowd stood and applauded with a warm, prolonged intensity which was an acknowledgment of the virtues which Yorkshiremen especially appreciate in a cricketer.

His batting, over nearly five hours of a tense and thrilling day, had a steadfast calmness and concentration of purpose remarkable in a young man of 21. He not only gave no chance, but his false strokes can be recalled on the fingers of one hand. Tall and slim, he is built to hit the ball off the forward foot.

The last English batsman to make a hundred in his first Test was S. C. Griffith.

Milburn goals win cup for Newcastle

By Frank Coles

PUBLISHED MONDAY 30 APRIL

Newcastle 2; Blackpool 0

Newcastle are FA Cup-holders for the fourth time in a glittering career. In defeating Blackpool in Saturday's not-so-distinguished final they completed a hat trick in Wembley wins –1924, 1932 and 1951 – and the latest triumph will always be known as Jackie Milburn's match. This tall, strapping young Tynesider is the fastest centre forward I have set eyes on. He won the game in the first ten minutes of the second half with two fine opportunist goals, and would have had more but for George Farm's sound anticipation between the Blackpool posts.

Milburn's first goal at the 50th minute was against the run of the play as inspired by the brilliance of Stanley Matthews. Blackpool had done most of the attacking in the first half. That they were not able to turn any of Matthews' streamlined centres to account was due to Brennan's complete bottling up of Stan Mortensen and the sure tackling of the wing halves, Harvey and Crowe.

All through the first half,

Milburn was a victim of Blackpool's offside tactics. As often happens, however, this dangerous trap recoiled on those who set it. Indeed it was the direct cause of Blackpool's downfall.

At the fifth minute after the interval Blackpool had eight men up in an all-out attack. A long clearance went straight upfield to Milburn only a few yards inside the Blackpool half, and he was away clear. Most of the crowd expected the whistle for offside but a linesman ideally placed to judge signalled onside. Milburn raced ahead, drew the goalkeeper out and fired a low shot into the net.

That surprise goal shook Hayward, Shimwell and the rest of the Blackpool defence to the roots and, before they could recover from the blow, Milburn scored again to settle all argument.

A finer goal has never been seen at Wembley. Little Taylor put the defenders off-balance with a back heeler to Milburn, and from 25 yards the Newcastle leader let fly with his left foot. The ball was in the roof of the net before Farm could move.

Many finals I have seen have produced a higher standard of skill, but those Milburn goals and the magnificence of Matthews will live in the memory.

Newcastle's Joe Harvey with the FA Cup and his victorious team.

1951

1951

South Africa give rugby lesson to the Scots

By E. W. Swanton

PUBLISHED MONDAY 26 NOVEMBER

Scotland 0 pts; South Africa 44

The South Africans have many triumphs to their name on the rugby football field, but they surely have never won a game against opponents of international class so brilliantly and so conclusively as that against Scotland at Murrayfield on Saturday.

The score, made up of seven goals, one dropped goal, and two tries, has been exceeded only once since the modern scoring values were adopted in 1905. This was in a match of a missionary kind played by Paul Roos's original Springboks against the French when rugby football in France was in its infancy. Modern history shows no parallel to the scoring of nine tries by one side in an international match since W. A. Millar's South Africans made ten against Ireland in 1912.

Almost from the moment of the first try there appeared between the two sides such a wide and ever-growing disparity that the game developed merely into an exhibition. The portents were slow to show themselves. In the first minute a footrush by the Scots would have led to an almost certain try by J. G. M. Hart, the new cap on the right wing, if he had been given a takeable pass.

What might have been the effect of such a start can only be conjectured. At all events, there followed 17 minutes which were not without occasions of peril to South Africa as well as to Scotland before the first try came. It was followed within two minutes by another, which was converted, and after five more by a third, converted likewise.

That was the end of the contest. There were two further scores before half-time, including a lovely left-footed dropped goal by J. D. Brewis, and Scotland changed over 19 hopeless points behind.

In the first 20 minutes of the second half South Africa touched down four times more. That gave them 39 points with still a quarter of the game to go.

But they seemed sated now and began to take such liberties that the Scots for a while were able to scramble out of their troubles, and even to instigate an odd attack or two. It was three minutes from the end when the ninth and last try came. For the 40 minutes in the middle of the game when the pressure was at its hottest, the South Africans ticked up virtually a point a minute.

Turpin wins world title for Britain

Randolph Turpin (on left), moves in on Sugar Ray Robinson in round one. Robinson had only ever lost one of his 131 fights before being beaten by Turpin.

From a Daily Telegraph *reporter*

PUBLISHED WEDNESDAY 11 JULY

Randolph Turpin, 23, the black boxer from Leamington Spa, at Earl's Court last night brought the world middleweight championship back to Britain for the first time since Bob Fitzsimmons won it at the end of the last century.

He defeated the American black holder, 'Sugar' Ray Robinson, 31, on points over 15 rounds.

Robinson was completely outfought in the biggest boxing upset for years. Turpin, who had lost twice in 43 bouts, dominated the contest from the start.

The crowd of 18,000 gave the victor a tremendous ovation. He looked completely unmarked. He said: 'Certainly Robinson hit me hard. He is a great puncher to the body. I was completely confident from the start that I would win. My idea was gradually to weaken him with my hooks and then, if necessary, knock him out. Unfortunately I couldn't catch him quite right.'

Robinson said: 'I have no excuses to make. Turpin proved himself the better man tonight.'

At the ringside were celebrities in all walks of life, society, politics, the stage, the Turf, and all other sporting spheres. Outside Earl's Court, as the decision was announced, a cheer rose from about 1,000 people clustered in groups around cars with radios tuned in to the broadcast of the fight.

Robinson received nearly £30,000 as his end of the purse. Turpin, as challenger, expected to get between £10,000 and £12,000. Robinson's purse is the biggest ever paid to a boxer in Britain.

MILESTONES

A golden age for English table tennis came to an end when Johnny Leach won the world table-tennis men's singles title for the second and last time. Japanese and Chinese players, introducing the pen-holder grip and thick sponge bats, now took a stranglehold on the game.

Faulkner is champion by two strokes

By Leonard Crawley

PORTRUSH, FRIDAY 6 JULY

Max Faulkner, the 34-year-old British professional who is not attached to any golf club, won the Open championship here at Royal Portrush this evening with the fine aggregate of 285, his four rounds being 71, 70, 70 and 74. A. Cerda (Argentina) was second with 287 and D. H. Ward of Little Aston, third with 290.

J. H. Taylor, who, if the golfing world lasts for a thousand years, will remain one of its greatest figures, once said that the best way to win a championship was to win it easily. Faulkner showed the wisdom of this observation today.

Faulkner, son of Gus Faulkner, a humble professional of the old school, learned much from his father in his early days, and until a few months ago was assistant to Henry Cotton at Royal Mid-Surrey. Cotton's teaching has had a great influence on his game, and for the last two years Faulkner has looked a golfer of the highest class.

But, he has often been a tragically weak putter, and this has cost him dearly in postwar tournaments and championships. Like all good, nay great, players, Faulkner is highly strung. He has tried to hide this very human weakness by dressing himself up in gaudy colours and pretending to play the fool as though this was the best way to get on with the job. This sort of behaviour is all very well if you are winning, as Walter Hagen used to in his prime, but if you are not, it all appears rather childish.

In serious mood and already wearing the mantle of Open champion, Faulkner played his fourth round in deadly earnest. He was out in 37, but par figures from the tenth to the 14th saw him well on his way. At the 15th a hooked tee shot cost him a five and one the other way in the rough on the right side of the 16th cost him another. A glorious drive, a magnificent brassie and a little pitch and a putt earned him a grand four at the 17th. At the last hole his second shot did not reach the green and he had to be content with a five, but he was home.

Laker is hero of the morning

By E. W. Swanton

PUBLISHED MONDAY 20 AUGUST

When time has blurred the memory of a great finish, it will be briefly observed that England beat South Africa by four wickets, and that England won the rubber by three matches to one with one drawn. But at least the exciting events of the last afternoon are safe in the minds of those who saw the battle ebb and sway from the time of England's going-in after lunch to make the 163 they needed, until the moment when J. Laker made the winning stroke at 20 minutes to six.

What a tossing and turning our emotions underwent in those three and a half hours! Towards three o'clock it looked so easy for England. Then within three minutes came the shock of L. Hutton's extraordinary dismissal on the grounds of obstructing the field, and the almost unnoticed demise of P. May, caught off pad and bat.

After the first innings neither side can have had any illusions as to the frailty of England's batting from number six onwards. When, after 50 exciting minutes D. Compton and Lowson both went their ways, and the score was still only 90 for four, the burden of England's hopes fell once again on the shoulders of their captain, F. R. Brown. W. Watson was batting like a rock, imperturbable and admirably efficient at the other end. But everyone sensed that to shift the fortunes of the game was needed something violent. The score at tea was 98 for four; 20 minutes after the interval it was 131 for four, and A. Rowan's last four overs had cost 27 of the 33 runs that had been made by Brown and Watson. Watson was caught behind off Chubb at 132 for an innings whose value the figures scarcely hint at.

Laker, who had been the hero of the morning with his bowling, now played his part fully, and although Brown was out when 12 runs were still needed, D. Shackleton's nerve did not desert him. It was indeed his full-blooded four over mid-off's head that preceded the leg-glance off Rowan with which Laker assured England both of the match and the rubber.

English off-spinner Jim Laker in action in the fifth Test. He took six for 55 in South Africa's second innings, giving him figures for the match of ten for 119.

SPORT IN BRIEF

MOTOR RACING

Argentinians Juan Fangio – in an Alfa Romeo – and Frollan Gonzales – in a Ferrari – are first and second in the Spanish Grand Prix at Barcelona. Giuseppe Farina of Italy is third in another Alfa Romeo. The race result confirms Fangio as winner of the world championship title.

FOOTBALL

Ten minutes from time in a match against Fulham in October, Arsenal have a comfortable 4–0 cushion. Fulham stage a miraculous recovery, scoring three goals within seven minutes. A desperately struggling Arsenal are lucky to come away with a win.

CRICKET

In the final Test against South Africa at the Oval, Len Hutton becomes the only Test batsman ever to be given out for 'obstructing the field' (see main text). Hutton tries to sweep Athol Rowan, the ball hits his bat and forearm and goes straight up in the air. Hutton tries to stop it dropping on his stumps by hitting it away again, but the wicketkeeper, Russell Endean, was trying to catch it, and Hutton is adjudged to have – albeit inadvertently – obstructed him.

FOOTBALL

The Austrian football team arrive at Victoria Station in London on 25 November. They have brought a supply of food including eggs and Vienna sausage, and a phrasebook. They have been warned not to smoke English cigarettes, because they are too strong, and the three players who smoke have brought their own. The Austrians are an impressive side, but England manage a 2–2 draw against them.

1951

1952

Karim cracks in squash final

By a special correspondent
PUBLISHED TUESDAY 8 APRIL

Hashim Khan, of Pakistan, is the British Open squash racquets champion for the second year. In the final at the Lansdowne Club last night he beat the Egyptian, Mahmoud Karim, 9–5, 9–7, 9–0.

I doubt if tougher squash has been fought in those first two games since the war. The ruthless precision of Karim, the graceful and deadly manner with which he killed the ball was like watching a squash automaton.

Yet all this high skill – and Karim has never played so well against Hashim – did not avail, despite a lead of 4–1 in the first game and one of 7–3 in the second.

Hashim ran and ran until it seemed a human being could do no more. Yet the man who tired was Karim. He cracked towards the end of the second game, putting down three shots running to lose it, and was not afterwards in the match.

Hashim is a sporting prodigy. In his native Peshawar, he plays mainly lawn tennis and little squash of high standard. Yet since his first British game last year this remarkable man has won all his 26 competitive matches.

His success comes from some oddity in his stocky physique that renders him fantastically mobile. Shots which would normally, at best, call for a flurried return, remain largely ineffective because his flashing footwork enables him to shape to the ball with relative deliberation.

Hashim's unique footwork is combined with some ungainliness of style, but fearsome speed of shot. Add this accomplishment to his infectious cheeriness – he often chuckles even during a hard rally, though this was not in evidence last night – and here is a personality squash is hardly likely to forget.

DID YOU KNOW?

Surrey won their first cricket county championship for 38 years under the astute captaincy of Stuart Surridge. With the help of fast bowlers such as Alec Bedser and Peter Loader and spin wizards Jim Laker and Tony Lock, Surrey went on to win the title a record seven consecutive times.

Lofthouse scores twice in Vienna

By Frank Coles
VIENNA, SUNDAY 25 MAY
Austria 2; England 3

A telling blow for British soccer prestige on the Continent was struck here this afternoon when England lowered the pride of Austria by winning 3–2 after appearing at one stage likely to be well beaten.

The winning goal was dramatically scored by Nat Lofthouse eight minutes from time, when Austria had put on severe pressure which had stretched a gallant defence almost to breaking point.

A long throw downfield by goalkeeper Gil Merrick was picked up by Lofthouse on the halfway line. With only one Austrian defender to beat, he burst through for goal.

Musil ran out to challenge and the two players fell in a heap. In the fraction of a second before falling, Lofthouse managed to get his boot to the ball and it was safely home.

Both Lofthouse and the goalkeeper were temporarily knocked out, and England's leader had to be carried off. It was not until he was picked up by his colleagues that Lofthouse realised he had given his country a glorious victory.

Austria had taken the knock-out blow, and when the end came there was an unforgettable scene. Hundreds of delighted British soldiers of the Occupation forces rushed on to the field and hoisted the English players shoulder high. Billy Wright and Lofthouse, both heroes, will remember this thrilling climax as long as they live.

Play ran so favourably for Austria in the opening 20 minutes that it seemed impossible they would lose. England were being overplayed, yet from their first promising attack the Austrian defence was pierced. A promising move between John Sewell, Elliott and Lofthouse ended with the last named finding the net with a left-foot hook shot which gave the goalkeeper no chance.

In the next minute Austria were level. The referee decided that Froggatt had tripped Dienst in the penalty area and Huber converted the kick.

No sooner had the game restarted than England were in front for the second time – three goals in a hectic spell of two minutes.

Sewell, making his first appearance in an international match on the Continent, pounced on a through pass from Wright and beat Musil with a splendid low drive.

Austria did not deserve to be behind again, and no Englishman present could complain when, three minutes before the interval, Dienst slipped through a big hole in the defence, raced on at top speed, and beat Merrick with an unstoppable shot.

Up to this point Austria had played the more attractive football. They kept the ball moving sweetly in the best Continental fashion and were more formidable in attack. The Austrians ruined more of their brilliant approach work by attempting to walk the ball into the net. This played into the hands of the English defence.

Unfortunately the game was fought in bad spirit. Rough play seemed to be the keynote and Froggat, Sewell and Lofthouse were all injured.

The unexpected victory will do British football a world of good. Naturally it was a great day for Lofthouse with his two splendid goals.

England goalkeeper Gil Merrick dives to save an Austrian shot in England's close-fought contest against one of the best sides in Europe. Lofthouse's dramatic late goal won him the nickname the 'Lion of Vienna'.

Amazing Zatopek lands great Olympic treble

By Lainson Wood

HELSINKI, SUNDAY 27 JULY

The curtain was rung down here tonight on the track and field athletics of the Games to celebrate the XVth Olympiad on the highest possible note. At the last but one victory celebration the man who this week has won the affection and esteem of the entire world stood proudly at the top of the rostrum.

Emil Zatopek, the amazing Czech, followed his victories in the 5,000 m and 10,000 m by winning the marathon. I predict it will be many years before another man takes home from the Olympic Games, wherever they may be held, these three long-distance gold medals.

It would, indeed, have been an achievement to have completed the course in all three. The 5,000 m was the

Emil Zatopek leads the field in the 5,000 m. The army officer was nicknamed the 'Czech Express'.

only event that presented any difficulties to the man who must now be acclaimed the greatest long-distance racer of all time.

Zatopek had received congratulations, kissed his wife at the side of the track, pulled on sweater and tracksuit and was chatting with friends when the next man, R. Corno from Argentina, swung through the gates of the arena. That was one measure of his victory. Another was his time of 2 hr 23 min 3.2 sec, easily a new record.

When this small, sandy-haired man ran on to the track the scene was unprecedented. He had three-quarters of the track to cover to the tape. He ran it amid the most deafening cheers I have ever heard in a sports stadium.

Miss Connolly, supreme and confident, wins through

By Lance Tingay

PUBLISHED MONDAY 7 JULY

To win the All-England championship at the first attempt is remarkable. To do so when only 17 is memorable, though not unique, and Miss Maureen Connolly, who accomplished that feat, will have a distinct niche in the game even if she never comes back to Wimbledon again.

'Little Mo' in fact intends to do so, and this being the case there seems every reason why this chirpy and irresistible Californian will go on winning the women's lawn tennis singles for a great number of years.

Her concluding triumph, executed in one of the best women's finals seen for years, came after much adversity. An injured shoulder was in itself a physical handicap.

The concomitant fuss, the difference of opinion with her coach, who for the best of motives wanted her to scratch, was an even greater mental one.

Miss Brough played her best lawn tennis of the championship. She used her wide variety of stroke, her strength of service and power of volley. Against this Miss Connolly replied with some net work that was relatively indecisive. It was the withering decision of her ground strokes that brought Miss Brough to defeat.

Miss Brough led 5–4 in the first set. The match, so tough up to that stage, was decided in the tenth game. Deuce was called three times before Miss Connolly won it.

Though Miss Brough's zest flickered anew at the end, it was merely delaying what was bound to come. Indeed, had Miss Brough after all won the first set, I think Miss Connolly would still have taken the match.

1952

1952

Heroic Rook completes course despite fall

By our special correspondent

HELSINKI, FRIDAY 1 AUGUST

By a tragic accident at the very finish of a gallant ride by Major A. L. Rook on Starlight, Britain were eliminated as a team from the three-day equestrian event, just when they seemed securely placed third to Sweden and Germany, with an excellent chance of a medal.

J. R. Hindley and A. E. Hill survive to ride the last phase as individuals, but as a team Britain, who had trained for six months at Porlock and had ridden today in accordance with long-term planning, are finished.

Only two countries had all three riders home with bonus points instead of penalties – in each case Sweden, the favourites, and Germany, the 1936 winners – when Rook set out, the last competitor of the day.

And what a chance Britain had! Hindley had scored bonus 34 and Hill bonus 69. Dashing horsemanship and the wonderful condition of the horses had put Britain in a position to challenge for the lead.

All news of Rook for nearly two hours was excellent, his steeeplechase in particular was fast. Then, with only a few jumps to go, Harry Llewellyn was seen running towards the finish in his shirtsleeves.

Rook was down. He had fallen, not at a jump, but on the flat, his horse tripping over a root on a sudden turn. Rook had been thrown heavily and had been out 30 seconds, but he was back in the saddle and finishing the course. He came in blood-streaked, muddy and dazed. In fact he knew so little where he was that he began to dismount before he had reached the paddock, and only warning shouts persuaded him back.

Then Rook's bonus points were announced as plus 60, in spite of the fall, a most gallant result and one which put Britain third for the day.

Britain's first gold medal

By our special correspondent

HELSINKI, SUNDAY 3 AUGUST

By her final effort in the last competition of the Olympic Games, Great Britain gained her only gold medal here today. It was won by a horse, and it went to the whole show-jumping team, in which Britain was most appropriately represented by an Englishman, a Welshman and a Scotsman. By his perfectly clear round of a very stiff course, Foxhunter, ridden by Colonel H. Llewellyn, made characteristic amends for a most uncharacteristic performance in the morning.

Had Foxhunter been in anything remotely like his real form we should have had a formidable team lead

Colonel Harry Llewellyn and Foxhunter, winners in the Olympic Grand Prix team jumping. Their medal chances in the individual event were ruined by a bad fall.

already, but he made a complete mess of it, and apart from nearly unseating his well-loved master, forfeited 16.75 points for errors he has never made since becoming a star and will probably never make again. Colonel Llewellyn said he could only suppose the horse was in some sort of pain, even if it was only indigestion.

When he came out for his second round the difference was magical, and he went like the champion he is to the emotional outburst of a crowd which had, in the morning, been struck dumb.

Jersey Joe Walcott to box again

From our own correspondent
PUBLISHED WEDNESDAY 24 SEPTEMBER

Jersey Joe Walcott today changed his mind about retiring. After losing his heavyweight championship to Rocky Marciano in the 13th round at Philadelphia last night he announced he had finished with the ring.

Second thoughts today must have persuaded him he had a chance of regaining the title. On his showing for 12 rounds there can be no gainsaying that.

So he is claiming his contracted right to a return contest, but waiving the clause which stipulates that it shall be within 90 days. This suits Marciano, who does not want to fight again until the New Year.

If Walcott loses the next time everyone will regret he did not abide by his original decision to retire. Then he would have gone out on a high note.

Sportswriters are unanimous he fought last night as none had ever seen him fight before. For 12 rounds he had out-thought and outmanoeuvred bull-like Marciano.

Forty-five thousand fans also saw Marciano prove he had guts. Despite the first knock-down of his career in the first round, Marciano doggedly marched forward and earned the hysterical mob-ovation that came minutes after the knock-out punch.

Marciano had two bad cuts on his forehead, a sore stomach and a substantial points deficit when the end came. He earned £33,000 for the night's work and Walcott £66,000.

The new champion plans a rest and a holiday before his return contest. Assuming he wins that, he is expected to try to cash in quickly on his title.

At the age of 28 he is a comparative veteran and he has little skill to fall back on when his reflexes slow and his strength fails. Also Marciano's manager, Al Weill, favours frequent fights with quick money-making.

Weill himself is likely to become as well known as Marciano. An ebullient character, he spent much time during the fight protesting his fighter had been blinded by chemicals rubbed on Walcott's shoulders.

The fight was also watched on television by spectators in 50 specially equipped theatres. This proved to be rather less than an outstanding technical success. The screen of the largest New York theatre was entirely blank during the first-round knock-down, and a riot might have developed if the fight had ended then.

The picture returned, however, and theatre television will live to transmit another fight. Fans in the theatre were just as noisy as those at the ringside. A constant stream of advice was given, although the fighters were 83 miles distant.

Jersey Joe Walcott on the ropes in the 13th round after a straight right from Rocky Marciano that became one of the best-known punches in boxing history. Marciano's victory in Philadelphia marked the beginning of his four-year reign as world heavyweight champion; he retired undefeated in 1956.

SPORT IN BRIEF

FOOTBALL
In July the Football Association announces that next season's FA Cup final will be broadcast and televised in full for the first time.

LAWN TENNIS
Australian Frank Sedgman, 24, wins the men's singles title at Wimbledon at his fifth attempt. He beats the former Czech, Jaroslav Drobny, who will go on to win the title two years later. Sedgman also wins the 1952 doubles title with K. McGregor.

MOTOR RACING
Ferrari dominate the season, while the BRM proves unpredictable and difficult to control. At Silverstone in August Froilan Gonzales **(on left with Alberto Ascari, below),** driving a BRM, is beaten by Ascari in a Ferrari. Ascari wins all six grands prix he enters, and is drivers' champion (as he will be next year too).

CRICKET
Five years after Partition, Pakistan play their first Test against India at Delhi. A. H. Kardar, who previously played for India as Abdul Hafeez, is Pakistan's first captain. India take the series 2–1 with one match drawn. Vinoo Mankad of India takes 25 wickets.

BOXING
In Johannesburg on 15 November, Australian Jimmy Carruthers knocks out world bantamweight champion Vic Toweel to become the first Australian to win a world title fight.

1953

Arsenal are champions for the seventh time

By a special correspondent
PUBLISHED SATURDAY 2 MAY
Arsenal 3; Burnley 2

Twelve minutes of frantic, triumphant and inspired teamwork which cut through and battered down their last obstacle won for Arsenal their seventh championship – a Football League record – by the most slender margin since they first established their jealously guarded supremacy in 1930.

Not in the 23 years they have endured could they have had to fight so fiercely as they did at Highbury last night against Burnley on a pitch more typical of the hazards of November than of the first day of May. It was something of an anticlimax when the police took up their touchline guard of honour to allow the champions to stagger from the field. For Arsenal had won the title merely by a goal average only 0.099 better than Preston's.

Irish forwards control game against England

By E. W. Swanton
PUBLISHED MONDAY 16 FEBRUARY
Ireland 9 pts; England 9

Whatever things were lacking in the match between Ireland and England at Dublin on Saturday, excitement was not one of them. The battle raged furiously for the full 80 minutes with never more than three points between the sides. Ireland led in all for only a bare minute, between the kicking of their second penalty and that with which Nim Hall brought England level again. Nevertheless, it was Ireland, inspired as ever by Jackie Kyle, who did fully two-thirds of the attacking.

The first moments of the game consisted of one Irish thrust after another. The first time England approached the Irish 25 they scored. England's hooker touched down near enough to give Hall quite an easy kick, which he missed.

The Irish forwards were constantly being put into short-range action by Kyle's kicking. There were long scrums almost on the goal-line. Yet somehow England weathered it all, and emerged with their precious three points.

The remaining 15 points, nine to Ireland, six to England, were scored in the space of 20 minutes. First with a long penalty Noel Henderson brought Ireland level. Then Hall, from something like 50 yards, regained the lead. Next came Ireland's try, a very good one scored by Mortell in the corner.

In preparing for the conversion Henderson touched the ball after it had been grounded, just as he had done at Belfast, and so there was no kick at goal.

The referee made a virtual present of three points to Ireland with a penalty against an England forward in the shadow of the goal, whereupon Hall promptly neutralised Henderson's goal with another magnificent long kick.

Henderson, instead of finding touch near the English line, now twice attempted penalties at goal, each from inside his own half, which merely gave England time and breathing space. These two kicks were the only minor tactical points of criticism that might be set against Kyle's transcendent skill in manoeuvre. As Ireland's captain he has come to his full influence and maturity.

> ### DID YOU KNOW?
> Legendary footballer Stanley Matthews was the son of a boxer, Jack Matthews, who was known as the 'Fighting Barber of Hanley'. In turn Stanley's son (also called Stanley) played tennis, representing Britain in the Davis Cup in 1971.

Gordon Richards ends Derby hoodoo on Pinza

By Hotspur
PUBLISHED MONDAY 8 JUNE

If the Queen's colt Aureole could not win the Derby on Saturday, as would certainly have been a fitting climax to Coronation Week, then a victory for Pinza, ridden by Gordon Richards, owned by Sir Victor Sassoon, bred by Mr Fred Darling and trained by Darling's former head lad, N. Bertie, was the second best result.

It was Gordon Richards' first victory in the race at his 28th attempt; having fulfilled a lifelong ambition, it may be that Pinza will prove his last Derby mount.

The start of the race was a good one, and among those soon conspicuous were City Scandal, Mountain King and Shikampur with Victory Roll, Star of the Forest, Nearula, Pinza and Aureole reasonably well placed.

After half a mile Shikampur had gone into the lead, and coming to the top of the hill he was followed by Victory Roll, Mountain King, Pinza, Nearula, Aureole, Pharel and Premonition among others.

From this point the pace increased noticeably, and before they had come to Tattenham Corner Shikampur and Pinza, on whom Gordon Richards was lucky to get a clear run, were out clear of the remainder, with Shikampur some four lengths ahead.

The positions were the same going into the straight with Pinza, in turn, four or five lengths ahead of a group which included Mountain King, Good Brandy, Star of the Forest, Pharel, Aureole and Nearula.

Mountain King, Good Brandy and Star of the Forest were in trouble a furlong later, while Gordon Richards was almost on the tail of Shikampur, waiting for the moment to challenge.

The champion jockey asked Pinza to win his race about a quarter of a mile from home. The colt drew up to Shikampur without ado, and with more than a furlong to go held a clear lead from Shikampur with his race apparently won.

The only danger now was Aureole, whom Carr brought to challenge wide of Pinza. Aureole ran on well but was not quite good enough and could not get to Pinza, who won decisively by four lengths.

Pinza, ridden by Gordon Richards, is led into the winners' enclosure. Richards had heard a few days earlier that he was to be knighted.

Matthews laughs at age and selectors

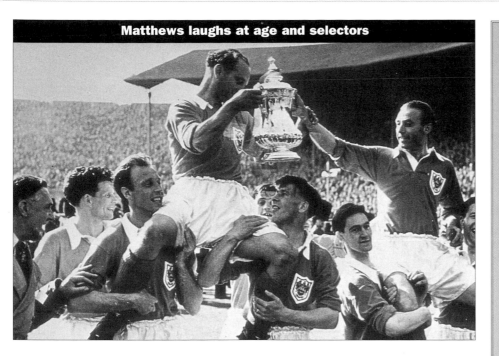

By Frank Coles

PUBLISHED MONDAY 4 MAY

Blackpool 4; Bolton Wanderers 3

Captain Harry Johnston (on left with Cup) and Stanley Matthews are feted by their Blackpool colleagues. It was Matthews' first Cup medal in 20 years' playing.

Coronation Year Cup final will be remembered for all time as the match Stanley Matthews won.

There has never been a Wembley final to match this one. On this never-to-be-forgotten afternoon there were half a dozen thrills, and in nearly all of them Matthews drew the 100,000 crowd to him like a magnet.

Matthews the Maestro. Matthews the Wizard. Old Man Matthews, thrown into the discard by the selectors – the captions have been used over and over again. Now it was Matthews the complete footballer who inspired the greatest rally Wembley has known in 30 years.

When, ten minutes after the interval, Eric Bell headed home Holden's cross from the right wing to put

Bolton 3–1 up, Blackpool's stock stood at zero. None but a player of genius could have saved this critical situation.

Blackpool's rally began with 23 minutes to go. Matthews placed the ball towards the far post; the next thing we saw was Stan Mortensen and the ball in the net.

In this final phase Matthews played the game of his life. Less than three minutes from time, Blackpool were awarded a free kick. Mortensen's terrific shot whistled into the roof of the net.

'Come on Stanley,' yelled the crowd. The magnificent Matthews touched the ball back to the onrushing Perry and into the net it flashed. Matthews (and Blackpool) had won the Cup at the third time of asking.

STANLEY MATTHEWS (1915–)

STANLEY MATTHEWS' EXTRAORDINARY PROFESSIONAL CAREER lasted 33 years, from his debut as a 17-year-old until his retirement in 1965. Throughout this time he played for just two clubs. Born in Hanley, Stoke-on-Trent, he was with his local team, Stoke City, from 1932 until 1947, returning there in 1961. In the intervening years he was at Blackpool, reaching the FA Cup final with them on three occasions. Blackpool lost the first two finals, but won in 1953, when the 38-year-old maestro played such a dominant role that it became known as the 'Matthews Final'.

Matthews' England career was equally illustrious. He made 54 appearances over 19 years for his country (1934–57), and also participated

in 29 wartime internationals. At every level, he mesmerised defences with his dazzling wing-play, which combined a magical body-swerve with perfect balance and ball control. 'Playing Stanley is like playing against a ghost', complained one of his despairing opponents.

Off the field, Matthews added something else to the game. With his modesty and sportsmanship – he was never cautioned by a referee throughout his entire career – he raised the status of football in the public eye. He was the first footballer to be honoured with a CBE (1957) and a knighthood (1965). After his retirement, Matthews managed Port Vale and coached in South Africa, taking their first all-black team on tour to Brazil.

FOOTBALL

Derek Dooley, Sheffield Wednesday's 23-year-old centre forward, breaks his leg when colliding with Preston's goalkeeper during a game. Gangrene sets in and Dooley's leg has to be amputated. It is a tragic end to a career that has seen Dooley score 46 goals in 30 games to help Wednesday to promotion last season, and 16 goals in 29 games in the First Division this season.

MOTOR RACING

A world championship is introduced for the manufacturers of sports cars. It covers seven races, including the Mille Miglia, the 1,000 km at the Nürburgring, Le Mans and the Carrera Panamericana. Ferrari – through Giuseppe Farina, Mike Hawthorn and Giannino Marzotto – win three of these races outright, and accumulate enough points to win the first championship title.

CRICKET

Derek Shackleton, the Hampshire medium-fast bowler, takes nine wickets for 77 runs against Glamorgan on 25 June. Shackleton will take more than 100 wickets a season for a record 20 successive years from 1949–68.

LAWN TENNIS

In an extraordinary third-round match at Wimbledon, Jaroslav Drobny and the 1950 champion Budge Patty engage in a five-set, 93-game battle. Drobny eventually emerges the victor, taking the match 8–6, 16–18, 3–6, 8–6, 12–10.

CYCLING

The green jersey, awarded to the leader of the race on points, is introduced in the Tour de France.

1953

1953

Cricket supremacy passes to England

By E. W. Swanton

THE OVAL, WEDNESDAY 19 AUGUST

The fifth Test, which had seemed to turn so sharply England's way when Australia were battling against the spin bowlers yesterday, duly ended in victory here shortly before three o'clock this afternoon: that elusive victory which has been awaited ever since D. R. Jardine's side won the Ashes 20 years ago. The margin of eight wickets was conclusive enough, but the result was not gained without a fight to the last ball.

W. A. Johnston bowled today without respite until A. L. Hassett came on, as at Melbourne in '51, to bowl a final comedy over at his end. R. R. Lindwall kept up a fast and accurate attack, until he gave the ball to A. R. Morris, off whom D. Compton hit the last four needed.

It took two hours and 40 minutes of resolute batsmanship to make the final 94 runs, P. May's wicket being the Australians' only reward.

All was as it should be, a hard struggle to the finish, and the final scenes were equally fitting. Some 15,000 clamoured in front of the pavilion, and the players were cheered **(above)** on their respective balconies.

England won the series 1–0; four of the matches were drawn.

Brilliant Hungarian footballers rout England

By Frank Coles

WEMBLEY STADIUM, WEDNESDAY 25 NOVEMBER
England 3; Hungary 6

England's proud record of never striking the home flag to a team from the Continent was shattered here this afternoon. The immense consolation in defeat is that the spell was broken by a Hungarian side playing English-style football at its choicest. For the first time a major match at Wembley produced nine goals, and six is the highest number scored against England for 72 years.

It was, indeed, a famous victory, achieved by the most brilliant display of football ever seen in this country. The Hungarians flashed before our eyes as fit and as fast as a track team. The mantle of masters rests gracefully on their shoulders. In scientific ball control of the highest degree, in speed and, above all, in shooting ability, they outmatched England. .

The crowd was given an immediate glance at the shape of things to come when, 90 seconds after the kick-off, the amazing Nandor Hidegkuti scored a goal which left English defenders and onlookers astonished, shooting the ball into the goal from 16 yards.

Twelve minutes later, John Sewell had the goalkeeper alone to beat, and this he did calmly and accurately.

The magnificent Magyars, led by Ferenc Puskas, walk out next to England at Wembley. The Hungarian team retained their unbeaten record, held since May 1950.

The pattern of the Hungarian attack was Hidegkuti playing hide and seek behind his inside forwards. In the 21st minute he stole from the debris of the English defence and it was Hungary 2, England 1.

Then began 20 minutes of spellbinding football by the Hungarians. Ferenc Puskas shot brilliantly into the goal after juggling the ball on to his left foot. Five minutes later it was 4–1. Five minutes from half-time Stan Mortensen squeezed a way past two Hungarians to shoot England's second goal, but 4–2 was a formidable score with which to start the second half.

England looked weary as they walked back, but the Hungarians played faster than ever. After seven minutes Joszef Bozsik drove into the goal a shot from 25 yards. Four minutes later the Hungarians scored their sixth goal. It was Hidegkuti again, and again it was that body swerve quickly followed by a powerful shot.

In the 13th minute the Hungarian goalkeeper pulled down George Robb by the legs and Alf Ramsey was called up to score with the penalty kick. That was 6–3 and, try as England did, the Hungarians played even better and narrowly missed scoring two more goals before the end.

DID YOU KNOW?

The defeat by Hungary at Wembley signalled the end of one England player's international career. His name was Alf Ramsey, and he played at right back. Thirteen years later he would return to Wembley as manager of the victorious England World Cup team.

British drivers triumph in two Rheims races

By W. A. McKenzie
RHEIMS, SUNDAY 5 JULY

British drivers had their finest hour in international motor racing today at Rheims. They won two of the chief events of the European calendar.

In the 12-hour sports-car race, Stirling Moss and Peter Whitehead won another brilliant Jaguar victory. They thus confirmed the Jaguar triumph in the 24-hour race at Le Mans three weeks ago, when these cars took first, second and fourth places.

Later Mike Hawthorn, the 24-year-old British engineering student who joined the Ferrari team six months ago, won the 310-mile Grand Prix of Rheims for his Italian firm in the closest-fought grand prix on record. His average speed was 113.6 mph, one second better than Juan Fangio in a Maserati.

Mr W. Lyons, head of Jaguars, had withdrawn his official team of cars. Rightly he thought it best to rest on his laurels after Le Mans. Nevertheless, he made available an old practice car for Moss to enter privately, and it was this which won the race.

It began with Umberto Maglioli putting the Ferrari into the lead with laps in the dark at over 112 mph. By the second hour Moss was in third place. Lap speeds were going up to 113 mph. Moss appeared to lack a dominating turn of speed on his 'hack' car, but his skill was contributing to his position among the leaders. Before the sixth hour Maglioli brought his Ferrari to the pits to refuel, but could not restart on the car's battery and pushed it. Immediately there was an uproar from the crowd. Push starts are not allowed, and the stewards decided to disqualify the car.

At this point the Italian pit staff refused to accept the disqualification. They cheered the driver on while the crowd booed him. Italian supporters joined in and the hubbub could be heard above the noise of the cars. Finally Maglioli was given the black flag to stop and, an hour after the trouble started, he did so and retired.

This left Fitch (Cunningham) in the lead with Moss just behind. Soon Moss took the lead and Fitch, straining to regain it, crashed but was unhurt. From that moment Moss never looked like losing his lead and finished 21 miles in front of the next car, Louis Rosier's Talbot. He had covered 1,274 miles at an average of 105.5 mph. Rosier (Talbot) and Cunningham (Cunningham) were second and third.

The 310-mile Grand Prix for stripped Formula II racing cars was notable, for the new Maseratis threatened the hitherto all-conquering Ferraris with defeat. But after the halfway mark, when Fangio took his Maserati into the lead, Hawthorn in his Ferrari was never more than two cars' length behind. Right to the last half-mile the result was in doubt. Then, as the two leaders swept at 160 mph to the finishing line, it was seen that Hawthorn, just behind when they last passed, was in front. Froilan Gonzales (Maserati) was third and Alberto Ascari (Ferrari), took fourth place.

'Unbeatable' Ben Hogan wins Open by four strokes

By Leonard Crawley
CARNOUSTIE, FRIDAY 10 JULY

Ben Hogan, of the United States, won the Open golf championship here this evening with the wonderful total of 282. Peter Thomson, of Australia; Frank Stranahan, the American Walker Cup player; Welshman Dai Rees; and Tony Cerda, of the Argentine, tied for second place with 286, and Robert de Vicenzo came next, one stroke further behind.

If Hogan did not bring this great course quite to its knees, his marvellous golf has at least humbled it, and his winning score will be unbeaten here for generations.

Hogan, who won his fourth American Open earlier this year, thus becomes the third American ever to have held the two major championships of the world at the same time. The others were the immortal Bobby Jones (1926) and Gene Sarazen (1932).

It will be seen from Hogan's four rounds of 73, 71, 70 and 68 that he gradually warmed up in preparation for his final triumph. He is undoubtedly the best golfer in the world today. He seems to have the indefinable quality of being able to bring himself to his supreme peak when the pressure is greatest. His great predecessor Walter Hagen was much the same, but whereas he was a genius at improvisation and would play a number of bad shots, Hogan is the nearest thing we have seen to the perfect golfing machine.

Hogan's fourth round, strangely enough, requires little comment. His four at the long sixth made one want to shout. An enormous tee shot, a gorgeous brassie, a chip and a four-foot putt. At the 13th he holed from 15 feet for a two. His second to the 14th was short and he took his only five of the round. The rest, superlatively good, meant a 68 and a record, and though Cerda finished gallantly in 71, nothing else really mattered.

SPORT IN BRIEF

GOLF
Ben Hogan, winner of the US and British Open titles, also wins the US Masters title this year. In what he himself believes are the 'best four rounds of golf in any tournament I've ever played in', Hogan achieves a record 14 under par for the Augusta course. The fourth of the 'major' titles – the US PGA – eludes Hogan: he cannot take part in it because it clashes with the British Open.

MOTOR RACING
Alberto Ascari **(left)** wins his second successive drivers' world championship title in a Ferrari after coming first in the Argentine, Dutch, Belgian, British and Swiss Grands Prix. Juan Fangio takes second place and Giuseppe Farina comes third.

CRICKET
In the second Test match at Lord's between Australia and England, Trevor Bailey and Willie Watson bat for most of the last day in order to save the match. Watson takes 346 minutes to reach his 109, and Bailey accumulates 71 in the 275 minutes that he is at the crease. The match is drawn.

FOOTBALL
England play the Rest of Europe in a match to celebrate 90 years of the Football Association. Thirty-eight-year-old Stanley Matthews is recalled to the national side. An untried European team drawn from six countries soon show their superiority. With time running out for England, Stan Mortensen is brought down in the box, and Alf Ramsey scores a last-minute penalty to earn England a very fortunate 4–4 draw.

1953

1954

Lester Piggott loses licence for six months

By Hotspur
PUBLISHED SATURDAY 19 JUNE

Lester Piggott, 18, the apprentice who won the Derby on Never Say Die (below), will not ride under Jockey Club rules again this season. The Stewards of the Jockey Club yesterday decided to withdraw his licence to ride.

The Stewards, Major-General Sir Randle Feilden, Lord Willoughby de Broke and Sir Humphrey de Trafford (acting for the Duke of Norfolk) made their decision before racing began as a result of a report by the Ascot Stewards on the King Edward VII Stakes on Thursday when Piggott rode Never Say Die.

At the moment Piggott is attached to his father's stable at Lambourn, Berks, and lives at home. I understand that Piggott is now required to attach himself to another stable.

There is no question of him being allowed to ride again for six months. He will miss the St Leger at Doncaster in September at which he was to have ridden Never Say Die.

In evidence Piggott said he had been unable to prevent Never Say Die hanging to the left at one period. The televised recording of the King Edward VII stakes showed Rashleigh, the mount of Sir Gordon Richards, veering sharply to the right soon after entering the straight. The offence apparently happened just before this incident.

DID YOU KNOW?

The winner of the 'golden boot' for most goals scored at the 1954 World Cup was Sandor Kocsis, member of the unlucky Hungarian team that lost to Germany in the final. Kocsis scored an incredible 11 goals in only five matches in the tournament.

Drobny wins Wimbledon at 11th attempt

By a Daily Telegraph *reporter*
PUBLISHED SATURDAY 3 JULY

Jaroslav Drobny, 32, the man with the reputation as the world's unluckiest lawn tennis player, became men's singles champion at Wimbledon yesterday when he beat Ken Rosewall, the 19-year-old Australian.

King Gustav of Sweden, Princess Margaret, and the Duchess of Kent were among the capacity crowd of 14,600 who saw Drobny win the most exciting final for years by 13–11, 4–6, 6–2, 9–7. It lasted 2 hours 36 minutes and was the longest singles final in the history of the championships.

Drobny was given a terrific ovation as one of the most popular winners for many years. He refused an order to return to Czechoslovakia in 1949, and later took up Egyptian nationality. Last year he married the former British lawn tennis international, Miss Rita Jarvis.

She watched every stroke of his long match from the front row of the competitors' stands, and Drobny's first action after winning was to look towards her and hold out his arms. They are expecting a baby in the autumn.

Drobny first played at Wimbledon in 1938. This was his 11th attempt there, and he was the No. 11 seeded player. Twice before he has reached the final.

He is the first left-hander to be champion for 40 years. Drobny won the French championship in 1951 and 1952 but has long been regarded in the lawn tennis world as the man who won all matches but the last.

He said afterwards: 'I'm delighted to have won. It has been my ambition for years. I shall defend my title next year but I doubt if I shall make a really serious attempt to retain it. I have no desire to turn professional.

'I felt I had to win this year at all costs. I'm sorry Rosewall, who is a fine player, had to lose, but he is young and will be able to win in the next ten years.'

Drobny wins at last; he was the first left-hander since Norman Brookes in 1914 to take the Wimbledon title.

England throw away 3–1 lead against Belgium

By Frank Coles
BASLE, THURSDAY 17 JUNE
England 4; Belgium 4

After leading by 3-1 with only a quarter of an hour to go, England threw their great chance away and allowed Belgium to draw level in their World Cup match here tonight. After an extra half-hour, an amazing struggle of ebb and flow ended 4–4.

England's display was extraordinarily inconsistent and in many respects disappointing.

Hesitancy by England's defence gave Belgium the first goal of the match after only six minutes. In the penalty area Coppens forced the ball through to Anoul, who hit the roof of the net with a rousing drive.

After Tom Finney had bungled a great chance from eight yards, Coppens raced through again and Belgium were within inches of being two ahead, the centre forward's shot whizzing just by the right post.

For 26 minutes England played incredibly poor football – a team completely at sixes and sevens. And then, against the run of play, Ivor Broadis equalised from close in as the goalkeeper challenged.

This equalising goal acted as a wonderful tonic to the sluggish Englishmen, and at the 37th minute England took the lead with a grand goal. Lofthouse dived low and headed into the net at tremendous speed. It seemed as though the death blow had fallen for Belgium half an hour before the end. Broadis ran on to Matthews' centre to shoot just inside the post from 20 yards.

But the Belgians came back into the game with a vengeance when Mermans went into the middle. Anoul followed up a long pass to reduce the lead and two minutes later Coppens made it 3–3 with a low shot and the game went into an extra half-hour.

Two minutes after the resumption of this hectic match, Lofthouse restored England's advantage with a shot which went in off the crossbar, but in the next breath Jimmy Dickinson headed through his own goal from Dries's free kick and it was 4–4.

Hero of the England side was Stanley Matthews, who outshone every other forward on the field. Billy Wright and Byrne were the pick of one of the poorest defences ever to represent England.

Roger Bannister runs mile in under four minutes

By Jack Crump

OXFORD, THURSDAY 6 MAY

The first four-minute mile in the history of athletics was accomplished here today by Roger Gilbert Bannister, a 25-year-old medical student, who was timed officially to run the distance in 3 min 59.4 sec. This was two seconds faster than the world record of Gundar Haegg, of Sweden, made in 1945.

This great triumph by an English athlete on an English track took the sporting world by surprise. It came at the start of an athletic season in America and in Europe, where several runners, notably John Landy (Australia), Joseph Barthel (Luxembourg), who beat Bannister in the 1952 Olympic Games, and Wes Santee (US) planned final assaults on the 'even time' mile.

Bannister's historic run was all the more remarkable because it was his first public race this season, and the chilly and blustering wind, varying between 15 and 25 mph, made conditions far from ideal.

During the winter he had trained almost secretly, and few knew that he had reached peak condition so early in the year. This was enough to attract a crowd of nearly

Bannister breasts the tape in record time. Landy of Australia and Bannister met later in the year in the 'Mile of the Century'. Bannister ran 3 min 58.8 sec, Landy 3 min 59.6 sec; it was the first time two men had run under four minutes in the same race.

2,000, who gathered around the track to see if athletic history would be made.

Roger Bannister's chances of succeeding in what he himself certainly had not publicly stated to be his target seemed very remote an hour before the race.

Luckily the weather improved and it was learned when the six runners in the race went to the starting line that Bannister and his great friend C. J. Chataway, were to attempt to run a 'really fast mile'.

I spoke to Roger Bannister soon after the race and he told me that the intermediate lap times of 57.5 seconds, the half-mile in 1 minute 58.2 seconds, and the three-quarter mile in 3 minutes 0.5 seconds were almost exactly as he hoped. He expressed the greatest delight, not merely on being the first man to achieve the coveted distinction, but also of having performed this feat on the track of the university where he was athletic president.

SPORT IN BRIEF

LAWN TENNIS

In June the United States score another Wightman Cup 'whitewash' by beating Britain in all six ties. Rain prevents the seventh tie being played. Maureen Connolly, who is one of the hardest hitters of the ball the women's game has ever seen, has a brilliant game against Miss J. Shilcock, which she wins 6–2, 6–2.

FOOTBALL

The Union des Associations Européene de Football (UEFA) is formed. Next year the national League champions from the 33 countries who belong to UEFA will play for the European Cup for the first time.

MOTOR RACING

On 4 July Germany's new Mercedes-Benz W196 cars eclipse the opposition in the French Grand Prix at Rheims. It is the first postwar appearance of the Mercedes-Benz team in a grand prix. In a thrilling race, Argentinian driver Juan Fangio and German Karl Kling set record speeds on the circuit, and finish almost side by side, with Fangio crossing the line 0.1 sec ahead of Kling in 2 hr 42 min 47.9 sec. Robert Manzoni is third, a lap behind, in a Ferrari. Fangio goes on to take his second world championship title.

GOLF

Mrs Mildred 'Babe' Zaharias, who returned to top-class golf after undergoing a colostomy operation last year, wins the American Women's Open for the third time.

RUGBY LEAGUE

Great Britain tour Australia. The match against New South Wales in Sydney ends in a brawl. It is abandoned in the 56th minute with New South Wales leading 17–6.

1954

1954

TOM FINNEY (1922–)

One of England's most gifted footballers, Thomas Finney was born on 5 April 1922 in the Lancashire town of Preston. His mother died when he was four and his father only managed to look after his six children with the help of friends and neighbours. Finney left school at 14 to train as a plumber and, in the same year, had a successful trial with his local team. Despite this, he continued to play as an amateur, so that he could complete his apprenticeship.

The Finney family lived within earshot of the roaring crowds at Deepdale, Preston North End's ground, and Finney spent his entire career with this club. Before beginning his army service in North Africa, he competed for Preston in the 1941 Cup final, but his first League appearance was not until 1946. From then until his retirement in 1960, he played 433 games for Preston, scoring 187 goals.

Finney's England career was equally distinguished. Between 1946–58, he won 78 caps for his country and scored 30 goals. During this time, he demonstrated his versatility by playing on either wing, or at centre forward. Inevitably comparisons were made between him and Stanley Matthews – especially since they were often rivals for the same place in the team.

Many people believe that the talent of the 'Galloping Ghost', as Finney was nicknamed, was greater. Tommy Doherty said of him: 'He was the perfect player. He had no weaknesses…. His skill was uncanny, his reading of the game superlative, his passing pinpoint in its accuracy.' Like Matthews, Finney was also admired for his sportsmanship.

Tom Finney was awarded the OBE in 1961 and the CBE in 1992.

MILESTONES

Tom Finney, Preston North End's leading goalscorer of all time, was awarded the Player of the Year award for the first time in 1954. He became the first player to be honoured twice when he was named Player of the Year again in 1957.

Shock victory for Germany in World Cup final

From our special correspondent
BERNE, SUNDAY 4 JULY
Germany 3; Hungary 2

Germany, the team which not even their own countrymen gave a chance of winning the World Cup, are the new international soccer champions.

They beat Hungary, odds-on favourites for the title ever since the competition began, 3–2 in the final here tonight, and they did it in the English style, with quick, long passes through the middle.

It was Hungary's first international defeat in four years, and it came after they had put themselves in a seemingly impregnable position with two goals in the first eight minutes.

Ferenc Puskas, the Hungarian captain who had missed the earlier knock-out matches because of an ankle injury, gave his side the lead in the sixth minute. Then outside right Zoltan Czibor, a live wire throughout, profited by a defensive error two minutes later.

A similar slip on the part of the Hungarian defence – a back-pass to the goalkeeper weakly placed – gave Max Morlock a chance to score for Germany after ten minutes, and seven minutes later outside right Helmut Rahn equalised following a corner.

The Hungarians, playing the same methodical football which twice routed England, hit the post three times in a great second-half victory bid when the Germans seemed to be tiring.

Then from a break-away six minutes from the end, Rahn, Germany's most dangerous forward, fired in a long, low shot which cut inches inside the far post for the winning goal.

The Germans owed much of their success to their new centre half, Werner Liebrich, a big, blond six-footer. His job was to block Puskas, obviously short of match practice, out of the game, and right well he did it.

Hungary paid the penalty for over-confidence. They repeatedly tried to dribble the ball into goal when first-time shooting would have been more profitable.

Captain Fritz Walter, who made two of Germany's goals, holds the Jules Rimet Trophy.

Chataway clips five seconds off world 5,000-m time

By a special correspondent
PUBLISHED THURSDAY 14 OCTOBER

Forty-five thousand people crammed in the White City arena last night – the gates were closed – rose from their seats and cheered the greatest athletics achievement of this year of great prowess. It was the revenge, in new world-record time, of C. J. Chataway over his Russian conqueror at the European Games in Berne recently, the world 5,000-m record-holder Vladimir Kuts.

Chataway won a magnificently judged, courageously maintained race by a couple of feet, passing the Russian barely ten yards from the tape after jogging behind him for the entire 12-and-a-bit rounds of the historic track.

The field of four broke up with little more than half the distance still to be run.

Kuts, in front from the the start, turned on the pace just as he had at Berne, but Chataway was prepared for the move. He accelerated too, though he still ran a yard behind the Russian, literally breathing down the back of his neck.

Immediately the field split in two, but though Kuts tried all manner of means to shake his rival off with sudden unexpected spurts and darts round the bends, Chataway responded to every one and allowed him absolutely no tether.

So the two went on, rapidly increasing the gap between themselves and the second strings who were toiling along, very soon half a lap behind.

At precisely the point now called 'Chataway's Corner', on the second bend about 300 yards from the winning-post, the tawny-haired Chataway lashed himself up from a canter into a gallop. At once Kuts did likewise and ran so strongly down the back straight that there was a momentary suspicion that Chataway was going to crack.

He was running all-out at the third bend and round the fourth into the short home straight, but still could not make up that yard that mattered. The pressure on Kuts, however, was tremendous, and even that magnificent runner could not quite stand it.

At last, so near to home, he was forced to give the contestable yard of ground and Chataway, dead game, came up level with him and finally accomplished a magnificent triumph. The packed stands were one confusion of terrific sound and tumult.

People in the dressing rooms beneath began to fear for their safety. And the cheering and stamping increased when, over the loudspeakers, Chataway's time – 13 min 51.6 sec – was announced. This was five seconds faster than Kuts's time in Berne, awaiting ratification as a world record, and 5.6 seconds faster than the established world record set by E. Zatopek.

Miss Connolly is a truly great Wimbledon champion

By Lance Tingay

PUBLISHED MONDAY 5 JULY

A great women's singles champion, a most worthy men's singles winner and some good doubles champions, such is my summary of the lawn tennis championships at Wimbledon. The mainly dull, grey weather could not suppress the throb and sparkle of a meeting well up to standard.

The finest champion was Miss Maureen Connolly. Of this there is no doubt, and why on Saturday her third successive singles victory was not more uproariously acclaimed I do not fully understand.

After winning last year Miss Connolly's first thought was to improve the weaknesses, if such relative lack of strength could so be termed, of her game. She now has no lawn tennis imperfections that can be properly described as such. She has the ability to flog and kill the ball from anywhere, whether running or still, off the ground or overhead, and from either wing.

Yet I thought Saturday's crowd less warm in applauding her achievement than they might have been. When in the course of the final Miss Connolly showed her human frailty and lapsed a little; when her opponent Miss L. Brough took this cue to play with skilled resolution reminiscent of her old championship quality and build a second-set lead of 5–2, the spectators understandably egged on the 'underdog' with frenzied zest.

Miss Connolly's even more splendid effort when she surged through to take the set was less zealously greeted. It was taken for granted that she should play like an easy-running machine.

It is, perhaps, one of the drawbacks of greatness that Miss Connolly's cold efficiency should be regarded as a personal characteristic. Off the court Miss Connolly is charming. She is remorseless only when she begins to play and has, by hard work, made herself the greatest lawn tennis exponent of two decades.

'Little Mo' Connolly stretches for a shot (far left) in the final of what would be her last Wimbledon (see Sport in Brief). As champion she received the Venus Rosewater dish (left) from the Duchess of Kent.

SPORT IN BRIEF

LAWN TENNIS
On 20 July Maureen Connolly, Wimbledon singles' winner for the last three years in succession (see main text), and star of America's Wightman Cup triumph, is badly injured in a riding accident when her leg is crushed against the lorry that scared her horse. The accident will end the career of 19-year-old 'Little Mo'.

FOOTBALL
After England's humiliating 7–1 defeat by Hungary in May, Wolverhampton Wanderers are delighted to score a 3–2 victory over Honved of Hungary. Honved are one of the best club sides in the world, supplying the Hungarian national side with seven of their current players, including Ferenc Puskas, the captain.

CRICKET
In the first Test match at Brisbane in England's 1954–5 tour of Australia, captain Len Hutton puts Australia into bat. They score 601 for eight; Neil Harvey gets 162 and Arthur Morris 153. Trevor Bailey scores 88 of England's first-innings total of 190; they are forced to follow on. Bailey is out for 23 in the second innings, caught **(below)** by wicketkeeper Langley off fast bowler Ray Lindwall. Australia win the Test by an innings and 154 runs.

Six more join Cotton's golf 'revolt'

PUBLISHED SATURDAY 27 NOVEMBER

Six more professionals have joined Henry Cotton's 'revolt' against the Professional Golfers' Association, last year's British Ryder Cup captain announced yesterday.

The latest development followed Cotton's announcement on Thursday that 24 had signed a statement that the playing section were not adequately represented on the committee.

None of the signatories, which included most of the last Ryder Cup team, would, it said, play in international matches sponsored by the PGA unless they were satisfied with the selection committee and the captain. The 'rebels' will meet next week to discuss their next step.

Cotton said yesterday: 'One logical solution to our complaints would be to create a players' committee to organise big events, pick their own Ryder Cup teams, and then allow those chosen teams to nominate their captain.'

J. Adams, the Wentworth professional, said they did not want to split the PGA. 'Even to the point of having to reorganise the constitution of the association, we desire a players' union,' he said.

1954

125

1955

England emphasise their Test superiority against Australia

From E. W. Swanton
SYDNEY, THURSDAY 3 MARCH

The final scoreboard of the fifth Test match may be slightly deceptive. Without an accompanying narrative, it will seem that Australia only struggled clear of defeat by the skin of their teeth. That was not quite the case, for, badly as Australia batted today, there was never quite the time for England to do the job.

Still, in that it illustrates the complete batting and bowling superiority of England over these last three days, the score is explicit enough. Not, indeed, since the Oval in 1938 have England looked, on the evidence of one match, so unmistakably the stronger team.

Australia this afternoon failed to avoid the follow-on by a single run. Len Hutton asked them to bat again, although there was a bare two hours remaining. At the end Australia had only four wickets left and were still 32 behind.

They began the second innings by losing three for 29 in three-quarters of an hour. After a further half-hour had passed, Hutton, acknowledging the inevitable, brought on Tom Graveney, who promptly got a wicket. The final comedy was a last over by Hutton, a wild swing to high heaven by Benaud and the ultimate entry in the scorebook, Benaud, b. Hutton, 22.

The Englishmen present appreciated this culminating joke, I think, slightly better than the Australians: at least than the Australians whose memories went back to better days, to Don Bradman and Stan McCabe let us say, if not to Charles Macartney, Victor Trumper and the giants of old.

I have never seen Australia bat so abjectly. It can only be hoped that away from their own exacting public and of the majority of their stern critics, the Australians rediscover in West Indies the cohesion and fighting spirit which has always characterised their cricket.

Johnny Wardle today took five for 79. He mixed his off-breaks with the googly, and scarcely anyone among the Australians seemed able to pick one from the other.

Strangely, with his varied assortment he kept a better length than in his less ambitious moods of the previous matches. Australia lost 14 wickets today for 257 runs, and Wardle took as many as seven of them.

England won the series 3–1; one match was drawn.

Disaster at Le Mans: France suspends all motor racing

From our own correspondent
PARIS, MONDAY 13 JUNE

Following a Cabinet discussion on the Le Mans disaster it was announced tonight that the government was provisionally suspending all motor racing in France.

A government spokesman stated that the ban would remain until new international rules could be drawn up. It was intended to make some suggestions on regulation to the international racing authorities.

The new regulations, it is proposed, should include:

1. Removal of the public stands and enclosures to a sufficient distance from racing tracks to ensure the safety of the spectators.

2. A ban on cars of widely differing capacities running in the same race.

3. Removal of refuelling pits to an adequate distance from the tracks.

It was stated at the Cabinet meeting that the inquiry had disclosed that the magnitude of the catastrophe was due to the use of magnesium in the construction of the Mercedes car which crashed into spectators.

The ministers hope that the new international regulations will be rapidly agreed and that the suspension of motor racing will be for only a short time.

The police have a cine film of the Mercedes crash taken by a spectator which may help their inquiries.

The death toll at Le Mans, when Pierre Levegh's burning Mercedes flew into the crowd (right), was the worst in the history of motor racing. Eighty-three people died, and more than 100 were injured. Despite the tragedy, the race continued for another 20 hours.

Newcastle enjoy Wembley luck

By Frank Coles
PUBLISHED MONDAY 9 MAY
Newcastle United 3; Manchester City 1

With the least notable of all their teams which have set up the magnificent unbeaten record of five Cup-final triumphs at Wembley since 1924, Newcastle United on Saturday defeated Manchester City, the favourites, by 3–1.

That the win was well and truly deserved everyone among the 100,000 crowd would agree, but the good luck which had marked United's progress to the 1955 final clung to them to the end of the story. A bitter end from the viewpoint of their rivals.

Nineteen minutes after the start, and when Newcastle were prospering under the influence of a snap goal by Jackie Milburn 45 seconds from the kick-off, Jimmy

SPORT IN BRIEF

CRICKET
After defeat by Australia in the first Test in Brisbane, England captain Len Hutton controversially drops bowler Alec Bedser, who dominated in the last series but is now unfit. His decision is vindicated as fast bowlers Brian Statham and Frank Tyson help England to victory: Statham takes five wickets for 60 runs in the third Test in Melbourne; Tyson takes seven wickets for 27 in the same Test, and 28 wickets in the series. Peter May also has a successful tour, scoring 351 runs, three fewer than Australia's top-scorer, Neil Harvey.

HORSE RACING
A new race for three-year-olds and upwards to be run over the Old Mile at Ascot is announced. It will be called the Queen Elizabeth II Stakes.

RUGBY LEAGUE
Britain lose to a faster and more penetrating French side at the Parc des Princes in Paris. Mick Sullivan, the 20-year-old Huddersfield centre, scores a try for Britain, but the French win 17–5. Sullivan will score a record total of 45 tries in international matches in a record 46 appearances between 1954 and 1963.

FOOTBALL
The Scottish Cup final is televised for the first time, and Celtic are tipped for an easy win over Clyde. Two minutes from time, Celtic lead 1–0, but a dramatic inswinging corner kick by Archie Robertson brings Clyde level. Clyde go on to win the replay 1–0 to gain their first Scottish Cup victory since 1939.

RUGBY UNION
Welsh lock Rhys Williams is a giant in the line-out in the British Lions' first Test against South Africa, and helps secure a tremendous 23–22 win for the Lions against the Springboks.

Meadows, Manchester City's right-back, fell in agonising pain. He had wrenched the ligaments of his left knee and took no more part in the match. The next sight the crowd had of Meadows was just after half-time, when he hobbled along to the trainers' touchline bench to watch the ten-man drama unfold itself.

Manchester City fought bravely to stave off the doom that seemed inevitable. With only three effective forwards they not only forced Newcastle back on their heels, but actually seized the initiative with a display of quality football reaching Wembley's top level.

The roar which heralded Bobby Johnstone's equalising goal with a header half a minute before half-time was spontaneous tribute to as gallant a bid to overcome odds as any Cup final has produced. But the immense strain it entailed had sapped City's stamina, and the penalty had to be paid.

Eight minutes after the interval Bill Spurdle, withdrawn from the right wing to fill Meadows's place at back, made his first misjudgment of the ball's flight, and Bobby Mitchell, the match-winner, drove past Bert Trautmann from a sharp angle.

Driven on by never-say-die attacking sallies headed by their wing halves, the City rallied once more, but six minutes later it was all over. Mitchell again outwitted rather ill-at-ease Spurdle, and the grateful George Hannah banged the winger's cross past the goalkeeper.

The last half-hour was an anticlimax, with a great Manchester City side struggling helplessly in the toils of cruel fate. The goal tally would have been doubled but for the superb skill of Trautmann, the flaxen-haired German, whose saves all through the afternoon stamped him unmistakably as one of the finest world-class goalkeepers the game has ever known.

1956

Britain regain the Curtis Cup

By Enid Wilson

PUBLISHED MONDAY 11 JUNE

There was a thrilling climax on Saturday to the Curtis Cup match at Prince's, Sandwich, the British Isles triumphing by five matches to four. Mrs Frances Smith, the British champion, won the deciding point by beating Miss Polly Riley on the 36th green.

Britain began Saturday a point down, having won one and lost two of the foursomes on Friday. To regain the cup and record their second success in the nine contests they needed four of the six singles.

Miss Pat Lesser, the American champion, began by hooking her second shot into a ditch. The hook persisted. Mrs Jessie Valentine streaked down an eight-yarder for a two on the 25th. That stroke settled Miss Lesser's fate.

Miss Philomena Garvey began the second round so ineffectually she provoked sturdy Miss Margaret Smith into letting fly a barrage of birdies. America's 19-year-old wonder golfer routed the eight-times Irish champion by nine and eight.

Miss Angela Ward and Miss Elizabeth Price played a very considerable part in the British victory by early establishing long leads over Miss M. A. Downey and Miss J. Nelson.

With Britain's tail so triumphantly aloft, the stage was set for the drama. Borne on the tide of the surging sea of spectators, Mrs Smith and Miss Riley left the 34th green all square. The destiny of the cup might now be decided on any stroke.

Like heroines they played the 35th stroke for stroke, foot for foot and inch for inch. So to the last hole. Here Miss Riley's approach faded and finished to the right of the green, below the bank. Mrs Smith followed with a controlled five iron within 15 feet of the flag. A truly magnificent stroke in a crisis and the match-winner for Britain.

MILESTONES

The first European Cup competition was held, and Real Madrid became the first winners of the trophy. Inspired by Argentine-born Alfredo di Stefano, Real Madrid come from 2–0 down to beat Rheims 4–3 in Paris.

Pirie smashes world 5,000-m record

By Jack Crump

PUBLISHED WEDNESDAY 20 JUNE

Gordon Pirie, of South London Harriers, achieved the finest performance of his remarkable career when, in a special 5,000-m race at Bergen last night, he smashed Hungarian Sandor Iharos's world record by the big margin of 3.8 seconds.

Pirie covered the distance in 13 min 36.8 sec, and beat into second place the Russian champion and former world record-holder Vladimir Kuts, whose time of 13 min 39.6 sec was also inside the previous world's best.

Pirie's participation in the race was an almost casual, last-minute affair. He has been spending a holiday with friends in Norway. Before he left England he sought and received official permission to compete in Norway if the opportunity should present itself.

It certainly did. The Russian touring team, who have already competed in Oslo, were running in Bergen last evening and Pirie, who has long cherished the hope of meeting Kuts over 5,000 m, seized the chance.

Pirie and Kuts ran together lap after lap, with Kuts always a yard or so ahead. Pirie tried to pass him several times, but Kuts would not allow him to until the last 300 yards.

Then came Pirie's final effort. A magnificent one it was as he made a devastating dash for the tape which Kuts was quite unable to match. Pirie, who won by about 20 yards, thus avenged the defeat he sustained from Kuts in the 10,000-m race in the Great Britain v Russia match in Moscow last September.

Pirie has once again confounded his critics. After an injury in the early part of last winter, he missed much of the cross-country season, which previously he had used as a building-up process for summer track competitions.

His insatiable desire to run led him to return to training rather prematurely, and subsequent injuries followed. These stopped him fulfilling the plans he had outlined as Olympic preparation. Indeed, his whole future in athletics was in jeopardy. With dogged determination and still greater emphasis on his already spartan training, he has clearly recovered his old form.

Devon Loch is unluckiest National loser of all time

By Hotspur

PUBLISHED MONDAY 26 MARCH

With 55 yards to go and the Grand National at his mercy, Queen Elizabeth the Queen Mother's Devon Loch **(below right, ridden by Dick Francis)**, clear of all opponents, stumbled, skidded, tried to keep his legs and stopped at Aintree on Saturday. It was, I think, the saddest and most dramatic event I have ever seen on a racecourse.

So ESB, ridden by D. V. Dick, strode on past him to win by ten lengths from the mare Gentle Moya, with the 1954 National winner, Royal Tan, a further ten lengths away third.

It is unlikely that anyone will ever really know exactly what happened to Devon Loch. It was all over in a matter of seconds, and occurred on the run-in from the last fence to the winning post, exactly opposite the water jump. My impression is that the horse was in pain.

One of the racecourse vets who examined Devon Loch immediately after the race thought he might have had a sudden attack of cramp. Another felt his behaviour might have been due to a small blood clot in a hind leg. The latter is known to cause paralysing pain and would explain the fact that Devon Loch appeared for a few moments to have no strength in his hind legs. Indeed, one's immediate reaction was that he had broken down. There is no doubt that Devon Loch was the unluckiest loser in the 120 years' history of the race.

Revie masterminds epic scoring in FA Cup

By Frank Coles

PUBLISHED MONDAY 7 MAY

Manchester City 3; Birmingham City 1

At last the FA Cup has been won by the brilliance of forward play as distinct from dour defence and, in accomplishing the great feat, Manchester City caused the greatest surprise since Portsmouth defeated Wolves in 1939.

Their three goals were of a standard unequalled at Wembley in a final, and were comparable with Scotland's Wembley Wizards of 1928 and the Hungarians' magic of 1953.

The result made history as well as being a repetition of 22 years ago when Manchester City gained the first of their two Wembley wins only 12 months after being beaten there. They lost last year's final to Newcastle by the same goal margin as on Saturday. In lifting the Cup, City have emulated United's triumph in the League and completed a unique Manchester Double.

In 1955 Jackie Milburn put City behind straight from the kick-off. City now followed suit with a shock goal through Joe Hayes in three minutes. When Noel Kinsey equalised with an in-off-the-post shot at the quarter-hour, the Manchester players must have felt qualms about the outcome of their carefully laid plot to strike swiftly.

At half-time, with the score 1–1, Birmingham were still very much in the game. Why did this team falter and then founder? The answers are in two names: Don Revie and Bobby Johnstone. These two international stars will remain the shining lights of the 1956 final long after all else is forgotten except the result. Revie was the grand

Little wonder that Manchester City's Bert Trautmann was described as 'holding his neck in pain'; he had broken it as he dived to save a shot from Peter Murphy (above). Roy Paul (left), captain of Manchester City, proudly clasps the FA Cup after his team's victory over the favourites, Birmingham.

master of ceremonies. I have never seen a forward more masterful in the ebb and flow of battle. Revie dictated the pace.

The Birmingham goal had escaped more than once by a hair's breadth when, in the 66th minute, Manchester took the lead with a goal by Jack Dyson, who snatched at his opportunity with a clean drive. Before his fellow defenders could ensure him safe protection, the goalkeeper was taking the ball out of the net for the second time in three minutes.

The third and decisive Manchester blow crowned Johnstone's day. When Dyson slipped the ball on to Johnstone, a quick-as-lightning goal was a certainty if the little Scot kept his balance and his head. He did both, and the shot flashed past Gil Merrick.

An injury to Trautmann led to the possibility of a dramatic climax. With 15 minutes left he was knocked out in a collision and staggered about in the goal area holding his neck in pain. He was in no condition to repel an all-or-nothing Birmingham rally. That alarming situation never arose, however, and the Cup was most worthily won.

SPORT IN BRIEF

WINTER OLYMPICS

A record 820 athletes from 32 countries compete for the winter Olympics in Cortina d'Ampezzo, Italy. It is the first winter Games to be televised. The Soviet Union win gold in the ice hockey, ending Canada's domination of the sport, and relegating them to bronze behind the United States.

BOXING

On 27 April, Rocky Marciano announces his intention to retire from boxing. The world heavyweight champion has won all of his 49 professional fights, 43 by knock-out. Born Rocco Francis Marchegiano, 'Rocky' enjoyed baseball and football at school and planned to pursue one of these sports professionally, before realising how much more he could earn through boxing. He is one of the fittest men in sport, enormously strong despite being only 5 ft $10^{1}/_{4}$ in tall and weighing 185 lb. He won the championship from Jersey Joe Walcott in 1952, and has withstood all six challenges for the title.

FOOTBALL

Manchester United top Division One at the end of the season, winning by a record-equalling margin of 11 points. The average age of players in the team is 23 years.

LAWN TENNIS

Australians Lew Hoad and Ken Rosewall face each other in three major tournaments during the year. Hoad beats Rosewall 6–4, 3–6, 6–4, 7–5 in the Australian Open to win his first Australian title. Hoad goes on to beat Rosewall again at Wimbledon, 6–2, 4–6, 7–5, 6–4, but loses to him in the US Open, 4–6, 6–2, 6–3, 6–3.

1956

133

1956

Laker takes 19 wickets for 90 runs

By E. W. Swanton
OLD TRAFFORD, TUESDAY 31 JULY

For many nervous hours since last Friday evening it has seemed that England would be robbed of victory in the fourth Test match. But Manchester expiated its sins of weather this afternoon, and it was in bright sunshine and tempering wind that the game ended in an innings win, which meant the safe-keeping of the Ashes until MCC next sail in their defence two years from now.

The only proper formal announcement of the result is that J. C. Laker defeated Australia by an innings and 170 runs. Laker followed his capture of nine first innings wickets with all ten in the second. What is left in the vocabulary to describe and applaud such a *tour de force*? It is quite fabulous.

Laker in 51.2 overs added a ten for 53 to his ten for 88 against this same Australian side for Surrey. And in this Test he has actually taken 19 for 90.

Laker's first innings performance was phenomenal enough, but its merit was perhaps clouded by the deficiencies of the Australian batting, as also by the palaver over the condition of the wicket.

There was no room whatever for argument regarding his bowling today. He bowled 36 overs, practically non-stop, all the time attacking the stumps and compelling the batsman to play, never wilting or falling short in terms either of length or direction.

Nor was he mechanical. Each ball presented the batsman with a separate problem. Laker never let up and neither for an instant could his adversary.

Applause for Laker, and applause also in a scarcely lesser strain for C. C. McDonald, who, in his long vigil, fought to win his side the respite of a draw.

The final Test at the Oval was drawn, as was the first at Trent Bridge. England won the series 2–1.

DID YOU KNOW?

Tony O'Reilly, who played for Ireland between 1955 and 1970, was the British Lions' top-scorer with six tries in ten Tests in 1955 and 1959. Recalled in 1970, he turned up for training in a chauffeur-driven Rolls Royce. He later became president of the Heinz Corporation.

Thomson, three shots clear, lands record treble

By Leonard Crawley
HOYLAKE, FRIDAY 6 JULY

Peter Thomson, 26, of Australia, won the Open golf championship here this evening for the third time in succession with a score of 286. Flory van Donck (Belgium) came second with 289 and Roberto de Vicenzo was third with 290. Gary Player, the Open champion of South Africa, was fourth with 291.

Since the championship has been played over 72 holes, no other golfer has performed a similar feat to Thomson's. I understand on the highest possible authority that James Braid, the most modest of all golfers, thought that he might have won here in 1907 for the third time in a row if he had not broken his braces at the eighth hole in the last round. But at any rate, braces or no braces, Arnaud Massy won that time and it was a good thing for the game.

So has been Thomson's third victory, since he is a young man of singular charm and modesty and sets a fine example in the matter of deportment and golfing manners to some of the strange, jumpy tournament professionals of today, many of whom have what we think of as the Hollywood temperament. That he is a more experienced player than ever is obvious, and he is certainly a more skilful one. His complete imperturbability is most noticeable, and it enables him to pull out the great shot when it is imperative for him to do so. His record in the Open is also of interest.

He was second in 1952, second again in 1953, and he won in 1954, 1955 and again this evening. I can find nothing comparable in the annals of the game.

He was first to admit this evening that he had had the luck of the draw which is so closely tied to weather conditions. This was emphatically the case, but his powers of concentration and his capacity to go on are such that I am not sure that he might not have won no matter which way his name had come out of that most important original hat.

Peter Thomson in action (below) and with the cup (left) after his third Open win. Thomson was the first Australian to win the British Open title.

Call-up may dash plans of heavyweight champion

From our own correspondent
NEW YORK, SUNDAY 2 DECEMBER

Floyd Patterson drove here today to see his new-born daughter following his surprisingly easy victory in Chicago on Friday night when he knocked out Archie Moore in the fifth round and won the world heavyweight championship.

At 21, he is the youngest boxer to win the title and, incidentally, he is also the only Olympic champion who has captured it.

Following the birth of his daughter less than five hours before the bout started – he was not told until it ended – his wife watched him on television from her hospital bed.

His manager said Patterson's immediate objective was to organise a lucrative contest in defence of the title, and he indicated that Rocky Marciano, who retired as undefeated champion last April, would be a most desirable candidate. Marciano, however, told friends last night that he had no intention of returning to the ring.

Moore, who is at least 39, said he was surprised that Patterson punched so hard. 'This boy is a good fighter, and he will probably be champion for a long time,' added Moore.

Patterson's plans are in danger of being upset by a summons to do his Army service, although his manager hopes that he may be deferred on the grounds that he is the sole supporter of a mother, father, eight brothers, a sister, a wife and a new baby.

World records tumble in Sydney relays

By Michael Melford

SYDNEY, WEDNESDAY 5 DECEMBER

Four world relay records were set up, two by the United States and two by Australia, during tonight's athletics match between the British Empire and Commonwealth and the United States. Yet what were probably the most remarkable performances of all will not find a place in any record books.

A fifth world record, one held by Britain, was beaten by 14.6 seconds by the Empire team of milers M. Halberg and N. Scott (New Zealand), I. Boyd (Britain) and J. Landy (Australia). But as they were not of the same country, no record can be claimed under the present laws.

Perhaps even more extraordinary was the long jump. A no-jump by about an inch by the American Olympic champion, G. Bell, spoiled an effort measured at 27 ft 4 in – nearly 8 inches further than Jesse Owens' world record, which has stood since May 1935. Bell won the event with over 26 ft.

The records broken by the United States were in the 4 x 220 yd and the 4 x 880 yd. The first was beaten by one-fifth of a second, the second by over 2 seconds despite a 1 minute 54 second first leg.

The Australian girls broke both world sprint records, though their 45.6 sec in the 440 yd is quite a bit slower than their 400-m time of Saturday.

The United States won their usual victory by 13 events to five (only men's events counting).

Miss Grinham wins gold medal by a touch

By Ossian Goulding

MELBOURNE, WEDNESDAY 5 DECEMBER

The Duke of Edinburgh was among the crowd which watched 17-year-old Judy Grinham, of Neasden, win a gold medal in the women's 100-m backstroke event in the new Olympic record time of 1 min 12.9 sec here tonight.

It was Britain's first Olympic swimming victory since Lucy Morton won the 200-m breaststroke in Paris in 1924. Moreover, it came on a day when we won one silver and two bronze medals for yachting.

Britain's young team of girl swimmers, none of the three over 17, will never want a closer, more thrilling finish than this.

Miss Grinham was clocked home in the same time as the silver medallist 16-year-old Caren Cone, of the United States, and won by the length of her fingers, while Margaret Edwards, who won a bronze medal for Britain, was only one-tenth of a second behind the American girl.

Britain's third contestant, Julie Hoyle, taking part in her first international race, returned the fastest time of her life to take sixth place.

The electric time recorders in use at Melbourne's Olympic Pool showed that all eight finalists finished within 1.1 second of each other.

It was obvious from the very start of the race that Miss Grinham was nervous and unsettled, for she was left trailing a bad last for the first half-length of the 50-m long pool. She and Miss Edwards gradually drew up to the leaders but at the 50-m mark it was Miss Hoyle who turned first.

Miss Grinham always swims a much stronger second length, and sure enough she came ahead after the turn, with Miss Edwards and Miss Cone neck and neck behind. Suddenly, 15 metres from home, her usual sustained

Grinham with her Olympic gold. She went on to win two Commonwealth golds in 1958 in the 110 yd and the medley relay, and a bronze in the freestyle relay.

finishing sprint faltered and it looked as though she was spent. But she came again with a second magnificent burst of speed, hurling herself at the end of the bath to win by a touch.

The manager of the British team, Mr Alfred Price, superintendent of Uxbridge Council Baths, said Britain's triumph was the result of two or three years of hard work – more work than the average swimmer ever dreams of. 'There is no easy road nowadays either to Olympic representation or to an Olympic medal,' Mr Price told me tonight. 'It is work, work, and more work, long after it has begun to hurt so much that you feel you cannot go on. But these girls have done it and are an example to British swimmers.'

SPORT IN BRIEF

OLYMPICS
The XVI Olympiad is marred by political controversy. China withdraw because Taiwan are competing at the Games; Egypt and Lebanon withdraw in protest at the invasion of Suez, and Liechtenstein, Holland, Spain and Switzerland refuse to participate as a mark of disapproval at the Soviet Union's invasion of Hungary.

In the 5,000-m, Vladimir Kuts of the Soviet Union beats Britain's Gordon Pirie into second place; Kuts also triumphs in the 10,000 m where he beats the Hungarian József Kovács in an Olympic record time of 28 min 45.6 sec.

CRICKET
Partnering the phenomenal Jim Laker (see main text) in the Test series against Australia is his fellow Surrey spinner, Tony Lock. In the third Test at Headingley, Laker takes 11 for 113 and Lock seven for 81, and England win by an innings and 42 runs. Lock has taken 100 wickets every year since 1951, and last year took a record 216. A popular chant among the English crowds issues a clear warning to the Australians: 'Ashes to Ashes, dust to dust; if Laker don't get you, Locky must.'

FOOTBALL
Nat Lofthouse of Bolton Wanderers is top-scorer in the First Division with 32 goals.

RUGBY UNION
After the comprehensive 4–0 Test defeat of New Zealand team by South Africa in 1949, the All Blacks score a gratifying 3–1 series win over the Springboks when the South Africans tour New Zealand. New Zealand are assisted by the inclusion at prop of the amateur heavyweight boxer Kevin Skinner.

1956

135

1957

Locke is Open champion again by three shots

By Leonard Crawley

ST ANDREWS, FRIDAY 5 JULY

South African A. D. Locke won the Open golf championship for the fourth time here this evening with a total of 279. His four rounds were 69, 72, 68 and 70. P. W. Thomson, of Australia, the holder, was second at 282, and E. C. Brown, the British Ryder Cup player, who led the field at the beginning of the day, was third with 283.

Locke's performance has not been equalled by any other contemporary player. He is 39 years old and, judging by his play this week, he can win again and again. He had a chance to win here in 1939 and again in 1946, but the 13th hole killed him on both occasions. He had another argument there this morning, but he forgot it and went on to finish in a glorious 68.

When the leaders went out again late in the afternoon the picture soon became clear. Very few could stand the pace. Thomson and Locke remained each with his chance.

Thomson, playing like a magician, without a care in the world, made a three at the long fourth but he missed his second to the long fifth and this cost him a six.

He made no mistake until the 17th, when for the second time in the day a poor tee shot left him in difficulties. This time he took five and then, when his putt of four yards at the last hole failed to drop, the door was wide open for Locke.

Locke went out in 34. A three at the fourth and another at the sixth, when he ran down a long putt of 18 feet, helped him on his way. When he played his second from near the road at the home hole he appeared to be aiming into the dining room at Russacks Hotel.

But he knows better than anyone else where he is going to hit them; his ball came to rest two feet from the hole and the championship was over.

MILESTONES

The first black player to win a Wimbledon singles title was Althea Gibson; the centre court was a far cry from her origins as daughter of a share-cropper in South Carolina. Gibson returned to defend her title successfully in 1958, and also won the US Open in 1957 and 1958.

Crepello's Derby odds are cut to 3–1

By Hotspur

NEWMARKET, WEDNESDAY 2 MAY

Crepello won the 2,000 Guineas clearly on merit today from Quorum and Pipe of Peace, and is now a 3–1 favourite for the Derby. If all goes well with him, he will start at shorter odds on the day of the race.

It is unlikely that Crepello will run again before Epsom, though he may be taken to York to get used to travelling and to have a gallop after racing.

Sir Victor Sassoon, owner and breeder of Crepello, has been a great supporter of English racing for more than 30 years. Today's success was his fifth in a Classic race. He won the Derby with Pinza in 1953, the 1,000 Guineas and Oaks in 1937 with Exhibitionnist, and last year's 1,000 Guineas with Crepello's half-sister Honeylight. Sir Victor is in Nassau, so missed seeing Crepello win a thrilling race.

Lester Piggott rode a cool race on Crepello, and certainly has the temperament for the big occasion. It is the first time he has finished in the first three in the 2,000, and his only previous success in a Classic race was on Never Say Die in the 1954 Derby. To my mind there is no doubt Crepello was a worthy winner, for Piggott had to move him on sooner than he wished in order to avoid interference from Tyrone. Further, Crepello seemed to come down the hill well and, in fact, ran rather lazily, perhaps because he had not had a preliminary race. It was an impressive performance.

On 5 June, Crepello and Lester Piggott won the Derby (right), again beating Pipe of Peace into third.

England just fail to win fabulous Test match

By E. W. Swanton

EDGBASTON, TUESDAY 4 JUNE

This has been a fabulous Test match. Writing a few moments after watching J. D. Goddard and young O. G. Smith fighting for their lives against J. C. Laker and G. A. R. Lock, with the English fieldsmen clustered round them like bees round a honeypot (and with the steel calypso band performing with smiles of relief on their faces in front of the pavilion), I cannot summon the memory or the knowledge of any previous game wherein the fortunes have changed with such utter completeness from one side to the other.

At noon yesterday P. May **(right)** and M. C. Cowdrey came together, as did at Sydney three years ago, knowing that only a day-long stand or thereabouts could bring England back into the match. A day and a half later West Indies surveyed a scoreboard showing 62 for seven, thanking their stars for an escape from defeat which could surely be measured only in minutes.

Laker and Lock set the West Indies batsmen indeed a testing problem enough. The root of the collapse this evening was, however, psychological. The change in events, catastrophic from their angle, combined with the long weary spell in the field made them always likely victims. Two hours and 40 minutes can seem an eternity.

The scoresheet will make it seem that England declared too late, and I believe they could have come in with complete safety half an hour earlier than they did, in fact when Cowdrey

SPORT IN BRIEF

FOOTBALL
For the second year running the Football League try to persuade the League champions not to enter the European Cup. Unlike Chelsea in 1955, however, Manchester United refuse to bow to their pressure. United manager Matt Busby argues that the 'European challenge should be met, not avoided', a position that is vindicated when United beat the Belgian champions Anderlecht 10–0. Manchester United are knocked out of the competition by Real Madrid, last year's winners, who go on to win again this year, 2–0 against Fiorentina.

RUGBY UNION
England win the Grand Slam outright for the first time since 1928. Influential in their victory is the second-row pairing of John Currie and David Marques, who made their debuts last year and will play together in 22 consecutive internationals.

BOXING
In a rematch against middleweight Gene Fullmer (who outpointed him in January), Sugar Ray Robinson, the underdog, manages to land what becomes known in boxing circles as 'the perfect punch'. The speedy hook connects with Fullmer's chin, knocking him out for the first time in competition. It is Robinson's fourth world middleweight title.

CRICKET
After the drawn first Test (see main text), England go on to win the series against the West Indies 3–0. At Trent Bridge Tom Graveney and Peter Richardson put on a record 266 runs for the second wicket, Graveney scoring 258. An elegant batsman, Graveney will score 4,882 runs in his Test career. Despite his talent, Graveney is not always a first choice for the Test side and is not picked between 1959 and 1962, or between 1963 and 1966. He plays his 79th and final Test in 1969.

was out. At this point West Indies could have been asked to bat for just over three hours, with 237 runs standing between themselves and victory. Yet in retrospect a draw seems perhaps the fairest answer, bearing in mind the various West Indian injuries which dislocated them so seriously at the crucial time.

For instance they bowled with the same ball for more than seven hours, since they had no one left to use a new one. In any case no one who has any conception of the strain imposed by an innings of ten hours will be disposed to blame May himself for not declaring earlier. With him I daresay times and figures were a blur in the mind.

May's batting, taking all the circumstances into consideration, deserves all the superlatives, so sadly overworked, which are part and parcel of a modern Test. It was an excellent innings from the technical viewpoint, an exemplary one in point of responsibility. This is the aspect, of course, which merits most praise. It may be

added that only four Englishmen have played bigger Test innings than this 285: Len Hutton, Walter Hammond, Andy Sandham and R. E. Foster, the latter by two runs. As a captain's effort, needless to say, it stands alone.

As to Cowdrey's innings, it had all the attributes of his captain in an only slightly less degree. Now that this remarkable innings has come in a Test at home, he must surely take the unquestioned place in the England side for which his talents qualify him.

The stand of 411 between May and Cowdrey is the highest ever made for England and the third highest in Test cricket. It is the best made by any country for the fourth wicket. May's 285 not out is the highest score ever made by an England captain, beating Hammond's 240 against Australia at Lord's in 1938. It is his own best in first-class cricket and the biggest individual score in all post-war Test matches.

The first Test was drawn.

1957

Fangio battles with two Britons for German race

By W. A. McKenzie

NÜRBURGRING, WEST GERMANY, SUNDAY 4 AUGUST

Juan Fangio, the Argentine, consolidated beyond further challenge his title to the world championship for 1957 when he won the Grand Prix of Germany here today. He was driving a Maserati.

Close on 47 now, world champion three times running before today, after holding the championship once previously, he put up on this 14 miles Eiffel Mountain circuit today the finest demonstration of skill and courage of his career. But he was good enough sportsman to say to me tonight: 'I was inspired, but the inspiration came from the dire necessity of catching two of the finest drivers I have ever raced against – your Englishmen, Mike Hawthorn and Peter Collins.'

Hawthorn took the lead at the start. Close behind lay Collins, with Fangio on his tail. These three had the race to themselves, away out in front of the field. Hawthorn and Collins were signalled to go flat out.

With only two laps to go, the Argentinian received wild applause as he passed the finish of the lap 150 yards behind Collins, who himself was on Hawthorn's tail. Half a mile farther on Fangio passed Collins, and halfway round the circuit squeezed past Hawthorn to finish the lap four seconds ahead. To do this he had put the record for the course to a still new speed of 9 min 17.4 sec on the 20th lap. He took the lead to win by 200 yards.

Ryder Cup triumph

By Leonard Crawley

PUBLISHED MONDAY 7 OCTOBER

The British Isles, led by D. J. Rees, won the Ryder Cup match at Lindrick on Saturday by seven-and-a-half to four-and-a-half matches. Rees himself won both his games and played like a tiger. He has always said that we could, and that we ought to beat the Americans over here, nor does he disagree with the view that it is nearly impossible for any British side to win in America.

His personal contribution to the British victory both as captain and player was immense. Harsh criticisms had been levelled at him overnight by H. Weetman, whom he left out of the singles, and cannot have helped him or his team when they set out to tackle the severe task before them on Saturday morning. It should be added that M. Faulkner, the other member of the side to be left out, raced around encouraging everyone and keeping them up to date with scores all down the line.

Having lost the foursomes by three to one on the first day, five-and-a-half matches were required from the eight singles, and very few people can have had much hope of a British victory.

Rees had every confidence in his men and declared publicly that they could still win. Rees has had a long and distinguished career as a professional golfer, having won everything but the Open championship in the country. Alas he is now in his middle 40s, and cannot conceivably go on much longer, either in Ryder Cup or tournament play. It is nevertheless very pleasant to reflect that such a splendid, indomitable character should achieve his greatest triumph of all leading a British side to victory against America for the first time for nearly a quarter of a century.

The British Isles won six singles, halved one and lost one, and each member of the team is to be congratulated on this truly remarkable performance never previously accomplished by a British side in Ryder Cup matches.

Dai Rees, captain of the British team, drives on the eighth (below), and (left) holding the Ryder Cup.

JUAN MANUEL FANGIO (1911–95)

ARGENTINA'S PREMIER RACING DRIVER, Juan Fangio dominated the early days of the Formula One championship. He was born at Balcarce, near Buenos Aires, on 24 June 1911. As a 17-year-old, he began work as a travelling mechanic on Argentina's long-distance road-races, before deciding to take up the sport himself in 1933. His parents were appalled, but supporters in his home town raised money to buy him a Chevrolet, with which he eventually won two national championships.

Fangio moved to Europe in 1948, where he purchased his famous blue and yellow Maserati. Known by his nickname of Cheuco ('bandy-legs'), he soon became a familiar sight at the major circuits. Accordingly, when the world championship was introduced in 1950, he was invited to drive for one of the leading manufacturers, Alfa Romeo, despite his comparatively advanced years.

Success was not long in coming. Fangio finished second in the opening year, winning the French, Belgian and Monaco Grands Prix. After this, he was virtually unstoppable, taking five of the next seven championships (1951, 1954–7). His tally might have been even higher, but for a horrific crash at Monza, where he broke his neck and was in plaster for five months.

Fangio retired in 1958, taking up a job with Mercedes-Benz. For many, he will always remain the greatest all-round driver in racing history. In addition to his successes in Formula One (he had won 16 world championship grands prix races by the time he retired), he also made his mark in long-distance races, such as the Mille Miglia (a 1,000-mile road-race, run between Brescia and Rome) and the Targa Florio in Sicily.

Lew Hoad wins Wimbledon

By Lance Tingay

WIMBLEDON, FRIDAY 5 JULY

The annals of the lawn tennis championships were distinctively inscribed today. Lew Hoad acquired a status rare in the history of the game by winning the men's singles for the second year running.

On the centre court today, where the grass is burned brown by the sun and worn to smooth bare patches by the battles of the last fortnight, Hoad became a champion plus by beating Ashley Cooper.

And what a beating he gave him! Hoad won by 6–2, 6–1, 6–2 in 56 minutes, and to find a parallel for such a display of inhumanly good power lawn tennis in the final one needs go back to 1932, when Ellsworth Vines, playing then as he never played again, trounced H. W. Austin in eight minutes fewer.

Afterwards Hoad averred that he believed he had once or twice played rather better, citing his defeat of T. Trabert in the Davis Cup challenge round at Forest Hills in 1955 as an example. I also saw that match, and if there be a difference between Hoad's form then and his

expertise this afternoon it was purely academic.

Hoad's service power was tremendous. His returns of service, which were the crux whereby he reduced the unlucky Cooper to ineffectiveness, were fantastic. It hardly seemed possible that eye and muscle could coordinate with such celerity.

One-sided finals are rarely interesting. It would, however, have been a cold-blooded observer who watched Hoad this afternoon and was not stirred by his virtuosity.

Cooper and Hoad (carrying the Challenge Cup) leave the centre court after Hoad's second Wimbledon singles victory in a row. Only two other men had successfully defended their singles titles: Fred Perry in 1935 and again in 1936, and Donald Budge in 1938.

SPORT IN BRIEF

FOOTBALL

Stanley Matthews plays his last game for England aged 42, although he will not retire from League football until 1965. Last year Matthews was the first recipient of the new European Footballer of the Year award.

CRICKET

Guyanan-born Lance Gibbs makes his Test debut for the West Indies against Pakistan, taking 17 wickets in four matches. In his next outing, against Australia, Gibbs takes three wickets in four balls in the Test in Sydney, and a hat trick in Adelaide, finishing the tour with a total of 19 wickets in three matches. In the West Indies' victory over India in 1958, Gibbs takes eight for six in 15.3 overs (though his final figures are eight for 38). Gibbs will go on to enjoy a successful first-class career with Warwickshire from 1967–73.

BOXING

On 29 July, Floyd Patterson defends his heavyweight title for the first time against Tommy 'Hurricane' Jackson. Jackson is floored in the first, second and ninth round; the fight is stopped in the tenth and Patterson declared the winner.

YACHTING

The Admiral's Cup competition is instituted by the 'admiral' of the Royal Ocean Racing Club in Britain, Sir Myles Watt. The perpetual challenge award is a biennial international event in which teams of three yachts take part in two onshore and two offshore yacht races, including the Fastnet Race. The Admiral's Cup will become the most important international ocean racing event in the world. Although the United States' *Carina* wins her second consecutive Fastnet Race, Britain wins the first competition by two points.

1958

Remarkable innings by 21-year-old Sobers

By Michael Melford
PUBLISHED MONDAY 3 MARCH

Garfield Sobers' 365 not out for the West Indies against Pakistan at Kingston, Jamaica, was a remarkable innings in a remarkable context.

Not only was this vast score his first innings of over 100 in a Test match, but it precipitated a unique scene when he made the single to pass Sir Leonard Hutton's Test record of 364. The crowd of 20,000 in Sabina Park swarmed on to the field, and, the West Indies having declared at the useful total of 790–3, carried the hero to the pavilion.

In the tumult they did so much damage to the pitch that the umpires ordered it to be repaired, and abandoned play for the day 55 minutes early.

The tall, left-handed Sobers batted from soon after tea on Thursday until Saturday evening, ten hours eight minutes (or three hours less than Hutton). At 21 he is seven months younger than Hutton was in 1938.

The innings seems to have been attended inevitably by a perfect wicket.

Though this is Sobers' first Test century, his achievement will be no surprise to the many in England who saw him making large scores last summer, particularly in May, who enjoyed his elegant driving, admired his resolution when pinned down by the best bowling, and reckoned him no doubt a great batsman in the making. He averaged 45 during the tour.

Sobers cuts for four runs during his record innings (far left). He was supported by Conrad Hunte, who scored 260. Their second-wicket stand of 446 was five short of the best for any wicket in a Test match – the 451 set by Don Bradman and W. H. Ponsford against England at the Oval in 1934.

England snatch dramatic victory against Wallabies

By E. W. Swanton
PUBLISHED MONDAY 3 FEBRUARY
England 9 pts; Australia 6

The game at Twickenham on Saturday, wherein England beat the Wallabies by a magnificent try scored in the last moments, will be remembered as one of the more extraordinary in the history of the rugby union ground.

The bare facts of the case were enough to impress themselves powerfully on the minds of all who were present, or who listened to the broadcast. England had twice pulled up from behind in spite of the loss of their stand-off half, J. P. Horrocks-Taylor, and the consequent strain on the depleted pack.

Yet in these final minutes (when all except those who had kept a stopwatch check covering the delays for injury must have thought that time was up), the last 14 men summoned their very last reserves of energy to mount a surging attack. P. B. Jackson completed it with a weaving, feinting run that deceived at least three men in his path before he threw himself over in the extreme right corner.

The climax would have been unforgettable in any circumstances. What made it especially so was that the crowd had been roused from unwonted indifference throughout a mediocre first half to an even more unusual fervour of partisanship.

This built up as the second half progressed, and finally expressed itself in hat-waving, cushion-throwing and a thunder of applause such as one scarcely remembers at Twickenham.

J. K. Lenehan, having missed two kickable penalties, scored from a third, and the Wallabies crossed over three points to the good.

The second half started with J. D. Currie going near with a penalty which hit the upright just below the bar. Then M. S. Phillips strode round his man magnificently and by sheer speed tore his way to the line.

The temporary laying out of P. H. Thompson by young Lenehan occurred just afterwards, and with the scores now level, the temperature rose both on the field and off.

Currie missed a fairly easy penalty, and then another longer one, awarded when K. J. Donald obstructed Thompson. J. Butterworth was brought down heavily, and there was some protracted first aid before he was lifted on to a stretcher. Then, just as one was wondering what on earth England could do now, Butterfield helped himself off the stretcher and carried on.

With a quarter of an hour to go, a desperate relieving kick by R. E. G. Jeeps was fielded by T. G. Curley, who took the ball on the run and dropped a lovely goal from out on the left. Three points down again.

England now made the rally which warmed all hearts, and kept the crowd keyed up to the highest pitch. In a furious onslaught on the Wallaby line, first R. W. D. Marques then Jackson and finally Thompson were pulled down just short, England throwing the ball about and backing one another up in the most thrilling way.

Five minutes after Curley's goal came another penalty against the Wallabies. J. G. G. Hetherington steered the ball just over the bar. Level again, and it was the Wallabies turn to thrust back.

But it was England who struck the final blow. After Thompson had been thrown into touch just outside the 25, England secured from the throw-in and the ball was flicked fast across the line to Jackson, who, apparently hemmed in, set off on the run that set the seal on the day. What commotion! And what a ferment when Mr R. C. Williams, whose handling of a difficult game had earned the admiration of all, blew his hard-worked whistle for the last time.

Munich air disaster: 21 dead

SPORT IN BRIEF

GOLF

Arnold Palmer takes the first of his record four US Masters titles at Augusta – he will win again in 1960, 1962 and 1964. At 28 he is the youngest winner of the tournament since Byron Nelson 21 years ago. Palmer will also win the US Open in 1960, and the British Open in 1961 and 1962, and will become the first golfer to earn $1 million in prize money from the tour.

SPEED SKATING

I. Voronina from the Soviet Union wins the second of her four women's world championship titles. She was champion for the first time last year, and will take the title again in 1962 and 1965.

FOOTBALL

Hearts win the Scottish League by 13 points from Rangers with a record 132 goals. The joint top-scorers in the Scottish First Division – with 28 goals apiece – are both Hearts players, Jimmy Wardhaugh and Jimmy Murray. Hearts have only suffered one League defeat this season.

RUGBY UNION

Hooker Ronnie Dawson makes his international debut against Australia in the city of his birth, Dublin. Dawson scores a try to ensure Ireland's first victory against a touring side, by nine points to six. Within a year Dawson has secured the captaincy of the British Lions on their tour of Australia and New Zealand. He leads his team to two wins – 17–6 and 24–3 – over Australia, though the Lions only manage one win in four Tests in New Zealand. Dawson will earn 27 caps for his country in his six-year career.

From Percival Banyard and John Adams,
Daily Telegraph *special correspondents*
MUNICH, THURSDAY 6 FEBRUARY

Seven players and three officials of Manchester United football team were among 21 people who lost their lives today when the British European Airways Elizabethan airliner bringing the team home from Belgrade crashed at Munich airport. Matt Busby, the team manager, and eight players are in hospital. Busby, who is also Scotland's World Cup team manager, has been put in an oxygen tent in a critical condition.

The plane was on charter. It crashed in a snowstorm while taking off at the third attempt late this afternoon. The Manchester United team were returning to Britain from Yugoslavia, where they had drawn 3–3 with the Red Star team in a European Cup match.

Of the 44 occupants of the plane, who included 11 sports writers, 20 were killed in the crash, and one, Frank Swift, former England goalkeeper, died in hospital. Swift was travelling as a guest of the Manchester United team.

Eyewitnesses at the airport said there was ice and snow on the runways. BEA confirmed in London that the

As snow continues to fall, officials and firemen stand amid the wreckage of the airliner that had been carrying the 'Busby Babes' home. Duncan Edwards died two weeks after the crash; Jackie Blanchflower and Johnny Berry were among the survivors who never played again. Matt Busby survived his terrible injuries.

plane first taxied out to take off, but returned. The reason for the return was uncertain. Shortly afterwards it taxied out again and attempted to take off but again returned. Describing the crash a BEA spokesman said: 'The plane passed over the threshold of the runway and ran into a wooden fence. The port wing-tip hit a small building and the plane then caught fire.'

BEA last night issued a complete list of the 21 dead in the crash: Footballers: Eddie Colman, Roger Byrne, Mark Jones, Billy Whelan, Tommy Taylor, Geoff Bent, David Pegg. Officials: T. H. Curry, trainer; H. Whalley, coach; Walter Crickmer, secretary. Journalists: Tom Jackson, Archie Ledbroke, H. D. Davies, Eric Thompson, Henry Rose, George Follows, Alf Clarke. Others: Frank Swift (former English goalkeeper), B. P. Miklos (travel agent), W. Satinoff, W. T. Cable (steward).

1958

Moss wins, but Hawthorn champion by one point

By W. A. McKenzie,
Daily Telegraph *motoring correspondent*
CASABLANCA, SUNDAY 19 OCTOBER

Stirling Moss today won the Morocco Grand Prix in a British Vanwall at a record speed of 116.2 mph. His close rival for many years, Mike Hawthorn, finished second in a Ferrari, but won the 1958 world championship by one point.

Fangio, the previous champion, retired this year. The manufacturers' world championship goes to Mr Tony Vandervell, maker of the Vanwall cars, which have won six grands prix this year.

Hawthorn could have lost the championship to Moss had he failed to finish within the first three places. He appeared to be making sure of the title, ignoring the temptation to fight out the race with the Vanwall. But he had to be careful not to fall too far behind and lose second or third place. He came 84 seconds behind Moss.

It was obvious from the start that the two were out to win the championship. But their tactics were very different. Moss was eight points down on Hawthorn before today's race, the last this season counting for the championship. To win that championship Moss would have had to finish first, scoring eight points, record the fastest lap, worth one point, and Hawthorn would have had to be fourth or worse.

Moss not only led from the second lap to the finish, but topped the lap speed record too. However, Hawthorn cantered in a comfortable second, scoring six points. But owing to the system of counting each driver's six best races only, he got the championship by one point, 42 to Moss's 41 points.

After the race Hawthorn **(below)** said that he was very happy and proud to become the first Englishman to win the world championship.

England girls smash world relay record

From our swimming correspondent
CARDIFF, FRIDAY 25 JULY

England's girl swimmers won the most thrilling final of the Games tonight when the 4 x 110-yd medley team beat Australia by a second in 4 min 54 sec. This was three seconds inside the world record.

The English girls led all the way. They knew they had to put their last swimmer, Diana Wilkinson, five seconds ahead of Australia's world record holder Dawn Fraser to be certain of victory. It was a desperate struggle, but they achieved their target magnificently.

Starting on the backstroke leg was Judy Grinham. She equalled her own world record, set up on Wednesday (1 min 11.9 sec) to put Empire breaststroke champion Anita Lonsbrough 4.3 seconds ahead of Barbara Evans.

Miss Lonsbrough increased the lead to 5.3 seconds. Then came Christine Gosden, who faced Empire butterfly champion Beverley Bainbridge. Australia gained a little, but the English girl touched exactly five seconds ahead.

Then the battle really began. Miss Fraser, fighting desperately for Australia, knew she must achieve the near impossible to carry her side to victory. The 'impossible' she did, swimming 110-yd freestyle in 60.6 sec (0.8 seconds inside her own world record) but it was not enough. For 14-year-old Diana Wilkinson, rising magnificently to the occasion, improved her personal best with a time of 64.4 sec.

Never before has England held a world swimming relay record of any kind.

DID YOU KNOW?

Denis Law, aged 18, made his debut for Scotland in a 3–0 victory against Wales. Law went on to become – with Kenny Dalglish – Scotland's equal leading scorer to date. Law scored 30 goals in 55 international games, while Dalglish took 102 internationals to reach the same total.

World Cup winners Brazil are real champions

STOCKHOLM, SUNDAY 29 JUNE

Brazil won the World Cup for the first time here today when they beat Sweden in the final with a brilliant exhibition of fast, artistic football. As Mr Arthur Drewry, president of FIFA, said in presenting the gold Jules Rimet Trophy to Bellini, the Brazilian captain, it was a game 'worthy of the world championship'.

The bronze medals were won by France, who beat Western Germany, the holders, 6–3 in Gothenburg.

Today's final opened encouragingly for Sweden when Liedholm scored in the fourth minute. Brazil soon struck back with a goal by Vava in the eighth minute, and they took the lead in the 32nd minute with a replica of the first goal, Vava again finishing off a move by Garrincha.

Though a goal down at the interval, Sweden were not out of the game and their attack still looked dangerous. But the Brazilians kept a firm grip on the match, and went further ahead with a great goal by Pelé. He lobbed the ball over the Swedish centre half before breasting it down and hitting it on the half-volley. This came after nine minutes of the second half, and 13 minutes later Mario Zagallo cut in to score the fourth.

Sweden got their second goal through centre forward Simonsson in the 79th minute, but just before the final whistle Pelé headed in a fifth for Brazil.

The Brazilians celebrate their 5–2 World Cup win over Sweden in Stockholm. Seventeen-year-old Pelé made his World Cup debut in the quarter finals, scoring six goals in the last three rounds.

Elliott runs fastest mile in 3 min 54.5 sec

By Jack Crump
PUBLISHED THURSDAY 7 AUGUST

Herbert Elliott **(below right)**, the 20-year-old Australian, set up a world mile record of 3 min 54.5 sec at Santry Stadium, Dublin, last night. The first four were all inside the official record of 3 min 58 sec, and Elliott finshed 15 yards ahead of his fellow-Australian Mervyn Lincoln. Elliott knocked 2.7 seconds off the previous world's best recorded time, set up by D. G. Ibbotson at the White City, which is still awaiting official recognition.

Albert Thomas, a third Australian, ensured a fast pace from the start by covering the first quarter mile in 58 seconds. He reached the half-mile in 1 minute 58 seconds. He finished in 3 min 58.6 sec.

Lincoln, who had run on Thomas's heels for much of the second lap, took the lead in the third lap with Elliott just behind him. The enthusiasm of the Irish crowd certainly seemed to inspire the runners.

Just after the three-quarter mile mark, reached in 2 minutes 59 seconds, with Lincoln in the lead, Elliott made his effort and went smoothly to the front. From then on it was a one-man race. He finished 15 yards ahead of Lincoln.

It had been considered that the limit for the one mile was likely to be 3 min 55 sec. But Elliott's time clearly establishes him as the greatest miler of all time.

Lincoln, who finished second and who has been a keen rival of Elliott for a long time, must consider himself unfortunate in finishing only second in the wonderful time of 3 min 55.9 sec.

SPORT IN BRIEF

HOCKEY
Hockey player Carsten Keller makes his international debut for Germany. Both his parents were international players; his father won a silver medal in the 1936 Olympics. Keller will play 123 matches for his country, represent Germany in three Olympic Games and, as captain, lead his team to the gold medal at the 1972 Munich Olympics.

FOOTBALL
In the Scottish League Cup final, Celtic score a staggering 7–1 win over Rangers. Two-nil up at half-time, Celtic's Billy McPhail scores a hat trick in the second half, adding to two goals from Neil Mochan and a penalty from Willie Fernie to ensure a crushing defeat over their old Glasgow rivals.

HORSE RACING
Fred Winter is champion jockey for the fourth time. He first won the title in 1951–2, when he rode 121 winners, a new record. He was last year's winning jockey in the Grand National, riding Sundew, and will win again on Kilmore in 1962. He will also ride two Gold Cup winners – Saffron Tartan in 1961 and Mandarin in 1962. After his retirement in 1964, Fred Winter will enjoy great success as a trainer.

RUGBY UNION
France take part in their first official tour to South Africa, and win one match 9–5 and tie the other, winning the series 1–0. The superb victory creates enormous excitement at home.

CRICKET
In the 1958–9 Test series against England in Australia, C. C. McDonald scores 520 runs in the series, the first Australian batsman to score more than 500 since Arthur Morris notched up 696 in 1948. Richie Benaud takes 31 wickets and A. K. Davidson 24 wickets in Australia's 4–0 win (with one match drawn) over England.

1958

1959

Brian London's defeat

By Donald Saunders
PUBLISHED MONDAY 5 MAY

Brian London, whose dream of becoming world heavyweight champion was shattered by the talented fists of Floyd Patterson on Friday night, will discuss his future during the next few days.

My advice to London is: Forget America. Catch the first plane home and make your peace with the British Board of Control.

The Board's opinion that the former British champion's challenge to Patterson was not in the interests of boxing was upheld when the battered and bemused London lay sprawled on the ring with his head cushioned on his left arm as the full count was tolled over him early in the 11th round of one of the most one-sided fights I have ever seen.

I understand that a queue of interested parties is eagerly waiting to sign him. I can already visualise their sales campaign: 'Here is the British guy who went 11 tough rounds with the world champion.'

MILESTONES

England's captain and centre half Billy Wright was the first footballer in the world to win 100 caps for his country. Wright had missed only three of England's 103 matches since the resumption of international football after the Second World War.

PUBLISHED FRIDAY 23 JANUARY

Mike Hawthorn, who was killed yesterday aged 29 in a road accident, had many escapes on the race-track during his spectacular progress to the forefront of British drivers.

World champion at the age of 29, Hawthorn announced in December his retirement from grand prix racing. In a Ferrari he won the title at Casablanca last year by a single point after coming second to his friend and rival, Stirling Moss, in the Morocco Grand Prix.

Hawthorn was deeply affected by the death of his friend and fellow driver, Peter Collins, in the German Grand Prix in August last year. Hawthorn, driving in the race, saw Collins hit a bank and turn over. Many felt that the loss of his friend was a factor in Hawthorn's decision to retire.

Tall, fair and genial, Hawthorn was immensely popular with his fellow-drivers. In 1952 he leaped into prominence by beating the great Argentinian driver, Juan Fangio, at Goodwood. Hawthorn drove BRM cars for a time, but in 1956 signed for Ferrari, the Italian firm, and by victories in race after race in many parts of the world established himself as a fearless and first-class driver.

W. A. McKenzie, *Daily Telegraph* motoring correspondent, writes: Mike Hawthorn was the most colourful and unpredictable personality in postwar motor racing. He was practically unheard of until the Easter Holiday meeting at Goodwood in 1952.

In a Cooper Bristol, and in the company of many of the world's leading drivers, he won two races and in a third finished second to the Argentinian, Gonzales.

His entry into grand prix racing was just as precipitate. He joined the Ferrari team and won the French Grand Prix at Rheims in 1953. For over 150 miles Hawthorn and Fangio were never more than a length apart. Hawthorn won. But the race was so close that Fangio and the equally famous Alberto Ascari and Froilan Gonzales all finished within less than three seconds of the winner.

One knew then that the big, flaxen-haired young Englishman had the courage and skill of a champion. He was 23 at the time.

Hawthorn was in the news again at Le Mans in 1955, when his car was involved in an accident with Pierre Levegh's Mercedes-Benz which disintegrated and killed 83 spectators.

I think that is the only time I ever saw Hawthorn's nerve shaken. He leapt out of his car, saying that he would not drive again. He was almost dragged back, and with the Mercedes-Benz opposite the pits an inferno, he went on to win the race.

Last year he lost his closest friend Peter Collins. His teammate Luigi Musso crashed fatally a few weeks earlier, and Archie Scott-Brown, another friend, lost his life during the season. Finally, Peter Whitehead died in a speed trial.

The wreckage of Mike Hawthorn's 3.4-litre Jaguar car lies beside the Guildford bypass (below). The car skidded on the wet road, hit a lorry and crashed into a tree.

England wreck disappointing Scots

By Donald Saunders
PUBLISHED MONDAY 13 APRIL
England 1; Scotland 0

Bobby Charlton came of age at Wembley Stadium on Saturday. With the instinctive timing of a great showman, this soccer prodigy from Manchester United chose English football's historic headquarters to demonstrate that he is ready to take his place among the honoured names of Britain's national winter game.

For Charlton it was a notable triumph, a victory for character as well as skill. I had seen him play many fine games. But never had I seen him so completely control a match as he did on Saturday. Every time Charlton moved on to the ball danger threatened Scotland and the pulse of the crowd quickened. He seemed to be everywhere, finding an unexpected opening, bursting through the astonished Scottish defence, or moving instinctively on to that patch of turf where the ball was next due to arrive.

Indeed, without Charlton this game would have been memorable only for the gallant stand of Bobby Evans, Scotland's defiant centre half, and the triumphal

departure of Billy Wright astride the shoulders of two teammates at the conclusion of his 100th international.

The Scots failed entirely to find the form expected of them. Their defence was sound, but their forwards rarely moved as a unit. The match became a battle of wits between England's attack and the Scottish defence.

We had to wait until the 60th minute for England to score the goal they had so often threatened. And what a glorious goal it was. Douglas curled a centre into the penalty area and there was Charlton, flinging himself upwards and forwards to head the ball down past the astonished Brown.

Several times thereafter they almost increased their slender lead. But the goal England needed for safety would not come. Thus Scotland were in the hunt with a chance right to the end. This narrow squeak may encourage England to remember in future that goals play an extremely important part in football matches.

Carried by teammates Ron Clayton (on left) and Don Howe, England captain Billy Wright celebrates victory against Scotland and the winning of his 100th cap.

1959

1959

Grand Prix won by Tony Brooks

By W. A. McKenzie
BERLIN, SUNDAY 2 AUGUST

Tony Brooks, of Britain, driving for Ferrari, won the Grand Prix of Germany on the Avus circuit today. Ferraris were also second and third.

Driving as leader of the Ferrari stable, he won both sections of the race, which was run in two halves of approximately 150 miles each. He completed the 309.5 miles in 2 hr 9 min 31.6 sec, an average speed of 143.6 mph.

The circuit is made up of two long straights with a steeply banked corner at the northern end, where the French driver Jean Behra was killed yesterday in the Berlin sports car Grand Prix.

In the first half of the race Brooks led for 24 of the 30 laps, and averaged 146.7 mph. He covered the second half, when there was no longer any need to press hard, at 134.961 mph.

Jack Brabham, of Australia (Cooper), leader in the world drivers' championship, retired in the 15th lap with engine trouble.

The BRMs were not suited to this kind of circuit, but put up a creditable show. The BRM of the German Hans Hermann spun on a turn and hit the straw bales. Hermann had an amazing escape. His car turned over after hitting the bales and he was flung out. The car then turned over several times and was so badly smashed that it is unrepairable.

Brooks made the fastest lap at 149.0 mph. This is a record, beating that of Juan Manuel Fangio of Argentina, 139.1 mph, set up in 1954. It earns Brooks an extra point for the world drivers' championship. He gets eight for winning. The world championship order now is: Jack Brabham, Australia, 27 points; Tony Brooks, Britain, 23; Phil Hill, America, 14. There are three more races which qualify for the championship: the Portuguese, Italian and American Grands Prix.

MILESTONES

France began a period of domination of the Five Nations tournament when they recorded their first ever outright win in the rugby union championship. The triumph comes in the last season in international rugby for Lucien Mias, their inspirational captain.

By Lance Tingay
PUBLISHED MONDAY 6 JULY

The 1959 lawn tennis championships, which ended at Wimbledon on Saturday, will stand bolder in the annals of the game than was expected by those who forecast an undistinguished meeting.

Not only did it produce two very good singles winners, but the emergence of A. Olmedo, a Peruvian, and Miss Maria Bueno, a Brazilian, as champions, emphasised a shift from the Australian–United States lawn tennis axis.

South America have produced notable players before, the Argentine E. Morea, the Brazilian A. Vieira, the still prominent Chilean L. Ayala, and, best of all, the professional F. Segura of Equador. Among women players I can only think of the Chilean, Miss Anita Lizana. Yet even among those aware of the growing strength of Latin-American nations, who would have been bold enough to declare the time would come when South America would claim both the singles champions at Wimbledon?

The great success of the 19-year-old Miss Bueno brought a chorus of 'I told you so.' It was obvious in Rome early last year, when she had her first European success, that a potentially splendid player had arrived.

While many have talent, it was clear that Miss Bueno, slight and trim, had genius. Her fluency and penetration of shot, produced from easy grace, is effortlessly brought about. Timing, not musclepower, is her secret, and that is something that can never be taught.

Brazilian Maria Bueno collects the Venus Rosewater dish from the Duchess of Kent after her 6–4, 6–3 victory over American Darlene Hard in the final.

The final in which she beat Miss Darlene Hard (who took her second defeat there with the air of jolly sportsmanship one expects from her) was too one-sided to rank as a great match. The outstanding aspect of Miss Bueno's performance was, I suppose, her service sting, for this produced a dominance normally only associated with men's matches. It is doubtful if ever a woman served better. The effect was a minor thunderbolt.

Defeat by Moore could be Bassey's last fight

From our special correspondent
LOS ANGELES, THURSDAY 20 AUGUST

Hogan Bassey has probably fought his last fight. He said today he was still thinking things over, but in the opinion of a lot of people besides George Biddles, his manager, he is fight-tired and should retire. Everything about the Nigerian's diastrous meeting here last night with Davey Moore for the featherweight title indicated that, quite suddenly, he had lost the urge to fight in the deep, hard sense of the word. Except for a period in the fifth round, he never looked like taking the title back from Moore.

Yet the end came as a shock. He had been resisting Moore's aggressions stylishly until the close of the ninth round, and in the early moments of the tenth he had Moore flurried. Then the fire died, and Moore began jabbing and punching him almost at will until he was wearily dodging blows in a daze as the round ended.

Yet he was still securely on his feet and, sportsman that he is, he turned and patted Moore's back as if to compliment his opponent before he turned and went to his corner.

Few expected the next development. As the bell sounded Bassey stayed sprawled on his stool. The referee went over and asked Biddles whether his man was coming out. Biddles said he wasn't. Bassey settled the matter dismally by telling the referee he did not wish to go on.

Then it could be seen that Bassey had indeed lost both physically and psychologically. His right eye was closed to a slit, blood was flowing from a cut beneath it, but, more significantly, his features were set in the lines of a man of sensitivity who knew within himself that the game was up.

George Biddles sensed that too. 'He has had too many injuries in too many fights,' he said. For a man of 27, Bassey's record of 67 fights tells its own story.

Nottingham Forest too good for Luton

By Frank Coles

PUBLISHED MONDAY 4 MAY

Nottingham Forest 2; Luton Town 1

The strange Cup final injury hoodoo, to which I drew attention on Saturday morning, again settled over Wembley and nearly ruined what had held every promise of developing into a spectacular struggle between Nottingham Forest and Luton Town, teams which were appearing at Wembley for the first time.

Fortunately, and as a gesture of justice to the victims, the result was not affected when Roy Dwight, Forest's lively right-winger, lay writhing in pain after a collision, was carried off and was found in Wembley hospital to be suffering from a broken right leg. The sad incident happened at the 33rd minute, after Forest had treated the crowd to a dazzlingly brilliant display of fast, controlled football. It cast a blight over two-thirds of the game. The sight of the men from Nottingham struggling

desperately to hold on to their two-goal lead afforded pleasure to neither friend nor foe.

Luton were in trouble from the first kick. The trite phrase, 'Class will tell', fitted the situation perfectly. Forest were the skilled craftsmen in their half-hour of glory, and while the two wingers, Dwight and Stewart Imlach, appeared to share principal honours for their full-scale attacks along the flanks, the side's strength really stemmed from the mastery imposed by the wing halfbacks, Whitefoot and Burkitt. The measure of Forest's early quality can be gauged from the fact that the game was 50 minutes old before Luton got in their first worthwhile shot.

What a tragic occasion it was for poor Dwight, the winger Fulham must be sorry they let go last year. A fine marksman, he had twice completed the hat trick this season and now showed his merit with a rousing first-time shot taken on the run which gave Forest the opening goal. Every time Dwight stole into the middle he looked a potential scorer, and fate could not have dealt a blow more cruel than when this happy wanderer became a stretcher case after colliding with Brendan McNally.

The third oldest club in the country – born 1865 – Forest have now won the precious trophy for the second time after an interval of 61 years.

David Pacey scores a consolation goal for Luton (below), but Forest were worthy winners of the Cup. Captain Jock Burkitt collects it (left) from the Queen.

1959

1960

Moss wins Grand Prix of Monaco

By W. A. McKenzie,
Daily Telegraph *motoring correspondent*
MONTE CARLO, SUNDAY 29 MAY

Stirling Moss, driving a Lotus-Climax, won the Grand Prix of Monaco here today in one of the most car-wrecking Formula One races in the history of the sport. At the end of the 200 miles race only four of the 16 cars that started were still running. The rest went out of the race after 'shunting' straw bales or walls or, the chief cause, transmission failure. Five of them 'motored in' afterwards to finish.

The course, which winds up and down the hilly streets of Monte Carlo, calls for 20 gear changes a lap, 2,000 in the 100-lap contest. It is as exhausting on the driver as on the car.

It was the first European race counting towards the 1960 world championship. Moss, who collected no championship points in the first championship event in the Argentine, picked up eight points by his win here. The Argentinian Grand Prix winner, Bruce McLaren, of New Zealand, earned eight points then. He scored another six today for finishing second to Moss and still leads in the championship. Moss is second and Cliff Allison of Britain third. McLaren, in a Cooper-Climax, also put up the fastest lap. At 73.13 mph, it was a record for this circuit.

Moss started off in third place behind Jo Bonnier of Sweden, BRM, and Jack Brabham of Australia, Cooper. By the fifth lap Moss had overtaken Brabham, and on the 20th lap had slipped past Bonnier to lead the field.

DID YOU KNOW?

Following Bill Slater's success in the FA Cup, and in winning the League championship in 1954, 1958 and 1959, he was honoured with the Football Writers' Footballer of the Year award. Unfortunately, he was also dropped from the England side on the same day.

A delighted Bill Slater, the Wolves captain, is carried by his teammates as he holds aloft the FA Cup. It was Wolves' fourth FA Cup victory – they also won the trophy in 1893, 1908 and 1949.

Real Madrid hit seven past Eintracht

By a special correspondent
GLASGOW, WEDNESDAY 18 MAY
Real Madrid 7; Eintracht Frankfurt 2

Real Madrid, winners of the European Cup every year since its inception, are still the holders. But they were given many anxious moments here at Hampden Park tonight, where only by football which rivalled the brilliance of the evening sun were they ultimately able to subdue the challenge of the German champions Eintracht Frankfurt.

Lacking such personality players as Ferenc Puskas, Francisco Gento and Alfredo di Stefano, Eintracht made up for such deficiencies by a display of

Hungarian exile Puskas scores Real Madrid's sixth goal.

fighting teamwork which repeatedly had Real reeling. It was a measure of Madrid's greatness that they could absorb the German attacks and the loss of an early goal without ever losing the power to launch their own counter-blows. Gento on the left was almost unstoppable, while Luis del Sol, di Stefano and Puskas forged and shot with unceasing venom. There was just no questioning Madrid's mastery. On this last performance they must be classed a team without peer.

At the end the entire Madrid team cantered round the track to a continuous roar of cheering seldom, if ever, equalled on any football ground. The 130,000 spectators had seen a brand of football never before displayed in Scotland.

Wolves win FA Cup

By Frank Coles
PUBLISHED MONDAY 9 MAY
Wolves 3; Blackburn 0

Norman Deeley, whose two brilliantly taken goals handsomely confirmed my prediction that he would be the Wolves 1960 FA Cup winner, will be the toast of the Black Country long after other incidents of the latest Wembley occasion are forgotten. His triumph in the role of Happy Wanderer in an attack which constantly changed pattern was also one more practical proof of the sound judgement of Wolves manager Mr Stanley Cullis as team selector.

Blackburn Rovers' misfortune in facing the second half without their left back David Whelan, who was carried off with a fractured shin bone after colliding with Norman Deeley three minutes

before the interval, was the cruellest of blows with the near certainty to follow of an unequal finish. But making light of the handicap, the Rovers fought back magnificently, and their three inside forwards, Peter Dobing, Derek Dougan and Bryan Douglas, entertained the crowd to some of the most delightfully constructive football of the game.

Only those with a close-up view of what happened realised that left half Mick McGrath had put the ball through his own goal to give Wolves the precious lead. The Wolves goal had two more lucky escapes after the interval, but the issue was settled at the 69th minute. Deeley was the scorer. A cross from Horne was pounced on by the right-winger from the edge of the penalty area and he promptly netted. Deeley's second and Wolves' third goal came two minutes from time.

The outburst of booing by Blackburn's supporters as Wolves' captain and his colleagues stepped up to receive the Cup and medals from the Duchess of Gloucester was completely unjustified and an injustice to the winners.

History made as Patterson regains title

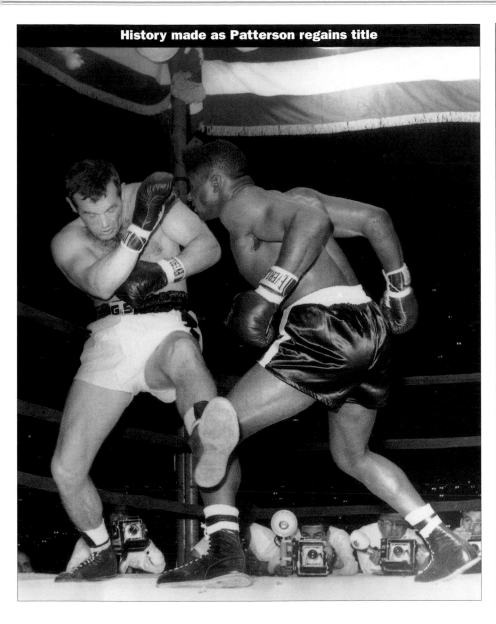

By Donald Saunders

NEW YORK, MONDAY 20 JUNE

Floyd Patterson, a 25-year-old from New York, made boxing history at the Polo Grounds here tonight. After one minute and 51 seconds of the fifth round he knocked out Ingemar Johansson of Sweden to become the first former holder of the world heavyweight championship to regain his title.

Patterson's victory was decisive beyond all possible dispute. Several minutes after he had been counted out Johansson was still unconscious. His stool had to be brought from his corner to the centre of the ring and he was then lifted on to it for further attention from his seconds and a doctor.

Patterson did all the early attacking, tearing into his opponent from the first bell. Twice Johansson was driven to the ropes and a red mark appeared over his right eye.

But Johansson retaliated with a hard right which just missed Patterson, who was fighting with amazing

Floyd Patterson first took the heavyweight title in 1956 when he knocked out Archie Moore. He defended it four times before losing to Ingemar Johansson in 1959 in the third round. He lost it for the second and final time in 1962 to Sonny Liston.

confidence for a man who had been knocked down seven times in their previous meeting.

Having taken three of the first four rounds with his speedy, skilful boxing, Patterson continued to take the initiative in the fifth. His left jabs repeatedly rapped Johansson in the face, and then suddenly a fierce left hook sent the champion flying to the floor with his heels flying in the air. He was up at eight – but Patterson tore after him.

Johansson looked desperately weary as the challenger tried to finish him off. The champion held on grimly, but could not escape another solid left hook to the chin and was sent sprawling to the canvas. There he lay helpless as the count was called over him.

SPORT IN BRIEF

CRICKET
South Africa tour England in the summer and England win the series 3–0 with two matches drawn. Geoff Griffin, a South African bowler, is 'called' for throwing. In the second Test at Lord's, he is 'called' 11 times, but nevertheless manages to finish off the England innings with a hat trick, taking the wickets of Mike Smith, Peter Walker and Fred Trueman. Despite this, England win the match by an innings and 73 runs.

MOTOR CYCLING
John Surtees wins his fourth 500-cc world title and his third 350-cc crown, with MV. He also makes his debut in motor racing in a Formula Junior Cooper for Ken Tyrell. Later he drives a works Lotus into second place in the British Grand Prix in only his second Formula One race. Less than a month later he wins the Isle of Man senior TT race on an MV. He now concentrates on driving cars, just beating Graham Hill and Jim Clark to win the Formula One world championship in 1964.

GOLF
The Centenary British Open at St Andrews is won by a 100–1 outsider, Kel Nagle from Australia. After opening rounds of 69 and 67, he is two behind leader Roberto de Vicenzo at the halfway point., but scores 71 for a two-stroke lead in the third. In the fourth round, postponed until the following day because of rain, Nagle retains his lead until Arnold Palmer, pursuing his attempt to win all four majors in the same year, cuts it to one shot. Nagle putts an eight-footer at the 17th and pars the 18th to take the trophy.

YACHTING
Finisterre, owned by C. Mitchell, wins the Bermuda Race for the third consecutive time. The race takes place biennially over a 635-mile course, starting from Newport, Rhode Island.

1960

1960

Two Britons killed in Grand Prix

By W. A. McKenzie,
Daily Telegraph *motoring correspondent*
SPA, BELGIUM, SUNDAY 19 JUNE

Two British drivers, Chris Bristow, 22, and Alan Stacey, 26, were killed in the Belgian Grand Prix motor race today. This followed serious accidents, in yesterday's practice, to Stirling Moss, 30, and Michael Taylor, 25.

The race, won by the Australian Jack Brabham, reigning world champion, at an average of 133.631 mph, was one of the fastest on any road circuit in the history of motor racing. Today's tragedies will arouse fresh controversy over the future of the sport.

Stacey's death seems almost certainly to have been due to a freak accident. A senior official of the circuit confirmed that a bird hit Stacey's face, smashing his goggles. It was at the spot called the Fountain of the Bird that Stacey, driving his Lotus at almost 140 mph, crashed. The car left the path, hit a bank and burst into flames. He died in the ambulance.

Bristow was well up, lying seventh in his Cooper, when, in the 19th lap, he took the long, fast bend known as Burneville at over 130 mph, accelerated and overtook another car. Then he seemed to lose control. The car shot off the road and somersaulted three times.

Chris Bristow was a promising driver, and had several successes. One of these was in a Cooper-Borgward which he drove as a member of the British Racing Partnership, winning the important John Davy Trophy at the August Bank Holiday meeting at Brands Hatch, Kent, last year, when he beat such stars as Jack Brabham and Roy Salvadori.

The accident in which Bristow was killed happened on the bend at which Stirling Moss in a Lotus came to grief yesterday. Moss has both legs fractured just below the knee, three broken ribs, a badly cut and broken nose, two black eyes and several superficial cuts.

DID YOU KNOW?

American athlete Wilma Rudolph won three gold medals in the 1960 Olympics – in the 100 m, 200 m, and running the anchor leg in the 4 x 100-m relay race. Her achievement was the more extraordinary since she had suffered from polio as a child.

Second British gold medal

By Michael Melford
ROME, WEDNESDAY 7 SEPTEMBER

Shortly before 7 o'clock this evening, Donald Thompson came into the floodlit Stadio Olimpico, weary but triumphant at the end of the 50-km walk. He completed a lap of the track and Britain had won their second gold medal of the 1960 Games.

Thompson had taken the lead just before halfway, but for the next two hours he could not shake off the gallant Swede Ljunggren, winner at Wembley in 1948, third at Melbourne in 1956 and now nearly 41 years old. Only in the last five kilometres along the road beside the grey Tiber did he open up a slight lead. He won in the end by 60 yards in 4 hr 25 min 30 sec, which beats the Olympic record by some two-and-a-half minutes.

Thompson, a 27-year-old fire insurance clerk from Cranford, Middlesex, who was turned down from National Service because of sinus trouble, had recorded the fastest time in the world this year, but little was known about the form of the Russians. In fact, the only Russian in the first six was fourth.

The Briton's victory was really won in his bathroom. It was there that for months on end Thompson sealed the

Don Thompson strides home 17 seconds ahead of John Ljunggren of Sweden. Italy's Abdon Pamich was third.

door and raised the temperature to a humid 90 degrees before going through a rigorous training schedule. No one in Britain's team could have tried harder to acclimatise himself to the Rome summer, and he reaped a worthy reward.

Miss Lonsbrough keeps strictly to plan

By Michael Melford
ROME, SUNDAY 28 AUGUST

Anita Lonsbrough's gold medal in the 200-m breaststroke last night was won after the sort of race which has normally unexcitable middle-aged citizens on their feet shouting like schoolboys. As a tonic and example to others who are to follow it was priceless.

Success here is very much a matter of producing your best at the right moment. Miss Lonsbrough **(below)** not only broke the world record but carried out with wonderful composure and self-discipline what cannot have been an easy plan.

In the previous round on Friday, Wiltrud Urselmann went off at a great pace, but seemed of somewhat suspect stamina over the later stages. Nevertheless she was nearly a second and a half faster than the English girl, and had the moral advantage of having relieved Miss Lonsbrough of the 200-m and 220-yd world records which she set up last year. It must have needed great patience and restraint to let the German build up an apparently unassailable lead, but Miss Lonsbrough bided her time

and swam her out of it over the second 100 metres.

The new champion, only the second British Olympic swimming champion (after Judy Grinham) that Britain has produced in 36 years, is 19. She was not in the best of health earlier in the season but has been in great form in recent weeks.

Like most of the English girls here she did not get the best of starts. The German was as fast away as she was on Friday and was a yard ahead at 25 yards. Halfway down the second of the four lengths she must have been three yards ahead of Miss Lonsbrough.

On the third length the race changed completely. Anita Lonsbrough almost closed the gap and turned no more than two feet behind the German who must have been suffering all the agonies of the fugitive as the hunt draws close. Halfway down the final length they were level, until the English girl was nearly a yard ahead with a beautifully judged race surely won.

In the last ten strokes, however, the German fought back, and there was an awful moment when it seemed that the British girl's hard-earned victory might be going to slip away at the last moment. But she held on and was clearly the winner.

Elliott runs away with 1,500-m title

By Michael Melford

ROME, TUESDAY 6 SEPTEMBER

Two world records were broken in half an hour today, one of them by Herb Elliott **(seen leading, below)**, who won the 1,500 m in a way in which he has always looked capable of winning it.

He won by over 15 yards, or nearly three seconds, from the Frenchman Michel Jazy, in 3 min 35.6 sec, which beat by two-fifths of a second his own world record made at Gothenburg during his European visit of 1958.

The other record was broken in the 400 m. The winner was the American Otis Davis, who beat the German Carl Kaufmann by inches. They became the first humans ever to run 400 m in under 45 seconds.

The first six in the 1,500-m final all beat Ronald Delany's Olympic record of 3 min 41.2 sec. Elliott has unusual gifts of strength harnessed to an equable temperament and sound judgement, but it was nonetheless a fine feat to present him at his best on the big day. Few, I imagine, would be prepared to dispute that on his form today he is the greatest middle-distance runner the world has known.

Drawn in lane three, Otis Davis did not start as fast as the South African, M. Spence, immediately outside him. Kaufmann, in the inside lane, may also have been a yard up on him after 200. Coming round the bend, however, he accelerated so swiftly that he had a lead of two yards coming into the straight. With 50 yards to go, Kaufmann was slowly closing the gap and Davis, tiring fast, was ominously upright. Yet somehow the American, with considerable resolution, kept going, and though Kaufmann threw himself at the tape, Davis had beaten him to it. The electric timing showed the difference between them as only one-fiftieth of a second.

Murray Halberg of New Zealand won the 5,000-m gold medal in Rome; he is flanked by Hans Grodotzki of Germany (left) and Kazimierz Zimny of Poland, who came second and third respectively.

SPORT IN BRIEF

OLYMPICS
An unknown Ethiopian soldier, Abebe Bikila, running barefoot, wins the marathon in an Olympic record time, claiming the first ever gold medal for his country.

CRICKET
Despite a slightly changed format, Yorkshire CCC win the county championship for the second successive year, with a total of 17 victories (out of 32 matches played). Fred Trueman takes 132 championship wickets; Ray Illingworth, Don Wilson, Mick Cowan and Brian Close take more than 60 each. Close also hits his highest county score, 198, at the Oval against Surrey.

MOTOR RACING
Jack Brabham wins five consecutive grands prix – the Dutch, Belgian, French, British and Portuguese – to take the world championship title for the second successive year in a revolutionary rear-engined Cooper-Climax. Teammate Bruce McLaren, who a year ago became the youngest driver (at 22) to win a grand prix, is second, and Stirling Moss third. British rear-engined cars have dominated the championship.

BOWLS
David Bryant wins the English singles title, aged 29, at Mortlake, beating Tom Fleming in the final. The son of an international bowler, Reg Bryant, David is unusual in taking the sport up at such an early age; most people who play the game are much older. He goes on to win the title a total of six times, and is world singles champion twice, world indoor champion three times, and Commonwealth singles champion four times.

1960

1961

England seek deputy for Greaves

By Donald Saunders

PUBLISHED MONDAY 17 APRIL

Is George Eastham, Arsenal's £45,000 inside forward, to be groomed as successor to Jimmy Greaves in the England team? Or, if the job becomes vacant, will it be given to young Johnny Byrne, of Crystal Palace? These questions arise from yesterday's announcement of the 19 players for next month's tour of Portugal, Italy and Austria and the possibility that Greaves will not be available to England if he joins Milan.

Both Eastham and Byrne are in the tour party as, of course, are Greaves and his ten colleagues who tore the Scots to shreds at Wembley on Saturday. Barring injury, Greaves is certain to play against Young England, against Mexico at Wembley and in all three tour games. But whether he will regularly be available next season, when England are engaged in two World Cup qualifying ties and are putting the finishing touches to their plans for the final stages of that competition, is another matter.

I understand that Milan have agreed to release Greaves whenever England want him. But as Wales have discovered since John Charles joined Juventus, Italian clubs have ways of breaking promises without appearing to do so. Indeed, the possibility that Milan will be as uncooperative to England as Juventus have been to Wales is probably team manager Mr Walter Winterbottom's only worry as he looks forward confidently to the World Cup finals in Chile next year. Cautiously he referred to the case of Juventus and Charles, then added: 'Unfortunately, players like Greaves do not grow on trees.' If they do have to replace this free-scoring little wizard, their choice is likely to rest between Eastham and Byrne.

Jimmy Greaves joins Milan for a fee of £100,000.

Scotland's footballers pay dearly for out-of-date ideas

By Donald Saunders

PUBLISHED MONDAY 17 APRIL

England 9; Scotland 3

As Johnny Haynes was borne in triumph off the Wembley pitch by jubilant England colleagues on Saturday, Frank Haffey, Scotland's goalkeeper, set out, head bowed, alone, on the long journey to the welcome darkness of the tunnel. Long before these two tired men had unlaced their boots at the end of Wembley's most amazing football match, they had become the central figures of a heated debate that can never be settled. Always the English will believe the genius of Haynes earned glorious victory; Scotsmen will for ever blame Haffey's shortcomings for ignominious defeat.

As a neutral Welshman, let me suggest Haynes's genius was aided by Haffey's shortcomings, then quickly add that England would have destroyed Scotland on Saturday whoever had been in goal. Their defence calmly repulsed early, optimistic Scottish raids; their forwards darted eagerly in and out of gaps only they had noticed.

It was Continental artistry backed by British thrust. And it contrasted so sharply with the Scotsmen's stereotyped, out-of-date football that England wisely began to discard in the autumn of 1958. With Bobby Robson linking perfectly with Haynes, England's football flowed from defence into attack, while Scotland wasted the brilliant unorthodoxy of Denis Law and the speed of Wilson by persisting with the old-fashioned pass to the wings and the inevitable cross to the far goalpost. By the end of the first half-hour their colleagues up front had gained such complete mastery over a too-rigid defensive system that a match-winning margin of three goals had been established.

Indeed Haynes and his men were so sure of themselves that even a couple of quick Scottish goals early in the second half did not throw them out of stride. They remained calm and confident. Within a few minutes they had halted all threat of a Scottish revival by scoring again themselves through Bryan Douglas.

A foul on Robson by Law so incensed England that they decided there and then to grind their opponents into the turf. The most devastating attack I have ever seen launched by an England forward line brought five goals in 14 minutes, the last four of them in a mere seven minutes. Amid this rush of English goals, we almost failed to notice one Quinn sneaked in for Scotland. But, then, it really made no difference.

Greaves scores England's third goal and his second. He went on to make a hat trick, one of a record six hat tricks that he would score for his country.

Australia scrabble to victory in fifth Test

By R. A. Roberts

MELBOURNE, WEDNESDAY 15 FEBRUARY

What a medical friend described as the 'coronary series' ended in another fantastic finish here this evening when Australia, after looking likely winners most of the day, faltered under pressure and scrambled in by two wickets.

In an unbelievable climax, even to those of us who have come to accept the unexpected in these tremendous games, Australia, having scored 200 of the 258 they needed to win, lost four more wickets, stumbling to 257. K. Mackay played one ball, then missed the next, which went through for the winning bye.

There was also another remarkable umpiring incident. When Australia needed four to win Grout shaped to late-cut Valentine. The ball ran towards the sightscreen as the batsmen crossed for two runs and the wicketkeeper, Alexander, pointed animatedly at a ball lying on the ground.

He was appealing that Grout was either bowled or had hit his wicket. Umpire Egar, at the bowler's end, consulted Umpire Hoy, at square leg, who indicated he had not clearly seen what had happened. The runs were allowed to stand and at least two of the West Indies' fielders flung themselves to the ground in vexation.

Captain Frank Worrell quickly ordered them to their feet and Grout was out in Valentine's next over without adding to his score.

The closeness of the result, however, indicates the importance of the two runs in dispute in the final count.

These happenings illustrate how so little divided the two teams and, indeed, it was a pity one side had to lose. Only a series like this could have provided such stupendous drama with the ball finally being swallowed by the advancing crowd singing 'For he's a jolly good fellow' as Worrell presented the trophy bearing his own name to a no doubt grateful Richie Benaud.

Australia won the series 2–1, with one match tied and one match drawn.

MILESTONES

Antonio Albertondo of Argentina achieves the first non-stop double-crossing of the English Channel when he swims from St Margaret's Bay near Dover, Kent, and back again in a time of 43 hr 5 min.

Football League give in: strike is off

By David Miller

PUBLISHED THURSDAY 19 JANUARY

The football debacle dissolved yesterday, and the way is now clear for the game to advance. The players have gained their final, and most important, concession. The strike on Saturday is off, League matches are on: the players have won.

At the joint meeting with the Football League and representatives of the Football Association at the Ministry of Labour, agreement was at last reached on the retain and transfer system, the outstanding point of difference. The alterations bear little difference from those negotiated on 21 December. The simplicity, and obviousness, of the new system make the past eight months' squabble seem sadly unnecessary.

Fundamentally, the players have been granted the right to change their club, the clubs the right to demand a transfer fee. The seven points drawn up yesterday protect both these essential freedoms.

Once a player has now been placed on the transfer list on 31 May, if he refuses to re-sign, the only problem lying between him and another club is the satisfactory settlement of the amount of the fee with the new club. The new scheme will also prevent a player 'choosing' his club. Once he has signified his determination to leave, he will be obliged to sign for any one of those clubs (he may choose which) which should meet the figure asked by the transferring club. At the same time a player can never again be retained on no wage, and he is assured of his retaining wage bearing some relation to the previous one.

It is indicative of the thorough, fair way in which the PFA have always conducted their cause – despite statements to the contrary, there is no questioning the advance their chairman, Jimmy Hill, has accomplished for soccer – that they suggested point No. 1 (no transfer during the term of a player's contract except by mutual consent of club and player), believing that a player should not be able to wriggle out of his contract before its expiration.

Jimmy Hill (with beard) talks to the press following a meeting to discuss proposals for ending the players' strike threat.

BOXING

Joe Brown, aged 35, retains his lightweight title for a record 11th time with a points victory over Bert Somodio. He won the title in August 1956, having been a professional fighter for ten years, and defends against top-class opposition. Nicknamed 'Old Bones', he will lose his title, also on points, to Carlos Ortiz in April 1962. He continues to fight, though, taking part in 45 more professional bouts and winning only 20 of them before hanging up his gloves in 1970. He later becomes a cab-driver in New Orleans.

ATHLETICS

Basil Heatley, the 27-year-old Bedworth gardener, joins the ranks of world record-holders when retaining his AAA title for ten miles at Hurlingham on 15 April. His 47 min 47 sec was 25 seconds better than Zatopek's time for the distance, which had stood for ten years, and more than 31 seconds better than the European record, also set by Heatley in this race last year.

MOTOR CYCLING

Mike Hailwood, aged 21, wins the 250-cc world championship on a Honda. At 20 he was the youngest rider to join a works team. He also wins three Isle of Man TT titles in one week – the senior, the lightweight and the ultra-lightweight.

CRICKET

Hampshire become county champions for the first time in their history when they beat Derbyshire by 140 runs. Hampshire's medium-fast bowler Derek Shackleton turns in a magnificent performance, taking six wickets for 39 runs.

1961

1961

Spurs complete the Double

By Donald Saunders

PUBLISHED MONDAY 8 MAY

Tottenham Hotspur 2; Leicester City 0

As Danny Blanchflower accepted the FA Challenge Cup from the Duchess of Kent at Wembley on Saturday afternoon, Len Chalmers lay on the treatment table in Leicester's dressing room, receiving attention to a badly injured right leg. That, in essence, is the story of how Spurs achieved the Double. Had Chalmers not been hurt in a clash with Allen after 18 minutes, Blanchflower might not have become the first captain this century to lead his team up the steps of the royal box to collect their Cup-winners' medals only a week after they had become League champions. That point will be argued heatedly for a year or two as each Cup final comes round. Then, when precise details of a disappointing match have been blurred by time, all that will remain clear in the memory is the indisputable fact that Spurs in 1961 created soccer history.

It could be said, with some justification, that they did not on Saturday look worthy of so great an honour. But during a long, exacting season they have sometimes scaled the heights of soccer artistry and never have they been less than efficient. Does it matter, therefore, that they completed the second half of the Double with their poorest performance of the season? Evidently Leicester did not think so. As Blanchflower and his men ran jubilantly round the pitch with the Cup held high, the ten survivors of Leicester's gallant battle against overwhelming odds lined up at the tunnel entrance to pay their tribute to their conquerors and a great achievement.

Two-and-a-half million spectators watched Spurs in their bid for the League and Cup titles: an average crowd of 67,766 attended the seven Cup games, the 42 League matches attracted a total of 2,037,671 spectators. The combined total of 2,512,034 is the greatest number of spectators in British soccer history to watch a club in League and Cup in any one season.

Stirling Moss wins Monaco Grand Prix

From W. A. McKenzie,

Daily Telegraph *motoring correspondent*

PUBLISHED MONDAY 15 MAY

The first of the 1961 world championship series grand prix races goes to a British driver and a British car. Stirling Moss, now 31, won the Grand Prix de Monaco today in one of the hardest battles of his career. Driving the privately owned Lotus, entered by Rob Walker, he finished 3.6 seconds ahead of the leader of a team of factory-entered Ferraris from Italy. With about 40 bhp above the power of the Lotus they finished in second, third and fourth places. A German Porsche was fifth.

Race enthusiasts from all parts of Europe came to see this contest. It was the first since the international grand prix formula was changed from an engine limit of 2½ litres to 1½ litres. They wanted to know whether the change would slow the sport to the point of ruining it. Instead they found themselves gripped for the whole of the 100 laps of this exhausting 1.9 miles 'round the houses' circuit, and found the winner averaging 70.5 mph, the highest race average in the 19 years' history of the contest.

Stirling Moss crosses the finishing line in Monte Carlo.

All the British cars were handicapped by the change in the grand prix formula. On the other hand, the change was ideally suited to the highly developed 1½-litre engines of Italy and West Germany. Perhaps on a faster circuit these foreign cars would be bound to succeed, at least until a British race sponsor can catch up on the development of smaller power units for the new formula. But here today the tortuous course gave them less advantage, and that advantage was resolved by the brilliant driving of Stirling Moss.

DID YOU KNOW?

Gary Sobers was one of three West Indies cricketers drafted in to Australian teams in their quest to wrest the Sheffield Shield from eight-times champions New South Wales. Sobers topped the averages for South Australia, but they failed to halt a ninth New South Wales triumph.

Palmer outclasses Player at St Andrews

By J. G. Campbell
ST ANDREWS, TUESDAY 4 JULY

With an impressive display of long, straight driving and a whole series of pin-splitting second shots, the great Arnold Palmer, of the United States, gained a decisive victory over Gary Player, of South Africa, in their $10,000 television golf match here today. Rounding off a polished performance with a brilliant run of three successive threes, Palmer holed the Old Course in 70 strokes, in a cold and troublesome northerly wind of considerable strength. Severely out-distanced and failing to hole his usual number of putts, Player took 75.

Thousands of holidaymakers watched the fun intermittently throughout the day, but as a contest it was as good as over after some two hours, by which time the carnival of camera crews and technicians had arrived at the fourth green. Here Player, who had taken the lead at the first, took three putts and completed a disastrous turnover of five strokes against him in the space of three holes. He fell further behind at the sixth, where Palmer got his second birdie three, and went six in arrears at the seventh, where he again took three putts. It was obvious that the fault did not so much lie with his putting as with his second shots, which were frequently so wide of the target as to leave him with insuperable problems on the huge and rather rough greens.

Player reached the turn in some four hours with a score of 41 against Palmer's 36. There the players, the press, the cameramen and hordes of technicians mercifully had a half-hour break for refreshment. St Andrews had never seen anything like this. Cameras were everywhere, purring, whirring, clicking. Palmer was less affected by the machine-shop atmosphere than was Player. He had the advantage that he was longer from the tee, and frequently lay out flat on his back, using his enormous golf bag as a rough pillow, while Player waited as patiently as he could for the tractors to nudge the unwilling crowd inch by inch from their objectives as they backed into position for the next 'take'. Just as the unfortunate South African was preparing to play his shot, someone was sure to run out of film.

At the start of the inward half Player made a determined effort to close the gap. But his counter-attack was repulsed as Palmer almost knocked the flag sticks from the holes with marvellously accurate iron shots.

Palmer leaves tonight for the Open at Birkdale.

Palmer chips onto the green at the British Open at Royal Birkdale; he won this tournament as well.

St Helens wins rugby League Cup

By Frank Chapman
PUBLISHED MONDAY 15 MAY
St Helens 12 pts; Wigan 6

The rugby League Cup final at Wembley on Saturday had sped by for 61 minutes with neither side having possessed more than a three-point lead when Large vindicated the decision of the St Helens selectors to recall him at right centre.

Four men took part in a 60-yard passing move, ending with Tom van Vollenhoven scoring a try, but Large did most to earn St Helens a deserved win over their more Wembley-experienced opponents. It was St Helens' second Challenge Cup success. Vollenhoven scored near the posts, and Austin Rhodes's conversion put St Helens 10–4 ahead at a vital moment when the next scorers were most likely to become winners.

After half-time Wigan enjoyed ten minutes of dominance, dictating play as clearly as they had in the first 20 minutes of the match. The warmest day of the year failed to evaporate the spirit of the St Helens pack. The rear trio were splendid grafters: Dick Huddart earned the Lance Todd Trophy as the game's best player.

In the 31st minute Huddart gave Alex Murphy a clear run through to the line. And he originated the match-winning try, carried on by Murphy and Large, whose final skilful inside pass gave Vollenhoven his chance.

Rhodes converted and soon kicked a penalty to make certain for St Helens. His three goals came out of ten attempts. Fred Griffiths kicked as many for Wigan; with as many chances he would have harvested victory for Wigan.

SPORT IN BRIEF

FOOTBALL

Jimmy Greaves, unable to settle in Milan and unhappy about his international prospects with England, is brought back by Spurs for £99,999, to avoid involving him in the added pressure of being Britain's first £100,000 player. This label is attached instead to Denis Law, who moves from Manchester City to Torino. He fails to stay long in Italy either; Manchester United pay a British record £115,000 to bring him back.

GOLF

The Ryder Cup is held in Lytham in Lancashire; matches are now played over one round instead of two, and the number of doubles and singles matches are doubled. Forty-nine-year-old Dai Rees leads Great Britain and Ireland for the fourth time. Rees first played in a Ryder Cup match in 1937 when he beat the great Byron Nelson and, with Charles Whitcombe, managed to halve his foursome against the awesome Americans Gene Sarazen and Densmore Shute.

FOOTBALL

With the maximum wage of £20 per week in the winter and £17 in the summer abolished as from the start of this autumn's season, Fulham offer their star player and England captain Johnny Haynes an unheard-of £100 a week in an effort to persuade him not to go to Italy. They are unable to match Milan's offer of £100,000, but Haynes decides to stay in England anyway.

RUGBY LEAGUE

New Zealand begin their tour with an excellent 29–11 win over Great Britain at Headingley. New Zealand lose the next two Tests, however, and only manage eight wins in 20 fixtures during the tour.

1961

1962

Goal-hungry England in World Cup

By Donald Saunders
SANTIAGO, SUNDAY 3 JUNE

The sun is shining at Coya today, the clouds of despondency have lifted from the England camp and a place in the quarter-finals now beckons Walter Winterbottom's men.

This transformation follows the impressive 3–1 victory over Argentina at Rancagua yesterday. It began indeed from the first moment of this hard, exciting battle when we saw that this was an England side in a far different mood from the one which went down to Hungary two days earlier.

They came on to the field determined to make amends for Thursday's drab display. The short period between the first two games had worried Mr Winterbottom but it turned out to be to their advantage.

They did not have time to brood over the failure against Hungary, but the period was short enough to leave them still smouldering angrily about the criticisms of those who had watched on Thursday.

Consequently, the tenseness that helped ruin their game two days earlier was replaced by firmness of purpose. They, and the excellent Russian referee, Latcychev, made it clear that if the Argentines tried to turn the match into a brawl, the penalty would be severe.

Their opponents were obliged to accept this ruling. The result was a good game of football in which England mastered one of the most useful sides out here.

Today the Chilean press described England's exhibition as the most fluent football seen since the campaign opened. Most of the World Cup ties have been defensive battles.

By contrast England went looking for goals from the start and maintained the search almost to the end, when minds and bodies were desperately weary.

In the quarter-finals England lost to Brazil 3–1.

DID YOU KNOW?

Edvaldo Izidio Neto, better known as Vava, of Brazil, was the only player to score in successive World Cup finals: he netted two in 1958 against Sweden and one against Czechoslovakia in 1962. He also shared in the 1962 'golden boot' award for most goals scored in the tournament.

Yugoslavs take lead in ending rough play

By Donald Saunders
SANTIAGO, MONDAY 4 JUNE

Yugoslavia have given a brave lead to the other 15 World Cup nations here in a drastic attempt to end the rough play which is threatening to ruin the competition.

Today they called their inside right, Mujic, before them and asked him to explain an incident which took place at Arica last week and which culminated in a player being sent off the field. They are evidently taking a strong line to curb their players and prevent further trouble arising. Let us hope one or two other countries, notably Italy, will follow this example and discipline their players. We might then see more football and less violence during the rest of the tournament.

It is highly significant that the five Communist countries have been among the best-behaved over here. With them I would bracket Brazil, Colombia, England and Mexico.

The villains of the piece so far have been the Italians. Indeed soccer as a whole is getting more than a little tired of this country which has contributed little to the game except scandal in recent years. Having lured some of the world's best players to their clubs with vast sums of money, they come out here with a team that is as representative of Italy as Spain's cosmopolitan collection of stars is of that country.

In a World Cup marred by violence and controversy, the match between Chile and Italy (which Chile won 2–0) was the most highly charged, with the players indulging in punching, kicking and arguments with the referee. By round two about 50 World Cup players had been injured; four were in hospital.

No cheers for Larkspur in chaotic Derby

By Hotspur (B. W. R. Curling)
EPSOM, WEDNESDAY 6 JUNE

The Derby, run in perfect June weather, was wrecked today by the falls of seven horses on the long hill down to Tattenham Corner. Victory among the survivors – and it seemed rather a hollow one – went to Larkspur, owned by the American Mr Raymond Guest, ridden by the Australian Neville Sellwood, and trained in Ireland by Vincent O'Brien.

Larkspur, a 22–1 chance and the outsider of O'Brien's two runners, was out clear a furlong from home and won comfortably by two lengths from the Boussac colt Arcor, who came from almost last to take second place close home from the fading Le Cantilien, with Escort fourth.

The sight of six riderless horses passing the stands stunned most of the vast crowd to silence, and there was more concern for the missing jockeys, lying perhaps seriously injured on the course out of view of the stands, than excitement over the winner.

There have been some sad stories to report in the 183 years' history of the Derby – the favourite Angers breaking his leg two years ago, and the race spoilt by a suffragette in Aboyeur's year (1913) – but there has been nothing as ghastly as the debacle on the hill on this sunny June afternoon.

It seems probable, but by no means certain, that Romulus, runner-up in the 2,000 Guineas, struck into the heels of a horse in front of him, bringing down Crossen. The favourite, Hethersett, was certainly brought down by the

In their two games to date they have been involved in the worst brawls of the competition, against Germany and Chile. The moral would seem to be that pampered stars who sell their nationality have no loyalty to any country or to the game which has made them rich.

It must be admitted that the Italians are the main target of the Chilean crowd for local political reasons. Consequently some of their vicious, ill-tempered actions are provoked. But it is time they learned to control themselves on the pitch. Not that the Italians are the only

bad boys out here. A growing list of casualties indicates that the theme so far is never mind the ball, get the man. Apart from Doubinski, of Russia, a Swiss player and Colombia's captain have broken bones. Two Spaniards have been sent home with severe injuries, and may soon be followed by another. One Argentinian is in hospital, an Italian has a broken nose, and two Bulgarians will be unable to take any further part in the competition. To these can be added many bumps, bruises, stud-marks and damaged muscles.

PELÉ (1940–)

PELÉ, THE BRAZILIAN FOOTBALLER, is widely regarded as the most skilful player in the history of the game. He was born Edson Arantes do Nascimento, in the township of Três Corações. The use of a one-word professional name is common among Brazilian footballers, while in Europe he was also known by the nickname of the 'Black Pearl'. His father, Dondhino, had been an unsuccessful soccer player, and as a result Pelé's youthful ambitions to follow in his footsteps were fiercely resisted by his mother.

In spite of this, he joined his first club, the Bauru Athletic Club of juniors, at the age of just 14. Two years later, he joined the famous Santos team, remaining with them until 1974. Under their

guidance, he developed the silky ball skills that would delight spectators round the world. 'Too many players think of a football as something to kick,' Pelé said. 'They should be taught to caress it and to treat it like a precious gem.'

Pelé made his debut for Brazil in 1957 and played a prominent role in their victorious World Cup campaigns in 1958, 1962 and 1970.

Pelé retired in 1974 and Santos dropped their number 10 shirt, realising that no other player could wear it with such distinction. Two years later, however, money troubles coaxed Pelé back into the game, and he ended his career in the US, playing for New York Cosmos.

SPORT IN BRIEF

RUGBY LEAGUE
Billy Boston **(above)** tours Australia with the British team, scoring 22 tries. He will play his last international match next year, when Great Britain thrash France 42–4 at Central Park in Wigan. Once dubbed 'the Peer of Wigan', Boston scores a total of 560 tries in his career, and plays in six Challenge Cup finals.

CRICKET
In the winter tour to India and Pakistan, Peter Parfitt scores his first Test century for England. England win one and draw two matches against Pakistan. Nari Contractor leads India to their first series win over England, with two Tests won and three drawn. During Pakistan's tour of England in the summer, Parfitt tops the averages with 113.33, scoring three hundreds. England take the series with four matches won and one drawn.

FOOTBALL
Tottenham Hotspur lose to Benfica in the semi-final of the European Cup. Trailing 3–1 from the first leg in Lisbon, Spurs put up a stirring display at White Hart Lane in front of 65,000 fans, but even Dave Mackay, Danny Blanchflower and Jimmy Greaves, who has a seemingly good goal disallowed, cannot quite make up the deficit. Spurs go out 4–3 on aggregate.

prostrate Romulus, and Pindaric in turn by Hethersett.

The others to fall were the rank outsiders Changing Times, Persian Fantasy and King Canute II, who broke a leg and had to be destroyed on the spot where he fell.

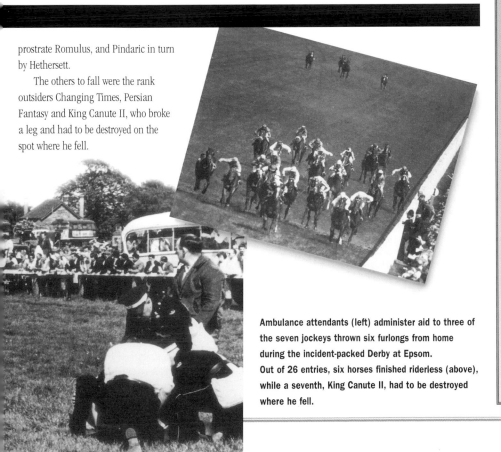

Ambulance attendants (left) administer aid to three of the seven jockeys thrown six furlongs from home during the incident-packed Derby at Epsom.
Out of 26 entries, six horses finished riderless (above), while a seventh, King Canute II, had to be destroyed where he fell.

1962

Rod Laver lands Grand Slam

From our own correspondent
NEW YORK, MONDAY 10 SEPTEMBER

Rod Laver completed his sweep of the world's four major amateur lawn tennis championships today for the first Grand Slam in men's tennis since Donald Budge, of America, in 1938.

In the final of the United States championship, Laver, 24, defeated his Davis Cup teammate from Australia 6–2, 6–4, 5–7, 6–4. Emerson was the holder.

Laver had defeated Emerson in the final of the Australian and French championships, and at Wimbledon, where Emerson had to default owing to injury, Laver beat Mulligan of Australia.

Laver was a sensation in the first two sets, with dazzling shots that brought gasps of approval from the crowd of 6,500. He was never really pressed though. Emerson got two breaks in the third set to put temporary breaks on the rout.

Rod Laver with the Wimbledon men's Challenge Cup; he went on to complete the Grand Slam.

Anquetil wins Tour de France

From our own correspondent
PARIS, SUNDAY 15 JULY

Jacques Anquetil **(below)** today won his third Tour de France and Tom Simpson finished sixth. They held these positions, first and sixth, when the 94 riders started this morning on the final stage of 168 miles from Nevers

to Paris. But whereas the last day is traditionally a 'promenade', with nothing much happening until the riders embark on the final miles into Paris, the 1962 race proved an exception.

After 100 miles there was a crash involving six riders, including three of the most notable men in the race, Charles Gaul (Luxembourg), Anquetil and Simpson. Fortunately none was badly hurt and they were quickly on their machines again, but it was an anxious moment for Anquetil and Simpson, who nearly had three weeks of great work wiped out.

The finishing sprint of the stage at the Parc des Princes is usually an exciting sight with riders jockeying for position on the steeply banked track. Today the stage finished in near chaos. Three riders came in with a one-minute lead over the main group, with Beneditti, of Italy, winning.

The main pack of 80 however slithered all over the rain-soaked track and Anquetil all but landed with his leader's yellow jersey in a pool of water. Simpson cautiously rode the stipulated lap on the grass just inside the track.

'Now the hard work starts,' said Simpson as his manager handed him his programme of races for the rest of the month. After his feat in taking over the *maillot jaune* [for one day], Simpson has been booked to ride in a series of remunerative road and track races beginning tomorrow at Evreux.

Arnold Palmer wins Open golf championship

By Leonard Crawley
TROON, FRIDAY 13 JULY

Arnold Palmer, of the United States, won the Open championship here this evening for the second year in succession and this time in the record total of 276; and he won it by six clear strokes from Kel Nagle of Australia.

If ever there was a great winner, it was Palmer today; and if ever there was a gallant loser it was Nagle, who finished in 282. Nagle won the Centenary Open at St Andrews in 1960, beating Palmer on the American's first visit to this country by two strokes. So Palmer has again had his revenge.

The previous best totals in the Open were by Peter Thomson at Royal Lytham in 1958 and Nagle at St Andrews in 1960, each with 278.

Palmer's victory here, as with many others in the long list of Open championships, was based on a magnificent third round of 67 to beat the record for the course by two strokes. Palmer's golf all day was of a brand no other player in the world that I know is capable on a great seaside course running quite fast and bumpy.

I cannot resist the temptation of pointing out that at about the same time as the unhappy Gary Player of South Africa arrived in New York today protesting at the unfairness of Old Troon as the cause of his failure to qualify in the championship, a far greater golfer triumphed over it with a record score likely to stand for a generation or more.

The American, Phil Rodgers, tied for third place with Brian Huggett, of Romford, in 289, Huggett being the only British player to finish in the first seven. That is a depressing thought, but all due credit to Huggett for a great performance.

The final shots in the championship were played in the middle of the most fantastic crowd scenes as 30,000 people pressed forward in a galloping mass.

Palmer was almost pushed into the clubhouse, while Nagle, caught in the mass, was cheered by the excited thousands. Then Palmer, trapped in a narrow passage of the clubhouse, could not move.

As people pressed in around him, one man was pushed through a window, a woman fainted and about ten people were pushed into a bunker by the side of the 18th green.

Sonny Liston wins title in two minutes six seconds

By Donald Saunders

CHICAGO, TUESDAY 25 SEPTEMBER

Sonny Liston became the new heavyweight champion of the world at Comiskey Park tonight by knocking out Floyd Patterson in only two minutes six seconds.

The fight was over almost before it had seemed to begin. Patterson had looked poor as he tried to grab and hold early in the first minute. Then Liston let go with two clubbing rights to the body. These clearly hurt Patterson and before he could recover he was caught with a right uppercut to the jaw. He seemed to stagger to the ropes and hold on with one arm and was a sitting target for the tremendous left hook to the chin. Down went the champion, rolling over on to his right side. There was never a hope of his rising. Indeed, he was still lying on his side as the count reached ten.

Pandemonium broke out at the ringside as dozens of Liston's supporters tried to reach the ring. The police managed to prevent many of them

getting under the ropes, but it was fully ten minutes before the ring was properly cleared. Then Patterson, now apparently completely recovered, walked away to the dressing room to reflect on the fact that he had been beaten. Not since Jersey Joe Walcott was stopped by Rocky Marciano in 1953 had a heavyweight fight ended in a first-round knock-out.

Floyd Patterson (below right) signs an agreement to defend his world title against Sonny Liston. Liston beat him (above) in the third fastest time in boxing history.

1962

SPORT IN BRIEF

FOOTBALL
Ipswich Town under Alf Ramsey win the First Division title in their first season in the top flight. They are only the fourth club to win the Second and First Division championship titles in consecutive years.

CRICKET
At Lord's, Fred Trueman (Yorkshire) leads the Players and Ted Dexter (Sussex) the Gentlemen in the last Gentlemen v Players match. Of the 137 matches played, the Players won 68, the Gentleman of England 41, and 28 were drawn. Next year the MCC will decree that all cricketers are now players, removing the distinction between amateurs (Gentlemen) and professionals (Players) that was the basis of these fixtures.

EQUESTRIANISM
Anneli Drummond-Hay wins Badminton on Merely-a-Monarch. A brilliant horse, one National Hunt trainer suggests he would be capable of winning the Grand National. As women are not yet allowed to compete in Olympic three-day eventing, Drummond-Hay becomes a show-jumper, though a near-fatal illness means that Monarch misses the showjumping event in the 1964 Olympics. In the 1968 European championships, however, Merely-a-Monarch and Drummond-Hay take the European title.

LAWN TENNIS
Karen Susman wins the women's singles title at Wimbledon, beating the unseeded Vera Sukova 6–4, 6–4. The latest sensation, 20-year-old Margaret Court (later Smith), is beaten in the first round by the young Billie Jean Moffitt (later King). Despite this setback, Margaret Court wins three of the four Grand Slam championships this year: the Australian, French and US Opens.

1963

Rangers land the Double

By Denis Lowe

GLASGOW, WEDNESDAY 15 MAY

Rangers 3; Celtic 0

Hampden Park was again the scene of a glorious Rangers triumph tonight when they beat Celtic, deadly rivals over the years, in the Scottish Cup final replay before a huge crowd of more than 120,000.

This success gave Rangers the cup for the 17th time – which equals Celtic's record in the competition – and also landed them the League and Cup double.

Rangers were always the masters. The ebullient Jim Baxter, a creative left half who was a model of coolness and dependability, prompted his eager forwards with superb passes. A lively attack, forcefully led by Jimmy Millar, posed continual problems for Celtic defence.

Ralph Brand, an inside left with a keen eye for a chance, scored twice in the seventh and 71st minute. His first came after a delightful four-man move, the second from a 25 yards drive. Wilson scored Rangers' other goal in the 44th minute after the Celtic goalkeeper, Frank Haffey, had parried yet another shot from Brand.

Clay defeats Cooper in fifth round – as predicted

By Donald Saunders

PUBLISHED WEDNESDAY 19 JUNE

Cassius Clay, the Louisville Lip, added another accurate prediction to his long list at Wembley Stadium last night, when he stopped Henry Cooper, the British heavyweight champion, in the fifth round, just as he said he would.

But victory did not come in quite the fashion the young American had expected. Tommy Little, the referee, was forced to intervene midway through the round, because blood was streaming from cuts over Cooper's so-often-injured left eye.

And a few minutes earlier, Clay had looked anything but 'the greatest', as he landed in an untidy heap on the canvas after taking a left hook flush on the jaw. The cocksure American, taking one chance too many, had walked into that punch in the dying seconds of the fourth round. He slumped to the boards and came to a rest with his head against the bottom rope. Mr Little continued the count under the new rule, until Clay heaved himself up at five, and walked poker-faced to his corner.

What might have happened had the round not ended then, no one can say. Clay looked more surprised than hurt, but who knows what might have been the outcome had he been obliged to meet the full fury of Cooper instead of being able to walk to the safety of his stool?

It is all very well to boast and brag outside the ring, but to underestimate the other man inside the ropes is to invite disaster. Unless Clay stops such childish antics as swinging his gloves loosely near his hips and sticking out his chin to taunt his opponent, he surely will run into serious trouble one day soon.

I thought it might end in the fourth when Clay once or twice cut loose with both hands. But then the 'Louisville Lip' remembered that he was supposed to be the greatest and pranced contemptuously in front of the half-blinded Cooper. Desperately Cooper let go a left hook and a second later Clay was sitting against the ropes.

But any hopes we had that Clay might have overstepped the mark ended here. He came storming out of his corner, tore into his opponent with both hands, and as blood spurted from perhaps the worst eye injury Cooper has ever suffered, Mr Little had no alternative but to step between the two men.

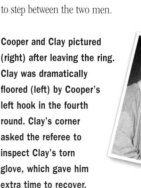

Cooper and Clay pictured (right) after leaving the ring. Clay was dramatically floored (left) by Cooper's left hook in the fourth round. Clay's corner asked the referee to inspect Clay's torn glove, which gave him extra time to recover.

Spurs back on top

By Donald Saunders

ROTTERDAM, WEDNESDAY 15 MAY

Tottenham Hotspur 5; Atletico Madrid 1

Britain's football prestige, down in the depths for a decade, soared skywards here tonight as Danny Blanchflower and his men trotted round the Feyenoord Stadium, proudly holding aloft the European Cup Winners' trophy.

Spurs had wrested this glittering cup from Atletico Madrid, the holders, with a superb display of skilful, fighting football that should make all those Europeans who saw it regard the British game with rather more respect henceforth.

Yet Spurs became the first British club to win a major European tournament without the assistance of Dave Mackay, for so long the backbone of their defence, and the inspiration of their attack. The Scottish left half failed a fitness test this morning, and was replaced by Tony Marchi.

When first we heard this news, few of us expected to see Spurs cheered to victory a few hours later. But perhaps it was this apparent blow to their chances that really goaded Tottenham back into full stride. At all events, they rose to the occasion like true champions.

Last autumn 25 teams from 24 countries entered this competition. Tonight Spurs proved themselves indisputably the best of the lot.

During the nervous opening stages they kept their heads and by half-time had moved methodically, calmly, into a two-goal lead. Then, having conceded a penalty two minutes after the interval, they were obliged to call on all their fighting spirit before they could sweep

Two years after winning the Cup and League Double, Tottenham Hotspur pose with the European Cup Winners' Cup. They beat Atletico Madrid 5–1.

arrogantly to victory over utterly demoralised opponents. This was, above all, a great triumph of team work. Yet, whenever I look back on the match, one name will immediately spring to my mind. For this was Terry Dyson's game.

The little Yorkshireman has never served Tottenham better than he did tonight. He not only scored two goals and provided the passes for two more, but by his example of tireless devotion to duty he inspired the other forwards, who had been out of touch for several weeks, to click back into top gear. Indeed, there were times tonight when this Spurs attack reached the heights they had scaled en route to the double two years ago.

Consequently, Madrid's defence, considered one of the strongest in Europe, was torn to shreds, with Dyson and Cliff Jones, who tortured poor Rodriguez for the greater part of 90 minutes, the chief executioners.

England beat Australia at the Oval

By Tony Goodridge

THE OVAL, TUESDAY 23 JULY

In the last over Miss Barker trapped Miss Marvell lbw and so brought England her first victory, by 51 runs, in the women's Test match series against Australia since the 1948–49 season in Australia.

They were almost thwarted, for throughout the last 35 minutes Mrs Kutcher and Miss Marvell, the last pair, doggedly resisted every blandishment which the England bowlers offered and remained impervious to nerves even with nine fieldsmen at times almost roosting on the bat.

It was a splendid finish to a match well fought by both sides. To Miss Duggan, England's captain, go particular congratulations for her part. She not only captained the side ably, but made a century in the first innings and bowled admirably in both.

The Australians, faced with the task of getting 210 runs in 225 minutes in the last innings, accepted the challenge with considerable zeal, and Miss Allitt and Miss Denholm produced 40 runs at the start in good time.

At the outset of the day, if a win was to come England's way, quick runs were essential, and then a declaration which would entice Australia into accepting a challenge.

Miss Brown and Miss Bragger produced 29 runs in the first half-hour before Miss Bragger, the nightwatchman, was caught at the wicket. Miss Brown, who had batted attractively, was drawn forward and stumped by Miss Jude and England were 74 for four, 123 runs ahead.

Miss Duggan immediately looked for runs, and with good strokes in front of the wicket and some splendidly timed cutting scored 32 in 25 minutes.

1963

1963

Jim Clark is youngest winner of world championship

By John Langley
MONZA, SUNDAY 8 SEPTEMBER

Jim Clark, 27 **(below),** became the youngest driver to win the world championship when he took the Italian Grand Prix in Monza today. Later he was interviewed by police about a crash in the 1961 race, in which the German driver Wolfgáng von Trips and 13 spectators were killed. Clark said today that the police wanted him to sign a form written in Italian. He understood this to mean he agreed to go to the police to make a further statement.

Clark won the 307-mile grand prix today in 2 hr 24 min 19.6 sec, at an average speed of 127.74 mph. Richie Ginther of the United States, in a BRM, was second and Bruce McLaren, of New Zealand, in a Cooper, third.

Clark, of Duns, Berwickshire, clinched the title by winning what is generally agreed tonight to have been the most hotly contested championship grand prix this year. The lead changed 23 times during the 86 laps.

Clark, who had been forced to use a less powerful engine than usual in his Lotus after having practice troubles with his regular engine, clung on grimly. One by one his rivals disappeared or dropped back with mechanical troubles. The championship finally came within his grasp on lap 62 when Dan Gurney spun his Brabham-Climax and was later forced to retire. By this time Clark had lapped every driver.

Although there are three more championship events, Clark has made sure of the title by winning five of the seven so far held.

Sussex win completes chapter of cricketing history

By E. W. Swanton
PUBLISHED MONDAY 9 SEPTEMBER

A new chapter of cricket history was given an exciting and altogether worthy climax at Lord's on Saturday. Sussex won the first Knock-out Cup and all credit to them; but credit, too, in fully equal portion for Worcestershire, who over the seven hours of the game fought an even fight and lost finally with a mere over and four balls to go, by 14 runs.

Where so much has been mediocre this summer, and the weather most of all, it is almost miraculous that both the Test series and this experimental competition should have passed off so well.

Often during Saturday's play one feared that the rain or the light or both would necessitate the game dragging on until this morning.

The atmosphere could not have been recaptured. However, though Sussex had a wet ball for their last seven or eight overs and Worcestershire a shocking batting light, the umpires were never called upon to make what would have been an unpopular decision.

Perhaps on a cold analysis the luck more or less evened out, for the pitch, which never flattered stroke-making, seemed to grow somewhat easier for batting as it dried. Runs always had to be earned against generally accurate bowling and a high fielding standard.

In the broad aspect this no doubt is to the good. Nothing is better to see than the ball hit hard and often when the conditions allow; but this 'instant cricket' is very far from being a gimmick and there is a place in it for all the arts of cricket, most of which are subtle ones.

That is why the day was so enjoyable, not only for the patriots with their banners and their rosettes 'up for the Cup' but for the practising cricketers, past and present, of all ages and types, who seemed to form the main bulk of the crowd.

Everyone seemed to be 'with it', and the only regret perhaps was that the weather uncertainty decided MCC against allowing in the extra 5,000 who could otherwise have been accommodated on the grass.

Ted Dexter, captain of Sussex 1960–65, and England 1960–64, was a batsman of great power and stamina. His authoritative manner earned him the nickname 'Lord Ted' among colleagues.

Geoff Strong heads equaliser to hold Spurs 4–4

By Donald Saunders
PUBLISHED WEDNESDAY 16 OCTOBER
Arsenal 4; Spurs 4

The final seconds of a great match were ticking away at Highbury last night when Arsenal's diminutive winger MacLeod curled a corner kick into Tottenham's penalty box, the fair head of Geoff Strong soared above friend and foe and the ball flashed into the net.

Thus did the 'Battle of London' come to its end, with honours even. And though there may be many a disappointed Spurs supporter who will not agree with me, I would not dispute the justice of its result.

True, Spurs had victory comfortably within their grasp. But their tired warriors relaxed too soon and fighting Arsenal stormed back to save the night. And what a night it was for the largest crowd crammed into Highbury since Spurs played there in February 1953. They saw 45 minutes of superb attacking soccer bring six

goals before half-time, and just when they thought a memorable game was stumbling to an understandably weary close with Spurs still kings of London's soccer, Arsenal came from nowhere to score two more and close the gap in the hectic last five minutes.

For over an hour Spurs looked the more mature, more skilled, more efficient team. Their forwards struck with devastating speed and accuracy, their defence, though often in trouble, overcame their difficulties with masterly calm.

Arsenal's refusal to give in was emphasised before the game was 20 minutes old. By then Jimmy Greaves had flicked a Danny Blanchflower free kick into the net for a 30-second goal, and Bobby Smith had thumped in another in the 18th minute. But, rallied by George Eastham and the hard-working Groves, Arsenal hit back.

In the 27th minute, George Armstrong was brought down by the enthusiastic Terry Dyson in the box and Eastham calmly stroked the penalty into the net.

Record win by Australia

By Bob Pemberton
PUBLISHED THURSDAY 17 OCTOBER
Great Britain 2 pts; Australia 28

Australia beat Great Britain in the first Test under the Wembley floodlights last night by the biggest margin they have gained since the series started in 1908. The game was a tragedy for butter-fingered Great Britain.

The Wembley hoodoo struck again for David Bolton, the Wigan and Great Britain stand-off half. After 20 minutes, Bolton, who was injured in last season's Cup final at Wembley, was taken to hospital with a shoulder injury. There was no injury to the bone and he was not detained.

Great Britain's chances of winning went with his departure. Bolton and Noel Murphy, the Great Britain halfbacks, were in great form until Bolton's injury caused the transfer of Eric Ashton from centre to stand-off half.

For the rest of the first half Bowman was withdrawn from the pack to play in the centre. After the interval Measures replaced him at centre and Bowman returned to the forwards.

Britain's 12 men played heroically and were often in the Australian half of the field, but they handled the wet ball so badly that Australia had often only to pick it up and run to score tries.

Great Britain's Neil Fox is brought down by Australian captain Walsh and centre three-quarters Langlands. Fox was unable to recreate his Wembley Challenge Cup final triumph of 1960, when he set an individual scoring record of 20 points (seven goals and two tries).

Two of their tries, one by Reg Gasnier from 60 yards and another by Ken Irvine after a pick-up near halfway, were the most spectacular efforts.

It was inevitable that big gaps should be left in defence and Australia, finely led by Ian Walsh, were alive to all their opportunities.

Vincent Karalius tried hard to rally the disorganised British pack but all his efforts were in vain, although he, Bowman, John Tembey and Tyson tackled hard.

One of the big Great Britain disappointments was the inability of Alex Murphy to hold Barry Muir, the clever Australian scrum half, although they were given equal chances by their hookers. The heroes of the Australian win were Graeme Langlands and Gasnier. Langlands gave Australia the lead in the 19th minute with a penalty goal and scored 13 points with a try and five goals.

Gasnier was quick to seize his chances and scored three tries. Fullback Ken Thornett came up to find a huge gap in Great Britain's defence to score a try and Irvine got the other. Neil Fox kicked Great Britain's penalty goal to level the scores in the 28th minute.

SPORT IN BRIEF

CRICKET
Yorkshire are winners of the county championship for the second season in succession. One of their new stars is Geoffrey Boycott **(right)**, who made his debut for them last year and will make his first Test appearance against Australia next year.

EQUESTRIANISM
Pat Smythe wins her third successive women's individual European showjumping championship on Flanagan. She also won in 1957 and was runner-up in 1959. At the Stockholm Olympics in 1956, when women were allowed to compete in the team showjumping event for the first time, she won a team bronze medal (coming tenth overall) on Flanagan. In 1967 in Aachen she becomes the British team's first woman *chef d'équipe*.

CRICKET
In the second Test against the West Indies at Lord's, England are chasing runs to win, and Brian Close has to face two of the most feared bowlers in the world, Wes Hall and Charlie Griffith. He makes 70 runs before being caught behind, keeping England in with a chance of victory. They have one wicket left, and need six runs off two balls to win. Next in is Colin Cowdrey, whose arm has already been broken by a Wes Hall delivery. Fortunately for the plastered Cowdrey, David Allen, at the other end, blocks both balls so that Cowdrey does not have to face a delivery, and the match ends in a draw.

FOOTBALL
Seventeen-year-old Irish player George Best makes his League debut for Manchester United in September. It is the first of his 349 League appearances for the club.

1963

1964

Footballers suspended for inquiry

By a Daily Telegraph *reporter*
PUBLISHED MONDAY 13 APRIL

Two Sheffield Wednesday footballers were suspended from the club last night while allegations of bribery made in a Sunday newspaper are investigated.

The two players are Peter Swan, the captain and centre half, and David Layne, centre forward. Mr Eric Taylor, the club's general manager, announced the suspensions in a statement on behalf of the directors.

Dr Andrew Stephens, chairman of Sheffield Wednesday, learned of the allegations while in Glasgow and travelled down immediately for talks with Mr Taylor. At the club he said: 'There was never any hint or suspicion of this.'

Today Sheffield police will start investigations. The allegations concern the First Division game between Sheffield Wednesday and Ipswich on 1 December 1962. Sheffield Wednesday lost 2–0.

A third player also mentioned in the article is the England international Tony Kay **(below)**, who was with Sheffield Wednesday at the time. He has since moved to Everton. 'It is a load of nonsense,' he stated.

Nash and Dixon set sights on second bobsleigh medal

By Howard Bass
INNSBRUCK, SUNDAY 2 FEBRUARY

Britain's sportsmen of the moment, Antony Nash and Robin Dixon, are not resting on their laurels. Most people who possess gold are not satisfied, and the new world and Olympic boblet champions are no exceptions.

In the four-man sled they hope to win another medal before this week is out. An up-to-date assessment of their chances must wait, for today no practice was possible on a melting track put out of action by the rising temperature.

Yesterday's magnificent achievement against the formidable Italian crews meant a rare moment of glory for Britain on the victors' rostrum, for theirs were only the fourth Olympic gold medal awards made to British competitors in winter sports.

The previous winners were the figure skater Madge Syers in 1908, the national ice hockey team in 1936 and another figure skater, Jeanette Altwegg, in 1952.

The total time Nash and Dixon took for their four winning runs over the 1,506-m course was 4 min 21.9 sec, precisely twelve-hundredths of a second better than the Italians, Zardini and Bonagura, who just pipped their teammates, E. Monti and S. Siopaes, for second place.

Tony Brooke, the British bobsleigh team manager, told me today that he has not yet finally decided on the composition of his two crews for the event on Thursday and Friday. He has 15 to choose from and several combinations are being tried out.

The one certainty is that Nash will pilot the main sled. Dixon, who is suffering from a badly strained back, is likely to be rested from further practice runs, and, though the odds are on his being fit enough to ride behind Nash, it may not be as brakeman. Andrew Hedges could get that assignment.

Winning Britain's first gold medal in the winter Olympics for 12 years, pilot Tony Nash and brakeman Robin Dixon race down the bob run in *Great Britain I*. *Italy II* and *Italy I* took the silver and bronze medals.

Five football divisions likely in two years

By Donald Saunders
PUBLISHED MONDAY 9 MARCH

Financial difficulties affecting an increasing number of clubs were discussed by the League management committee yesterday and will shortly be raised at a meeting of First and Second Division chairmen.

Alan Hardaker, the League secretary, said last night that a number of members were concerned about the high wages being paid by some clubs since the lifting of the maximum wage nearly three years ago.

The problems will no doubt have been considered by the committee when they discussed the revised form of player's contract, expected to come into operation next season, and the new 'pattern of football' which will be put before the clubs later this year.

I understand that more and more clubs favour a moderate basic wage and increased incentive bonuses. This may have been written into the revised agreement.

In turn, the Professional Footballers' Association are likely to have negotiated a form of contract that will prevent clubs taking up an option for a longer period than that for which a player is originally engaged.

The new pattern of football proposed a slight reduction in the size of the present four divisions, the formation of a fifth and the extension of the season to the end of May.

These modest changes have failed to gain sufficient support hitherto; but there is now a real prospect of their being reluctantly accepted.

The need for reorganisation of the League and extension of the season has again been underlined in the past week by a significant transfer request and by the fixture congestion facing one of the most successful teams in the country.

When Fred Pickering asked Blackburn for a move he made no bones about his reason. 'I want to better myself,' said Pickering, who today may be named as the Football League's centre forward against the Scottish League at Sunderland on Wednesday week.

This makes it quite clear that even leading First Division clubs are finding it more and more difficult to keep star players when they cannot match the high wages and bonuses offered by their richer brethren.

Liston beaten by Clay after six rounds

By Donald Saunders

MIAMI BEACH, TUESDAY 25 FEBRUARY

Cassius Clay pulled off one of the greatest surprises in the history of boxing at the Convention Hall here tonight when as a 7–1 underdog he took the world heavyweight title from Sonny Liston, the man so many had thought to be invincible.

Liston retired at the end of the sixth round with a shoulder so badly injured that he was unable to continue. At the time one judge had Clay leading on points, the other thought Liston was in front. The referee scored them even.

So Clay, the brashest, most talkative young man boxing has seen for many a day, kept his promise to take the title.

Whether he would have won the title but for Liston's injury no one can say. But certainly up to then he had boxed at great speed and with considerable skill to keep out of trouble. He had also opened a cut under Liston's left eye and had made the champion look slow and old.

Liston went straight into attack but Clay made him miss three times with jabs before countering smartly with a good left hook.

Suddenly Liston looked to be in trouble in the third round as blood began to trickle from a cut under his left eye. Clay made the injury the target for his left hand and the eye looked ugly.

At this stage Clay was certainly keeping his promise to 'fly like a butterfly and sting like a bee'. Liston was being made to look slow and clumsy.

Clay came out for the fifth round blinking. Then Liston cornered him and let go half a dozen thumping blows to the body. Clay took them without flinching and he also absorbed two long lefts to the face without apparent concern.

Liston was clearly puzzled by Clay's conduct, especially as the challenger let go some stiff left jabs at the start of the sixth. The champion's other eye was now swelling and he looked none too happy when Clay confidently hooked and jabbed him without difficulty.

Suddenly great cheers broke from the crowd and hundreds tried to invade the ring when it was seen that Liston was not coming out for the seventh round.

It was a strange finish to a strange fight and one that will be debated hotly by all who saw it for many years to come.

Liston, his pride shattered that he, the Iron Man, had been forced to quit, stood sadly in his corner shaking his head. And to add to his misery he had to listen to the crowd's boos as he made his way to the dressing room.

Before the match (below) few believed Clay could successfully challenge the reigning heavyweight champion. But Clay's speed and skill made him look sluggish (left), and Liston was knocked out in the seventh round.

1964

SPORT IN BRIEF

FOOTBALL
In the worst soccer disaster in history, 318 people are killed and 500 injured in crowd riots caused by a disallowed goal during a match between Peru and Argentina in Lima.

RUGBY LEAGUE
Brian Bevan, one of the greatest rugby league players, retires from the game aged 40 after 16 years with Warrington and the last two with Blackpool Borough. With his receding hair and his thin legs, he may not look the part, but he is the greatest try-scorer in the history of the game, with 796 tries in English rugby. He twice scored seven tries in a match, and has also made 69 hat tricks. His speed, change of pace and body-swerve are feared by opponents. Born in Sydney, Bevan was formerly a stoker in the Australian navy, signing for Warrington in 1945.

BOXING
Emile Griffith retains his world welterweight title against Luis Rodriguez. This is their third meeting – Rodriguez defeated Griffith for the title in March 1963, but Griffith won it back in June that year. Griffith goes on to win the world middleweight crown by defeating Dick Tiger in April 1966. In all, Griffith is world champion at welterweight and middleweight five times before he retires in 1977 after 112 fights.

RUGBY UNION
Scotland are joint winners of the Five Nations championship with Wales; it is their first international championship title for 35 years. It will be a further 20 years before Scotland win the Five Nations competition outright again. Scotland have enjoyed a successful season: they were the only home nation not to be beaten by the All Blacks in their tour earlier this year, drawing 0–0 with them at Murrayfield.

1964

Injuries, Blunstone and Mackay

By Bryon Butler

PUBLISHED WEDNESDAY 18 SEPTEMBER

Frank Blunstone, 29, the Chelsea winger, who has twice broken his left leg and who has twice been told his playing days were over, hopes to be match-fit by December.

Blunstone, a former England international, had an operation three months ago after damaging an Achilles tendon during Chelsea's Caribbean tour. He will be examined by a specialist today and expects to be given permission to increase the tempo of his training. 'I have been very pleased with my progress,' he said last night.

Blunstone first broke a leg in January 1957, while playing against Spurs at White Hart Lane in the FA Cup. He broke it again the following August and was told, for the first time, that he would not play football again.

But he did, successfully too, until his injury on tour last summer. That was when the second gloomy and, it would seem, second incorrect prophecy was made about his future.

Dave Mackay, 29, the Spurs and Scotland wing half who broke his left leg for the second time last Saturday, has entered hospital for a minor operation.

Mackay can take hope from Blunstone's case; but there is one important difference. The Chelsea player was only 23 when he broke his leg twice. Mackay will be 30 before he can contemplate another comeback.

Back in training at White Hart Lane in December, with teammate Terry Medwin (left), Dave Mackay recovered fully and went on to a successful career as player and manager.

Marathon hat trick in 1968, says Abebe

By Donald Saunders

TOKYO, WEDNESDAY 21 OCTOBER

Shortly after Abebe Bikila had achieved the greatest triumph in Olympic history by retaining the marathon championship here today, he announced that he intends to complete a hat trick of victories in this classic event four years hence.

This spare-framed little sergeant of the Ethiopian Imperial Bodyguard, who only five weeks ago had an appendix operation, explained that he is certain to win the race in Mexico City in 1968, when he will be 36, because the climatic conditions will be identical with those to which he is accustomed at home. 'I expect an easy victory,' he said. 'After all, Mexico City is 7,000 feet above sea level – just like the hills around Addis Ababa, where I train.'

No one was prepared to challenge this bold statement, for Abebe, though he had covered the course of 26 miles 385 yd at an average speed of just under 12 mph, looked as fresh as a man who had just returned from a brisk walk down to the shop on the corner.

Abebe's second consecutive marathon gold medal overshadows all other achievements in these Games. Few runners have even dared to enter twice for this most gruelling of all Olympic events, and until today none had won it more than once.

Yet he was so sure of himself that he took over the lead less than half an hour after the start and was never headed again.

Abebe strode relentlessly on to break the tape more than four minutes ahead of Basil Heatley, of Coventry, in the world's best time of 2 hr 12 min 11.2 sec, which is more than three minutes better than his winning time in Rome. Though this runaway victory may suggest a procession rather than a race, the 1964 marathon fully lived up to the traditions of this ancient trial of stamina and courage.

None of the million spectators who lined the pavements of Tokyo and its suburbs from early this morning will forget the sight of this lonely little African pounding along the cleared streets behind three white-helmeted motor-cycle outriders.

At the stadium the clock showed ten minutes past three as a great cheer greeted the entrance of the triumphant champion. Not once was the little sergeant's rhythmical stride disrupted as he lapped the track before breaking the tape with a triumphant flourish of his arms.

Abebe had time to pick up his hand towel, wipe his face and bow ceremonially to all four sides of the arena before the loudest cheers of the games heralded the arrival of Kokichi Tsuburaya of Japan. But the weary little Japanese had scarcely begun his final lap when the stocky Heatley came striding powerfully into view. One could almost hear the silence as the anxious crowd held their breath while the Briton set about the task of stealing what would have been Japan's only athletics silver medal.

Heatley clinched the issue 200 yards out, and while he forged on to the finishing line, the broken Japanese was left to struggle home for a bronze.

Abebe Bikila of Ethiopia heads for his second Olympic marathon gold.

Surtees wins world driving championship

By a Daily Telegraph *correspondent*

MEXICO CITY, SUNDAY 25 OCTOBER

John Surtees, 30, of Britain, took the world championship title from Jim Clark, also of Britain, when he came second in the Grand Prix in Mexico City today.

Clark, 27, was winning until the last lap of the 65-lap race. Halfway through this his Lotus sprang an oil leak. Dan Gurney, of California, won the race in a Brabham. Lorenzo Bandini of Italy, in a Ferrari, was third.

The six points earned by Surtees gave him a total of 40. Graham Hill was struck in the tail by Bandini in the 31st lap and retired with a broken exhaust. Bandini allowed Surtees to pass him in the final lap to make up the points needed to win the championship.

Clark told correspondents after the race: 'It has been a season of it. It is all in the jampot.'

He was awarded fifth place for finishing 64 laps. This put him in front of Pedro Rodriguez of Mexico, in a Ferrari, who finished fifth. Mike Spence of Britain was fourth in a Lotus.

World record and gold for Mary Rand

By James Coote

TOKYO, WEDNESDAY 14 OCTOBER

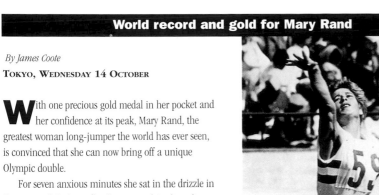

With one precious gold medal in her pocket and her confidence at its peak, Mary Rand, the greatest woman long-jumper the world has ever seen, is convinced that she can now bring off a unique Olympic double.

For seven anxious minutes she sat in the drizzle in the centre of the huge floodlit National Stadium here tonight before knowing that her world record-breaking leap of 22 ft 2 in had made her the first woman athlete to earn for Britain the supreme Olympic award.

Celebrations had to be restricted to a glass of champagne. On Friday Mrs Rand, 24, a Henley housewife, begins her gruelling five-event campaign in the pentathlon.

All day in the rain Mrs Rand never put a foot wrong. From her first qualifying jump this morning of 21 ft 4³/₄ in she led the field at such a pace that no one could keep up. Her greatest rival, Tatyana Shchelkanova, of Russia, the former world record-holder, crumpled under the strain.

It was left to the young, slim, Polish girl, Irena Kirszenstein, to keep up the pressure until the last second. Mrs Rand confessed afterwards that she was worried until the result of Miss Kirszenstein's final jump was flashed on the electric sign board.

With a world-record jump (left) Mary Rand took the Olympic gold. She went on to win silver in the pentathlon (above) and a bronze medal in the 4 x 100-m relay. A popular sportswoman, Mary Rand was voted BBC Sports Personality of the Year and in 1965 was awarded the MBE.

Dawn Fraser makes it a golden treble

By Pat Besford

TOKYO, TUESDAY 13 OCTOBER

Dawn Fraser, the magnificent Australian, made swimming history tonight by winning the Olympic 100-m freestyle title for the third successive time. No man or woman has ever achieved such a feat.

Britain's swimmers were not in the golden Fraser class, but Linda Ludgrove and Jill Norfolk, in the 100-m backstroke, and the men's 400-m freestyle relay squad, qualified for tomorrow's finals.

Miss Fraser, 26, the immaculate technician, did not sail away in isolation to her victory as she did in Melbourne in 1956 and Rome in 1960. Susan Stouder, 15, a Californian who was only seven when Miss Fraser won her first Olympic gold, stayed at her side almost the whole of the race. But not for a single moment did it seem likely that the Australian would lose. She shot away from the gun and touched at half-distance in 28 seconds, a foot ahead of Miss Stouder.

Amazingly she did not swoop into a fast tumble turn, but did a slow open swivel surface turn, and this enabled the American to close the gap.

Up the last length it was experience versus youthful determination, and experience told. Miss Fraser broke the Olympic record she set in a semi-final clocking 59.5 sec (only six-tenths outside her world record).

Miss Stouder had the deserved honour of becoming only the second woman to break the minute with 59.9 sec for her silver medal place.

1964

1965

Runaway win by Clark in Indianapolis

By Henry Miller

INDIANAPOLIS, MONDAY 31 MAY

Jim Clark, of Scotland, won the Indianapolis 500-mile race today in record time.

His Lotus-Ford led for all but ten early laps. He is the first overseas driver to win the race since Mario Resta, of Italy, in 1916.

The defending champion, A. J. Foyt, also in a Lotus-Ford, was forced out by transmission failure on the 115th lap of the 200-lap race.

Clark's terrific pace took its toll mechanically of many cars. Twenty-two broke down, and at the 400-mile mark only 11 cars were strung out.

Clark's average speed was 150.686 mph, breaking the old record of 147.350 mph set by Foyt last year. His time was 3 hr 19 min 5.34 sec.

A former winner, Parnelli Jones, also in a Lotus-Ford, was second. Third place went to Mario Andretti, in a Brabham-Ford car.

In a Lotus designed specifically for the race by Colin Chapman, Jim Clark was the first European to win the Indianapolis 500 for 45 years.

DID YOU KNOW?

When England and Surrey batsman Ken Barrington played in the first Test against New Zealand at Edgbaston, he took over seven hours to reach 137. At one point Barrington had faced 20 overs while remaining on 85. Barrington was dropped for the rest of the series, but returned to hit three centuries against Pakistan in the 1967 series.

Sealey's goals clinch West Ham triumph

By Bryon Butler

PUBLISHED THURSDAY 20 MAY

West Ham 2; TSV Munich 1860 0

Ron Greenwood's team brought the European Cup Winners' Cup back to England and back to London at Wembley last night. Two goals in 90 seconds by Alan Sealey, midway through the second half, were too much for the brave, virile but finally outplayed Munich.

This was a magnificent climax to three years of passionate work, and clear thinking by West Ham. But, more than that, it was a triumph for football itself.

West Ham's rise out of the wastes of mediocrity to the same dizzy heights achieved by the 1963 Spurs owes nothing to damp, safety-first tactics or to 'traditional' English theories.

West Ham have travelled far to see and learn. They have believed in themselves and their ideals. And, last night, they got their just reward for all their hard work.

Bobby Moore and company used Wembley's green carpet as an artist uses his canvas. Their movements were precise, their designs bold and imaginative. They were a credit to themselves and to English football.

But the crowd, too, made its contribution to this memorable night. More people paid more money than ever before to watch a floodlight match in England.

Yet there was another difference. This was a crowd of genuine football supporters, who obviously cared passionately about the teams and about the game. A happy contrast to much of the crowd that attends the FA Cup final each May.

'I'm forever blowing bubbles,' they sang when West Ham took the lead. Then came 'Sea-ley, Sea-ley,' a moving tribute to West Ham's right-winger, a player who has rarely been sure of his first-team place.

And, finally, the sound of 'Ee-eye-addio, we've won the cup,' filled the stadium. They could be forgiven for getting their lines crossed with the members of Liverpool's Spion Kop club.

Munich? It takes two teams to make such a match as this. They were hard, industrious, mobile, fair and, during moments in the first half, looked more than capable of becoming the first German club to win a major European trophy.

Bobby Moore holds the European Cup Winners' Cup aloft before cheering fans who greeted the triumphant team on their arrival for a civic reception at Newham town hall.

Government aid for World Cup matches

By Donald Saunders

PUBLISHED WEDNESDAY 10 FEBRUARY

The government's offer to provide money towards the organisation of next year's World Cup finals and to set up an inquiry into the problems of League football indicates that the importance of professional soccer has at last been recognised at Westminster.

After announcing the two decisions in the House of Commons yesterday, Denis Howell, the minister responsible for sport, said the government had taken the initiative over the matter of financial aid because they realised how necessary it was for the World Cup to be properly staged.

I suspect, however, that interest in the problems of League football has been aroused in the House only after patient lobbying by the League secretary, Alan Hardaker, Mr Howell, and a small band of other soccer-following Members of Parliament.

One would expect Mr Howell, a former League referee, to understand the urgency with which the World Cup problem must be tackled and the need for some inquiry into League soccer.

The most important factor to emerge from yesterday's announcements is that he has persuaded his colleagues that both matters are deserving of more than vague electoral promises.

Money, he said, would be forthcoming if a case were made out, and it was he who would have to present that case to Parliament.

Consequently, he will make a fact-finding tour of the provincial World Cup centres – Sheffield Wednesday, Manchester United, Middlesbrough, Everton, Sunderland and Aston Villa, starting on Friday. He will then meet representatives of the FA, the League and FIFA, to decide what aid is needed.

Asked how much he thought would be made available he replied, 'I cannot put foward a reasonable sum until I have put forward a reasonable case. But we do place great importance on the competition. It is the second most important international sporting event after the Olympic Games.'

Matthews returns in unique match

By Bryon Butler

PUBLISHED SATURDAY 6 FEBRUARY

Fifteen full internationals and nearly £1 million worth of talent at White Hart Lane...Stanley Matthews, 50 last Monday, jinking inimitably along Stoke's right wing once more. Time and money in soccer are given a new dimension today.

Spurs are fourth in Division One, Manchester United are third; much will hang on this meeting of giants. Yet as surely as this is the match of the day, Matthews is the man of the day.

Stoke's fixture with Fulham would normally provide an ordinary game between ordinary sides and a crowd of 25,000. But today nearly 40,000 spectators are expected at the Victoria Ground – many of them bent only on earning the right to say: 'I saw Matthews play at 50.'

Stanley Matthews hangs up his professional football boots. In his farewell match, Stoke beat Fulham 3–1.

It may not be a great match but it is certainly unique. And it will be remembered when the Spurs–Manchester United result is just another line in the record book.

What the result of the game at White Hart Lane will be is almost imponderable. Spurs, the only side in Division One unbeaten at home, will be unchanged. Manchester United, seven points ahead, will be at full strength.

Both sides have eight internationals in their ranks. Jimmy Greaves, Alan Gilzean and Cliff Jones can win matches with lone shafts of genius; but so, too, can Denis Law, Bobby Charlton and George Best.

It will be hard and it should be close, but I think Spurs' ground advantage will be decisive.

1965

1965

By Leonard Crawley

BIRKDALE, FRIDAY 9 JULY

Peter Thomson, of Australia, won the Open golf championship here at Royal Birkdale this evening for the fifth time. Thus he becomes the first of a modern race of highly specialised and full-time tournament golfers to do so.

Also he joins the exalted company of James Braid and J. H. Taylor, each of whom won five times. At 33 he will surely go on for a few more years in an endeavour to equal or even surpass the record of Harry Vardon, who won six British Opens and one American.

As surely as long, straight hitting won the US Masters tournament for Jack Nicklaus in the early spring this year, and fine straight driving from the tee enabled Kel Nagle to tie for the US Open, so Thomson's driving swept him triumphantly through a representative international field.

It was the most closely contested Open championship for many years and we may rejoice that two of our own golfers, Brian Huggett and Christy O'Connor, tied in second place. And we salute Tony Lema, the American holder, paired with Thomson today, who surrendered his crown only at the very end.

It is reasonable to suggest that a golfer of Lema's calibre is not interested in second prizes in great events any more than was Walter Hagen and that he could have finished second had he not been compelled by his adversary's brilliance to take risks in the closing stages.

Peter Thomson receives the trophy at Birkdale, winning with a total of 285 over the 72 holes.

Pollock's glorious 125 saves South Africa

By E. W. Swanton

TRENT BRIDGE, THURSDAY 5 AUGUST

An innings was played here today by Graeme Pollock which in point of style and power, of ease and beauty of execution, is fit to rank with anything in the annals of the game.

Pollock came in when after 50 anxious minutes South Africa's score stood at 16 for two. Between this point and lunch he batted easily and without inhibition or restraint while two more wickets fell, and his companions struggled in every sort of difficulty against some very good swing bowling by Tom Cartwright.

When the afternoon began the scoreboard showed 76 for four, Pollock 34. An hour and ten minutes later it said 178 for six, and Pollock was walking back with 125 to his

English batsman Barber is caught for one by Lindsay on the third day of the second Test. Graeme Pollock's superb 125 ensured victory for South Africa in this Test and a 1–0 series victory.

name, and the crowd standing in salute to a glorious piece of batting. In cold fact this young man of 21 had made then 125 out of 162 in two hours and 20 minutes, and in the 70 minutes since lunch 91 out of 102. In his whole innings were 21 fours, and the two of these that came off the edge from Cartwright's bowling were the only false strokes of any kind that I saw.

The other 19 were either hit with a full, easy swing of the bat, or glanced or cut to every point of the compass. No one could find any way of containing him because he uses every stroke.

Keino threatens world mile record

By James Coote

WHITE CITY, MONDAY 30 AUGUST

A new era of mile-running was begun here today when before a jubilant 25,000 crowd Kipchoge Keino, 25, a Kenyan police instructor, became the first African to break four minutes by clocking 3 min 54.2 sec – the third-fastest time ever recorded.

Only Michel Jazy of France (3 min 53.6 sec) and Peter Snell of New Zealand (3 min 54.1 sec) have run a mile faster, and so furious was the pace of this race that the first four home set national records.

The standard can be gauged by the fact that Rotherham's Alan Simpson lowered his own national

time by nine-tenths of a second to 3 min 55.7 sec yet was disappointed because he was third.

Second was his old Czechoslovakian rival, Josef Odlozil, with 3 min 55.6 sec and fourth the East German, Jürgen May, who, by recording 3 min 56 sec became the 66th athlete to break the four-minute barrier.

It was Derek Ibbotson who, with Keino, helped the early pace while the rest struggled to keep up. The Yorkshire man led the first lap in 56.4 seconds with Keino next in 57 seconds, May in 58.6 seconds, Odlozil in 59 seconds and Simpson in 59.2 seconds.

Keino kept up this remarkable pace in the second lap and a flabbergasted Ibbotson said: 'I thought he was going flat out, yet he swept away. It was unbelievable.'

GARFIELD SOBERS (1936–)

ONE OF THE FINEST ALL-ROUNDERS *that cricket has ever seen, Garfield St Aubrun Sobers was born in Bay Land, Barbados, on 28 July 1936. He was the fifth of seven children and his father, a merchant seaman, was killed in 1941, when a German submarine torpedoed his ship. As a youngster, Gary adored playing 'knee' cricket (where batsmen kept one knee on the ground) and, by the age of 12, was giving net practice to senior players at the local club. They would place a 50-cent coin on the middle stump and give it to him if he bowled them. Needless to say, he was rarely short of money.*

As a teenager, Sobers joined the police team in the Barbados League, holding the nominal position of bugler in the police band. His Test debut came in 1954, when he was picked to face England, and he soon became a regular in the squad. In all, he went on to represent the West Indies in 93 Tests, 39 of them as captain. During this time, he scored more than 8,000 runs, took 235 wickets, and made 109 catches.

Don Bradman described Sobers as a 'captain's dream'. In the field he could move with the grace and agility of a panther. As a bowler, he was astonishingly versatile: he could open the attack

with swing, bowl orthodox spin with his first finger, or googlies with his third. Most impressive of all, perhaps, was his batting. His innings of 365 not out, made when he was just 21, remained a world record until broken by Brian Lara in 1994.

In 1975, Sobers received a knighthood for his services to cricket.

England win solves no problems

By E. W. Swanton

EDGBASTON, TUESDAY 1 JUNE

England's delayed victory arrived this morning at quarter to one after the minimum of excitement on a slightly warmer day, the job being done with calm efficiency by Bob Barber and Geoff Boycott, who in their eighth Test partnership exceeded 50 for the fifth time.

Barber was caught in the deep field by Graham Vivian, the 12th man, going for the winning hit, thus bringing in Ted Dexter who was not required to take guard since a four by Boycott next ball finished the game.

The result notwithstanding, I imagine the New Zealand camp will be rather more satisfied with their team's performance than the English.

Almost every one of their side made a contribution with which they could be pleased, and in particular the less experienced men proved to themselves that there is nothing intrinsically different or more awesome about a Test match.

England, by contrast, are faced with the same problems as heretofore with nothing encouraging to show. The outcricket generally was uninspired, with only the bowling of Fred Titmus and Barber to brighten the picture.

If David Allen had been chosen it is inconceivable that New Zealand would have made nearly as many as they did in the second innings. When in doubt selectors always pick a quicker man for the last place. They never, never, never pick a spinner too many, often one too few.

Barber and Boycott set about the job in hand each in his characteristic way. Boycott no doubt feeling that this was a heaven-sent chance of doing something to find the form that has eluded him so far this season.

He is the sort of player who, when batting well, can look attractive enough, as was to be seen for instance in his 100 against Australia at the Oval last August. In his present groove, on the evidence of his play in both innings here, he is full of inhibitions.

Not that his has been the sort of wicket to encourage stroke-making. It was sluggish from the very start and has progressively lost pace, and I hope and trust that its restoration now becomes the Warwickshire club's major priority.

New Zealand's bowling was ill-suited by the pitch, their faster men today making even less impression than they had done in the first innings. The game, therefore, proceeded placidly to its conclusion.

England won the series 3–0.

BOXING

Laszlo Papp of Hungary, European middleweight champion, is forced to withdraw from a world title challenge against Joey Giardello when the communist government reneges on its agreement to let him fight for money. He was originally granted this concession after winning three Olympic gold medals (at middleweight in 1948, and light-middleweight in 1952 and 1956).

GOLF

In the US Masters in Augusta, Georgia, Jack Nicklaus returns a record score of 271 to take his second title and the green jacket. Nicklaus also equals Loyd Mangrum's record 18-hole score of 64, and Arnold Palmer's three rounds under 70 in 1964. Palmer can only manage second place this year, with Gary Player in third.

EQUESTRIANISM

Show-jumper Marion Coakes (later Mould) has an excellent year on her 14.2-hands Irish-bred pony Stroller. She is the youngest winner of the Queen Elizabeth Cup at the Royal International Horse Show, beating Alison Westwood on The Maverick by a tenth of a second. She and Stroller go on to win the world championship, and are members of Britain's three victorious Nations Cup teams.

MOTOR CYCLING

Mike Hailwood **(below)** wins a further world title at 500 cc, completing a run of successes since 1961. He will win a total of 76 grands prix races between 1961 and 1967.

1965

Henry Winter

Football, the world and the legacy of 1966

SCANDAL AND DISASTER, record transfers and fabulous football: the opening decade of the 20th century provided enough material to dominate tap-room tittle-tattle until the Millennium. These tales of the unexpected never ceased, spreading in unstoppable waves from the shores of Great Britain around the world. The force that is football had been unleashed.

Those first ten years presaged events throughout the century. Illegal payments saw Manchester City and Middlesbrough punished. Poor stadium design took 25 lives at Ibrox. Alf Common's £1,000 move from Sunderland to Middlesbrough drew gasps of disbelief. Tottenham Hotspur won a momentous FA Cup final. *Plus ça change*, as they have learnt to say in the modern, foreigner-filled English Premiership.

England taught the world to play and then discovered the pupils graduating to embarrass an ageing professor.

Yet the real story of the 20th century has been the ebbing of English influence, football reflecting political reality. England taught the world to play and then discovered the pupils graduating to embarrass an ageing professor. Like an erratic clock, England were ahead of the time and then behind it.

England's initial impact on the rest of the world is undeniable. Each of the national associations, from the Libyan Arab Jamahiriya Football Federation to Soccer New Zealand, carries the country's identity in its title. Not England. It boasts the Football Association. The FA had already been established 37 years when the century dawned. The English, proving hugely inventive, had been busy. By 1900, the FA Cup had been going for 29 years, the shin-pad for 26 seasons, and floodlights, admittedly pretty crude ones, for 22 years. As the 20th century was ushered in, professionalism had been legal for 15 years, penalties and linesmen in force for nine years, while promotion and relegation had been quickening pulses for two seasons.

Evolved in southern public schools and northern mill towns, football was ripe for export. Nation after nation fell for its obvious charms, its cheapness and simplicity. British wayfarers and manufacturers proved unintentional footballing missionaries, dropping anchor or business roots and then introducing locals to the joys of association football.

The most impassioned footballing strongholds acknowledge their debts to England. Travellers to Latin America will come across English-sounding clubs, such as Newell's Old Boys and Corinthians. Some European clubs take English, rather than local, spelling, such as Athletic Bilbao (as opposed to Atletico Madrid).

Italy, home to the world's most powerful club football, number in their illustrious ranks a famous club called AC Milan, whom Mussolini insisted be Italianised in the Thirties. So they became Milano but, on Il Duce's death, swiftly returned to their Anglicised origins. Juventus's black-and-white stripes stem from those of Notts County, the world's oldest League club.

England was both cradle and catalyst. Passage from one century to another heralded the game's global expansion. Genoa, Juventus and Barcelona were formed as one century closed and another opened, marked by the formation of Real Madrid and FIFA, football's international brotherhood.

As the century unfolded, even the world's most sceptical outposts were seduced by the 'beautiful game' as Pelé, the game's greatest player, called football. Even in Uncle Sam's backyard, where Pelé finished his phenomenal career and where the hoop, puck, base and end-zone traditionally dominated, soccer has proved a healthy kick in the grass. Even 'soccer', a heretical word in many purists' eyes, boasts strong English and historical links, being a public school corruption of the 'association' in association football.

Not content with endowing the cradle of the game, the proud if arrogant parents of England had to play the innovator, displaying an originality soon to be copied around the world. In 1933 numbers adorned shirts in the FA Cup final: Everton wore 1–11, Manchester City 12–22. The 1938 Cup final between Preston North End and Huddersfield Town was televised live. Today Wembley, tomorrow the world.

But come half-time in the century's course and a gradual shift in power could slowly be detected. In 1950, England lost to the United States, a result that would bring apoplexy now but was even more sensational at a time when English self-esteem reigned supreme. Worse followed. In 1953, the Magical Magyars of Hungary came to Wembley and led England a merry dance, prevailing 6–3, inflicting upon the Mother Country the first defeat by a non-British team on home soil. Within a year, England had been thrashed 7–1 in Budapest.

A trend seemed to be developing. In 1956, while England were marvelling over the first proper floodlights at a League match (Portsmouth versus Newcastle), and preparing to celebrate Everton's experimentation with an electrified frost-beating pitch, weightier matters were afoot on the Continent. The European Cup began with Real Madrid to the fore. Colonel Blimp did not realise it, but Johnny Foreigner was catching up. Continental leagues grew in prestige and power, a reality intimated when Torino paid £100,000 for Denis Law from Manchester City in 1960.

But any thoughts of a national decline were soon placed on hold. Along came a generation of players whose supreme talent and temperament brought the Jules Rimet Trophy to England. Home advantage at the 1966 World Cup finals undoubtedly helped, as did a sympathetic linesman who decreed Geoff Hurst's shot had crossed the line against West Germany, but there can be no questioning the quality and blend of Alf Ramsey's 'wingless wonders'.

Bobby Moore was England's greatest defender, a generous, self-effacing soul who wiped his sweaty palms before shaking hands with the Queen as he stepped up to receive the World Cup. Next to Moore, Jack Charlton was defensive obduracy personified. Behind Moore, Gordon Banks's alertness and athleticism frustrated opposing forwards while, further forward, Bobby Charlton and Hurst provided some special goals. In between, Alan Ball worked his socks off so much they often appeared down by his ankles. Wembley, the Venue of Legends, lived up to its grandiose name.

The legacy of 1966 And All That was two-fold. A feel-good factor seized the sport, the nation even, encouraging attendances to spiral. This was a golden age when the Three Lions appeared rampant. In 1968 Manchester United won the European Cup, the first English club to do so, a year later Celtic led the way for Scotland. Although England faltered in the 1970 World Cup finals, an understandable belief prevailed that this side were even stronger than the Boys of '66.

Yet such successes seduced the English into illusions of long-lasting grandeur. A shift was occurring. England were not sliding back – far from it, as the teams of Ramsey and Matt Busby indicated – but the overseas threat was gathering pace. Even in football politics, England's global influence was on the wane with Sir Stanley Rous, the very English president of FIFA, being replaced by Joao Havelange, the Brazilian autocrat.

England still had plenty to feel proud about, though. The European Cup was dominated between 1977 and 1984 by Football League clubs with Liverpool, heavily indebted to non-English players, Nottingham Forest and Aston Villa leading the charge. The national team were struggling, but solace could easily be found in club colours.

A shift was occurring. England was not sliding back – far from it, as the teams of Alf Ramsey and Matt Busby indicated – but the overseas threat was gathering pace. Even in football politics, England's global influence was on the wane.

As so often in English football, tribulation followed triumph. Halfway through the Eighties, another cloud, another emission from the cradle of the game rained on England's parade. Hooliganism, named after a troublesome London family, had long been known as the 'English disease', but sadly it spread worldwide. England's history of excess remains the worst, primarily because it is the only country to export violence, as the citizens of Luxembourg, among other defiled venues, will attest. Brussels too. When 39 fans died at Heysel in 1985 after Liverpool supporters had run riot, football League clubs were rightly banned from Europe.

Embarrassment was only half the problem. The ensuing loss of high-level competition ensured that English clubs were left behind their Continental counterparts. England stood still while the rest raced over the horizon. Technically, tactically, even physically, English clubs were overtaken by the likes of Milan, Juventus and Borussia Dortmund. Only the emergence of a new crop of young talents, like David Beckham and Michael Owen, allowed England to conclude the century with anywhere near the self-belief it had begun it.

1966

Victory for Billie Jean King

By Lance Tingay
Wimbledon, Saturday 2 July

The lawn tennis championships, which ended for the 80th time on Saturday, will be remembered by me as the occasion when good manners and sportsmanship came back to Wimbledon, thanks mainly to Manuel Santana, the men's singles champion.

The new women's singles champion, Billie Jean King, the 13th American to take the title, won a final against the Brazilian Maria Bueno that was disappointing because the loser played so far below her best. 'I have never played worse in my life,' said the Brazilian afterwards, and though she played the odd rally, when her beautiful economy of penetrating shot reminded one that she was the champion in 1959, 1960 and 1964, she rarely did so twice running.

American strength on the one side and Brazilian frailty on the other did not make for a good match. It ended in 67 minutes. Mrs King's volleying was superb throughout, and her tight, tidy, forceful game was worthy of a Wimbledon champion. At the age of 22 Mrs King won at her sixth attempt. She has proved herself a tremendous grass court player. It would be interesting to see her put her skill to the test of the famous hardcourt championships of Italy, France and Germany.

A triumphant Billie Jean King holds the Venus Rosewater dish at Wimbledon, after beating Maria Bueno of Brazil 6–3, 3–6, 6–1.

MILESTONES

The first woman in Britain to be granted a racehorse training licence was Florence Nagle, who had taken her case to the Court of Appeal. The court ruled against the Jockey Club, which had refused to licence women trainers. Norah Wilmot was also granted a licence at the five-minute hearing; she had been training horses for 35 years under the name of her head lad.

Clay retains heavyweight title in sixth round

By Donald Saunders
Published Monday 23 May

As 12 stitches were inserted in a jagged wound over Henry Cooper's left eyebrow yesterday, British boxing sighed deeply and settled down again to await the long overdue return to these shores of the heavyweight championship of the world.

The deepest, ugliest and unkindest cut Cooper has suffered during a battle-scarred career, gave Cassius Clay a sixth-round victory at Highbury on Saturday night, for little purpose.

It left Cooper facing the fact that all he now has to fight for is the comparatively modest distinction of becoming the first heavyweight to own three British championship belts.

The prospect of adding a third notch to a third belt later this year is probably all that prevented him, during the bitterness of defeat, from abandoning, at 32, a trade that has too often exposed the frailty of the skin round his eyes.

Clay's victory was predictable enough. We guessed he would cut Cooper, but expected the wounds to be opened gradually as jabs, hooks and crosses left their mark. No one thought misfortune would strike so suddenly. It all happened in a flash when they moved into a neutral corner in the first minute of the sixth round. Clay countered sharply with a left hook to the jaw, then chopped at Cooper's face with his right. Almost simultaneously, their bobbing heads met.

As they separated, blood streamed in half a dozen rivulets over Cooper's face and down on to his chest. There was a red patch, too, high on Clay's forehead. The referee, George Smith, moved quickly between them, to assess the damage, but after a brief examination told them to box on.

I have little doubt that Mr Smith would have ended the bout when he first looked at the wound, had Cooper's camp not pleaded earlier that they were the best judges of eye injuries.

In a last desperate effort to win a title that he now knew in his heart could never be his, Cooper charged across the ring, swinging wildly with both gloves.

Shortly afterwards Mr Smith walked firmly forward, waved his arms and indicated to Cooper that it would be dangerous to allow a lost cause to be further pursued.

Cooper's vulnerable eye area is exposed again by his opponent. Clay said later that he could barely stand the sight of Cooper bleeding so badly. 'Blood scares me,' he admitted.

Santana's artistry clinches title

By Lance Tingay
Wimbledon, Friday 1 July

Castilian skill and charm conquered in the lawn tennis championships today. Manuel Santana beat the American Dennis Ralston 6–4, 11–9, 6–4 to become the first Spaniard to take the crown.

There has been no more popular winner since Jaroslav Drobny beat Ken Rosewall in 1954, not a better men's singles final since that year. Wimbledon finals have a tendency to be an anticlimax if only because of the tension under which the players perform, but Santana took his victory by displaying his artistry in full.

Equally Ralston's defence against Santana's fine craft was forthright and able. The contest was in every way worthy of the occasion.

Ralston played so well against Santana that he will probably forgive me if I say the right man won. The competence of the American was superb and his conduct during the match earned him plaudits he might not have gained at the start.

If, during the 104 minutes the final lasted, Ralston earned a reputation as a good sportsman, Santana merely furthered his. Last year he won the United States singles title, the second of the outstanding grass court championships, and his fine hard court skill was proven when he took the French title in 1961 and 1964.

He now stands indubitably as the No. 1 amateur of the world, a mastery based on a wonderful forehand, a stroke where for sympathy of touch between ball and racquet strings he has no equal. He also has the capacity to raise his game and find an outstanding shot in a moment of pressure and crisis.

He is 28, the age usually assessed as when a man reaches his peak, and since he began his career as a ball-boy in Madrid, he can be said to have made his own way in the lawn tennis world.

Indeed it must have been quite a moment for Santana, with his wife watching him from the competitors' stand, when he went to receive his trophy from Princess Marina. Not only did he bow low but, in accordance with Spanish custom, he kissed her hand.

Killy skis to victory

GOLF

American Jack Nicklaus makes sporting history when he takes the US Masters title at Augusta, Georgia, for the second year running and the third time in all. Nicklaus earns the green jacket after a three-way play-off with Tommy Jacobs and Gay Brewer.

CYCLING

Tour de France cyclists stage a protest against the random dope tests that have been carried out overnight in Bordeaux. Three miles after the start of the ninth stage, 122 riders get off their bikes and walk for 100 yards. World champion Tom Simpson says, 'I think it was stupid. It is French law and it is pointless protesting.'

ATHLETICS

Russian sisters Irina and Tamara Press retire just before the 1966 European championships. Tamara, the elder sister (below), was world record-holder six times in both shot and discus, and won three European titles. Irina won the pentathlon gold at the 1964 Olympics with a world record score (her eighth in the event). She was fourth in the 80-m hurdles (she won the gold in 1960) and sixth in the shot. It is rumoured that sex-testing of women before all international competitions has prompted the sisters' retirement.

By Howard Bass

PORTILLO, SUNDAY 7 AUGUST

Jean-Claude Killy, 22, of France, competently survived a sporting test of fitness and stamina to win a fearsome-looking men's downhill race when the world Alpine ski championships continued here today.

With an extra-pronounced forward lean from the waist, Killy was the hero of chapter two in a championship series already emphasising the success of French style and training.

His time was 0.4 seconds faster than his compatriot, Leo Lacroix, and two more Frenchmen, Pierre Stamos and Bernard Ocrel, came fifth and sixth. The heavily built West German, Franz Vogler, made effective use of his weight to take the bronze medal.

After gold medal successes at the world championships and the 1968 Olympics, Jean-Claude Killy (above, on left), went on to become skiing's first millionaire.

Three of the 69 starters failed to finish. Jeremy Palmer-Tomkinson came 42nd, one place behind the Australian, Malcolm Milne.

The conditions were perfect but it was a tribute to their expertise that none of the leading group fell.

A belated disqualification in the women's slalom means that Gina Hathorn and Divina Galica finished 20th and 22nd, each a position higher than was originally announced.

I have previously suggested that any British place in the top 20 would be heartening, yet both girls reproached themselves for being more cautious than usual.

1966

Chichester arrives at Sydney

By a Daily Telegraph *correspondent*

SYDNEY, MONDAY 12 DECEMBER

Francis Chichester, 65, is sailing in towards Sydney harbour this morning, 107 days after leaving England on his single-handed sail round the world.

He was met outside the Heads by many yachts, some of whom had been waiting since Saturday. A large crowd waited at the quayside.

He radioed a message last night to his wife Sheila, who is waiting in Sydney to greet him. It read: 'Regret unable to get in today. Estimate time of arrival 10 am tomorrow.'

Unfavourable winds slowed his run up the New South Wales coast and forced him to tack over 20 miles out to sea last night.

Mr Chichester had hoped to complete this first half of his round-the-world sail in 100 days, the average time taken by the old sailing clippers.

Gipsy Moth IV **nears Sydney harbour. Francis Chichester's single-handed voyage from England had taken 107 days. The return voyage to Plymouth, via Cape Horn, took 119 days.**

Jack Brabham claims third world championship

By John Langley

ZANDVOORT, SUNDAY 24 JULY

Jack Brabham, 40, driving his own green-and-gold Repco-Brabham, romped home at an average speed of 100.1 mph in the Dutch Grand Prix here today to record his third successive world championship win.

His hat trick puts him securely in the lead for the drivers' championship, with a total of 30 points, more than twice as many as his nearest rival, Graham Hill. Hill (two-litre BRM) was second, and Jim Clark (two-litre Lotus-Climax) third.

From the results sheet today's race looked like another comfortable win for the Australian. But the race-long duel between Clark and Brabham made this the best championship contest so far this season.

Jack Brabham drives to a third world title. Brabham also won the constructors' championship in 1966.

Clark, in his lower-powered car, harried Brabham mercilessly for the first 26 laps of the 90-lap race, then took the lead with a dazzling display around the tricky curves of this 2.6-mile seaside circuit. With the race two-thirds over, Brabham began really motoring as his car settled down with its lighter fuel tanks. He whittled away Clark's lead, passing him 14 laps from the end.

It seemed that Clark could do nothing about this – and the reason became clear when Clark rushed into the pits with an overheated engine. Hill had been a lap behind the two leaders, but Clark's pit-stop allowed him to get within striking distance, and he pounced into second place.

West Indies round off three great years

By E. W. Swanton

LEEDS, MONDAY 8 AUGUST

The overwhelming victory of the West Indies here this afternoon brings their exploits of the last few years to a wonderful climax. Since 1963 they have beaten England in two rubbers, Australia in one, and this is easily the most comprehensive success of the three.

The West Indies have, perhaps, owed more to Garfield Sobers than any Test side has ever owed to any one player, let alone any captain. He has scored 641 runs in the four games, taken 17 wickets, and held a bagful of catches. He has not lost a tactical trick, and has taken a good many that were by no means obvious.

The captain has held the centre of the stage from first to last, and to some extent has eclipsed the other stars in his distinguished side. But that this has been a notable team effort was always clear enough from the West Indies' performance in the field.

The plain fact is that England have been outmatched. There is no disgrace in losing to a side

of such calibre, but the manner of today's defeat was indeed disappointing.

Sobers won the awards for the best bowling and best batting. The point cannot be too often made – as it was indeed by Sobers after the game – that until English players are consistently able to bat and bowl on true pitches of this sort they will be at a hopeless disadvantage against those who have been brought up on them.

DID YOU KNOW?

The Jules Rimet trophy, stolen before the World Cup competition began, was dug up in a garden in Norwood, South London, one week after its disappearance. The unlikely sleuth was a black-and-white mongrel called Pickles; his astonished owner found him unearthing a parcel which turned out to contain the cup. Pickles became the hero of a nation for his detective work.

England twice fight back for greatest triumph

BY DONALD SAUNDERS
LONDON, SATURDAY 30 JULY
England 4; West Germany 2, after extra time

Now the Jules Rimet trophy is safely in England's keeping for the next four years, Alf Ramsey and his world champions can at last put up their feet and briefly enjoy the privileges due to all-conquering heroes. Let me pay tribute to 11 Englishmen and 11 West Germans for their contribution to the sagging prestige of international sport, during the most exciting final the World Cup competition has produced in 36 years.

For two hours that strained the emotions of all who watched, both teams played with dogged persistence, supreme courage and methodical efficiency.

It took a man of character and judgement to lead England back into the game after Ray Wilson had nodded the ball down to the feet of Helmut Haller, who promptly slammed it past the unsighted Gordon Banks. In that dreadful 12th minute Bobby Moore rose calmly, quietly, but firmly to the occasion; he decided he could and should risk playing a more attacking role. Though Moore's move forward caused some anxiety behind him, it helped produce the pressure that ultimately relaxed the Germans' grip in midfield.

Within six minutes England were level, Geoff Hurst racing ten yards to head in a free kick from Moore, while the Germans mistakenly kept close watch on the Charlton brothers.

After the break England's forwards found their touch. The German defence looked less and less sure of themselves, and 13 minutes from time their failure to clear a corner kick allowed the alert Martin Peters to force the ball past Hans Tilkowski. Now it was the Germans' turn to call on their courage. Tenaciously they fought to deprive England of possession, and 30 seconds from the end of normal time they snatched the equaliser. The referee, Gottfried Dienst, signalled a goal, and seconds later the end of the first 90 minutes.

As his troops flopped disconsolately to the turf, trying to absorb this blow, Mr Ramsey moved among them, assuring them with a smile here, a pat on the back there, that England would still win the cup.

They believed in him and, inspired by the calm authority of Moore, and young Alan Ball's tremendous energy, they again took control.

With three minutes of the first period remaining, Hurst thumped a cross from Ball straight at goal and Tilkowski pushed it against the underside of the bar, whence it rebounded to the turf. The Germans will forever claim the ball did not cross the line. The Russian linesman ruled otherwise.

Even now these plucky Germans did not give in. During the second period of extra time they forced their leaden legs forward in a desperate effort to overcome opponents who were as close to exhaustion as they were.

But England refused to be robbed of their well-deserved prize twice in the same match.

With the referee looking at his watch, Hurst trundled on to a through pass and drove home a goal that earned him the distinction of becoming the first player to score three times in a World Cup final, and confirmed England as undisputed champions.

England captain Bobby Moore shows off the Jules Rimet Trophy after the closely fought final at Wembley.

1966

1967

Vicenzo's fight ends in victory

By Leonard Crawley
PUBLISHED MONDAY 17 JULY

Roberto de Vicenzo **(below)**, of Argentina, won the Open championship at Hoylake on Saturday with the grand total of 278 over four rounds, two strokes ahead of Jack Nicklaus, the American holder.

Clive Clark, of Sunningdale, tied with Gary Player, of South Africa, for third place on 284. Another up-and-coming British player, Tony Jacklin, of Potters Bar, finished fifth on 285.

It is seldom that the gods who control the destinies of the world's greatest players ever forgive one who has failed to grasp the golden opportunity to win the British or American Open championships or the Masters tournament at Augusta.

Vicenzo, who is 44, had been second once and third five times over here, and one feared that he was heading for the title of the greatest player of all who never won any of the three most coveted titles.

For years, it has been my pleasure describing the splendour of his game. He has been so good that he has never been out of the running.

But there is all the difference in the world between winning a championship and losing one, and, in this connection, I recall the sad story of British-born Harry Cooper, the greatest professional player in America during the early Thirties.

He couldn't win the Open there and then, in 1936, when at last he appeared to have won, he was sitting back triumphantly at Baltusrol when Tony Manero, an unknown player, went mad at the end of the day and beat him on the post. Cooper packed his bags and went home never to play again.

Those who watched Vicenzo at Hoylake on Saturday will never forget his Olympian calm and the manner in which his last round of 70 was compiled.

Here was the character of a great man who was able to forget the past and rise to the hall of fame in which for so many years he has belonged by right.

Celtic make soccer history in Lisbon

By Bryon Butler
LISBON, THURSDAY 25 MAY
Inter Milan 1; Celtic 2

The European Cup, like the World Cup, has come home. Celtic tonight became the first British club to win the world's toughest club competition because brilliantly, emphatically, they overcame the toughest defence in the world.

Inter Milan converted a penalty after six minutes, and then wretchedly tried to hang on to their lead. They succeeded for an hour. Play was confined to the Italians' half of the field, and every person present who respected football poured down resentment on to their heads.

But Celtic proved themselves magnificent competitors, and in the second half they succeeded in breaking the unbreakable. Goals by Tommy Gemmell and Steve Chalmers gave them the European Cup to add to the Scottish League Championship, Scottish Cup, Scottish League Cup and Glasgow Cup.

The final whistle acted like a starting pistol. An army of Celtic supporters – about 8,000 of them – whooped

Billy McNeill, the Celtic captain, is presented with the European Cup. It was the final triumph in a season of trophy wins for Celtic.

Foinavon goes home to champagne

By Guy Rais
PUBLISHED MONDAY 10 APRIL

Foinavon, the 100–1 shock winner of the Grand National, returned from Aintree to his stables at the tiny village of Compton, Berkshire, yesterday, cheered by hundreds of people.

As soon as the dark bay entered his box he was given a sip of vintage champagne and a packet of mints with-a-hole, the 'sweets he loves', by Mrs Patricia Kempton, wife of his trainer, John Kempton. Each week Foinavon consumes a dozen packets of the mints.

When the horsebox bringing Foinavon back turned into the narrow lane leading to the stables, scores of children waved Union Jacks and banners on which were written the words: 'Well done, Foinavon.'

First out of the box was Susie, a white goat which accompanies Foinavon on all his travels. Then came Foinavon, ears pricked.

He seemed to enjoy the excitement of the cameras, and showed his teeth several times as the glass of champagne was placed under his nostrils.

There to greet him were his owner Mr Cyril Watkins, 58, and Mr McIntyre Bennellick, 49, who up to nine months ago had a share in the horse.

Mr Watkins admitted he was so nervous on Saturday that he did not watch the final stage of the race on television. 'In addition to the £15,000 prize money, six of us had £16 each way, and netted about £10,000,' he said.

After a dramatic pile-up at one of the fences, April Rose, riderless (below), leads the remaining pack. The winner, Foinavon, was ridden by John Buckingham (inset right).

their way off the terraces and, just as the Scots had done at Wembley, swarmed like ants on to the pitch. Fifty thousand other spectators stood transfixed.

Turf was dug up as souvenirs, players had to hold on grimly to their shirts, and flags everywhere were snatched and pocketed.

Then suddenly the pitch was cleared as the Scots gathered in a giant half-moon below the main terrace. Billy McNeill, the Celtic captain, a tiny figure beneath the white pillars of the National Stadium main building, held the European Cup high above his head.

It was a precious moment, for this was the cup that even such sides as Manchester United and Tottenham Hotspur failed to win. But not only that: it meant defeat, and shame, for a club whose influence on football is wholly bad.

DID YOU KNOW?

The captain of Ireland's rugby union team, Tom Kiernan, earned his 33rd cap on tour in Australia this year, equalling the world record for a fullback. He also scored his 100th point in internationals. By his retirement in 1973, Kiernan had captained Ireland a record 24 times.

True, Inter were without Luis Suarez and Jair, and might even conceivably have had their sights on a replay on Saturday in the hope that one or both would be fit.

But Inter's philosophy, their play-acting, their time-wasting and irritable temper, lost them thousands of would-be friends.

It meant, of course, that Celtic's problems were halved. They were able to ignore the fact that most sides are asked to prevent goals as well as score them.

Inter's defence is no ordinary one. It employs up to ten men, and is a devious, complex, immensely physical thing in which everything and everybody are sacrificed in the cause of survival.

They failed this time because they could do nothing to relieve the pressure and because in Celtic they had opponents who more than matched them for class, and strength, and persistence.

The pity of it all was that Inter were given the one encouragement they most needed – an early goal, and that a penalty. Jim Craig made a messy attempt at tackling Cappellini, and the referee was quick enough to award a penalty from his position 40 yards away. Valentino Mazzola shot to the left, Ronnie Simpson dived to the right.

Inter promptly retreated into their shell, and the pattern of the match was irredeemably established.

SPORT IN BRIEF

AMERICAN FOOTBALL

On 15 January, in the Memorial Coliseum in Los Angeles, the first Super Bowl is contested. In front of 61,946 fans, the Green Bay Packers of the National Football League (NFL) beat the Kansas City Chiefs of the rival American Football League (AFL) 35–10. The Chiefs' owner, Lamar Hunt, has been the guiding force behind the setting up of this NFL/AFL showdown. The organisations have been engaged in a spiralling transfer war in order to lure the best players to their own clubs, and it is agreed that this competition will determine the 'world championship of professional football' between the two leagues.

BOXING

After Muhammad Ali was stripped of the WBA heavyweight crown in 1965 for agreeing to an immediate return bout with Sonny Liston, Ernie Terrell took the vacant WBA title, while Ali made several successful defences of his WBC crown. In February this year a 15-round fight between Ali and Terrell is staged for the undisputed title. It turns into a grudge fight. Terrell insists on using Ali's 'slave name', Cassius Clay; in response Ali – totally outboxing him – lands punches as he repeatedly asks, 'What's my name?' Although Ali takes the unified title, he is stripped of it two months later when he refuses to be drafted into the US army, famously observing, 'I ain't got no quarrel with them Viet Cong.'

FOOTBALL

In the first all-London FA Cup final held this century, Spurs enjoy a 2–1 win against Chelsea. Dave Mackay has come back from suffering broken legs in two separate incidents to lead them to their third Cup win this decade. Their previous triumphs were in 1961 and 1962.

1967

Laver proves he is the best tennis°player in the world

By Lance Tingay

PUBLISHED TUESDAY 29 AUGUST

Rod Laver of Queensland, 29 years old, became the first man to win as a professional at Wimbledon when he beat Ken Rosewall 6–2, 6–2, 12–10 in a splendid singles final of the BBC 2 tournament yesterday.

It was fitting that Laver, the last of the amateur Wimbledon champions to turn professional, should thus distinguish himself. A superb player, the outstanding left-hander of all time, I suppose nobody will deny Laver his standing as the best player in the world today.

A high-quality final was won by a high-quality player. For the consistently good quality of shot-making it surpassed anything done at amateur Wimbledon for many years.

In one department only did Rosewall surpass his masterly opponent. That was in lobbing, when Rosewall's facile hoisting was breathtaking, but in all else Laver was the better.

The most marked aspect of Laver's superiority was his service. Rosewall, of course, never was a fast server, and he has held his own for years in the finest company by the depth and cunning of his placements rather than on any power.

Yesterday at Wimbledon Rosewall's own serving standards let him down and the proportion of first deliveries he got into court was small. After taking the opening game he lost no less than five service games running and soon was two sets behind.

Laver netted £3,000 for his win, so from his three singles matches he earned £40 a game, a reward as awesome as his skill.

There was a crowd of about 13,000 to watch him yesterday, and with all seats sold on Saturday as well, Wimbledon's first all-professional venture was as successful as anyone dared to hope.

DID YOU KNOW?

After an outbreak of the highly infectious foot-and-mouth disease in Britain, horse racing was banned until early 1968. In a more bizarre twist, the New Zealand All Blacks rugby union game with Ireland was also cancelled because of the risk of spread of the disease.

Higgs and Arnold topple Pakistan for 140

By E. W. Swanton

TRENT BRIDGE, THURSDAY 10 AUGUST

The thunderstorm which reduced the field to a lake around five o'clock this afternoon in a few vivid, deafening minutes was the most violent I have seen since the 1946 Brisbane Test of indelible memory.

There were no hailstones like golfballs here, nor were there tarpaulin wicket covers to float briskly downwind until halted by the boundary fence. But the noise was scarcely less, and there was a flash slap in front of the BBC quarters that reduced four selectors and several professional talkers to a moment's unwonted silence.

Looking out at the swamp with an occasional small green island standing out in the waste of water, one wonders whether there can be any cricket tomorrow.

The crease covers are in position, but by rule the business part of the pitch cannot be covered until the umpires have decided further play is impossible. Strictly speaking this issue could have been determined within a few seconds of the downpour, but the point swiftly became academic: something of a joke.

But the deluge must not submerge the merit of England's performance. The new combination of Geoff Arnold and Ken Higgs, with a help not recognised in the analysis by Basil d'Oliveira and one timely intervention by Derek Underwood, bowled out Pakistan on an easy paced wicket.

Saeed and Majid apart, Pakistan batted as though mistrustful of the wicket, perhaps in view of the moisture that had penetrated overnight at one end on Tuesday. One could not, however, detect any difference as between one end and the other, and not a ball misbehaved.

One need not waste much space speculating as to what may happen when the game is continued. The wicket could well be slow and easy for quite a long time.

The first strokes of the match were made by Saeed: polished persuasions off his legs and some wristy hits square to the off. Higgs's first overs were a little ordinary by his standards but suddenly he moved one away and Ibadulla edged it to Alan Knott. Within half an hour, both new boys had got their names into the scorebook.

England won the series 2–0.

Hulme first at record average of 101.47 mph

By John Langley

NÜRBRUGRING, SUNDAY 6 AUGUST

Denis Hulme and his Repco-Brabham got a firmer grip on the lead of the 1967 world championship here today by winning the gruelling German Grand Prix at a record average speed of 101.47 mph. His team leader, world champion Jack Brabham, was second.

The other winner here today was that tortuous, bumpy 14.1-mile cirucuit. Car after car, including the entire Lotus, BRM and Eagle teams, cracked up under the hammering they received before the fast and reliable Repco-Brabhams had completed the 212-mile race. Only eight of the 17 Formula One cars were finishers.

Hulme, 31, from New Zealand, who had already won the Monaco Grand Prix this year, drove a fast, steady race. He was never lower than second.

But until two laps from the end it was Dan Gurney, in his Eagle-Weslake, who looked a certain winner. After setting a lap record of 103.15 mph, Gurney had built up a 45-second lead and was still pulling away when his dark blue car was put out by engine trouble.

At the start, Jim Clark's Lotus-Ford pounced into the lead followed by Hulme, Bruce McLaren in the Brabham and John Surtees' Honda. Following cars had to swerve wildly to avoid Graham Hill's Lotus which spun across the track during the race into the first corner.

The next 30 minutes produced a thrilling wheel-to-wheel duel between Clark, Hulme and Gurney. After 25 minutes flat-out racing Clark was still only less than half a second ahead of the New Zealander.

On lap four, Clark's Lotus dropped out with a broken front suspension. On the same lap, Gurney moved ahead of Hulme into the lead he held until his retirement.

With the Eagle-Weslake out of the way, world champion Brabham took over second place, and coolly held off a tremendous challenge from Chris Amon.

Denny Hulme (left) went on to win the world drivers' championship; Jack Brabham (right) was runner-up.

Simpson dies in Tour de France

From our correspondent

CARPENTRA, THURSDAY 13 JULY

Tommy Simpson, the British professional cyclist, collapsed while racing on the Ventoux Mountain in today's stage of the Tour de France. He died in hospital at Avignon where he was taken by a police helicopter.

Simpson, aged 29, had kept with members of the leading group of riders, including the race leader, Roger Pingeon, of France, until three miles from the summit of the 5,550-ft mountain, known as the 'Giant of Provence'.

The Englishman then dropped back and was seen to be pedalling with extreme difficulty. Eventually he fell by the roadside. The British team car, driven by Ken Ryall, a cycle dealer of Twickenham, was immediately behind and Harry Hall, a mechanic, went to help Simpson.

Simpson said he wanted to continue, remounted and rode a further half-mile under the scorching sun –

Tom Simpson (leading, above), was found to have been taking amphetamines to enhance his performance. These, combined with the heat and physical strain of the race, caused his death.

temperatures were in the 90s. He fell again and when the Tour doctor arrived within a minute or so Simpson was already unconscious.

At the start of today's stage, Simpson was seventh in the overall placings. Mr Alec Taylor, British team manager, said tonight that the British team would race tomorrow.

Tommy Simpson was the most successful road-racing cyclist Britain had produced, winning the world professional road championship in 1965. His other victories included the Bordeaux–Paris (1963), Tour of Flanders (1961), Milan–San Remo (1964), and the Tour of Lombardy (1965) classic races.

SPORT IN BRIEF

LAWN TENNIS

In the last amateur Wimbledon, held two months before the all-professional tournament won by Rod Laver (see main text), John Newcombe is the only seed to survive in the men's singles, and beats Wilhelm Bungert in a one-sided final. Newcombe, a hard-hitting Australian, also wins at Forest Hills, and is thus the last amateur to win Wimbledon and the US Open championships.

MOTOR RACING

Jim Clark wins the final Grand Prix of the season at Mexico City in his Lotus-Ford **(below)**, giving his team second place in the constructors' championship. The team introduced the new Ford Cosworth DFV engine at the Dutch Grand Prix at Zandvoort in June, in the Lotus 49 designed by Colin Chapman; in a day of mixed fortunes for the Lotus drivers, Graham Hill suffered engine failure while Jim Clark won the race. Although the reliability of the new engine is initially suspect, Clark goes on to win the British Grand Prix at Silverstone for the fifth time in six attempts, as well as the United States Grand Prix, and the Ford Cosworth proves itself a highly successful Formula One engine.

1968

MPs join wave of protest at d'Oliveira omission

By a Daily Telegraph *reporter*

PUBLISHED FRIDAY 30 AUGUST

Protests grew yesterday over the omission of Basil d'Oliveira **(right)**, the Cape coloured cricketer, from the MCC team to tour South Africa this winter.

One member of the MCC for more than 30 years, Mr Ivor Montagu, resigned his membership in protest. Mr Charles Loughlin, Labour MP for West Gloucestershire, resigned from the county club. 'I do not wish to be associated even indirectly with the MCC,' he said.

Several MPs joined the protests and one of them, Mr Ivor Richard, Labour MP for Barons Court, suggested that the case might come under the Race Relations Act. He has asked the Race Relations Board to investigate the matter 'as a matter of urgency'.

Mr Howell, the minister responsible for sport, said: 'As minister I am supposed to be speechless on the question of team selection – and I certainly am.'

The MCC offices at Lord's received telegrams and telephone calls of protest. The MCC stuck to its statement that the decision was purely on grounds of d'Oliveira's form.

In Johannesburg, Mr Jack Plimsoll, manager of the South African team which toured England in 1965, said there would have been cricketing reasons behind the decision, not political considerations, 'although his present performances seemed to justify his selection'.

Australians end tour with flurry of runs

By Michael Melford

LORD'S, TUESDAY 3 SEPTEMBER

The Australians finished their tour in the grand manner here early this afternoon when Bill Lawry and Ian Redpath made the last 71 runs needed in 50 minutes, and the Rest of the World were beaten by eight wickets. Redpath has been the outstanding batting success of the tour and, suitably, he was the dominant figure in the final stand which began when the Australians, needing 101, were 13 for two. Once again, he drove with much elegance to either side of the wicket and, if he had not endeared himself to the spectators before, he did so when he ran a hurried single to allow his captain the distinction of making the last run of the tour.

Doug Walters, opening the innings on this occasion, finished a disappointing tour by being lbw playing across a full toss from Wes Hall. John Inverarity was caught at third slip in Hall's third over. There was too much coming and going among the Rest bowlers for them to look as if they were going to press the Australians hard in the last innings.

Farewell scenes: Derek Underwood (on left, inset left) is congratulated on his seven for 50 in the final Test at the Oval. Tour captains Bill Lawry of Australia (on left, below) and Colin Cowdrey greet the crowd after the five-match Ashes series ends in a 1–1 tie with three matches drawn. The Australians rounded off their tour with a match against the Rest of the World.

Player joins giants of Carnoustie

By Leonard Crawley
Published Monday 15 July

Gary Player, of South Africa, won the Open championship for the second time on Saturday and so joined the immortal band of Tommy Armour, Henry Cotton and Ben Hogan.

Considering the prospects at the beginning of last week, I suggested that, whatever happened, we were bound to get a worthy champion. Only a player of consummate skill could win over such a course.

Byron Nelson, one of the great United States players who competed at Carnoustie in 1937, declared over the air at the halfway stage that it was the toughest examination of a modern golfer in the world.

Peter Thompson, five times winner of the Open, added when still in contention that the course was so difficult, the

winner was likely to come from behind on the final day. This is exactly what happened.

It would be hard to imagine a more worthy winner, since Player has already won all the major titles, and it may be that he is now beginning a second cycle.

He is the complete golfer. Small of stature and immensely strong, a picture of physical fitness, he is blessed with an iron nerve. But above all, it was his capacity to hole the telling putts that brought him ahead after four gruelling days.

He never wavered, despite the fact that he was partnered by mighty Jack Nicklaus who, with his tremendous physical advantages, was ready to strangle him over those last devastating holes

A winning smile: Gary Player lifts the claret jug after regaining the Open title.

Lions lose series as chances go begging

By John Reason
Cape Town, Sunday 14 July
South Africa 11 pts; British Isles 6

For the first time in the series, the British Isles' forwards held South Africa in the scrums and beat them in the line-outs, and they had their opponents under pressure as never before in the first 20 minutes of the second half here yesterday.

South Africa were then leading 8–3, and if the Lions were to win they had to make two scores. They created three clear chances, but missed them all.

Inevitably, a reaction set in. South Africa came back and scored another three points, the Lions adding a penalty goal, to win by a goal and two penalty goals to

two penalty goals. They also won the series, with the last international, at Johannesburg, still to be played.

Maurice Richards has been one of the most quick-witted players on this tour, and immediately he saw that Bob Taylor was unmarked at the back of the line-out, Richards snatched up the ball and threw it to him.

All Taylor had to do was to catch the ball and fall over the line, but he lost sight of it in the flat rays of the late afternoon sun which was just dipping behind the towering Table Mountain, and he knocked on.

The other two missed chances were when C. Gibson failed with a drop at goal and Roger Arneil was stopped two yards from the line. If Arneil had put his head down, gritted his teeth and pumped his legs, he must have scored. Instead he looked for support.

Britain limited to four Open tennis meetings

By Lance Tingay
Paris, Sunday 31 March

Concessions had to be made, but in the balance the British lawn tennis revolution, brought about last December when the authority of the International Lawn Tennis Federation was flouted, was successful.

The historic emergency session of the Federation here yesterday capitulated to the British *fait accompli*. It created new amateur rules which, while allowing for amateurs and 'registered players' for those who want them, permits self-determination by nations.

With this freedom Britain's abolition of the amateur-professional status was legalised. Britain emerged from the meeting still a member of the international game.

This was undoubted victory. At the same time, Britain yielded ground and accepted a limitation on the number of tournaments open to all classes of players, and such events must now be sanctioned by the management committee of the ILTE.

Britain was today granted four open tournaments: Wimbledon, the hard court championships at Bournemouth, the Kent championships at Beckenham and the London championships at Queen's Club.

SPORT IN BRIEF

Winter Olympics
In the 20th winter Olympic Games in Grenoble in February, Jean-Claude Killy wins all three Alpine skiing events, the downhill, the slalom (held in thick fog) and the giant slalom. In doing so he emulates the achievement of Austrian Toni Sailer in 1956. The home crowd are thrilled by the Frenchman's exploits; the Games are nicknamed the 'Killympics' in his honour. Killy also wins the overall World Cup in its first two seasons, 1967 and 1968. He turns professional this year, aged 24.

Golf
In the US Masters at Augusta, Roberto de Vicenzo takes 65 for his final round which puts him into an 18-hole play-off with Bob Goalby for the title. De Vicenzo gets a birdie at the 17th (witnessed by spectators and television viewers); unfortunately it is marked on his card as a par four, giving him a final round of 66. Rushing away at the end of the contest for a TV interview, de Vicenzo signs the card without checking. He thereby signs away his title since, according to the rules, the 66 has to stand. A generous sportsman, he accepts the situation without demur. 'I am a stupid,' he confesses.

Equestrianism
Marion Coakes on Stroller becomes the first woman to win an Olympic show-jumping silver medal, beaten only by the great Bill Steinkraus on Snowbound. Stroller develops an abscess on his back tooth shortly before the competition and is only passed fit to jump the day before. In the team event, however, the pony finds the huge treble too much, refuses twice and unseats his rider. The British team are eliminated.

1968

1968

Clarke dominates day of British brilliance

By James Coote

PUBLISHED TUESDAY 3 SEPTEMBER

Britain's athletes reached almost Olympian heights at the White City yesterday with a series of performances that can only give encouragement for Mexico. Indeed the girls beat their Polish counterparts for the first time ever by the surprisingly wide margin of 64 points to 46 before a crowd of 20,000.

Dominating all the individual feats by the British athletes was Ron Clarke's majestic 5,000 m in 13 min 27.8 sec, another All-Comers record and the fastest time in the world this year.

The Australians rated the run as his finest performance ever, better even than any of his 17 world records. Such is the measure of his own high standards.

In three races since the Saturday before last, with conditions never perfect, Ron Clarke (above) has set a world two-mile record and run the fastest 5,000 m and 10,000 m seen this year.

What a build-up he is having for his Olympic 10,000-m challenge!

Tomorrow, he travels to South Lake Tahoe, Nevada, the American altitude camp, for training and, perhaps, a race or two before meeting up with the Australian squad in Mexico.

Clarke's time yesterday was only 11.2 seconds outside the world record he set two years ago – and only three men have bettered the performance. It was almost frightening to see how he made some of the best men in Britain look like 'also-rans'.

DID YOU KNOW?

Ivan Robinson scored the only goal in a Division Three match between Barrow and Plymouth Argyle. Unfortunately he was the referee. Robinson deflected a shot from George Maclean from 15 yards out, beating the Plymouth goalkeeper, Pat Dunne.

Black Power displays at the Olympics

By Donald Saunders

MEXICO CITY, FRIDAY 18 OCTOBER

Three coloured American athletes, who took the three medals in the 400 m tonight, made a protest at the victory ceremony when they appeared wearing black berets and making the Black Power salute.

Lee Evans, gold medallist and one of the leading advocates of the Black Power movement, Larry James and Ron Freeman removed their berets during the playing of 'The Star Spangled Banner'.

They had been warned that 'the strictest disciplinary action' would be taken against them if they staged any political or racial demonstration.

Earlier Tommie Smith and John Carlos, the coloured American sprinters who gave the Black Power salute when receiving their medals on Wednesday, were given 48 hours to leave Mexico by the United States Olympic committee.

The two athletes, who finished first and third in the 200 m, were suspended from the American team and ordered to remove themselves from the Olympic Village. They will be sent home today.

Mr Avery Brundage, president of the International Olympic Committee, criticised the violation by American athletes of the Olympic 'no politics' principle.

This has given rise to unconfirmed reports that the Americans' entire Olympic team will be thrown out of the Games if they do not control their competitors.

After a record-breaking win in the 4 x 400-m relay, the American team display the clenched fist salute of the militant Black Power movement.

Hemery wins gold with world record in hurdles

By James Coote

MEXICO CITY, TUESDAY 15 OCTOBER

Britain won her first gold medal of the Olympics today with a world-record run in the 400-m hurdles by David Hemery, 24. Another Briton, John Sherwood, finished third to take the bronze medal.

Hemery's time was 48.1 sec – exactly one second faster than the listed record of Gert Potgieter, the South African. Just a month ago, Potgieter's 49.1 sec was lowered to 48.8 sec by Geoff Vanderstock (America).

Hemery has a book in which every performance and every time between hurdles of his rivals is recorded. He

was once a high-hurdler and won the Commonwealth Games 120-yd hurdles title in 1966 in Kingston, but because of repeated injury switched to the intermediates.

Hemery, a lean, fair-haired six-footer with an American accent, seemed to pause for a split second after the starting gun. But then it was so smooth that there appeared to be no hurdles at all.

Within two flights, he had overtaken Ron Whitney. It seemed impossible that Hemery could continue to increase his lead – but he did.

Striding to victory, David Hemery breaks the world record in the 400-m hurdles.

Three world records shattered at Mexico Olympics

By James Coote

MEXICO CITY, FRIDAY 18 OCTOBER

Three athletics finals; three world records. The level of performances this afternoon reached a new peak. The most important mark to go from Britain's point of view was in the long jump.

The long-legged American, Bob Beamon, shattered the world record and won the gold medal with a fantastic 29 ft 2½ in. Beamon, who takes off from either foot, is no stylist, and has no knowledge of the finer points of jumping. But he has the spring of a kangaroo and the longest legs imaginable. 'They almost come under his chin,' Ron Pickering, Lynn Davies's coach, once told me.

Beamon's leap left Davies, the reigning Olympic champion and British record-holder, with 27 ft, with an almost impossible deficit to recover.

American Bob Beamon leaps to a world record of 29 ft 2½ in (8.9 m). The jump became the oldest record in athletics, standing until 1991, when fellow American, Mike Powell, jumped 8.95 m.

Lee Evans, like Beamon, a Black Power supporter, cut a fifth of a second off the world's fastest 400-m time despite a morning of mental and physical anguish. His time was 43.8 sec.

At one point Evans, the premier advocate of the Black Power movement among the athletes, was led from the American headquarters on the point of collapse.

The third world record came in the women's 200 m. Irena Kirszenstein-Szewinska came through in the last 60 metres to overtake the Australian pair, Raelene Boyle and Jenny Lamy, thus shutting out for the first time the American girls from any of the first three places.

SPORT IN BRIEF

OLYMPICS

Top Czech gymnast Vera Caslavska wins four gold medals at the Olympic Games. The recent Soviet invasion of Czechoslovakia has made the women's gymnastic competition an emotionally charged event, with a packed stadium backing Caslavska and her team. The Soviet Union win the team competition, Natalia Kuchinskaya of the USSR takes the beam, but Caslavska wins the combined exercises, the vault, the asymmetric bars and – to a standing ovation from the crowd – the floor exercise (jointly with Larissa Petrik of the USSR). In a moving gesture on her return to Czechoslovakia, Caslavska presents her gold medals to the leaders deposed by the Soviets.

SPEEDWAY

Ivan Mauger wins his first world individual speedway title. Barry Briggs, who comes from the same city in New Zealand, is second. This is the start of an unprecedented run. Mauger wins six world individual titles, three of them in succession. From 1968 to 1974 he is never out of the first two places. He and Barry Briggs ride together in the Great Britain team this year to win the world team championship; later Mauger will ride for New Zealand.

MOTOR RACING

It is a tragic season in motor racing with four fatal accidents: Jim Clark inexplicably crashes during a Formula Two race at Hockenheim; Jo Schlesser dies at Rouen; Mike Spence in practice for the Indianapolis 500; and Lodovico Scarfiotti, former Italian Grand Prix winner, in a hill climb. Graham Hill battles on for Lotus after Jim Clark's death and wins the title from Jackie Stewart in a Matra. Lotus win the constructors' championship.

1968

1969

Gonzales turns boos to cheers after marathon victory

By Lance Tingay at Wimbledon
PUBLISHED THURSDAY 26 JUNE

Ricardo Gonzales (below), 41, who has never won the singles at Wimbledon and almost certainly never will, yesterday put himself into the annals of the championships as predominantly as a champion ever did.

On Tuesday night, Gonzales was booed as he left the centre court. Yesterday afternoon, when the same player had won one of the most memorable matches of all time, they cheered him as few have been cheered before.

They could hardly have done less. The mighty Gonzales came through a Wimbledon match that broke records of every sort.

He completed his unfinished business of the night before, when he was left trailing against fellow-American, Charles Pasarell, 22–24, 1–6. The road back was a long one and Gonzales, a hero in every step, made it.

He won the third, fourth and fifth sets on an unforgettable afternoon. He won a match in which he never led until the last two games, in which he was seven times within a shot of losing, and which on its completion gave Wimbledon the longest singles both in number of games and duration.

It was a contest of pristine quality. Despite its heroic quality, it was only a first-round match. It is one of the tragedies of lawn tennis that Wimbledon never saw Gonzales at his peak.

He was immature when he played as an amateur. By the time the game had opened up, this superb performer was too old to have a hope of taking a title he more than anyone had deserved. But even at 41, Gonzales, as he awesomely indicated yesterday, makes other players look puny. When he is in action it is almost impossible to take cognisance of the other player, no matter who it is.

This restless, fidgety giant dominates the court, his opponent and the whole scene. He has power, he has touch and his judgement of the flight of the ball, in knowing what shots to let go by him, seems unparalleled.

At Wimbledon yesterday afternoon, Gonzales dominated the centre court for two hours 52 minutes and a fine player 16 years younger than himself. With lost sets behind him he could afford to yield nothing; and nothing did he yield during the course of the next three tremendous sets.

Never-say-die Ann Jones is Wimbledon queen at long last

By Lance Tingay at Wimbledon
PUBLISHED SATURDAY 5 JULY

Ann Jones gave British lawn tennis one of its finest moments in the championships yesterday when she beat the American Billie Jean King 3–6, 6–3, 6–2 to become the women's singles champion

A splendid triumph and a rare one! The only other British singles champion at Wimbledon in more than three decades was Angela Mortimer, in 1961.

The three big wins she had to take her crown were, first, against Nancy Richey; second, against Margaret Court, this being the match in which she played her most splendid game, and yesterday against Mrs King, the champion of the three preceding years.

All this was brought about at her 14th challenge and at the age of 30, a time when lawn tennis skill is generally held to be diminishing.

There were doubtless many factors that brought success at long last to Mrs Jones, and certainly one of them was the fervent wish of about 15,000 spectators that she would pull it off. There was a time during the final when the patriotic zeal of the crowd threatened to be less than fair. Indeed, I have the feeling that when Mrs King's game began to fall apart, it was because she was tired not only of playing against Mrs Jones, but almost every person in the stands as well.

In the first game of the third set, when the crowd was becoming so loud and vociferous in its partisan support, Mrs King expressed her feeling by ironically courtseying to a section of them.

Then, when it was obvious that Mrs King was not resenting their partisan outlook, and obvious, too, that Mrs Jones could win the title, the crowd warmed to the American almost more in the imminence of her defeat than they ever did in her previous victories.

Mrs Jones brought off her victory in 71 minutes. The quality of the play was mixed, as it so often is in a match on which so much depends, and the victor played less well than she did last Wednesday when she beat Mrs Court in the semi-final.

Nor did Mrs King reach the same standard of play as she did in any of her last three finals. But it was a contest of rapt excitement nonetheless. Afterwards Mrs Jones summed it up by saying: 'I got better and she got worse.' She could not have been more accurate.

Displaying grim determination, Briton Ann Jones battles her way to victory, depriving American Billie Jean King of her fourth successive Wimbledon crown.

Ricardo 'Pancho' Gonzales (left) performing in one of the greatest matches ever seen at Wimbledon. He won 22–24, 1–6, 16–14, 6–3, 11–9 against Charlie Pasarell in a match that lasted five hours and 12 minutes.

MILESTONES

British sailor Robin Knox-Johnston completed the first solo non-stop voyage around the world. The trip, in his yacht *Suhaili*, took him east from Falmouth via the Cape of Good Hope, New Zealand and Cape Horn on a 30,123-mile journey lasting 313 days.

Stewart unlucky as Hill wins fifth Monaco Grand Prix

By John Langley in Monte Carlo
PUBLISHED MONDAY 19 MAY

Britain's world champion, Graham Hill, won the Monaco Grand Prix yesterday – as usual. It was his fifth success in the event – a record.

He took the lead at just over a quarter distance when Jackie Stewart's Matra-Ford fell out just as the Scot seemed set to win his third world championship event in a row.

Stewart, who had built up an apparently impregnable lead of almost half a minute, suffered a broken universal joint. Driving his works Lotus-Ford with clockwork precision, Hill, 40, then pulled steadily away and was never seriously challenged.

Only seven of the 16 starters finished the 80-lap race around the 1.95-mile street circuit. Two former world champions, Jack Brabham (Brabham-Ford) and John Surtees (BRM) were eliminated when their cars touched.

At the start of the race Stewart pushed his Matra straight into the lead ahead of Chris Amon's Ferrari, Jean-Pierre Beltoise in the second Matra, and then Hill.

He was pulling away at the rate of about a second a lap from Amon when the New Zealander's Ferrari broke down after 16 laps. At 20 laps, Stewart had a commanding 28-second lead over Hill's Lotus.

A magnum of champagne is poured over the winning Lotus-Ford as Graham Hill celebrates his fifth Monaco victory in seven years (1963–9).

But, only three laps later, the Matra's race was run when both Stewart and Beltoise were put out of the race by similar trouble. With Surtees and Brabham already out of the way after their collision, in a tunnel, the main interest centred on the fight for second place between two of the younger drivers, Piers Courage, and Belgium's Jacky Ickx in the second works Brabham.

Hill sailed serenely on to victory at an average of 80.1 mph. It was a sweet moment for the Londoner after his crash in the Spanish Grand Prix a fortnight ago.

Brilliant batting takes Australia near victory against West Indies

By Henry Calthorpe in Adelaide
PUBLISHED MONDAY 27 JANUARY

One of the most entertaining day's play of the series saw Australia's batsmen take their side to an almost impregnable position in the fourth Test against the West Indies in Adelaide on Saturday.

Almost 400 runs were scored in the day and, at 424 for six, Australia are 148 runs ahead, so that the West Indies look likely to be forced to bat for two days to save this match and the series.

The most exciting batting came during the afternoon when Ian Chappell and Ian Redpath, facing Gary Sobers and Lance Gibbs, added 78 exhilarating runs in 53 minutes, repeatedly coming down the wicket so that the bowlers were in effect made to bowl where the batsmen wanted.

Redpath matched Chappell for footwork and power and certainty of stroke and there appeared to be nothing that Gibbs and Sobers could do about it.

They were driven repeatedly through the covers and when they dropped short the batsmen were quick to get on the back foot and cut or force. This stand broke the back of the West Indies effort, for although Chappell and Redpath got out within six runs of each other, the bowlers could not regain the control to restrict Doug Walters and Paul Sheahan.

It is a mark of the tremendous improvement of the Australian batting during this series that none of the West Indies bowled especially badly. It was simply that their best was not good enough to contain such exciting hard-wicket players.

Chappell and Redpath's magnificent stand ended when Chappell turned Gibbs round the corner and Sobers' reflexes enabled him to take an amazing catch at backward short leg. Six runs later Redpath was lbw sweeping at Joey Carew, and it seemed as if the West Indies might keep Australia's lead within bounds.

But Walters, in his concentrated, almost workmanlike way, and Sheahan, upright and elegant, saw to it that the West Indies had no relief.

Doug Walters averaged 116.5 on the five-match tour, which Australia won 3–1.

1969

1969

Stewart triumphs in wheel-to-wheel duel

By Colin Dryden at Monza
PUBLISHED MONDAY 8 SEPTEMBER

Jackie Stewart, of Scotland, driving a Matra-Ford, clinched the world championship at Monza yesterday after a wheel-to-wheel fight to the finishing line with Jochen Rindt to win the Italian Grand Prix by inches. He now has an unassailable lead with 60 points.

It was one of the closest grand prix races – only just over a second separating the first five cars after 60 of the 68 laps of the terrifyingly fast Monza circuit.

Stewart completed the distance in 1 hr 39 min 11.26 sec, at a record average of 146.97 mph.

Rindt (Lotus-Ford), was timed at 1 hr 39 min 11.34 sec. But the fastest lap, a record, was put in by Jean-Pierre Beltoise at 150.97 mph. The French Matra-Ford driver finished third.

Stewart was in the lead for 59 laps, but the result was not certain until the chequered flag fell. Rindt, second for the first six laps, led on lap seven followed by Stewart, Denny Hulme (McLaren-Ford), Piers Courage, Jo Siffert (Lotus-Ford) and Bruce McLaren.

Courage kept well up with the leaders in a brilliant drive throughout the race to finish fifth, but Hulme and Siffert were forced to drop back with mechanical troubles.

As the race went on, fiercely fought lap by lap, Graham Hill wormed his way through the field to challenge Stewart and Rindt. He was fourth on lap 25 and third on lap 36. Ten laps later, he was second behind Stewart, and leading his Lotus teammate Rindt.

Hill, the reigning world champion, looked almost certain of second place until he slipped back to third five laps from the end, and then disappeared from the race altogether with a broken drive shaft.

In the closing stages, Rindt was harrying Stewart every inch of the way. The Scot and the Austrian took the finishing flag side-by-side, followed by Beltoise.

MILESTONES

In Australia the first one-day cricket competitions were held this year. In Britain overseas players calling themselves the Cavaliers entertained crowds to 40-over matches on a Sunday; their popularity led to the establishment of the Sunday League competition.

Threat to step up Springbok protests

PUBLISHED WEDNESDAY 24 DECEMBER

Mr Peter Hain, chairman of the Stop the '70 Tour Committee, said yesterday that demonstrations against the Springbok rugby tourists would no longer be confined to the remainder of their matches.

His warning followed a threat by Mr Corrie Bornman, the South Africans' manager, that the tour could be called off.

Mr Hain said: 'With increasing security on the game itself, the Springboks can expect direct action protests. Demonstrations will no longer be confined to matches.'

The current campaign against racialist sport in general had proved that opposition to apartheid in sport was widespread and massive, and certainly not confined to 'long-haired students', as the supporters of racialism claimed.

'We believe that it is the extent of this anti-apartheid feeling throughout the country which has affected the white South African team psychologically, and so affected their performances,' said Mr Hain.

The Bishop of Coventry, Dr Cuthbert Bardsley, is to take part in a protest march when the Springboks visit Coventry on 6 January – but only if there is no violence. The Bishop said yesterday: 'I dislike South Africa's apartheid policy intensely.'

Demonstrators show their contempt for the South African regime by giving the fascist salute during the game between South Africa and Oxford University.

England forwards pave way to historic victory at Twickenham

By John Reason
PUBLISHED MONDAY 22 DECEMBER
England 11 pts; South Africa 8

No one watching South Africa's forbidding forward domination in the first quarter of an hour of this international, in the gloom and the mist of Twickenham, would have given England any chance of overhauling a lead of eight points.

After half an hour South Africa led by a goal and a penalty goal, and yet the England forwards fought back so magnificently that they scored two tries themselves and gave Bob Hiller the chances to kick a penalty goal and conversion to win the match.

It was the first time that England had beaten South Africa since the two countries first played each other, 63 years ago.

Instead of being penalised for an early tackle, South Africa were allowed to play on. Nigel Starmer-Smith and Hiller fumbled the ball between them, D. Walton snatched it up and spun to feed Piet Greyling, who was tearing down the left touchline.

Greyling scored in the corner, and Piet Visagie converted the try with a beautiful kick. Visagie had already kicked a penalty goal, when K. Fairbrother was penalised for barging in a line-out.

The England front row kept the scrum steady and the strikes against the head down to 3–2, and they all had a day to remember in the loose.

The crowd sensed it and began to chant 'England, England'. The England forwards then not only lit the blue touch paper but they went off with such a bang that they dominated the match for the next 40 minutes.

The Springboks arrive at London airport at the beginning of their tour which, dogged by protest and controversy, was to be their last until the 1990s.

Two-stroke triumph puts Jacklin on road to £250,000

By Leonard Crawley
PUBLISHED MONDAY 14 JULY

Tony Jacklin, 25, whose attitude to golf has been based on courage, a spirit of adventure, rigid self-discipline, patience and character, won the Open championship at Royal Lytham and St Annes on Saturday by two strokes from Bob Charles, of New Zealand.

Jacklin's total of 280 came from rounds of 68, 70, 70 and 72. Two former champions of great distinction, Peter Thomson (Australia) and Roberto de Vicenzo (Argentina), tied for third place on 283.

Thus, on a great day for British golf, Jacklin became the first British player to win an Open since Max Faulkner's victory at Royal Portrush in 1951. I confidently predict that Jacklin has a great golfing future.

He has kept himself in superb physical condition, though the temptations of the tour have proved too great for lesser mortals. His early, almost precocious success in America, surpassing anything Britain's Henry Cotton ever achieved there, led people to think prematurely that Jacklin had arrived.

Tony Jacklin, son of a Scunthorpe steelworker, shouldered the weight of British expectations as he tackled the course at Royal Lytham.

It is interesting for me to reflect that his triumph at Lytham comes so soon after our recent meeting at Houston, Texas, during the United States Open. Then he confided that he was emerging from a period in the doldrums. It was at this critical period that Jacklin decided to begin all over again, and he began on his backswing.

The slowing down of his backswing began to work wonders, and there was, at Houston, a majesty about his game that was new and impressed me and my colleagues. Though he was never really in contention, when the pressure came on towards the end of the championship, he struck me as having real possibilities at the time.

No one watching him at Lytham, in the flesh or on television, could have been other than confident in our man. I have watched no more solid and inspiring performance than Jacklin's since Henry Cotton was at the height of his powers in 1937.

Rocky Marciano, lion of the ring

By Terry Godwin
PUBLISHED TUESDAY 2 SEPTEMBER

Rocky Marciano **(below)**, who was killed in an air crash on Sunday, had the punch strength and streak of victories to be acknowledged as the greatest heavyweight champion of all time.

Marciano became champion of the world in 1952 and retired four years later with a record of 49 wins in a total of 49 contests.

Few fighters before him, and none since, gained such success so quickly, for his career spanned only eight years and his earnings exceeded $1,750,000. If

these are the statistics that are the measure of a great champion, not even Jack Johnson, Jack Dempsey, Gene Tunney, Joe Louis or Cassius Clay can be compared.

To most people, Rocky Marciano would be the greatest champion of all time because, no matter who the opponent, and regardless of his style, strength, punch, cleverness or durability, this lion of a man usually mauled him to defeat inside the distance.

The lion of the ring was the lamb out of it. Boxing, which has had so many heroes, has had very few who made the transformation so completely; and there will be many who will remember this great fighter for that alone.

SPORT IN BRIEF

CRICKET
After the cancellation of the tour to South Africa, Colin Cowdrey leads an England tour to Pakistan. All three Tests are drawn, but the first and third are marred by disturbances among the spectators. The third Test in Karachi is abandoned after three days because of rioting. Alan Knott – on 96 not out – is denied his first Test century.

BOXING
In July Mashiko 'Fighting' Harada is controversially defeated on points by Australian Johnny Famechon for the world featherweight title in Sydney. Harada had Famechon down three times, but referee Willie Pep, himself a former featherweight champion, declared the fight a draw before admitting to an error and giving the decision to Famechon.

GOLF
In an exciting Ryder Cup match at Royal Birkdale in September, Jack Nicklaus meets Tony Jacklin – the new British Open champion. As they approach the final tee, the match score is $15\frac{1}{2}$ points each. Jacklin putts short, then Nicklaus has a putt for a birdie, but misses, holing it in the next shot for a par. He picks up Jacklin's ball rather than see him miss – and the match is drawn 16 all. As holders, the Americans keep the trophy.

FOOTBALL
In October Celtic win their fifth successive League Cup. In the final they face St Johnstone, who put up a good performance, but lose 1–0, the only goal being scored by Celtic's Bertie Auld.

GOLF
The United States win a twelfth successive Walker Cup competition against Britain and Ireland, 10–8. The Ryder Cup is the professional equivalent of this amateur event.

1969

189

1970

Springboks chief tells of bomb death fear

By a Daily Telegraph *reporter*

PUBLISHED MONDAY 2 FEBRUARY

Mr Corrie Bornman, manager of the South African rugby party which flies home tonight, spoke yesterday of his fears of 'a madman' planting a bomb on their coaches or planes during the tour.

'I could never have lived with myself had one of the players been killed,' said Mr Bornman. He was explaining for the first time how he felt as demonstrations against the Springboks increased.

Mr Bornman, who has consistently refused to comment on the effect of the anti-apartheid demonstrations on the team, admitted the threats of violence were worrying.

Asked whether he had considered cancelling the Irish part of the tour, Mr Bornman said: 'Had the British rugby officials told us it would be dangerous to go to Ireland we would not have gone. But I think we would have been cowards not to have gone to Dublin.'

After all the threats and demonstrations at Dublin and Bray, the tourists had one of their 'nicest visits' at Limerick. 'There was an intense rugby atmosphere, which was like a balm on our nerves.'

Of the players he said: 'They showed courage in coming back every time. There were a lot of outside influences, and yet they always tackled each new game with absolute determination.' He added that the tour organisers could 'not have done better', considering the demonstrations.

The last contest – one with words – was being fought last night, with both rugby officials and demonstrators claiming victory. Mr John Tallent, chairman of the Home Union tours committee, said, 'We faced a challenge – and rugby football won the day.' Peter Hain, 19, chairman of the Stop the '70 tour commented, 'We would have settled for a tenth of the impact.'

DID YOU KNOW?

Austrian Jochen Rindt, who was killed during practice for the Italian Grand Prix, was the first driver to win the Formula One world championship title posthumously.

Joe Frazier ranks with the best, but lacks challengers

By Donald Saunders in New York

PUBLISHED WEDNESDAY 18 FEBRUARY

The world has found itself a good, new young heavyweight champion, possibly in the nick of time, perhaps a little too late, to save boxing from extinction as a major spectator sport.

If, three years ago, Joe Frazier, now 26, had been throwing his left hook with the power and precision that destroyed 29-year-old Jimmy Ellis at Madison Square Garden on Monday night, there now would be no doubt about the health of this ancient sport.

En route to victory over Ellis, who failed to come out for the fifth round, Frazier suggested he would have given Cassius Clay, otherwise Muhammad Ali, a hard enough fight to persuade even the sceptics that boxing has a future.

Alas, as he succeeds to the throne, he is in danger of finding himself ruler of a barren kingdom. Only if Clay is allowed, or wishes, to return to the battlefield shall we discover just how good Frazier is.

By the second round it was clear that he was going to be too strong, too persistent, for his older rival. But no one among the 18,000 spectators could have imagined that the battle would be won and lost inside five rounds.

The turning point came in the third when Ellis landed his 'sneaky' right bang on target. Frazier merely shrugged his shoulders and grinned.

'I told him then, "Cissy, you can't hit. I can take anything you throw and you won't hurt me",' Frazier later explained. How prophetic were those words.

Before Ellis knew what was happening he was trapped on the ropes and hooked savagely to the jaw. Then came a hail of lefts and rights to head and body. Bravely Ellis took his punishment and came out for more in the fourth. He did not have to wait long.

A left hook stretched him full length on the canvas for six, the further two seconds he was allowed on regaining his feet were not enough to clear his head.

Though he held on desperately, he could not get away from that left hook. Frazier threw it again – and once more Ellis crashed to the boards. As the bell sounded the timekeeper had reached seven. At nine Ellis struggled up and staggered to the sanctuary of his stool.

Angelo Dundee, perhaps the greatest corner man in the world, tried to talk him back to reality. 'There was no response,' confessed a sad Dundee later. So, as the buzzer warned them to prepare for the resumption of hostilities, Dundee waved his arms wide in surrender.

Frazier indisputably was the king.

Davis Cup disaster

PUBLISHED MONDAY 11 MAY

The kindest thing to say about Austria's 3–2 victory over Great Britain in the first round of the European zone of the Davis Cup in Edinburgh is that it was their best win and Britain's worst defeat of all time.

The Austrian captain, Kurt Schwendenwein, was frank enough before the tie to assess his country's chance as no better than a 30 per cent probability of winning.

Now, having come through, this minor lawn tennis nation is caught on the wrong foot at having to arrange a tie against France, for which they never bargained.

Granted the merit of Britain pulling back to level terms after the original deficit of 2–0, it was still a sad performance.

The pity of it was that Scotland staged their first Davis Cup tie with the utmost efficiency, only to have the affair marred by bad weather and a poor home performance.

There is no point in recrimination, even if the omission of David Lloyd from the team was a hot talking point. The fact is that at present a strong Davis Cup side for Britain does not seem a possibility.

Britain have as much to gain as most nations in wanting the competition made open to contract professionals. In any case, the prestige of the Davis Cup as a whole calls for such reform.

Brabham second to Rindt after crash on last corner

By Colin Dryden in Monte Carlo
PUBLISHED MONDAY 11 MAY

Jochen Rindt of Austria (Lotus 49C) won the Monaco Grand Prix yesterday with a storming finish after Jack Brabham, the leader, had crashed on the last corner.

Brabham limped in second with a smashed nose-cone on his Brabham BT33, and Henri Pescarolo, of France, drove his Matra-Simca with great dash for third place. Denny Hulme of New Zealand was fourth in a McLaren-Ford.

It was one of the greatest Formula One races Monaco has seen.

The incredible Graham Hill, 41, five times a winner, and starting fourth from the back of the grid in a borrowed Lotus he had not seen before, was fifth. Pedro Rodriguez, of Mexico, brought a Yardley BRM into sixth place.

Rindt's record-winning time was 1 hr 54 min 36.6 sec, a speed of 81.6 mph. In his desperate attempt to catch Brabham he set up a lap record of 1 min 23.3 sec The tigerish Austrian, 27, cut back an 11-second deficit in four laps of the twisting 'round-the-houses' circuit.

Brabham was baulked by back-markers on the last corner of the last lap. Undecided as to which side to pass, and with Rindt breathing down his neck, he went past his braking distance for the gasometer curve.

Then Brabham's brakes locked and the car struck a barrier, damaging the front fins and nose-cone. It was bad luck for the Australian triple world champion. Although robbed of victory, however, Brabham's second place gives him the lead in the world championship with 15 points against Jackie Stewart's 13 points.

Stewart was unfortunate, like the other March drivers except Petersen. Stewart led the race for the first 27 laps and was pulling away from Brabham and Chris Amon (March-Ford) until he had to go into the pits with rotor arm trouble. He struggled on in tenth place, and finally retired his Tyrell March-Ford with ignition problems.

The Monaco Grand Prix was the first of five won by Jochen Rindt (above) in 1970. He went on to take the Dutch, French, British and German Grands Prix before being killed in practice at Monza.

191

1970

SPORT IN BRIEF

FOOTBALL
Manchester City end a successful season by winning the League Cup final – beating West Bromwich Albion 2–1 – and the European Cup Winners' Cup. In the final of the European competition they face the Polish team Gornik Zabrze. Neil Young scores City's first goal, and is in with another clear scoring chance when he is brought down by the Polish goalkeeper. Francis Lee scores from the penalty spot. Although Gornik pull one goal back midway through the second half, City win 2–1.

BASKETBALL
Bob Cousy is elected to basketball's Hall of Fame. The 'Houdini of Hardwood' began his professional career with the Boston Celtics in 1950, playing with them for 13 years. The 6 ft 1 in Cousy amazes opponents and audiences with his extraordinary sleights of hand and dazzling play. In his first season with the Celtics he helps them to 39 victories (they had won 22 games the season before), and from 1957 until his retirement in 1963 Cousy inspires his team to six championship titles.

CRICKET
A tour of England by the South African cricket team is cancelled eight days before it was due to begin. Although the Cricket Council intended to go ahead with the tour, James Callaghan's government has requested that it should be called off. Twelve African Commonwealth countries – which had been threatening to boycott the Commonwealth Games in Edinburgh because of the Springboks' tour – will now compete. The Cricket Council issues a statement deploring 'the activities of those who, by the intimidation of individual cricketers and threats of violent disruption, have inflamed the whole issue.'

1970

Piers Courage dies in grand prix crash

By Colin Dryden

ZANDVOORT, HOLLAND, MONDAY 22 JUNE

Piers Courage, 28, the racing driver, was burned to death when his car crashed and caught fire in the Dutch Grand Prix at Zandvoort yesterday.

His Italian Formula One de Tomaso car left the track on the 23rd lap, hit a bank and rolled over. Dutch firemen tried desperately to release him, but he was trapped in the blazing wreckage.

Mr Courage's wife, the former Lady Sarah Curzon, who was watching the race from the pits, was led away by Mr Louis Stanley, secretary of the Grand Prix Drivers' Association, and a woman friend.

Lady Sarah, a daughter of the late Earl Howe, himself a former racing driver, married Mr Courage, son of Mr Richard Courage, head of the Courage brewery business, in 1966. They have two sons, Jason, three, and Amos, one.

As smoke billowed over the circuit an official announcement said that the car had crashed but that the driver was all right. Organisers said later that the announcement was a mistake, due to the smoke and confusion.

The heat from the blaze was so intense that surrounding woodland was completely destroyed.

Four minutes of magic shatter Italian dreams

By Donald Saunders

MEXICO CITY, SUNDAY 21 JUNE
Brazil 4; Italy 1

Brazil proved beyond all possible doubt that they are the greatest soccer nation in the world, sweeping to handsome victory over Italy at the Aztec Stadium in Mexico City yesterday.

The gifted Latin-Americans experienced greater difficulty reaching the safety of the dressing room after winning their third World Cup final in 12 years than they had in wrecking the Italian defence. Within seconds of

An emotional Pelé celebrates Brazil's victory over the European champions with his teammates.

the final whistle, the Brazilian players were dragged to the turf by deliriously happy supporters and stripped of their yellow and green jerseys.

With more than an hour gone, nobody would have been prepared to bet on which of these teams was to earn the distinction of becoming the first outright holders of the Jules Rimet Trophy.

Even after Brazil had jumped ahead in the 18th minute, with Pelé heading home a perfectly placed cross from Rivelino, I was still uncertain of a Latin-American triumph. But the six greatest footballers in the world refused to be harnessed. Pelé, Jairzinho, Tostao, Rivelino, Gerson and Clodoaldo, decided the Italian defence could be shattered. Midway through the second half they proved their point with four minutes of magic.

Two goals in that crucial period left Italy without a hope of becoming the first European nation to win the World Cup on the western side of the Atlantic.

Then, as the stadium clock ticked to within four minutes of the final whistle, Carlos Alberto, Brazil's captain, raced upfield to score his first goal in the tournament.

Taylor ends Laver decade as seeds go tumbling

By Lance Tingay at Wimbledon

PUBLISHED MONDAY 29 JUNE

The lawn tennis championships at Wimbledon begin their second week today with the probability of an all-Australian men's singles final between John Newcombe and Tony Roche, in contrast to a week ago when the expectation was of a title match between Rod Laver and Arthur Ashe.

There can have been few endings to the opening week so full of conflicting emotions. Sadness that the dominance of so superb a player as Laver should come to an end on Saturday was balanced by the patriotic delight that a Briton, Roger Taylor, had brought about that spectacular downfall.

Regret that Britain's Virginia Wade failed in melancholy fashion to justify her seeding at No. 3 was compensated by the joy that another Briton, Winnie

Shaw, had won a quarter-final place against the odds.

The demise of the brilliant Ashe, who deserved to be at least a finalist, was occasioned by the Spaniard, Andres Gimeno. One may reflect that justice of sorts was done in this, since Gimeno, a player of the finest touch, has never before quite met with his deserts at Wimbledon.

I suppose Roche will play Newcombe in the final next Saturday, with the lesser possibility that Ken Rosewall or Clark Graebner might do so instead.

Taylor has already brought off one miracle, so his chances of survival must not be ignored. Indeed, the omens are by no means poor, for he beat Graebner at Forest Hills last year, and early this year he brought down Roche in Australia.

Win or lose, Taylor has already accomplished enough this year to link his name with the 1970 Wimbledon. He was the instrument, a most able one, that brought the invincibility of a decade to an end.

DID YOU KNOW?

Brazil's victory in the 1970 competition was their third World Cup success, and earned them the right to keep the Jules Rimet Trophy in perpetuity. From 1974 a new FIFA World Cup was presented to the winners.

Jacklin wins the US Open

PUBLISHED MONDAY 22 JUNE

Tony Jacklin, 25, the British Open golf champion, yesterday won the US Open at the Hazeltine National course, near Minneapolis. He's the first Englishman to capture the title since Ted Ray in 1920.

Starting the fourth round four strokes ahead of Dave Hill, the American Ryder Cup player, Jacklin, who had led in every round, scored a final 70, two under par to take the title by seven strokes, with Hill second on 288.

Jacklin's victory brought him a prize of £12,500, but his potential earnings as double Open champion run into hundreds of thousands of pounds from advertising contracts, exhibition matches and the like.

He finished yesterday's final round like a true champion, with a bold, long putt into the 18th hole for a birdie three.

Jacklin, with his arm around his wife, Vivienne, said afterwards: 'I'm very proud to be an Englishman.' He added that he had not felt confident of winning till he had a par on the 17th hole.

'I thought about that treacherous dog-leg all last night and all through all the play today,' he explained. 'When I had a par I thought: "The Open is mine, it really is mine."'

Tony Jacklin drives to glory in the US Open; he had taken the British Open title less than 12 months before.

Mrs Court earns triple crown in memorable final

By Lance Tingay
WIMBLEDON, SATURDAY 4 JULY

Margaret Court, of Australia, won the women's singles crown for the third time in the lawn tennis championships at Wimbledon yesterday by beating Billie Jean King, of the United States, 14–12, 11–9. Had Mrs King won the title, for the fourth time, equal justice would have been done.

The general course of the women's singles this year had been flat and unspectacular. The event was retrieved by a final that was magnificent and memorable, one of the finest ever played.

Not only that, it was the longest. The 46 games played between Mrs Court and Mrs King exceeded by two the previous record of 44, set in 1919 by Suzanne Lenglen and Dorothea Lambert Chambers.

And the 26-game opening set was not only the longest played in a women's singles final but the longest of any Wimbledon singles final, men or women. How can one talk of the weaker sex? From start to finish each player strove to impose her game on the other.

It was the demanding serve-and-volley technique all the way. The cut and thrust of attack was pushed back by defence, with one fine shot being countered by another that was even better. One could not see how the issue could be resolved.

It is academic whether there have been better finals. Perhaps there have been one or two. This, though, was among those that will be long remembered and, as I have said, had the American instead of the Australian got the decision, sporting prowess would have been just as well rewarded.

Following victory at Wimbledon, Mrs Court went on to win the US Open, becoming only the second woman after Maureen Connolly in 1953 to win the Grand Slam.

SPORT IN BRIEF

FOOTBALL

The World Cup, held in Mexico City in June, is one of the most exciting and entertaining to date. Teams are allowed to field substitutes for the first time; a rule change that has a direct bearing on England's fortunes. After going 2–0 up against West Germany in the quarter-finals, Bobby Charlton is substituted, and the game turns West Germany's way. Franz Beckenbauer and Uwe Seeler bring the score back to 2–2, and the game goes into extra time; eight minutes later West Germany's Gerd Müller puts his team 3–2 up and into the semi-finals.

GOLF

In the fourth round of the British Open at St Andrews, pre-qualifier Doug Sanders needs to hole his putt at the 18th to record a superb victory, but misses. Tied on 283, he and Jack Nicklaus meet in a play-off over 18 holes. Nicklaus's enormous drive of more than 350 yards to the 18th hole sets him up for a birdie and the title.

ATHLETICS

At the Commonwealth Games in Edinburgh, outstanding Kenyan athlete Kipchoge Keino (**below**) wins gold in the 1,500 m. Kip Keino has already broken world records in the 3,000 m and 5,000 m, won gold medals in the one-mile and three-mile races in the 1966 Commonwealth Games in Jamaica, and a gold medal in the 1,500 m in the 1968 Olympics.

1970

1970

Newcombe power triumphs over Rosewall finesse

By Lance Tingay
PUBLISHED MONDAY 6 JULY

'It's real misery,' declared John Newcombe, 26, after winning the men's singles at Wimbledon for the second time. He was referring to being on the centre court with everyone expecting him to win but hoping that his opponent, Ken Rosewall, would do so.

This was the slightly cynical reaction of a real professional, and I doubt if the Wimbledon singles was ever won by a more utterly professional player; able, dedicated, realistic, powerful and uncompromising.

Sentiment was with Rosewall almost 100 per cent. He played enough of his superb backhand strokes, usually as breathtaking passing shots, and enough of his immaculate volleys to stress anew the satisfaction he gives to the connoisseur. But he could not prevent Newcombe's overpowering skill from thwarting him. Newcombe's winning score was 5–7, 6–3, 6–2, 3–6, 6–1.

Rosewall won the first set after saving a set point at 4–5. Newcombe, now asserting his intimidating power with smooth efficiency, took sets two and three commandingly. He led 3–1, 30–0 in the fourth set and poised himself for victory.

The sequence that followed was one of the most unusual I have witnessed. Newcombe fell into a kind of daze. He afterwards confessed that the strain of playing not only the match but against the sympathy of the crowd had numbed him.

At one stage he was so confused that he tried to serve without a ball. Rosewall pounced into the victory area that was opened up. He collared the next 12 points in sequence and 20 out of the next 23. It gave him five games for the loss of three points only and squared the match at two sets all.

Newcombe recovered himself and that was that. This entrancing final lasted two hours 43 minutes, the longest for many years.

MILESTONES

The first New York City Marathon for men and women took place in 1970. The winner of the men's race was G. Muhrcke, who finished in 2 hr 31 min 38 sec; there was no woman finisher in the first year.

Nijinsky earns a place among immortals

By Hotspur
PUBLISHED MONDAY 14 SEPTEMBER

Nijinsky may not have beaten a great field when landing his Triple Crown with a St Leger win at Doncaster on Saturday, but this was no empty triumph for Mr Charles Engelhard's champion.

A truly great horse, he needs not only skilled training and jockeyship to place him among the immortals, but he needs to be raced with fearless sportsmanship as well.

Mr Engelhard, on the advice of his trainer, Vincent O'Brien, behaved in just such a manner when subjecting Nijinsky's stamina to the St Leger's uncompromising 14½ furlongs.

Nijinsky's commercial value would have suffered not one whit had his stable kept the colt to mile-and-a-half races following his Derby triumph. By resisting such temptation they have now given recorded proof that Nijinsky possesses a versatility matched only by that of Ribot among postwar European champions.

Nijinsky, who has won at all distances upward from six furlongs, settled a truly run St Leger with that customary burst of speed which took him ahead one-and-a-half furlongs from home.

My own opinion, not generally shared, is that he was tiring towards the finish. He is now a 5–2-on chance for the Prix de l'Arc de Triomphe.

Nijinsky had already taken Lester Piggott to his fifth Derby win, running the course faster than any horse since Mahmoud in 1936. The Prix de L'Arc de Triomphe proved too much for him, though; he lost by a head.

LESTER PIGGOTT (1935–)

THE LEADING BRITISH JOCKEY of the modern era and one of the most successful riders in Turf history, Lester Keith Piggott was born on 5 November 1935 in the town of Wantage, near Newbury. Racing was in his blood. His grandfather had ridden three Grand National winners, and his father was a prominent trainer. Piggott made his debut in a public race when he was only 12.

Piggott rode his first winner a few months later at Haydock Park in 1948. After this his rise was meteoric. In 1954, he gained the first of his record-breaking 30 victories in the Classics, romping home in the Derby with Never Say Die. From the outset,

his passion for winning was all too apparent, leading to suspensions and fines for reckless riding.

From 1954–6, Piggott enjoyed a fruitful partnership with the trainer Noel Murliss. Then he went freelance. It proved a shrewd move, and he became one of the richest sportsmen in Britain. Many of his subsequent rides, including Nijinsky in 1970, were for Vincent O'Brien.

Piggott retired in 1985, but was charged with tax evasion two years later and spent a year in jail. After his release, he took up racing again. In 1992, now in his late 50s, Piggott won the 2,000 Guineas riding Rodrigo de Triano.

Regazzoni roars to Monza triumph

By Colin Dryden in Monza
PUBLISHED MONDAY 7 SEPTEMBER

Clay Regazzoni, 30, the Swiss-Italian driving a Ferrari, won yesterday's thrilling Italian Grand Prix in Monza, the lead changing hands 30 times, to the delight of 100,000 spectators. Jackie Stewart (March-Ford), the reigning world champion, was second, and Jean-Pierre Beltoise (Matra) third.

It was Ferrari's first victory on their home ground for four years. A newcomer to grand prix racing this season, Regazzoni won his first Formula One victory at his fourth attempt.

The event was clouded by the death of Jochen Rindt in practice on Saturday, and none of the Lotus-Ford team were on the grid for the start.

The world championship after Rindt has Stewart level with Brabham on 25 points, closely followed by Hulme with 23, Regazzoni with 21 and Jacky Ickx with 19.

Surtees, in his Surtees TS7, got going two laps late but soon dropped out and the early pace-setters were Jacky Ickx, Pedro Rodrigues (Yardley BRM), and Stewart, leading from Regazzoni and Jackie Oliver (Yardley BRM).

With a third of the race gone and Stewart leading, Brabham crashed, when lying seventh, on the same bend as Rindt. Brabham walked away from the wreckage.

Ten laps from the end of the 68-lap event, the pace having taken its toll, it was still anybody's race. Then, on lap 60, Regazzoni managed to shake off the pack and pulled clear to win by just over six seconds.

New-style Ali gives Frazier clear warning

By Terry Godwin in Atlanta, Georgia
PUBLISHED WEDNESDAY 28 OCTOBER

Muhammad Ali, the emphatic three-round conqueror of Jerry Quarry in Atlanta on Monday night, will seek one, perhaps two other contests before inducements are offered to Joe Frazier to settle once and for all the world heavyweight championship.

Frazier is officially recognised as champion, but now that Ali is re-established the pressure will be on the unbeaten New Yorker to prove not only that he has been a worthy caretaker in Ali's enforced absence, but that he is honour bound to give Ali a chance to regain a title that was not lost in the ring.

The most influential factor in bringing about a Frazier–Ali meeting, of course, will be financial. Both men would become rich overnight from the fight that, with all its implications, is likely to be the biggest money-spinner in boxing history.

In boxing terms we gleaned not overmuch from the short three rounds, except that Ali is a different fighter, as I suspected he might be. No longer does he float like a butterfly and sting like a bee. He has matured seemingly into a bludgeoning power man that might make even the most ardent admirers of the rugged Frazier wonder who would come off best toe to toe.

Quarry was a stone lighter, shorter in reach and height and possibly a victim of calculated intimidation. One could not help feeling sorry for him.

As referee Tony Perez mumbled instructions, Ali subjected Quarry to the long stare. As Perez intoned, Ali leaned massively forward, glaring threateningly. Quarry, the white All-American boy lost that one, too. He blinked several times.

Quarry managed only two real punches, both to the body, and neither made Ali puff or blink. The rest was

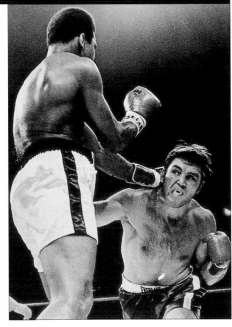

Ali lands a left to Quarry's jaw in his first fight for nearly four years. Having refused to do national service, Ali had been stripped of his title and sentenced to jail; the conviction was finally quashed in June 1971.

painful subjection. The master belligerent thumped Quarry to his body and reddened his features so quickly that it was clear the fight would not take long.

In a way Quarry escaped a more severe hiding when midway through the third round Ali struck home a short chopping right which opened up a two-inch cut over Quarry's left eye.

His trainer saw no reason or hope for heroic acts when he got the unsteady Quarry to his corner at the end of that third round. A look at the damaged eye was enough. The referee merely confirmed the retirement.

1970

195

1971

By Donald Saunders in New York

PUBLISHED WEDNESDAY 10 MARCH

A breathless hush has fallen on the professional ring as Muhammad Ali, the king who once ruled a rugged empire so firmly, nurses a badly damaged jaw, severely wounded pride and, perhaps, a broken heart.

Ali, who began life as Cassius Clay, was confident he could defy sport's oldest maxim that 'they never come back' by taking the heavyweight championship of the world from Joe Frazier after spending most of the last four years lecturing because no one would let him box.

At Madison Square Garden on Monday night he discovered the awful truth that he was wrong, as they led him away to hospital, beaten for the first time in his career, his 'pretty' face grotesquely swollen, the voice that had launched a thousand quips silenced at last.

Though battered, bruised and almost exhausted, 'Smokin' Joe' Frazier had shown us that the butterfly that had once floated so beautifully cannot now fly fast enough and the bee that stung so savagely is no longer spiteful.

Going down but not out: despite his battering, in 1974 Ali would prove he was still 'the greatest', beating Frazier in a rematch, then George Foreman, to regain his heavyweight title.

Uproar as Bugner steals Cooper's triple crown

Bugner raises his arm in triumph after a narrow and controversial points victory over Henry Cooper.

By Donald Saunders

PUBLISHED WEDNESDAY 17 MARCH

A glorious era in the history of British heavyweight boxing ended sadly, noisily and controversially at Wembley Pool last night when the European, British and Commonwealth titles passed from the veteran hands of Henry Cooper.

The triple crown was grasped by young Joe Bugner amid a storm of booing, the like of which the arena has rarely heard before. Afterwards, Cooper announced his retirement from the ring.

When the fight ended, Cooper turned in anticipation towards the referee, Harry Gibbs. Like the rest of us he suffered a tremendous shock as the official promptly held aloft Bugner's right glove.

I simply could not believe it. Nor could most of the crowd. Yet Mr Gibbs, one of the most experienced referees in Europe, made Bugner the new champion by $73\frac{3}{4}$ points to $73\frac{1}{2}$ – the narrowest possible margin.

On my card, Cooper had won this fight with several of the 15 rounds comfortably in hand. He seemed to me to outbox, out-think and outlast a man who is nearly 16 years his junior.

Obviously most of the paying customers, who had been chanting 'Cooper, Cooper' in the closing rounds, shared my views.

But Henry Cooper, always the gentleman, stood there poker-faced, taking his bitter disappointment in his stride before going over to congratulate the man who now sits on the throne he has occupied for most of the last 12 years.

Half-an-hour later the sad message filtered through that Cooper had decided to retire from the sport he had served so nobly since 1954.

But, as we say thank you and farewell to a great king, let us spare a moment for the young man who succeeds him. Who knows, one day Bugner's ascension to the throne may be seen as the dawn of another glorious era.

MILESTONES

The one-day international was born in 1971 when rain washed out play between Australia and England in the fourth Test. The 40-over match that replaced it was a great hit with the Melbourne crowd; Australia won by five wickets.

MUHAMMAD ALI (1942–)

BORN IN LOUISVILLE, KENTUCKY, on 17 January 1942, *Cassius Marcellus Clay was named after an anti-slavery campaigner. He started boxing at the age of 12 and, at the Rome Olympics of 1960, won the gold medal in the light-heavyweight division. Four years later he took the world heavyweight crown when he outclassed a lumbering Sonny Liston.*

Clay soon made his mark as a public entertainer, composing humorous, highly immodest rhymes. Rivals dubbed him 'the Mouth', but Clay had the talent to back up his boasts. At his best, he coupled dazzling footwork – the 'Ali shuffle' – with rapier-like combinations of punches.

After converting to the Black Muslim faith, Clay changed his name to Muhammad Ali and refused to do military service on religious grounds. The ban from boxing that followed was quashed in 1971. In the same year Ali suffered his first professional defeat after a bruising encounter with Joe Frazier. Undismayed, Ali won the rematch and in October 1974 regained his heavyweight title by beating George Foreman in Zaire in the 'Rumble in the Jungle'. He took the title for a record third time in 1978, but probably delayed retirement too long. In 1984 he was diagnosed as suffering from Parkinson's syndrome.

Knott just fails to score second century

By Michael Melford in Auckland
PUBLISHED TUESDAY 9 MARCH

What had been a splendid Test match for most of the first three days died away disappointingly yesterday when England fought a long rearguard action to save the match but did nothing towards winning it.

Alan Knott, who had survived a stumping chance on Sunday evening before he had scored, batted for five hours, and was last out when four runs short of becoming the first England batsman to make two hundreds in a Test match since Denis Compton in 1947.

The concentration which saved a series in Guyana three years ago was turned on again, and it was not until well after lunch that he made any attempt to accelerate.

By contrast, Colin Cowdrey, who made 41 of the day's first 51 runs, played fluently for the second time in the match, though now he had a heavy cold as well as the damaged hamstring which required Brian Luckhurst's services as a runner.

Once Cowdrey and Knott had come comfortably through the first hour, the odds were heavily against England being bowled out in time. But there was still a fair chance that they could come near to winning if Ray Illingworth timed his declaration right. But none was forthcoming and Knott was allowed to continue his advance towards his second hundred. The dullness of play caused some comment from the 5,000 crowd.

There will inevitably be post-mortems. Would New Zealand have won if Bob Cunis had not been taken off on Friday when England were 148 for six? If the batting on Saturday had been more purposeful? But overall there have been encouraging signs for New Zealand cricket in the two-match series and indeed the other matches.

England won the series, 1–0.

Ibrox crowd fell like pack of cards after equalising goal

By Daily Telegraph reporters
PUBLISHED MONDAY 4 JANUARY

An equalising goal near the end of the game between Rangers and Celtic at Ibrox Park, Glasgow, on Saturday, was followed by Britain's biggest soccer ground disaster in which 66 people died.

There had been no scoring in the match, watched by 80,000, until the 88th minute when Celtic went one up. Disappointed Rangers fans were pouring out from the ground when a huge roar announced an equaliser.

Supporters already on their way down the steep steps from the terraces tried to turn back, but they were engulfed by a wave of jubilant fellow supporters leaving at the end of the game.

Victims of Britain's worst soccer tragedy are laid out on the pitch at Ibrox Park. An inquiry into the disaster led to legislation on ground safety.

It happened at the Copland Road end of the ground – the traditional end for Rangers' supporters. People living in a nearby block of flats overlooking the ground said the 'crowd fell like a pack of cards'.

The pressure of the surging mass of people caused metal barriers on the steps to collapse, people fell, were trampled, crushed against stanchions and many were suffocated as hundreds fell on top of them.

Supporters leaving the ground were unaware of what was happening and continued to press forward, pushing more people on to the pile of bodies.

Soon the terracing and pitch looked like a battlefield. Dead and injured were carried on to the pitch and a line of bodies was laid out from one of the goalposts to a corner flag. Ambulances took 108 injured to hospitals.

Mr Willie Waddell, manager of Rangers, said yesterday that the gate of 80,000 was 30,000 short of the ground capacity and he was satisfied with the stewarding of the crowd.

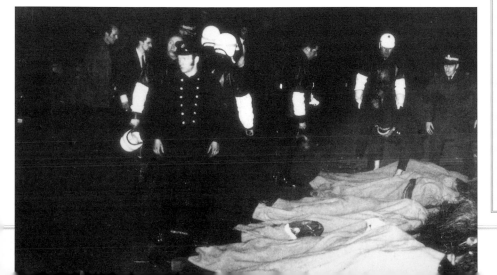

SPORT IN BRIEF

BOXING
The defeat of Henry Cooper by Joe Bugner, and his subsequent retirement (see main text), brings to an end a professional career that has spanned 18 years. Cooper has held the British and Commonwealth world professional heavyweight titles from 1959 to 1970, and has won the European title three times. He has also won three Lonsdale Belts. His tendency to develop cuts easily is the source of his nickname, 'Bleedin' 'Enry'.

FOOTBALL
Pelé scores his last international goal when he plays for Brazil in a friendly match against Austria. It comes 14 years after his first goal for Brazil, which was scored against Argentina in 1957. Pelé retires with a record tally of 77 goals in 92 internationals.

CRICKET
Sunil Gavaskar, playing in his first Test series, makes 774 runs in eight innings against the West Indies in India. 'The little master' makes four hundreds in the series, and his highest score is 220. He completes the four-match series with an extraordinary average of 154.80, helping India to their first victory over the West Indies, and a series win.

GOLF
In 1969 Texan Charles Coody bogeyed the last three holes at the US Masters tournament in Augusta, finishing fifth behind George Archer on 281 and Billy Casper, George Knudson and Tom Weiskopf, all tied on 282. In April this year he is able to lay the ghost of that memory when a first round of 66 sets him up for a Masters win. He finishes on 279, two strokes ahead of Johnny Miller and Jack Nicklaus, who both take 281.

1971

1971

By Donald Saunders
PUBLISHED MONDAY 10 MAY
Arsenal 2; Liverpool 1

Now Arsenal have become the second club of the 20th century to win the FA Cup and League Championship in the same season, they inevitably will be compared with Tottenham, the only other footballers to achieve that distinction since 1897.

This is one notable occasion when comparison is rendered odious by the drastic changes the game has undergone. It is as difficult to measure, fairly, the Spurs of 1961 against the Arsenal of 1971, as it would be to decide whether Charlie George's long hair is more outrageous than was the length of the shorts worn by his illustrious predecessor, the late Alex James.

There was a graceful ease about Tottenham's twin triumph. Arsenal have earned their successes by strength of character in the face of adversity. So who is to say which of these achievements is the greater?

Though my preference always would be for the smoothly skilled football Spurs perfected, I must admit that Arsenal have provided the soccer scene with more dramatic moments.

Few clubs have left a championship triumph so late. None had previously gone home from Wembley with the FA Cup after being a goal behind in extra time.

The Arsenal of 1971 have been a mutual aid society that utilised individual ability and suppressed personal ambition in the interests of the team.

This policy enabled them to snatch the Cup out of Liverpool's eager grasp when it seemed destined to return to Anfield for the second time in seven seasons.

Arsenal captain Frank McLintock (right), surrounded by delighted teammates, lifts the FA Cup. He had already led his team to victory in the European Fairs Cup in 1970, Arsenal's first major trophy for 17 years.

MILESTONES

In an effort to limit the length of matches, Wimbledon introduced the tie-break, to come into operation at 8–8. Marathon encounters such as the two-day, 112-game match between Charlie Pasarell and Pancho Gonzales in 1969 had been causing disruption to tournament schedules.

By a special correspondent in Brisbane
PUBLISHED WEDNESDAY 12 MAY

The British Lions face really hard opposition right at the start of their tour of Australia and New Zealand. Queensland, their opponents in the first match in Brisbane today, beat Scotland last year.

There are five Wallabies in the team, and all but two of the others have played in the State side for some time. It is a greatly improved team, and at present highly confident of success against the tourists.

In fact there is a refreshing atmosphere of expectancy and enthusiasm in Brisbane. Queensland are in the forefront of the new publicity policy to attract the crowds who have stopped watching rugby league and soccer.

'I'm rapt in rugby', is the slogan Queensland have adopted, and their bold, fresh outlook is reflected in the performance of their teams.

The Lions management, while also exuding a fine determination and confidence, are fully aware of the magnitude of the task. Dr Doug Smith, the manager, Carwyn James, the coach, and John Dawes, the captain, pointed out that much of the talk they had heard during these two days had been of New Zealand, but these two games in Australia – they meet New South Wales in Sydney on Saturday – are both difficult for a team that have not had time to find their feet.

However, Dawes believes that the Lions have a better team than the one Wales sent out after winning the championship two years ago. Up front the management no doubt have great expectations from Sean Lynch, the devastating Irish prop, and from Peter Dixon, at last recognised by England as a top-class No. 8.

The Lions lost their first match 11–15 to Queensland, but won 14–12 against New South Wales.

Britain and Ireland clinch it with thrilling 6–2 singles triumph

By Michael Williams, St Andrews

PUBLISHED FRIDAY 28 MAY

Amid some of the most emotional scenes in the history of golf, the Great Britain and Ireland team **(below right)** yesterday won the Walker Cup. They beat the United States 13–11 at St Andrews, scene of their previous solitary triumph back in 1938.

What better time to do it than in this jubilee year of the first match between the two countries. It was a marvellous performance, achieved against all the odds after America had led by a point after the first day and by two with only the eight singles to come. This meant that to win outright Great Britain had to win six of the eight singles; that they did it, under greater pressure than any of them have faced in their lives, speaks volumes not only for their class as golfers but for their character, too.

Michael Bonallack, the captain, afterwards in a choking voice declared it 'the most amazing day of my life', and I have not the slightest doubt that of all the countless triumphs that have come his way in a glittering career, this was the one that gave him the greatest satisfaction.

At lunch on this last day, the Americans led overall 9–7. When Bonallack went four down after six holes to some superlative golf by Lanny Wadkins, the team as a whole had the worst possible start.

It was, as Bonallack modestly remarked later, a 'victory achieved despite their captain.' For Wadkins showed no mercy and beat his man on the 17th green.

But Bonallack's leadership, encouragement and confidence in his team ultimately had its effect.

Playing their very best golf at absolutely the right time, they kept at their American opponent. Marsh's long shot to the Road Hole may have been the finest shot of his life; certainly it was the most critical and certainly it brought the greatest cheer. It found the heart of the green; Marsh got his four, and at that moment Britain had won the Walker Cup.

Weary Ajax clinch Dutch double with late goal

By Donald Saunders

PUBLISHED THURSDAY 3 JUNE

Ajax 2; Panathinaikos 0

Ajax of Amsterdam made sure that the European Cup will remain in Dutch hands for another year by scoring in the opening and closing minutes of a noisy, disappointing final against Panathinaikos, the plucky Athenians, at Wembley last night.

As Vasovic, the Ajax captain, already the possessor of two runners-up medals in this competition, came down from the royal box with the trophy held aloft, scores of youngsters jumped over the barriers and raced on to the pitch to mob their heroes.

Poor Vasovic and several of his colleagues were in danger of being crushed beneath the feet of their eager well-wishers – until they were escorted, at the double, into the tunnel by a posse of policemen.

Meanwhile, as the band of the Corps of the Royal Engineers marched away, the hallowed turf of Wembley was taken over by hundreds of Ajax supporters, all of them, it seemed, waving red and white flags or banners.

Well they did have something to celebrate! A few years ago, Holland were a second-class soccer nation. Now, for the second consecutive season, they have produced the champion club of all Europe.

Ajax did not look potential world-beaters last night. Having snatched an early lead, they tossed away several golden chances of increasing it, then ran out of stamina and had to hang on grimly until a somewhat lucky goal settled the issue a few minutes from time.

Ajax delighted us early on by producing sharp, enterprising football. But, towards the end, my sympathies went out to Panathinaikos, the rankest outsiders ever to play in a European Cup final.

The Greeks lacked the ability to win this match, but their determined rally after the interval saved it from dying. Moreover, in my view, they provided the man of the match, in Elefterakis, a skilful, diligent player, who controlled the middle of the pitch during the second half.

The first Ajax goal should have been the signal for a hatful. Instead Panathinaikos were allowed back into the game. The Dutch must have sighed with relief when Haan hammered a shot forward and saw it twist into the net off the boot of Kapsis a few minutes from the end.

Ferenc Puskas, the Greeks' manager, said: 'The result was fair – Ajax scored twice and football is played for goals. Ajax played from first to last in a self-contained manner. My team took 20 minutes to settle, then did magnificently.'

SPORT IN BRIEF

HORSE RACING

Brigadier Gerard, trained by Dick Hern and ridden by Joe Mercer, wins the 2,000 Guineas at odds of 11–2. Brigadier Gerard becomes one of the few horses to beat the legendary Mill Reef, who finishes three lengths behind. It is the only meeting of these great horses. Like Mill Reef, Brigadier Gerard also enjoys a sparkling career, being beaten only once in 18 races.

FOOTBALL

In June Leeds United take the Inter-Cities Fairs Cup for the second time, beating Liverpool 1–0 on aggregate in the semi-final before overcoming Juventus in the final. The first leg, played in Italy, ends in a two-all draw, Paul Madeley and Mick Bates scoring for Leeds. The second leg also finishes in a draw – 1–1 – with Allan Clarke scoring for Leeds. Leeds win the trophy, the first team to take the cup on the away goals rule (in the event of a tie, goals scored away from home are worth twice as much). The Inter-Cities Fairs Cup will be replaced next year by the UEFA Cup.

EQUESTRIANISM

Princess Anne is winner of the European three-day event title on her horse Doublet. She is awarded the title of BBC Sports Personality of the Year.

YACHTING

British yachtsman Chay Blyth returns to Hamble in August to a hero's welcome from thousands of well-wishers. He has travelled 'the wrong way' round the world, single-handed, in his yacht *British Steel*. The trip began in November 1970, and has taken him west around the globe via Cape Horn, New Zealand and the Cape of Good Hope. He completes the trip in a record time for a single-hulled sailing vessel, 292 days.

1971

1971

Evonne is queen

By Lance Tingay

PUBLISHED SATURDAY 3 JULY

Wimbledon had a storybook finish to the women's singles yesterday when Evonne Goolagong, charming, fresh and only 19, beat the title-holder Margaret Court to make herself the most popular overseas champion since the Brazilian Maria Bueno won for the first time in 1959.

Miss Goolagong is by no means the youngest player to emerge as Queen of Wimbledon, not even the best, for Maureen Connolly was both younger and more efficient.

In terms of popularity, measured by appeal of personality rather than national sentiment, this engaging Australian has had few equals.

Mrs Court, denied winning the event for the fourth time, must have felt she was competing not only against her doubles partner but 14,000 spectators.

Vic Edwards, the Australian trainer who has been a virtual foster-father to Miss Goolagong for many years, was bold enough last year to declare that she might win Wimbledon by 1973.

He was two years wrong in his forecast. Nor did he hint that she might take the French championship into the bargain, a feat she accomplished a month ago.

Evonne Goolagong lifts the Venus Rosewater dish after beating fellow Australian Margaret Court 6–4, 6–1.

Tireless Trevino joins ranks of great champions

By Michael Williams in Southport

PUBLISHED MONDAY 12 JULY

It was entirely appropriate that the 100th Open golf championship should have been won at Royal Birkdale on Saturday by someone rather special. Lee Trevino is certainly that.

At the still young golfing age of 31, goodness knows how many more peaks Trevino will conquer.

Certainly he now stands alongside Jack Nicklaus as one of the world's two supreme players, but, unlike Nicklaus, his mind remains uncluttered with theories and technicalities.

He also retains a freshness of approach that knocks on the head all the laws of averages. The more he plays, the more he enjoys it, and consequently the pressure he should have felt as he neared the unprecedented hat trick of the two major Opens and the Canadian as well, all in four weeks, never materialised.

His seven at the 17th, where he drove into the left sandhill, was not the result of a poor stroke but a too-perfect one. He always allows for a slight fade, but this one went like an unwavering arrow.

Having earlier gone to the turn in 31 to stand five strokes clear of his nearest challenger, it nevertheless now meant that with three strokes at least to spare over his partner, the delightful Liang Huan Lu, he had only one. As his score was changed from 15 under par to 13, a great buzz of anticipation swept the multitude of spectators from every vantage point they could find round the 18th green.

But Trevino, with a drive and a six-iron at this 513-yard hole, reached the back of the green, and his first putt was close enough to make the second a certainty, even though Lu's matching birdie left him with that for the championship.

At 278 for 72 holes, Trevino was 14 under par and six strokes inside Arnold Palmer's previous record at Birkdale of 284 in 1961. In fact no less than six players beat Palmer's score. 'Mr Lu', as he will for ever be known, was second on 279; Tony Jacklin third on 280; another Briton Craig deFoy fourth on 281, and Jack Nicklaus and Charles Coody equal fifth on 283.

At 70,076 the overall attendance was a record for an Open in England.

DID YOU KNOW?

Lee Trevino was only the fourth man in the history of the game to have won the Opens of the United States and Britain in the same year. Bobby Jones in 1930, Gene Sarazen in 1932 and Ben Hogan in 1953 were the others.

Trevino swings into action in 1971. In 1972 he won the Open for the second time; at this point he had taken three of the previous five major championships he had played.

Last-match draw seals Lions' historic triumph

By John Reason in Auckland

PUBLISHED MONDAY 16 AUGUST

New Zealand 14 pts; British Isles 14

Making history is an agonising business. Few of those British people who lived through the Lions' first victory in a series abroad will ever want to repeat the coronary strain of this last battle at Eden Park.

This applied as much to the Lions as it did to their supporters, because the strain was evident through every dragging minute of the second half. In any normal game the Lions would have coasted home.

They had recovered magnificently from a beginning in which they had presented the All Blacks with eight

All Blacks pile in as Lions scrum half Gareth Edwards clears the ball. Although New Zealand won the first Test, the Lions won two and drew one to take the series.

points. By half-time, they had won back all the lost ground. With the brisk wind behind the Lions in the second half, the winning of the match looked a formality.

They added a penalty goal and a dropped goal to the goal and the penalty goal they had scored in the first half, but their play was uncharacteristically constrained, and each time the All Blacks came back.

New Zealand scored a penalty goal and a try to add to their first-half goal and penalty goal and so the match was drawn.

Mill Reef sets record in superb Arc triumph

By Hotspur

PUBLISHED MONDAY 4 OCTOBER

Mill Reef, ridden in copybook style by Geoff Lewis, set a new time record for Longchamp's mile and a half when winning the Prix de l'Arc de Triomphe yesterday by three lengths from Pistol Packer.

Mill Reef has now won 10 of his 12 races and a European record of £256,000 in first prize money, but yesterday provided his finest hour and emphatically placed Mr Paul Mellon's tough little bay colt among the great horses of modern times.

Mill Reef was never out of the first six and never more than four lengths behind the leader, Ossian. He established a position on the rails and did not leave it until approaching the straight. He then pulled out a little and found a gap through between Ortis and Hallez.

Lester Piggott on Hallez had held a brief lead, but the older horse possessed no answer to Mill Reef's acceleration. Mill Reef struck the front just under two furlongs from home. Lewis rode him right out to win in a time which beat by seven-tenths of a second the record set by Levmoss in this race two years ago.

In one season the extraordinary Mill Reef – ridden (right) by Geoff Lewis – came second in the 2,000 Guineas, then went on to win the Derby, the Eclipse in a record time, and the King George VI Stakes, before setting another record in the Prix de l'Arc de Triomphe.

1971

1972

Ireland pack make England pay

By John Reason

PUBLISHED MONDAY 14 FEBRUARY

England 12 pts; Ireland 16

Kevin Flynn, the Irish centre, took a pass from a set scrum and ran straight past David Duckham on the outside to score the winning try for Ireland at Twickenham. It was in the last movement of a match that had laboured along so painfully it seemed as if neither side was capable of winning.

Flynn's try put Ireland ahead 14–12, and Tom Kiernan's simple conversion gave his team victory by a goal, a try, a dropped goal and a penalty goal to a goal and two penalty goals.

Ireland deserved their victory, if only for their forward discipline, and not surprisingly field an unchanged team against Scotland in Dublin on 26 February. Like Wales, whom they play also in Dublin on 11 March, they are unbeaten.

The match was divided by a chill northwesterly wind blowing down the pitch into one half of attack and one half of defence for each side.

England had the help of the wind in the first half and, with Chris Ralston supreme, their forwards overwhelmed Ireland to such an extent in the line-out that they attacked almost incessantly.

They did this despite the failings of the England midfield players, and despite the inflexibility of their kicking tactics, which denied their backs the ball.

With England leading 12–7, both sides gave the impression that they had despaired of their ability to create anything more. The surprisingly patient crowd had arrived at a similar state of mind some time before, but England managed to make two more mistakes in the last eight minutes to lose the match.

Then Duckham missed his tackle and Flynn ran on strongly to plant the ball behind England's posts.

DID YOU KNOW?

The Five Nations rugby union tournament was abandoned in 1972 when Scotland and Wales refused to travel to Ireland. The Bloody Sunday killings in January had brought Northern Ireland to the brink of civil war, and the teams feared for their safety. Ireland had already defeated England and France, but were denied a bid for the title.

Dominant Germans prepare World Cup challenge

By Donald Saunders in Brussels

PUBLISHED MONDAY 19 JUNE

Russia 0; West Germany 3

West Germany became champions of Europe for the first time, and established themselves as early favourites for the 1974 World Cup, with a wholly convincing, highly attractive victory over Russia at the Heysel Stadium in Brussels yesterday.

Indeed, the hysterical reception the German supporters gave their heroes, at the end of the first final of true quality the European championship has produced, suggested that they are already satisfied that the World Cup will not be taken out of Munich two years hence.

With five minutes still to go, thousands of fans, waving a forest of black, red and yellow flags and blowing on klaxons and horns, surged from the terraces.

One or two more fervent characters ran on to the pitch near the German goal and were promptly bundled off by the angry Sepp Maier, who clearly was worried that the match might be abandoned and the trophy dashed from Germany's hands.

For 28 minutes Khurtsilava, the veteran Russian captain, marshalled his troops. Then a shot by Günter Netzer bounced off the bar, Heynckes hammered the ball back, Rudakov pushed it away and Gerd Müller popped it into the net. I have a suspicion that Müller handled the ball, but any doubts we had about Germany's right to be in front disappeared in the 52nd minute with their second goal, from Herbert Wimmer, who drove it into the corner of the net.

On the hour, Müller struck again. From then we were treated to an almost arrogant demonstration of superb soccer by the confident Germans.

For Germany this was the greatest day in their football history since they won the 1954 World Cup. Now, perhaps, only Brazil, the current world champions, could match the Germans.

Frenzied fans put Rangers' European future in danger

By Robert Oxby

PUBLISHED FRIDAY 26 MAY

Rangers 3; Moscow Dynamo 2

The bitter aftermath of the battle of Barcelona left UEFA authorities counting the cost in soccer prestige, and Rangers facing the prospect not only of losing their newly won Cup Winners' Cup, but of being barred from Europe for a long time.

Moscow Dynamo, beaten 3–2 in a match which ended in a riot, have lodged a formal protest, with the full support of their national association, on the grounds that the match was deliberately broken up by 'drunken Scottish fans'.

Although I would question the terms of the protest, there is no doubt that the Russians have a strong case. No club can ever before have been forced to play an important match in such an unnatural atmosphere.

The pitch was invaded four times – at the start, when the players appeared; in the 24th minute, when Colin Stein scored Rangers' first goal (Willie Johnston got the other two in the 40th and 49th minutes); two minutes from the end, when it was thought that the referee had blown for time, and immediately after the final whistle. Each time, Russian players were manhandled and

Two late goals from Eshtrekhov and Mahovikov of Moscow Dynamo failed to ruffle an impressive Rangers, who retained their composure while their fans wreaked havoc. One person died and hundreds were injured in the rioting after the match. Rangers were banned from European competition for a year.

insulted by jeering mobs, and Szabo, the Dynamo midfield player, was struck by a flying bottle. I also saw another Russian player lying unconscious on the pitch.

There can be little criticism of the behaviour of the Rangers players themselves. I saw several of them pleading with their fans, and the manager, Willie Waddell, and his training staff frequently attempted to remove people from the pitch.

There is clearly something dangerous about a situation in which a club can attract such fanaticism, and the authorities – remembering also the appalling scenes in Lisbon after Celtic won the European Cup in 1967 – may feel forced to take action.

To say that a club is not responsible for the behaviour of its fans is to miss the point. Because of the presence of Rangers and their supporters in Barcelona, thousands of innocent people were put in peril from flying bottles and swinging clubs.

Football cannot afford such behaviour, whoever is responsible. It would be wrong, for instance, to blame the Barcelona club for not taking proper precautions, because the behaviour of the Rangers supporters was completely outside their experience.

It is easier to blame the violence on the police. After showing considerable forbearance, they appeared to go berserk, and their wild clubbing of guilty and innocent alike provoked the hail of bottles from the stands.

Whether the match is replayed; whether Rangers keep the first European trophy they have ever won; whether they are barred from Europe…all these issues are irrelevant to the central theme, which is that mesh fences and barbed wire are now necessary on European grounds.

Buchanan bows out in chaos

By Henry Miller in New York

PUBLISHED WEDNESDAY 28 JUNE

An after-the-bell blow or kick in the groin cost Scotland's Ken Buchanan his world lightweight crown at the end of the 13th round of his clash with Roberto Duran of Panama, in New York.

It was one of the most chaotic and undignified climaxes to a title fight ever witnessed at Madison Square Garden. The irony is that Duran was so far ahead of the champion that he could have gone on to win without any of the stigma that now surrounds his victory.

Controversy arose the moment Buchanan fell in obvious agony. My ringside view was obscured by the referee, John Lobianco, but many agreed with Buchanan's trainer, Gil Clancy, that it was a knee to the groin that put Buchanan out of the fight.

Duran, however, claimed it was a punch to the abdomen, and the referee concurred.

What is indisputable is that the crippling blow was delivered after the bell when both fighters were still battling against the ropes with the referee desperately trying to separate them.

Buchanan begged the referee to let him continue, but Mr Lobianco told him: 'I'm not letting you go on. You are in no condition.'

Later, Buchanan was critical of the referee, saying that throughout he had allowed Duran to use his head.

Apart from the controversial ending – which sent Duran's flag-waving compatriots wild with glee but which seemed to numb the majority of the 18,800 crowd – the truth is that the young Panamanian had given Buchanan a thrashing.

Only rarely did Buchanan get on top. He won perhaps three rounds but the rest were unquestionably Duran's, with one even. But Buchanan can look forward to a re-match with Duran in November, by which time he may be better prepared to withstand a constant pounding.

SPORT IN BRIEF

RUGBY UNION

In an effort to encourage the playing of more open rugby, the scoring system is changed. A try is now worth four points instead of three. The try's value has been increasing steadily: originally worth one point, it was raised to two in 1892; and in 1905 it became worth three points.

FOOTBALL

In one of the most extraordinary upsets in FA Cup history, non-league Hereford United knock out First Division Newcastle United in the third round of the competition. They also score one of the best goals in FA Cup history when Ronnie Radford crashes the ball home from 40 yards. The game finishes 2–1 in Hereford's favour, Ricky George scoring the late winner. Hereford are no strangers to the FA Cup; they have appeared in the first round for 17 consecutive years since 1956, a record for a non-league club.

RUGBY LEAGUE

Great Britain win the rugby league World Cup for the third time, following their victories in 1954 and 1960. In the course of the competition they beat New Zealand 53–19 in one of the highest-scoring games in international rugby league history.

HORSE RACING

Roberto, trained by Vincent O'Brien and ridden by Lester Piggott, wins the Epsom Derby. It is Piggott's sixth Derby win, following his sucesses on Never Say Die in 1954, Crepello in 1957, St Paddy in 1960, Sir Ivor in 1968 and Nijinsky in 1970.

FOOTBALL

In the first all-English European final, Tottenham Hotspur win the UEFA Cup when they beat Wolverhampton Wanderers 3–2 on aggregate.

1972

1972

Trevino shatters Jacklin's dream

By Michael Williams at Muirfield
PUBLISHED MONDAY 17 JULY

Lee Trevino **(below left)** became on Saturday only the fourth American to have won the Open championship in successive years. The others are Bobby Jones, Walter Hagen and Arnold Palmer – rich company that Trevino fully deserves to join.

To have come to Muirfield, a course he had never seen in his life, 48 hours before the championship began, and conquer it with a six-under-par 278, reminds one of the late Tony Lema, who did the same thing at St Andrews in 1964. What is more, he was barely out of convalescence after a strength-sapping attack of viral pneumonia.

Altogether, he holed out four times from off the green. The last of these was at the 17th on Saturday afternoon; it provided the final twist to one of the most enthralling final days in the history of the event.

The man who made it so was Jack Nicklaus. He will go down in the record books simply as runner-up, one stroke behind on 279. It will conceal one of the bravest challenges of even his remarkable career. Six strokes behind when he went into the final round, he did a 66 and failed to catch his man by one stroke.

By James Coote
PUBLISHED TUESDAY 5 SEPTEMBER

How the American sprinters must detest coming to compete in Europe! The last time the United States did not win either the 100-m or the 200-m Olympic title was in Rome 12 years ago.

Yesterday in Munich, Valeri Borzov of the Soviet Union filled their cup of unhappiness by adding the 200-m title to the 100-m crown and thus became the first man since Bobby Morrow in 1956 to complete the double.

The weather was cool and gusty, but it did not stop Borzov from running so fast that he cracked Pietro Mennea's newly set European record of 20.2 sec with a run electronically timed at 19.99 sec, rounded off to 20 sec for the record book.

Borzov only held his own round the bend as the two Americans, Larry Black and Larry Burton, arms pumping fiercely, fought to gain an advantage. But as they entered the straight the Russian seemed to relax, and effortlessly overtook the Americans.

Valeri Borzov (above right) sprints to his double victory. Borzov was European champion from 1969 to 1976.

MILESTONES

Indoor handball made its first appearance in the 1972 Olympic Games; Yugoslavia won the gold medal. Archery was also included again, 52 years after it had last featured. John William and Doreen Wilber of the United States took the golds. There were now 195 Olympic events.

Spitz makes it a world-record seven swimming medals

By Pat Besford in Munich
PUBLISHED TUESDAY 5 SEPTEMBER

Mark Spitz, of the United States, made Olympic history by winning his seventh gold medal last night, but even this tremendous achievement was overshadowed by the news that America were ordered to withdraw one of their swimmers from a final because of a drug offence and may lose a gold as a result.

Rick DeMont, 16, from San Rafael, California, winner of the 400-m freestyle on Friday, was barred from starting in the final of the 1,500 m, at which he was the world record-holder, because a drug test following his earlier victory had proved positive.

DeMont, an asthmatic, takes efedrine to combat breathlessness and this is one of the drugs banned by the International Olympic Committee.

In DeMont's absence, the 1,500-m gold medal went to defending champion Mike Burton of the United States, chosen only as a third string for this event, but who came home in a world record time of 15 min 52.58 sec.

The record gold medal tally by Spitz was a feat never achieved by any other competitor in any other sport in the 76 years of the modern Games.

Mark Spitz (left) swims into the record books. His gold medals came in the 100-m and 200-m freestyle, the 100-m and 200-m butterfly, the 4 x 110-m and 4 x 200-m freestyle relays and the 4 x 100-m medley relay.

Mary Peters takes pentathlon with world record

BY JAMES COOTE
PUBLISHED MONDAY 4 SEPTEMBER

Mary Peters, of Britain, at 33 the 'doyenne' of the pentathlon, capped an amazing career to win the Olympic gold medal in Munich yesterday by the slenderest of margins, ten points, in a world record-breaking total of 4,801.

This is a 26-point improvement on the previous record, held by Burglinde Pollak, of East Germany, who could not match the Belfast secretary's amazing two days, and finished third with 4,768.

This was the third Olympics for Miss Peters, who has had 14 years of international competition. She was fourth in Tokyo behind the silver medallist Mary Rand, who was in the stadium yesterday to see her win the gold, and in 1968 Miss Peters finished ninth. The best she has attained in a European championship is fifth in 1962.

So close was yesterday's event that everything hinged on the 200 m, the final event.

Miss Peters made a perfect start and held her own against the faster girls for the first 120 metres. Then the sprinters came through. But Mary struggled on to finish fourth and no one dared guess whether she had won.

At last the scoreboard flashed this message – 'Peters, Mary, 24.08'. We knew then that Britain had won the Olympic pentathlon for the first time, and that Mary had become only the third British girl to win an athletics Olympic gold.

Miss Peters started with a superb hurdles of 13.29 sec to gain a 33-point advantage over Miss Pollak. Then with 53 ft 1³/₄ in the shot putt, she increased her lead by another six points. In the high jump Miss Peters cleared the bar at 5 ft 11³/₄ in. In the long jump Miss Pollak recovered 50 points. Miss Peters narrowly avoided a no-jump to return 19 ft 7¹/₂ in.

Peters (on left, below) gets the start she needs in the 200 m to claim the Olympic pentathlon gold medal. Her points total bettered her British record by 171.

SPORT IN BRIEF

CRICKET

In an exciting Ashes series, Australia and England tie on two matches each, with one match drawn. Australian fast bowler Dennis Lillee begins to show the extent of his talent, taking six wickets for 66 runs in the first Test at Old Trafford. Lillee enjoys an excellent series, taking 31 Test wickets at an average of 17.87, which beats the record for the number of wickets taken by an Australian in England. The Australian fast bowler Bob Massie also makes a spectacular debut, taking 16 for 137 in the second Test at Lord's.

LAWN TENNIS

After a dispute over payments to players between the International Lawn Tennis Federation and the World Championship Tennis organisation, the ILTF bans WCT players, and WCT member John Newcombe is unable to defend his title at Wimbledon. Playing in his first Wimbledon final, Romanian Ilie Nastase faces American Stan Smith. Smith eventually prevails, taking the trophy after winning an epic match 4–6, 6–3, 6–3, 4–6, 7–5.

CHESS

In a highly publicised and bad-tempered match in Reykjavik, Iceland, 29-year-old American Bobby Fischer defeats Boris Spassky of the Soviet Union to take the world chess championship. Fischer is, according to the ranking system, the greatest chess player of all time.

HOCKEY

Australian Ric Charlesworth wins his first hockey cap. A talented cricketer as well, he opened the batting for Western Australia before opting to concentrate on hockey. He will play in three Olympic Games and five World Cup tournaments.

1972

1972

Two golds for little Olga

PUBLISHED SATURDAY 12 SEPTEMBER

Russia and East Germany each landed two individual gold medals in women's gymnastics today.

Olga Korbut, 17, the tiny Russian, won the balance beam and floor exercise events, and Karin Janz, 20, took the golds for the uneven bars and the horse vault. She also took a bronze in the balance beam to add to her silver in the all-round individual.

The all-round title and gold medal went to Russia's Liudmila Tourischeva, and the Russians emerged as the top team.

MILESTONES

The first Benson & Hedges Cup was held. The one-day, limited-overs knock-out competition was won by Leicestershire, captained by Ray Illingworth, who beat Yorkshire by five wickets in the final at Lord's in July.

Shorter's marathon triumph breaks bleak spell

By Donald Saunders, Munich

PUBLISHED MONDAY 11 SEPTEMBER

Frank Shorter, born in Munich just after the war, became the first American to win the Olympic marathon for 54 years when he crossed the finishing line at the Olympic Stadium yesterday more than a lap ahead of Karel Lismont, of Belgium, and Mamo Wolde, the Ethiopian gold medallist in 1968.

Not since John Hayes was awarded one of the most famous marathons of all time, in London in 1908 after Dorando Pietri, of Italy, had been disqualified, has the United States won this Olympic classic.

On that occasion, Pietri reached the Shepherd's Bush stadium first, collapsed several times on the final lap, and was helped over the line by officials. Ultimately, Hayes was promoted from second to first place.

Even this time, the Americans were not allowed to enjoy the satisfaction of seeing their hero enter the stadium first.

As the band played a fanfare of welcome for Shorter and the 80,000 spectators began cheering, a fair-haired youth, wearing blue shirt and orange shorts, with the number 72 pinned on his back, dashed up the tunnel and onto the track.

While officials looked on helplessly, the lad, later identified as Norbert Sudhaus, a German student, sped down the straight. Spectators, informed by the scoreboard that Shorter was leading, at first were puzzled.

Then, as the American appeared at the tunnel entrance, the crowd realised that the other runner was a hoaxer.

Eventually, the youth, who had kept some 80 metres ahead of Shorter, disappeared into the arms of a posse of security police, after completing a full lap.

Though this tasteless prank deprived Shorter of the welcome he deserved, it did not prevent the crowd according him the tumultuous acclaim Olympic marathon winners so richly merit – and always receive.

The young American, whose father was serving as a doctor in the US forces at the time of his birth, had been with the leaders from the start and dominated the race after 15 kilometres.

Minute by minute he widened the gap between him and the rest. By the halfway stage he was more than 65 seconds ahead of his compatriot Kenneth Moore, and Wolde, with Lismont trailing by another 20 seconds. As the race moved on through the suburbs and back towards the stadium, Shorter's grip on the gold medal tightened.

First Moore dropped back to fourth, then Wolde faltered. Though Lismont moved into second place, he never looked like catching Shorter.

Indeed the American strode firmly on through the stifling hot streets to complete the 26 miles 385 yd as fresh as though he had been out for a morning spin around the block.

Worldwide horror at massacre of 11 Israeli hostages

PUBLISHED THURSDAY 7 SEPTEMBER

Amid worldwide condemnation at the murder of 11 Israeli Olympic hostages by Arab guerrillas, West German authorities opened an inquiry last night into their ambush rescue plan that ended in disaster. German police admitted firing first after the terrorists and nine hostages touched down in helicopters at Fürstenfeldbruck air base. Police marksmen failed to kill all the terrorists in their opening burst, and in the battle that followed nine hostages, a policeman and five gunmen died.

As detectives questioned the three Arabs who were captured after the battle and bitter recrimination raged over fixing the blame for the airport disaster, it was claimed that the marksmen fired at the order of an unidentified police captain.

He gave the order after two of the terrorists had left the helicopters to inspect the Boeing 727 airliner which they had demanded should fly them to Cairo.

One of the terrorists was shot dead. Another was wounded. As he fell he fired his Russian-made sub-machine gun, killing a policeman. The other guerrillas promptly killed the hostages.

A second storm raged around West German ministers and officials because of the long delay in admitting that the hostages had been killed.

The captured Arabs, Ibrahim Badran, 20, Abd es Kadir el Dnawy and Samer Mohamed Abdulah, 22, said they were students. Their nationalities are not known but they said they last lived in Jordan and Syria.

Police are investigating how the ringleader of the massacre was able to work as an engineer on an Olympic building site. Two of the terrorists also worked as a gardener and a cook in the Olympic village where two Israelis were killed at the start of Tuesday's siege.

The Games were resumed yesterday after a memorial service which filled the Olympic Stadium. Tunisia was the only Arab country to attend. Some athletes followed the lead of the Israeli and Egyptian teams in withdrawing, but the mood of many was summed up by David Hemery, the bronze medallist, who said: 'If something that is basically awful stops what is basically good, that makes two wrongs. And two wrongs do not make a right.'

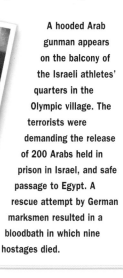

A hooded Arab gunman appears on the balcony of the Israeli athletes' quarters in the Olympic village. The terrorists were demanding the release of 200 Arabs held in prison in Israel, and safe passage to Egypt. A rescue attempt by German marksmen resulted in a bloodbath in which nine hostages died.

Fittipaldi streaks in for Monza Grand Prix and world title

By Colin Dryden at Monza

PUBLISHED MONDAY 11 SEPTEMBER

Motor racing has its youngest world champion with Emerson Fittipaldi's victory yesterday in the Italian Grand Prix. At 25, the Brazilian **(above and right)** took the title in his John Player Lotus after only three years as a grand prix driver.

His rise to the top has been one of the quickest in the history of motor racing, and at 25 he obviously has many more years as champion ahead of him. It is Lotus's fifth team title.

He drives with a determination, flair and a calmness that recalls Jim Clark, probably the greatest grand prix driver of all time, and one of his predecessors with Lotus.

Jackie Stewart surrendered his title on the start line. He needed to win at Monza and in the United States and Canada with Fittipaldi not finishing in three races – a forlorn hope.

The field stormed away – all but Stewart on the second row. Those behind streamed round him while the 005 Tyrrell-Ford, which is having an ill-starred baptism in races, limped up the track and pulled off at the chicane, its race run.

Race speeds are not comparable with previous years because two chicanes have been installed. Fittipaldi's average was 131.61 mph compared with the 150.75 mph last year by Peter Gethin in a BRM.

Mike Hailwood, many times motor-cycle world champion, scored his best grand prix result to come second in his Brooke-Bond Surtees. Denny Hulme (Yardley-McLaren), runner-up in the championship table, was third.

SPORT IN BRIEF

MOTOR RACING

Brazilian Emerson Fittipaldi finishes the season 16 points clear of Jackie Stewart in the drivers' championship.

MOTOR CYCLING

Giacomo Agostini wins his seventh successive 500-cc world championship and his fifth consecutive Isle of Man Senior TT race.

CYCLING

Eddy Merckx of Belgium wins the Tour de France **(below)**, equalling the record of Jacques Anquetil by winning his fourth successive Tour. 'The Cannibal' has also won the world professional road-racing championship twice, and will win it for a third time in 1974.

1972

Bugner turns on best British show since Cooper

By Donald Saunders

PUBLISHED WEDNESDAY 11 OCTOBER

Joe Bugner, who has heard more boos than cheers during the last two years, was given a standing ovation by a delighted crowd at the Royal Albert Hall last night after knocking out Jürgen Blin to win back the European heavyweight title.

With precisely a minute of the eighth round gone, Bugner unleashed a short right, probably the best punch of his career, landed it flush on Blin's jaw, and saw the West German crash to the boards.

Blin, tough and brave, rolled over on to his side and tried desperately to struggle upwards. But the shattered champion was still in the act of rising on unsteady legs

when the Italian referee, Mancello Bertini, waved his arms wide and shouted 'Out.'

The poor German stumbled against the ropes; then was helped to his corner.

So Bugner reclaimed the title he had lost ignominiously to Jack Bodell, who clearly outpointed him over 15 tame rounds at Wembley Pool 13 months ago.

Now, no doubt, his target will be the British and Commonwealth championships which also passed to Bodell that night, and since have moved on to the Irish-born boxer Danny McAlinden.

For the moment, however, let us remember the most impressive performance by a British heavyweight since the heyday of Henry Cooper. Bugner not only knocked out Blin, he outclassed him.

1973

Power punching of Frazier may end Foreman's dream

By Donald Saunders in Kingston, Jamaica
PUBLISHED MONDAY 22 JANUARY

Joe Frazier, the 1964 Olympic heavyweight champion, and George Foreman, who won the gold medal four years later, will meet at the National Stadium in Kingston tonight to decide which of them has since become the better professional boxer.

At stake will be the heavyweight championship of the world, currently held by Frazier, and the prospect of a multi-million-dollar defence against Muhammad Ali within the next 12 months.

This is the first time two former Olympic heavyweight champions have contested one of sport's richest prizes.

It is also the first world heavyweight title bout to be staged in the Caribbean since Jess Willard ended Jack Johnson's reign in Havana nearly 58 years ago.

I doubt whether tonight's battle – the 120th for this ancient championship – will leave as lasting an impression on the sport as did Willard's accession to the throne in 1915.

With the odds on a Frazier victory now 2–5, most punters are forecasting only the round that will bring the end of Foreman's dream of becoming the champion.

Apart from the challenger's close friends, few believe Foreman can do what the great Muhammed Ali failed to accomplish when he shared a ring with Frazier in New York nearly two years ago.

Though Frazier is three and a half inches shorter than his 6 ft 3 in opponent, is out-reached by five inches, will be about 10 lb lighter and is five years older, I believe he will out-punch and outlast Foreman.

I believe that, eventually, he will get close enough, often enough, to wear down Foreman. Frazier may not knock out the magnificently proportioned giant from California, but I shall be surprised if the referee does not have to come to Foreman's aid before the final bell.

In a shock result, Foreman knocked out Frazier (above, in foreground) in the second round.

Carwyn James plots memorable Barbarians win

By John Reason
PUBLISHED MONDAY 29 JANUARY
Barbarians 23 pts; New Zealanders 11

Carwyn James talked to the Barbarians for 20 minutes and in that time he convinced them that they could go out at Cardiff Arms Park and play just as they had when they were Lions in New Zealand.

He convinced them that they could beat the All Blacks in the last match of the tour, despite their crippling lack of match practice, and he convinced them they could do it with no compromises to their own supreme brand of 15-man football.

The 12 Lions in the team believed him, and with Tom David, Phil Bennett and Bob Wilkinson, they went out and did exactly what he said they could do. The task seemed impossible, because Gerald Davies had withdrawn from the match with a slight hamstring and Mervyn Davies could not play either because of a heavy cold.

How could the British Lions in this Barbarians team possibly recapture the magic of 18 months ago?

Carwyn James told them: 'You will be playing two games, one when Sid Going is on the field and one when his ankle injury gets so bad, he has to go off. The All Blacks will not know quite how to meet the game you will play, because with Sid Going in their side they have got out of the habit of playing it.'

From the way his words came true, they might have been written in tablets of stone. The All Blacks' attempts to meet the spirit of the occasion were thoroughly praiseworthy, but they were as rusty as the much-applauded Haka they performed before the match.

DID YOU KNOW?

The Barbarians rugby union club was founded in 1890. The club has no ground or clubhouse; it is an invitation-only side whose members aim to play fun and entertaining rugby. One uncapped player is always included in the team; the players wear their own club socks.

The ball goes loose during the Barbarian–All Black match. The first Barbarian move went from one end of the pitch to the other and finished with a Gareth Edwards try. The match, one of the most exciting in rugby history, ended in a thrilling win for the 'Baa-baas'.

Wales are masters in the rucks

By Rupert Cherry

PUBLISHED MONDAY 22 JANUARY

Wales 25 pts; England 9

England will not beat Wales until their forwards have mastered the art of rucking – for it is an art, and as both New Zealand and now Wales have demonstrated to the English pack, it is by far the most important one in the modern game.

Four of the five tries this splendid Welsh side scored at the National Stadium, Cardiff, came with the ball obtained in rucks or mauls. It mattered little that England were able to achieve near parity in the line-out and scrum.

Wales's possession was always better than England's, for the ball came to Gareth Edwards swiftly and precisely, sometimes shooting yards back from the ruck to him while England were hastily reforming their defence.

Behind the scrum, the Welshmen had the imagination and flair to use half a dozen different ploys that caused further disarray in the England ranks, and then to run in swiftly with an easy *coup de grâce*.

England, by tackling their hearts out – a great improvement on the New Zealand games – stood within one score of Wales until the 40th minute of the second half, a feat for which one is happy to pay tribute to a brave young team. They were not all the failures that such a drubbing might make them out to be.

The drubbing, it must be said, however, might easily have been much more severe had Phil Bennett kicked accurately at goal. He missed three penalties and three conversions, some probably due to trouble he had with his foot and a change of boots.

By scoring ten points in injury time, however, Wales achieved a true reflection of their domination of most of the game. The margin was a goal, a penalty goal, and four tries against a dropped goal and two penalty goals.

Wales played probably as well as they have done since the war. Their forwards were superb, particularly Derek Quinnell, who could never be stopped by fewer than three men, or so it seemed, and Dai Morris, who drove forward like any Lion.

Edwards, happy with the way the ball came to him, gave his backs easy opportunities to display their guile. There were always loops and scissors and variations of direction to delight the singing crowd.

Towards the end Wales ran with such gay confidence and constancy at a tired, desperate defence, drawing them expertly out of position, that one marvelled at England's holding out so long.

Perhaps England's greatest achievement was in stopping John Williams. It was quite a change to see his powerful bursts checked, even though he was another who required three men to pin him down.

England had possession of a sort from tapping down at the line-out. A. R. Cowman, however, seldom got his line moving. He preferred to kick. Whether it was by orders or of his own volition, it seemed tactically wrong, with John Williams always waiting for the ball with safe hands and determination to counter-attack.

England began in adversity; they could not kick themselves out of trouble and seemed fearful of running the ball. They managed to reach the Welsh 25, however, and Cowman, with his three-quarters nicely aligned, dropped a goal. Six points would have been better than three. The thought was echoed when Quinnell burst from a ruck and John Bevan scored the first Welsh try. Then Gerald Davies coasted in with a try from Bennett's well-placed kick.

S. A. Doble got a penalty goal despite crowd noise, but Edwards scored the third Welsh try after D. J. Lloyd had shot away from a maul. John Taylor and Doble exchanged penalty goals, and England tackled and tackled until injury time. Then Alan Lewis, in a scissors with Bennett, scored a try that Bennett converted, and finally Bevan scored again.

Wales are obviously well ahead in the coaching of modern techniques. England's young players, and some of the older ones too, have a lot to learn and to practise.

1973

209

1973

Red Rum and Crisp restore prestige to National

By Hotspur (Peter Scott)
PUBLISHED MONDAY 2 APRIL

The Topham family's long association with Aintree and the Grand National climaxed on Saturday with Red Rum's win from Crisp in a race that restored the prestige of this famous steeplechase to its highest point for some years.

Crisp's name will be remembered with such gallant Grand National losers as Prince Regent and Easter Hero. L'Escargot and Spanish Steps, the other two 'class' horses of Saturday's field, ran well enough to encourage others of their calibre to take part in future.

Red Rum sustained an over-reach during the race, so amid sympathy for the heavily weighted Crisp must go credit to a winner possibly feeling some pain.

Fast ground and the presence of so many natural front-runners suggested a record time, but none could have anticipated that Saturday's winner would be almost 19 seconds inside Golden Miller's record, set 39 years ago.

Grey Sombrero led until Becher's on the first circuit. Crisp then went ahead to dominate so much of the race with his speed and a boldness of jumping that made those great fences look easy.

Early on the second circuit Red Rum went past a group that included Spanish Steps, Rouge Autumn and Black Secret to take second place. By the Canal Turn, Red Rum had drawn clear of the rest, but was making no ground on Crisp.

Brian Fletcher's hopes of a second Grand National win rose between the last two fences, when Crisp started to tire.

Crisp jumped the last fence with a longer lead than did Prince Regent in 1946 but, like Prince Regent, his weary legs were carrying him slower and slower. Red Rum went ahead less than 100 yards from home, almost at the point where Devon Loch threw the 1956 race away.

DID YOU KNOW?

The Charlton brothers, Bobby and Jack, retired from football on 28 April 1973. Each had played more than 600 times for their respective clubs, Manchester United and Leeds United. Bobby went as player-manager to Preston North End and Jack as manager to Middlesbrough.

Norton breaks Ali's jaw

Ken Norton (on left) heads for a split decision win against Ali, who endured ten rounds with a broken jaw.

By Mabel Elliott in New York
PUBLISHED MONDAY 2 APRIL

Muhammad Ali, his jaw broken in the most unexpected defeat of his boxing career, was expected to leave hospital in San Diego last night or today.

But he will have to wear a wire support round his jaw for two or three weeks, and will not be able to talk normally for about six weeks, his trainer, Angelo Dundee, said yesterday.

There would then be a training period, perhaps interrupted for hospital visits and treatment. It was almost certain he would not be fit to go back into the ring for three months.

Ali, 31, was taken to hospital on Saturday after losing the 12-round bout to Ken Norton, 28. He underwent a 90-minute operation and yesterday the surgeon, Dr William Lundeen, said: 'I see no reason why he can't fight again after it heals.'

Dr Lundeen said the former heavyweight champion's jaw was broken on the lower left side – 'a clean break, all the way through. He was in considerable pain. If he broke it in the second round, as his manager says, I can't fathom how he could go the whole fight like that.'

It is only Ali's second defeat in 43 fights since 1960, the first being to former world champion Joe Frazier.

Hulme dashes past on final straight

By Colin Dryden in Anderstorp
PUBLISHED MONDAY 18 JUNE

Denny Hulme, the former world champion, won the Swedish Grand Prix in Anderstorp yesterday in one of the best races of the season after Ronnie Peterson, the local hero, had led for 70 of the 80 laps.

Hulme, who had been playing a waiting game in fourth place for most of the race, suddenly surged past on the last straight as the Swede slowed with a deflating tyre.

It was Hulme's first grand prix victory since March last year and a fitting present for his 37th birthday today.

It was a fantastically lucky win because the New Zealander was about to call in to the pits with his Yardley McLaren after his throttle slides became jammed by dirt thrown up when Jackie Oliver's Shadow went off the track in front of him.

'For three corners I was helpless, just flicking the ignition switch, when suddenly the jammed throttle cleared and I was able to press on,' Hulme said.

Neither of the two top world championship contenders fared well. Stewart ended in fifth position while Fittipaldi had to give up on the last lap when the brakes failed and the gearbox disintegrated.

But the Brazilian still has a slender two-point lead over Stewart in the battle for this year's championship. Stewart's teammate, François Cevert, finished third.

The main feature of the race was the domination achieved by Peterson and Fittipaldi in the two Lotuses. For lap after lap they led, pursued by Stewart. But trying all he knew, Stewart was unable to get past.

Hulme was in close attendance and, after overtaking Cevert, he started harrying Stewart. With the whole 50,000 crowd willing Peterson to win his first grand prix, the Swede held off every challenge from Stewart.

Then everything happened in the last two or three laps to upset what seemed a certain Lotus one-two. Fittipaldi and Stewart dropped back with mechanical troubles and Hulme, always waiting his chance, pounced, so Peterson was robbed again.

Miller shatters all opposition at US Open with record 63

By Michael Williams in Pittsburgh

PUBLISHED MONDAY 18 JUNE

Johnny Miller **(below)** yesterday snatched the United States Open Championship at the Oakmont Country Club with probably the most remarkable finish of all time. He had a last round of 63 – eight under par.

It was a record for the championship in any round; after going into the final day six strokes behind, Miller won by a stroke with a 72-hole aggregate of 279 from John Schlee, who had a last-round 70.

Miller had nine birdies, four in the first four holes, and just one blemish– three putts at the par-three eighth for a four.

The decisive moment, he said, was at the long 12th where, after being in thick rough, he hit a four-iron third shot to within five yards and holed out for a birdie four.

Yet the destiny of the title had for a long time been obscure as one player after another – six in all – took, shared and then lost the lead.

For instance, it was not until the last few holes that Jack Nicklaus, who finished level with Lee Trevino and Arnold Palmer on 282, got even faintly into contention.

As many as ten players were in a position to win when the last round began and they soon became 11 when Miller, three over par for three rounds, began with four birdies in the first four holes.

As the front-runners approached the finish, any mistakes were now crucial. Miller missed from eight feet at the 17th, Palmer from four at the 11th – but soon Miller was in with his 63 to a standing ovation and only minutes after a 65 from Lanny Wadkins.

So Miller had his score of five under par safely in, and suddenly it seemed as if the news had filtered back to break the hearts of the rest.

Palmer dropped three strokes in three holes; Schlee three-putted the 13th but then hit back with a two at the 16th which meant he needed a birdie in the last two holes to catch Miller.

Tony Jacklin had a final round of 77 to finish on 300, 21 strokes behind Miller. He was out in 40, but pulled himself together over the inward half. It was nevertheless his highest round of the championship.

SPORT IN BRIEF

MOTOR RACING
British driver Mike Hailwood averts tragedy at the South African Grand Prix in March when he rescues Swiss driver Gianclaudio 'Clay' Regazzoni. Regazzoni has fallen unconscious after crashing his car; Hailwood pulls him from the flames to safety. He is awarded the George Medal for his bravery.

FOOTBALL
Sunderland become the first team since the war to win the FA Cup while playing in the Second Division. They beat Leeds United 1–0 in the final with Ian Porterfield scoring the all-important goal. The Sunderland hero, though, is goalkeeper Jim Montgomery, who makes a series of outstanding saves to deny Leeds.

LAWN TENNIS
Billie Jean King, a vociferous campaigner for better prize money for women tennis players, is challenged to a five-set exhibition match by Bobby Riggs, 55, the last prewar Wimbledon champion, who feels that the women's game is vastly inferior. The match is billed as the 'Battle of the Sexes' and staged at the Houston Astrodome with a television audience of millions. Billie Jean King wins the strange encounter 6–4, 6–3, 6–3.

GREYHOUND RACING
In June Patricia's Hope wins the English Greyhound Derby at the White City Stadium. Having won the race in 1972, he becomes only the second dog to win the race twice, after Mick the Miller in 1929 and 1930. Patricia's Hope also won the Scottish and Welsh Derbys in 1972, and is one of only three dogs to complete the 'triple'.

1973

1973

By James Coote in Lausanne
PUBLISHED SATURDAY 23 JUNE

Two brave Britons, Dave Starbrook and Keith Remfry, went beyond the limits of exhaustion to bring home two bronze medals after the first day of the world judo championships in Lausanne last night.

Starbrook, silver medallist at the last Olympics and in the European championships, drew on all his experience and produced some unexpected and unorthodox moves against the tough Russian, Evgeniy Solodukhin. Six minutes later he went back to the mat to face former world champion, Nobuyuki Sato from Japan, for the silver medal. But he was so weary he could offer little resistance against the greatest floor fighter in the world.

Remfry, who also won a silver in the last European championships, had an uncompromising contest with the giant Dutchman, Peter Adelaar, which was distinguished by the Dutchman's losing his temper, and with it control of the fight.

MILESTONES

The first integrated boxing match held in South Africa was between black world light-heavyweight champion Bob Foster and white local man Pierre Fourie. Foster beat Fourie on points in the 15-round fight, which was staged in front of a segregated audience.

Peterson wins US Grand Prix as Stewart ponders future

PUBLISHED MONDAY 8 OCTOBER

Ronnie Peterson, of Sweden, driving a John Player Lotus, won the United States Grand Prix at Watkins Glen yesterday. James Hunt (Britain) in a March, was second, and Carlos Reutemann (Argentina), in a Brabham-Ford, was third.

The race was the 16th and last in this year's world championship, already clinched by Britain's Jackie Stewart. Stewart and Chris Amon, of New Zealand, withdrew following the death in practice on Saturday of their Tyrrell-Ford teammate, François Cevert, of France.

Immediately there was speculation that Stewart, 34, who had already made sure of recapturing the world title, would retire from the sport. Many of his close friends, including Jim Clark and Jochen Rindt, have died in crashes.

Stewart, badly upset, described the accident of Frenchman Cevert, 27, whose Elf Tyrrell-Ford hurtled into a crash barrier then bounced across the track into another one as a 'terrible, terrible thing'.

Peterson led throughout the race, hotly pursued by Hunt, who crossed the finishing line only half a second behind. Hunt, in his first season of Formula One racing, set a record of 1 min 41.45 sec on the 40th lap.

Peterson averaged 118 mph for his first US Grand Prix victory.

Jackie Stewart, winner of the 1973 world championship, competing in the British Grand Prix at Silverstone (far right) and (right) with teammate Cevert, who was lying third in the championship table, and was the 12th international driver to die this year.

Crisis at Wimbledon: 69 players to boycott championship

By Lance Tingay
PUBLISHED FRIDAY 22 JUNE

The Wimbledon authorities continued to play it cool yesterday, in the midst of the greatest crisis they have ever faced, with their chairman, Mr Herman David, going to watch the Test match at Lord's, and the referee, Captain Mike Gibson, as yet having received no withdrawal from any player.

The draw is due to take place at 11 o'clock this morning, 48 hours later than usual. So far as Wimbledon are concerned, the deadline for withdrawals is one hour and a quarter before then.

The Association of Tennis Professionals (ATP) have undertaken to deliver withdrawal forms, signed by those

players pulling out in support of their boycott, by that time. The number is believed to be 69.

Yesterday, the men's singles part of the qualifying competition at Roehampton was postponed because of the condition of the courts.

It is assumed that the men's qualifying competition will resume today. But in the event of 69 withdrawals, there will be no point in continuing them, because those players still unbeaten will take the vacant places left in the championship proper.

There are 32 men still unbeaten, and it is expected that the 32 losers in the last round will make up the balance to complete the full draw. A ballot comprising the losers in the round before that could also be made if necessary.

A new seeding list will have to be prepared. Since Ilie Nastase is a certain starter, he will obviously head the new list, and one may suppose that the Czech, Jan Kodes, will be the No. 2.

The same criteria apply to the men's doubles and to the mixed doubles. The boycott involves the top three seeds in the men's doubles – Bob Lutz and Stan Smith, Tom Okker and Marty Riessen, and Cliff Drysdale and Roger Taylor. The fourth seeds are Jim Connors, the American, who is not an ATP member, and Nastase. They must be promoted to top position.

In the mixed doubles, the top seeds are Nastase and Rosemary Casals. Nothing changes there, but the No. 2 position has one of the boycott men, Riessen, with Margaret Court.

SPORT IN BRIEF

FOOTBALL
Liverpool win the UEFA Cup, beating Borussia Moenchengladbach in the final. Two goals from Kevin Keegan and one from Larry Lloyd give them a 3–0 win in the first leg at Anfield. However, Moenchengladbach score two first-half goals in the second leg and Liverpool are fortunate to hang on to take the trophy 3–2 on aggregate.

ATHLETICS
On 13 July David Bedford sets a world record of 27 min 30.8 sec in the 10,000 m. His time is nearly eight seconds faster than Lasse Viren's previous record. An outstanding distance runner, Bedford has also won the national cross-country championship this year for the second time.

RUGBY UNION
In one of the greatest shocks in the history of the sport, the Tongans, on a tour to Australia, beat the Wallabies 16–11 in Brisbane.

CRICKET
The West Indian tourists beat England 2–0 to win the Wisden Trophy. In the last Test at Lord's, West Indies run up a massive score of 652 for 8. Three of their players – Rohan Kanhai, Gary Sobers and Bernard Julien – make centuries.

FOOTBALL
On 17 October England fail to qualify for the 1974 World Cup when they only manage a 1–1 draw against Poland at Wembley. Poland score in the 58th minute through Domarski; eight minutes later Allan Clarke equalises through a penalty. But England cannot break through the Polish defence, spearheaded by goalkeeper Jan Tomaszewski, who was labelled a 'clown' by Derby County manager Brian Clough.

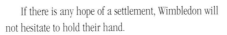

If there is any hope of a settlement, Wimbledon will not hesitate to hold their hand.

Pilic said at his home in Split last night that the Yugoslav authorities were not willing to go back on their decision – despite the fact that he had apologised to them. 'The situation has become complicated,' he added.

Nikki Pilic had been disciplined for not playing in a Davis Cup match, with the ILTF ruling that he should be suspended for a period after the French Open. Pilic continued to play; Wimbledon refused to let him enter the championship; the ATP protested and asked their players to withdraw. The Czech Jan Kodes (left) won the boycott-hit event, taking the final 6–1, 9–8, 6–3 against Alex Metreveli of the Soviet Union.

1974

Filbert Bayi sets world record

By James Coote

PUBLISHED MONDAY 4 FEBRUARY

The finest 1,500 m in the history of athletics and a last-minute rush of medals by English competitors combined to produce an unparalleled ending to the tenth Commonwealth Games in Christchurch on Saturday.

Filbert Bayi's world record will be the most lasting memory of the Games. The 20-year-old Tanzanian soldier from the foothills of Mount Kilimanjaro gave the most impressive display of front running for years.

He ran the equivalent of a 3 minute 50 second mile (Jim Ryun's record is 3 min 51.1 sec), with the promise of more to come.

Bayi had served frequent notice in 1973 of his talents with some spectacular front running, which he used to avoid a repetition of Munich where he had been boxed in.

On one occasion he covered the first 800 metres in 1 minute 50 seconds compared with Saturday's 1 minute 52 seconds, before dying on his feet before the line.

On Saturday, Bayi rushed through the first lap in 54.5 seconds, 800 metres in 2 minutes 51.9 seconds. But Mike Boit, the 800-m silver medallist, also played his part.

He shepherded the rest of the field just fast enough to maintain contact, but not so fast that they would fade before the line. By keeping their hopes alive, Boit insured that they would be sufficiently inspired to 'have a go'.

Thus the excited crowd were treated to the sight of seeing two of their own runners, Rod Dixon and John Walker, chasing Bayi home. Ben Jipcho, seeking his third gold of the Games, and Graeme Crouch of Australia were also significant participants.

First Dixon surged along the back straight, then Walker let fly with a final sprint that he did not believe he could produce to finish runner-up inside the old world record. The results play havoc with the rankings. Even Brendan Foster in seventh place was fast enough to set his second British record of the games, with 3 min 37. 6 sec.

DID YOU KNOW?

Industrial action and the 'three-day week' led to a football League match being held on a Sunday for the first time. It took place on 20 January; Millwall beat Fulham at home 1–0. Due to Sunday trading laws, the club could not charge spectators an entrance fee.

Spirited Germans' commonsense lands World Cup

Overath (on left) and Gerd Müller lift the World Cup after their 2–1 win over Holland. The knock-out quarter-finals were replaced this year by a further round-robin group stage, the final and the third-place play-off being the only sudden-death matches in the tournament.

By Donald Saunders in Munich

PUBLISHED MONDAY 8 JULY

West Germany 2; Holland 1

West Germany became champions of the soccer world for the second time and first holders of the new trophy with a spirited, intelligent performance that enabled them to outsmart Holland in a highly dramatic, often ill-tempered final at the Olympic Stadium in Munich yesterday.

The Germans came back with great courage after conceding a first-minute penalty, equalised from the spot in 25 minutes, moved in front before half-time, then withstood tremendous pressure to secure football's most coveted prize.

Their commendable demonstration of skill, teamwork and commonsense thoroughly merited success. Yet they might have been deprived of victory if Holland had been less arrogant initially and more disciplined later.

The Dutch, like so many teams before them, forgot that the West Germans are great competitors. After snatching that early goal they assumed their hands were already on the trophy. Instead of immediately putting their opponents under heavy pressure, Johan Cruyff and his men foolishly decided to play possession football.

The intention presumably was to prove they were more sophisticated than the Germans. If so, they were guilty of a dreadful miscalculation.

If any one man can fairly be singled out to shoulder the blame for Holland's defeat it must be Cruyff, their captain. He set the arrogant early pattern, was among the first to lose control of his temper, and ultimately failed to provide the inspiration needed to save his team because he could not shake off Vogts, his tenacious, effective shadow.

Indeed, this great footballer did a true captain's job only after the final whistle, when he called together his downcast colleagues, patted one or two on the shoulder, then led them in a salute to the crowd.

In contrast, Franz Beckenbauer led his troops with the skill, inspiration and authority of a great general. He uplifted them during that morale-shattering opening period, guided them smoothly back into the game, and then into the lead, and finally held them together when the Dutch launched their big push.

Speed serves its purpose for England in India

By E. W. Swanton at Edgbaston

PUBLISHED TUESDAY 9 JULY

The game duly took its inexorable course, and there were few moments when one felt that the Indian batting, despite the perfection of the pitch, would be capable of extending it into the last day.

Just before tea, all was over, England's victory by an innings and 78 runs completing a series hat trick – a thing that has not happened since the last Indian tour but one in this country, seven years ago.

Only once in England, by the way, has a Test been lost and won with the fall of only two wickets of the winning side: one needs to go back to a Lord's Test against South Africa, as long ago as 1924.

Tony Greig got a couple of wickets in the afternoon, and it was a welcome sight to see him at work in the style on which English hopes must much depend in Australia. But it was the fast and fastish bowlers who, at a torpid over-rate, bored their way through the Indian defences.

It is not a glamorous form of attack, and we saw its full limitations against high-class Test batsmen in the West Indies. However, in this series, it has been sufficient for the job, and that is all that has to be said.

England won the series against India 3–0.

Fierce Connors too powerful for Rosewall

By Lance Tingay

PUBLISHED MONDAY 8 JULY

Wimbledon 1974 will be remembered most of all because the singles titles were won by two young Americans engaged to marry, Jim Connors, 21, and Chris Evert, 19 – each of whom is double-fisted on the backhand – and because of that the coaching manuals can hardly be the same again.

A nostalgic memory will be of the man who fell at the last fence, Ken Rosewall, 39, contesting the men's final for the fourth time without success. There was a sad overtone to the singles final on Saturday when Connors beat him 6–1, 6–1, 6–4.

One cannot deny that Rosewall played badly. One could have wept for the simple shots he missed. Equally, one cannot dispute that Connors performed superbly. If ever a player turned round the sympathies of a centre court crowd by the sheer quality of his game, it was this rather brash young man.

What a fierce and compelling game this left-hander played. It was surging, dynamic stuff. Practically every shot he hit was a bold one taken early, aimed fast to the lines with minimal margin of error, and he missed extraordinarily few.

He pulverised an off-form Rosewall utterly. The Australian took the opening game but lost the next six and won only seven points in the course of them.

The punishment continued. Connors went to 4–0 in the second set, this making a sweep of ten games running though, as it happened, Rosewall got more points – eight of them – in the long opening game to the second set than he had in the six preceding it.

Only in the third set did Connors' *tour de force* lose momentum. There was a brief spell when Rosewall hinted that he might come back. He managed to lead 2–1 and three times came within a point of advancing to 3–1. Artistic shots, especially from the backhand, hinted at his old brilliance with the return of service.

Connors, nonetheless, got that game and the one that followed. He began to project his mighty winners once more.

The match lasted 93 minutes and, though far short of being the most one-sided men's singles final played at Wimbledon, it was not a contest in which the loser had shown any hint of winning.

Poor Rosewall! Tremendous Connors!

Connors demonstrates his double-handed backhand as he powers towards his first Wimbledon singles title.

SPORT IN BRIEF

HORSE RACING
Red Rum **(above)**, ridden by Brian Fletcher, clears the final fence in the Grand National on his way to a second successive win. Red Rum will come second in the race in 1975 and 1976, and win for a third time in 1977.

FOOTBALL
Haiti become the first team from the Caribbean to take part in the final stages of the World Cup. However, they fail to win a game, and finish bottom of their group. Although they take the lead in their first game, against Italy, they lose 3–1. This is followed by a 7–0 defeat at the hands of Poland, and a 4–1 drubbing by Argentina.

LAWN TENNIS
Chris Evert **(below)** takes the women's singles title at Wimbledon, before going to watch her fiancé Jimmy Connors win his match against Rosewall (see main text). Evert wins the final against Olga Morozova 6–0, 6–4. Chris Evert has already met Olga Morozova in another final this year; Evert beat her 6–1, 6–2 to take the French Open title.

1974

1974

Lions' scrum power is bitter blow to South Africa

By John Reason in Port Elizabeth
PUBLISHED TUESDAY 16 JULY

'The greatest Lions team in history,' was the description Alun Thomas, the tourists' manager, gave the side after they completed a hat trick of wins in the international series against South Africa.

Such enthusiasm is understandable. England felt just the same after they had beaten the Springboks at Ellis Park in 1972. Yet England went back home and lost all four matches in the international championship in the season that followed. All things are relative.

They still are, and the fact of the matter is that South Africa's rugby has never been more barren than it is at this time. South Africa have used 32 players in the three internationals in a series of desperate permutations, but these have only revealed with ever increasing clarity their lack of playing talent and their lack of organisation.

The thing that has hurt South Africans most has been the total eclipse of their scrummaging, traditionally their greatest strength. Deficiencies first revealed by England two years ago have been fully exposed.

Lions robbed of clean sweep by disputed try

By John Reason in Johannesburg
PUBLISHED MONDAY 29 JULY
South Africa 13 pts; British Isles 13

The British Isles retained their magnificent unbeaten record at Ellis Park on Saturday before a crowd of 75,000 and came within an ace of making a clean sweep of the international series and the tour.

Right at the end of the match they thought that Fergus Slattery had scored the try needed to give them victory when he crashed over the Springbok line.

But referee Max Baise, although agreeing that Slattery may have grounded the ball, said that by then he had already blown his whistle for a five-yard scrum.

'As Slattery went over the line he was held by Cronje,' he said. 'The ball was stopped on Cronje's leg and I don't like allowing mauls to develop in that sort of situation. As soon as I saw that the ball was stopped I blew my whistle and ran back to take up position. Slattery may have got the ball down after I had blown the whistle but I didn't see it.'

There is not much doubt that Slattery did get the ball down because Cronje was just as convinced that Slattery had scored as Slattery was himself. The photographic evidence supports both these opinions. However, there is not much doubt either that the movement of the ball did happen in the two stages described by the referee, and few British supporters would argue about the justice of the eventual result.

The Lions scored a goal, a try and a penalty goal and South Africa scored a try and three penalty goals. It was the last match of the tour and the first one the Lions had failed to win.

It was a miserable niggling game which lived constantly on the edge of war. The Lions looked weary beyond words, but they are due to return to London Airport tomorrow and are assured of a hearty welcome.

Mervyn Davies breaks from the scrum during the Lions' successful tour of South Africa. A superb No. 8, he took over the Welsh captaincy on his return and led them to their 1976 Grand Slam triumph.

GARETH EDWARDS (1947–)

*GARETH OWEN EDWARDS **(opposite right)** was born at Gwaun-cae-Gurwen, Swansea, on 12 July 1947. He was educated at Pontardawe Grammar School and at Millfield, where he set a new British junior record for the 200-yd hurdles.*

In 1967, while still a student, Edwards gained his first Welsh cap in a match against France. This was the start of a run of 53 consecutive international appearances – 13 as captain – a record for a scrum half. Edwards earned his final cap against France in 1978.

During his career Wales enjoyed a glorious spell of success, notching up seven championships, five

Triple Crowns and two Grand Slams. Edwards' jinking runs and his memorable halfback partnerships with Barry John and Phil Bennett lay at the heart of these triumphs. In all he scored 20 tries for Wales, a record at the time.

Edwards took part in three British Lions' tours – to South Africa in 1968 and 1974 and to New Zealand in 1971, where the Lions won their first series victory against the All Blacks.

Edwards retired at the peak of his form. He was awarded the MBE in 1975.

Dahlia's £337,500 breaks Mill Reef record

By Hotspur (Peter Scott)

PUBLISHED MONDAY 29 JULY

Dahlia **(below right)**, back to her 1973 brilliance and now the only horse ever to win Ascot's King George VI and Queen Elizabeth Stakes twice, has beaten Mill Reef's European record for first-prize money earnings. Her total stands at more than £337,500.

Mr Bunker Hunt, elated by Saturday's win, revealed that an autumn campaign in America was under consideration for his champion filly. I hope this idea is dropped and that the Prix de l'Arc de Triomphe is made Dahlia's next target. She still has a score to settle with Allez France, who has beaten her in all their six clashes so far. Tennyson has finished ahead of Dahlia in three of their four previous meetings.

Neither Allez France nor Tennyson ran at Ascot. Other absentees were English Prince and Dibidale, winners of the Irish Sweeps Derby and Irish Guinness Oaks.

Dahlia's time on Saturday was almost three seconds slower than she returned in last year's race. Hippodamia kept the early pace moderate, Snow Knight and Buoy lay close behind Hippodamia and the gallop did not really quicken till halfway through the race.

It did so just as Dankaro was being eased back from a good position and M. Boussac's colt turned for home with only two behind him. Snow Knight had a slight lead over Hippodamia entering the straight, with Buoy third and Dahlia going easily in fourth place.

Hippodamia soon dropped back and, just as Buoy was mastering Snow Knight, Dahlia swept nonchalantly past both with that smooth flow of acceleration that stamps a really outstanding horse.

Highclere struggled on tenaciously into second place. Dankaro looked the only possible threat, but he could not sustain this effort when coming under real pressure and came in third.

SPORT IN BRIEF

BASEBALL
Hank Aaron of the Atlanta Braves hits his 715th home run, breaking the record set by Babe Ruth in 1935. By the time of his retirement in 1976, Aaron will have scored 3,771 hits and 2,174 runs, a total exceeded only by the legendary Ty Cobb, who played with the Detroit Tigers (1905–26) and the Philadelphia Athletics (1926–8).

FOOTBALL
Victories over Grasshoppers, Aberdeen, Dynamo Tbilisi and Cologne take Spurs to the UEFA Cup final and two legs against the Dutch champions Feyenoord. The first leg at White Hart Lane finishes in a 2–2 draw; Feyenoord win the second leg in Rotterdam 2–0 to take the trophy 4–2 on aggregate. Once again there is violence among the English supporters, and Dutch police mount baton charges.

EQUESTRIANISM
Captain Mark Phillips wins the Badminton Horse Trials on Columbus. It is his third win in four years; he won in 1971 and 1972 on Great Ovation. Captain Phillips's run was interrupted in 1973 by Lucinda Prior-Palmer, who came first on Be Fair.

FOOTBALL
In one of the most one-sided FA Cup finals in years, a Kevin Keegan-inspired Liverpool overwhelm Newcastle United 3–0. It is a particular disappointment for Newcastle's Malcolm Macdonald, who until now has scored in every round of this season's competition.

ATHLETICS
Running at a meeting in Gateshead on 3 August, Brendan Foster breaks the world record for 3,000 m, recording a time of 7 min 35.2 sec. The Englishman also holds the world two-mile record at 8 min 13.68 sec.

1974

1974

Plans to counter hooliganism at Twickenham

By John Reason
PUBLISHED WEDNESDAY 30 OCTOBER

The Rugby Union have made plans to counter hooliganism on the terraces at Twickenham in case the serious crowd disorders which disfigure so much of soccer should spread to rugby. They have bought a closed-circuit radio system to guide a staff of crowd controllers, who have been specially recruited to assist the police in case of trouble.

'Incidents at the end of the match between England and Wales in March gave us all cause for concern,' admits Rugby Union secretary Air Commodore Bob Weighill. 'We realised then that rugby football could not necessarily assume that the problem of hooliganism on the terraces would not spread to our own game.'

The rather benevolent system of stewarding which has served the Rugby Union so well in the past might not be adequate for the needs of the future.

Ambulance workers will also be equipped with two-way radio.

The Rugby Union are well aware that there is nothing to stop spectators gaining easy access to the playing surface at Twickenham, because there are no fences to be climbed. There is a low rim of wooden paling with a rail on top to stop the ball rolling off the grass at the sides of the ground, but it is not even knee-high.

At the moment the Rugby Union have no intention of building fences round the pitch at Twickenham. They are naturally reluctant to change the easy-going tradition of the ground and the game. However, they realise that they cannot take these traditions for granted, and they accept that a proportion of spectators are now attracted to the game by the prospect of seeing a punch-up.

The other great problem concerns dissent at the referee's decisions. There is no doubt that this is spreading in rugby football as well, and it all has a deleterious effect on the behaviour of crowds.

DID YOU KNOW?

When Muhammad Ali went to fight George Foreman in Zaire, his corner were convinced that Ali would be seriously injured – or worse. They had a plane standing by at Zaire's Kinshasa airport ready to fly him to hospital in Europe.

By David Saunders in Paris
PUBLISHED MONDAY 22 JULY

Eddy Merckx, of Belgium won the Tour de France, which ended in Paris yesterday, for the fifth time.

Merckx was the eventual winner of the 22nd and final stage of the 91 miles from Orléans to the stadium at Vincennes, on the outskirts of the French capital, although he finished second in the big bunch sprint behind Patrick Sercu.

There was a protest that Sercu had switched his line in the final 50 metres, which he certainly did, and Sercu was put down to third place for the infringement, which gave Merckx another victory.

Merckx had tried desperately to create a record of nine stage wins, having equalled the present record of eight wins back in 1970. But the odds proved too much for him after he won the first section of Saturday's stage of 73 miles from Vouvray to Orléans. The Belgian was hoping to win the time trial over 23 miles at Orléans later

Eddie Merckx celebrates his fifth Tour de France win, which equalled the record set by Frenchman Jacques Anquetil in 1964.

that day, which would have given him successes; but his chances were ruined by ten seconds, the margin between him and a young Belgian rival, Michel Pollentier.

Pollentier won the stage but – more important – veteran Raymond Poulidor, who took fifth place on the time trial, moved in to second overall position with a much better time than Vicente Lopez-Carril.

It left only one second separating the two men at the start of the final day. With bonuses to be won at the two hot-spot sprints on the stage, the Gan-Mercier team not only protected Poulidor but got him a second place.

This meant he ended with a five-second advantage over the Spaniard, while his British team colleague Barry Hoban carried off the overall prize in the hot-spot section. That, plus his stage victory, was a fine achievement by the British rider.

Ali's artistry and power crushes 'bewildered bear'

By Donald Saunders in Kinshasa
PUBLISHED THURSDAY 31 OCTOBER

If anyone has $10 million he would like to invest in a worthy cause he should get in touch with Muhammad Ali, now restored to his rightful place as king of all the heavyweights after six frustrating years among the commoners.

After climbing back on to the throne when George Foreman's brief reign came to a spectacular end in the eighth round at the May 20th Stadium in Kinshasa, Ali let it be known he was prepared to listen to offers of that magnitude for a contest with Joe Frazier, the only man to beat him in a championship bout.

One promoter called that figure 'ridiculous', but the sweet truth is that Ali is no ordinary heavyweight champion. Most of the world is now coming round to his long-held view that he is the greatest of them all.

Ali is not just a superb athlete, he is a symbol of hope to millions of less privileged and less gifted members of his race. Surely no one else from any sport, with the possible exception of Pelé, could bring a city to the fever of excitement he inspired in Kinshasa.

As those who had been privileged to watch the champion demonstrate his magic drove home through the grey dawn, barefoot boys and girls, nursing mothers and off-to-work fathers lined the new champion's expected triumphal route to the city in their thousands, chanting with joyful relief, 'Ali, Ali, Ali.' In these days when so much of sport is a business, that was a scene worth travelling to Africa to see.

So was Ali's victory. Of his dozen high-standard championship performances over the past ten years, this was easily the most accomplished. We saw not the arrogant dancing master indulging himself, but the dedicated artist producing a boxing masterpiece.

Ali stripped the massive Foreman of his frightening power by refusing to follow the expected path to slaughter. Instead of running away until his legs were drained of stamina, he backed slowly on to the ropes or into corners, smothering, spoiling, slipping or simply absorbing the champion's heaviest punches and countering with jolting accuracy and bewildering speed.

Poor Foreman, whose mind worked as ploddingly as his feet and hands moved, just could not understand what was happening. Though, initially, he thumped away to the body with the clubbing blows that had destroyed Joe Frazier, Joe Roman and Ken Norton inside 15 minutes, this opponent would not crumble.

In the eighth Ali let loose a decisive barrage of short punches, finishing with a right that sent Foreman sprawling to the canvas like a bewildered bear.

The new champion left the ring for the dressing room where honour was duly paid him by those who had doubted his ability to become the second heavyweight to regain the title. Floyd Patterson shares that, but little else, with the man whom I am more than happy to call the greatest heavyweight of my time.

Mad scramble for points is driving football fans from grounds

By Donald Saunders
PUBLISHED MONDAY 30 DECEMBER

As a difficult year draws to its close, the most widely competitive League championship struggle since the war shows no signs of luring soccer's missing millions back to the stands and terraces.

Although gates on Boxing Day and Saturday were swelled by Christmas holidaymakers, they did not approach the total needed to encourage belief in the continued existence of League football in its present four-division, 92-club form.

Indeed, it is becoming increasingly clear that the open nature of the championship is provoking the tough, physical type of game that the more discerning fan simply will not pay to watch.

Recently, Ron Greenwood and Tony Waddington, two of the most respected managers in the First Division, have emphasised their distaste for some of the tactics now being employed in the desperate search for points.

Tommy Docherty, Manchester United's manager, is saying much the same about the ruthless competition among the Second Division's promotion challengers.

Mr Docherty urges referees to give players greater protection and the media to play a more prominent part in putting the finger on guilty teams and players.

There has been a tendency this season for those in the press box and on the television panel to lose sight of the basic roughness of League soccer amid the scramble for points.

Teams have been readily complimented for adding 'steel and professionalism' to their game, when they should have been strongly criticised for becoming far too willing to follow the example of those who kick, trip and manhandle opponents, argue with referees, waste time and generally break the laws.

Even if the dirty teams are exposed, however, refereeing will have to be much more consistently strict to persuade players that skill is more reliable than strength for obtaining success.

So the situation is unlikely to improve, at least until the championship challengers have been reduced to two or three. By then, many former customers may have lost the soccer-watching habit.

1974

219

1975

Leeds scrape home with own goal

By Donald Saunders
PUBLISHED TUESDAY 11 FEBRUARY
Wimbledon 0; Leeds United 1

Wimbledon bade a defiant farewell to the FA Cup at Selhurst Park last night with a spirited performance that left mighty Leeds sighing with relief when the final whistle sounded.

The Southern League club's giant-killing exploits are over, largely because their skill and endeavour were not supported by the good fortune they deserved.

At the end, all that separated them and their illustrious opponents was a goal for which Leeds were duly grateful; but in which they are unlikely to take much pride.

It was scored in the 50th minute of a fourth round replay, which – until then – Wimbledon had dominated by sheer impudence and purpose.

Johnny Giles collected a pass some 20 yards out and let fly hopefully: Dickie Guy seemed to have the shot covered but, at the last moment, the ball was deflected off Dave Bassett just wide of the goalkeeper's left hand and into the corner of the net.

Even that misfortune failed to deflate Wimbledon. They kept searching with sufficient intelligence and determination to leave Leeds a bag of nerves.

Cooke all but did the trick ten minutes from time. Alas for him and his colleagues, his angled shot struck a Leeds boot and was deflected for a corner.

So, eventually, Wimbledon had to settle for a standing ovation from the large crowd. Meanwhile, Leeds must prepare themselves for the fifth-round battle at Derby on Saturday. I have a feeling that the League champions will tackle that job rather less nervously than they undertook last night's task.

Leeds were quick to congratulate their non-league opponents for a performance that will surely put Wimbledon high in the ranks of FA Cup giantkillers.

MILESTONES

The first professional female jockey to ride in Britain was apprentice Jane McDonald, aged 21, who rode Royal Cadet into 11th place at Doncaster in the Crown Plus Two Apprentice Champion Handicap Stakes.

Klammer's sixth shatters record

By Alan Smith in Innsbruck
PUBLISHED MONDAY 27 JANUARY

Franz Klammer made it six out of six World Cup downhills on the pre-Olympic course at Igls yesterday, shattering the five-in-a-row record set by Jean-Claude Killy eight years ago.

Surprisingly, it was the old downhill champion, Switzerland's Bernhard Russi, winner of the world title in

1970 and the Olympic gold in Sapporo, who gave him most to do.

This snaking, icy course, manmade and set between patches of snowfree mud, had been thought by some less likely to suit Klammer than one or two of his rivals, but his superb line, held with great strength, won the day.

Klammer, 20, came down third, immediately after Italy's Herbert Plank, who had been widely rated his biggest danger, but the Austrian was always just in front.

Russi, 26, had been 'written off' by most Swiss fans even before last year's world championship, and his 13th place there did nothing to prove them wrong. But yesterday he was faster than Klammer almost everywhere – except where it matters.

After that passing excitement for the Swiss it was the Italian's turn. Plank had been beaten, but late in the second group came Gustavo Thoeni, three times winner of the world cup, gold medallist in Sapporo and world champion on both slalom and giant slalom in St Moritz.

At the first timing point he was behind Klammer, but two-thirds of the way down he had gone ahead. Then he, like Russi, took one sweeping turn too wide and went down too low into juddering ice that slowed him from first to a final fourth.

Franz Klammer (left) wins his sixth consecutive World Cup downhill. He went on to win an Olympic gold in front of his home crowd at Innsbruck in 1976.

Nicklaus, Weiskopf and Miller provide fantasy finish

By Michael Williams in Augusta, Georgia
PUBLISHED TUESDAY 15 APRIL

Even though the dust has settled and the superlatives have run dry, it is still difficult to appreciate that the manner of Jack Nicklaus's fifth victory in the United States Masters at Augusta is fact and not fantasy.

How else to describe the climax as three of the finest golfers in the world fought it out toe-to-toe: Tom Weiskopf and Johnny Miller coming up the 18th fairway line abreast, on the very heels of Nicklaus, and both with putts to tie?

All the world now knows that both missed. But what a battle it had been, one that those privileged to be there will never forget.

From the moment Nicklaus split the field wide open with opening rounds of 68 and 67, to Weiskopf's third round of 66, which changed everything, to Miller's unparalleled finish of 65, 66, this was an exceptional US Masters.

Nicklaus's five-iron tee shot to the pin at the back of the 16th was not especially good, at least 13 yards short of

the flag. 'But there are moments,' Nicklaus said afterwards, 'when you have a vision that you are going to hole a putt, and this was one of them.'

Nicklaus has written too many pages of golf history to need to prove a thing. What this Masters did prove, however, is that Weiskopf, runner-up at Augusta now on four occasions, and Miller may be talked of in the same breath. For all his low-scoring feats in tournaments, Miller had to settle unjustified doubts that both these and the 63 that won him the 1973 US Open were not flukes.

It is to be hoped that Weiskopf is not to be a fated golfer at Augusta, in the same way, for instance, that Arnold Palmer has never won the PGA or Sam Snead the US Open. No swing as pure and majestic as his can fail to conquer the game's highest peaks.

If anything, Weiskopf said he felt almost too relaxed. He must have been the only one who did.

As he and Miller emerged round the elbow of the 18th fairway, four results – barring the fluke of a holed second shot – were still possible; one three-way tie, two two-way ties, or outright victory for Nicklaus. You cannot get closer than that.

L'Escargot rounds off great treble for Raymond Guest

By Hotspur (Peter Scott)
PUBLISHED MONDAY 7 APRIL

L'Escargot flew home to Ireland within hours of Saturday's Grand National triumph. His victory breakfast at Dan Moore's stable yesterday included champagne and a dozen eggs. Red Rum took more normal nourishment in Don McCain's Southport yard.

Celebrations apart, an important reason for their different diets was that L'Escargot will almost certainly never race again, whereas Red Rum could well run either at Ayr on 19 April, or Sandown Park seven days later.

'Red Rum is in both the Scottish Grand National and Whitbread Gold Cup. I hope to make some plans later this week but they would still be subject to ground conditions nearer the day,' says McCain. Saturday's race was unique in Grand National history because not since its 1839 foundation had the same horses taken first and second places two years running.

The all-important difference of revised positions was accepted with sportsmanship by Red Rum's stable. Dan Moore's attempts either to ride or train a Grand National winner go back to Royal Danieli's head defeat by Battleship in 1938.

L'Escargot became the first Irish-trained Grand National winner since Mr What in 1958. Remarkably, they have the same breeder, Mrs Barbara O'Neill of Co. Westmeath. L'Escargot's dam is half-sister to Mr What. Mrs O'Neill sold L'Escargot as a foal. Three years later,

still unnamed, he went up for sale again and Mr Raymond Guest became his new owner.

L'Escargot's Cheltenham Gold Cup triumphs of 1970 and 1971 have been followed by four Grand National appearances. Knocked over early in the 1972 race, he finished third and second in Red Rum's triumphant years before Saturday's well-deserved win.

L'Escargot has now joined with Sir Ivor and Larkspur in doing for their American owner what Golden Miller and Straight Deal accomplished for the late Miss Dorothy Paget. These are the only owners to have had their colours carried successfully in the Derby, Grand National and Cheltenham Gold Cup.

Tommy Carberry, whose riding triumphs in the last month have included the Gold Cup, Irish Distillers' Grand National and now the Grand National itself, had his worst moment on Saturday when L'Escargot blundered badly at the seventh fence.

He soon worked back to a position near the leaders, and three fences from home L'Escargot and Red Rum began to draw clear. They jumped the last just about level, but Carberry then shook up L'Escargot and the battle was over.

Red Rum, though finishing 15 lengths behind L'Escargot, still beat Spanish Steps by eight lengths for second place. Red Rum has now equalled Cloister's feat of finishing first or second in three consecutive Grand Nationals, but Red Rum has won twice, whereas Cloister was twice runner-up before his 1893 triumph.

Reactionary Rugby Union reject main Mallaby reforms

By John Reason
PUBLISHED TUESDAY 15 APRIL

The Rugby Union have produced a report which rejects all the major alterations proposed by the Mallaby Committee. If it is accepted, this report on the Mallaby recommendations will much reduce the likelihood of any significant reform of the game in England in the foreseeable future.

The Mallaby Committee was set up to investigate the state of the game in England.

It proposed that the Rugby Union should be reorganised into an enlarged council with a policy-making executive, and that the present county championship should be superseded by an area championship.

It also suggested that the constituent bodies should be reshaped and that the major clubs, the referees and other organisations should be given direct representation on the Rugby Union, with a reduction in the representation of the Armed Forces and Oxford and Cambridge universities.

None of these suggestions has been adopted. Instead, the Rugby Union propose to reduce the county championship from five groups to four.

The Rugby Union also propose to form a major clubs sub-committee, although it has decided against giving either the clubs or the referees direct representation on the Rugby Union. The Armed Forces will continue to have two representatives each on the Rugby Union, Oxford and Cambridge universities one each, and the schools representation will be increased from one to two.

It is hard to see how any of this can be acceptable to the major clubs. They field more than 200 teams each week, nearly all of them of a far higher standard than those fielded by the 23 colleges of Oxford and 20 colleges of Cambridge. The major clubs have now been trying to achieve changes in structure of the game in England for six years.

It took three years to arrive at the Mallaby Committee and three more years to reach a conclusion which puts the clubs back almost exactly where they were when they started. The Rugby Union have adopted only the minor recommendations made by the committee.

SPORT IN BRIEF

RUGBY UNION
Scotland beat Wales 12–10 in a Five Nations championship match at Murrayfield. The crowd number is officially recorded as 104,000, setting a world record for attendance at a game of rugby.

BOXING
By beating Jim Watt for the British title and Antonio Piddu for the European title, Ken Buchanan earns the right to challenge Japanese boxer 'Guts' Ishimatsu Suzuki for the WBC world lightweight championship. In their fight on 27 January, and despite the Scot's best efforts, Guts wins on a points decision after 15 gruelling rounds.

FOOTBALL
Leeds United meet Bayern Munich in the European Cup final. The final proves a match too far for Leeds. Roth and Gerd Müller score two goals for Bayern Munich in the last 20 minutes to take the trophy to Germany. Yet again English 'fans' react violently; Leeds are banned from Europe for three years.

CRICKET
England finish their Ashes tour of Australia, which Australia win by four matches to one, with one drawn. Dennis Lillee and Jeff Thomson (who does not play in the final Test) have taken 25 and 33 wickets respectively; Another Australian, Greg Chappell, tops the batting averages; he has scored 608 runs in the series.

GOLF
American Tom Watson wins the British Open at Carnoustie. It is the first time he has won one of the major tournaments. After completing the four rounds in 279 strokes, he goes on to a play-off against the Australian Jack Newton. Watson wins by one stroke.

1975

1975

Thomson injures batsmen

PUBLISHED THURSDAY 12 JUNE

Jeff Thomson, the Australian fast bowler, caused two Sri Lanka batsmen to retire hurt in yesterday's Prudential World Cup match at the Oval.

The tiny Duleep Mendis ducked into a rising ball and was hit on the head, and Sunil Wettimuny played another riser on to his body and was hit on the instep by the next ball. As he staggered out of his crease Thomson threw down the wicket appealing for a run-out. It was disallowed, and the Sri Lankan fans booed Thomson persistently from then on. Both batsmen went to hospital for precautionary checks while their compatriots replied to Australia's 328 for five wickets with 276 for four.

Van Impe rounds off triumphant Tour de France

By David Saunders in Paris
PUBLISHED MONDAY 19 JULY

Lucien Van Impe, the little Belgian, took overall victory in the Tour de France which ended in Paris yesterday. The Belgian champion, Freddy Maertens, was denied the record of nine stage wins at the very end of the 22nd and final stage.

Gerben Karstens, of Holland, prevented that by scoring his second stage victory in much the same manner as his first, at Bordeaux last Wednesday, breaking away just inside the final kilometre of the 56-mile stage.

Karstens earned the British TI Raleigh team their third stage win and so managed to wipe out some of their disappointment at losing world road champion Hennie Kuiper through an accident when he was well placed.

It has been a splendid tour, full of incident and courage. Van Impe is a worthy winner because he not only used his natural climbing talent to the full but also guarded his lead and became a true rider of quality as a result.

Joop Zoetemelk, of Holland, had to be content with second place for the third time in his career. What a pity the quiet, forceful Dutchman suffered a saddle boil in the closing stages. I always felt that had Zoetemelk been fit, Van Impe was far from safe while time trials and mountains lay ahead.

After winning Saturday's stage to Versailles, despite a crash in torrential rain, this victory gave Freddy Maertens the chance to set the record of nine wins in one tour. But nine wins in one tour is a lot to ask, and although his team rode themselves into the ground to protect him, the escape from Karstens could not be matched.

MILESTONES

Italian driver Lella Lombardi became the first woman to gain Formula One championship points when she finished sixth in the Spanish Grand Prix at Montjuich, driving a March-Ford.

Gritty Australians bow to Lloyd in thrilling final

By Michael Melford
PUBLISHED MONDAY 23 JUNE

All day Saturday, as the Prudential World Cup final unfolded at 14 overs an hour amid the clank of cans, the honk of horns and other less-than-tranquil visitations of cricket 1975, Australia were on the losing side.

But to their great credit they kept going, so that it was always possible some heroic individual feat might turn the match for them. When it was all over, just before a quarter to nine, they had lost by only 17 runs.

England supplied a lovely summer's day; West Indies and Australia fought an historic battle and though West Indies always looked the stronger side, the 'ifs' which might have brought Australia victory were numerous.

If they had not put West Indies in…one wondered about the wisdom of this decision on a sunny morning, even when West Indies were 50 for three.

If Clive Lloyd had been caught when 26…this was perhaps the decisive event, for Lloyd, with his immense power, is a cruel opponent for a fielding side once he gets going. At 26, he mistimed a pull and Ross Edwards dropped the catch. As it was, Lloyd made 102.

If only the Australians, after reaching 81 for one in the 21st over had not begun to run themselves out…five run-outs, the first three costing the precious wickets of Alan Turner and the Chappell brothers, were evidence of the pressure which Australia were under to keep up the required rate.

Test of stamina though it was, it all seemed to be greatly enjoyed and it did much credit to Clive Lloyd, the inevitable Man of the Match, the other 21 players and the two umpires, Tom Spencer and Harold Bird.

Whether it did the crowd so much credit is doubtful, though the police worked wonders in keeping them within bounds for most of a thirsty day's watching.

As a final compliment to the Prudential for their great contribution, one can applaud the fact that when it was all over, there were no speeches, just the presentation of the cup and cheques for £4,000 and £2,000. Perhaps, Prince Philip's dinner, like that of many others, was being kept hot in the oven at home.

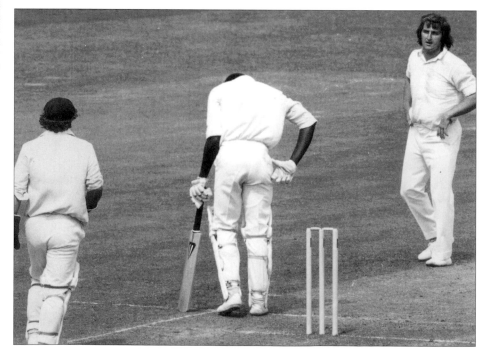

Captain Clive Lloyd heads for the pavilion, caught Rodney Marsh, bowled Gary Gilmour, for 102 runs.

Brilliant Sheene beats bewildered Agostini at post

By George Turnbull in Assen
PUBLISHED MONDAY 30 JUNE

Barry Sheene, 24, the brilliant Suzuki works rider from Wisbech, produced all his world-class ability to score a spectacular victory in the Dutch TT 500-cc Grand Prix in Assen on Saturday. It was Sheene's first 500-cc grand prix victory.

He won by a wheel's length from 14-times world champion Giacomo Agostini after 16 laps of the five-mile circuit, in one of the most exciting races for years.

In the process the ebullient London-born rider out-fought and upstaged not only the Italian ace, but also the reigning world champion, Phil Read, who was third.

Sheene brought the 135,000 spectators to their feet and received a tremendous ovation as he flashed over the line just ahead of a bewildered Agostini, who thought the race was his when leading only 300 yards from the chequered flag. Throughout the race Sheene had played a brilliant cat-and-mouse game with Agostini.

Read and his MV Augusta set the pace for the first four laps, but then Agostini took over on his quicker and better-handling Yamaha. With Sheene tucked on his tail,

Agostini (above), beaten by Sheene in the Dutch Grand Prix, recovered to win his eighth 500-cc world championship later in the year.

they eventually left Read some 45 seconds behind.

Agostini led the field for another four laps but, despite all his roadcraft, was unable to shake off a very cool and confident Sheene, who stayed within a machine's length of his rival.

Sheene took the lead for a couple of laps or so, only to lose it again to Agostini, who must have felt he had the edge as he kept glancing over his left shoulder to see where the young Cockney was lying.

As they hurtled into the last bend only 300 yards from the flag, Agostini was again leading, with Sheene in his slipstream. He again glanced over his left shoulder, and it was then that Sheene acted. He unleashed the full power of his Suzuki-4, feinted to the right of the Italian, and then swooped on the left to take the flag and the tributes of the crowd.

Agostini could not believe it. He admitted later: 'I did not think anyone, but anyone, could have passed me in that short distance from the corner to the flag.'

Ali defeats Bugner in searing heat

By Donald Saunders in Kuala Lumpur
PUBLISHED WEDNESDAY 2 JULY

Shortly after Muhammad Ali had outboxed Joe Bugner over 15 wearying rounds in the blistering heat of Kuala Lumpur, he predicted that his British victim would be the next heavyweight champion of the world. 'After me he is the greatest,' declared Ali, who kept the title by earning a unanimous decision from the judges.

Turning to Bugner, as they sat side by side, sweat still dripping from their tired bodies in the blissful coolness of the air-conditioned interview room, the champion emphasised that he would not be around much longer.

'I am barely hanging on to one rope,' Ali said. 'So stay in shape. You are the next in line for the crown.'

Few could believe he will ever match the earning capacity of Ali. Still, as Bugner rightly reminded us, he is only 25. 'I will be back,' he promised.

SPORT IN BRIEF

HOCKEY
The World Cup in Kuala Lumpur is affected by torrential rain. In the semi-finals Pakistan beat West Germany 5–1; India's game against Malaysia is abandoned after the pitch becomes completely waterlogged; India win a replay 3–2. India go on to beat Pakistan 2–1 in the final, with a disputed second goal from Ashok Kumar. West Germany come third.

CRICKET
Londoner Graham Gooch makes his Test debut for England. In his first appearance against the Australians at Edgbaston, he is out for a duck in both innings, and Australia win the Test by an innings and 85 runs. Desperate for a batsman who can brave the pace of Dennis Lillee and Jeff Thomson, England call up David Steele, a grey-haired 33-year-old who plays for Northamptonshire. In six innings in three Tests, Steele scores 365 runs at an average of 60.83. His highest score is 92 in the second innings of the third Test at Headingley. England hold the Australians to draws in the final three Tests.

HORSE RACING
Grundy, trained by Fulke Walwyn and ridden by Pat Eddery, wins the King George VI and Queen Elizabeth Diamond Stakes. In a thrilling race, Grundy and Bustino race neck and neck for the final furlong before Eddery's mount pulls away to win by half a length.

GOLF
France win the women's European team golf championship for the fourth time since its inception in 1959, beating Spain by $4^1/_2$ matches to $2^1/_2$ in the final in St Cloud.

1975

223

1975

Ashe's clever tactics take crown from bemused Connors

By Lance Tingay

PUBLISHED MONDAY 7 JULY

There are many things by which the lawn tennis championships could be remembered, but none so striking as the climax of the main event – the men's singles final – where Arthur Ashe nobly and cleverly made himself a first-time Wimbledon champion.

His 6–1, 6–1, 5–7, 6–4 victory over his fellow American, Jim Connors, took little more than two hours. It was not a particularly long match and it was not the first time a black player had become the champion, for Althea Gibson took the women's singles title in 1957 and the doubles the year before.

It was not one of those heroic affairs where the title was won from the brink of defeat. Nor was it one of those rare great matches, such as that between Stan Smith and Ilie Nastase in 1972, when a superlative standard of play was maintained by both sides from first to last over the maximum distance.

It was, though, about the most intellectual victory seen within recent memory, and the outcome was against every predicted possibility. But that Ashe **(below left)** is now Wimbledon champion and that Connors has been deposed was because Ashe assessed what shots and tactics would negate his power and put his theory into effective action.

Connors began the final an overwhelming favourite. It would have been foolhardy to have regarded him otherwise, for his command of killing shots had taken him through all his other matches with ever-increasing domination. Ashe, 31, had played and lost to Connors, 22, three times before.

Ashe can hardly have played better or a more disciplined match than he did on Saturday. He served wide of Connors, who, at full stretch, was made to return ineffectively. He varied his pace beautifully; against the slower balls Connors became very human with his errors.

It was an absorbing and human contest. It was not only Ashe that beat Connors; Wimbledon itself proved greater than him.

By Lance Tingay

PUBLISHED SATURDAY 5 JULY

It was a great day for the United States in the All-England championships yesterday, which was Independence Day, for both the titles that were decided, the women's singles and the men's doubles, went to them.

For Billie Jean King, who took the singles, it was as splendid a moment as she has had in her 15 years as a competitor at Wimbledon. She gained her sixth singles title, and that was her 19th Wimbledon title in all.

She now stands as a record-maker, equal arithmetically with her fellow Californian Elizabeth Ryan. But since Miss Ryan won no singles titles, the place of Mrs King as the premier monarch of Wimbledon must be undisputed.

Yet it was a sad day for Wimbledon also. No one begrudged Mrs King her fine glory, for so good a player as she certainly deserved it in every way. But no player so richly talented as Evonne Goolagong-Cawley, and assuredly no player so well loved as she, deserved to suffer so calamitous a fate as befell her on the centre court.

She was routed 6–0, 6–1 in a women's singles final that was almost pathetic for its one-sidedness. How could a player so good as Mrs Cawley perform so badly?

One has seen her cast away matches in a dream before. Indeed, such has often been the case with her, and 'walkabouts' and Evonne Goolagong are a commonplace of the story of the game in recent years. On this occasion it was not that Mrs Cawley played in a hazy kind of

Evonne Cawley (above) won only one game on her own serve and a total of 24 points during Billie Jean King's 39-minute dash to victory.

dream, rather it was that she just played poorly. But when she returned service it was an open invitation to Mrs King to volley away a winner.

Mrs King played well. She made hardly an error on her own account, she was sharp and her concentration never faltered, not even when it became obvious that her opponent was never going to make a real match of it.

A bewildered and almost grieving centre-court crowd watched Mrs King swallow the first ten games of the match without her opponent even reaching points for a game. When at last Mrs Cawley broke her duck, there was a cheer.

The crowd, perhaps still hopeful that one of their best-loved players might yet show something of her proper form, exuded sympathy. But Mrs Cawley got her solitary game and that was all.

DID YOU KNOW?

The golfer Lee Trevino was still not stuck for words, even after being struck by lightning at the Western Open in Illinois in 1975. 'There was a thunderous crack,' he recalled afterwards, 'and I was lifted a foot and a half off the ground. Dammit, I thought to myself, this is one helluva penalty for slow play.'

Lauda beats Hunt to tighten grip on drivers' title

PUBLISHED MONDAY 7 JULY

Austria's Niki Lauda, driving a Ferrari, swept to his fourth victory this year in the French Grand Prix yesterday, but his triumph was far harder than it looked.

'My front tyres started giving trouble 20 laps from the end, and I had to drive to my absolute maximum to keep out ahead,' said Lauda, who increased his lead in the world drivers' championship. 'But I had the psychological advantage of being the leader,' he added, 'and I didn't think James Hunt could catch me.'

The British driver, who broke Lauda's string of wins in Holland two weeks ago in his gleaming white Hesketh, moved into second place after only eight laps of the race, but he never looked like catching the Austrian, even though he was only about one and a half seconds behind at the finish.

After some drama in the opening laps, Lauda led Hunt, West Germany's Jochen Mass and his McLaren teammate and reigning world champion, Emerson Fittipaldi – and that order remained unchanged.

With this victory Lauda has opened up a 22-point lead at the top of the drivers' table in the race for the title.

Lauda won five grands prix and took Ferrari to their first championship win since 1964.

Battered Ali demolishes Frazier

By Ian Ward in Manila

PUBLISHED THURSDAY 2 OCTOBER

Exhausted, aching all over and uncharacteristically subdued, Muhammad Ali yesterday savoured his retention of the world heavyweight boxing crown, praised the defeated Joe Frazier as the world's toughest fighter and speculated that he may have fought his last fight.

For 14 gruelling rounds, Ali had pounded his relentless challenger with a shattering combination of punches to the head; for 14 rounds the champion absorbed shattering lefts and rights to the body, as Frazier, burrowing under the champion's longer reach, sought to sap Ali's strength and skills.

Time and again the 25,000 fans jamming Manila's Philippine Coliseum rose to their feet and roared Ali in for the kill; on each occasion, sheer guts and stamina saw Frazier over the crisis.

Frazier's courageous boring-in tactics earned him the crowd's admiration — yet they proved his undoing.

By the 14th round Frazier, tired and cruelly battered about the head, walked into a series of lefts and rights to the face and jaw, and was knocked almost unconscious on his feet by 15 blockbusting blows inside 45 seconds.

Clinging on through little more than instinct, Frazier saw out the round; but, as he shuffled wearily to his corner, the challenger presented a tragic picture.

The left side of his forehead had been pummelled until a massive swelling stretched his eye upwards into a grotesque slant. Eddie Futch, his manager, took one look at Frazier and told him: 'No more; that's it. That's enough.'

Frazier started to protest, but Futch motioned to the referee that they were conceding victory to Ali.

Members of Ali's entourage leaped around their idol. But Ali fell to the canvas and had to be assisted to his feet.

Frazier lands a left on Ali in the 'Thrilla in Manila', one of the greatest of all heavyweight fights. 'He's the toughest man in the world,' Ali afterwards said of Frazier.

SPORT IN BRIEF

MOTOR RACING
In November the former Formula One champion, Indianapolis 500 and Le Mans 24-hour race winner Graham Hill dies in a plane crash after running into thick fog near Elstree airport in north London. Hill was piloting the plane himself; with him were five other members of his team, who are also killed in the accident.

FOOTBALL
Only a fortnight into the football season, violent scenes are reported around the country as football hooliganism takes hold. In a match at Luton, as Chelsea go three goals down, Chelsea supporters attack players, police and ground staff. Violence spills out into the streets, and 100 people are arrested. Other disturbances take place at Ibrox and at Stoke's ground.

RUGBY LEAGUE
A new nine-month home-and-away tournament is designed to decide the World Cup. When England lose 12–7 to Wales in Brisbane, it is decreed that Wales are the home side; so despite enjoying a win and a draw against Australia, England finish one point behind them.

BOXING
Carlos Monzon retains the world middleweight title for the 12th time, when he wins by a fifth-round knock-out against Gratien Tonna of France.

GOLF
The United States win the Ryder Cup tournament easily at Laurel Valley, Pennsylvania, by 21 points to 11. Great Britain and Ireland's only high point comes when London-born Brian Barnes beats Jack Nicklaus in the singles – twice – by four and two and two and one.

Mihir Bose

The emergence and re-emergence of sporting nations

THE ROMANCE OF SPORT lies in its sheer unpredictability: the injury-time goal that changes the destiny of a match, even a season; the last-ball wicket, run or the incredible putt that turns a loser into a winner.

Nothing, though, has been as romantic as the unpredictable rise of countries who even a few short years ago were considered little more than minnows and did not figure in anyone's calendar. Add to that the re-emergence as a sporting giant of one country, all but dead internationally, and you have a remarkable sporting revolution.

That country, of course, is South Africa. A decade ago men in white coats would have taken away anyone suggesting that South Africa would re-emerge among the civilised sporting nations. Locked in the terrible grip of apartheid, a totalitarian system which extended to all walks of life, there seemed no way back for a country of such talent and such brutality.

A decade ago men in white coats would have taken away anyone suggesting that South Africa would re-emerge among the civilised sporting nations.

This was emphasised in the summer of 1989 when Ali Bacher, then head of the white South African cricket organisation, shocked the world by announcing in the middle of an Ashes series that a rebel tour of South Africa, led by former England captain Mike Gatting, would take place that winter. The tour was met not only by protests outside South Africa, common for such sporting visits, but for the first time well-orchestrated protests within the country which led to its curtailment.

However, in the middle of the tour Nelson Mandela was released from prison after 27 years, and soon South Africa was transformed from a pariah white country into a rainbow one that everyone wanted to embrace. Eighteen months after Gatting and his men had been forced out, a South Africa team flew to India to make their return to international competitions after two decades of isolation. It was an historic flight. South Africa, where in the days of apartheid contact with non-white countries had been shunned, were playing India for the first time in any sport – they had only met once before in a Davis Cup match in a neutral city in Europe in the Sixties. Indeed it was the first time a South African plane had even flown to India. The pilot, who had often flown F. W. De Klerk, the president of South Africa, on international visits, was so unfamiliar with the flight plan he kept checking it on the route from Johannesburg to Calcutta.

Although that one-day cricket series ended in defeat for South Africa, within a few months other South African sports were back on the international calendar. Just before isolation, in 1970, white South Africa had produced a brilliant cricket team, who beat the Australians 4–0 at home. They have not quite reached those heights again on their return, though the first time they played in the World Cup, in Australia in 1992, only the peculiar rules governing rain-affected matches prevented them beating England and reaching the final. Yet led by the magnificent pace bowling of Allan Donald, widely seen as the fastest white bowler in the world, and the fielding of Jonty Rhodes, who at one stage was rightly considered the greatest fielder in the game, they have shown themselves to be not far behind Australia, probably the best cricket nation of the last decade of the 20th century.

It is in rugby and soccer that in different ways South Africa truly surprised the international sporting world. Rugby had always been the game of the Boers, the Dutch-descended white South Africans who designed and implemented apartheid. Perhaps because they were never ostracised by the rugby authorities during the years of isolation – rugby internationals were played for many years after other sports had ended all contact – South Africa maintained their standard. This was emphasised when the rugby World Cup was held in South Africa in 1995. Then, with Nelson Mandela wearing the Springbok jersey, marking the reconciliation of the Boer and the blacks, South Africa under François Pienaar won the competition, wearing down the more gifted All Blacks, who included the player of the tournament, Jonah Lomu.

South Africa's emergence in soccer has taken a bit longer. Just as rugby is the great white game in South Africa, soccer is the great black game. As South Africa re-entered the sporting world, much was made of the riches South Africa would bring to soccer. However, it was only with their appearance in the 1998 World Cup finals in France that it could be said that South African soccer was a force on the African continent.

One reason South Africa have struggled to become pre-eminent in soccer is that the competition on the continent has been severe, and the past decade has seen a near revolution in African soccer. When Pelé suggested that an African country could win the World Cup before the end of the century, it was seen as the sort of all too fallible and risible comments even the great can make. However, in 1990 and 1994, Africa showed that the continent had the talent. What held them back was a lack of belief that they could defeat the more established nations. This was emphasised by the quarter-final between Cameroon and England during Italia 90, and the match between Nigeria and Italy in USA 94.

A drab World Cup in Italy was lit by the skills of the Cameroon side, who announced themselves in the first match of the tournament when they beat the reigning champions, Argentina. In the quarter-final against England, after falling behind, Cameroon went on to lead 2–1. Even the England players conceded Cameroon were playing the better football, but two defensive blunders cost them penalties and hastened their defeat. In USA 94 a similarly gifted, if more muscular Nigerian side were within minutes of beating Italy when they lost their nerve and allowed Roberto Baggio to equalise. Italy went on to win and were only denied by Brazil in the final in a penalty shoot-out.

So remarkable has been the progress of African soccer since then that there is hardly a top team in Europe who do not have some African input. As far as football scouts are concerned, Africa is the place to search for talent, and they descended in unprecedented numbers on the African Nations Cup in Burkina Faso in 1998. Africa had become the newest, most exciting place on the soccer map.

If Africa has taken the limelight in athletics in the last three decades, in 1993 it was overshadowed by the world's most populous country announcing itself in startling fashion. In September that year, Chinese women competing in the national championships shook the world with extraordinary records. Wang Junxia, 20, who in April had run one of the world's fastest marathons, set three world marks and had a hand in a fourth. Her 10,000-m record of 29 min 31.78 sec, and the 3 min 51.92 sec for the 1,500 m equalled the times of the male B-string international. In the 3,000 m she ran 8 min 6.13 sec, only two seconds slower than Ireland's Frank O'Mara in the 1987 world indoor championships. As one commentator noted: 'This was record-breaking on the grand scale. It was Paavo Nurmi crossed with Flo-Jo mixed with a dash of Bob Beamon.'

As the world tried to take in the news, Wang's coach Ma Junren insisted that Wang's success was due to old-fashioned hard work. However, since then there have been suggestions that her performances were enhanced by the use of drugs. These rumours were apparently substantiated when seven Chinese swimmers in the 1998 world championships tested positive. The results cast a deep shadow over Chinese achievements.

No such shadow hangs over perhaps the most surprising sporting achievements of recent times: the emergence of Sri Lanka as a major cricketing nation, at least in one-day cricket. In 1975, when the first World Cup was held in England, Sri Lanka were minnows waiting to be slaughtered and mocked. They had an horrific match against Australia where they were terrorised by the pace bowling of Jeff Thomson; one of their batsman had to be sent to hospital. The injured player was asked by a policeman how he had hurt himself, and when told it was in a cricket match the policeman wondered if he wanted to press charges. Ian Chappell, the Australian captain, dubbed Thomson 'our ambassador to Sri Lanka'. It showed a certain contempt for Sri Lankan cricket.

The older countries will have to accommodate the new if they are not to be left behind in the race for sporting supremacy.

Two decades later, in 1996, Sri Lanka, now a recognised Test-playing country, won the World Cup in Lahore in grand style. During their triumphal progress they twice beat India in India, so devastatingly in the semi-final in Calcutta that angry Indian fans rioted and the match was abandoned. The Sri Lankan success was based on brilliant batting, particularly by the opener S. T. Jayasuriya, splendid fielding and remarkable spin bowling. It was all part of a ten-year Sri Lankan plan to become the top cricket nation.

However, the rise of such minnows also poses problems. Despite Sri Lanka's status they have yet to play a full series in England, where existing commitments to countries such as Australia means there is little space on the calendar. This will have to change. As new countries emerge with their vibrant sporting talent, the older countries will have to accommodate them if they are not to be left behind in the race for sporting supremacy.

1976

Curry lands Britain's first gold

By Howard Bass in Innsbruck
PUBLISHED THURSDAY 12 FEBRUARY

Magnificent John Curry has done it. Last night in Innsbruck, with the most brilliant performance of his career, he became the first Briton ever to win an Olympic gold medal for men's figure skating.

With the majestic finesse which nobody has yet succeeded in imitating, each of his deliberate and unhurried movements was perfectly placed and everyone knew that, although his major rivals had still to skate, none could possibly beat him.

His three triple jumps – loop, salchow and toe-loop – were never allowed to upset the rhythmic continuity of an always elegant, shrewdly devised programme perfectly timed to ideally chosen music from 'Don Quixote'.

Among the mighty fallen were Sergei Volkov, the reigning world champion, Jan Hoffmann, the 1974 world champion, and Vladimir Kovalev, who lost his European title to Curry last month.

In tenth place, Robin Cousins, of Bristol, a most worthy heir-apparent to Curry's national crown, cleanly landed no fewer than five triple jumps and also underlined his growing versatility in spins.

John Curry said of his success last night: 'It's the perfect start to my professional career – I hope.'

Asked if he was disappointed not to receive a perfect six from any of the judges, he said: 'No, I skated too early in the programme to have a six, because it wouldn't have been fair to the skaters who came after me.'

He said he expected to live permanently in the United States, 'for professional reasons and because I just love it. I am very happy in America. It's been a long road and the last two days have been the longest and slowest of my life. I've been wanting to get out and skate, and I just had to wait.'

MILESTONES

Twenty-one-year-old Tony Miles, a mathematics student from Edgbaston, Birmingham, was the first British chess player to be officially recognised as an international Grand Master.

Austrians roar Klammer on to famous victory

By Alan Smith in Innsbruck
PUBLISHED FRIDAY 6 FEBRUARY

Franz Klammer gave his fellow Austrians the start they had dreamed of to the winter Olympics in Innsbruck yesterday, but how he had to fight to take the downhill title from the Swiss veteran, Bernhard Russi, by just over three-tenths of a second!

A draw that the organisers could not have bettered had they fixed it themselves had Klammer going last of the first group, after all his main rivals.

Russi, at 27 five years Klammer's senior, was third to go down this hard, sometimes icy, piste, and although most of the mountainside was bathed in sunshine, at the top gale-force winds added to the problems. On every inch of it Russi was attacking.

Klammer (on right of picture) with Philippe Roux and René Berthod, before his hair-raising dash for gold.

Although he won the world championship in 1970 and the gold medal in Sapporo four years ago, Russi, whose father once trained the British Army langlauf team, has been consistently underrated, not least by some of his fellow countrymen.

His run yesterday was that of a true champion, fast and exactly on line, so that when he raced through the finish in 1 min 46 sec, well over nine seconds faster than Klammer's winning time 12 months ago, the Austrian could be forgiven for thinking he had been set an impossible task. He said afterwards that that was what he did think: 'I did not consider it possible to ski this course in under 1 min 46 sec, but I knew I had to try.'

Try he did – without his new holed 'magic' skis. On this brilliant day, the course looked almost the colour of the yellow and black Austrian uniforms, the rays of the sun edged by the excited crowds who had climbed every goat-track to get a higher, better view of their hero.

They roared their massive approval as Klammer's first intermediate time was announced, fractionally faster than Russi, murmured in wanton disbelief when the second was heard to be slower. Klammer went perilously close to missing a gate, and then really turned it on.

'I gave myself some terrible frights,' he recalled later. 'I was in the air so often I was sure I would fall.' Downhill races of this class, though, are only won by a skier on the edge of being out of control, and Klammer kept from going over the brink.

Klammer's reward was a richly deserved gold medal.

West Indies' recovery hopes ruined

By Ray Robinson, Melbourne
PUBLISHED THURSDAY 5 FEBRUARY

Three good wickets in four overs by fast bowler Dennis Lillee blighted West Indies' blossoming chance of a valiant rearguard action in the final Test against Australia at Melbourne Cricket Ground yesterday.

Lillee struck his telling blows in mid-afternoon, when Vivian Richards and Alvin Kallicharran were right on top of the Australian bowling with a century stand.

Their mastery looked so complete that West Indies' remote hope of going on to score 492 was ceasing to be inconceivable. Australia's declaration at 300 for three had left them 491 behind with ten hours to go.

Five times in his first 22 runs Richards pounded drives off the back foot past Jeff Thomson and Gary Gilmour to each side of the sightscreens. He showed no liking for sharp singles when there were fours to be hit

with the confidence bestowed by three hundreds and a half-century among his last five innings

When Lillee came on for the eighth over, Richards drove him twice to the sightscreen, too. He had made himself a celebrity in three weeks; with superlative stroke-play in his 13th Test, he was demanding admittance to the upper echelon of international batsmen.

Nine fours off 48 balls in 76 minutes won him a prize for the fastest 50 of the Test. Kallicharran backed him well in raising 170 for only two wickets, the little left-hander sticking to his unaccustomed role of supporting partner for an hour and three-quarters.

Captain Clive Lloyd, who had come in fifth, saw five partners fall to Lillee and Mallett. In this dispiriting procession four of them managed only 26 – Rowe 6, Murray 5, Boyce 11, and Holding 4.

Australia won the six-match series 5–1.

Southampton's triumph is a tonic for soccer backwaters

Donald Saunders
PUBLISHED MONDAY 3 MAY
Southampton 1; Manchester United 0

A jubilant Southampton team celebrate their victory in the FA Cup. Founded 91 years before, the club had never visited Wembley, or won a major honour.

Southampton's first FA Cup triumph is shining like a beacon of hope across the quiet backwaters of English soccer, where success has so long been regarded as the monopoly of London, the Midlands and the industrial North.

As convoys of jubilant supporters drove home along the M3 on Saturday evening – their cars, mini-buses and coaches festooned with scarves, rosettes and banners – every motorway bridge was manned by kindred spirits saluting the good news from Wembley.

Not since 1939, when Portsmouth also ridiculed the odds by defeating Wolves, had the south of England so much to shout about on Cup-final day.

Though there will be much weeping and gnashing of teeth in scores of Manchester United supporters' clubs, this turn up for the book can only be good for the game.

Southampton took home the Cup because they produced, at Wembley, the sound, honest football of which they are capable. United failed because they did not remotely approach the heights scaled earlier this season.

Tommy Docherty's task is to find out why things went wrong before United set out on another arduous domestic season and a UEFA Cup campaign. He will not need telling that only Martin Buchan, an elegant captain, and Brian Greenhoff, whose alert, truly competitive performance must have impressed Don Revie, reached their normal standard.

As those two central defenders were busy enough to attract our regular scrutiny, it is clear that Manchester United did not swarm all over their opponents as most of us had expected.

Indeed, United failed utterly to demonstrate that the reintroduction of a pair of conventional wingers is the answer to English soccer's prayers. Mr Docherty ultimately abandoned the policy, by pulling off Hill after 66 ineffective minutes and replacing him with David McCreery.

Though United's manager, understandably, felt that he must do something to prevent his team surrendering tamely under the steadily increasing pressure in the second half, this substitution may well have been a psychological error.

Southampton, whose confidence had been growing as Jim McCalliog gradually took midfield control away from the quietly fading Lou Macari and Gerry Daly, now sensed that their opponents were seriously worried.

So they pushed forward even more purposefully with the eager Bobby Stokes, surprisingly industrious Peter Osgood, and fleet-footed Mick Channon frequently harassing United's defence and testing the watchful Alec Stepney.

At last, seven minutes from time, Stokes raced on to a beautifully judged through-pass from McCalliog and calmly placed his low, firm left-foot shot wide of the diving goalkeeper and inside the far post.

SPORT IN BRIEF

WINTER OLYMPICS
Twenty-five-year-old Rosi Mittermaier of West Germany, who during ten years of top-flight skiing has never won a World Cup downhill, wins gold in the women's downhill and slalom skiing events. She just fails to take a unique treble, however, when she comes second in the giant slalom, Kathy Kreiner of Canada denying her a third gold.

LAWN TENNIS
Sue Barker becomes the first English player since Ann Jones in 1966 to win the French Open women's title. She beats Renata Tomanova in the final 6–2, 0–6, 6–2.

CRICKET
Greg Chappell enjoys a successful series against the West Indian tourists. His 702 runs in six Tests are a record for Australia against the West Indies.

BOXING
Londoner John Stracey, having won a sensational fight against José Napoles of Cuba in December last year, now holds the WBC world welterweight title. In March this year he makes his first defence against Hedgemon Lewis, winning with a knock-out in round ten. Against Stracey's better judgement, his manager persuades him to fight again within three months, and in a match against Carlos Palomino of Mexico he loses by a knock-out in round 12. Stracey **(below on left, with Palomino)** never wins a big fight again.

1976

1976

Borg subdues the genius of Nastase

By Lance Tingay

PUBLISHED MONDAY 5 JULY

The tournament by which the All-England lawn tennis championships completed 100 years of history will go down as the hottest and driest in living memory. It will also be remembered as one in which youth was dominant.

Björn Borg won the men's singles title for Sweden with a meteoric display against the Romanian, Ilie Nastase, on Saturday, to succeed at the age of 20, the third youngest of all time.

This year's tournament, the 90th meeting, can only be known as Borg's Wimbledon. He was a revelation, not so much in his consistency of form in the early rounds, but in his *tour de force* in the final. For Borg it was a dream performance.

Yet when the contest started the signs were that this sort of performance was going to be put forward by Nastase. The pace of the rallies, aided by the lightning surface of the court, was that of a frenzied knock-up.

Out of this exchange of electric pace Nastase emerged in the lead by 3–0. Borg saved himself from a crippling deficit by at last holding his service in the fourth game. The Romanian's dominance was then checked and later thrust back. Borg took the lead for the first time at 5–4, initiating his break of service with a brilliant backhand passing shot that became his typically killing weapon.

What had become a one-sided final revived into one of exciting uncertainty when Borg served vainly for the match at 5–4 in the third set. For four games the match held some hope of Nastase recovering. Then he dropped his service in the next game.

Born won 8–7, boomed out the following service game to love and was singles champion of Wimbledon.

Björn Borg, above right, serves his way to his first Wimbledon title. He did not lose a single set during the tournament.

BJÖRN BORG (1956–)

BJÖRN RUNE BORG was born in the Swedish town of Södertälje on 6 June 1956. His first love was ice hockey, but he was soon introduced to tennis by his father, who was one of Sweden's leading table-tennis players. At the age of 11, Borg won his first tournament, the Sormland country championship, playing his shots using both hands because he found his racquet too heavy. Coaches eventually persuaded him to change his forehand so he could gain more topspin, but the two-handed backhand remained one of the trademarks of Borg's game.

The Swede began to make an impact on the senior circuit in the early 1970s, winning his first Grand Slam tournament, the French Open, in 1974. His golden-haired good looks attracted mobs of teenagers, but he always appeared unflappable, on court and off, and was nicknamed 'Ice Borg'.

His returning was awesome; as fellow player Vitas Gerulaitis said, 'He's the world's best counter-puncher; Björn does more with the ball, more often, than anyone else in the game's history.'

These qualities led him to six French titles (1974–5, 1978–81) and five consecutive Wimbledon wins from 1976 to 1980. Borg retired prematurely in 1983; several comeback attempts proved unsuccessful.

Miller times victory run in Open championship

By Michael Williams

PUBLISHED MONDAY 12 JULY

For a naturally aggressive golfer, Johnny Miller had to steel himself to be patient before, with a final flood of peerless strokes, he won the Open championship at Royal Birkdale on Saturday by six strokes.

Ultimately, he did it in the true Miller manner, his 66 being the lowest winning last round in the championship's history, as, too, was the 63 that brought him triumphantly home in his only other major championship, the 1973 US Open at Oakmont.

For those with romance in their hearts, I suppose there will be a touch of regret that the captivating, smiling young Spaniard, Severiano Ballesteros, could not keep the lead he had held for three days. But he repaired a round that was fast falling apart with a wonderful finish of three birdies and an eagle in the last six holes.

The cool chip-and-single-putt he played at the 18th to tie with Jack Nicklaus for second place rightly and properly raised the roof.

Talking frankly afterwards, Miller commented that he thought it was probably as well for Ballesteros – who had

Miller kisses his first Open trophy (right); his winning margin was the highest since Arnold Palmer's six-stroke victory 14 years earlier.

begun championship week as caddy for his brother, Manuel, in the pre-qualifying – that in the long run, he had not won. 'So much would have been expected of him,' he said, 'that it would have been nearly impossible to live up to it.'

Miller compared it with his own experience when he was 23 and came second to Charles Coody in the US Masters. 'I could have won,' he said, 'but I now know I wasn't ready for it.'

Great swim for golden Wilkie

By Pat Besford in Montreal

PUBLISHED MONDAY 26 JULY

David Wilkie's four years of dreaming, toiling and hoping, which culminated in his gold medal for the 200-m breaststroke in Montreal, earned Britain her first swimming victory by a man since 1908, and the first individual gold in these Games.

Now, with every major title – world, European, Commonwealth and Olympic – in his possession, the Scot quits big-time swimming for a more leisurely life and, perhaps, a job in promotions and public relations.

The way Wilkie, 22, beat his rival, John Hencken, in the apparently impossible time he had forecast two weeks earlier, a world record of 2 min 15.11 sec, 3.1 seconds inside the two-year-old figures by the American, earned him lavish compliments from experts here.

Top American coach Pete Daland said: 'That must be one of the greatest swims of modern times.'

The Briton's majestic, surging last 50-m effort left Hencken, already a metre in arrears, trailing home in second place four metres behind. And though the American was inside his old record, with 2 min 17.26 sec, it was a performance in little consequence in the wake of the flying Scot.

Africans stage walkout

By Donald Saunders in Montreal

PUBLISHED MONDAY 19 JULY

The withdrawal of African and Arab nations from the 21st Olympics is likely to have greater effect on the development of sport within the Third World than it is on the Montreal Games.

The absence of such outstanding athletes as Mike Boit of Kenya and John Akii-Bua of Uganda will obviously lower the standard of competition, and all who have the interests of international sport at heart are sad to see so many young men and women denied the opportunity to test themselves at the highest level.

But the plain fact is that to make a real impact, black Africa needs the support of the Warsaw Pact countries. The Soviet Union are due to stage the 1980 Olympics in Moscow, and their multi-million rouble plans to make these Games the greatest show in history are already in an advanced state. In such circumstances, the Russians would be highly unlikely to rock the Olympic boat.

Even those of us who sympathise with the broad principles of the campaign – to persuade South Africa to permit multiracial sport at all levels – are becoming impatient with the Supreme Council for African Sport and its political manipulation.

1976

Greig magnificent

By Michael Melford at Headingley
PUBLISHED WEDNESDAY 28 JULY

West Indies won the fourth Test at Headingley, by 55 runs, and with it the series 2–0, but defeat is less sour after a magnificent cricket match from which England emerged with much honour and renewed hope.

Several reputations have been re-established, not least that of the captain, because Tony Greig's 76 not out yesterday, following 116 in the first innings, will go down as one of the great innings which failed.

The honour lies not in running West Indies so close, but in doing so after they had made the morale-breaking score of 330 for two by tea on the first day, and after England's own reply to a score of 459 (which eventually reached 387) had stood at 32 for three on the second day.

Foster struggles to bronze

By James Coote in Montreal
PUBLISHED TUESDAY 27 JULY

Brendan Foster became only the second man in Olympic history to win a 10,000-m medal for Great Britain when he finished third in Montreal last night.

The title went to Lasse Viren, of Finland, who became the second man to retain his 10,000-m title since the Games began, and the silver medal went to a gallant little Portuguese, Carlos Lopes, who cut out the pace that cracked the entire field with the exception of Viren.

The race started encouragingly with Tony Simmons, the British No. 2, and Bernie Ford setting a perfect pace – the first kilometre in 2 minutes 53 seconds, the second in 2 minutes 51 seconds, and the next two each in 2 minutes 49.4 seconds. The pace steadily increased and the slower runners wilted.

Just after the 5,000-m mark, Foster looked to be set for one of his famous breaks; but it did not happen. With eight-and-a-half laps remaining, Lopes made a little burst, looked around, and knew that the gold medal was between himself and Viren.

Viren was obviously wanting to spring, but he held on as late as he dared. Then, when he went, there was a sudden display of Finnish flags throughout the stadium.

Foster wearily hauled his body round the final lap; Simmons almost caught him with a brave last sprint.

Lasse Viren was the first athlete to defend successfully his 10,000-m and (below) 5,000-m Olympic titles.

Moses and Juantorena produce world record times

By James Coote
PUBLISHED TUESDAY 27 JULY

In a significant day's athletics on Sunday, the East German women relinquished their sprint supremacy, an American ran a 'perfect' 400-m hurdles in a record 47.64 sec, and a Cuban confirmed the enormous potential now being realised in his country.

Annegret Richter of West Germany, who set a world 100-m record in the semi-finals of 11.01, three-hundredths of a second faster than the time set by her compatriot Inge Helten last month, won the gold medal by a wide margin. Miss Richter defeated the reigning Olympic and European

champion, Renate Stecher, from East Germany, by two-tenths of a second, showing complete supremacy. Miss Helten took the bronze.

Ed Moses, a slim, bespectacled black athlete from Dayton, Ohio, achieved what hurdlers have been attempting since this event began – a fluid stride pattern with no change of leading leg throughout and 13 strides between each hurdle.

Such a feat was not accomplished by Dave Hemery when he won his gold medal in a world record time of 48.12 sec eight years ago, nor by John Akii-Bua in his world record gold at Munich of 47.82 sec.

Alan Pascoe had based his training on such a world record eventuality – though by Akii-Bua, not by Moses. The Ugandan was, of course, absent because his country joined the boycott. Pascoe ran out of steam and almost came to a full stop at the last hurdle. There was no way a man who has spent so much time injured can match seven other fit men. American Michael Shine got the silver medal and Yevgeniy Gavrilenko (URS) took bronze.

Alberto Juantorena must be a certainty to become the first man in Olympic history to record a 400-800 double in the same Games after his shattering 800-m world record of 1 min 43.5 sec.

After breaking the world record in the 800 m, Juantorena (in white, left) went on to win the 400 m.

Niki Lauda critical after crash at German Grand Prix

By Colin Dryden
PUBLISHED MONDAY 2 AUGUST

Niki Lauda, the Austrian world-champion driver, was critically ill last night after being trapped when his Ferrari crashed and caught fire during the German Grand Prix at Nürburgring.

As flames leapt round him three drivers, Guy Edwards, Brett Lunger and Arturo Merzario fought desperately to free him. Edwards, whose hands were burned in the rescue, said that it took them over a minute because his belts were jammed. 'We were trying like hell to get Niki out, but we couldn't get the seat belts undone and the fire was getting hotter and hotter.'

One of the drivers dashed for a fire extinguisher and played in on the flames and Lauda was finally freed. Edwards added 'Niki was conscious after about 10 seconds and he was screaming "Get me out." The skin was coming away from his face and his hands. He was sitting in a sea of flames.'

After treatment at a burns unit Lauda was transferred to an intensive care ward of the Mannheim University clinic. Doctors were still battling to save his life, mainly because of the effects of inhaled fumes and flames.

Lauda made a remarkable recovery from terrible burns (above), returning for the Grand Prix in Fuji in October.

Hunt is world champion as heroic Lauda retires

By Colin Dryden in Fuji, Japan
PUBLISHED MONDAY 25 OCTOBER

The vital Japanese Grand Prix, to decide the world championship between the 1975 champion Niki Lauda and his challenger James Hunt, was won yesterday by Mario Andretti, the first win by Lotus since 1974.

Patrick Depailler (Tyrrell) was second, while Hunt, after a dramatic pit stop in the closing laps, fought back to third place.

Lauda, despite his heroic return to the cockpit after near-fatal injuries and burns received in the German Grand Prix in August, was unable to cope with racing in the atrocious weather conditions. He described them as 'suicidal' and pulled into his pit after one lap.

The race was postponed for over an hour and a half because of the appalling wet and misty conditions, and most of the drivers, including Hunt, did not want to race.

But Hunt had the great advantage of starting the race from the front row alongside Andretti, which meant that until slower cars were overtaken, he was not blinded by the great plumes of spray being thrown up by the open-wheeled cars.

After the race, drinking a can of beer, Hunt said: 'Conditions were very difficult and it was extremely dangerous. My start was not brilliant, but it was good enough…. It was my lucky day. I just drove as hard as I could.'

James Hunt gets up into third place at the Japanese Grand Prix to ensure his first – and only – world championship win, by one point, from Niki Lauda.

SPORT IN BRIEF

CRICKET
Despite rallying slightly in the fourth Test (see main text) England suffer a comprehensive defeat at the hands of the West Indies. Viv Richards has a superb series, scoring 829 runs in four matches at an average of 118.42. He twice makes double centuries, scoring 232 at Trent Bridge (in his first match against England) and 291 at the Oval. The West Indies fast bowlers also enjoy an excellent tour: since his Test debut last year, Michael Holding has developed into a daunting opponent. At Old Trafford he takes five for 17 as England crash to 71 all out, and in the final Test at the Oval he takes eight for 92 and six for 57.

LAWN TENNIS
American tennis player Chris Evert, who is still only 21, becomes the first woman to make a million dollars (£600,000) from the sport when she wins the Colgate lawn tennis tournament at Palm Springs in October. Evert beats Françoise Durr 6–1, 6–2 in the final to collect the winner's cheque for £27,000 and top the million-dollar mark. She has not lost a match since April this year, and has won five major championships, including the US Open.

1976

Virginia triumphs and Wimbledon crowd goes wild

By Lance Tingay

PUBLISHED SATURDAY 2 JULY

The centenary championships and the Queen's Jubilee year could not have combined better in the women's singles at Wimbledon yesterday, when Virginia Wade **(left)** celebrated Her Majesty's presence by winning the crown for Britain.

At just about two o'clock, immediately before the Queen sat down, they played 'Land of Hope and Glory' and there was the atmosphere of a festive occasion, rather like the last night at the Proms.

An hour and three-quarters later, the cheer that went up could have been heard in Putney High Street, so loud, prolonged and frenzied was it.

Miss Wade had beaten Betty Stove, of Holland, 4–6, 6–3, 6–1, to ensure that a British player was queen of Wimbledon again.

Miss Wade was expected by many to beat Miss Stove easily. She did not do that. The fact is made evident by the score, and when she lost the opening set after 38 minutes the earlier euphoria of the crowd was dimmed.

I say she lost the opening set because that is what she did. Equally, Miss Stove lost the second set. And then the Dutch girl lost the third set. It was that sort of match.

In the decider Miss Wade led 4–0 as the quality of the play became more reasonable. The crowd warmed to the situation; every winning shot by Miss Wade, and every losing one by Miss Stove, was greeted with acclamation.

The Dutch girl won the fifth game, but by then Miss Wade was too close to the title to be deterred. She lost one match point but took the second with a forehand return that forced Miss Stove to volley to the net.

Miss Wade has now collected her finest lawn tennis crown. Her other major triumphs were the US Open in 1968, the Italian in 1971 and the Australian in 1972.

Red Rum joins in hometown celebrations after third National win

By Trevor Bates

PUBLISHED MONDAY 4 APRIL

Red Rum's home town of Southport counted its winnings and nursed even bigger hangovers yesterday after a night of parties to celebrate the horse's third Grand National win and his place among racing's immortals.

With one local hotel-keeper scooping £39,000 in winnings and hundreds of other townspeople backing Red Rum to achieve the history-making treble, it was certainly a night to remember.

The swing doors were taken off their hinges at the Bold Hotel, a mile from the horse's stables in Upper

Tommy Stack is overcome with emotion after riding the phenomenal Red Rum to his third Aintree victory.

Aughton Road, Birkdale, so that the champion could make a grand appearance in the ballroom.

Red Rum, who romped home by 25 lengths at Aintree on Saturday, seemed to love every minute of the fuss and adulation heaped on him by the sporting world and local residents. He celebrated with a munch of his favourite mint-with-a-hole titbits and by kicking and jumping his way around a local paddock.

In the end his trainer, Mr Don 'Ginger' McCain, had to call it a day and lock him away for a quiet afternoon. 'We have had a tremendous number of visitors – so many that police had to be called to control them,' said Mr McCain, who plans to enter the champion in next year's National. Bookmakers, who are believed to have lost hundreds of thousands of pounds on Red Rum, have already shortened the odds on him winning the 1978 Grand National to 16–1.

Red Rum's owner, Mr Noel Le Mare, 90 this year, who had been unwell, braved strong winds to watch his horse romp into the record books with a total of £114,000 jump prize money, not to mention the three wins and two second places that Red Rum has achieved in the National since he bought him five years ago.

Grand National Day attracted a crowd of 51,000, the biggest attendance for many years.

DID YOU KNOW?

Willie Duggan of Ireland and Geoff Wheel of Wales were the first players to be sent off during a Five Nations rugby union tournament. The pair were ordered off the pitch after exchanging blows.

Tartan riot ends with 289 arrests

By Frank Robertson

PUBLISHED MONDAY 6 JUNE

A total of 289 Scottish football fans were arrested in and around Wembley Stadium and in the West End during the weekend, after their team's 2–1 victory over England and the gigantic invasion of the pitch which followed it.

Yesterday Mr Howell, Minister for Sport, called for an inquiry into the hooliganism surrounding the match. He is to discuss measures to combat hooliganism with Wembley officials.

Some of those arrested will appear at Bow Street today on charges ranging from malicious damage to obstructing police and drunkenness. Others will come up at Marlborough Street tomorrow.

Mr Howell said there had been massive gate-crashing. He called the pulling down of goal posts and tearing up of the pitch 'idiocy'.

Scotland's Kenny Dalglish keeps his eye on the ball despite Watson's acrobatics. Dalglish scored Scotland's second goal in an unpleasant match that ended in the destruction of the pitch by drunken fans.

The whistling during the National Anthem, he said, suggested 'that we were present at a tribal occasion rather than a sporting fixture'. Hundreds of Scots escaped arrest because the 2,000 officers on duty could not stem the Tartan torrent.

Mr Ted Croker, Football Association secretary said: 'It was the worst pitch invasion I have ever seen. We dare not allow this sort of thing to happen again.'

Behind hastily repaired gates yesterday, groundsmen were busy picking up broken glass and other missiles from the pitch. Work on repairing holes torn in the carefully nurtured turf is to begin on Wednesday. Anti-riot fencing should be in place at Wembley before England's World Cup qualifier against Italy in November.

SPORT IN BRIEF

CRICKET

To celebrate 100 years of the Ashes, England take on Australia in the Centenary Test, which is played in Melbourne in March. The Australians set England 463 to win; Derek Randall scores 174; but despite this England are all out for 417, Australian fast bowler Dennis Lillee taking 11 wickets in the match. In a remarkable coincidence, the winning margin of 45 runs is the same as in the inaugural Test in 1877.

RUGBY UNION

France win the Grand Slam, beating Wales 16–9, England 4–3, Scotland 23–3 and Ireland 15–6.

LAWN TENNIS

American player Tracy Austin is accepted to play at Wimbledon. She is aged 14, and is the youngest player to appear there for 90 years. Austin has not been beaten by anyone her own age for seven years, and is known as 'Superstarlet'. The youngest player to become champion at Wimbledon – so far – is Lottie Dod, who won there in 1887, aged 15 years and 285 days.

CRICKET

Chris Old, playing for Yorkshire against Warwickshire at Edgbaston, makes a century off just 72 balls. His innings includes four sixes and twelve fours.

BOXING

On 30 July, Argentinian Carlos Monzon and Colombian Rodrigo Valdes meet in a middleweight title rematch in Monte Carlo. Monzon had won their last fight in the 15th round. Valdes scores an early hit, knocking Monzon down, but Monzon comes back to take the title in the 15th with a unanimous points decision. It is the end of an era: Monzon retires straight after the fight.

1977

1977

FA should grasp nettle and go for Clough

By Robert Oxby

PUBLISHED WEDNESDAY 13 JULY

The surprise resignation of Don Revie, the England team manager **(below)**, who was expected to remain at least until the decisive World Cup qualifying match against Italy in November, has brought waves of speculation as to his likely successor.

Bobby Robson, the successful manager of Ipswich, despite his club's narrow failure to win a major trophy, has been named by the bookmakers as the front-runner – as he was when Sir Alf Ramsey was dismissed in 1974.

Another leading candidate is Dave Sexton, released as manager of Queen's Park Rangers last weekend, and thought likely to join Arsenal as coach.

Other names that spring to mind are Jack Charlton, who resigned as manager of Middlesbrough at the end of last season, Ron Saunders, of Aston Villa, and Terry Venables, of Crystal Palace.

There have been suggestions that a young man such as Mr Venables could team up with Ron Greenwood, 56, a respected establishment figure, who is still manager of West Ham.

The best choice, in my view, would be Brian Clough, the often controversial manager of Nottingham Forest, whom he took back to the First Division last season. Mr Clough has made it known that a move to the FA is the only managerial step he would now take.

Whatever brushes he has had with authority in the past – and they have been many – Mr Clough has shown

a completely responsible attitude since his controversial 44-day reign as manager of Leeds in succession to Mr Revie in 1974.

Mr Clough's inspired leadership enabled Derby to return to the First Division in 1969 and to win the championship three years later. Subsequently, his flair for publicity got him into hot water and he resigned in 1973.

Such was the impression he left on his playing staff that there was a serious danger of a strike by Derby players. He has inspired similar loyalty at Forest and, apart from making the club solvent, has brought them unexpected success.

Watson stakes claim as successor to world 'supremo'

By Michael Williams

PUBLISHED MONDAY 11 JULY

In adding the Open championship to the US Masters he won in April, Tom Watson may finally have achieved what Lee Trevino, Tom Weiskopf and Johnny Miller all threatened to do; namely dethrone Jack Nicklaus as the world's supreme golfer.

Watson is, at 27, not only the youngest of them all but ten years the junior of Nicklaus. At this level of the game that is significant, for, as Arnold Palmer discovered, it is in the late thirties that nerve can begin to fail. Watson is far too gracious and modest a person to make any such claim.

Indeed, after his superb culminating round of 65 for a record-breaking total of 268 at Turnberry on Saturday, he made a point of describing Nicklaus's resistance as 'the mark of a great champion'.

It is nonetheless inescapable that twice this year, first at Augusta, now at Turnberry, Nicklaus's supremacy has been successfully challenged by the same man when he alone was in the best position to defend it.

Watson is congratulated by his caddie on taking his second British Open title in three years.

In the Masters, Nicklaus fired a final round of 66 at the heir to a throne he has occupied with such distinction. Watson answered with a 67 and won by two strokes.

At Turnberry, in the most captivating two-man duel in the long history of the Open championship, Nicklaus was given the chance of a rematch. Side by side throughout the last two days over 36 holes they slugged it out, punch for punch, birdie for birdie. Nicklaus had his man on the canvas three times, but finally it was he who was felled.

MILESTONES

Charlotte Brew created history when she became the first female jockey to ride in a Grand National. She enjoyed an excellent ride until the 26th fence, at which her horse, Barony Fort, refused.

236

Botham bewilders Australia with five for 74

By Michael Melford at Nottingham
PUBLISHED FRIDAY 29 JULY

The top of the Australian batting was respectable enough. So was the bottom. What went in between, when six wickets fell for 24 runs in 50 minutes on a good pitch, defied belief on the first day of the third Test at Nottingham today.

From 131 for two, the innings subsided bewilderingly to 155 for eight before it was picked up again by Kerry O'Keeffe, who, with Jeff Thomson and Len Pascoe, eventually produced a total of 243.

Five of the wickets (for 74) fell to Ian Botham **(below right)** who, in his first Test, moved the ball just enough to inspire strokes of marvellous irrelevance and at one time took four for 13 in 34 balls.

The England catching and fielding were again of a high standard, improved if anything by the return of Mike Hendrick and Geoffrey Boycott.

But I fear that the prediction in these columns yesterday that Australia could not bat as feebly as at Old Trafford was grossly inaccurate. They could – and did.

However, other things had changed. Boycott, on coming in to play out three overs with Mike Brearley, was welcomed back as an old friend who had seen the light.

Earlier, when Jeff Thomson came in, his defection from the Packer circus was marked by a standing ovation all the way to the wicket.

After lunch, at 101, Hendrick moved another ball away from Rick McCosker and this time found the edge, the ball just carrying to Brearley at first slip. Then, until the mid-afternoon break for drinks, Greg Chappell and D. W. Hookes batted with what looked ominous safety against Hendrick and Bob Willis.

Yet in two overs after the break both were out. Botham, replacing Hendrick, bowled the first ball which kept a little low and was dragged on to the stumps by Chappell giving the young bowler a notable first Test victim.

Hookes was miraculously caught by Hendrick, bowled Willis, in a lightning dive to his left in the gully.

Twenty minutes later Hendrick held a more straightforward low catch off Botham and off an unlovely stroke played far away from the body.

Robinson had begun with some desperate-looking strokes, and when he launched another at a wide ball from Tony Greig, Brearley took a good high catch at first slip. In Botham's next over Rodney Marsh was lbw and, in his next, Max Walker, playing a similar stroke to that of Walters, found the inevitable Hendrick, this time at third slip.

O'Keeffe, as usual, batted sensibly and stubbornly and Thomson shared in a ninth-wicket stand of 41 in 40 minutes before he was caught at the wicket slashing at Botham.

England won the third Test at Trent Bridge by seven wickets.

Top umpires reject Packer

By Ray Robinson in Sydney
PUBLISHED FRIDAY 29 JULY

Two top Australian umpires, Max O'Connell and Lou Rowan, have declined invitations to join the Kerry Packer cricket circus. This follows hard on the news that Jeff Thomson, Australia's fast bowler, has quit the Packer camp.

There have also been reports that Viv Richards, Somerset's West Indian batsman, is ready to pull out, although yesterday he said his contract still stood.

In Port of Spain last night Deryck Murray, vice-captain of West Indies, said he hoped that the West Indies Board of Control would not go along with the ICC decision to ban all players who signed for Packer.

The Thomson decision, made because he renewed his contract with a Brisbane radio station, must be a real threat to Packer's plans. The *Sydney Sun* said: 'It is the most serious blow, with the possible exception of Dennis

Lillee, that the Packer circus could suffer.'

Lillee said yesterday: 'There's no way I'll be trying to wriggle out of my contract. We all knew what the consequences might be and nobody signed without giving it a lot of thought.'

But Thomson said: 'I should not have done it. I was with a bunch of lads when we signed. We did not think it would interfere with our cricket careers.'

His manager, David Lord, who is in Nottingham for the Test match, said: 'It took a lot of guts for Thommo to do what he has done. He was one of Packer's biggest drawing cards. Now he has had the courage to pull out. I hope others will follow suit.'

Lord, who also acts for Viv Richards and fellow West Indian Alvin Kallicharran, also emphasised: 'I shall be offering them the same advice I have given to Jeff.'

Meanwhile in Sydney, Packer has issued a writ claiming libel damages against Australian Test selector Neil Harvey.

1977

1977

By Alan Smith
PUBLISHED MONDAY 15 AUGUST

Eddie Macken proved his complete mastery of the Hickstead course yesterday by taking the first two places in the British Jumping Derby on Boomerang and Kerrygold, and collected £4,500 for his trouble.

The Irishman, 27, won last year on Boomerang and is only the second rider to win this classic in successive years. He is the first to finish first and second here, but this was no novelty; at the Hamburg Derby last year Macken won on Boomerang and was runner-up on Boy.

Boomerang had to go first against the clock and his brilliant rider gave the opposition a desperately hard target, flying over the last with inches to spare. Only Kerrygold could match his faultless jumping and he clocked an excellent time as well – 86.2 sec to the winner's 85.8 sec.

DID YOU KNOW?

Colour television, coupled with the 'in-the-round' setting at its new home, the Crucible Theatre, Sheffield, gave snooker a massive boost. Millions watched John Spencer beat Cliff Thorburn to claim his third world professional crown.

'Artisan' Lions waste power of superb pack

By John Reason in Suva, Fiji
PUBLISHED TUESDAY 16 AUGUST

Half an hour after New Zealand had snatched a late try to win the final Test and the series against the British Lions, Fran Cotton, the Lions' loose head, sat in the dressing room at Eden Park still unable to believe that it had happened.

Twenty-four hours later, he was in the departure lounge at Auckland Airport, still as bemused. 'After the hammering we gave the All Black forwards in the last two Tests, I still can't believe that we are going to walk through that door having lost both those games and the series,' he said.

Cotton shook his head ruefully. Then he grinned philosophically. 'Ah well,' he said, 'it's just like playing for England.'

Indeed it was. The British Lions in New Zealand in 1977 eventually mastered the All Black forwards as never before, and yet, because of the inadequacy of their back play, lost both matches in which their forwards were most dominant, and with them the series.

There could have been no more cutting indictment of British back play and of the deterioration which has taken place in the last four years.

The day that the Barbarians beat the All Blacks at Cardiff in 1973 was the end of an era lasting more than 70 years. The artists have departed and we are left with the artisans.

The artisans in the 1977 Lions' backs could have been made much more effective, but the collapse of confidence in midfield and the curious omission of Peter Squires after the first Test meant that the enormous potential of Andy Irvine was never realised in the Test matches. The Lions needed stars and Irvine could have been one.

From the point of view of British rugby, the tragedy of the 1977 tour was that New Zealand have only half a team and they know it.

'We are not a good team,' said J. J. Stewart, one of the All Black selectors, 'and we are not saying we are. Our great days of the Sixties have come to an end.'

The 1977 Lions were only half a team as well, but they could have been so much better than they were. They had appalling luck with injuries and the weather, but they did not make the most of their resources.

The management were always self-conscious about the success of the 1971 Lions who had preceded them, and they went so far out of their way to be different that they neither developed the individual skills nor the teamwork necessary to win the crucial first Test.

The selection policy leading up to this game was so strange in an attempt to preserve the delusion of equality of ability that the Lions ended up with neither a first team nor a second team and lost two matches in five days.

Long before then, though, it had been obvious that the Lions were suffering from limitations at halfback and in midfield which would have to be faced if Irvine and J. J. Williams were to become Test-match winners.

Sadly, those limitations were not acknowledged, even if they were recognised. The pattern of coaching work necessary to correct the faults was not adopted, and the selection options which could have made an improvement were not taken either.

All black: British Lions and New Zealand juniors in a line-out. Captained by Phil Bennett, 18 of the players included in the 1977 Lions squad were from Wales.

Judge rules 'ban on Packer players would be unreasonable'

PUBLISHED SATURDAY 26 NOVEMBER

To ban cricketers from English county and Test matches because they had signed for Mr Kerry Packer's 'World Series' matches would be an unreasonable restraint of trade, Mr Justice Slade ruled in the High Court yesterday.

He rejected the argument that it was morally wrong for players to sign for Mr Packer and held that the ban proposed by the International Cricket Conference and the Test and Country Cricket Board was void.

The judges saw no reason why the players – 'with the possible exception of Tony Greig' – could be criticised on moral grounds for secretly signing contracts with Mr Packer.

Giving judgment, Mr Justice Slade said the case raised issues of importance to everyone who played or aspired to play cricket at first-class level and was of concern to everybody interested in the game.

'The issues have already produced an acute division of opinion throughout the cricketing world, and may perhaps continue to be debated so long as the game is played,' he said.

Kerry Packer, Australian media tycoon; his rival 'super-Test' matches revolutionised cricket.

He could see the force of criticism against Tony Greig, who signed when he was still generally regarded as the England captain. But the judge said that to deprive, by a form of retrospective legislation, a professional cricketer of the opportunity of making his living in an important field of the game was a serious and unjust step to take.

He went on: 'The public will be deprived of a great deal of pleasure if it is to be deprived of watching these talented cricketers play in those many official Test matches which do not clash with World Series Cricket matches, and for which they would otherwise be available.'

Boycott's 100th century puts England in charge

By Michael Melford at Headingley
PUBLISHED FRIDAY 12 AUGUST

Only the most macabre imagination could have pictured Geoff Boycott failing to make his 100th hundred on his return to Test cricket at Headingley, and at ten minutes to six yesterday evening the feat for which one and all were waiting was duly accomplished. The day's play thus ended amid tremendous scenes of jubilation. The churlish might say that 67 runs after tea was a poor haul on a splendid batting pitch.

For once, however, England have time on their side and do not need to take risks; moreover, only 87 overs were bowled. In this context, of course, they had the ideal batsman in charge in Boycott, with his massive concentration and unflagging technique.

He was all but caught at the wicket when 22, but otherwise played with a look of permanence which made the occasional mishap at the other end seem of minor concern.

The gates were closed before the start of play on a superb cloudless morning. England, as expected, left out Miller and Australia preferred the brisk left-arm spin of R. J. Bright to the wrist spin of Kerry O'Keeffe.

Whatever effect this Australian change may have had

on England's batsmen, it relieved their bowlers of having to probe the near impregnable defence of O'Keeffe which can be irksome late in the innings, especially if someone is batting well at the other end.

After tea, when the fourth wicket had added 96 in 105 minutes Tony Greig was out in a not unfamiliar way, bowled driving outside a ball from Jeff Thomson which came back to hit his off stump.

Graham Roope in his early stages would not be recommended watching for those of a nervous disposition, but nothing seemed likely to dislodge Boycott as he made five in 45 minutes after tea and moved on towards the inevitable moment of glory.

A hook off Len Pascoe produced another four, but Max Walker, in a fine spell of ten overs for 14 runs, made him work hard and it was a straight drive to the football stand off Greg Chappell which eventually brought about the historic event.

The ball was not halfway to the boundary when the hero's bat was raised and, amid a rare hubbub, small boys were converging on him from all over Yorkshire.

Boycott scored 191, and England won the fourth Test by an innings and 85 runs. England won the series against Australia 3–0; two matches were drawn.

SPORT IN BRIEF

MOTOR CYCLING

Britain's Barry Sheene. riding for Suzuki, wins his second successive 500-cc world championship title. During the season, riding at Spa-Francorchamps in Belgium, he sets a record for the fastest average speed achieved in a world championship race, 217.37 km/h, 135.07 mph. Sheene will win 15 grands prix for Suzuki between 1975 and 1981, and four for Yamaha.

CRICKET

Kerry Packer, Australian tycoon **(left)**, wins a court case against the English cricket authorities, who are found guilty of 'restraint of trade' when they ban English players signing for Packer's World Series Cricket. Packer has signed up most of the current Australian team, many of the key West Indies players, and others from sides such as South Africa and Pakistan. Packer's bid to show Test matches on his television station has been rejected by the Australian Board, so he has decided to offer the public a rival spectacle. 'Packer's Circus', as the team becomes known, stays on the road for two seasons before agreement on televising Tests is reached. Jeff Thomson **(below)** is one of the players who is torn between ambition and loyalty to his country: he joins Packer's 'circus', leaves, and then rejoins.

1978

Shilton ensures Forest triumph

By Roger Malone
PUBLISHED MONDAY 24 APRIL
Coventry 0; Nottingham Forest 0

The championship finally won, Brian Clough – usually unavailable after matches – invited us graciously into the Nottingham Forest dressing room and opened up warmly about the long, hard road he and his players have journeyed so successfully.

He began to believe that Forest could win the championship in their first season after promotion, he said, after they had played everybody once.

'We'd done badly in London, losing at Arsenal and Chelsea and drawing no score at West Ham, but we knew we could do better,' he said. 'We've worked very hard, and got our just result.'

On next season's European Cup, he said: 'It's something we very much wanted to get into. Now we look forward to pitting our skills over there.'

As he talked his faithful assistant, Peter Taylor, stood discreetly to one side, every now and again making a joke to lighten the atmosphere. What of their special chemistry? 'No chemistry, purely talent,' boomed Clough.

Peter Shilton's was the performance that earned Forest the final point they needed, against a virile, dominant Coventry, and everyone was still drooling over one superb save from Ferguson's 36th-minute header.

Characteristically, Mr Clough soon put a stop to any over-emphasis on one player: 'Shilton has been able to "coast" for seven months. Just lately he's been able to earn his money.'

Ferguson, hardly able to believe that he hadn't scored, said: 'His secret was he didn't sell himself one way or the other, like most keepers would have to, when I shaped to make my header, which I could have sworn had to go in.'

Forest, without Tony Woodcock and John McGovern, were not at their best on the attack, but that one point made it a marvellous day for supporters who swelled Coventry's gates to a season's best of 36,881.

DID YOU KNOW?

When Liverpool beat Nottingham Forest 2–0 at Anfield, it ended Forest's incredible record sequence of 42 matches unbeaten in the League, which began in November 1977.

Phil Read puts on the style in Formula One race

By George Turnbull
PUBLISHED TUESDAY 2 MAY

Phil Read, eight times world champion, but nudging 40, yesterday showed that despite advancing years he has lost none of his grace or skill on two wheels with a magnificent victory in the Formula One race at Oulton Park, Cheshire.

Riding the big and beautifully prepared 888-cc production Honda, he swept to victory in the ten-lap race at an average speed of 94.62 mph, more than five seconds ahead of Tony Rutter.

Read was left trailing at the start, and it was his Honda team colleague Ron Haslam who shot ahead of the pack to build up a substantial lead, only to lose it when harassed by Read.

He went wide at Esso and came off on the third lap. Haslam remounted and forged through the field from 16th place, but there were not enough laps left for him to get back into contention.

Stan Woods on a Suzuki rode a superb race to win the junior event less than 24 hours after he and Charlie Williams were victors in the 600-km race at Zandvoort, Holland, on a works Honda.

Dave Potter, circulating like clockwork on his big 750-cc road Yamaha, won the senior race with consummate ease, but the hero of the 20,000 crowd was Mick Grant, who finished second on a Kawasaki, despite breaking a bone in his right foot during Sunday's Austrian Grand Prix.

Phil Read gets the feel of his new machine; he was lured out of retirement to ride this works Honda. Read had won the Formula One world championship for Honda in 1977; in the same year he had taken his eighth Isle of Man TT race trophy. In 1979 he was awarded the MBE.

Botham tears up the record book and Pakistan

By Michael Melford at Lord's
PUBLISHED TUESDAY 20 JUNE

The fall of Pakistan's last eight wickets for 43 runs yesterday morning, seven of them to Ian Botham, and the loss of the second Test by an innings and 120 runs looks miserable on paper, but they were up against something out of the ordinary.

For no obvious meteorological reason, on a cloudless morning, the ball swung prodigiously, and Botham, in an astonishing piece of bowling, beat the bat with three or four outswingers an over.

He bowled the full length required with great accuracy, received the best possible help from Bob Taylor, Graham Roope and finally Graham Gooch, and in 13.5 overs took seven wickets for 14. There has never been an all-round performance like his in a Test match.

In the past selectors have been profoundly grateful for all-rounders. Ian Botham has played in seven Test matches. He has made three hundreds and a 50 and has taken five wickets or more in an innings five times.

And he is only 22.

Ian Botham (far right) is clapped into the pavilion after his astonishing performance. His eight for 34 were the best figures by an England bowler since Jim Laker's nine for 37 and ten for 53 at Old Trafford in 1956.

Paolo Rossi is brightest new talent in World Cup tournament

By Donald Saunders in Buenos Aires

PUBLISHED TUESDAY 27 JUNE

With Argentina returning, perhaps reluctantly, to normal, it is time to look back on the 1978 World Cup finals and ask just what they have accomplished.

For the host nation, quite apart from victory on the field, the obvious answer is a sense of pride and

Argentina celebrate as Mario Kempes scores in the 3–1 win over Holland. The competition was used as a propaganda weapon by General Jorge Videla, who had established a brutal regime after a coup in 1976.

satisfaction at staging a great international sports festival with commendable efficiency, colour and charm, an achievement few of us believed remotely possible only a few weeks ago.

This, in turn, probably will have strengthened the immediate position and popularity of the military government, though they would be wise to live through the anticlimax that inevitably follows the closure of this great tournament before coming to any firm conclusion.

But, as the last of the teams, the manager, the media and the fewer-than-hoped-for foreign fans leave for home, soccer should be able to find a clue to its future.

Alas, the finals have left the game in an even greater state of confusion than it was when they began three-and-a half weeks ago. No pattern has emerged – certainly nothing to match the 4–2–4 revolution the Brazilians began in 1958, the 'wingless wonders' with whom Sir Alf Ramsey won the 1966 competition, or the 'total football' Holland introduced before losing the 1974 final.

Pelé in 1958, Garrincha and Zagallo in 1962, Bobby Moore, Bobby Charlton and Geoff Hurst four years later, Pelé and Gerson in 1970, and Franz Beckenbauer and Johan Cruyff last time, left lasting impacts on the competition and the game.

To me the most interesting footballer on view these past weeks has been Paolo Rossi. This young Italian has moved with the grace and speed of a gazelle amid the chopping tackles and painful body-checks that have been an all-too-familiar feature of the World Cup.

Rossi's goals have been brilliantly taken, his reaction to attempted physical intimidation courageous, his self-discipline under frequent provocation strict, and his spirit unquenchable.

1978

1978

Borg's all-round mastery crushes Connors

By Lance Tingay
PUBLISHED MONDAY 10 JULY

The climax to the lawn tennis championships on Saturday, when Björn Borg **(below left)** won the men's singles for the third year running by beating Jimmy Connors 6–2, 6–2, 6–3, set new standards in a meeting which has always weaved rich design in the tapestry of the game's history.

There have been some fine men's singles at Wimbledon over the years, in which the winner has played punishingly well, but I doubt if such overwhelmingly good tennis was ever before produced to crush so fine a player.

When in the first set, Borg, having trailed 0–2, won the next six games in a row, it was, so far as Connors was concerned, like seeing a contender for the world heavyweight title taking a count of eight in the opening round.

One must give Connors credit for the fight he put up. It was obvious that had Borg relaxed in any way, the American would have come back at him and charged ahead. But Borg never fell short of his own tremendous standards. In attack he was superlatively good, delivering a service that was often unreturnable – a cannonball. He played stop-volleys and acutely angled volleys that were breathtaking in their touch and audacity. In defence, and Connors was always counter-attacking him, his backhand passing shot across the court was a dream.

Connors, put out of the match once he lost his starting lead of 2–0 in the opening set, was not allowed to get back into it. For 119 minutes Borg strode the centre court triumphantly.

The Swede is not the most elegant of players and, in grace and style, there have been finer champions. But for rugged effectiveness and all-round mastery of every shot it could be that he has no equal; how one would have liked to see him matched against Rod Laver at his best!

Borg, who despite his skill and enormous earnings remains a pleasantly modest young man, has now won 21 singles matches at Wimbledon without defeat; his three championships in as many years equal the record set by the then British Fred Perry in 1936.

Scotland keep MacLeod as manager

By Robert Oxby
PUBLISHED SATURDAY 8 JULY

Ally MacLeod, the Scotland team manager, has survived the inquest into the World Cup failure in Argentina. Ernie Walker, the Scottish FA secretary, announced last night that Mr MacLeod is to keep his job.

The SFA committee met for four-and-a-half hours in Glasgow yesterday, and they are to reconvene on Monday. Mr Walker revealed that there had been a motion to remove Mr MacLeod from his post but it had been defeated.

There had been persistent reports of misbehaviour by players, and Willie Johnston, of West Bromwich Albion, was sent home after a drug test proved positive following the 3–1 defeat by Peru in the opening match in Córdoba.

Subsequently Don Masson (Derby) and Lou Macari (Manchester United) were associated with newspaper articles concerning events in Argentina, and it can be anticipated that the SFA will consider disciplinary action next week.

Meanwhile Mr MacLeod has the opportunity to learn from his disastrous Argentine expedition, and to profit from his experiences in time for the European championships final in 1980.

Mr MacLeod, whose stewardship saw Scotland through to the World Cup finals, has clearly made mistakes. He may well have been saved by the unwillingness of any suitable candidate, such as Jock Stein, former manager of Celtic, to take over.

MILESTONES

The first woman to sail around the world single-handed was Naomi James of New Zealand, who set off from – and returned to – Dartmouth in southern England in *Express Crusader*, a 53-foot cutter. The trip took 272 days.

Joe Davis, supreme champion of snooker

PUBLISHED TUESDAY 11 JULY

Joe Davis, the man whose name has been synonymous with snooker for 50 years, died yesterday aged 77 at a Hampshire nursing home.

Born at Whitwell, a village near Chesterfield, he took up billiards after watching customers play at his father's hotel. By the time he was 12, he had compiled his first 100 break.

In the mid-1920s, when already established as an outstanding billiard's player – he was world champion four times – he was the first to foresee the possibilities of snooker. Invented in 1875, it was still being played as a lighthearted fill-in by the professionals.

Davis soon realised that it was a crowd-pleaser and, in 1927, persuaded the then governing body, the Billiards Association, to sanction the first world professional snooker championship. Acting as promoter and organiser as well as competitor, Davis took the title and cash prize of £6 10 s (£6.50). He held the championship, unbeaten, for 20 years.

During those two decades, the game increased in popularity to the extent that, after the 1939–45 war, it had overtaken billiards. The top players had made billiards too easy-looking and repetitive, and the public turned to snooker.

Davis himself constantly worked on his own game and developed the techniques now taken for granted in modern break-building and positional play. His mastery of the delicate stun shot, and ability to think many moves ahead in the manner of a chess master, were unequalled.

His first 100 snooker break came in 1928, his 500th in 1953, and his skill was often employed for charity, for which he raised nearly a million pounds.

Many of his triumphs were scored with a cue he bought for 7s 6d at a church institute in 1931. He offered £50 for its return when it was lost in 1948 – and got it back.

He retired from championship play in 1947, having won the snooker championship on all 15 occasions it had been held.

Joe Davis (on right of picture) discusses a shot with brother Fred before the Open snooker championship in 1974. Joe Davis was the only player to hold the world professional snooker and billiards titles simultaneously.

Martina claws her way to title from nadir of misery

By Lance Tingay

PUBLISHED SATURDAY 8 JULY

The lawn tennis championships acquired a new women's singles champion yesterday and one worthy of the honour – the Czechoslovak Martina Navratilova, 21, who beat American Chris Evert, a narrow and generous loser, 2–6, 6–4, 7–5.

Wimbledon, which was blessed with warmer weather, lived up to tradition with a women's final that was better in playing standards than many, and enthralling in some of its excitement.

It lasted one hour and 43 minutes, and until the final two minutes not even the most fervent supporter of one side or other would have presumed to foretell the winner, so even was the battle.

Perhaps it was ordained early this year when Miss Evert, queen of lawn tennis for so long, indicated that she was to compete less.

Martina Navratilova celebrates her first victory at Wimbledon. It was the first time the women's title had been won by a Czechoslovakian player.

Miss Navratilova, a No. 2 and never a No. 1 until this season, dominated the early American scene to a striking degree.

Those who watched the BP Cup matches at Torquay five years ago, when she was 16, could hardly fail to take notice of the super athlete from Czechoslovakia. Her penchant for the super aggressive serve-and-volley game betokened both ambition and skill beyond the normal.

Her subsequent career was not without setbacks, for as a young Czechoslovak in America the delight of Western life were tempting. She was left to her own devices without normal family guidance when she became a refugee.

This season, with no fitness problems, Miss Navratilova's skill came into its own. Yesterday, on Wimbledon's centre court, she proved her supremacy where it mattered most – and against the one player most fitted to dispute it.

There have been greater women's singles finals, but not many. The mistakes that were made did nothing to lessen the excitement of a rousing contest. At the end Miss Evert ran to her conqueror and affectionately stroked her hair. What a generous gesture by the former champion.

SPORT IN BRIEF

SNOOKER
Forty-five-year-old Ray Reardon wins his sixth and final world championship. He is the oldest ever winner of the title. Reardon is ranked No. 1 in the world, and will help Wales to snooker World Cup wins in 1979 and 1980. Reardon's win this year has been enacted under the full glare of the cameras; the BBC have covered all 17 days of the tournament.

BOXING
Ken Norton defends the WBC heavyweight title, which was handed to him earlier this year when Leon Spinks failed to defend it. Norton faces Larry Holmes, who has not been beaten in 27 fights. The judges still cannot separate them at the end of the 14th, but a bruising 15th round is awarded to Holmes, and he walks away with the world heavyweight title.

HOCKEY
The fourth World Cup is held in Buenos Aires, with 14 nations competing. Pakistan score 31 goals in their first six games, including seven against the home side, Argentina. Holland face Pakistan in the final; although at one point they take a 2–1 lead, Pakistan storm back to claim a 3–2 victory and their second World Cup.

CRICKET
David Gower makes his Test debut against Pakistan at Edgbaston. He hits the first ball he is bowled for four. Later in the summer, playing against New Zealand, he scores his first Test century at the Oval. Gower will average more than 50 in three out of his first four series.

1978

243

1978

Wells' time equals record

By *James Coote*

PUBLISHED MONDAY 10 JULY

Alan Wells, 26, a marine engineer from Edinburgh, yesterday equalled the oldest British athletics record in the book, Peter Radford's 100-m time of 10.29 sec, set 20 years ago.

Wells, competing in the Philips Gateshead Games, thus put himself in line for a Commonwealth Games medal. But had he not raised his hands in triumph, thus checking his momentum, a couple of feet from the line, the record would undoubtedly have been his alone.

Yet Wells's forte is 200 m, and he had not trained for five days because of a hamstring injury. The injury forced him to withdraw from the 200 m, won by James Gilkes (Guyana) in 20.74 sec, and indeed he was doubtful for the 100 m until the last moment.

However, his win has made him even more confident of beating the British 200-m record held jointly by Dick Steane and David Jenkins on 20.66 sec, probably in the UK Closed Championships at Meadowbank next weekend, assuming he has recovered from his injury.

The best aspect of Wells's race was that he finished first ahead of three world-class sprinters, Gilkes (the PanAm title holder), James Sanford, the AAA champion, and Don Quarrie, the Jamaican Olympic 200-m gold medallist.

Two United Kingdom All-Comers' records were broken. In the women's mile, the World Cup champion, Greta Waitz (Norway) ran an excellent 4 min 26.9 sec.

In the men's 400-m hurdles the American Olympic champion Ed Moses romped home in 48.55 sec. Alan Pascoe, who held the previous record of 48.85, was second in 50.45.

An exciting mile was won, not unexpectedly, by Dave Moorcroft, in 3 min 56.6 sec. This was a personal best, though he has run faster over 1,500 m. Local hero Brendan Foster was second in 3 min 56.97 sec.

MILESTONES

The first black football player to represent England in a full international was Viv Anderson of Nottingham Forest. The fullback won his first cap in England's 1–0 win against Czechoslovakia at Wembley on 29 November.

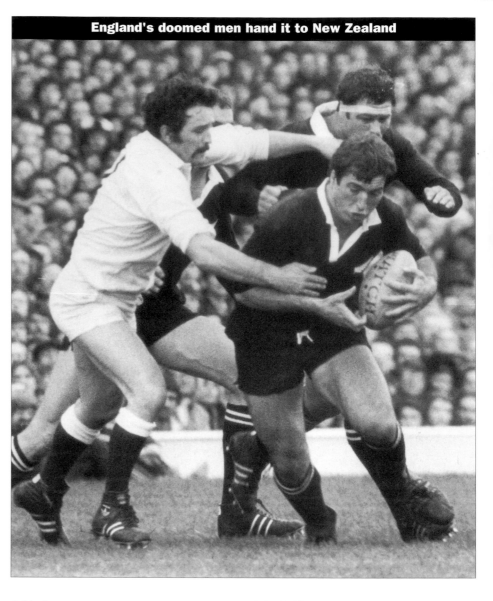

England's doomed men hand it to New Zealand

By *John Reason*

PUBLISHED MONDAY 27 NOVEMBER
England 6 pts; New Zealand 16

The entirely predictable poverty of the England pack enabled New Zealand to win at Twickenham despite making so many mistakes in attack that they threw away at least 15 points in the first half alone.

Condemned by the selectors to play without a scrummage and without a line-out – surely a resignation issue – England found their opponents apparently doing their best to play down to the English level.

It was as if the All Blacks could not bring themselves to walk off with the family jewels, even though the front door had been left open and a series of polite and clear instructions left directing them to the open safe.

New Zealand had the opportunity to score at least three tries of their own creation, but missed them all because of poor angles of run which forced them to kick, and in the end only won with two tries from England throws at defensive line-outs.

England's Mike Slemen goes for the ball as Lawrie Knight gets into his stride for the All Blacks. Flanker Graham Mourie captained the New Zealand side to their first Grand Slam against the four home nations.

As one of those was scored from an All Black knock-on, and the other from an all-too-familiar England tangle in their line, which could have been avoided, it was not exactly the stuff of which heroes are made.

New Zealand's goal-kicking was not convincing either. However, in the middle of some embarrassing miskicks, Brian McKechnie did have three successes, including one from a distinctly improbable rebound, and so the All Blacks won by a goal, a try and two penalty goals to a dropped goal and a penalty goal.

The All Blacks have now beaten Ireland, Wales and England, but if they do beat Scotland in a fortnight's time, I cannot help feeling that it will be not so much a Grand Slam as a rather apologetic and tentative closure, like someone quietly shutting the door on four patients on their death-beds.

Spurs will resist all pressure on Argentinian signings

By Robert Oxby

PUBLISHED TUESDAY 18 JULY

Tottenham yesterday unveiled their historic £750,000 signings from Argentina – Osvaldo Ardiles **(below)** and Ricardo Villa **(right)** – and the two young men made a profound impression upon the crowded press conference at White Hart Lane.

Articulate and soft-spoken, the two World Cup players said they were delighted to be joining Spurs and foresaw no problems in settling into the English League game.

Asked why they chose England, Ardiles said: 'It is always difficult to leave one's country, but we could not miss the chance of coming to the cradle of world football. Now we have met our future colleagues, we are conscious of the great welcome we have received from everyone connected with the club and know we shall be happy.'

The two players had only five hours' sleep after being delayed on their 28-hour flight from Buenos Aires, but they arrived at White Hart Lane before ten am. After passing their medical examinations, they completed formalities relating to their contracts.

Sidney Wale, the Spurs chairman, said that the club would withstand any pressure to debar the two Argentines from playing for the club. 'We owe that to our supporters,' he declared.

'I cannot see how anything can go wrong,' he told me. 'The Football League approved conformity with the requirements of the Treaty of Rome at their annual general meeting last month, and our enterprise has been greeted enthusiastically by many people in the game.'

Ardiles revealed that French and Spanish clubs had made unofficial approaches to them even before the World Cup was won. 'We did not consider them because we did not want our minds diverted,' he said. 'Now that we have signed for Spurs, we are satisfied with the deal and we are not interested in any other possibilities.'

Ali is the master again

By Donald Saunders in New Orleans

PUBLISHED MONDAY 18 SEPTEMBER

One morning, probably later rather than sooner, Muhammad Ali will wake up and decide he no longer can carry the crippling burden of being the most important black man on earth.

For nearly 20 years, Ali has been a symbol of hope, pride and defiance to an entire race. Now having re-established himself as the greatest heavyweight in the world, he knows he is obliged to remain, at least a little longer, up there on the pedestal to which his millions of worshippers have lifted him.

As he stood in the ring at the New Orleans Superdome following his historic triumph over Leon Spinks, the stunning enormity of his responsibility must have struck him harder than any blow delivered by his opponent during the previous hour.

Gigantic though his ego is, he surely felt a twinge of fear as 70,000 half-crazed spectators screamed 'Ali, Ali, Ali' from the floor, the stand, the boxes – and seemingly even from the huge dome that dominates the largest and highest arena in the world.

And Ali needed only to glance across at the television cameras to realise that millions more were – or soon would be – sharing that hysterical joy in the black ghettoes of his country's larger cities, in the shanty towns of Africa and Latin America, in the slums of Asia and the Middle East.

When, eventually, he had been escorted through the biggest 'live' crowd to watch a fight since Louis knocked out Schmeling at Yankee Stadium more than 40 years ago, to the relative peace of his dressing room, perhaps the new champion pondered over the unfairness of the situation in which he now finds himself.

Ali knows he can remain a truly great world figure only as the heavyweight champion. And that his body simply will not allow him to hang on to that title much longer. Now he is approaching 37, even a man of his depth of character and determination cannot regularly whip himself into the superb condition that enabled him to dance his way to a decisive points victory over Spinks.

In his moment of triumph, Ali could not resist asking critics who had written him off as a champion: 'Did I look like I need to retire? Did I look like I was all washed up? Did I look nearly 37 years old?'

The answer to all three questions must be 'no'. But Ali knows, as well as I do, that he cannot go through the agonies of preparation needed to reach that peak of condition many more times.

1978

245

1979

Clough and Taylor to chase more glory for Forest

By Donald Saunders
PUBLISHED FRIDAY 1 JUNE

Brian Clough and Peter Taylor, who guided Nottingham Forest to their first European Cup triumph in Munich on Wednesday, are staying at the City Ground to mastermind the defence of the title next season.

Despite persistent rumours that Mr Clough and Mr Taylor might seek fresh fields to conquer, notably at Sunderland, it is clear they intend to continue at Nottingham to try to build

Trevor Francis (here in Birmingham City colours) was the first £1-million footballer, signing for Forest in February and inspiring them to a European Cup victory. Francis scored the only goal in their 1–0 win against Malmö in Munich.

Forest into one of the super-clubs.

As the new European champions flew home from Munich yesterday with the mammoth silver cup, Stuart Dryden, Forest's chairman, disclosed that the most successful managerial partners in English soccer history had accepted new four-year contracts.

'They signed them three or four months ago,' said Mr Dryden, who was largely responsible for Forest's seeking Mr Clough as their manager 4½ years ago.

This indicates the intention of Mr Clough and Mr Taylor to consolidate Forest's remarkable success since they reformed their partnership at the City Ground in the summer of 1976.

It also should discourage potential poachers, who would be obliged to pay compensation of more than £750,000 to lure the pair away from Forest.

Obviously, Mr Clough and Mr Taylor believe there is much satisfaction to be gained from playing leading roles in the development of Forest into a club that can take its place alongside such traditional giants as Liverpool, Manchester United, Arsenal and Tottenham.

The amazing progress achieved since Forest climbed, somewhat luckily, back into the First Division two years ago has created a healthy enough financial situation for them to go ahead with expensive ground improvement schemes, within a few months of becoming the first British club to spend £1 million on a player.

Undeterred by the fate that befell Chelsea and Sheffield United when they spent heavily on modernising their grounds, Forest expect to have their new £2.6 million stand open by December.

Forest's Munich triumph will help strengthen the financial position, since it qualifies them for another European campaign. The revenue from last and next European campaigns will allow Forest to pursue their policty of strengthening the team.

Asked if Forest could buy another £1-million player so soon after the purchase of Trevor Francis, Mr Dryden replied: 'If pressed to give an answer, I would have to say yes. But we are expecting to sign another prominent player within the next week or two — and he will not cost £1 million. There also will be a few departures.'

Hailwood wrecks the opposition

By George Turnbull
PUBLISHED TUESDAY 5 JUNE

Mike Hailwood yesterday more than justified his 'living legend' title when in two hours of pure racing magic he hurtled to his 14th TT victory on the Isle of Man at a record average speed of 111.75 mph.

Hailwood, now nudging 40 years of age, finished more than two minutes ahead of Tony Rutter in 2 hr 3 min 39.4 sec, and if he had been pushed there is little doubt that the whole of the TT record book would have needed rewriting.

As it was, the rider who is still regarded as the greatest the world has ever seen, set a new lap record for a senior event at 114.02 mph on his third circuit of the frightening 37¾ mile mountain course – while slowing down to take on more fuel in the pit.

Writers have run out of superlatives for the achievements of Hailwood, who has ten world championships to his credit, and it is almost impossible to capture in words the emotion that grips the 50,000 fans and hard-bitten observers as 'the Bike' wrecked the opposition with a ride of sheer brilliance.

It was as if the clock had been put back more than a decade to the halcyon days of the 1960s as Hailwood, the most immaculate rider of all time, peeled off the laps with a display of precision riding that is never likely to be seen again.

This is to be Hailwood's last year in competitive riding and his final TT appearance. He only returned to the island last year after an absence of 11 years, and six years out of the sport altogether.

No one could have possibly anticipated a more fitting final curtain.

Mike Hailwood (left) powers his way towards another TT victory on the Isle of Man, riding the ex-Barry Sheene works Suzuki.

Troy wins 200th Derby

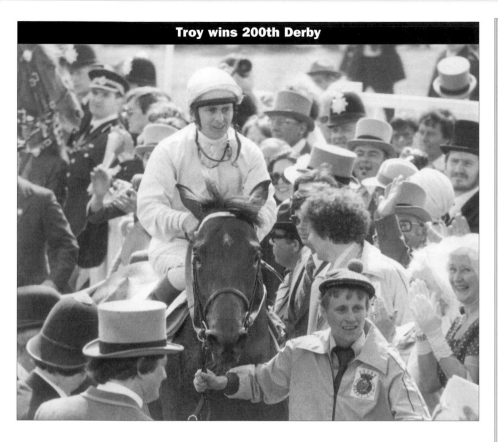

By a Daily Telegraph *reporter*

PUBLISHED WEDNESDAY 6 JUNE

Troy, at 6–1 one of the best-backed horses, coasted home seven lengths clear in the 200th running of the Derby yesterday. It was the biggest winning margin for 54 years.

Dickens Hill, the Irish challenger, was second, and France's 66–1 outsider Northern Baby finished third.

Worth £153,000 to the winner, it was the world's richest race and was watched by the Queen whose Milford could only finish tenth.

Riding for Dick Hern, champion jockey Carson gained his first victory in a Derby on Troy.

After a run fraught with problems, Troy at last found daylight two furlongs from home and in a few long strides he burst clear of his rivals.

The result emphatically vindicated the judgement of Willie Carson, who had the choice of Troy and the Queen's Milford. Carson said: 'I planned to lay up among the leaders early on, but Troy had no pace so then I had to weave my way through. Once we found room, though, he flew. He's the best colt I've ever ridden.'

Hoban protests as Barras triumphs in cycling championships

By J. B. Wadley

PUBLISHED MONDAY 25 JUNE

Sid Barras (Carlton-Weinmann) yesterday won the National Professional Road Cycling championship he has been after for ten years, but the moment of victory was hardly as sweet as he had dreamed.

After a hurried judges' consultation, Barras was declared the winner amid a storm of cheering and jeering from the crowd. But as Barras mounted the podium, a white-faced and furious Barry Hoban forced his way out of the chaos and refused to accept his second position.

Six riders were involved in the finishing sprint at the end of 156 miles racing at Telford, Shropshire. Rounding the final corner for the 400 yards slightly uphill, into-the-

wind showdown, the contestants loitered at touring pace. Then the six exploded into action. Barras powered towards the line, with Hoban on his right.

Barras made a switch towards Hoban, forcing him into the crowd; and as Barras crossed the line, Hoban was already sitting up and waving his fists towards the judges' stand. He made a rapid U-turn and lodged his verbal protest, encouraged by about half the large crowd.

When, half an hour later, Hoban had showered, changed and cooled down, he said: 'It was a regrettable finish to a fabulous race. I don't claim that I would have beaten Barras, but there would have been only inches in it either way.'

Barras said, 'The switch was involuntary. In an uphill finish it is difficult to keep a straight line.'

SPORT IN BRIEF

GOLF
After four years on the US tour, Frank 'Fuzzy' Zoeller wins his first tournament, the San Diego Open. This makes him eligible for the US Masters, which he wins at his first attempt, only the first man since Gene Sarazen in 1935 to achieve this feat. In the first sudden-death play-off staged at Augusta, Zoeller faces Ed Sneed and Tom Watson. Zoeller wins at the second extra hole.

CRICKET
England's Ashes tour of Australia continues, with England winning the final three matches. Australia's Rodney Hogg tops the bowling figures; he has taken 41 wickets, a record for an Ashes series in Australia, with best figures of six for 74 in the first Test. While dwindling crowds watch England win the official series 5–1, more than 50,000 watch 'Packer's Circus' play a day/night game in Sydney. The Australian Cricket Board finally do a deal with Kerry Packer, granting his Channel Nine exclusive rights to televise Tests for ten years – on the proviso that World Series Cricket is disbanded.

FOOTBALL
Last year's FA Cup losing finalists, Arsenal, contest this season's final with Manchester United. They are 2–0 up with five minutes to go when Gordon McQueen and Sammy McIlroy put United back in the game. But a last-gasp effort from Arsenal's Alan Sunderland ensures a win for them this year.

RUGBY UNION
In Ireland's tour of Australia, the Irish fly half Ollie Campbell kicks over 50 points in four Tests to ensure a victory for the tourists. His tally includes 19 points in one Test against Australia, beating the existing Irish record for points in an international by five.

1979

1979

By Lance Tingay

PUBLISHED MONDAY 9 JULY

Wimbledon 1979 will need a bigger entry than usual in the annals of lawn tennis for records were written anew, the chief one being the achievement of Björn Borg in winning the singles for the fourth successive year and establishing himself as outstanding even among the titans.

What a mighty player is Borg. He is 23 and he has won four Wimbledons in a row, involving 26 consecutive singles victories, the French championship four times, including this year and last, and the Italian championship twice.

Is there anything more for him to do? There is. Yes, he still has to take the US Open championship – and how Jimmy Connors will battle to prevent him doing that – and he has yet to win the Australian title.

He has not yet approached the achievement of the Grand Slam, which is simultaneously holding the championships of Australia, France, Wimbledon and America. No one could doubt his ability to do so and the question is just if and when he will.

Borg won the final against Roscoe Tanner by 6–7, 6–1, 3–6, 6–3, 6–4. It was a very good match and reflected great credit on Tanner. One may take Björn Borg's conduct of it for granted, and it was a champion's performance.

Tanner lived for nearly three hours against the Swede, led by one set to nil, led by two sets to one, and I dare say had he been able to implement his threat to make it four games all in the final set he could have taken the All-England Championship.

The excitement of the final reached crescendo when Borg serving to make himself 5–3 in the last set, trailed 15–40. Tanner perpetrated a forehand error, because he tried too hard, and then was forced to take a volley lower than he liked and his backhand found the net.

Borg took the next two points like the giant he is. When, two games later at 5–4 he served for the match, Tanner resisted Borg's initial lead of 40–0, and it was not until five points later that the Swede was allowed to clinch victory.

It was a splendid climax to the championships. The sporting spirit displayed by both warmed the heart, for each delighted to confront skills which they sought to overcome.

By Michael Melford

PUBLISHED MONDAY 25 JUNE

There were numerous ways in which England might have been beaten by the West Indies in Saturday's Prudential World Cup final at Lord's, but the manner in which they did lose was frustrating – and was, to some extent, avoidable.

In hindsight it was not the England batting which needed strengthening, but the bowling, perhaps – in the absence of the injured Bob Willis – by bringing in Miller.

The three bowlers used to fill up the fifth allotment of 12 overs, bowled too short and too near West Indian legs. Their 12 overs yielded 86 runs and helped to launch the match-winning partnership of 139 between Vivian Richards and Collis King.

A look at the West Indian score shows how near England were to reaching the end of the really dangerous batting when King came in at 99 for four and played from the first with confidence.

For a time, as King made 86 out of 139 in 21 overs, even the superb Richards was outshone, though he stayed to finish the innings that showed his extraordinary eye and reflexes. Mike Hendrick's full-pitched delivery on the

---

middle stump would have limited most mortals to one run; Richards stepped outside the off stump and hit it behind square leg for six.

But if one or both of these batsmen, who made 224 of the 286 total, had been contained or winkled out by a good fifth bowler early on, West Indies would barely have made enough runs.

By the time England batted, the easy-paced pitch put 230 well within their range. But in aiming to build a solid base for attack, Geoffrey Boycott and Mike Brearley dug in too deep. If Boycott had been caught at mid-on at 107 in the 34th over, there might still have been time for batsmen with greater weight of stroke to come in and establish themselves. Clive Lloyd dropped the catch.

As it was, Brearley was not out until the 38th over and Boycott the 40th. The score was only 135 after 40 overs but the younger batsmen were expected to come in and make 152 in 20 overs.

Graham Gooch's 32 in eight overs did him the greatest credit. Derek Randall's running between the wickets showed what the fleeter-footed batsmen might have done.

There were fielding moments to savour: Brearley ran 25 yards away from the wicket at full tilt and judged a horrible skier perfectly. Richards, rounding off his day, raced along the long-on boundary to take an improbable catch from a well-middled lowish drive by Ian Botham.

After this catch, the crucial and colourful 138 not out of a great batsman, and his largely unmolested bowling, the £300 award to the Man of the Match was easily made.

West Indies bowler Joel 'Big Bird' Garner in full flight against England. He took five for 38 in the final.

Buccaneer Seve wins hearts at golf Open

By Michael Williams

PUBLISHED MONDAY 23 JULY

Severiano Ballesterors (**right**), the first continental golfer to win the Open championship since Arnaud Massy, for France in 1907, has given the game not only a fillip in Europe but an almost new dimension as well.

The fairways have little to do with his buccaneering, captivating style of play. At Royal Lytham and St Annes on Saturday he found only one fairway with his driver, yet he still had a 70 for a 72-hole aggregate of 283 to win by three strokes from Ben Crenshaw and Jack Nicklaus.

So, once more, Lytham preserved its record of never having yielded an Open to an American professional. Bobby Jones, in 1926, remains the only conqueror from the United States, and he was an amateur.

Spanish Ballesteros may be, but the acclaim he received as he strode into the arena of the 18th green was every bit as heartful, warm and emotional as it had been for Tony Jacklin ten years before.

At 22, he is the youngest winner of the Open this century. He 'arrived' three years ago when he finished second in this same championship to Johnny Miller. He has been there ever since.

He has won the Harry Vardon Trophy as leader of the European order of merit for the past three years, and is now in line to do it for a fourth time, which would equal the record of Peter Oosterhuis from 1971–75.

A truly international golfer, Ballesteros last year won seven tournaments as far afield as Kenya, Japan, America, Switzerland and Woodcote Park. The Open, his first major championship, is his 17th victory in four years.

Provided his back holds up, it is unlikely to be his last, either; though as Hale Irwin, the American champion who had charmingly waved a white hankerchief of surrender to the multitude around the 18th green, remarked to me: 'I cannot understand how anyone can drive as badly as that and still win an Open championship.'

It was, I think, said more in disbelief than criticism. No wonder. Starting from the 13th, Ballesteros did not hit a single fairway from the tee. Yet it was typical of him that he still played those last holes in one under par.

That is his game, always has been and probably always will be – an adventurous flirtation with disaster interspersed with breathtaking recoveries.

Great win for Ireland in ladies' golf championship

By Elizabeth Price in Dublin

PUBLISHED MONDAY 9 JULY

Despite a wet afternoon, the Irish crowds flocked to Hermitage Golf Club, near Dublin, to see their side win the European Ladies' Team championship, beating Germany in the final 6–1.

Not since 1907 in the days of the Hezlet sisters have Ireland been successful in a series of international matches. Their best finish in recent years in this tournament was third place in Paris in 1975. Yesterday the Irish were superb. After sharing the foursomes they took all five singles in convincing fashion.

Mary McKenna, the Irish champion, beat Germany's number one Marion Thannhaeuser by six and five. She won five holes in a row from the ninth in pars.

Maureen Madill began to show more of the skill which won her the British championship. She has been playing diffidently, a reaction to her title win, but in this match she was more positive. She had three twos in her round but Barbara Boehm stayed with her. The Irish girl was four up after ten holes.

She lost the 11th and 12th but then scored her third two. Three putts lost her the 14th but a good one for a birdie made amends and she won on the next green.

Only one more match was needed. Susan Gorman was three up after nine on Sadine Blecher, the German amateur champion, and ran out by three and one.

The Germans are not used to playing before such big crowds, and can be proud of their team who were far from overawed.

England, the holders, were beaten into fourth place by France, who took both foursomes. So England ended without a win in the form of golf they are supposed to enjoy most.

The Scots finished sixth and the Welsh tenth.

1979

249

1979

By Alan Smith in Luhmuhlen
PUBLISHED MONDAY 3 SEPTEMBER

Nils Haagenson, 24, a student at Copenhagen University, riding Monaco, took the individual honours, and the Irish became team champions after a fraught weekend at the European three-day event in Luhmuhlen, Germany. It was the first time that either a Dane or the Irish had claimed the titles.

Lucinda Prior-Palmer and the British team lost their chance of retaining their titles when Badminton winner Killaire had to be withdrawn before yesterday's show-jumping phase.

Rachel Bayliss and Gurgle the Greek took the individual silver behind Haagenson, a thoroughly deserving winner who led the dressage and was fastest across country, while the British team took second place to Ireland.

Lucinda and Killaire had been lying third after Saturday's cross country, less than one show-jumping fence behind the leader, but after giving so much, the courageous Killaire was lame, possibly in a shoulder.

Peter Scott-Dunn, the team vet, could not make a positive diagnosis at that stage, and although it might have been possible to patch Killaire up so he could jump, neither Lucinda nor Malcolm Wallace, the team manager, to their great credit, even considered such action.

Luncinda's reaction was typically sporting. 'It was my turn for some bad luck but I'm sick about the team.'

While Killaire's score counted, Britain had an almost unassailable lead, but without it they went into yesterday's show-jumping 37 penalties behind Ireland, a deficit they could not quite overcome.

'Tiger' Smith, stumper extraordinary

By E. W. Swanton
PUBLISHED SATURDAY 1 SEPTEMBER

E. J. 'Tiger' Smith, of Warwickshire, the oldest Test cricketer and, in particular, the patriarch of the county ground at Edgbaston, died at Birmingham yesterday, aged 93.

After six years' apprenticeship, Smith's career as Warwickshire's wicketkeeper lasted from 1910 to 1930, and it was in 1926 that he became the first man in history to make seven dismissals in an innings – which happened against Derbyshire at Edgbaston.

The late A. T. W. Grout, 30 years later, achieved eight in a state match at Brisbane but only seven other Englishmen have taken seven in an innings, including Bob Taylor twice.

'Tiger' Smith rose to fame with the Warwickshire XI of 1911 who, having been admitted to first-class status only in 1904 and been bottom but two of the championship in 1910, astonished the cricket world under F. R. Foster's inspiring leadership by winning the title the next summer.

Both Foster and Smith (the latter replacing another Warwickshire keeper A. A. Lilley), were chosen for the MCC side under Plum Warner which recovered the Ashes in Australia in 1911–12, and he played in the 1912 Triangular Tournament and also for MCC in South Africa in 1913–14.

His dismissals numbered 782 and he was no mean bat, with 15,901 runs to his credit. On his retirement, Tiger became a first class umpire and stood in Test matches. When that was done he returned as county coach to Edgbaston, where he did faithful service for many years.

Veteran Mauger clinches title

PUBLISHED MONDAY 3 SEPTEMBER

Veteran rider Ivan Mauger, of New Zealand, won the world speedway championship in Chorzow, Poland, yesterday, for a record-breaking sixth time. Zenon Plech, of Poland, was second, only one point behind the New Zealander, and Briton Michael Lee was third.

Mauger had made sure of his title by the 17th race and Plech clinched his silver medal a race later, but Lee had to ride an additional race to take the bronze.

After 20 races, four riders – Kelly Moran (US), Billy Sanders (Australia), Ole Olsen (Denmark) and Lee – had each scored 11 points. So there was a run-off for the third place. Lee won the additional event, ahead of Sanders, Moran, and Olsen, who did not finish.

Sixteen riders from England, New Zealand, West Germany, Poland, Australia, Czechoslovakia, Denmark, the United States, and the Soviet Union competed in the championships.

Record-breaker Ivan Mauger, here practising for Britain's speedway golden jubilee, won his sixth world championship 11 years after winning his first.

Chaos as McEnroe defeats Nastase

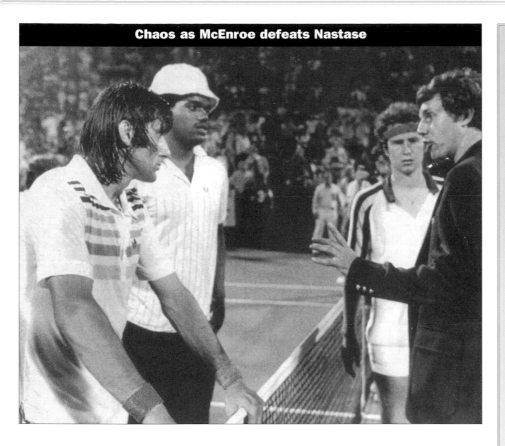

Ilie Nastase receives a stern word from an official during the bad-tempered second-round match at the US Open. McEnroe went on to win the championship.

By Lance Tingay, New York

PUBLISHED SATURDAY 1 SEPTEMBER

American lawn tennis in general, and the United States Open championships in particular, had to endure moments at Flushing Meadow, New York, that they would rather forget.

If the behaviour of Ilie Nastase, combining with the opposition of John McEnroe, was no more than normally provocative, that of a midnight crowd sank to a new low.

One was critical the other year in Rome when an Italian emerged as the finalist in his own championship after the spectators, more used to soccer than to lawn tennis, had more or less forced the retirement of a Spaniard.

But under the floodlights at the National Tennis Centre, one realised that the surging popularity of the game in America as a mass spectator sport also has its drawbacks.

No one could have been proud of what took place, and if the basic problem was the way the crowd took the side of Nastase and resented the discipline imposed on him, I cannot say that officialdom emerged with high credit.

The official referee, Mike Blanchard, said yesterday when tempers had cooled; 'Commercialism triumphed, as it tends to do today.'

What happened before McEnroe, the No. 3 seed, emerged as second-round winner over Nastase by 6–4, 4–6, 6–3, 6–2 – an outcome one more or less took for granted now that Nastase is beyond his best

may be briefly put.

There were two fine sets to start, for Nastase's touch was good and young McEnroe played beautifully too.

Then Nastase, hardly for the first time in his career, began to have interchanges with the crowd. This came to a climax in the fourth set, around midnight, which had the umpire, Frank Hammond imposing first a penalty point and then a penalty game against Nastase for delaying play.

Hammond's apparent militancy towards Nastase angered the crowd and brought the climactic uproar. As Nastase delayed more Hammond announced 'game, set and match to McEnroe', the ultimate sanction under the rules.

There was pandemonium, with beer cans and coins thrown on to the court. But Hammond's ruling was not allowed to stand and under instructions from the tournament director Bill Talbert, referee Blanchard took the place of Hammond in the umpire's chair.

The match had been declared ended, but neither the crowd nor, for that matter the players, admitted to the fact. The score was actually 3–1 to McEnroe in the fourth set and was eventually resumed at that stage with, as it happened, a reasonably peaceful finish.

This may have been Nastase's last appearance in the United States Open. If so, it will rank as quite a swan-song.

SPORT IN BRIEF

CRICKET
In the first Test against India at Edgbaston, David Gower scores 200 not out, his maiden first-class double century. England win the match by an innings and 83 runs.

MOTOR RACING
The Formula One world championship is won by American Jody Scheckter, driving for Ferrari. It is the ninth time that Ferrari have produced the champion's car. To complete the Italian constructor's triumph, Gilles Villeneuve claims second place for the team. Australian Alan Jones, driving for Williams-Ford, has had a highly successful last few months, winning four of the final six races of the season.

BOXING
In November Sugar Ray Leonard wins the WBC welterweight world championship, his first world title, from his fellow American, and 7–2 favourite, Wilfred Benitez. In the 15th round, Leonard knocks down Benitez with a left uppercut, and the referee stops the fight with only six seconds remaining on the clock.

YACHTING
Disaster strikes in the Fastnet Race when winds reach Force Ten as the yachts approach the Fastnet rock off the southwest coast of Ireland. Lifeboats and helicopters are used to help crews to safety, but 15 people die in the storm.

BOXING
'Marvellous' Marvin Hagler challenges Vito Antuofermo for the middleweight world championship. Although Hagler has been a professional since 1973, it is his first world title fight. The close contest ends in a draw, allowing Antuofermo to keep the title.

1979

1980

Unique feat by Heiden

PUBLISHED MONDAY 25 FEBRUARY

The accomplishments of Eric Heiden, the speed skater, during the past two weeks read like something from schoolboy fiction. To win four events in seven days and then, two days later, eclipse all by breaking the world record for the 10,000 m is comparable to a track sprinter winning the marathon.

Heiden is truly king of the Lake Placid Games, the only person to gain five gold medals in one winter Olympics. His world record for the 10,000 m was 6.2 seconds inside the previous best, set at Medeo in 1977 by Viktor Leskin, of the USSR.

Heiden, world champion for the past three years, yet only 21, announced afterwards that this would be his final season. He is studying to be a doctor of medicine. 'After next month's world championships, I shall continue to skate, but never again in competition.'

Brutality scars rugby's image as England head for 'Slam'

By John Mason
PUBLISHED MONDAY 18 FEBRUARY
England 9 pts; Wales 8

Budge Rogers, chairman of England's selectors, hinted broadly yesterday that, though no formal decision has been made, he was thinking of an unchanged team to meet Scotland at Murrayfield on 15 March.

At stake next month will be the Calcutta Cup, the Triple Crown, the Five Nations championship and the Grand Slam. Whatever happens, England – having won three matches – are bound to share the championship.

Rogers and skipper Bill Beaumont believe the Grand Slam, which England last achieved 23 years ago, is in reach; but they are mindful that Scotland vividly found their feet against France on Saturday.

England's victory over Wales by three goals to two tries was as miserable an advertisement for rugby football as the triumph of Scotland was encouraging. Success on a major sporting occasion need not equate with a degrading war of attrition.

It was gratifying yesterday morning that the decision of David Burnett, the referee, to send off Paul Ringer was vigorously upheld.

Now for 'treble' says Olympic hero Robin Cousins

By Howard Bass at Lake Placid
PUBLISHED SATURDAY 23 FEBRUARY

Robin Cousins, despite an error in the triple jump, won Britain's first gold medal of the winter Olympics, claiming the figure-skating title with a free-skating programme which just beat his arch-rival Jan Hoffmann of East Germany late on Thursday evening.

'It was one of the closest results ever,' Cousins said afterwards. 'After I made that mistake I knew I had to do something special.' His next target is the world championships next month.

Cousins' victory at Lake Placid will be a great fillip to figure skating in Britain and is bound to stimulate a much increased call on ice rinks already bursting at the seams. It is hoped public authorities and private enterprise alike will be inspired to invest in the extra arenas needed if worthy successors to Cousins and John Curry are to be produced.

Jan Hoffmann lost by a slender margin but there was no doubt that the right man had won, a fact which Hoffmann and third-placed Charlie Tickner sportingly acknowledged.

Hoffmann had begun his free skating with a distinct points advantage from the figures. Cousins whittled that away and could still afford a mistake and win – that is the measure of his world superiority in free skating today.

Cousins mesmerised the crowd with a spellbinding succession of difficult manoeuvres, all interlinked and presented so smoothly and artistically that it looked easy. He leads a revised thinking in free skating; that mighty leaps are not the be-all-and-end-all.

Robin Cousins (left) beat Jan Hoffmann by a narrow margin to win Olympic gold, but Hoffmann avenged his defeat in the world championships the following month.

He deliberately did not overload his programme with triples, but emphasised versatility and all-round competence in every department, not least the spins, the true art of which he has resurrected and advanced.

Cousins succeeded with three great triples, two cherries and a salchow, but two-footed a triple loop – almost certainly the reason he gained no 'six', for the rest was sheer perfection. Even so, eight of the nine judges saw fit to award 5.9 for presentation and three of them gave a similar high mark for technical merit.

Cousins has confirmed his intention to compete in the world championships in Dortmund next month and expressed the hope that he might emulate the 1976 triple crown triumph of John Curry.

Apart from Curry in 1976, the only other British Olympic gold medallists for figure skating have been Madge Syers in 1908 and Jeannette Altwegg in 1952.

DID YOU KNOW?

In November the world's fast bowlers faced a speed camera to establish who was the fastest. Michael Holding of the West Indies bowled at 87.76 mph, but Jeff Thomson of Australia recorded an amazing 99.688 mph.

Mr Burnett twice spoke to the captains about incidents of foul play. Still the nastiness simmered and the rugby suffered. So, too, did Wales in a match of 34 penalties. As Wales received only a third of those awards and as the match hinged upon penalty goals, the last of which Dusty Hare kicked in the 41st minute of the second half, the only inference can be that the wounds to Welsh pride were self-inflicted.

That they were the better team was patently obvious. With 14 men for all but 13 minutes of 87 minutes 10 seconds' playing time, they out-thought and out-fought England and, to boot, scored two tries by turning opposition errors to rich profit. Only in the matter of goal-kicking did Wales come seriously unstuck.

On another day, five kicks would have been successful. Even more galling for Wales, whose supreme run in domestic competition has ended so sourly, was that Hare, though missing four kicks, put over three to keep England firmly on course.

Welshman Paul Ringer is ordered off the pitch because of a late and dangerous tackle on England's outside half, John Horton. Ringer was the first player since Cyril Brownlie of New Zealand in 1925 to be sent off in an international at Twickenham.

Battling Arsenal are beaten in penalty decider

By Robert Oxby in Brussels
PUBLISHED THURSDAY 15 MAY
Valencia 0; Arsenal 0, after extra time
Valencia win 5–4 on penalties

Valencia won the European Cup Winners' Cup at the Heysel Stadium in Brussels last night, beating Arsenal by the dubious deciding factor of penalty kicks. Graham Rix was the unlucky player to miss in this cruel, sudden-death affair.

The players had battled through 120 minutes of tense but indecisive football before five chosen from each side lined up to try their luck from the spot.

Pat Jennings, the Arsenal goalkeeper, instantly raised British hopes by saving from Mario Kempes, but immediately Pereira did likewise with Liam Brady's effort.

The deadlock continued as Solsona, Pablo, Castellanos and Rainer Bonhof succeeded for the Spaniards, and Frank Stapleton, Alan Sunderland, Brian Talbot and John Hollins slotted the ball home for Arsenal.

After Arias put the Spaniards 5–4 ahead, Graham Rix had his shot saved by Pereira. The Valencia players rushed to their goalkeeper in delight as Rix, inconsolable, dropped to his knees in despair.

Jimmy Armfield, the former England captain, said: 'What a way to lose a final: they might as well toss a coin.

Why on earth don't they play on until a goal is scored?' The bitter truth is that Arsenal were denied the trophy despite being unbeaten in all their European matches this season. Suddenly, their hopes of winning two Cup finals in four days have been left in ashes.

Fears that Arsenal would show fatigue in their 68th match of the season were dispelled by a gallant and industrious performance in the match proper. They were, however, thwarted constantly by an unexpectedly secure Spanish defence.

For the entire 120 minutes, there was little to choose between the sides, but Arsenal grew stronger and more menacing as the match progressed and they deserved at least one goal in the second half.

But the outcome remained finely balanced until the critical series of penalty kicks, which determined that Arsenal now have only a UEFA Cup place to chase as they face two more First Division matches back home — away to Wolves and Middlesbrough.

A horrified Rix can only watch as Pereira makes the crucial save that gives Valencia the trophy.

1980

By Lance Tingay

PUBLISHED MONDAY 7 JULY

Wimbledon, 1980, will be remembered for its jewel of a climax. This was a men's singles final that lies with a handful of matches in being classed as the most enthralling and richest in quality of all time.

Björn Borg began the meeting as a lawn tennis hero. He ended it an even greater one, now in possession of the singles for the fifth consecutive year at the age of 24.

It takes two to make a notable lawn tennis match. It became an outstanding singles final because John McEnroe, 21, resisted so superbly. This young American was booed as he went out to play, and cheered for his gallantry as a loser three hours 53 minutes later.

Borg beat McEnroe by 1–6, 7–5, 6–3, 6–7, 8–6. It must be said that at the start, for all of the first set, and for much of the second, the Swede was untypically frail. McEnroe was venomously sharp.

Borg, after nearly two hours' play, led two sets to one towards his fifth championship. The fourth set came to the tie-break. Theoretically I would say that this abbreviated sequence is too much of a gamble on which to risk a Wimbledon championship.

Yet its excitement in such a situation transcended most thrills in sport, and for the 20 minutes or so during which this tie-break endured on Saturday, tested the heart of all who saw it. Borg, 6–5 and then 7–6, had two more match points which he was not allowed to win. McEnroe, at 8–7 and 9–8 had two set points. Borg at 10–9, 11–10 and 12–11, had three more match points. Then came McEnroe's third, fourth, fifth and sixth set points.

McEnroe finally won his seventh set point. It gave him the sequence 18–16, and every shot in the course of these throbbing exchanges was positive by both men.

In the fifth set Borg was in the ascendancy throughout. The end came in the 55th game of the match when Borg broke service to win. Characteristically, his closing shot was a searing backhand that won his eighth match point.

Borg thus won his fifth championship and 35th successive match at Wimbledon. The unique record of the Swede is 105 sets won, 19 lost, 742 games won, 475 lost.

For McEnroe it should be said that his resistance was heroic. Who else has saved seven match points in a Wimbledon final? What a fighter! What a champion who beat him!

By Nigel Wade and Roger Heywood in Moscow

PUBLISHED MONDAY 21 JULY

Spectacular pageantry failed to disguise the impact of the Afghanistan crisis on the opening of the Moscow Olympic Games, although Russian television tried to hide it from millions of ordinary Russians.

Seven of the 81 teams taking part in the Games took no part in the opening parade.

In each case a Russian girl in a red cape carried the team's name-board, followed by a Russian man in red jacket and white trousers holding the Olympic flag.

These teams, which had demanded to be represented in this way, were those of Belgium, France, Italy, Luxembourg, the Netherlands, San Marino and Switzerland. Britain, Ireland and Portugal were each represented by one of their own officials carrying the Olympic flag.

Athletes from Andorra, Australia, Denmark and Puerto Rico followed the Olympic flag, and sportsmen from New Zealand and Spain marched behind the five-ringed flags of their national Olympic associations.

In New Zealand's case four athletes and one official who took part in the parade were all who were left from an original squad of about 90 which was almost completely wiped out by protest withdrawals before it left for Moscow.

A total of 65 Olympic member countries are not competing in Moscow, chiefly because of the American-led boycott in protest at Russia's invasion of Afghanistan.

A Russian commentator explained the little that Russian viewers were allowed to glimpse of the protests as 'strange' conduct contrary to the tradition of the Games. He referred to the American boycott as 'a foolish venture by Washington which has failed'.

With the big American, Canadian, West German and Japanese contingents missing, in addition to the abstentions by several competing teams, the whole procession lasted only just over one hour.

This compared with at least 90 minutes at Mexico and Munich where more than 100 teams took part. Eighty-eight countries were at Montreal four years ago, when an African boycott was enforced.

Tanzanian team members jerked into a ragged goose-step as they gave President Brezhnev the eyes-right. Russian soldiers dressed as civilians also goose-stepped down the track, clutching 22 white doves symbolising peace. The *Soviet Military Review*, published on the opening day, repeated Russia's claim that 'the decision to host the Games was recognition of the Soviet Union's merits in the struggle for peace as well as its contribution to the world Olympic movement.'

DID YOU KNOW?

Playing for Ipswich Town in the First Division, goalkeeper Paul Cooper set a remarkable record. He faced ten penalties during the course of the season and managed to save eight of them.

The Soviet Union team parades around the Lenin Stadium at the boycott-hit Moscow Olympics.

Touch of bronze marks perfect end to day of golden Goliaths

By Ken Mays in Moscow

PUBLISHED MONDAY 28 JULY

The showdown is nearly over, the battle almost won. Steve Ovett is emerging as the Goliath of the Lenin Stadium track after his rough, tough victory over the world's top 800-m runners that brought him one of the most talked-about gold medals of the Olympic Games in Moscow on Saturday.

The brash young man from Brighton provided the most glittering triumph for British athletics as he beat off world record-holder Sebastian Coe.

Then Daley Thompson clinched another gold of the highest quality in the decathlon, and Gary Oakes finished off a marvellous day with a bronze in the 400-m hurdles.

Thompson, 21, proved the master at the ten-event competition. Oakes was both surprising and outstanding, but the 800 m was the focus of interest, and it ended in utter bewilderment for most of the 100,000 Russians who had come to see the much-discussed showdown.

Ovett, 24, not everyone's favourite man, ran the race of a true champion to deserve the gold in an event that he was only 50 per cent confident of winning.

Coe ran like a raw novice who had somehow managed to get on the track just to taste the atmosphere and was totally overcome by it all.

Ovett, as usual, refused to talk about his race afterwards, but even he must have been surprised at the way the challenge from his great rival never materialised until the final straight. Over that distance no one in the world will beat Ovett.

Coe avenged his 800-m defeat by winning the 1,500-m final (above) in which Ovett could only manage bronze. Allan Wells (left) won Olympic gold in the 100 m by a whisker; at 28 he was the oldest ever 100-m champion.

There were two laps of sheer guts and determination from Ovett who, according to times produced during the preceding six months, looked a possibility to finish outside the medals. But there was no accounting for experience and brute strength. He was shut in on the back straight, and surely must have been in some danger of disqualification as he elbowed his way out into the open.

He was again in trouble during the 1 min 45.4 sec it took him to pick up the gold, but he followed the strong Nikolai Kirov out of the final bend and then swamped the Russian with his usual power.

It was only then that Coe, 23, who had never been in contention, came into the running for a medal, but there was never any chance that he would be more than second best – and the Loughborough student did not deserve any more.

Ovett did not wave. He did not even look over his shoulder until he hit the finishing tape, with the grin on his face stretching from ear to ear and his one finger of victory held high for all the doubters to see.

Coe was a clear half-second behind, a dejected, well-beaten runner-up, and clearly shattered by the experience.

Coe admitted afterwards that he had made a disaster of the whole thing. 'Some days you run well, some days you don't,' he said. 'I didn't cover the break with speed, thought or movement.'

1980

1980

Johnny Owen dies after 46 days in coma

By Roger Heywood, sports correspondent

PUBLISHED WEDNESDAY 5 NOVEMBER

Johnny Owen, the British and European bantamweight champion, died in a Los Angeles hospital yesterday, nearly seven weeks after being knocked out by Lupe Pintor of Mexico in a world title fight.

Owen, 24, had two major brain operations, but never regained consciousness after his knock-out. The hospital said death was due to respiratory complications resulting from his prolonged coma.

Only a life-support machine had kept him alive since he was knocked out by Pintor in the 12th round of their fight on 19 September.

Reports in America said that Owen had such a thin skull that he should never have been allowed to fight. But this was said to have been discovered only after he was taken to hospital unconscious.

Dr Adrian Whiteson, senior medical officer to the British Boxing Board of Control, said yesterday: 'I believe that the fight would probably have been stopped in this country when Owen was knocked down the first time in round 12.' Pintor knocked Owen down in the ninth round and then again in the 12th, a minute before the final blow after two minutes 35 seconds of the round.

The referee, Marty Kenkin, said afterwards: 'The ninth round, he was hit and went down. I talked to him. I asked: "John, how do you feel?" He said: "Yes, sir, I'm okay." He never lost his politeness, his gentleness.'

Owen, affectionately known as the 'matchstick man,' was a boxer of extraordinary quality and strength. He appeared the antithesis of a fighting man, being so thin that he adopted the skeleton as his trademark. No one was more dedicated to boxing than this modest little Welshman. As a triple champion – British, European and Commonwealth – he should have been a fashionable name, but outside his beloved Wales, fame had not quite caught up with him.

DID YOU KNOW?

Stuart Lane had the briefest of careers with the British Lions rugby union team. The Cardiff and Wales flanker tore his knee ligaments after 45 seconds in his debut match; he had to come off, and never played for the side again.

By Donald Saunders

PUBLISHED MONDAY 29 SEPTEMBER

Now British boxing has been dragged to depths of degradation previously plumbed only by British soccer, it faces the prospect of being condemned by both international authorities as a pariah.

Even in the best of circumstances Alan Minter's defeat by Marvin Hagler midway through the third round of their world middleweight title bout would have been a severe blow to the British boxing ring. The ugly crowd scenes that followed Alan Minter's dethronement by Marvin Hagler have caused the once 'noble and manly art' to sink painfully to its knees.

Ironically, the Wembley disturbances came only a few days after Ray Clarke, the British Board of Control's general secretary, had publicly demanded the removal of the Los Angeles Olympic auditorium from the list of world championship venues. Mr Clarke complained that the Mexican-American crowd had behaved with intimidating hostility before, during and after Johnny Owen had made his ill-fated challenge to Lupe Pintor, the world bantamweight champion.

The Los Angeles fans, who even cheered lustily when the gravely injured Welshman was carried to the dressing room, behaved despicably, but, unlike the Wembley hooligans, they did not endanger the life and limb of boxers or spectators.

Hagler raises his arms in delight as Minter's corner concede the world middleweight title fight in the third round. Minter retired from boxing in 1981.

During more than a quarter of a century of ringside reporting I cannot recall more violent or sinister behaviour by a British boxing crowd. Bottles and cans thudded and splashed into the ring and onto press, radio and television desks around it, forcing us to take what cover we could.

Within a minute of achieving the ambition of a lifetime, Hagler was obliged to cower in his corner, spread-eagled between a loyal second who lay protectively over him. 'It was sickening', declared Pat Petronelli, Hagler's other joint manager, when they reached the dressing room 20 minutes later.

Why did it happen? The simple answer is that the hooligan element who have long plagued soccer have now turned their attention to the ring. They have brought with them the crude chants, banal songs, contemptuous attitude towards all visitors and inability to understand that defeat is as integral a part of sport as victory.

In the seven-and-a-half minutes that this contest lasted, Hagler cut his opponent to ribbons. In Las Vegas last March Minter won the title with a coldly disciplined performance against Vito Antuofermo. He is only too bitterly aware that he might have been equally successful on Saturday had he employed a similar policy.

Jones wins by seat of his pants

By Colin Dryden in Montreal
PUBLISHED TUESDAY 30 SEPTEMBER

After celebrating winning the world championship, a relaxed Alan Jones said yesterday that he would rather drive for Frank Williams' team than any other.

'I have had a couple of offers that I have to think about but I really want to stay with Frank and make it two in a row with Saudi Leyland Williams,' said Jones. He added that he would be signing his new contract after the final race of the season at Watkins Glen next Sunday.

Drinking black coffee and Vichy water the morning after winning the Canadian Grand Prix and clinching the championship, Jones said he knew he would win because his lucky underpants had arrived on Saturday night. They were sent out specially by his wife Beverly and he had worn them at all the races he had won last year.

Very superstitious, Jones admitted that he had only really started to relax since Nelson Piquet overtook him by one point at the Italian Grand Prix.

'I have always lost championships in the past when I have been leading right up to the last round. I was twitchy in Zandvoort and Imola, but I have been relaxed here and I knew everything would work out when the underpants arrived in time,' he added.

Jones was disappointed that the race had to be restarted and that he would have to 'do it all over again.' He accepted that obviously the race had to be stopped. 'Nelson Piquet was driving very well, but all along I knew one of us was going to have some sort of mechanical ailment,' he added.

The new world champion insisted he was not going to give up his fight to have his win in the 'illegal' race in Spain reinstated. 'I am more determined than ever now; I can legitimately scream and yell about it as champion.'

Jones said he was disappointed that his rival Piquet had not congratulated him after the race. 'I would have said something to him if he'd won, even if I didn't mean it,' said Jones.

A measure of the man is that, before leaving Montreal as the new champion, he is visiting Jean-Pierre Jabouille, who is in hospital here with a badly broken leg after crashing in his Renault-Elf turbo-charged car during the race on Sunday.

The final race of the 1980 season takes place at Watkins Glen, New York State, on Sunday, but Jones is secure as champion because, even if Piquet wins, the Brazilian has to discard points under the complicated scoring system. The grand prix season is divided in half and drivers' points count for only five races in each half. Piquet has scored in the second half in Britain, Germany, Austria, Holland and Italy. He therefore has to discard his lowest score – two points won in Austria.

Even if Piquet won nine points in Watkins Glen, his total of 63 would have to be reduced to 61 – one point less than Jones's total after the Canadian Grand Prix.

Alan Jones wins the British Grand Prix at Brands Hatch. Because of disagreements between the motor racing federations FISA and FOCA, the Spanish Grand Prix – which Jones also won – did not count towards the championship this year.

SPORT IN BRIEF

ATHLETICS
In August, running in Koblenz, West Germany, Brighton runner Steve Ovett breaks the world record for the 1,500 m. He completes the course in a time of 3 min 31.36 sec.

LAWN TENNIS
Czechoslovakia beat Italy 4–1 in the Davis Cup final to take the trophy for the first time. Italy were runners-up last year as well, when they lost 5–0 to the United States.

RUGBY UNION
The British Lions' tour of South Africa ends in a 3–1 Test series win for the Springboks after four hard-fought games. It is indicative of the narrow gap between the two teams that the Lions, led by Bill Beaumont, run up 68 points over the four games compared to the 77 points scored by the Springboks.

GOLF
Jack Nicklaus wins the US Open at Baltusrol, New Jersey, when he completes the course in a four-round total score of 272 strokes, a record for the event. He wins by two strokes from Isao Aoki, who also breaks the old record in his attempt to become the first Japanese player to win a major championship.

CRICKET
A match (not a Test) is played at Lord's between Australia and England to celebrate the centenary of the first Test match played in England. Ian Botham captains the side for the first time, but has a disappointing match. Geoff Boycott scores 201 runs in reply to the Australians' 385 for five declared, but the rain-interrupted match ends in a draw.

1980

Robert Philip

Sporting tragedies

THE SPORTING WORLD WITNESSED many terrible tragedies in sports stadia across the world in the 20th century – in Lima, for example, where 301 people were killed and over 500 injured fleeing a riot at a Peruvian football match in 1964 – but no one who had any personal experience of the events at Ibrox, Munich, Bradford, Heysel or Hillsborough was the same again....

Ibrox, Glasgow, 2 January 1971

As Ne'erday Old Firm games go, this particular episode of the world's oldest club fixture appeared to have passed off reasonably peacefully, both on the field and among the crowd of 80,000 spectators on the terraces. With 90 seconds remaining, Celtic were leading 1–0 as vast numbers of Rangers fans, resigned to another defeat against their bitter rivals, headed for the exits; on stairway 13, a steep 80-foot incline of concrete steps and steel handrails, a human stampede was sweeping downwards when Ibrox erupted in a mighty roar. Rangers' centre forward Colin Stein had equalised.

Fatally, hundreds turned back in the hope of belatedly joining the celebrations just as the main vanguard of supporters began their descent at the sound of the final whistle. Somewhere in the middle, a barrier collapsed under the strain of pressing bodies, sending a human avalanche hurtling down the stairway; within seconds, Exit 13 had been hideously transformed into a huge mound of dead, dying and injured.

Men, women and children who had escaped the crush – some wearing the blue of Rangers, some the green of Celtic – clawed at the tangled mass of bodies, frantically searching for friends and loved ones until they were gently led away.

On the news desk of the *Sunday Post* in Glasgow, where I was employed as a trainee, the death tally on the following morning's front-page headline rose with every succeeding phone call from the reporters on the scene. In all, 66 people died – mostly by suffocation – and 145 were injured.

Munich, 5 September 1972

The running, jumping and swimming resumed with cynical haste, allowing Lasse Viren, Olga Korbut and Mark Spitz among others to seize the opportunity of inscribing their deeds in the book of Olympic legend. Few could begrudge them their medals or their sporting immortality, even though the spiritual flame of the 1972 Olympics was surely extinguished when 11 Israeli athletes and officials were massacred by Arab extremists from the 'Black September' organisation.

Two were shot dead in the initial attack; their nine teammates, who had been held hostage within the Olympic village compound for 15 hours while West German Chancellor Willy Brandt attempted to secure their release through negotiations, were killed during a gun battle at Fürstenfeldbruck NATO airbase, where the terrorists had demanded a plane be waiting to fly them to a sympathetic Arab country.

That the slaughter of 11 innocent Jews, who had journeyed to Germany to compete as sportsmen, should take place just a few miles from the remains of Dachau, merely added to the sense of global despair; yet there should have been despair, too, at the International Olympic Committee's decision to allow the Games to proceed even as the bodies of the slain were being returned to Israel for burial.

But it was not only President Avery Brundage and his IOC acolytes who were guilty of gross insensitivity. As Herr Brandt desperately strove to reach a peaceful settlement with the terrorists barricaded inside Block 31 of the Olympic Village throughout the afternoon preceding the bloody climax, courting couples (fellow athletes of those being held hostage less than 50 yards away) sat cuddling and laughing on the grass in the very midst of the crisis. 'Should the Games continue?' pondered one American fencer, '...don't ask me to decide – I'm through to the finals.'

As a salve to its collective conscience, the IOC held a memorial service in the Olympic Stadium before the (fun and) Games resumed; the 11 empty seats in the section reserved for the Israeli team were both a symbol of man's inhumanity to man, and a reminder that no matter what atrocities may befall some of their members, as far as the so-called Olympic family are concerned, the show must go on.

Bradford, 11 May 1985

Television pictures showed it starting with a single, deceptively innocent wisp of smoke in the far corner of the main grandstand. In the blink of an eye, the entire wooden structure housing around 40,000 spectators was ablaze from end to end; within minutes, 40 people would lose their lives and 150 suffer serious injury. Some died of their burns, some of smoke inhalation; some were simply trampled to death in the panic.

The cameras had been at Valley Parade that Saturday afternoon to film the Bradford City–Lincoln City Third Division encounter due to be shown the following day on ITV's *Big Match* programme. Instead, their images of the inferno were broadcast around the world: spectators fleeing on to the pitch with their hair and clothes afire, blazing rafters crashing down on helpless fans below, 100 firemen fighting the raging flames while bodies were still being dragged out, a sobbing policemen describing 'people wandering around in a daze shouting the name of their loved ones'.

Though various theories abounded, including that it might have been started by a smoke-bomb or an arson attack, it is thought the fire was ignited by a discarded cigarette-end setting light to years of accumulated litter underneath the grandstand; thereafter, smoking at all British football stadia, and indeed at the majority of sports events, was banned on the grounds of safety.

Father Danny Flanagan, who travelled to Bradford from his parish in Dublin to join what he hoped would be City's promotion party, spoke for the nation when he said: 'The loss of life is overwhelming. It is heartbreaking to think that a few hours earlier we had gathered at Valley Parade in an atmosphere of happy anticipation to see City crowned champions. Now scores of families have been devastated. What can I say to comfort them, what can I say…?'

Brussels, 29 May 1985

Forty-one fans of Juventus were trampled or crushed to death before the European Cup final when a wall collapsed under the weight of charging Liverpool supporters.

In Britain, the usual excuses were trundled out as the marauding hordes skulked home defiantly: the Heysel Stadium was a crumbling antique and unsuitable for such an important game…European football officials were to blame for allowing Italian and English supporters on to the same section of terracing…the Belgian police goaded the Liverpool innocents into violence.

I was there, reporting on what should have been the climax of the football season for Reuters. I saw what happened. I saw young men in the red and white of Liverpool – many of them drunk – attack the family groups of Italians with flagpoles, metal batons fashioned out of safety barriers, lumps of concrete, bottles, cans, anything and everything. I saw the charge of the Liverpool brigade, I heard the apocalyptic *Crack!* as the wall gave way. I counted the dead as they were brought in to a makeshift

canvas chapel in the car park at the front of the stadium where a priest delivered the Last Rites.

Sickeningly, the 'game' was allowed to proceed (Juventus winning 1–0, as if anyone cared); Austrian TV screened pictures but no commentary, merely a caption explaining, 'This is not a football match, it is an exercise in crowd control.' An American TV reporter described it as '…a sickening sight from the Middle Ages.'

They banned English clubs from Europe for a while as a token punishment, but the shame will last for ever. When I left Brussels airport 48 hours later, the Belgian policeman at the security checkpoint spat on my picture before handing me back my British passport.

Sheffield, 15 April 1989

Hillsborough continues to take its sickening toll; 93 died within the stadium and in nearby hospitals, more have since been allowed to slip away following the switching-off of the life-support systems which had kept them 'alive' for years afterwards.

The recriminations, too, go on. The Merseyside families of those who were crushed to death on the Lepping Lane terraces shortly after the start of the Nottingham Forest–Liverpool FA Cup semi-final will not rest until another public inquiry has been held and anyone found accountable brought to justice.

At the time, police said a huge contingent of Liverpool fans – around 3,000–4,000 – arrived less than ten minutes before kick-off and that a gate which had earlier been shut was reopened to ease the crush. The families of the victims claim the fans were packed into a section too small to accommodate them and had the life squeezed out of them when forced against the anti-hooligan perimeter fencing.

Anfield was turned into a shrine in the days that followed as fans from all over Britain visited Liverpool's stadium to leave flowers, scarves, bobble hats and shirts representing every team in the land. Every news bulletin carried reports of the latest funeral attended by grieving friends, family and Liverpool players.

Some day, the truth may be known, thereby affording those who survived or those left to mourn a measure of comfort, but the memory of the anguished faces trapped behind the Hillsborough fencing will never fade. Above one such harrowing photograph, a headline writer managed to sum up the full horror in just four words: The Gates of Hell….

1981

Mike Hailwood, master of the track

By George Turnbull
Published Tuesday 24 March

Mike Hailwood **(above)**, 40, who died yesterday from injuries received in a car accident in which his daughter was killed, was universally regarded as the finest exponent of the art of motor-cycle racing. Hailwood had been fighting for his life at Birmingham's accident hospital since suffering severe head injuries in the crash on Saturday. His son David was slightly hurt.

Hailwood, who was fetching fish and chips, collided with the back of a lorry on the A435 at Portway, only two miles from his home at Tanworth-in-Arden, Warwicks.

In a career spanning some 21 years and at a time when competition was at its toughest, Hailwood, who became known as 'Mike the Bike', won nine world championships and a record 14 Tourist Trophy races over the notorious mountain course on the Isle of Man.

His world championship tally would have no doubt been much higher, but for the decision at the height of his motor-cycle racing career to switch to car racing.

It was said that Stanley Michael Hailwood was born to race motor cycles. Certainly with a millionaire father, he had no need to enter such a demanding and dangerous sport. But from the day he made his debut as a 17-year-old at Oulton Park on Easter Sunday, 1957, it was evident that Hailwood had followed his right instincts.

Less than two months later, he won his first race, a 125-cc event, and from that point his flair and rapidly developing natural talents took him to grand prix championship successes.

He won the 250-cc world championship in 1961 and was double 250- and 350-cc champion in 1966 and 1967. In between, he won the supreme title, the 500-cc championship, four times in succession.

Hailwood achieved the rare distinction for a motor cyclist of becoming a worldwide, household name. But success and fame never rested easily on his shoulders. An extremely modest, even shy man, he was embarrassed by praise and tended to reply to compliments with a quip which was often misunderstood for aloofness.

Hailwood quit full-time two-wheel racing in 1968 and turned to cars, and although he became a competitive Formula One driver, he never achieved the success he sought. He was awarded the MBE in 1968.

A 100-mph crash brought his car career to an end at Nürburgring in 1974, two years after he had been awarded the George Medal for bravery in pulling fellow driver, Clay Regazzoni, from his blazing car during the South African Grand Prix. He never talked about this.

His countless fans, however, had not seen the last of Hailwood. In 1978 he returned from New Zealand to enter the TT, just for the fun of it.

And amid jubilant scenes never before witnessed on the Isle of Man, he won the Formula One race after an 11-year absence. A year later he won the senior TT, and ended an extraordinary career a few days later with a win at Mallory Park.

Bob Champion and Aldaniti: two heroic fighters

By Hotspur (Peter Scott)
Published Monday 6 April

Saturday's Grand National blazed an example of courage and perseverance round the world when Aldaniti and Bob Champion provided a miraculously triumphant ending to the tale of a crippled horse and a cancer victim.

Aintree has not yet won its own battle to survive, but Saturday's heroism, added to so many played out on its historic turf, must strengthen the resolve not to let this hard-pressed warrior die a financial death.

Champion, 32, was given eight months to live when the doctors diagnosed cancer in July 1979. Two bouts of tendon trouble and a fractured hock-bone made Aldaniti's own prospects of Aintree glory appear remote.

Horse and rider began their partnership in January, 1975, when Aldaniti won a novices' hurdle at Ascot on his racecourse debut. Now he has become the first Grand National winner since Sundew in 1957 to lead throughout the final circuit.

Mr John Thorne's own example of supreme fitness at the age of 54 may not have ended in victory, but it certainly ended in triumph. Mr Thorne and his beloved Spartan Missile made up many lengths to finish second.

Royal Mail was a name added to the Grand National's winning roll in 1937. The New Zealand-bred namesake of that horse made a gallant effort to match his predecessor's achievement, but Royal Mail's sustained challenge to Aldaniti started wilting with a blunder two fences from home.

Josh Gifford's wonderful training achievement with Aldaniti is matched on a more personal basis by loyalty to an employee. Champion's long fight against pain and near despair was made that little more bearable by Gifford's repeated promise that Champion's job as stable jockey would be there on his return.

Aldaniti was bred by Mr Thomas Barron at his Harrowgate stud near Darlington, County Durham. Alistair, David, Nicola and Timothy, Mr Barron's four grandchildren, each provided part of Aldaniti's name. The horse was sent to Ascot sales in May 1974, when Josh Gifford bought him for 3,200 guineas on the advice of his father-in-law, George Roger-Smith.

Triumph against the odds: Bob Champion (on left, below) and Aldaniti celebrate their victory at Aintree. Champion's successful career as a jockey and his fight against cancer became the basis of the film *Champions* (1983), in which John Hurt starred.

Aga Khan colt gallops to magnificent Derby win

By Hotspur (Peter Scott)
PUBLISHED THURSDAY 4 JUNE

Shergar made yesterday's Derby the most one-sided of modern times. His ten-length winning margin was the widest officially recorded for a race founded in 1780, and the result was a foregone conclusion long before he took command early in the straight.

The Irish Sweeps Derby on 27 June should provide a similarly easy conquest for the Aga Khan's superb colt, who will face a much more informative test against the leading older horses in Ascot's King George VI and Queen Elizabeth Diamond Stakes on 25 July.

Shergar's time of 2 min 44.21 sec was the slowest since Airborne won in 1946, but yesterday's Classic was run on softer going than usual.

Riberetto and Silver Season, tracked by Shergar, set a strong early gallop which had the field beginning to string out after half a mile. While his two fellow leaders rounded Tattenham Corner under pressure, Shergar was lobbing along, with young Walter Swinburn standing up in his irons.

Shergar went on to win the King George VI and Queen Elizabeth Diamond Stakes at Ascot in July.

Riberetto and Silver Season then gave way to Scintillating Air, Shotgun and the Queen's Church Parade, who became the favourite's closest pursuers as he nonchalantly drew clear.

Glint of Gold looked a hopeless prospect two furlongs out, but he finished strongly and wore down Scintillating Air to take second place by two lengths.

Shotgun finished fourth. Lester Piggott reported that the distance was too far for his mount against a colt of Shergar's calibre, but Shotgun will face weaker opposition in the Mecca Bookmakers' Scottish Derby at Ayr.

With Shergar bound for the Irish Sweeps Derby, Glint of Gold will next tackle the 15-furlong Grand Prix de Paris at Longchamp. His autumn target is the St Leger.

Glint of Gold was involved in an early scrimmage with Kalagow and Kind of Hush, neither of whom ever promised to recover the lost ground.

Lydian was withdrawn after what the Epsom stewards described as unruly behaviour before the start. His French

stable, who did not consider that Lydian had been appropriately handled, will be sent to Italy for the Gran Premio di Milano on Sunday week.

Meanwhile, the Aga Khan will seek another Derby at Chantilly on Sunday, when his unbeaten colt Akarad opposes Recitation and No Lute in the French equivalent, the Prix du Jockey-Club. Mr Nelson Bunker Hunt, with Empery and Youth, landed this particular double in 1976.

Michael Stoute, who has handled Shergar with such skill, became only the second Newmarket trainer to saddle a Derby winner since 1961. Sir Noel Marless, with Royal Palace in 1967, was the other.

Stoute's stable is among four to house the Aga Khan's massive team of 137 horses in training. His bloodstock empire, inclusive of mares, yearlings, foals and stallions, approaches 450.

Master Willie, Mrs Penny and Prince Bee, three possible opponents for Shergar at Ascot on 25 July, meet in today's Coronation Cup at Epsom.

Master Willie, second in last year's Derby, after an interrupted preparation, is my nap.

SPORT IN BRIEF

CRICKET
Ian Botham is captain for the 1980–1 winter tour of the West Indies, which the home team wins 2–0. The tour is marred by an attack on the pitch in the first Test and the death of England's manager, Ken Barrington, during the third Test.

HORSE RACING
In March Sea Pigeon, trained by Peter Easterby and ridden by John Francome, wins the Champion Hurdle at Cheltenham for the second year running. The horse also came second in 1978 and 1979.

ATHLETICS
The first London Marathon is staged; 7,055 runners enter the race, which begins from Greenwich Park, and more than 6,000 complete it. American farmer Dick Beardsley and Norwegian physiotherapist Inge Simonsen (**right**) cross the finish line hand in hand. British runner Joyce Smith wins the women's race.

1981

1981

Graham is first Australian to take US Open

By Michael Williams in Philadelphia
PUBLISHED MONDAY 22 JUNE

David Graham, 35, yesterday became the first Australian to win the United States Open championship when he had a final round of 67 at Merion to beat George Burns and Bill Rogers by three strokes.

Graham's aggregate of 273 was seven strokes inside the record for Merion, and it was his second major championship win. Two years ago he took the PGA at Oakland Hills and this latest performance, when he was three behind Burns going into the last round, confirmed him as a golfer of the highest class.

Two birdies in the first two holes gave him the impetus he needed. His smooth swing never quickens and he saw off not only Burns but passing challenges from Rogers and Jack Nicklaus.

Over the last nine holes it was mostly a three-horse race between Graham, Burns and Rogers. And the Australian's birdies at the 14th and 15th holes, on one of the most difficult finishes in championship gold, was a fitting climax.

On a hot, sultry afternoon, it was obvious that Burns, who had established a three-stroke lead on Saturday,

needed a solid start to leave everybody else to do the work. In fact, it took Graham only four holes to draw level.

The Australian, as composed and unhurried as ever, did most of the work. At the first, having driven into the left rough, he holed a putt of a good six yards for a three. Then, at the second, Graham played three perfect strokes.

Burns did not look shaken but his first error soon followed. The flag at the long fourth was tucked right down, and Burns caught the top of the bank with his pitch and was lucky his ball did not topple into the water.

He nevertheless dropped a stroke by missing a putt of some eight feet, and shrieks from further up the course announced that Nicklaus was on the move. He holed for birdies at the fifth and sixth, which partially made up for the chance he had failed to take at the fourth.

Any sense of elation Graham felt at catching the leader so early did not last long. The green at the fifth has a wicked slope and, putting downhill, Graham saw his ball run far enough for him to miss the one back.

Nicklaus's sudden thrust was not maintained. Though he played a fine pitch up to the seventh green, giving him the chance of a third successive birdie, he slightly overcooked the putt and, to a groan from the crowd, missed the return as well.

However, he perked up with a birdie at the ninth to be out in 34 and then, down that treacherous slope at the 12th, took three putts for the second time.

Rogers was then only one behind both Graham and Burns, who had also got into trouble at the tenth and dropped a shot where he would have been hoping to look for a birdie. Burns had not been finding the fairway exactly regularly and, at the 14th, where he again did well to scramble a par, Graham finally overtook him with a lovely mid-iron to around six feet from where he holed without any apparent tremor.

There was by now not much threat from elsewhere either, for Rogers suddenly fell three behind when he hooked his drive into the rough at the 16th. Almost immediately Graham struck again, this time holing from perhaps eight feet for another birdie. That put him in the comfortable position of being two ahead of the field with three holes to play.

Of course, you never know at Merion, but though Burns with a final flourish chipped in for two at the 17th, Graham did not weaken and finished in the style of a true champion.

David Graham was the first foreign player to win the US Open championship since Tony Jacklin in 1970.

Carl Lewis leaps 28 ft 7¾ in

By Ken Mays
PUBLISHED MONDAY 22 JUNE

Carl Lewis, 19, from Alabama, once more issued a warning to his World Cup rivals in Rome in September, when he produced the second best long jump in history at the United States National championships in Sacramento at the weekend.

Lewis was deprived of the world 100-m record in Florence earlier this month when his run, first timed at 9.93 sec, was corrected 20 minutes later to 10.13 sec.

This time, Lewis won the 100 m in a legitimate 10.13 sec and produced a remarkable 28 ft 7¾ in (8.73 m) in the qualifying round long jump but, like the 28 ft 3¼ in he did recently, it was ruled out because of a strong following wind and he had to settle for victory at 28 ft 3½ in (8.62 m).

Bob Beamon, another American, holds the world record at 29 ft 2½ in, which he set in the 1968 Olympics in Mexico.

Thierry Vigneron of France became the first pole-vaulter to clear 19 ft when he set a world record of 19 ft ¼ in (5.80 m), to improve the mark set by Poland's

Wladyslaw Kozakiewicz in the Moscow Olympics by three-quarters of an inch.

It helped France beat Great Britain by 49 pts to 34 in the jumps match in Macon where Roy Mitchell of Enfield won the long jump with 25 ft 8¾ in (7.84 m) and Birchfields' Aston Moore the triple jump with 53 ft 11 in (16.43 m). France also beat Britain by 21 pts to 15 in the women's match.

While still at Houston University (1979–82), Carl Lewis showed potential for all-round athletic brilliance, which was to blossom at the 1984 Los Angeles Olympics.

MILESTONES

During the Olympic Congress of 1981, the expression 'Olympic amateur' was taken out of the Olympic Charter. This allowed sports associations to decide for themselves who was eligible to attend the Olympic Games.

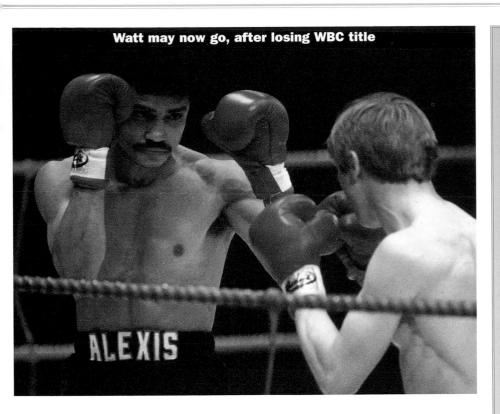

Watt may now go, after losing WBC title

By Ken Mays

PUBLISHED MONDAY 22 JUNE

Jim Watt will take the next few days to consider whether to continue his boxing career following the loss of his World Boxing Council lightweight title to Alexis Arguello of Nicaragua after 15 hard-fought rounds at Wembley Arena on Saturday night.

The Glasgow car dealer, although a clear points loser of a title that he had won two years ago and defended successfully four times since then, surprised many of the spectators and sport's experts by still being on his feet at the end of the match.

Despite a few cuts around his slim features, this is what may convince him that he is still the second best at the weight and that a return fight with Sean O'Grady, this time for the World Boxing Association version of the title, is worth holding out for.

There was no doubt that the Scot lost Saturday's contest and even he, in the solemn surrounds of a loser's dressing room, admitted that he was defeated by possibly four or five rounds.

But the margin given by American judge, Dick Young, who awarded Arguello 147 points to 137 – meaning that Watt had won three rounds and the challenger 12, one by two points – was nowhere near correct in my opinion.

Watt had been off his feet in the seventh round, when a left forced him to take a count of eight. 'It was a good punch and he hit me with a lot of those,' confessed Watt. 'But I was still clear-headed.'

Arguello dominated the fight from start to finish with Watt's best round coming in the eighth as the Miami-based challenger took a breather and, although Watt came back strongly in the final few rounds, it was not enough to sway the judges.

The new champion summed up his facial injuries – which did not require stitching – by saying: 'I'm in the car business and if I had to give an estimate on it, I think I'd write it off.'

Arguello was the aggressor throughout and American judges like aggression, which could explain Young's scoring. Although Watt tried to out-smart his opponent, and he did succeed at times, he could not capitalise on his rare successes.

Arguello now goes into the record books as a winner of three world titles, the featherweight and junior lightweight before Saturday, and as Watt said: 'It wasn't a palooka who took my title and I'm just glad that I lost it to a great fighter.'

It will take a great fighter to depose Arguello who, after a build-up and a contest that was a credit to the sport, said: 'Watt is a great boxer and he fought like a man ten years younger to hold on to his crown. I am proud to have beaten him.'

Charlie Magri, the European flyweight champion from Stepney, who has just been reinstated as No. 1 challenger in the world, made short work of José Herrera in the chief supporting contest, having the Mexican down three times before he was counted out after only 105 seconds of the first round.

After scoring a 15-round victory over Jim Watt, Alexis Arguello (left) became boxing's sixth three-title champion, holding the featherweight and junior lightweight as well as the WBC lightweight title.

SPORT IN BRIEF

FOOTBALL
In May Ipswich Town win the UEFA Cup when they beat AZ 67 Alkmaar of Holland 5–4 on aggregate in the final, winning 3–0 at home but losing 4–2 away. The Ipswich midfielder John Wark creates a record for goals scored in the competition, scoring 14, including two in the final.

SQUASH
Australian Geoff Hunt wins the British Open for the sixth time in succession and the eighth time in all; he won in 1969, 1974 and from 1976–81, He has also won the World Open championship four times in succession, 1976–9.

FOOTBALL
On 27 May a goal from left-back Alan Kennedy in the 82nd minute against Real Madrid gives Liverpool the European Cup for the third time in five years. Bob Paisley's side are the first British team to win it three times.

MOTOR RACING
John Player and Lotus unveil their Type 87 car at the Spanish Grand Prix on 21 June. Nigel Mansell and Elio de Angelis **(in the car, right)** will be the Lotus drivers this season; they come fifth and sixth in the race at Jarama.

ATHLETICS
Sebastian Coe breaks the world record for the 800 m in Florence, completing the course in a time of 1 min 41.72 sec. In August he goes on to break the world record for the mile in Zurich, where he records a time of 3 min 48.53 sec.

1981

1981

By Michael Melford at Headingley
PUBLISHED WEDNESDAY 22 JULY

Just occasionally in life the unbelievable does happen. It happened on the last day of the third Cornhill Test at Headingley yesterday when England, who had seemingly been within a few minutes of defeat on Monday afternoon with Ladbrokes offering 500–1 against them, bowled out Australia for 111 to win by 18 runs.

Ian Botham hauled them up from the depths on Monday and, having made 149 not out, took the first wicket when Australia batted yesterday.

But the 130 which Australia needed was very little on a pitch still producing the unpredictable ball. At 56 for one indeed Australia seemed to be cruising home.

Then Bob Willis, having switched to the Kirkstall Lane end, began to bowl as straight and as fast as at any time in the long career which has been miraculously extended after injury. He has only once produced better figures than eight for 43, but not in a Test match.

His inspired spell began 20 minutes before lunch when he took the first of three wickets in 11 balls. It ended 70 minutes after lunch when he knocked out Bright's middle stump and England incredibly had levelled the series.

The inspiration was not confined to Willis, for England threw themselves frantically about the field and, until the last few seconds, held all their catches, while Mike Brearley conducted operations with the unflappability which has coped successfully with numerous tight limited-over finishes in the past.

Twenty-four hours earlier England were 135 for seven, still needing 92 to avoid an innings defeat.

Only once in more than 100 years of Test matches has a side following on been victorious: England won by ten runs in Sydney in 1894–95. That makes it an extraordinary feat, but it is more extraordinary still to win from the sort of situation in which England found themselves before Botham and Graham Dilley took over.

England's innings lasted another ten minutes yesterday morning before Willis was well caught at second slip by Allan Border in Terry

Alderman's second over with the new ball. Botham had driven Alderman handsomely past cover in his first over and five runs had been added.

The last wicket stand had made 37 in 31 minutes during which Willis received nine balls. The last three wickets had added 221 and, as at Trent Bridge, Alderman, who had not played in a Test before this series, had taken nine wickets in the match.

On a lovely fresh sunny morning, the new ball swung little and the Australians set off as if the task was trifling, Graeme Wood hitting Botham's first two balls for four.

In Botham's second over Wood drove and apparently hit ground and ball at the same time, Bob Taylor taking the catch. The score then advanced uneventfully to 56 before Willis, in the second over after changing ends, made a ball lift and lob up from the handle of Trevor Chappell's bat.

Kim Hughes played a form of steer towards third man fairly profitably in the first innings, but now he met a ball from Willis which lifted, and Botham dived at third slip to catch him two-handed to the left.

Three balls after Graham Yallop fended off a ball towards Gatting at close short-leg, Gatting was back on his heels

All-round brilliance: Botham took six wickets for 95 in the first innings (below left) and scored 149 runs in the second innings of an unforgettable Test.

but recovered to scoop the ball up near his toes.

At that, they went in for lunch with the score 58 for four and an England win suddenly in sight if the inspiration could be sustained afterwards. It was.

The first wicket after lunch was the valuable one of Border. In Willis's next over Dyson, hooking, was caught at the wicket. In his next Marsh hooked off the top edge and Graham Dilley held the catch safely chest high. In Willis's following over Lawson touched a wide one to Taylor and Australia were 75 for eight.

Australia decided to hit straight and often, and the match was slipping away again when Lillee miscued a stroke off his legs and Gatting caught it.

Willis then produced a yorker, Bright drove over it, and a never-to-be-forgotten Test match was won and lost.

DID YOU KNOW?

In the third match between Australia and New Zealand in the World Series final, Australian Trevor Chappell bowled the crucial final ball underarm. Though legal under Australian rules, his action was 'deplored' and it was made illegal the following week. Australia won the match.

Protest battles as Springboks open tour

By Ian Ward in Gisborne
PUBLISHED THURSDAY 23 JULY

Brawls involving police, rugby fans, and anti-apartheid demonstrators marked New Zealand's 'Day of Shame' yesterday as the visiting Springboks played their first match in the town of Gisborne.

Violence spread to five cities, and in Gisborne police and protesters fought in the mud as the game went on amid the worst protests since the Vietnam war.

The South Africans beat Poverty Bay 24–6, and afterwards the country's police commissioner threatened a crackdown on demonstrators.

The beginning of the 16-game tour was dubbed a day of shame by opposition groups who have split the country. As the match began, 400 screaming and chanting protesters repeatedly charged at the wire fence surrounding the ground. The under-strength police were pushed back and part of the fence collapsed.

About 10,000 spectators who had been jeering the demonstrators punched, kicked and pushed them until police reinforcements arrived.

Police clubbed demonstrators with batons and pushed them down an eight-foot bank, trampling on those who fell. Several police, including women in plain-clothes,

mingled with the fans when the trouble began. But police generally displayed discipline and self-control, despite much provocation. There were a number of arrests and at least three people were treated for minor injuries.

Springbok fly half Errol Tobias, 31, the first and only coloured player to win a place in the South African side, was one of the stars of the game. He scored the Springbok's second try. Protesters have tagged him an 'Uncle Tom'.

In Christchurch, on the South Island yesterday, 8,000 demonstrators marched peacefully through the city. Further south, at Dunedin, several hundred gathered outside the National party offices and eight broke in and chained themselves to furniture.

In the capital, Wellington, on the North Island, 24 demonstrators took over the National party offices, flinging files, leaflets and books into the street. It took police two-and-a-half hours to enter the building.

In the North Island's largest city, Auckland, 1,000 protesters last night attacked the Eden Park ground, home of the city's rugby union, and venue for one of the three South Africa v New Zealand rugby Tests.

Last night, Commissioner Robert Walton said police had the lawful right to protect themselves from violence when maintaining law and order.

Hunt loses world title to Jahangir

By D. J. Rutnagur in Toronto
PUBLISHED MONDAY 30 NOVEMBER

Jahangir Khan of Pakistan, 18 next month, relieved Geoff Hunt of Australia of the world squash racquets Open title, winning Saturday's final in Toronto in a manner which showed him clearly superior and predicted a long reign as champion.

However, the beaten champion, a great player in his own right, will dispute Jahangir's supremacy next April in the British Open, which he has won eight times. Hunt certainly has no immediate plans for retirement.

The final, won 7–9, 9–1, 9–2, 9–2, by Jahangir in 110 minutes, did not provide the thrills and the swings of fortune of their Bromley battle earlier this year. But for quality of squash racquets, it excelled even that particular encounter. Hunt himself was a contributor to this opinion. The higher levels were achieved by the advance of the new champion, both as a more seasoned competitor and as a player.

The success of youth is stirring because freshness and fragility are part of being young, but Jahangir played with confidence and insight, his calm undisturbed by Hunt winning a first game of 56 minutes. Hunt, too, declared his class in playing thoughtful and versatile squash racquets to win the opening game.

Jahangir Khan built on his Open success with a win in 1982 in the International Players' Association competition, beating Maqsood Ahmed. In doing so Khan became the first player to win a major final without losing a point.

The capture of this game would have been of greater use to Hunt had he taken it on his first game ball, rather than fifth, after many gruelling rallies. The strains of the tussle imposed on his stamina both physical and mental.

Hunt's agitation was expressed in an outburst when a penalty point was awarded against. Hunt screamed his protest. For the rest of the match, the former champion was Canute trying to hold back the tide of genius.

SPORT IN BRIEF

LAWN TENNIS
Chris Evert-Lloyd wins Wimbledon for the third time when she defeats Hana Mandlikova of Czechoslovakia in the final 6–2, 6–2. It is the American's first victory since 1976, although she was a losing finalist in 1978, 1979 and 1980.

FOOTBALL
Manchester United break the British transfer record when Ron Atkinson signs Bryan Robson from West Bromwich Albion for £1.5 million. The hard-tackling midfielder has scored 39 goals in his 198 games for the Midlands side.

GOLF
The United States, captained by Dave Marr, win the Ryder Cup against a Europe team led by John Jacobs. The competition, played at Walton Heath in Surrey, is won easily by the Americans, $18^1/_2$ to $9^1/_2$.

FOOTBALL
Bill Shankly dies in hospital in Liverpool aged 67. Shankly joined Liverpool as manager in 1959, after spells at Carlisle, Grimsby, Workington and Huddersfield, and proceeded to build the club into a huge force in domestic and European football. Three years after his arrival, Liverpool won the Second Division title, and by 1964 had topped the First Division, which they did again in 1966 and 1973. Liverpool also lifted the FA Cup in 1965 and 1974, and the UEFA Cup in 1973. Shankly was awarded the OBE in 1974; he passed the stewardship of his beloved club to Bob Paisley in the same year. Under Paisley the club is enjoying further triumphs.

1981

265

1982

By Roger Heywood

PUBLISHED THURSDAY 1 APRIL

Geoff Boycott and the so-called English cricket rebels were greeted with a police escort when they flew into Heathrow airport in London yesterday after their controversial tour of South Africa.

A Heathrow official revealed that the police were asked to meet the party because Boycott had been told that anti-apartheid extremists 'were out to get him'.

Police said later: 'Our officers were there to prevent any nasty scenes blowing up between players and the press. We were requested to keep an eye on the situation.'

Boycott, beardless and tanned, simply said: 'Good morning chaps,' and then disappeared into a taxi. Later at the London International Press centre where he met Peter Houston, the British dominoes champion, for a game, he faced his inquisitors but, in a good Yorkshire fashion, said nowt.

'How long was the flight from South Africa?' Boycott looked pained, glanced at his watch and replied: 'I don't honestly know.' Did he enjoy the trip? He smiled. Will he go back to South Africa? Another smile.

Meanwhile Graham Gooch, who captained the English players in South Africa, was his usual genial self. 'I'm glad to be back,' he said passing through the airport with his wife Brenda. 'There's no place like home. Yes, I enjoyed myself. I'm not prepared to say anything else.'

The players who returned home yesterday were Gooch, Boycott, John Emburey, Chris Old, Geoff Humpage, Arnold Sidebottom, Les Taylor, Peter Willey and Mike Hendrick. Bob Woolmer arrived separately.

After a meeting in Westminster Mr John Carlisle, chairman of the Conservative Backbench Sports Committee, said legal action was 'being considered' against the Test and County Cricket Board for banning the rebels for playing for England for three years.

MILESTONES

Queens Park Rangers were the first British club to play a League game on an artificial surface. Oldham Athletic, Luton Town and Preston North End followed suit, but by 1994 the Football League had banned the pitches, on the basis that they gave the home team an unfair advantage.

The rebels – the 'Dirty Dozen' plus three – in South Africa. Geoff Boycott and Alan Knott were among those whose Test careers were ended because of the tour.

Veteran Saunders turns back clock

By Tony Stafford

PUBLISHED MONDAY 5 APRIL

History will record the 1982 Grand National as one won by the oldest jockey and in which a woman jockey completed the course for the first time.

But behind the scenes a poignant moment was provided by Diana Henderson, wife of Lambourn trainer Nicky and daughter of the late John Thorne.

Twelve months ago she was part of the group that received her father and Spartan Missile as they returned to unsaddle in second place.

Joy and pride, rather than disappointment, was the theme of that little party.

On Saturday Diana Henderson was one of the first to greet Dick Saunders and Grittar on their way back to the winner's enclosure.

Saunders had been encouraged by John Thorne to continue riding almost 20 years ago, when he was ready to give up for the second time. The first break had been his own decision, with the ambition of building up his own farming interests, which he realised to the full.

He said: 'I had just lost three horses in three weeks and wanted to hang up my boots, but John said, "Come and have a drink" and talked me into keeping going. And that was just after Nigel, his only son, had died.'

The parallels between Spartan Missile and Grittar are remarkable. Both were ridden by Midlands farmers well into middle age, and on the day each was a nine-year-old carrying 11 st 5 lb.

But for the intervention of Saturday's first-fence fallers Aldaniti and Bob Champion in 1981, this would have been a carbon-copy, for both Spartan Missile and Grittar are champion hunter chasers and winners of the Cheltenham and Liverpool Foxhunters'.

Grittar's owner-trainer-breeder, Frank Gilman, disagreed with the view of those who believed Grittar's chance had been lessened by the fact that the course had dried out. In fact, Grittar recorded the second-best time for the race.

'If it had been heavy, I don't think he would have had the stamina to last out four-and-a-half miles,' Gilman said. 'He looked to be going well all the way.'

Grittar runs with the same economy and jumps with the precision that enabled Red Rum to win three Grand Nationals. Only Red Rum has clocked a faster winning time, and only Red Rum in the past quarter century has carried a higher weight to victory.

If the Grand National is saved, Grittar, with two or maybe three more attempts before him, may be thought of in the same class as Red Rum.

There are many who believe that Grittar would not have beaten Loving Words, who conjured an astonishing rally into third place after unseating his rider, Richard Hoare, at the fourth last.

Hoare took quite a time to get back in the saddle and stormed after the others to such good effect that he gained third place and at least a share of the honours with Dick Saunders and Mrs Geraldine Rees on another epic day at Aintree.

Dean and Torvill strike gold again

By Howard Bass in Lyon
PUBLISHED SATURDAY 6 FEBRUARY

Chris Dean and Jayne Torvill enthralled a rapt audience in Lyon last night to retain their European ice-dance title with no serious challenge in sight.

Eight of the nine judges gave them maximum six marks for presentation – the highest ever from one set of marks in any skating event – and they got three more sixes for technical merit.

Simple superlatives cannot adequately describe their degree of finesse. Their superbly matched free legs moved as one graceful unit, and even their heads inclined to right or left in incredible unison.

Aptly chosen music, shrewdly interpreted with exceptional choreographic skill, coloured a performance rich in original, intricate steps which looked deceptively easy. With their golden Olympic goal still two years away,

Dean and Miss Torvill have already reached a pinnacle of technical efficiency to warrant bracketing with such all-time greats in other sports.

Betty Callaway, their Nottingham coach, modestly attributed their success to their abnormal dedication in training, but her importance as the third member of a triumphant team may be gauged by the fact that she also coached their world title winning predecessors, Any Sallay and Kris Regoczy of Hungary.

Trailing helplessly in the champions' wake were the Soviet runners-up, Andrei Bukin and Natalia Bestmianova, who for the first time outpointed their third-placed compatriots, Andrei Minenkov and Irina Moiseeva, the winners in 1977 and 1978.

Torvill and Dean's performance earned them 11 maximum sixes at the European championships. They went on to win the world title as well this year, scoring another five sixes with their Mack and Mabel routine.

SPORT IN BRIEF

FOOTBALL
Victories over Valur Reykjavik, Dynamo Berlin, Dynamo Kiev and Anderlecht take Aston Villa to the European Cup final, where on 26 May they beat Bayern Munich 1–0, thanks to a goal from Peter Withe. They are only the fourth English team to win the trophy, after Manchester United, Liverpool and Nottingham Forest.

MOTOR RACING
In a tragic year for Ferrari, Gilles Villeneuve **(with Didier Pironi, below)** dies as a result of injuries sustained in an accident. The Canadian driver is taking part in final practice for the Belgian Grand Prix at Zolder in May, when Jochen Mass's March strays into the Ferrari's path, causing it to flip over. The track in Montreal, Canada, will be renamed after Villeneuve; he won the first world championship race held there in 1978. Patrick Tambay now joins Ferrari.

FOOTBALL
Twenty-four teams take part in this year's World Cup, held in Spain. Scotland bow out after the first round. Northern Ireland reach the second round after a 1–0 win against Spain; England progress to round two as well, but both teams are knocked out at this stage. In a highly dramatic confrontation between France and West Germany in the semi-final, the sides are one-all at the end of normal time. France go 3–1 up, but Germany level the score; West Germany win the penalty shoot-out 5–4, and go on to meet Italy in the final.

1982

267

1982

Double triumph for Britain

By Roger Heywood, sports correspondent

PUBLISHED MONDAY 10 MAY

Hugh Jones, a modest 26-year-old student, and Joyce Smith, a 44-year-old mother-of-two, sealed a double win for Britain yesterday in the second London Marathon. Jones ran the 26 miles 385 yards from Greenwich to Westminster Bridge faster than anyone before. And Mrs Smith broke the British women's marathon best time in 2 hr 29 min 43 sec.

Britain completed a hat trick of wins when their 'B' team of Mike Gratton, Dave Clark and Derek Stevens took the men's Nations Cup.

Organisers said 16,350 started the race and 15,758 completed it. The last competitor home recorded a time of 6½ hours.

Jones, born in Liverpool and last year's AAA marathon champion, recorded a time of 2 hr 9 min 25 sec, beating his own personal best by well over a minute. Jones, who is studying in Budapest, led from start to finish and only just missed out on Ian Thompson's eight-year-old national best time by 13 seconds.

He finished nearly three minutes clear of Oyvind Dahl, from Norway, who had a tussle with Mike Gratton, of Canterbury, to take second place.

Jones has already been selected for the European championship in Athens and was helped in the first eight miles by Grenville Tuck, but then was left by himself for a solo run. He said: 'I felt pretty good up until 16 miles but then the pace began to tell and I really had to concentrate hard. I misjudged how far I had to go near the finish but I don't think I could have gone any faster.'

Mrs Smith also misjudged the pace. Her time was an improvement of 14 seconds on her previous best and she finished 6½ minutes ahead of her closest rival, Lorraine Moller from New Zealand.

Tambay has first grand prix victory after Piquet is put out

The injuries sustained in practice by Pironi (left) finished his motor-racing career. The tragedy-hit Ferrari team still won the constructors' championship with 74 points, ahead of McLaren-Ford.

By Colin Dryden at Hockenheim

PUBLISHED MONDAY 9 AUGUST

Patrick Tambay, 33, of France, scored his first Formula One victory, only three months after joining the Ferrari team, in the German Grand Prix at Hockenheim yesterday.

Disaster had hit the team on Saturday when Didier Pironi, Tambay's compatriot, was seriously injured in a crash during practice in heavy rain. Tambay joined Ferrari in May after the death of Gilles Villeneuve.

With Pironi, the world championship leader, now out of contention, John Watson, of Great Britain, in second place with 30 points, was unlucky not to improve his position.

The Ulsterman was in a comfortable third place when he crashed out of the race after his Marlboro McLaren's front suspension broke nine laps from the end. He was not hurt.

Rene Arnoux (Renault Turbo), winner of the French Grand Prix a fortnight ago, was the only driver on the same lap as Tambay at the finish.

Mixed fortunes for the turbo-engined brigade enabled Cosworth-powered cars (Keke Rosberg's Saudi Williams

and Michele Alboreto's Tyrell) to fill the next two places. Bruno Giacomelli (Alfa Romeo) was fifth and Marc Surer (Arrows) came through to sixth place from the back row.

Nelson Piquet, the world champion, was unlucky yet again. Running with half-full fuel tanks and soft tyres to enable the Brabham pit team to try out their fast refuelling and tyre-changing technique, he had built up a lead of 24 seconds after only 17 laps.

But back-marker Eliseo Salazar (ATS) collided with Piquet's Brabham Turbo at the controversial new chicane on the Ostkurve. Both drivers climbed out of their cars unhurt and, according to the race organisers, Piquet then 'hit Salazar heavily on his helmet and chest'.

Piquet said afterwards: 'That is not my normal reaction but Salazar had already cost me a hell of a lot of time. I was just too upset.'

To add to the Brabham team's misfortunes, Riccardo Patrese suffered yet another engine breakdown, this time at one-quarter distance when he was lying fourth.

Alain Prost, another of the early leaders in his Renault Turbo, also had a short race because of fuel injection problems.

With Piquet out of the race Tambay took over the lead on the 19th of the 43 laps and was able to keep Arnoux's Renault at a comfortable distance.

Brian Henton (Tyrrell) was the first British driver to finish, in seventh place, followed by Nigel Mansell (JPS Lotus), ninth, and Derek Warwick (Toleman Turbo), tenth. Tambay's victory came in only his fourth race for Ferrari and his 53rd grand prix in all.

Rossi hero again as Italians complete eclipse of Germans

By Donald Saunders in Madrid

PUBLISHED MONDAY 12 JULY

West Germany 1; Italy 3

Italy won the World Cup for the third time, at the Bernabeu Stadium in Madrid last night, scoring three goals in an exciting 24-minute second-half spell before allowing West Germany to reply only once.

But although Italy ultimately sent their supporters home glowing with pride, this was one of the worst finals in history until the last half-hour. Each side endeavoured to prevent the other from playing. Consequently gifted attacking players such as Paolo Rossi, Bruno Conti, Marco Tardelli, Karl-Heinz Rummenigge, Pierre Littbarski and Klaus Fischer were allowed little opportunity to demonstrate their art.

Within eight minutes, Graziani had been removed from the match, for good, by a heavy tackle by Dremmler. Graziani's early exit – with an injury – upset some of his

Italy celebrate after Marco Tardelli scores their second goal. Italy joined Brazil as the only other three-times winners of the World Cup.

colleagues and Dremmler became the target for a succession of rough tackles and crunching body checks.

The Germans began to retaliate, and there were times when one wondered why the ball had been taken on to the pitch. Arnaldo Coehlo, a remarkably tolerant Brazilian referee, did little to halt the kicking, tripping and charging.

Things began to come right for Italy in the second half. Their first hero was Rossi, who became the tournament's leading marksman by heading home Antonio Cabrini's centre, in the 57th minute, for his sixth goal in the finals. That goal was enough to persuade Italy to show us how well they really could play.

Although Germany replaced Dremmler with Horst Hrubesch in the 68th minute, Italy widened the gap one minute later. This time Tardelli thumped the ball into the roof of the net.

The Germans responded by pulling off Rummenigge, who clearly was not fully fit, and sending on Hansi Müller. But it was too late.

In the 81st minute Alessandro Altobelli put the trophy beyond Germany's reach by scoring Italy's third goal from a well-judged cross by Conti.

1982

269

1982

Australians overrun Britain in rugby league Test

By Paul Rylance

PUBLISHED MONDAY 22 NOVEMBER

Great Britain 6 pts; Australia 27

Five tries and six goals with only 12 men, a record-equalling sixth straight Test victory, the last three without conceding a try, and retention of the Ashes with a match to spare was the latest chapter in Australia's all-conquering tour in the second Dominion Insurance Test at Wigan on Saturday.

Add to that Mal Meninga's 15 points to bring his total in eight games to 100, Ray Price pipping all his teammates for the Man-of-the-Match award, and the failure of Britain's full complement to penetrate Australia's 25 line, and the miserable catalogue of British inadequacy is complete.

It was not a happy birthday for coach J. Whiteley, but he must shoulder some of the blame for his defenders allowing the Australians space to hit them at top speed instead of moving forward to stop them at source.

Thank goodness for Mumby. The young Bradford fullback was immaculate in defence. He saved another five tries and landed three goals from three attempts.

Nevertheless, the 23,000 crowd could not help but wonder at the brilliance of Australia and, after Meninga's sixth goal had completed the massacre, they accorded the tourists an enthusiastic ovation.

Frank Stanton, Australia's coach, was magnanimous enough to advise Britain's selectors to choose players with imagination and unpredictability for Sunday's final Test 'It is the only way to trouble our defence,' he said.

Colin Hutton, Britain's manager, said: 'They are light years ahead of us. Hopefully the Australians will force us to change our system. But there are still many people at club level who are quite satisfied to plod along.'

Surely no one will put their heads back in the sand after being shown the way out of the desert.

DID YOU KNOW?

In the men's 10,000 m in the 1982 Brisbane Commonwealth Games, Cayman Islander David Bonn was lapped twice by the field. When the winner breasted the tape he still had seven laps to complete. He ploughed on alone to finish in 41 min 21 sec – to great applause from the crowd.

By Ken Mays in Athens

PUBLISHED THURSDAY 9 SEPTEMBER

The incredible Daley Thompson, the finest all-round athlete that Britain has ever produced, won the European championships decathlon gold medal and recaptured the world record in the electrifying atmosphere of the Olympic Stadium in Athens last night.

Thompson, who had seen the record he set in Gotzis, Austria, in June, tumble to Jürgen Hingsen **(below)** last month, came back to score a total of 8,774 points, breaking the West German's best by 21 points.

So Thompson goes down into the record books as only the second Briton to complete the Grand Slam of Olympic, European and Commonwealth titles, joining long jumper Lynn Davies on the pedestal.

Astonishingly, the Greeks failed to announce to the crowd that Thompson needed just 4 min 26.5 sec in the final event, the 1,500 m, to break the world record, and they had streamed away from the stadium in their thousands.

Those who stayed behind, including hundreds

Flying the flag: after coming seventh in the 1,500 m, Thompson knew he had enough points to break the decathlon world record and take the gold.

of Union Jack-waving supporters, saw Thompson chase his way to 4 min 23.17 sec to easily surpass the necessary 612 points.

Thompson had ended the first day with a lead of 114 points over the 6 ft 6 in Hingsen, confident of winning, but uncertain that he could recapture the world record.

It was after the discus event, the seventh on the schedule, that he knew he had the chance of both and went for it like the superb athlete he is.

Yet he had looked in trouble in that event, his lead being whittled down to just over 40 points on Hingsen's third throw of 146 ft 9 in (44.74 m), but he came back with his final effort of 149 ft 2 in (45.48 m) to snatch victory and capture 108 valuable points. Thompson, who had opened the day by winning his heat of the 110-m hurdles, went on to win the pole vault with 16 ft 4¾ in (5 m) and produce 208 ft 6 in (63.56 m) in the javelin to put the record and the title within his reach.

Americans ease to final 4–1 victory in Davis Cup

By John Parsons in Grenoble
PUBLISHED MONDAY 29 NOVEMBER

Arthur Ashe, the United States tennis captain, described John McEnroe as 'the most complete tennis player of the Open era' after his outstanding contribution to America's 28th victory in the Davis Cup in Grenoble yesterday.

Few among the 15,000 French partisans privileged to view McEnroe's exciting repertoire of strokes as he and Peter Fleming beat Yannick Noah and Henri Leconte to give the United States a winning 3–0 lead in Saturday's doubles would disagree.

Such was McEnroe's eminence during a 6–3, 6–4, 9–7 victory, that in ten service games there were only 11 points against him, and not one due clearly to an error on his part, while his parade of perfectly timed touch and reflex winners was endless.

On the other hand, McEnroe and Ashe realise that this triumphant weekend alone will not automatically lift the essentially mental block which this brilliant left-hander still needs to conquer whenever he plays on clay.

The indoor court, specially laid down by the French in the hope that it might just prove a match-turning stumbling block for McEnroe, was by no means as slow as those at Roland Garros, for instance. The 32 aces by McEnroe and Noah in Friday's singles illustrated that.

'I just hope that one day John will win the French title so that he can go down with the all-time greats in winning on all surfaces,' said Ashe. 'He certainly has to win in Paris to achieve that accolade.'

In yesterday's meaningless reverse singles over the best of three sets, Noah beat Gene Meyer 6–1, 6–0 in 51 minutes, but McEnroe had too much pride to allow Leconte any such hollow satisfaction. His 6–2, 6–3 victory made the United States 4–1 overall winners.

Where this fourth Davis Cup win in five years should particularly assist McEnroe, who, as a junior, regarded clay as his best surface, is in convincing him that his inner fears are groundless.

Grisly afternoon leaves England cricketers in dire trouble

By Michael Carey in Adelaide
PUBLISHED MONDAY 13 DECEMBER

England produced another batting collapse in the third Test match at Adelaide Oval yesterday, when, after negotiating the first session without mishap, they lost eight wickets between lunch and tea.

The last seven of these went down for 35 runs in some 15 overs and so, on a largely blameless pitch, England were all out for 216 and followed on 222 behind. The immediate departure of Chris Tavare then put David Gower and Graeme Fowler under enormous pressure.

Though not without problems, they prevailed against bowlers wearying in temperatures approaching the 100 mark, and England finished 132 behind.

After today's rest day, Australia's bowlers will resume refreshed and England face a struggle to save the match which no observer could have envisaged when Allan Lamb and Gower walked in together at lunchtime.

They had not only survived an entire session together, a luxury hitherto not enjoyed by either side in this series, but by their very discipline and restraint had suggested that in these testing conditions Australia's attack might ultimately be made to look very plain.

The second ball of the afternoon removed Gower; given Lamb's growing certainty, however, and the sight of a purposeful, controlled Ian Botham, there seemed no cause for alarm until Lamb hooked at a short ball. With only another 58 required, this seemed a slight hiccough,

but two balls later Geoff Lawson produced a yorker removing Derek Randall. Miller's stroke flew off the edge to the gully where it struck a surprised Bruce Yardley on the chest. He managed to snatch up the rebound at ankle height, and three overs later reduced England to 199 for seven when Chappell, at slip, took a tumbling catch to remove Bob Taylor.

When Thomson followed, Botham, seizing on a ball of full length, failed to control his drive, and Kepler Wessels held a good low catch at mid-wicket, whereupon Thomson finished the grisly afternoon off by bowling Eddie Hemmings and Bob Willis.

Thomson took 22 wickets in the series, which Australia won 2–1. They won the third Test by 8 wickets.

1982

271

1983

Hooliganism: Dutch police switch tactics

By Colin Gibson
PUBLISHED TUESDAY 1 FEBRUARY

Football hooliganism, it seems, is no longer just a British disease but has now spread to other European countries, especially Holland, and in a much more sinister form.

The Dutch hooligan has added the bomb to his menacing armoury, and three weeks ago a fan at the Ajax versus Den Haag game in Amsterdam nearly lost his life when one was thrown.

The spectator had serious leg and stomach injuries and was only saved by the quick attentions of a policeman. Even so, he still nearly bled to death before reaching hospital, where 20 other fans were also treated for injuries after the outrage.

The Dutch Football Association, which has seen both Utrecht and Haarlem involved in major European soccer violence in the last two seasons, were so concerned by the broadening of crowd trouble, they have appointed Robert De Bakker as a security officer to try to combat the growing problem.

One of the major changes to be enforced has been the move to preventive policing in Holland. No longer are large numbers of riot and uniformed police on hand to deal with the violence when it starts.

Instead plain-clothes police are mingling with fans on trains and on the way to and inside the stadiums. One plain-clothes police officer arrested two of the people involved in the Ajax bombing. The hooligans are now facing an attempted murder charge.

'We seem to be fighting the symptoms rather than the disease itself,' says Mr De Bakker. 'It is obvious now that the causes of football hooliganism are not connected with the game. It is a social problem.

'If we in football manage to combat our part of the disease, then the problems, unless solved on a social level, will only reappear in the form of street vandalism or muggings. Football alone cannot solve the whole problem,' he added.

Sports seek more from TV

By Roger Heywood, sports correspondent
PUBLISHED WEDNESDAY 9 FEBRUARY

Sporting governing bodies want to end the 'monopoly' of the BBC and ITV in screening major events, like the FA Cup final and Test matches.

This was agreed unanimously at a meeting of the major spectator sports division of the Central Council of Physical Recreation yesterday.

The sports concerned – soccer, rugby union, cricket, golf, showjumping, motor racing, motor cycling, athletics and swimming – said 'action should be taken radically to alter the current television negotiating agreements which limit the ability to generate finance.'

With many sports suffering declining attendances and problems in raising sponsorship, cable television is seen as one way of solving financial problems.

The nine sports also said they would meet again to discuss 'the opportunities for sporting coverage which would become available if the recommendations of the Hunt inquiry into cable expansion and broadcasting policy were accepted by the government'.

Mr Peter Lawson, general secretary of the central council, said: 'British sport is in a parlous financial state. Though we welcome the expertise and dedication of the television companies that currently bring sport into the homes of the British people, we feel the current structure, which lacks a competitive edge, is injurious to the financing of sport.

'We cannot agree that sport should be singled out for monopoly arrangements. If this policy means that long-standing sacred cows must be sacrificed, then so be it. We shall be taking our case to the British public and to Parliament.'

High drama and low farce in Shergar hunt

By Kenneth Clarke and A. J. McIlroy
PUBLISHED FRIDAY 11 FEBRUARY

The hunt for the kidnapped multi-million pound stallion Shergar **(left)** continued on both sides of the Irish border yesterday amid elements of farce and high drama.

There were rumours that the horse had been killed, that its ears had been cut off and, for a change, that it had been seen trotting down a country road close to the border. None proved accurate.

In the Republic, there was an unanswered question over a 12-hour delay in the reporting of a telephoned ransom call demanding £2 million to police.

The call was taken early yesterday by Mr Ghislain Drione, manager of the Ballymany Stud near Newbridge, Co. Kildare, from which Shergar was stolen. But it was not reported until lunchtime.

According to Chief Supt. James Murphy, leading the hunt in Eire, 'there has been a language barrier. Mr Drione is a Frenchman and while he speaks reasonable English he might have had some difficulty understanding fully. But the contact made no threat about Shergar if the money was not paid.'

Police, north and south, had their most promising lead since Shergar was stolen early on Wednesday by five armed and masked men who raided the stud farm, when intermediaries in Ulster were contacted several times by a man claiming to represent the thieves.

He said the original ransom demand of £2 million was now only £40,000 – the equivalent of £1,000 for each of the 40 shares in the horse, six of them held by the Aga Khan, who also owns the stud farm.

A call was made to the *Belfast Newsletter* by a man with a 'Southern Irish accent'. He said that if any one of three English racing journalists flew to Belfast and waited at the Forum Hotel, negotiations for Shergar's release could begin.

All three went. They were Lord Oaksey of the *Daily Telegraph* and racing correspondent of the *Sunday Telegraph*, Peter Campling of the *Sun* and Derek Thompson of Thames Television.

Lord Oaksey had been contacted by the Northern Ireland intermediaries in the affair, Mr Jeremy Maxwell and his wife Judith, who train horses at Downpatrick and to whom a man using the codename Arkle made several telephone calls.

Today, acting in the belief that the Aga Khan was prepared to negotiate, Arkle telephoned the Maxwells, offering photographic proof of Shergar's captivity.

Shergar, whose current stud value is more than £10 million, was retired to stud in 1981 after he had won both the Epsom and Irish Derbys and the King George VI and Queen Elizabeth Diamond Stakes at Ascot.

DID YOU KNOW?

In March Michael Dickinson achieved one of the greatest feats in horse-racing history; he trained the first five horses home in the Cheltenham Gold Cup: Bregawn, Captain John, Wayward Lad, Silver Buck (1982 winner) and Ashley House.

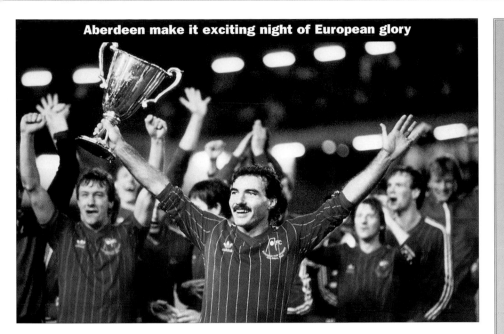

Aberdeen make it exciting night of European glory

By Denis Lowe in Gothenburg

PUBLISHED THURSDAY 12 MAY

Aberdeen 2; Real Madrid 1

John Hewitt, 20, a late and lively substitute, scored the extra-time goal against Real Madrid in rain-swept Gothenburg last night to bring Aberdeen their first European trophy and take the Cup Winners' Cup back to Scotland for the first time since 1972.

Hewitt, a Scotland Under-21 international, notched his fifth and most valuable goal of the competition with a neat diving header in the 112th minute.

So Aberdeen, who went ahead through Eric Black in the sixth minute, and then conceded a penalty for Juan Juanito to equalise, gained reward for a magnificent

Aberdeen were the sixth British club to win the Cup Winners' Cup and the first Scottish victors since Rangers defeated Moscow Dynamo in 1972.

season. They have made tremendous strides under Alex Ferguson's shrewd management and are still in the hunt for two other trophies, the Premier Division title and the Scottish Cup.

Making their first appearance in a European final, as compared to Real Madrid's 11th, Aberdeen made most of the running on a saturated pitch.

This was a triumph for teamwork as Aberdeen, blending skill with strength, mounted dangerous raids through the power supplied by Gordon Strachan and Peter Weir, outstanding in midfield and on the left wing.

Stagnation of British badminton

By a special correspondent

PUBLISHED FRIDAY 13 MAY

Badminton, probably the most popular participatory sport in England, is suffering stagnation as a spectator and a readership sport.

Sponsors this season have been lost, one major event has been dropped, and no domestic grand prix has been revived. Yet this vacuum coincides with the start of the game's most lucrative international grand prix – sponsored by Pro-Kennex for one million dollars.

The contrast between badminton in an international and a British setting recently caused several well-known players to complain publicly to the Badminton Association of England.

Soon afterwards, the association's chief executive, Air Vice-Marshal G. C. Lamb, announced that he had been given supreme powers to put things right. Shortly after

that the association parted company with its development and publicity officer.

One of the big problems has been that there has been no regular way for the most talented players to parade their skills in Britain, and therefore none for the young players to ply their trade against the most talented.

Lamb himself is now overseas negotiating a sponsorship, but there is still no publicity officer, and the sport's media coverage, at an important stage of its development, inevitably deteriorates.

Supreme powers or not, the chief executive has been unable to make an appointment. Part of the reason for that lies with the association's fiercest and best known critic, Gillian Gilks, the former world No. 1 and winner of ten All-England titles. Mrs Gilks' High Court case against representatives of the Badminton Association will be heard at the beginning of June, and the loser – whoever it may be – must be prepared to pay large costs.

1983

273

1983

Nelson edges home from Watson

By Michael Williams in Pittsburgh
PUBLISHED TUESDAY 21 JUNE

Larry Nelson yesterday became one of the more surprising winners of the United States Open when he completed the last three holes of his interrupted fourth round at Oakmont in level par.

It gave him a 67 for a total of 280, four under par, and victory by a stroke from Tom Watson, the defending Open champion.

Watson had been level with Nelson overnight but dropped one stroke, taking a five at the 17th.

Though the whole thing took only 55 minutes, after a severe thunderstorm on Sunday evening had delayed the climax, it was an eventful hour for Nelson and Watson.

Both had been in position long before the siren sounded at 10 am on a still, damp morning, and Nelson promptly hit a four-wood to the 16th green before holing a putt of fully 20 yards for two.

Watson, who had resumed action with an approach putt on the 14th green, was consequently immediately behind but, when Nelson took three putts on the 18th green for a five, the odds were very much on a play-off.

However, barely had Nelson, his shoulders drooping in disappointment, turned to look at the scoreboard than Watson missed a short putt at the 17th.

The defending champion bunkered his approach at a hole where he must have been thinking in terms of a birdie and, though he came out well, the putt that would have kept him level slid by.

That left Watson with a three to tie but he went through the green with a seven-iron second shot at the 18th and only got his four by sinking a long putt. He was consequently round in 69.

It was a remarkable win by Nelson, who now adds the US Open to the PGA championship he won at Atlanta two years ago. His final round of 65 and 67 were almost unbelievable golf on this course, particularly by someone without a shred of current form.

MILESTONES

The first professional American Football match to be staged in Britain was held at Wembley Stadium. The Minnesota Vikings and the St Louis Cardinals battled for the Global Cup; the Minnesota Vikings won 28–10.

Ruthless Indians punish confident West Indies

By Michael Carey
PUBLISHED MONDAY 27 JUNE

India won the Prudential Cup for the first time at Lord's on Saturday, beating the holders, West Indies, by 43 runs, and in the process turning what had seemed a straightforward and predictable final into one of increasing drama and, ultimately, much emotion.

They were put in and bowled out for 183 in 55 overs, which, though not the lowest winning total in a Lord's final, looked inadequate against the West Indies' batting on a good pitch.

Indeed, as West Indies swept effortlessly — a shade too effortlessly, perhaps — to 57 for two from only 14 overs with Viv Richards at his most imperious, it looked as if the anniversary of Custer's Last Stand was to have an inappropriate ending with the Indians put to flight.

At that point, Richards, who had struck Madan Lal for three fours in one over, paid the price for either underestimating the merits of the medium-pacer or for losing his concentration when Clive Lloyd called for a runner.

The West Indies captain had aggravated his strained groin at the start of his innings and when, in increasing discomfort, he failed to time an off-drive soon afterwards they were 66 for five.

By the end of the game India's dream had become a glorious reality. In a remarkable game no batsman made 50, no bowler took more than three wickets, yet the outcome was a perfect climax to a competition regularly punctuated by the unlikely and the unexpected.

With Prudential's sponsorship of £500,000 now over, the competition's future will be debated this week by the International Cricket Conference, who will no doubt have in front of them confirmation from the Test and County Cricket Board that they would be happy to stage it again provided financial arrangements are adequate.

Kapil Dev's triumphant team celebrating victory (below), and (above) lifting the Prudential World Cup.

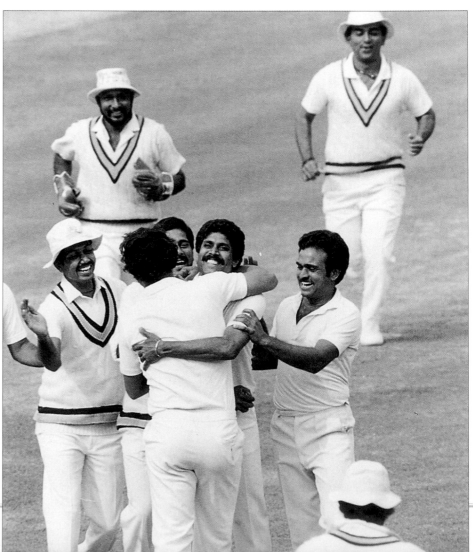

Mighty Moses puts rivals in place

By Ken Mays in Helsinki
PUBLISHED WEDNESDAY 10 AUGUST

Edwin Moses, the American who brings a combination of poetry in motion to athletics that has seldom been seen in the sport, stretched his unbeaten run to six years and 81 races when he won the 400-m hurdles gold medal at the world championships in Helsinki yesterday.

Moses, who last tasted serious defeat in August 1977, recorded 47.50 sec, the ninth fastest time ever, and he has been responsible for eight of those since he sprang from obscurity to win the 1976 Olympic title in Montreal.

The world record-holder from Laguna Beach, California, who takes the hurdles as though they were not there, literally destroyed the opposition by the 300-m mark, leaving them trailing by ten metres at the line.

The man who followed him home for the silver medal was Harold Schmid, the West German who was the last man to beat him, but there was never any danger of that yesterday with Russian Alex Kharlov snatching the bronze medal.

Upset about missing the 1980 Olympics through the American boycott, and then all of last season because of injury, Moses, 28, is now hoping for another 19 wins so that he can switch to racing over 800 m.

Before the event began yesterday the three Americans who reached the final went into a huddle for which Moses

Jubilation for Moses after another 400-m hurdle victory. The 1976 Olympic champion dominated this event for ten years from 1977 to 1987.

explained: 'We were praying that we did not get injured and wishing everyone in the race best of luck.'

But for his two colleagues who had followed him off the final bend, luck deserted them, and André Phillips was fifth and Dave Lee sixth.

Lewis grabs two more golds and a world record

By Ken Mays in Helsinki
PUBLISHED THURSDAY 11 AUGUST

Carl Lewis, the giant American, and Jarmila Kratochilova, the Czechoslovak girl with the bodybuilder's physique, became the golden athletes of the world championships in Helsinki yesterday when they added three more titles and two world records to their earlier spoils.

Lewis, 22, a Houston student who had won the 100 m on Monday, interchanged between the long jump and the sprint relay to come away with two more golds, as well as a world record in the latter.

He ran the opening heat to qualify for the relay before dashing across the track to produce a first leap of 28 ft ³/₄ in (8.55 m) that destroyed all his rivals.

He then teamed up with Emmit King, Willie Gault and Calvin Smith to run away with the relay gold in a world record 37.86 seconds.

Lewis had been given a good enough lead over the Italians, anchored by Pietro Mennea, the Russians and the East Germans. But the sight of his powerful frame and unbelievable long strides had the 55,000 crowd

urging him home and even producing a banner that read 'Carl Lewis for president'.

Miss Kratochilova, one of seven children from Prague, missed the bus as an eight-year-old on the first step of her athletics career, arriving late for a junior race but taking part and winning the senior event.

There was no chance yesterday of her missing anything; she waited until the last bend to outpace her rivals over the final 100 metres, crossing the line in 47.99 sec to beat the previous best of 49.15 sec set by East Germany's Marita Koch. Tatiana Kocembova and Maria Pinigina came home behind her.

With the 800-m title won on Tuesday, she now goes for a third gold in the 4 x 400 m. 'It has been so tough I would have preferred to go home,' she said. Her rivals wish she had.

Lewis makes an explosive start in the 100-m heats.

SPORT IN BRIEF

LAWN TENNIS
John McEnroe wins the Wimbledon men's singles title for the second time, having met New Zealander Chris Lewis in the final. Lewis has exceeded expectations to reach this stage, but McEnroe is too strong for him and wins in straight sets, 6–2, 6–2, 6–2.

GOLF
Tom Watson wins the British Open for the second year running and the fifth time in total. He has now won the title on five different courses: at Carnoustie in 1975, Turnberry in 1977, Muirfield in 1980, Troon in 1982, and at Royal Birkdale this year.

CRICKET
England play New Zealand in a four-match Test series. England win the series 3–1, taking the final Test by 165 runs, thanks to centuries from Ian Botham and Allan Lamb. When Richard Hadlee bowls England tail-ender Norman Cowans in the second innings, it is the New Zealander's 200th Test wicket.

ATHLETICS
The International Amateur Athletic Federation hold the first world championships in Helsinki, Finland, in the Olympic Stadium. Juha Vaatainen of Finland wins gold in the 10,000 m; in the women's javelin competition, Finnish thrower Tiina Lillak, willed on by the home crowd, throws 70.82 m in the final round to snatch gold from Fatima Whitbread of Britain.

1983

1983

'Superman' Daley Thompson

By Ken Mays in Helsinki
PUBLISHED MONDAY 15 AUGUST

Daley Thompson (below) has once more proved that he is without equal in the decathlon when he added the world championship gold medal – the first for Britain – to the Olympic, European and double Commonwealth titles that he already holds, in Helsinki on Saturday.

Thompson disposed of a three-pronged West German attack with little difficulty, winning by 105 points from Jürgen Hingsen, the world record-holder, with a total of 8,666 points.

But, according to Thompson, the West Germans helped bring defeat on themselves by not talking to him in the athletes' village, thus motivating him at a time when he most needed it.

Thompson lost points on the 1,500 m, the final discipline of the ten which stretched over two days. But he felt that once he had moved into the front on Friday in the opening event, the 100 m, he would not lose.

'It all went better than I expected,' he explained, 'because at one stage there was a chance I would not compete. But once it started I was not in any pain that was too much for me.'

Around Christmas, Thompson will be off to his usual training ground in San Diego. He will compete in only one more decathlon, in the United States, before defending his Olympic title in Los Angeles next year.

'Winning the Olympics would be special because only one man, Bob Mathias, has done it twice before, and I will still be young enough to attempt the hat trick in Korea in 1988.'

Unless a country can produce another superman like Thompson, the Briton is unlikely to have any serious competition. In the past five years he has beaten every challenger – not once but five times in Hingsen's case.

Cram takes gold to leave Ovett back at fourth

By Ken Mays in Helsinki
PUBLISHED MONDAY 15 AUGUST

Steve Cram, once the pretender to the throne of Brendan Foster as Gateshead's favourite son, followed the advice of the old master to become the 1,500-m gold medallist on the closing day of the world championships in Helsinki yesterday.

Cram, already the European and Commonwealth champion, is now no longer haunted by the shadow of Sebastian Coe and Steve Ovett. He produced a scintillating last 100 metres of 13.2 seconds to beat off American Steve Scott, with Said Aouita of Morocco third and Ovett fourth.

The time of 3 min 41.59 sec reflected the slowness of the earlier pace, but for Cram it did not matter as he took command after the 200-m mark to outrun the rest like the champion he is.

Cram, who spent several days training with Foster, now working for BBC television, said: 'I took Brendan's advice on how to handle the race and it paid off.

'I kept thinking that the others were going to come up. I felt that I still had a bit extra left if I needed it, but you never know how much until you're tested.'

After winning the 1,500m, Cram, a Newcastle Polytechnic student, declared: 'I don't care if I never break a world record in my life; those with records would love to have what I have got now.'

Europe lose thrilling Ryder Cup by just a point

By Michael Williams in Palm Beach, Florida
PUBLISHED MONDAY 17 OCTOBER

The United States yesterday retained the Ryder Cup in the most thrilling finish there has ever been in America, beating Europe by a single point, $14^1/_2$ – $13^1/_2$ at PGA National – and never have the Americans been more relieved.

Throughout the three days there was never more than a point between the two sides and, right until those last few throbbing minutes, Europe were in with a chance. They faltered only at the last gasp when a tie, at the very least, seemed to be within their reach.

Level at the beginning of the day at 8–8, the Americans took the final series of singles $6^1/_2$–$5^1/_2$, and, for Europe, it was very much a case of so near but so far.

With ten of the day's 12 singles completed, the two sides were still locked together, at 13–13, but José-Maria Canizares, from Spain, was one up with one to play against Lanny Wadkins, and Bernard Gallacher one down with two to play against Tom Watson.

Had it stayed that way it would have been a tie, as it had been 14 years ago at Royal Birkdale, and if only Gallacher could have drawn level with Watson, Europe were even in a position to have won.

But it was not to be. Canizares, earlier three up, was well placed just short of the 18th green in two shots.

But his pitch to a flag tucked behind a bunker was marginally under-hit and the Americans jumped feet into the air when Wadkins pitched his third shot to within a yard of the hole.

Poor Canizares could not hole his chip or subsequent putt, and that half-point was a crucial loss.

For all the enormous European disappointment, not least for their captain, Tony Jacklin, who had got just about the best possible out of his troops, it had nevertheless been a most gallant try.

DID YOU KNOW?

When tennis player Bill Scanlon beat Marcos Hocevar 6–2, 6–0 in Florida, he did not lose a single point in the final set. It was believed to be the only time in a professional tennis tournament that a player has won all 24 points in a set.

Perth celebrates

By our Perth correspondent
PUBLISHED WEDNESDAY 28 SEPTEMBER

As Perth began to recover from an almighty but glorious hangover and lack of sleep yesterday, it heard that a successor to *Australia II*, the America's Cup winner, is already on the drawing board.

Mr Stephen War, who built *Australia II* and the first *Australia*, said there would be changes in design because of problems with the victorious 12-metre yacht, which he built in his own boatyard in the suburb of Cottesloe.

He believed new yacht plans would give a future Australia greater speed to fight off challengers attempting to wrest the America's Cup from the Royal Perth Yacht Club in 1986 or 1987.

Mr Alan Bond, 46, the multi-millionaire Perth businessman who headed the winning syndicate, reached Australia on a migrant boat from England 32 years ago. By 26 he had made a million in land deals. He lost it and fought his way back.

He has been determined to win the America's Cup since he made his first attempt in 1974. He had a metal plate placed in the Royal Perth Yacht Club and said that was where the cup would reside. His prediction will soon come true and the cup will be bolted into place there.

The euphoria in Perth is still high. New parties are breaking out and champagne and Bond's beer – the local Swan brew – is flowing swiftly.

Piquet reigns but Renault to battle on

By Colin Dryden in Kyalami
PUBLISHED MONDAY 17 OCTOBER

Before the cars were packed away after the finish of the South African Grand Prix at Kyalami on Saturday, the Brabham-BMW turbo of Nelson Piquet **(below)** was carrying the world champion's coveted No. 1.

The transfer had been unpeeled from the Williams-Honda turbo car of Keke Rosberg, the previous champion, and handed over in a little private ceremony.

For the last four seasons the world championship has been held alternately by drivers from the British Williams and Brabham teams – Alan Jones, Piquet, Rosberg and now Piquet again.

To the chagrin of the French Renault-Elf team the challenge of Alain Prost, who had led Piquet by two points before the start of the final race, had ended in the pits before the halfway mark.

Despite having started the turbo-charged revolution at Silverstone in 1977 and the expenditure of many millions of francs, Renault have not produced the first French world champion.

Undaunted, Jean Sage, the Renault team spokesman, said: 'Naturally we are very disappointed but there is no question of our withdrawing from grand prix racing – we want that championship.'

With the fine form of Piquet, who will have a new Brabham-BMW within days for testing, plus the promise of the Williams-Honda and the McLaren-TAG turbo teams, Renault's task now seems even harder.

Piquet's race for the championship was planned meticulously by the Brabham team and went like clockwork. The 1981 world champion leapt to the front from the start, followed by the eventual winner, his teammate Riccardo Patrese.

The two blue and white Brabhams were obviously the fastest cars on the hot, dusty circuit near Johannesburg.

1983

1984

'Beagle' keeps Green on top

By Alan Smith
PUBLISHED MONDAY 16 APRIL

Lucinda Green rejuvenated the 14-year-old Beagle Bay to score an unprecedented sixth victory in the Badminton three-day event, going clear in the show jumping to clinch success after leading from the start.

But she immediately stamped upon the suggestion that the grey might be a possible reserve horse for the Olympic Games. 'He is brilliant, but he is too old,' she said. 'It will have to be Regal Realm or nothing.'

History repeated itself for Mrs Green. Twelve months ago she won the Whitbread Trophy on her world champion Regal Realm with Beagle Bay fifth, and yesterday she again also filled fifth place with Village Gossip, who is two years older than Beagle Bay and the doyen of the S. R. Direct Mail team.

Since John Burbridge's firm took over the sponsorship of Mrs Green and her husband in the winter of 1982–83, so preventing their enforced retirement, he has had exceptional rewards – including two Badminton wins and a European championship silver medal.

DID YOU KNOW?

In the men's slalom in the winter Olympics at Sarajevo, American twins Phil and Steve Mahre both competed for the title. Amazingly they came first and second; Phil Mahre claimed America's first gold medal in this event.

Highbury face fences order over violence

By Michael Calvin
PUBLISHED MONDAY 16 APRIL

Highbury, scene of the latest outbreak of crowd violence, has little prospect of remaining an FA Cup semi-final venue unless fences are erected to control aggressive team supporters.

The Football Association will, in June, consider the implications of Saturday's disturbance, when police with dogs and horses struggled to separate hooligans who staged running battles on the pitch after Everton's victory over Southampton.

Referee George Courtney was in the dressing room at the time of the incidents, so will have little to offer the inquiry led by Bert Millichip, chairman of the FA. But A. D. 'Mac' McMullan, his vice-chairman, will provide eyewitness evidence.

The supporters were successfully segregated, but could invade the pitch with ease before celebrations turned sour in a sadly familiar way.

Mr McMullan, who saw the trouble from the directors' box, admitted the FA cannot order Arsenal to erect fences. But he said: 'We can consider whether Highbury should be awarded a semi-final if there are no fences in place. Few major venues these days do not have fences and I have raised the point often that there is a risk without them. It will obviously be a central part of our deliberations.'

By James O'Brien
PUBLISHED TUESDAY 17 APRIL

Thousands lined roads and crowded into the Old Market Square, Nottingham, last night to give Jayne Torvill and Christopher Dean a 'home town' welcome.

The world and Olympic ice-dancing champions were unable to make themselves heard on a balcony at the Council House.

Torvill and Dean perform their dazzling *Bolero* routine at the European championships.

The public climbed onto any available vantage point and cheered the city's two idols who arrived at the Council House to the music of Ravel's *Bolero*.

Christopher, a former policeman in Nottingham, and Jayne, who worked in an insurance office in the city, were both bronzed after their holiday in the Caribbean. Later at a reception Christopher said: 'This was a terrific welcome. The last time there were crowds like this I was in a policeman's uniform trying to hold them back.'

The cheering and chanting crowds drowned their attempts to thank their fans for their support. Later they attended a civic reception attended by 300 people.

Four years ago while they were both still at work, before their ice-skating talents enthralled millions of people all over the world, they received an £8,000 grant from the city council. This was followed by two annual grants of £14,000 each, and last year it was increased to £18,000 to cover inflation.

The money has enabled the couple to undertake the full-time training required to make them amateur world champions. A council official said last night that the couple would not have achieved such success without it. 'It has paid off for the city,' he added, 'incredibly so.'

Fullback Hewson kicks 19 points

By a special correspondent in Auckland
PUBLISHED MONDAY 25 JUNE

New Zealand's fullback Alan Hewson proved the difference as the All Black rugby union team beat France 31–18 in a free-flowing Test to take the series 2–0 on Saturday.

Jean-Patrick Lescarboura, the French fly half who set a goal-kicking record in the Five Nations championship, missed eight attempts at goal, but Hewson grabbed 19 points from five penalties and two conversions.

The first half was marked by scrappy play and the scoring was dominated by penalties. Hewson put the All Blacks 6–0 up after 13 minutes, converting two penalties given for French rough play.

Bruce Smith took it to 10–0, scoring a try by the posts when a long Hewson penalty fell short, and Hewson converted two other penalty attempts.

New Zealand appeared to have the game well wrapped up when captain Andy Dalton ran in for a try converted by Hewson to make it 22–6, but the French came alive and Philippe Sella cut through on the inside near the All Black line, flicked to Lescarboura on the inside, who went over for his first try.

Hewson took the score to 25–10 with another penalty, but France went back on the attack, marching the All Black pack back in a scrum near the line to allow scrum half Pierre Berbizier to come through on the blind side and switch it again to Lescarboura for his second try, bringing the score to 25–14.

With ten minutes remaining, France won a line-out on their goal and, instead of kicking clear, Serge Blanco and Sella attempted to run inside the French goal area, but Sella was put down, the ball ran free, and Warwick Taylor crunched down to score the All Blacks' third try, putting them ahead 31–14.

French triumph is boost for soccer

By Donald Saunders in Paris
PUBLISHED THURSDAY 28 JUNE
France 2; Spain 0

France scored a major triumph for the future of soccer at the Parc des Princes in Paris last night overcoming fierce Spanish resistance to win the European championship for the first time.

Under the enlightened management of Michel Hidalgo, the French have remained in the forefront of the move away from the sterile, defensive school of soccer – despite cruel setbacks.

So, this victory – greeted with a fervour few European stadiums have seen or heard since the war – will surely advance the cause of those trying to turn soccer back into a game players and spectators can enjoy.

Yet, despite the apparent decisiveness of the margin of victory, this was neither a great performance nor a good final. Indeed, France were given a generous helping-hand by Luis Arconada, the luckless Spanish captain and goalkeeper.

In the 57th minute, Arconda got down smartly at the far post to a free kick from Michel Platini – then allowed the ball to trickle through his arms into the net. That was just about Platini's sole contribution to this disappointing final. Like so many of his colleagues, this great footballer failed to find his true touch on the most important night in his international career.

For a long time, France allowed the hard-tackling of the Spaniards to throw them out of their stride.

No doubt, French supporters will find poetic justice in the fact that this all-important first goal came from a free kick. Yet, although some of the Spaniards' football reached the depths of cynicism for which their League is notorious, they also produced some excellent attacking.

However, once Platini had put them in front, they began to demonstrate the skill and imagination which has made them Europe's outstanding team during the past two years.

Spain responded with great spirit and their fair share of skill during the exciting closing stages but, despite the replacement of Julio Alberto, they could not find the target.

Heading for victory: Platini towers above the defence. He scored a record nine goals in the championship.

SPORT IN BRIEF

AMERICAN FOOTBALL
On 22 January in Tampa the Los Angeles Raiders take on the holders, the Washington Redskins, for the Super Bowl. The Redskins are unable to hang on to the title as the Raiders win by the biggest margin in the history of the competition, 38–9. The Raiders' running back Marcus Allen wins the Most Valuable Player award.

FOOTBALL
Liverpool **(below)** record their fourth successive victory in the League Cup when they beat Everton 1–0 in a replay after the first game finishes 0–0. Their previous victories had come over Manchester United in 1983, Tottenham Hotspur in 1982 and West Ham in 1981.

1984

1984

Ballesteros is champion with flair and dash

By Michael Williams
PUBLISHED MONDAY 23 JULY

When it came down to it Severiano Ballesteros had the shots and Tom Watson did not, as the Spaniard **(below)**, finding again all his old flair and dash, won the Open championship for the second time in five years over the Old Course at St Andrews yesterday.

But finishing with a four at the dreaded 17th, his first there indeed of the week, and a birdie three at the last for a final round of 69, Ballesteros, with a 12-under-par total of 276, beat Watson and Bernhard Langer, who tied second, by two strokes.

Watson – the principal figure with Ballesteros on this captivating final afternoon before more of the enormous crowds that helped to make this a thoroughly memorable Open championship – on the other hand finished with a five and then a four for 73.

That was the difference between them, just two holes, as they slugged it out shot for shot, first one and then the other in the lead until they moved a line abreast with only six holes to play.

And all the time, close on their heels, waiting for a slip that in the end came only from Watson, was Langer as he dogged the steps of the two front-runners and, with a three at the last, caught Watson at the last gasp.

As I wrote before a ball had been hit, 'one never can tell with Ballesteros' and though he came to St Andrews short of both form and confidence, he leaves it having set a record aggregate for the Old Course, beating by two strokes Carl Nagle's 278 in the Centenary Open in 1960.

'It is a funny game, even a strange one,' said Ballesteros, once he had calmed down after his joy at holing that birdie putt on the 18th green. What put him on the right lines again was, it seems, two practice rounds with Jaime Gonzalez and Vicente Fernandez.

They told him that he was swinging 'round the ball rather than through it' and a new light dawned in the mind of Seve Ballesteros. While he had been moody for much of the year, some of the old humour began again to emerge.

England sag as Marshall takes five for 35

By Michael Carey at the Oval
PUBLISHED SATURDAY 11 AUGUST

England underwent their ordeal by fire at the hands of the West Indies fast bowlers in the fifth Cornhill Test at the Oval yesterday and had their work cut out to make 162 all out, the tourists finishing 43 runs ahead with all second innings wickets standing.

Every run had to be grittily earned, not least against Malcolm Marshall who, bowling with great pace, took five for 35, but also must have gone close to transgressing the bounds of legality by use of the short-pitched delivery.

No warning under Law 42 was forthcoming, and on a pitch that afforded pace and bounce, England's innings followed an uneven course from the moment Graeme Fowler retired hurt with a bruised forearm early on.

He returned to make the highest score, 31, but the loss of Ian Botham and Allan Lamb in five deliveries to Marshall effectively ended England's hope of a lead, and now it may be the turn of their bowlers to toil.

Paul Terry, batting with a broken arm in the fourth Test. Terry was one of the victims of the West Indian fast bowlers Joel Garner, Michael Holding, Malcolm Marshall and Eldine Baptiste, in the 5–0 series 'blackwash'.

Thompson lets record slip in stroll to gold

By Ken Mays in Los Angeles
PUBLISHED SATURDAY 11 AUGUST

Daley Thompson proved without doubt that he is the greatest all-round athlete the world has seen when he won the Olympic gold medal in the decathlon for the second time in Los Angeles on Thursday.

Thompson amassed a total of 8,797 points that left his greatest rival, Jürgen Hingsen, the West German and world record-holder, 123 points adrift at the end of the ten-event competition.

But Thompson mystified his supporters by running such a slapdash 1,500 m to finish off two days of hard work that he missed taking the world record by a fraction.

In what appeared to be total disregard of what he achieved in nine previous disciplines, Thompson ran like a jogger on a training spin to record 4 min 35 sec in sixth place, a time that cost him the record by one point and one-tenth of a second.

With a personal best 4 min 20.1 sec, Thompson had only to show interest in the record to have broken it for the fourth time, yet he ambled nonchalantly round the track and then had the audacity to look at the clock in disbelief when he found he had not cracked it.

At a press conference afterwards in front of possibly the biggest gathering to see an athlete, except that commanded by Carl Lewis, Thompson denied that he had come to America to set a record, and said that the gold medal was his sole target.

'I believe that I can take the world record anytime, but what I have won here has been worth the hours of seclusion and all the training I have put in. Getting the record would have been an extra, but it was not that important.'

Thompson said that his only thought in the 1,500 m was that 'the sooner I got it over, the sooner I could do the lap of honour'.

DID YOU KNOW?

The 5–0 series victory by the West Indies cricket team over England was sandwiched between six consecutive defeats of Australia. The West Indies' 11-match run of victories was the longest winning sequence in Test cricket history.

British athletes reach finals in Los Angeles

By Ken Mays in Los Angeles
PUBLISHED SATURDAY 11 AUGUST

Britain's big three, Sebastian Coe, the 1980 Olympic 1,500-m champion, Steve Cram, the world champion, and Steve Ovett the world record-holder, all won through to today's final of the Blue Riband event in Los Angeles last night.

Coe qualified by finishing third in the first semi-final behind Abascal, of Spain, in 3 min 35.71 sec. In the second race Cram raced into first place in 3 min 36.31 sec, with Ovett fourth.

Just before the semi-finals there was a shock when Joachim Cruz, the Brazilian winner of the 800-m gold, withdrew from the event, apparently because of influenza.

Shirley Strong, the Commonwealth Games champion from Manchester, won her way through to the 100-m hurdles final when she finished second in her heat to Kim Turner of the United States. Miss Strong was never in any danger of not reaching the final.

For Miss Strong, who finished fifth in the world championships in Helsinki last year, her qualifying was a welcome relief, because she had been eliminated at the semi-final stage in Moscow four years ago.

Britain storm back to take hockey bronze

By Chris Moore in Los Angeles
PUBLISHED MONDAY 13 AUGUST

David Whitaker, the Great Britain hockey coach, believes he can pinpoint the precise moment when he realised that his side, losing 2–1 to Australia in their final match of the Los Angeles Olympics, could still win the bronze medal.

'It was about seven minutes before half-time,' said Mr Whitaker. 'We were taking a tremendous hammering but I thought we could still beat them if we weathered the storm.'

Britain staged an exciting second-half revival to beat Australia, once considered near-certainties for the Olympic title, 3–2 to take their first medal of any colour since 1952.

Many feel that the arrival of Richard Leman and Kulbir Bhaura as second-half substitutes provided the turning point.

The superb goal-line stop by Sam Martin from Walsh in the seventh minute of the second half was also a major factor. If Australia had gone 3–1 ahead at that time the bronze medal would have slipped beyond Britain's grasp.

But Britain played as they had done since arriving in Los Angeles, with determination, knowing that they had to produce something special to take home a medal.

After Richard Dodds, fending off two defenders and Neil Snowden, the goalkeeper, had opened the scoring for Britain from a fourth-minute short corner, Britain had their backs to the wall as the Australians threw everything into attack.

They forced 13 short corners by Britain's defence, positioning superbly and covering well, held firm until the ninth Australian attempt in the 18th minute, when Davies at last found the gap and slammed his shot home.

Ten minutes later Parmore put Australia ahead with a first-time shot from a Ric Charlesworth free-hit.

But the crowd of 13,000, expecting to see the Australian goal-machine move into even higher gear, were in for a shock. In the second half it was Britain's turn to put the pressure on from short corners, with Paul Barber driving home the equaliser in the 48th minute.

With ten minutes left and Leman and Steve Batchelor, the British wingers, tantalising the Australian defence, yet another short corner led to the winner from Sean Kerly, Britain's leading Olympic marksman.

An intricate move involving Batchelor and Bhaura ended with Kerly tipping his shot over Snowden and into the net. 'I mis-hit my shot,' Kerly confessed afterwards. 'It was the best mis-hit of his life,' countered Roger Self, the team manager. Britain ended the Olympics as they had begun — as the surprise team of the tournament.

1984

1984

Budd returns with no blame attached

By Ken Mays

PUBLISHED MONDAY 13 AUGUST

Zola Budd, the little girl who came to the Los Angeles Olympics with the idea of gaining a medal, will return to Britain today cleared of blame in one of the most controversial incidents in a modern Olympics.

Miss Budd, 18, who was eventually to finish seventh in the 3,000 m, had to go through the trauma of being booed by a hostile crowd after Mary Decker, the American darling, had fallen. Miss Budd was then disqualified for causing the incident. But after enough TV reruns of the clash to make one giddy, little Zola was reinstated to her proper position.

She was accused of cutting in too soon on the American girl who then ran her spikes into Zola's left leg almost causing the Briton to go over as Decker herself crashed onto the grass verge.

Miss Decker was clearly upset that Zola had 'tripped her,' which was strange when she had been behind.

Drama on the track: Budd (centre) and Decker (right) before their controversial clash in the 3,000 m.

Several girls further back showed little sympathy for the American by saying that she should have avoided trouble, instead of trying to get through on the inside.

Miss Budd returned to the athletics private area in tears and was then whisked away by those most interested in her welfare, namely a Fleet Street newspaper.

The American audience were almost equally upset as Miss Decker and Miss Budd, but then they have achieved the almost daunting task of being even more biased than the crowds in Moscow four years ago.

The incident overshadowed the fact that Miss Decker was not certain to win even if she had stayed on her feet, for I doubt whether she could have beaten the tough Maricica Puica, from Romania, who took the gold.

MILESTONES

The inaugural European football championship for women took place in 1984. The two-legged final was contested in Gothenburg and Luton between England and Sweden. The tie went into penalties, and Sweden won the penalty shoot-out 4–3.

Carl Lewis takes four Olympic golds

By Ken Mays

PUBLISHED MONDAY 13 AUGUST

Carl Lewis succeeded in establishing himself as the greatest athlete in American track-and-field history when he completed his schedule of four gold medals and shared in the only world record of the Los Angeles Olympics on Saturday.

Lewis, who had earlier won the 100 m and 200 m as well as the long jump, finished off his magnificent achievement by anchoring the 4 x 100-m relay team to the gold and world record of 37.83 sec.

So Lewis, 23, had emulated the feat of Jesse Owens at the Berlin Olympics in 1936 of winning four titles, but the similarity will end there, for Lewis is likely to be the most sought-after athlete in the history of the sport with about £7,600,000 to be earned.

'If I can make 50 dollars or 50,000 dollars it does not make any difference. I have four golds and nobody can take that away from me. I have the same feeling for Jesse Owens, he is still the legend, I'm just a person,' he said. 'I am very exhausted,' he went on, 'but I am not injured in any way.'

Star of the Los Angeles Olympics: Carl Lewis's four-medal haul was only surpassed by the 17-year-old Romanian gymnast, Ecaterina Szabó, who gained four golds and one silver.

Lauda takes world championship by half a point

By a special correspondent in Estoril

PUBLISHED MONDAY 22 OCTOBER

Niki Lauda, of Austria, won the world drivers' championship by half a point when he finished second to Alain Prost, of France, his Marlboro-McLaren teammate, in the Portuguese Grand Prix at Estoril yesterday.

'I want to win the championship for a fourth time,' said Lauda, after describing the race as the hardest he had driven. 'The back-markers were more difficult than I can ever remember.'

Lauda was champion in 1975 and 1977 and was badly burned at the old Nürburgring in 1976, being given the last rites. He retired in 1979 but returned to grand prix racing in 1982.

Alain Prost, who finished first in the Portuguese Grand Prix – and in six other grands prix during the season – was second to Lauda in the drivers' championship.

Prost started on the front row of the grid yesterday and Lauda had to work his way up from 11th, needing second place to win the title if Prost won the race.

Lauda's half a point margin was the smallest in the drivers' world championship since the series began 34 years ago, and a Frenchman has still to win it.

Lauda said his car was not right during Saturday's practice but he was untroubled after an engine change after yesterday morning's warm-up.

Prost drove impeccably and forcefully to take over the lead after nine laps from Keke Rosberg, who passed Nelson Piquet and Prost at the start in his Williams.

Melville given captaincy on England rugby union debut

By John Mason

PUBLISHED MONDAY 22 OCTOBER

Nigel Melville, the resolute survivor of a string of depressing setbacks in the past 20 months, will captain England against Australia at Twickenham on Saturday week, his international debut. He is 23.

Not since January, 1947, when Joe Mycock led England against Wales, has an Englishman been captain on the occasion of his first cap.

Melville, of Wasps, Yorkshire and the North, is one of five new caps in England's side, the others being Rob Lozowski (Wasps), Stuart Barnes (Bristol) and the Bath forwards Gareth Chilcott and Nigel Redman.

Compared with England's last international match – the defeat by South Africa on 9 June – there are 12 changes. Only Gary Pearce, tight-head, John Hall, flanker,

and Chris Butcher, No. 8 reappear.

Ironically, Richard Hill, who did not cease in his efforts on England's behalf throughout a difficult summer tour, is among those to go. But he does become Melville's deputy at scrum half.

While Hill remains in contention for the foreseeable future, John Scott, England's captain on tour and again against the President's XV on Sept 29, steps down after 34 caps. He does so at his own request.

The contribution of Scott in all capacities – he first played in a national trial when 17 – has been vigorously wholehearted. His loyalty to those he approves is legend. Those he does not, know so.

The rise of Chilcott and Redman, who was in a state of delighted shock yesterday, can be linked to the continuing successes, discipline and organisation of the Bath club.

SPORT IN BRIEF

FOOTBALL
Tottenham Hotspur reach the UEFA Cup final, where they play Anderlecht. After two legs the score is level at 2–2 but Spurs win the penalty shoot-out 4–3. Danny Thomas misses for Spurs, but neither Morten Olsen nor Gudjohnsen can beat Spurs' keeper, Tony Parks.

HORSE RACING
In June the running of the Epsom Derby brings a surprise when Secreto, ridden by Christy Roche and trained by David O'Brien, wins the race at 14–1. The hot favourite, 8–11 El Gran Señor, only manages second.

LAWN TENNIS
In an awesome display of tennis, the Wimbledon men's championship is won by John McEnroe. In the final he destroys Jimmy Connors 6–1, 6–1, 6–2, echoing Connors' destruction of Rosewall in the final of 1974.

GOLF
Lee Trevino wins the US PGA championship at Shoal Creek when he completes the course in a four-round total of 273 strokes, having played every round in fewer than 70 shots. It is his first major win since he won the same tournament in 1974.

CRICKET
England tour India during the winter. Three days after they arrive the Indian prime minister, Indira Gandhi, is assassinated. Also killed is the British Deputy High Commissioner to Western India, who has played host to the England team the day before his death. On the field the 18-year-old spinner Laxman Sivaramakrishnan takes six wickets in every innings; despite this amazing achievement, England win the series 2–1.

1984

1985

Fire engulfs stand at Bradford City

By Guy Rais

PUBLISHED MONDAY 13 MAY

As the bandaged and blistered survivors of the Bradford soccer fire relived the terror of their escape yesterday, one repeated theme emerged clearly – sheer disbelief among the hundreds fleeing the blazing grandstand that disaster could be overwhelming them amid the carnival air of a promotion celebration.

It seemed inconceivable that what started as a small fire at the back of the stand opposite one penalty area could have erupted at such speed that within four minutes the whole building was engulfed.

'At first, some in the stand just stood staring at the smoke, not realising it was spreading rapidly under the seats,' said Mr Arthur Martin, a home supporter.

There were about 3,000 people packing the 77-year-old wooden stand at Valley Parade, enjoying the last match of a triumphant season which had seen Bradford City win the Third Division championship, and with it promotion to the Second Division.

The visitors, lowly Lincoln City, were holding the champions to a goalless draw. But the home supporters were elated. This was their day.

Supt. Barry Osbourne, standing by the players' tunnel waiting for the teams to come off at half-time said: 'At first I thought it was a smoke bomb,' then he realised it was something worse. 'I could see people standing up from their seats. Within seconds flames appeared and then the whole of the roof at the back of the stand was well alight and the stand was rapidly engulfed.'

The burnt-out remains of the stand at Valley Parade in Bradford. The fire claimed 52 lives and over 200 people were injured. A row about safety standards ensued.

By David Millward and Donald Saunders in Brussels
PUBLISHED THURSDAY 30 MAY

Forty-one people were killed – many of them trampled to death – when a wall and a safety fence collapsed during rioting by Liverpool and Juventus football fans before the European Cup final in Brussels last night. More than 350 were injured.

It was believed early today that 33 Juventus supporters were among those killed when hooliganism turned to thuggery and then to tragedy in the Heysel Stadium. The dead also included seven Belgians, one of them possibly a member of the Brussels Anderlecht youth team which had played as a curtain-raiser before the Cup final.

Police said that no Britons were killed and that it was unlikely that any had been injured by the wall collapse, although some were believed to have been hurt in the fighting earlier.

A police spokesman said the wall collapsed when British fans charged towards Italian supporters of Juventus of Turin after rival supporters had fought a series of battles with each other and with policemen.

The deaths were a hideous climax to a night of rioting during which fans, many of them drunk, had used flagpoles and metal torn from safety barriers as weapons and had hurled fireworks, bottles and cans and pieces of concrete.

Bodies were piled high in two tents outside the main gates of the stadium as helicopters and ambulances with sirens carried the injured to hospitals.

The first hint of trouble came more than an hour before the match – which Juventus won 1–0. Italian supporters began throwing fireworks at police, who hurled them back and beat the nearest spectators with batons. Then Liverpool supporters began hurling cans and bottles at Juventus fans, separated from them only by

Police confront drunk and rioting fans at Heysel. The FA withdrew English clubs from European competition, but the authorities still resisted measures such as banning the sale of alcohol at grounds.

a wire fence. A few Liverpool supporters encroached into a section of the terracing occupied by Italians, an action which the stadium authorities had not anticipated.

Immediately the police charged forward in battle formation. Hundreds of Liverpool fans surged out of their area to join the battle.

According to witnesses close to the clashes many Italians tried to climb over a wire perimeter fence and a wall. Dozens of them were seen to have fallen 40 foot from the back of the terracing when the wall collapsed under them.

Bloodstained, battered and bewildered supporters of both nationalities wandered around in a daze, not knowing whether their friends had survived. Inside the dressing rooms the players were not told of the deaths.

A united Ireland hails McGuigan

By Charles Laurence

PUBLISHED MONDAY 10 JUNE

The rival communities of Ireland on both sides of the border and the religious divide joined forces yesterday to celebrate the stunning world championship victory of featherweight boxer Barry McGuigan (below, in background).

After thousands celebrated in a night of parties in pubs and streets, both the Lord Mayor of Belfast and the prime minister of the Republic congratulated the 24-year-old boxer on his contribution to unity and reconciliation.

Dr Garret FitzGerald, Eire's premier, telephoned McGuigan soon after he beat the Panamanian Eusebio Pedroza on Saturday night at Queen's Park Rangers football ground in London – despite an injury which prevented maximum use of his left hand.

'Like everyone else in Ireland I watched the fight with bated breath but with mounting confidence round by round. I and everyone else in Ireland is proud of Barry McGuigan for what he stands for. He is making an enormous contribution to the cause of reconciliation in Northern Ireland,' said Dr FitzGerald.

In Belfast, traditionally rival Ulster Unionist and Irish Nationalist councillors came together to plan a civic reception to mark McGuigan's return from London, probably on Wednesday.

The Belfast reception is expected to equal that given to Mary Peters in 1972 when she was cheered by Protestants and Catholics alike through the city streets after her gold medal success in the Olympic Games.

The Lord Mayor, Alderman John Carson, said he will organise a motorcade through the city and a civic reception at the City Hall.

'It is difficult to unite people in Northern Ireland from both sides of the divide, but Barry McGuigan has managed to do just that. He is a great ambassador for Northern Ireland,' he said.

President Reagan was among the thousands who sent their congratulations.

DID YOU KNOW?

In the wake of the events at Heysel, the Football League put forward a ten-point plan to reduce violence at matches. Margaret Thatcher was 'deeply unimpressed' with the proposals, which rejected her idea for ID cards and appeared to be demanding more government funding at a time when transfer fees were still huge.

SPORT IN BRIEF

SNOOKER
The world championship is won by Dennis Taylor, who beats Steve Davis 18–17 in the final at Sheffield's Crucible Theatre. In front of an estimated television audience of 18.5 million Taylor wins the final frame on the black.

CRICKET
On 10 January, playing in a match between Bombay and Baroda, the Indian all-rounder Ravi Shastri becomes the first player to emulate Gary Sobers' record of hitting six sixes from a six-ball over in a first-class match. The unfortunate bowler is Tilak Raj.

AMERICAN FOOTBALL
On 20 January the San Francisco 49-ers defeat the Miami Dolphins 38–16 to take the Super Bowl. The 49-ers quarter-back Joe Montana wins the Most Valuable Player award for the second time, having won it in 1982 when the 49-ers beat the Cincinnatti Bengals 26–21.

HORSE RACING
The Grand National springs another surprise with a long-priced winner. This time Last Suspect, ridden by Hywel Davies and trained by Tim Forster, is first past the post at 50–1. Corbière appears in the places for the third time, finishing third at 9–1.

GOLF
In April Bernhard Langer becomes the first German player to win the US Masters at Augusta when he completes the course in a four-round total of 282 shots. Severiano Ballesteros, Raymond Floyd and Curtis Strange finish tied for second place.

1985

Popplewell recommendations for football reform

By Roger Malone

PUBLISHED THURSDAY 25 JULY

Mr Justice Popplewell's suitably hard-hitting recommendations to tackle hooliganism and improve crowd safety drew undiluted enthusiasm from many of the rich in football, but worried concern from League headquarters, the guardians of the poor among the 92 clubs.

On the day Everton's fee to buy Leicester's Gary Lineker was set at £800,000, and Liverpool announced an improved after-tax profit of £433,000 – despite a record wages bill of more than £2 million last season – the Popplewell report was welcomed by John Smith, the Anfield chairman.

Mr Smith, one of the game's most experienced and respected chairmen, commented: 'It makes a valuable and thoughtful contribution to solving the problems which have been in football for too long.' He went on: 'The commonsense and practical approach throughout the report should be welcomed by everyone, regardless of the sport they follow.

'The sooner the suggestions are put into operation the better, not only for the good of sport in general but also for players and spectators in particular,' added Mr Smith, who is also chairman of the Sports Council.

At League headquarters, spokesman Andy Williamson said: 'A large proportion of the report makes a great deal of sense.' But he added that its recommendations could lead to several clubs in the lower divisions being forced out of existence.

The costs of membership-cards for spectators, perimeter fencing and closed-circuit television vigilante systems would 'widen the number of clubs in danger, and increase the risk of them going out of business'. He went on to paint a bleak picture at the top of football, besides the lower reaches, if Popplewell becomes law and the government continues to refuse financial help.

Boris Becker, 17, makes Wimbledon history

By John Parsons

PUBLISHED MONDAY 8 JULY

Boris Becker, the 17-year-old West German, rewrote the Wimbledon record books yesterday when he defeated Kevin Curren to become the first unseeded champion and the youngest-ever winner.

A packed centre-court crowd, which included Becker's parents who had flown from their home in Leimen, near Heidelberg, rose to the strapping 6 ft 1 in West German after his 6–3, 6–7, 7–6, 6–4 win.

It was a remarkable performance. Becker, who first came to prominence in Britain when he won the Young Masters in Birmingham last January, had beaten three other seeded players to reach the Wimbledon final. No other German has ever won the championship.

Becker wrote himself into several Wimbledon records. Apart from being the first unseeded champion, no other unseeded finalist has even taken a set.

A year ago Becker left Wimbledon in a wheelchair after being injured in the third round. He needed an operation which kept him out of tennis for two months.

This time, in the gleaming sunlight, the match began slowly but became a three-hour 18-minute thriller.

Curren, who had knocked out former champions John McEnroe and Jimmy Connors, said: 'He certainly could become the best player in the world. He has a tremendous talent and, although I have faced harder servers, I have not played one who places it better.'

To underline the new champion's youth, Becker is in fact four months younger than Leonardo Aavalle, of Mexico, winner of the junior boys' singles contest.

It was an extraordinary and exhilarating climax to a Wimbledon which, despite all its problems with the weather in the first week, ended on time and with record total attendances.

A powerhouse of strength, speed and agility, Boris Becker retained his Wimbledon title in 1986 and won the championship for a third time in 1989.

Brilliant Spencer triumphs twice

By George Turnbull in Francorchamps, Belgium
PUBLISHED MONDAY 8 JULY

Freddie Spencer was the toast of Francorchamps last night after winning both the 250-cc and 500-cc races at the Belgian Grand Prix in devastating style.

It is some time since the Belgian enthusiasts have been treated twice in an afternoon to such a display of racing artistry by one man, and the 120,000 crowd rose to the American.

Spencer, 23, from Louisiana, snatched the lead from the outset on his 500-cc Rothmans-Honda and had soon built up a commanding lead on the beautiful four-mile circuit that winds through the Ardennes.

Freddie Spencer's 250-cc win was his sixth junior classic victory of the season.

His arch-rival in the world championship chase, Eddie Lawson, the current champion, had some difficulty in getting his Marlboro-Yamaha to fire and was unable to get on terms with Spencer throughout the 20-lap race.

Spencer led from start to finish of the 16-lap 250-cc race on his small but very fast Honda to enhance even further his considerable points advantage in the 250-cc championship.

Spencer gracefully swept his way through the Ardennes forest, leaving Anton Mang and Carlos Lavado to squabble for the runners-up position.

Piquet and Brabham back in top form

By Brian Allen at Le Castellet
PUBLISHED MONDAY 8 JULY

Nelson Piquet, twice world champion but an also-ran after this season's first six world championship rounds, and the Brabham team, stormed back to winning form in the French Grand Prix at Le Castellet yesterday.

It was in June last year, in Detroit, that the Piquet–Brabham combination previously won a grand prix. This season they switched to Pirelli tyres and until yesterday had struggled to achieve competitiveness.

Piquet's victory, the 13th of his career, was a tribute to the Brazilian's sympathy for both car and tyres. It was also a tribute to good teamwork as Piquet had to make a late switch to his spare car after his regular mount developed a vibration just before the start.

He chose a hard tyre compound to last the race, cornered circumspectly to preserve the tyres, and was able to control the race from the front after overtaking Keke Rosberg's Williams-Honda on the 11th lap.

Yet it was a close call. Piquet said afterwards that he drove the last five laps with his rear tyres almost finished.

The Brabham win injects renewed interest into the grand prix scene. Goodyear, the tyre company, dominant this season until yesterday, will be fighting back hard.

For Pirelli, whose previous grand prix win was at Monza in 1977, and who returned to grand prix racing five years ago with scant success, the win at the Paul Ricard circuit is a real morale-booster.

It also paid off a huge testing programme carrried out by the Brabham team at Kyalami, in South Africa, several months ago.

SPORT IN BRIEF

FOOTBALL
Everton enjoy a 3–1 win over Rapid Vienna in the final of the European Cup Winners' Cup final on 15 May. Everton's goals come from Andy Gray, Trevor Steven and Kevin Sheedy; Hans Krankl replies for the Austrian team.

HORSE RACING
John Francome rides 101 winners in the season to become National Hunt champion jockey for the seventh time. He first achieved the feat in 1975/6 when he rode 96 winners, but his most successful season was in 1983/4 when he finished ahead of the field 131 times. One of the greatest jump jockeys of all time, he is also a great sportsman: in the 1981/2 season, when fellow jockey Peter Scudamore was put out of the championship through injury, Francome matched his points total and then stopped competing, so that the two men could share the title.

GOLF
The British Open, played at Sandwich, is won by Sandy Lyle in a four-round total score of 282 strokes. On the last day he does not move into the joint lead until the 15th hole but is then able to secure the title, despite bogeying the last hole. Payne Stewart finishes in second place.

CRICKET
On 7 September the NatWest Trophy (previously the Gillette Trophy) final is contested between Nottinghamshire and Essex. Essex bat first, running up 280 for two off their 60 overs, with Brian Hardie making 110. In an exciting finish Nottinghamshire require 18 off the last over. Derek Randall scores 16 from the first five balls of the over, but is caught on the sixth, and Nottinghamshire finish on 279 for five. Hardie takes the Man-of-the-Match award for his century.

1985

Torrance putt brings Europe historic win

By Michael Williams

PUBLISHED MONDAY 16 SEPTEMBER

At precisely five minutes past four yesterday afternoon, Sam Torrance holed a putt across the 18th green at the Belfry that echoed around the world, for with that birdie and the defeat of Andy North, Europe, at last, won again the Ryder Cup.

Not since Lindrick in 1957 had the United States been beaten by the then Great Britain and Ireland team, but the point that Torrance brought home after standing three down with eight to play put the Europeans finally out of reach.

Ahead 9–6 going into this momentous final day, they got the $5\frac{1}{2}$ points they needed from the first seven singles matches and, in the end, won by $16\frac{1}{2} – 11\frac{1}{2}$, which was more comprehensive than even the most optimistic had envisaged.

Not for 28 years has there been such excitement and such scenes at a Ryder Cup; most of the 27,500 spectators there yesterday, bringing the total for the three days to nearly 80,000, seemed to ring the 18th hole for a glimpse of the magic moment.

No sooner had Torrance's putt disappeared from sight than he was engulfed by the other team members, led by the captain, Tony Jacklin, for whom victory was every bit as sweet as it was when he won the Open championship in 1969 and the US Open the following year.

Of Torrance's finish, Jacklin said: 'You dream about that sort of thing. It was just great to be a part of it.

'The team was my inspiration and it shows the world how good we really are. We have so much talent, more perhaps than even we realise.'

Hardly had he spoken, as his joyous team sprayed champagne over the crowd from the roof of the hotel, than Concorde thundered low overhead, making two runs over the course and dipping its silver wings in salute as it did so.

Torrance, arms aloft, after his birdie at the 18th clinched the Ryder Cup for Europe for the first time in nearly 30 years.

The man who made Celtic

By Denis Lowe

PUBLISHED WEDNESDAY 11 SEPTEMBER

Jock Stein died a few minutes after a match at Ninian Park, Cardiff, where Wales and Scotland drew 1–1.

Jock Stein, who was 62, made his excellent reputation in the game as the man who steered Celtic to a record nine Scottish League championships in succession.

He had been his country's manager for almost seven years, taking over the post in 1978. He guided Scotland to the World Cup finals in 1982.

A former miner, who was highly respected and widely admired throughout the world of football, he gave Celtic excellent playing service for many years as a centre half and captain. He had also played for Albion Rovers and Llanelli before joining Celtic.

When he first entered club management Mr Stein became successful with Dunfermline and returned to his favourite Parkhead club in 1965 after a period in charge at Hibernian.

With Celtic he moulded the magnificent team which became the first British club to win the European Cup – InterMilan were beaten in Lisbon in 1967 – and went on to take the Glasgow club to nine successive Scottish League titles between 1966 and 1974.

He retired from management with Celtic when his health suffered after a serious car crash, but later moved to England to become manager of Leeds United for three months in 1978 before being recalled by Scotland to succeed Ally MacLeod.

Laura Davies set for big pay-day

By Michael Williams

PUBLISHED WEDNESDAY 4 SEPTEMBER

Just as Kitrina Douglas tended to steal the show in her first season on the WPGA circuit last year, so another rookie, Laura Davies **(right)**, has been doing the same thing in this long, damp summer.

In 1984, Miss Douglas was leading money-winner almost until the last minute when Dale Reid just about doubled her earnings by finishing equal second in the inflated prize fund that was then attached to the British Women's Open championship.

Now it is Miss Davies who leads the way as the women's professional circuit arrives in Kingswood, Surrey, today for the IBM European Open, an event worth £35,000 with a first prize of £4,500.

Miss Davies, with the sort of British Curtis Cup team which lost narrowly to the US at Muirfield last summer, has already accumulated prize money of £17,200. She leads by £1,694 from Jane Connachan, with Beverly Huke a close third.

All this is just the stimulant the WPGA circuit needs, for there is nothing like new blood succeeding. It prompts a continuing supply of talent from the amateur ranks, just as it does in men's golf.

Miss Davies, with the sort of mighty hitting which turns most par fives into fours, also attracts spectators, and each week she already tends to be looked upon as the player to beat.

Gillian Stewart, who won her first event as a professional, the Ford Classic at Woburn in May, has made more sedate progress, though her fifth place in the Ring and Brymer Order of Merit would have been higher had she won the recent Delsjo Tournament held in Sweden.

She was leading in the fourth round when a downpour brought play to a halt, and Cathy Panton was declared the winner on the three-round scores.

Miss Stewart is, nevertheless, in the unusual position of being the IBM defending champion, having won the event last year as an amateur at the Belfry.

> ### MILESTONES
>
> The first Intercontinental Cup match is held in Paris. In an outstanding performance, France beat Uruguay 2–0 to take the Artemio Franchi Trophy. The goals are scored within 55 minutes by Rocheteau and Toure.

Mansell and Prost share Brands Hatch glory

By Brian Allen

PUBLISHED MONDAY 7 OCTOBER

The victory of Nigel Mansell, a British driver, in the Canon-Williams, a British car, in yesterday's Shell Oils Grand Prix of Europe at Brands Hatch overshadowed Alain Prost's winning of the world drivers' championship.

An estimated 90,000 spectators saw Mansell, 31, though suffering the effects of incidents in the two previous grands prix, forget the aching ribs as he forged into the lead on lap nine of the 75-lap race and coolly held his advantage to the finish.

He comfortably beat off a challenge from Marc Surer, of Switzerland, which ended when, 13 laps from the finish, the Brabham BMW expired in flames.

Prost, by finishing fourth, became the first Frenchman to win the championship. With only two races left he cannot be caught.

Michele Alboreto, of Italy, his only challenger, saw his hopes disappear in huge clouds of smoke as his Ferrari engine blew.

But Prost had his worries on the way. He was clearly ill at ease in the opening stages, and opted to come in for fresh tyres, which cost him valuable time but transformed his McLaren's handling.

From eighth place he made a strong charge to take three points and put himself out of Alboreto's reach.

Ayrton Senna, of Brazil, mercurial in qualifying, had to be satisfied with second place in his JPS Lotus, 21.4 seconds behind Mansell.

England take an absorbing series 3–1

By Michael Carey at the Oval

PUBLISHED TUESDAY 3 SEPTEMBER

England completed victory over Australia with rather more ease than could have been expected in the sixth Cornhill Test at the Oval yesterday, capturing their last six wickets for 58 runs to triumph by an innings and 94 and win an absorbing series 3–1.

From the third day at Edgbaston, England have proved unstoppable with bat and ball, and before lunch David Gower had joined the ranks of England captains who have stood on the Oval balcony celebrating the return of the Ashes.

For him, the moment was particularly sweet, coming as it did some 12 months after the annihilation by the West Indies, or, if you like, following suggestions from some quarters this summer that he should resign because of his chequered form.

Since those unhappy days, however, he has completed 732 runs in the series and become only the second England captain, after Douglas Jardine, to win a series in India and regain the Ashes, and in less than a year.

Gower was unsurprisingly named Man of the Series by Tony Lewis, and Graham Gooch collected the Man-of-the-Match award for his 196 after Richard Ellison, with four wickets in eight overs, Ian Botham and L. B. Taylor had completed the *coup de grâce*.

For Australia, the cool, overcast morning, which helped Ellison particularly to move the ball about, was an all-too-familiar reminder of the gloomy weather that has haunted them, and us, more or less since they arrived.

The crowd, some perhaps recalling Trevor Bailey and Willie Watson in 1953, might have half wondered if Allan Border and Greg Ritchie, another left- and right-hand combination, might also achieve something remarkable but, in more daunting circumstances, it was not to be.

Once Ritchie had gone, getting the faintest of touches to Ellison's outswinger, the ball regularly found the edge, the catches stuck, with a particularly good one by Botham, and Taylor had the pleasure of completing victory with a return one off Murray Bennett.

England thus took a series which somehow survived miserable weather, was often played to capacity crowds, and which both sides probably felt would be much closer.

The key was that, although bowlers win matches, as England's subsequently did, the platform was the consistency as a unit of the top six batsmen who were unchanged, unprecedentedly, throughout the series.

Gower (right arm raised, far right), who had scored 215 in the first innings, catches Ritchie in the fifth Test. Australia lost the match by an innings and 118 runs.

SPORT IN BRIEF

BOXING

Larry Holmes defends his IBF world heavyweight championship against Michael Spinks. After 15 rounds Spinks wins a points decision, ending Holmes's hopes of emulating Rocky Marciano's record of 49 unbeaten fights. Holmes is just one short of his goal.

RUGBY UNION

Fiji tour Britain. They suffer a narrow defeat against Ireland at Lansdowne Road, 16–15, but lose heavily to Wales, 40–3.

CRICKET

New Zealand travel to Australia for a three-match series. New Zealand fast-bowler Richard Hadlee takes a total of 33 wickets (including nine for 52) as New Zealand head for their first series victory over Australia. Between 1978 and 1987 Hadlee plays for Nottinghamshire; his 100 wickets in the 1981 season helped them to their first county championship win since 1929. This season he has also taken eight for 41 against Lancashire.

1985

289

Sue Mott

Women in sport

'WOMEN HAVE BUT ONE TASK, that of crowning the winner with garlands….' When Baron Pierre de Coubertin said that in 1902, he probably didn't expect a rugby prop forward to come and spit her disagreement (and teeth) in his face. But, hey, how was he to know that women, those fluffy things with headaches, would embrace liberty, equality and gum shields by the end of the 20th century?

The Baron was the founder of the modern Olympic movement long before women had the vote or those wrap-around sunglasses in which Marleen Renders of Belgium came fourth in the London Marathon. Marathon? In 1928, women were only just allowed to run 800 m and when a few of the athletes collapsed at the finish, the men gleefully told them it was far too great a distance for their silken, feminine little limbs.

The marathon itself was barred to women until as recently as 1984, when the winner was Joan Benoit, an American who had to overcome a sense of shame in her chosen pursuit. 'When I first started running I was so embarrassed I'd walk when cars passed me. I'd pretend I was looking at the flowers.'

The whole century of sport has been characterised by male concern at the expending of female energy. Which is a bizarre twist. In every other field – over the twin-tub, in the labour ward, on the school run, in the brothel – energetic women are to be thoroughly applauded.

In fact, the whole century of sport has been characterised by male concern at the expending of female energy. Which is a bizarre twist. In every other field – over the twin-tub, in the labour ward, on the school run, in the brothel – energetic women are to be thoroughly applauded.

Ah but, that is because that is where men put them. It was still evidence of docility and dependence. But when women put themselves in the Arsenal women's line-up, all tangible evidence of a 'weaker sex' broke down.

When Babe Didrikson, perhaps the world's greatest example of a tomboy grown up, won three medals at the 1932 Olympics, in hurdles, javelin and high jump, she was still asked by the American press to reveal her 'beauty diet'. 'I eat anything I want – except greasy foods and gravy,' she replied heroically. 'I pass the gravy. That's just hot grease anyway.'

Even the heavyweight entities who compiled the *New York Times* (banned, in the 1990s, from mentioning the size of Monica Seles's knickers, which consumed the British tabloid press in the summer of 1996) were keen to hear of Babe's feminine pursuits. 'Naturally athletics has not left me much time for household tasks. I don't care about them. If necessary, I can sew and cook. One of my dresses won first place in a Texas state contest in 1930.'

That was all right then. A homemaker was revealed. What a difference two decades were to make. In a word: none.

When Fanny Blankers-Koen – a 30-year-old mother of two – won four gold medals at the London Olympics in 1948, the London *Daily Graphic* was moved to headline its story: 'Fastest Woman in the World Is an Expert Cook.' It would be a bit like *The Sun* reporting: 'Benazir Bhutto Makes Mean Chapatis'…which, come to think of it, they might, so perhaps we had better leave the analogy alone. Even so, the desperation of the mid-century man to cajole, jolly and, if that didn't work, then force women back to the hearth clangs like a knell of doom in that *Daily Graphic* headline. For doomed it certainly was.

When Fanny Blankers-Koen won four gold medals at the London Olympics in 1948, the Daily Graphic *was moved to headline its story, 'Fastest Woman in the World Is an Expert Cook.'*

The runner-up to Blankers-Koen in the 80-m hurdles was Maureen Gardner…'the shyest girl at the Games, more excited about 11 September than about her record-breaking run. It is her Wedding Day'. Now, if any gnarled old hack with a cigarette-butt welded to his sneering lip dared write about shy girls or weddings today, he'd be subbed, sacked and probably prosecuted by the Equal Opportunities Commission.

As the century has progressed, so has women's inalienable right to bear racquets and what-not on the field of sporting combat with less wailing and gnashing of teeth from their deserted menfolk. So it is better but it is not great.

The Marylebone Cricket Club voted to maintain their ban on women members in 1998 on the grounds, established 200 years ago, that they should be at home blacking the fire grate. That, in a sense, was not a bad thing for women. By becoming such a clearly-defined enemy of equality and common sense, the MCC, bless their suspenders, became a marvellous focal point for justified female contempt. Feminism would have been less rampant without them, just as the Tories were now floundering without socialism.

Far more insidious was the remnant chauvinism that, for instance, found Chris Evert so much more palatable than Martina Navratilova. For years and years, almost two decades, Navratilova laboured at Wimbledon in the slim, pert, blonde shadow of her rival whose cutesy, apple-pie content was never in the least contaminated by a string of dates from Burt Reynolds to Adam Faith (which ought to have been enough to expunge her from the record books regardless of those 18 Grand Slam singles titles).

Navratilova was grudgingly admired rather than passionately supported. She had muscles and girlfriends, that's why.

Navratilova, despite being by far the more extravagantly gifted and exhilarating player, was grudgingly admired rather than passionately supported. She had muscles and girlfriends, that's why. Polite English society was not ready for this, and only in the twilight of her supremacy, when she was winning Wimbledon a record ninth time, did the recalcitrant public warm to the privilege of watching one of the greatest women athletes of the century. Never mind. As Richard Krajicek, the 1996 Wimbledon winner, said so gallantly: 'They're all lazy, fat pigs anyway.'

There must be a reason why the Krajiceks cower behind the barricades of abuse, or the all-male 19th hole or the testosterone-injected post-match pub. And there is. Sport is a field that men have had almost exclusively to themselves since Neanderthal times (which is pretty recently in the case of Leeds United supporters), but I mean in the historical sense. When women encroach on sport, they are exuding confidence, competitiveness, aggression, freedom, strength and, in the case of the English women's goalkeeper, Pauline Cope, even appearances before the FA Disciplinary Committee. We are talking seriously equal here.

There are down sides. An equal right to ingest anabolic steroids, especially in the late state-induced programmes of the iron-curtained countries, proved to be a hideous abuse of women. Almost as hideous as the humiliating sex tests upon which the International Olympic Committee insisted to prove that a female champion was not actually some fella in a dress.

Tamara and Irina Press, of the then Soviet Union, were always cited as examples of the hairy blokes-in-disguise theory, when they won the pentathlon, hurdles, discus and shot-putt between them. But whether they were actually Tom and Ira, ingeniously packaged, must remain forever in doubt. They dropped out of the competition when sex-testing was about to start. And what testing. You took your kit off and someone looked at you. If we were all judged by that scientific method, there would be an awful lot of 'don't knows' walking around. And an awful lot of volunteers to check out Anna Kournikova.

In the 1990s sex testing is obviously defunct. If any man is willing to share a locker room with girl-power he probably deserves every medal upon which he can lay his trembling hands.

In the 1990s sex-testing is obviously defunct. If any man is willing to share a locker room with girl-power he probably deserves every medal upon which he can lay his trembling hands.

By late 1998 the newly feminised Marylebone Cricket Club had finally opened its Pavilion doors to women members. But the change has not been without its teething problems. Former England women's cricket captain Rachel Heyhoe-Flint went to the ladies there just after her enrolment as a fully-fledged MCC member, and found a gent coming defiantly out of the door.

1986

Rangers move for Souness

By Roger Malone
PUBLISHED TUESDAY 8 APRIL

Graeme Souness, Scotland's World Cup captain, appears set to move from Sampdoria to become player-manger of Glasgow Rangers.

Rangers, who parted company with manager Jock Wallace 'by mutual agreement' yesterday, said through David Holmes their chief executive last night, 'We are hoping to finalise a deal with Sampdoria in the next 24 hours. We are in negotiations with them.'

Souness left Liverpool for the Italian club in a £700,000 transfer two seasons ago. Now 34, he may cost Rangers considerably less, although his contract is likely to be highly lucrative, especially as his ambition to move into player-management may have attracted competitive offers.

His contract with the Genoese club has one year remaining, but he is understood to have agreed with Sampdoria that he can leave at the end of the season. He was in Glasgow last night, ostensibly to attend a social function with Scottish international colleagues.

Mr Wallace said: 'I did the job to the best of my ability but it has not gone right.'

Graeme Souness signed for Rangers on 8 April.

Late surge brings glory for Jack Nicklaus

By Michael Williams in Augusta, Georgia
PUBLISHED MONDAY 14 APRIL

Jack Nicklaus, 46, that seemingly fallen colossus of golf, climbed heroically to his feet yet again yesterday when, with a marvellous last round of 65, he won his sixth US Masters at Augusta National.

With an astonishing inward half of 30, he beat Tom Kite and Greg Norman, of Australia, by a stroke, with a 72-hole total of 279, nine under par.

Both Kite and Norman had putts to tie at the 18th, but both missed, the Australian indeed taking a five after hitting his second shot into the gallery.

Seve Ballesteros, who had led going into the 15th hole, finished third while Sandy Lyle, the Open champion, was equal tenth, a stroke ahead of Bernhard Langer, the defending champion.

After the grey and rather humid weather of Saturday, when Norman had taken a one-stroke lead from Price, Langer, Ballesteros and Hammond, the sun shone brilliantly again yesterday and there was always a chance that someone could come out of the pack to set a target.

As the leaders went through the turn Norman, who was out in 35, had been caught by Ballesteros. Ballesteros brought the biggest roar so far when, having played the first six holes in par and broken the deadlock with a birdie at the seventh, he holed a pitch from 45 yards at the eighth for an eagle three.

Nicklaus began shedding the years with a run of three birdies from the ninth to move to five under par and only two strokes off the lead. The great man's spurt was temporarily checked at the short 12th, where he failed to get down with a chip and a putt from some distance. Scenting for the first time a genuine chance of victory, the Spaniard cut loose with a glorious drive round the corner at the 13th, hit a medium iron to around six foot and in went the putt for an eagle, his second of the day.

But one never knows at Augusta, and suddenly the whole picture changed.

After a glorious drive down the 15th, Ballesteros mis-hit into the water, took six and thereby fell back into a three-way tie with Nicklaus and Kite, the latter having a four at the same hole.

Now it was Nicklaus who was at full speed ahead as he collected yet another birdie at the 17th. It meant he needed a three at the last for 29 home, and though the putt was long, he all but got it. However, he was round gloriously in 65 and with a total of 279.

Nicklaus chips out of a bunker on his way to a sixth US Open title. It was also his 20th championship title.

Rampant Richards scores 100 in 56 balls

Michael Carey in Antigua
PUBLISHED WEDNESDAY 16 APRIL

Vivian Richards, with a massive display of virtuosity, hit a century from only 56 deliveries against England's world-weary bowlers in the final Cable and Wireless Test yesterday – the fastest in Test history in terms of balls received.

With scarcely a flawed stroke, and lifting a six off only his second ball, Richards made his first 50 off 35 deliveries, his second off a mere 21, and the carnage ended only when he declared after needing only 41 scoring strokes to achieve the 20th and most memorable Test hundred of his career.

At that point England, having avoided the possibility of following on earlier, were left to make 411 – or to bat for six hours 50 minutes to save the game – and a totally compelling day's cricket ended with them, not too surprisingly, at 33 for two.

In making an unbeaten 110 out of 136, Richards was at the wicket for 81 minutes, but it is more pertinent to measure his feat in terms of balls received in an era when over-rates are slow, and England with times and runs important to their chances of survival, were hardly racing through their overs.

Hitherto, the fastest Test hundreds recorded in this manner were Jack Gregory's made from 67 balls for Australia against South Africa at Johannesburg in 1921–22, and Roy Fredericks', made from 71 deliveries for West Indies against Australia at Perth in 1975–76.

Gregory's was timed at 70 minutes, while others who have beaten Richards in terms of time only were Gilbert Jessop (75 minutes against Australia in 1902), Richie Benaud (78 minutes against West Indies in 1954–55) and James Sinclair (80 minutes, for South Africa against Australia in 1902–3).

It was possible to sense that something historical was in the offing when Richards, appearing first wicket down in the interests of adding to a lead of 164 as quickly as possible, struck his second ball from John Emburey effortlessly for six.

He then picked up a perfectly decent delivery from Richard Ellison for six over mid-wicket, and with much purposeful running (there were 18 singles as well as six sixes and seven fours) quickly made it impossible for anyone to bowl at him.

Viv Richards pauses for breath during his record innings. In his Test career, Richards scored 8,540 runs and appeared in 121 matches, a record for a West Indies cricketer.

Senna pips Mansell on the line

By Brian Allen in Jerez, Spain
PUBLISHED MONDAY 14 APRIL

The closest finish for years saw Ayrton Senna just beat Nigel Mansell across the line in yesterday's exciting Spanish Grand Prix.

What at one time seemed destined to be a professional race, with hardly any change of positions, flared suddenly to life as Mansell, in his Williams-Honda, began to close on Senna's JBS Lotus.

On lap 40, with just over half the race run, Mansell took over the lead from the rival with whom he clashed on the first lap of the recent championship round in Brazil. This was the signal for a classic duel between two supreme drivers, with Mansell trying all he knew to keep Senna at bay while preserving his tyres and keeping a tight watch on his fuel consumption.

Senna finally threw caution to the winds, badgering Mansell at almost every corner and once taking desperately to the grass. Mansell refused to give way but, with nine laps to go, much against his will, he was pulled in by his team to change tyres.

When he came out of the pits he was more than 20 seconds behind Senna, with Alain Prost's McLaren sandwiched between. But with fresh tyres Mansell's car was rejuvenated and, as soon as they warmed up to working temperature, he began to cut the gap.

His attack on Prost probably cost him the race, for it took him some two-thirds of a lap to get by on the twisty Jerez circuit.

Then it was Senna in his sights. The Brazilian, teetering on the edge of disaster on badly worn tyres, went into the last corner sliding slightly as Mansell loomed large in his mirrors.

As they both accelerated hard for the line, Mansell nearly had more traction, but his effort came just too late. Senna won his third grand prix by less than a car's length.

1986

293

1986

Flawless Leng takes double gold

By a special correspondent, Gawler, South Australia
PUBLISHED MONDAY 26 MAY

Britain won both team and individual gold medals at the world three-day event championships, thanks to two faultless rounds across country from Virginia Leng, who took the individual gold on Priceless, and Lorna Clarke, who collected the individual bronze with Myross.

New Zealand's Trudy Boyce with Mossman followed their second place in the corresponding event last year, when it was a qualifying competition for Australia and New Zealand riders, with the silver medal.

This was a highly appropriate medal as the New Zealand team led at the end of the cross-country, with Tinks Pottinger and Volunteer, the winners here last year, well ahead.

But at yesterday's final veterinary inspection, Volunteer had a swollen knee, the result of hitting one of the cross-country fences, and failed to pass.

Mrs Pottinger's time on the cross-country course – she was the only rider given no time penalties – must be suspect, though; for Ian Stark, like her held up by an accident ahead of them, was credited with the second fastest time with Oxford Blue, even though he had a fall on the flat after the fifth fence. Going third of the British team, he went slowly for the next few fences to allow Oxford Blue to regain confidence. Yesterday in the show-jumping arena, it was obvious that Oxford Blue was feeling the after-effects when he had four fences down.

Clarissa Strachan, who went first for the team, fell at the water complex. The two individual British riders, Anne-Marie Taylor with Justyn Thyme VI, and Mandy Orchard with Venture Busby, both performed with credit throughout.

Miss Taylor had three fences down in yesterday's show jumping which cost her the bronze medal. Miss Orchard did not present Venture Busby at yesterday morning's final veterinary inspection as he had knocked himself.

DID YOU KNOW?

In May Real Madrid beat Cologne 5–3 on aggregate to become the first team to retain the UEFA Cup. Although Barcelona and Valencia had both won the competition two years running as well, it was then known as the Inter-Cities Fairs Cup.

Liverpool complete the Double after Merseyside final

By Donald Saunders
PUBLISHED MONDAY 12 MAY
Liverpool 3; Everton 1

The City of Liverpool, condemned throughout the world as the capital of soccer hooliganism following the Brussels tragedy last June, can be proud of their footballers and supporters this morning.

Liverpool and Everton provided an FA Cup final of superb quality and their followers added the noise, colour, humour, passion and sportsmanship required to turn it into a truly big Wembley occasion.

So a season on which English clubs had embarked so apprehensively has ended triumphantly. For that we must largely thank the two Merseyside giants. They gave us the most exciting League championship for at least ten years. Now, they have provided an FA Cup final that can be compared favourably with Everton's 3–2 triumph over Sheffield Wednesday in 1966 and Liverpool's 2–1 defeats by Arsenal in 1971 and by Manchester United in 1977.

Though always an enthusiastic believer in the importance of UEFA and their tournaments, I have enjoyed this season far more than many that have included matches between English and European clubs during the past 30 years.

This and the widely publicised activities of less disciplined Merseyside fans in London over the weekend lead me to suggest that League clubs should not press too hard for a return to Europe in 1987.

From Everton's

viewpoint, this was a final they lost; Liverpool will see it as an historic victory earned by Jan Molby's persuasive midfield generalship, the devastating finishing touch of Ian Rush and one spectacular save from Bruce Grobbelaar.

For the first 57 minutes, Everton dominated the match. They deservedly moved in front, with Gary Lineker accelerating past the surprised Alan Hansen to plant the ball in the net at the second attempt.

Then, in the 57th minute, Stevens inadvertently transformed this one-sided Merseyside derby into a classic Cup final by pushing the ball straight on to the feet of a grateful Ron Whelan. Whelan's pass was swept on to Rush, who took the ball round the stranded Bobby Mimms before placing it in the net.

Liverpool still looked none too sure of themselves. Yet, in the 63rd minute, they snatched the lead through Craig Johnston. From that point, Molby commanded the midfield, and with Howard Kendall pulling off the demoralised Stevens and sending Adrian Heath to join his attack, Everton became increasingly vulnerable.

With six minutes left, Rush took Whelan's cross in his stride and drove the ball firmly home to ensure that Liverpool became the first club to complete the Double since 1971.

The impressive Danish international Jan Molby (above, with arm raised) dominated the midfield in the FA Cup final. Alan Hansen lifts the FA Cup for Liverpool (below), only the third club to achieve the Double this century.

Uruguay face threat of expulsion

By Donald Saunders in Mexico City
PUBLISHED MONDAY 16 JUNE

Uruguay, who came to Mexico as second favourites for the World Cup but reached the second round only by the skin of their teeth, are now threatened with expulsion from the tournament. The South American champions have been fined for misconduct by their players and officials.

So far, this has been a miserable tournament for the Uruguayans, who were expected to play the most technically accomplished football. Instead, they are now branded as the most violent team in Mexico.

Following their first game against West Germany, some of their officials were reported to FIFA for misbehaving during the routine dope testing. Early in their second game against Denmark, Miguel Bossio was sent off for a vicious foul. Uruguay's scoreless last group match, against Scotland, was only 50 seconds old when Jose Batista, another defender, was shown the red card for a scything foul on Gordon Strachan.

Their manager, Omar Borras, was so incensed by this dismissal that, at the subsequent press conference, he called Joel Quiniou, the French referee, a 'murderer'.

Uruguay lost 1–0 to Argentina in the second round.

Argentina are back on top of the world

By Donald Saunders in Mexico City
PUBLISHED MONDAY 30 JUNE
Argentina 3; West Germany 2

Argentina became the soccer champions of the world for the second time in eight years, at the Aztec Stadium, Mexico City yesterday, after withstanding a typically brave, determined comeback by West Germany that almost snatched the cup from their grasp.

Leading 2–0, with only 17 minutes to go, the Latin Americans seemed to be cruising to the comfortable victory their commendably sensible all-round team performance so richly deserved.

Then, as so many other nations have discovered in World Cup battles over the years, Argentina found themselves trying to cope with a German onslaught.

In eight memorable minutes that kept this capacity crowd of 115,000 on tenterhooks, Franz Beckenbauer's defiant men surged upfield and drew level.

This final might well have slipped into extra time and beyond the control of Argentina during those exciting minutes. But in their moment of crisis Diego Maradona calmly made his final, crucial contribution to a tournament he had dominated – and European hopes of a first success in this hemisphere were shattered.

As the Germans overreached themselves with a last-gasp effort to win, the Argentine genius caught them on the break with a beautiful pass to Jorge Burruchaga. Burruchaga raced some 50 yards through unguarded German territory, calmly drew Toni Schumacher – then planted the most important goal of his life into the far corner of the net.

Even the Germans were now forced to accept the inevitable. Three or four of them collapsed to the turf, holding their heads in sheer disbelief. A few minutes later cascades of silver foil were floating down from the ecstatic spectators to greet the most spectacular, exciting victory this great competition has ever staged.

Victory was no more than Argentina deserved. Until that late rally by Germany, they had controlled the game with their most accomplished all-round performance of this tournament.

It could be said, with some justice, that Maradona carried his country into the final, with a series of virtuoso performances. He resisted any temptation to turn this great occasion into a one-man show, and quietly played his part as a responsible member of the team.

Though closely marked by the dogged Matthaeus, the Argentine captain found enough space to help his colleagues patiently build neat moves that eventually wore down the tight, well-organised German defence.

Argentina's captain, Diego Maradona, lifts the World Cup. Maradona's inspiring and brilliant play dominated the tournament. England witnessed the other side of the Argentinian's mercurial temperament, however, when a goal scored, so Maradona claimed, by the 'hand of God', put them out of the tournament.

SPORT IN BRIEF

BASEBALL
Having begun his baseball career in 1963, Peter Rose finally retires from the sport. He holds the record for the most base hits, having hit 4,256 in his 23-year career.

MOTOR RACING
Nigel Mansell **(above, on right)** celebrates a win over Alain Prost **(on left)** in the French Grand Prix at Paul Ricard. Mansell, driving a Williams-Honda, has already won the Belgian and Canadian Grands Prix; he will go on to take first place in the British and the Portuguese Grands Prix, too.

HORSE RACING
Dancing Brave dominates the Flat season. Although as favourite he finishes second behind Shahrastani in the Epsom Derby, he wins the 2,000 Guineas, the Eclipse Stakes, the King George VI and Queen Elizabeth Stakes and the Prix de l'Arc de Triomphe.

MOTOR RACING
The British Grand Prix, held on 13 July, ends in disappointment for French driver Jacques Laffite. He is injured in an accident at the start of the race and is forced to retire from racing. Ironically, he only needed to begin one more race to overtake Graham Hill's record of 176 grands prix started.

1986

1986

A dream goes up in sparks for Nigel Mansell

By Michael Calvin in Adelaide

PUBLISHED MONDAY 27 OCTOBER

Nigel Mansell exhibited all the signs of a man in shock as he sought refuge in a scruffy white six-berth Swagman deluxe caravan situated behind the Williams pit.

His shoulders sagged and there was a distant air in his voice as he asked: 'What happened? I just can't believe it.'

Washed and changed but still glassy-eyed, he submitted hesitantly to reliving the split-second when a shower of sparks signalled the end of his world championship ambition.

'How do I feel?' he inquired, echoing the inevitable first question. 'Oh quite tremendous. In fact, I might not have been here, I might not have been alive.'

He was travelling in sixth gear at close to 200 mph on the long Jack Brabham straight when his left rear tyre exploded. In that instant the most basic of human instincts overwhelmed his other priorities.

'When something like that happens self-preservation is the only thing on your mind,' he reflected. 'The car went out of control and started to dance from one side of the track to the other.

'I had to correct it and if it was not for the fact that I was in a straight with a good run-off area there could have been a massive accident.'

The prize offered supreme self-fulfilment, sporting immortality and millions beyond his comprehension when he cleaned windows to augment the family income.

Finishing as runner-up in the championship with two points fewer than Prost's total of 72 represented failure. As he consoled his wife Rosanne, the enormity of his lost opportunity was achingly clear.

A statement by the Williams team stressing they had intended to call him in for a tyre change soon after the accident was greeted with some scorn.

Greg Norman wins Open at last

By Michael Williams

PUBLISHED MONDAY 21 JULY

Greg Norman, so near, and yet so far, so often on golf's great occasions, at last crossed the threshold at Turnberry yesterday when, with a display that showed no sign of nerves, he won the Open championship and, with it, a first prize of £70,000.

A final round of 69 for a total of 280 brought him safely home by five strokes from the Yorkshireman Gordon J. Brand, while Ian Woosnam of Wales and Bernhard Langer of West Germany tied for third place, another stroke away.

Norman is the first Australian to win the title since the great Peter Thomson took the last of his five titles at Royal Birkdale in 1965, while his five-stroke margin was one of the biggest in postwar years.

Only Johnny Miller, at Royal Birkdale in 1976, and Arnold Palmer, at Troon in 1962, have won by more – six strokes in each case.

But that will not matter to Norman, 31, who had begun to look like the man who might never win a major championship. That he had the game for it had long been clear. It was his nerve that was more questionable.

Two years ago, in the US Open at Winged Foot, he was beaten in a play-off by Fuzzy Zoeller after that infamous second shot which went into a grandstand that nearly cost him a tie at the 18th.

Then, in the Masters earlier this year, he came to the last hole needing a birdie three to win, but instead took five after a similarly wild second shot and lost to Jack Nicklaus.

Opportunity beckoned again in the US Open at Shinnecock Hills only last month, but again he could not hold on to a one-stroke lead going into the final round and faded quietly away.

All these things must have been playing on Norman's mind yesterday as he again went into this final round a stroke ahead of Tommy Nakajima, of Japan, who could not sustain his challenge.

But Norman, an imposingly tall figure with a handsome swing to match, always knew he could do it, while nothing spurred him more than the support he received from other players.

He wanted to play well, and he did, even if there was a tinge of disappointment in that he did not break par for the four rounds. 'I wanted to prove that the Royal and Ancient had not built a monster,' he said.

Greg Norman, the Great White Shark, battled stormy weather at Turnberry to take his first British Open title by a convincing margin.

Tyson brings back nobility to boxing

By Donald Saunders in Las Vegas
PUBLISHED MONDAY 24 NOVEMBER

The noble and manly art of boxing can at last cease worrying about its immediate future, now it has discovered a heavyweight champion of the world fit to stand alongside Jack Dempsey, Gene Tunney, Joe Louis, Rocky Marciano and Muhammad Ali.

Mike Tyson has won a reprieve for this ancient and much-abused sport by taking the WBC title from Trevor Berbick with a performance of great distinction at the tender age of 20.

Tyson's second-round victory, at the Hilton Centre in Las Vegas, was achieved in such awesome style that a significant decline in the worldwide popularity of boxing surely will now be arrested.

Following Marciano's retirement in 1955, 20 heavyweights had called themselves world champion before Berbick's annihilation on Saturday night.

Having enjoyed the opportunity to study all but two least distinguished of those 20 during nearly 40 title bouts, I have no hesitation in concluding that Tyson is a more devastating fighter than any of them.

Looking back over the five minutes 35 seconds his first title bout lasted, it is difficult to appreciate that the new WBC champion is a novice.

Tyson walks away from a floored Berbick. The second-round destruction of his opponent gave Tyson the WBC heavyweight crown.

Those who believe boxing is rather more than simply a matter of one man battering another to the boards were exhilarated by the speed and skill with which Tyson delivered his deadly hooks and uppercuts.

It was like watching that great middleweight, Sugar Ray Robinson, punching with the lethal power of Joe Louis, one of the most distinguished of all heavyweights.

A combination of lefts and rights sent Berbick stumbling to the canvas in the second round and, although he got up, he was soon in trouble again. Tyson sank a savage right to the body, then brought up a sickening left hook to the temple, stepped back and shoved the helpless Berbick to the floor.

A few moments later, Tyson was excitedly declaring: 'I'm the youngest heavyweight champion of the world – but I'm going to be the oldest!'

Australians punish Britain

By Graham Tait
PUBLISHED MONDAY 27 OCTOBER
Great Britain 16 pts; Australia 38

It was hardly a secret. Despite a general rise in playing standards, Great Britain are not as good as the Australians, who went into this first Whitbread Trophy rugby league Test at Old Trafford feeling confident but expecting a sustained challenge to their authority.

What they did not take into account was charity. The tourists must have been amazed at Great Britain's contribution to their own downfall.

The home side fumbled their way through an opening 40 minutes of tactical ineptitude littered with any number of handling errors. Supposedly taking advantage of a strong blustery wind at their back in the first half, Britain persisted in running the ball from defence when the most simple of agricultural methods would have sufficed.

On the credit side, there were ten minutes early in the second half when the home side showed their potential but, after a brilliant try by Joe Lydon, charity allowed the Australians back, Henderson Gill making a hash of Wally Lewis's kick-off and the tourists scoring almost from the drop-out. That was the end of the home cause.

1986

SPORT IN BRIEF

ATHLETICS
In the European Championships in Stuttgart, Jürgen Hingsen **(below, putting the shot)** and Daley Thompson indulge in another epic battle in the decathlon. Once more Hingsen fails to overtake Thompson, who takes gold.

CRICKET
On 6 September the NatWest Trophy final is contested between Sussex and Lancashire. Lancashire bat first and make 242 for eight, but Sussex reply with 245 for three. Sussex all-rounder Dermot Reeve takes the Man-of-the-Match award after taking four for 20 in the Lancashire innings.

FOOTBALL
Following a riot by Millwall supporters Luton decide to ban away supporters in an effort to combat hooliganism. However, as a result of their initiative they are banned from playing in the League Cup.

1987

England complete remarkable cricket treble

By Peter West

PUBLISHED THURSDAY 12 FEBRUARY

In acclaiming England's victory over Australia last night by eight runs in a gut-wrenching finish, I think we should recall what the mood was on the eve of the first Test in November.

England's cricketers then looked back on three successive Test series lost against West Indies, India and New Zealand and not a single victory in 11 matches.

Their form leading up to the first Test inspired no confidence to say the least. There had been no greater problem than finding a successful opening partnership.

And yet, since that stunning victory at Brisbane, England have won the Test series 2–1, retained the Ashes, won the quadrangular Perth Challenge and now, for the first time, the Benson and Hedges World Series Cup without the need of a third encounter at Melbourne.

Had England scored enough (187 for nine) after Gatting had opted yesterday to bat first – even though the Sydney pitch is never quite predictable?

It hardly seemed so after Geoff Marsh and Allan Border had launched Australia's reply – not without a good deal of luck against Graham Dilley and Philip De Freitas – with 55 for their first wicket by the tenth over. Border certainly lived dangerously.

It was Botham, with three wickets for seven runs off 27 balls and limping slightly, who turned the tide. But S. P. O'Donnell brought Australia within 18 runs of victory when the last over began. It was bowled by Neil Foster. Taylor obtained a single off the first ball; O'Donnell could manage only four twos off the last five. His brave innings of 40 not out came from 27 balls.

There could be only one man for the Player-of-the-Final Award. Botham's all-round contribution yesterday, allied to his 71 in the first game as well as nine tidy overs, left him without a rival for the prize.

DID YOU KNOW?

The unfortunate Gary Mabbutt, who scored at both ends in the Cup final, was the third player to do so. Charlton's Bert Taylor did the same in 1946 when Derby won; and Manchester City's Tommy Hutchinson scored both goals in their 1981 draw with Spurs. Spurs won the replay.

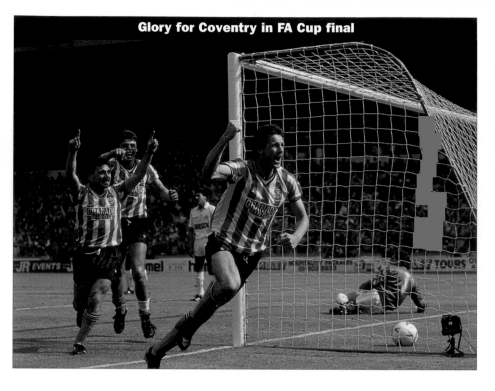

Keith Houchen netting Coventry's second goal (above) and (below), with Dave Bennett, lifting the cup. It was Coventry's first FA Cup win.

By Donald Saunders

PUBLISHED MONDAY 18 MAY

Coventry 3; Tottenham 2, after extra time

The FA Cup has reconfirmed, in front of millions of assenting fans, its unchallengeable right to remain the most distinguished competition in the ever-changing world of club soccer.

Protecting its illustrious reputation with the vigilance of the Privy Council, this ancient tournament has rejected Tottenham's claim to become the first club to win it eight times.

And Coventry have been permitted, at last, to join the other 40 holders of this coveted trophy. No one can gainsay the justice of these decisions, taken at Wembley, in a final of the highest quality.

Spurs did not play well enough and long enough to deserve retention of their undefeated FA Cup final record or stretch their triumphs beyond Aston Villa's seven.

Coventry, though twice behind, responded with such purpose to the demands of this great occasion – their first appearance – that the prize they have sought for 104 years could no longer be denied them.

For the jovial, deceptively shrewd managerial team of George Curtis and John Sillett, Coventry's success is an outstanding achievement.

Defeat is a bitter disappointment for David Pleat, Tottenham's manager. Mr Pleat is too honest to avoid facing the unpalatable truth. He understands the Spurs did not do enough in any of the domestic competitions when it mattered most. Mr Pleat has encouraged a style that depends heavily on a high standard of individual skill within a sophisticated tactical system. So, there is always a danger when key players fail that the rest will quickly lose their way.

This is what happened on Saturday. Twice Tottenham moved in front, in the second and 40th minutes; twice they failed to prevent Coventry hitting back.

Thereafter, Coventry's less gifted but more resolute footballers took control and marched to the most exhilarating FA Cup final victory since Everton beat Sheffield Wednesday by the same margin 21 years ago.

As they trooped despondently into the tunnel, Spurs might have been tempted to blame Gary Mabbutt who, having scored their second goal, achieved the unsought distinction of putting Coventry's winner into his own net in the sixth minute of extra time.

But a solitary mistake by a tired player does not explain this result. In truth, Coventry found two men of the moment on an afternoon when Spurs were let down by two of their most distinguished players. Lloyd McGrath and Dave Bennett won this match for Coventry as surely as Glen Hoddle and Richard Gough lost it for Tottenham.

That old magic gives 'Sugar' Ray Leonard victory

By Donald Saunders in Las Vegas
PUBLISHED WEDNESDAY 8 APRIL.

'Sugar' Ray Leonard has flown home to Maryland with the world middleweight title packed safely in his baggage and the old cliché that they 'never come back' buried deep beneath the sands of the Nevada desert.

Boxing for only the second time since a detached retina forced his premature retirement five years ago, Leonard brought a welcome touch of magic back to a tired old sport, before ending Marvin Hagler's seven-year reign as champion on a split decision.

'Now I want to go away and enjoy this accomplishment,' he pleaded, brushing aside all inquiries about his future.

Until the closing rounds of a gruelling battle drained the strength from his legs, Leonard gave a virtuoso performance which left the fans still dazzled as they shuffled out of the car park of Caesars Palace, Las Vegas, an hour later.

During the most absorbing contest I have seen since Joe Frazier outpointed Muhammad Ali, at Madison

Square Gardens in 1971, Leonard scaled heights of brilliance that must have earned a nod of approval even from the incomparable 'Sugar' Ray Robinson.

His footwork was balletic; his tactics intelligently planned and executed to perfection; his punching so accurate, so fast that he might have been in the gym sharpening up on the speedball.

Yet, I must agree with Hagler that Leonard did not really win this fight. Though the new champion danced away with the early rounds, his quickfire flurries and 'show-boating' in the later stages did not accumulate as many points on my card as did Hagler's persistent, if unspectacular, aggression.

In short, I believed the artist painted the prettier picture, but the street fighter did the more effective job over the 12 rounds.

Two of the judges thought otherwise, one of them by the ludicrous margin of ten rounds to two.

Perhaps it was this inept judgment that caused Hagler – so long a champion of honour and dignity – to complain loudly of robbery.

When he has had time to absorb a dreadful blow to his pride, Hagler might regret his hasty words. Even to hint at a 'fix' is to devalue a memorably sporting occasion to which he has made a major contribution.

Sugar Ray Leonard (in white shorts, below) took the WBC middleweight title on a split decision.

SPORT IN BRIEF

AMERICAN FOOTBALL

On 25 January in Pasadena, the New York Giants take on the Denver Broncos for the Super Bowl championship. For the first time in their history the Giants take the prize, winning 39–20; their quarter-back Phil Simms takes the Most Valuable Player award.

YACHTING

Dennis Conner's *Stars and Stripes* **(above)** wins the America's Cup for the United States. Alan Bond and John Bertrand had taken the cup to Australia four years earlier, but do not reach this year's final. Kevin Parry's *Kookaburra III* sails for Australia, but loses 4–0 to *Stars and Stripes*.

GOLF

In April Larry Mize claims the US Masters at Augusta, after a play-off against Greg Norman and Seve Ballesteros. Mize wins at the second extra hole, when he holes a running pitch from 140 feet. It is a very popular win: Mize was born in Augusta.

RUGBY UNION

The Pilkington Cup is won by Bath for the fourth year in succession. In a repeat of the 1986 final, Bath play Wasps, this time winning 19–12, having won 25–17 last time. In 1985 they beat London Welsh 24–15, and in 1984 Bristol were their victims, by a narrow 10–9 margin.

1987

1987

PUBLISHED WEDNESDAY 22 JULY

New Zealand recorded one of the biggest rugby league surprises of recent years by beating Australia 13–6 yesterday.

The scoreline did scant justice to the young New Zealand side's superiority. They displayed courage in recovering from an early shock when the game's unofficial world champions went ahead with a superb try by scrum half Peter Sterling, set up by a surging run from captain Wally Lewis, with Michael O'Connor converting. But a quick converted try by prop Ross Taylor, and another effort by winger Gary Mercer put New Zealand in front.

Mercer added a drop goal just before half-time for a 13–6 lead to New Zealand at the break.

Australian Dale Shearere crossed the line in the 75th minute but his try was disallowed.

Lewis had few excuses after the game. 'We didn't play well enough on the night. But full credit to the Kiwis, they deserved their win.'

France squeeze past Australia in epic semi-final

By John Mason

PUBLISHED MONDAY 15 JUNE

Of the many things that France and Australia accomplished in a superlative exhibition of rugby skills, the most important was to sweep away the last lurking doubts about either the validity or the future of rugby's World Cup.

The irrefutable truth of a sporting occasion that played havoc with the emotions was that a match of wit, intelligence and competitive endeavour was possible no matter how important the prize.

The contest hijacked the senses from the start. Even a day later it was difficult to absorb everything that happened, so varied were the exchanges, so subtle the nuances, so emphatic the cut and thrust.

France, though outscoring Australia by four tries to two, required Serge Blanco at his most bold to settle the match and secure France a place in the final of rugby's first World Cup - a try in the left-hand corner barely two minutes from time. The prospect of extra time to decide the issue did not appeal to the French.

Victory by four tries and two penalties to two tries, a dropped goal and three penalties was a fair result of a match in which the only disappointment had to be the

In a gripping semi-final (below), France and Australia played a game of the highest quality.

thin attendance of 17,000. In Sydney rugby union has many hills still to climb.

It would be hard to exaggerate the drama and excitement of the proceedings which began with a stylish dropped goal and a penalty goal from Michael Lynagh in the opening seven minutes.

Philippe Sella, probably the best centre in the world, Alain Lorieux, who wrestled the ball from Troy Coker at the lineout, and the speeding Patrice Lagisquet scored the other tries for France and the tidy, unobtrusive Didier Camberabero kicked six goals from eight attempts.

David Campese, establishing a world record for tries in internationals, and David Codey, the replacement for Campbell, scored Australia's tries in a memorable encounter during which Lynagh claimed another 16 points — a dropped goal, three penalties and both conversions. If you get a chance to see the match on film, take it.

MILESTONES

Lincoln City became the first team to be automatically relegated from the football League. In previous years the team that finished bottom of all four divisions could apply for re-election. This rule was used most frequently by Hartlepool United, who successfully reapplied 14 times.

Nigel Mansell snatches dramatic victory

By Brian Allen

PUBLISHED MONDAY 13 JULY

Shortly before he stepped into the cockpit of his Williams-Honda on the grid before the British Grand Prix yesterday, Nigel Mansell declared: 'I expected a very interesting race.'

Interesting it certainly was, but little did he know just how he would have to battle for his tenth GP victory.

On the first Silverstone circuit the two Williams of Mansell and Nelson Piquet were quite uncatchable. It was a tense and exciting duel between two talented drivers striving to demonstrate who was No. 1.

After his criticism of Mansell a few days earlier, and his avowal that his motivation was still strong, Piquet was determined to prove a point. He led from the start and, though he did not make a significant break, he seemed able to control his advantage over Mansell.

In front of an enthusiastic home crowd, Mansell drives his Williams-Honda to his third win of the year.

Around halfway, Mansell began to make a charge but on lap 35, with 30 to go, he stormed into the pits for a rapid tyre change. It cured a serious vibration caused through a lost balance-weight but, despite the slick work by his mechanics, it cost him nearly half a minute.

Piquet drove with all the nerve of a twice world champion, but Mansell remorselessly closed the gap. With eight laps to go the margin was under four seconds and on lap 63 with 21 remaining, Mansell slipped through on the inside of Piquet at Stowe Corner. There was nothing Piquet could do to reply, and he had to be content with second place, 1.9 seconds behind Mansell.

It was an epic battle, a fitting climax to the intense duel they fought during qualifying. The support of the crowd Mansell described as 'unbelievable'.

The draw that left us all exhausted

By Peter Deeley at Edgbaston

PUBLISHED WEDNESDAY 29 JULY

In a marvellous finale to what had been for four days a pedestrian Test, England failed by 15 runs – and Pakistan by three wickets – to snatch victory.

So it was the draw everyone had predicted, but one of those games without result that left everyone privileged to watch the final hours emotionally drained, players and spectators alike.

This final day in the fourth Cornhill Test saw no fewer than 17 wickets fall for 276 runs. That statistic alone tells something of how the balance swung from caution to full-blooded aggression.

By bowling Pakistan out for 205, England were always in the driving seat in the final run chase. That

they were ever in such a position was due largely to Neil Foster, four for 59, supported by Ian Botham and Graham Dilley, who each took two wickets.

In their quest for the 124 runs needed for victory, England faced a task which might have been on in a one-day game. But Pakistan's bowlers, Imran Khan and Wasim Akram, had the benefit of being able to bowl both short and wide, a measure which would have been denied them in the lesser competition.

With Bill Athey and John Emburey there, 17 were needed off the final six balls. But run-out disasters, Emburey off the first ball and Phil Edmonds off the third, signalled the end.

Pakistan won the series 1–0; four Tests were drawn.

1987

1987

Cool Davies putts way to history in US Open

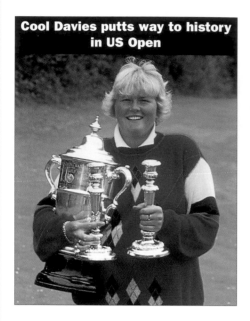

By Lewine Mair in Plainfield, New Jersey
PUBLISHED WEDNESDAY 29 JULY

Laura Davies became the first British player to win the United States women's Open **(above)**, finishing two shots ahead of that master of the short iron, Ayako Okamoto, and three shots clear of Jo-Anne Carner.

The English golfer, 23, had a good night's rest before the play-off. She then began as she finished on Monday, making awkward little putts at each of the first three holes.

At the fourth she moved into a clear lead for the first time, holing from seven yards.

The Japanese girl showed early signs of cracking at the 181-yard fifth when she hit her tee shot into a lily pond. She made the most gallant of fours but at the next, dropped a further shot to go two behind Miss Davies.

Miss Davies has made a greater impact than any other, and no remark is more telling than that from Nancy Lopez.

As she watched Davies in the closing stages, Miss Lopez turned to her friend Lori Garbacz and said, 'If this girl were to play over here next year she'd be our leading money-winner.'

Roche tops season with world cycling title

By a special correspondent in Villach, Austria
PUBLISHED MONDAY 7 SEPTEMBER

Ireland's Stephen Roche, 27, crowned a remarkable season by winning the world professional road-race title in Austria yesterday to add to his victories earlier this summer in the Tour de France and Tour of Italy.

The Dubliner timed his effort to perfection at the climax of the 170-mile race, sprinting away from four breakaway companions just 300 yards from the line to win by three lengths from the defending champion, Morino Argentin of Italy.

'It was all or nothing,' said Roche. 'I knew if I waited any longer I would only be fourth or fifth, so I took the bull by the horns.'

Only 12 months ago Roche's whole career was threatened by a knee injury.

The race at Villach, which began in heavy thunderstorms, only came to life in the last 35 miles, and Roche and compatriot Sean Kelly were in a group of 13 riders who escaped at the start of the last seven-and-a-half mile lap.

There were several attacks at the front until Roche found himself clear of other riders, but they slowed in the closing stages, allowing the others to regain contact as Roche flashed across the line. Kelly was awarded fifth place.

Ireland's Stephen Roche with the mayor of Dublin. Roche's victory put him alongside Belgian Eddy Merckx as the only rider to win the Tours of France, Italy and Austria in the same season.

Europe hold on to Ryder Cup

By Michael Williams in Dublin, Ohio
PUBLISHED MONDAY 28 SEPTEMBER

After a day of almost unbearable excitement, Europe successfully defended the Ryder Cup at Muirfield Village yesterday, when they defeated the United States by 15–13.

After their handsome five-point lead going into the last series of singles, it was however an absolute cliff-hanger as the Americans fought to their last breath, which is so typical of them.

They took the singles by six games to three, with another three halved, but this was the only one of the five series of games that they won.

Never before have the Americans been beaten at home, and the European Ryder Cup team therefore follows in the footsteps of the Curtis Cup team, which won in the States last year.

It is a significant triumph for Tony Jacklin, the European captain, who has now led two successive winning teams. He arranged his batting order perfectly, for his two strongest players, Severiano Ballesteros and Bernhard Langer, came up trumps as the pack of cards was in danger of collapsing.

Ballesteros, relishing the challenge of playing Curtis Strange, led at one point by three up, but was brought back to one with five to play.

However, he took the 14th, and a four at the 17th closed his man out, seconds after Langer had made sure of at least a tie against Nelson.

Langer had been three down with seven to play against Larry Nelson, but came back with a string of birdies and did not falter again.

Other crucial contributions came from Howard Clark and Eamonn Darcy, both of whom won, against Dan Pohl and Ben Crenshaw, while valuable half points came from Sam Torrance and Gordon Brand Junior.

But, by goodness, it was touch and go, uncomfortably so, and all credit to the Americans, whose pride very nearly tipped the scales.

Tony Jacklin, the European captain, gets a lift from Ian Woosnam after Europe's great Ryder Cup victory.

MILESTONES

Welshman Ian Woosnam became the first golfer to earn more than £1 million in a year. He won five tournaments, including the World Matchplay, and also topped the European earnings with £439,075.

Ian Woosnam takes Wales to World Cup victory

By Richard Bright in Hawaii
PUBLISHED MONDAY 23 NOVEMBER

Ian Woosnam, winner of last month's World Matchplay Championship, clinched the World Cup for Wales with his partner, David Llewellyn, in Hawaii after a play-off with Scotland. Both players made par at the second extra hole and collected $100,000 each.

Woosnam won another $50,000 for the best individual score of the tournament – a magnificent 14-under-par 274.

'I've never played better in worse conditions,' said a soaking-wet Woosnam after a par 72 in the final round played in heavy rain and a high wind.

The title went to Wales for the first time when Sam Torrance, of Scotland, three-putted at the second extra hole after Sandy Lyle had safely made par. 'I just hit the ball too hard,' explained Torrance after shooting his first putt five feet too far and just missing the return.

Llewellyn, who struggled for most of the week, saved his best golf for the last day. He parred his way round the final nine holes, saving par from a greenside bunker at the last for a 76.

There was no disputing who was the outstanding player of the tournament, though, 'Woosnam has got to be the best player in the world right now,' said Llewellyn. 'I've never seen golf played like that.'

Even the unassuming Woosnam said: 'I played pretty solid. Fourteen under is pretty good in those conditions.'

Wales and Scotland both finished with a total of 574, two under par for the 6,761-yard Bay Course of the Kapalua Bay Golf Club, which was buffeted by strong winds and rain throughout the four-day tournament.

Despite a final round of 71 by Howard Clark, England slumped to a total of 288, 14 behind Wales and Scotland.

The United States team of Ben Crenshaw and Payne Stewart shot even par for the tournament to finish in third place on 576.

Umpire accuses Gatting after angry exchange

Michael Austin in Faisalabad
PUBLISHED WEDNESDAY 9 DECEMBER

Shakoor Rana, the umpire, last night threatened to pull out of the second Test in Faisalabad unless he received an apology from Mike Gatting, the England captain, following a war of words just before the end of yesterday's play.

Mr Rana, 54, said after the close of play: 'I am reporting Gatting to the Test and County Cricket Board, the tour manager Peter Lush and the Pakistan Board for using foul and abusive language. No captain has spoken to me like that before.'

Later Mr Rana said he would not take the field today unless Gatting showed contrition, prompting fears that the whole tour could be in jeopardy.

A productive day in cricket terms for England was especially prosperous for John Emburey who took three for 26 as Pakistan struggled to 106 for five in reply to 292, Chris Broad making 116 in seven hours and Iqbal Qasim returning five for 83.

In other respects, a more unsavoury saga would be difficult to imagine. It ended with Gatting and Mr Rana exchanging words almost eyeball to eyeball during the final over, and being separated by Bill Athey, who ushered away his captain.

Sadly Gatting, having urged his tour party to keep their heads in controversial circumstances, lost his during a finger-wagging, heated argument with Mr Rana, who had earlier given two dubious decisions against England.

The triviality of the cause and the violent verbal aftermath sums up the powder-keg on which this three-match series sits. A five-match programme would probably not last the course.

Mr Rana, umpiring at square leg, intervened when Eddie Hemmings was running in to bowl because he believed that Gatting was changing his field behind the back of Salim Malik, the batsman.

Gatting, who was fielding at backward short leg, said: 'I had already informed Salim that I was bringing in Capel, the deep square leg fielder, and when Hemmings was running in I indicated to Capel with my hand that he had come in far enough. Obviously the umpire thought I was cheating. A few words passed between us but I am not saying what because I don't want a slanging match.

'I just felt that it was not his job at square leg to inform the batsman what I was doing.'

Gatting and Shakoor Rana call a truce after 65 hours of negotiation and an apology from Gatting. The England captain had engaged in a finger-wagging row with the umpire during the second Test in Pakistan.

LAWN TENNIS
British pairing Jeremy Bates and Jo Durie claim the Wimbledon mixed doubles title. Durie is the first British woman to win a Wimbledon title since Virginia Wade won the ladies' singles in 1977. Bates is the first British man to take a Wimbledon title since John Lloyd won the mixed doubles with Australian Wendy Turnbull in 1983.

BASKETBALL
Playing for the Chicago Bulls in the National Basketball Association league, Michael Jordan finishes as the season's highest points scorer for the first time. He scores 3,041 points in 82 games.

LAWN TENNIS
Australian Pat Cash meets the losing finalist from 1986, Ivan Lendl, in the Wimbledon men's singles final. Lendl suffers disappointment again (the Wimbledon title will always elude him) as Cash comes through 7–6, 6–2, 7–5. In an athletic celebration, Cash climbs up to the box from which his family are watching before returning to claim the trophy.

CRICKET
In the cricket World Cup held in India and Pakistan, Australia meet Pakistan in Lahore in the semi-final, and win by 18 runs. Australian Craig McDermott takes five for 44. In the other semi-final, England meet India in Bombay. Graham Gooch scores 115, and Eddie Hemmings bowls well to give England a win by 35 runs. In the final in Calcutta, a 70,000-strong crowd watch a close battle between Australia and England. Australia win by just seven runs, and captain Allan Border lifts the trophy.

RUGBY UNION
New Zealand score the highest number of points in an international when they beat Japan 106–4 in Tokyo.

1987

1988

Witt elated as Thomas fails ultimate test

By Michael Calvin

PUBLISHED MONDAY 29 FEBRUARY

Thankfully Debi Thomas did not linger after delivering her solemn words of self-justification. The sight of Katarina Witt giggling like a naughty schoolgirl would have been too much to take.

The East German champion, obliged to drink beer for the first time in her life in the doping control area, was high on a mixture of alcohol, adrenalin and a sense of achievement. As only the second girl successfully to defend an Olympic figure-skating title, she can look forward to being allowed to pursue a lucrative professional career outside the Eastern bloc.

But, in the Olympic Saddledome, material rewards were put into perspective. Witt's greatest satisfaction came from the knowledge she had resisted the most severe personal pressure international sport has to offer.

'I wanted to show the world that I was best,' she said. 'I saw Debi was very nervous. She showed me she is not a miracle.'

Thomas, beaten by Elizabeth Manley of Canada for the silver medal when she had an outstanding chance to win the gold, will have a void in her life no amount of philosophical reflection can fill.

Her desperation to win the Olympic title was so painfully obvious that watching her struggle through her free programme was rather like an intrusion into private grief. The stage smile might have remained intact but inside Thomas was numb.

'I just wanted to get off the ice,' she said. 'When that first jump was not there my heart was not in it. I don't know if the pressure got to me but I was not comfortable with myself.'

The American did not require any reminding that she had disappointed a nation which craves Olympic success. Thomas must now learn to live with the stigma of being the girl who failed the ultimate test.

DID YOU KNOW?

Twenty-one-year-old Graeme Hick, playing for Worcestershire against Somerset at Taunton, made the eighth highest individual score of all time when he scored 405 not out. He faced 469 balls and set his team up for a winning 628–7.

Hopes of returning to Europe are hit by convictions

By Donald Saunders

PUBLISHED SATURDAY 16 APRIL

The conviction of two England footballers in a Glasgow court yesterday on charges of disorderly conduct and a breach of the peace, during a Rangers–Celtic match, will inevitably further damage British soccer's already badly tarnished reputation.

Though Terry Butcher and Chris Woods have been found guilty of offences while playing for a Scottish team, their misconduct will scarcely enhance the prospects of a return to European competition by English clubs next season.

UEFA, hearing that two England players have been involved in a fracas on the pitch – albeit in Scotland – must now seriously doubt whether English fans can be trusted to behave themselves if League clubs are allowed back into Europe.

The Glasgow police clearly detected a connection between trouble on the pitch and subsequent violence on the terraces. They had every right to prosecute.

The Shrewsbury magistrates took a similar view, 24 hours earlier, when Chris Kamara, a Swindon player, was fined £1,200 for causing grievous bodily harm to Jim Melrose of Shrewsbury.

Even so, it must be hoped that the outcome of these two cases will not encourage regular use of the law, either in Scotland or England, when footballers are involved in a punch-up.

I shudder to think what might happen on the terraces if a posse of police officers invaded the pitch to haul a misbehaving local hero off to the local nick.

Nevertheless, the news from Glasgow and Shrewsbury this week contains a clear warning to footballers. Violence on the pitch is now, officially, as grave an offence as violence on the terraces.

Tomba la Bomba leads all the way

By Alan Smith

PUBLISHED FRIDAY 26 FEBRUARY

Italy's Alberto Tomba lived up to his reputation, and his nickname 'Tomba la Bomba', when he turned the Olympic giant slalom into a solo tour of honour at Nakiska yesterday.

In a sport where results are usually measured in hundredths, he had more than a second to spare in 2 min 6.37 sec.

Austria's Hubert Strolz, the combined winner, was second, and in this battle of champions the downhill gold medallist, Pirmin Zurbriggen, of Switzerland, took the bronze.

Tomba, 21, the extrovert son of a textile millionaire from Bologna, has burst upon the ski scene this season, winning four out of five World Cup slaloms and three of five giant slaloms.

Built more on the lines of an operatic tenor than an athlete – though he lost a lot of weight before the start of this season – he is nevertheless lightning fast on his feet, with an instinctive feel for the slopes.

Roberta Siorpaes, former Italian international who trained him in his early days, said: 'He caresses the snow like a big cat.'

His overwhelming enjoyment of the adulation that goes with success has endeared Tomba to many. Before and after a race, or even between runs, he strolls among 'his people', hugging and kissing them – the older women as well as the pretty young ones.

In full flight, Tomba 'la Bomba' skis towards giant slalom gold. He also won gold in the slalom.

SPORT IN BRIEF

RUGBY UNION

At the age of 22, Harlequins centre Will Carling is appointed England captain by coach Geoff Cooke. The choice of such a young captain is vindicated when, in Carling's first match in charge, England beat Australia 28–19.

FOOTBALL

A Holland side including Ruud Gullit, Marco Van Basten and Frank Rijkaard win the European Championship when they overcome the Soviet Union 2–0 in the final. The goals come from Gullit and Van Basten. Earlier in the tournament a hat trick from Van Basten had seen England's hopes of success ended.

ATHLETICS

David Jenkins, winner of the 400-m gold in the 1971 European championships, is sentenced to seven years in jail and fined after being found guilty of smuggling steroids. He will be released after serving ten months, in return for providing information to the American goverment.

Magnificent birdie gives Sandy Lyle the Masters

By Michael Williams

PUBLISHED MONDAY 11 APRIL

Sandy Lyle **(below right)**, with a magnificent birdie at the final hole, became the first British golfer to win the United States Masters at Augusta yesterday.

After losing a lead of three strokes with nine holes to play, Lyle had two birdies in his last three holes for a final round of 71 and a pulse-raising one-stroke victory over the American Mark Calcavecchia.

At the 18th Lyle, knowing he needed a birdie to win, drove into a fairway bunker, but then hit a magnificent seven iron to eight feet and sank the putt. His rounds of 71, 67, 72, 71 gave him a seven under par total of 281.

'After dropping three shots at 11 and 12 I knew I had two par fives to come, and wanted to make birdies at them,' said Lyle. 'It was a bit disappointing that I didn't, but I just had to keep going.

'I was not too sure of the line on the last putt, but I got it just right.'

Craig Stadler, the 1982 champion, snatched third place with a 68 in the final round for a 283 total.

The two other British contestants disappointed, Nick Faldo finishing with 296 and Ken Brown with 298.

Greg Norman set the standard on the last round with a 64 – only one shot outside the course record – which lifted him into a share of fifth place.

The leading money-winner in America this year, Lyle takes his earnings for the year to more than half a million dollars and career earnings on the US circuit to close on one million dollars.

He won the Phoenix Open in January and the Greater Greensboro Open last week. The last player to take the Greensboro and Masters titles in successive weeks was Sam Snead in 1949.

Thirty-year-old Lyle, a member last year of the first European team to win the Ryder Cup in America, is only the fourth overseas player to triumph in the Masters, the first of the year's 'majors'. The others are Gary Player, who has won three times, Seve Ballesteros (twice) and Bernhard Langer.

Shropshire-born of Scottish parents, Lyle won the Open Championship in 1985 and the American Players' Championship in 1987.

1988

Laurels to Senna, accolades to Mansell

By Brian Allen

PUBLISHED MONDAY 11 JULY

The rain-soaked crowd at Silverstone were warmed to fever heat as Nigel Mansell brought off a surprise second place in yesterday's British Grand Prix.

There was generous tribute to Ayrton Senna, who finished 23 seconds ahead of Mansell to capture his fourth victory this season and the tenth of his career. As in his first grand prix win at Estoril in 1985, McLaren's Brazilian again proved his tremendous talent in the rain.

But applause for Senna was nothing to the roars from the appreciative crowd who accompanied Mansell's skilful and courageous drive as he tore through from 11th place on the grid.

Senna has now drawn to within six points of his McLaren teammate in the drivers' championship.

But the day belonged to the man who came second. The satisfaction glowed all over Mansell's face.

Don Howe's blueprint paves way for Wimbledon

By Colin Gibson

PUBLISHED MONDAY 16 MAY
Liverpool 0; Wimbledon 1

Wimbledon's astonishing and most unlikely victory in the FA Cup final was plotted, fittingly, in the most unlikely of places.

The blueprint for Wimbledon's success was drawn up by their coach Don Howe in a motorway traffic jam.

Trapped on the M25 last week, Mr Howe grappled with the disturbing evidence of the club's final Wembley training session when Wimbledon's reserves ripped apart the first-team defence. The plan that he and manager Bobby Gould had formulated to combat the skill and trickery of John Barnes was in tatters.

A young reserve, asked to copy Barnes's style, ran Alan Cork and Goodyear ragged. A new approach was needed. Mr Gould and Mr Howe agreed that Cork should be switched with the effervescent and diminutive figure of Dennis Wise. The young winger did his job magnificently.

So well, in fact, that Barnes failed, until the last minute, to produce a run of any menace. With him went Liverpool's dreams of their second League and Cup double in three seasons.

Sanchez beats Liverpool keeper Bruce Grobbelaar to take Wimbledon to an outstanding Cup victory.

Wimbledon, with their interests in such experienced hands, stuck to the principles which had carried them to Wembley from the Southern League in 11 years.

They arrived at the old stadium with a billing that would have had Satan consulting the libel laws. They left with the Cup, a whiter than white image and a message of hope for every under-privileged member of the footballing community.

Wimbledon demonstrated that if Liverpool cannot be outbought, then at least there are rare days when they can be outthought and outfought.

When Lawrie Sanchez scored his memorable goal from Wise's free kick in the next attack, it was clear that the gods had decided it was time to embarrass Liverpool.

That feeling was cemented on the hour when Mr Hill unjustly ruled that Goodyear had fouled John Aldridge in the penalty area. Aldridge watched in horror as Dave Beasant plunged to his left to save.

DID YOU KNOW?

Dave Beasant's penalty save was the first to be made in a Wembley FA Cup final, but the second within a month in a Wembley final. In the League Cup final Luton's Andy Dibble had saved a penalty; Luton went on to beat Arsenal 3–2.

US Open is a Strange experience

By Michael Williams in Brookline, Massachusetts
PUBLISHED THURSDAY 16 JUNE

Nick Faldo's dream of adding the United States Open championship to the British title he already holds ended in disappointment yesterday when he was beaten by four strokes at the Country Club in a play-off against Curtis Strange.

It is for Strange, 33, his first major title in a career more notable for his consistency as a money-winner, but yesterday he rose to the occasion with an accomplished round of 71, level par, to Faldo's 75.

Perhaps one might have expected something slightly better on such a 'heavyweight' occasion, but the wind was

Restoring American pride, Curtis Strange took the US Open in the play-off. He went on to win again in 1989.

blustery and the greens slippery on a golf course that is acknowledged as being one of the finest in the United States.

It was never vintage Faldo, and not once did he have his nose in front. He had put too much pressure on himself around the greens, which he just kept missing, but for the Americans it is something of a relief.

The golfer they have begun to believe is the best in their country has at last proved it, and after Ryder and Curtis Cup defeats and Sandy Lyle's victory in the Open, the pendulum has tipped back the other way.

Ballesteros conjures extra inspiration to take third Open

By Michael Williams
PUBLISHED TUESDAY 19 JULY

A quite magnificent final round of 65 at Royal Lytham and St Annes yesterday gave Severiano Ballesteros **(below)** his third Open championship when he got home with two strokes to spare from Nick Price, of Zimbabwe.

Ballesteros's 65 equalled the lowest winning round in the 117-year history of the Open, the other being by Tom Watson at Turnberry in 1977. The Spaniard's 72-hole total of 273, 11 under par, was a record at Lytham by four strokes.

In a sense one could say that Ballesteros, 31, has 'come in from the cold', for it is four years since he won a major championship, the Open at St Andrews in 1984. It was, of course, here at Lytham in 1979

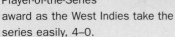

that Ballesteros won his first Open, and such was the warmth of his reception as he received the trophy that there is no doubt he holds a special place in the hearts of the British sporting public.

Yet brilliantly though Ballesteros had played, the ultimate two-stroke margin tells nothing of the magnificent resistance put up by Price who, for the second time in his career, finds himself runner-up.

The other occasion was at Royal Troon in 1982 and yesterday, as then, Price stood on the 18th green with a putt to tie. Ballesteros, already with a one-stroke lead, had chipped exquisitely dead from the back of the green to be sure of his four.

Price had to go for it. He went too far past and missed the one back. It was not really a sad end, for by then it did not matter whether he took four, five, six, seven or even eight; second place was assured.

SPORT IN BRIEF

CRICKET
On the rest day of the first Test match against the West Indies at Trent Bridge, allegations of sexual misconduct are made against the England captain, Mike Gatting. Despite the fact that Gatting's denial of any impropriety is apparently believed by the selectors, Gatting is sacked from the captaincy to be replaced by Middlesex spinner John Emburey.

MOTOR RACING
In June Britons Johnny Dumfries and Andy Wallace combine with Dutchman Jan Lammers to win the Le Mans 24-hours' race. Driving a Jaguar they complete 394 laps of the circuit, driving a total of 3,313.540 miles between them.

CRICKET
Malcolm Marshall **(right)** enjoys an excellent tour with the West Indies. At Old Trafford 'Mr Whippy' takes seven for 22; his tour figures are 35 wickets at a cost of just 12.65 runs each. Marshall wins the Player-of-the-Series award as the West Indies take the series easily, 4–0.

BOXING
Thomas 'the Hit Man' Hearns challenges for Sugar Ray Leonard's WBC super middleweight title. Since being beaten in the 14th round by Leonard seven years ago, Hearns has been determined to avenge his defeat. Leonard is the favourite, but Hearns presses him hard and Leonard just manages to hold on to his title in a split 12th-round draw.

1988

1988

By Ken Mays

PUBLISHED FRIDAY 30 SEPTEMBER

Al Joyner, husband of Florence Griffith-Joyner and brother of Jackie Joyner-Kersee, yesterday defended the two Olympic gold medallists after accusations that they had used illegal methods to obtain their successes.

Mrs Joyner (below) added the 200-m gold medal to the 100 m she won on Saturday, and twice broke the world record in the process.

Mrs Kersee, already the Olympic heptathlon champion and record-holder, came from behind to win the long-jump gold medal.

But following the Ben Johnson drug scandal it seems that every successful athlete is under suspicion.

'The trouble with some people is that if they see success, then they have to point the finger that it was not done above board,' said Joyner.

He was reacting to a television interview in which Joachim Cruz, the Brazilian who won the Olympic 800-m gold in Los Angeles, said that Mrs Joyner looked like a man. What she achieved could not have been achieved legally, he said.

'He implied that Flo was using something. It is simply not true. I have always been the one to argue that there should be random tests at training camps as well as in competition,' said Joyner.

On the track Mrs Joyner looked every inch the glamour girl when she shattered the record of 21.71 sec shared by Marita Koch and Heike Drechsler, with an amazing 21.56 sec in the semi-final.

Johnson tragedy signals salvation for the honest

Johnson (on left, above) finishes ahead of Carl Lewis in the 100-m final. He was later exposed as a cheat.

By Michael Calvin

PUBLISHED TUESDAY 27 SEPTEMBER

The shrill sound of telephone calls waking Seoul at five this morning, local time, signalled salvation for the honest sportsmen and -women of the world. For as the sleep of the Olympic family was broken by news of the disgrace of sprinter Ben Johnson, it began to realise that the fight against drug abuse in sport is serious and increasingly successful.

It is important to look beyond the human tragedy of the Canadian, who, with one 75-millilitre sample of his urine, taken after the 100-m final, found himself branded as the most notable cheat in sports history.

His positive drug test added substance to the rumours which have dogged him ever since he emerged, heavily muscled, to push back what we hoped were the boundaries of human excellence.

The significance of his downfall is heartening to those like Britain's Sir Arthur Gold who have insisted that sport's obligation is to protect its future generations.

When he estimated that 50 per cent of Olympic competitors had been involved in some form of drug misuse, some accused him of alarmist talk. His comment that those discovered cheating in Seoul would be 'either careless or ill-advised' was, however, unanswerable.

Johnson represented the justification for the pollution of one's body with performance-enhancing chemicals. He had fame, money and medals. Too many of his contemporaries were willing to ignore the suspicion that those were acquired under false pretences.

The risks in so doing may now become prohibitive. What must happen — perhaps through a development of the anti-doping charter being processed by the International Olympic Committee — is that the initiative be seized. Juan Antonio Samaranch would make many enemies but a million friends if he suggested such sanctions as banning from the Games sports which are known to be tainted by widespread drug abuse.

The weightlifting competition has been scarred by the exposure of the Bulgarian squad as wholesale cheats. From Sweden and America comes news of athletes involved in anabolic steroid smuggling rings.

Sport may still reflect the ills of a society in which it exists. But sportsmen must also live with themselves. Today Ben Johnson will find that unbelievably difficult.

DID YOU KNOW?

After an absence of 64 years, tennis reappeared among the disciplines in the Seoul Olympic Games. Table tennis was included for the first time; Yoo Nam Kyu of Korea won the men's title, and Jing Chen of China the women's.

Refined Sugar makes it record five world titles

By John Hiscock in Las Vegas
PUBLISHED WEDNESDAY 9 NOVEMBER

Sugar Ray Leonard **(in foreground, right)** added two more world titles to his collection when he knocked out the WBC light-heavyweight champion Donny Lalonde, of Canada, in the ninth round at Caesars Palace, Las Vegas, on Monday.

Now he is assured of his place in boxing history after winning a record five world titles at different weights.

In a display of courage and ability Leonard, 32, twice came back from the brink of defeat to out-punch and out-muscle the bigger, stronger Lalonde.

He recovered from a fourth-round knockdown to fight his way back and establish supremacy over Lalonde, 28.

Yet Lalonde was no push-over. He showed why he was the world light-heavyweight champion by stunning Leonard several times with powerful right-hand punches.

In the end Leonard's refined ringcraft saw him through against a brave, strong opponent who responded to the occasion by putting on the fight of his life.

Best to come from all-conquering Steffi Graf

By John Parsons
PUBLISHED MONDAY 12 SEPTEMBER

Steffi Graf celebrated her Grand Slam triumph 35,000 feet over the Atlantic, knowing that the sky is the limit as far as her potential achievements in world tennis are concerned.

Next in line is an Olympic gold medal, and she will be heading for Seoul later this week after a few days at home in West Germany with her family.

Almost as important, though, is the fact that, at 19, she now had nothing to prove bar durability, and there is

excitement that the best is yet to come from a player who moves like Maureen Connolly.

The late 'Little Mo' became the first woman to join the exclusive Grand Slam club in 1953. Its founder member, Don Budge (1938), joined in the ceremony.

Now Graf also stands alongside Rod Laver, Margaret Court and Martina Navratilova.

Steffi Graf's win at Wimbledon (below), and wins at the French, Australian and US Opens gave her the Grand Slam. At the Olympics Graf again beat her opponent in the US Open final – Gabriela Sabatini – to take gold.

LAWN TENNIS

Swede Mats Wilander dominates the men's tennis scene, winning the Australian, French and US Open championships. Unlike Steffi Graf, though, he fails to clinch the Grand Slam; his game is not well suited to the grass courts of Wimbledon.

OLYMPICS

In the Olympic equestrian individual three-day event, Ginny Leng **(below)** finishes third behind Mark Todd of New Zealand and Ian Stark of Britain to claim a bronze medal. She also wins a silver when Britain come second in the team three-day event. West Germany win the team event and New Zealand are third.

HOCKEY

Great Britain win their first Olympic hockey gold medal, beating West Germany 3–1 in the final.

CRICKET

In September Middlesex and Worcestershire contest the NatWest Trophy final at Lord's. Middlesex overhaul Worcestershire's total of 161 for nine with three wickets to spare. The Man-of-the-Match award goes to young Middlesex batsman, Mark Ramprakash, who makes 56.

MOTOR RACING

On 11 September the Italian Grand Prix at Monza is won by Gerhard Berger, driving for Ferrari. The win is very popular among Italian race fans; every other race of the season has been won by either Ayrton Senna or Alain Prost in a McLaren.

1988

1989

Widnes fight back to keep title

By David Mankelow
PUBLISHED MONDAY 17 APRIL
Widnes 32 pts; Wigan 18

Widnes retained the Stones Bitter championship with a tremendous second-half display in which they fought back form an early 12–4 deficit to take control with three tries in eight minutes.

They finished strongly, despite having only 12 men for the last 23 minutes after second row Koloto was sent off for a high tackle on Potter.

With a rich array of talent from Wales, New Zealand and Australia on view, it was a Londoner and a Scotsman who led the way for Widnes in a match that lived up to all expectations, despite the teams' obvious fatigue after a surfeit of matches in the last month.

Martin Offiah, with his sixth try hat trick of the season, and the steady Alan Tait were the pick of a splendid Widnes effort in the final 40 minutes, when Jonathan Davies moved to stand-off from the wing after injuries to David Hulme, and to his replacement Dowd.

Sorensen, McKenzie, Grima and Eyres all played their part in putting Widnes back on course after Wigan were unfortunate to only have a 12–10 interval lead, with Offiah's 39th-minute try providing the turning point.

Referee Holdsworth waved play on after O'Neill's pass looked as if it might have gone forward. The ball ran loose to Offiah who touched down under the posts leaving Davies with an easy goal.

In the 46th minute, McKenzie sent Sorensen over, and within four minutes Offiah raced past Steve Hampson for his 54th try of the season.

Paul Hulme completed the purple patch in the 54th minute, with Eyres supplying the pass for the scrum half to score the try that ended Wigan's hopes.

The superb Ellery Hanley put Wigan within range again with a splendid break to touch down 15 minutes from time.

McKenzie capped a fine match with Widnes's final try three minutes from time, allowing Davies his sixth goal.

Wigan, whose Grand Slam dream has ended, looked in total control early on after the lift of a try from Andy Platt in the opening minute. Offiah replied with a try but Wigan restored a healthy advantage when Andy Goodway brushed past tackles by Offiah and Tait.

Two goals from Joe Lydon, who finished with three successes, gave them a hold which looked unshakeable before Offiah took over.

Desert Orchid's courage decisive in Gold Cup

By Hotspur (Peter Scott)
PUBLISHED FRIDAY 17 MARCH

Desert Orchid yesterday summoned every ounce of courage for his finest hour. He wore down the equally gallant Yahoo in a Tote Cheltenham Gold Cup battle that was made gruelling by the heavy ground.

Mr Richard Burridge, Desert Orchid's principal owner, had considered withdrawing him, but left the final say to trainer David Elsworth, who decided to go ahead.

Neither Elsworth nor jockey Simon Sherwood had feared dead ground, but hours of rain turned it heavy. Snow started falling at breakfast time in neighbouring areas, so Cheltenham were lucky to race.

Ten Plus's death marred what was otherwise a great occasion. Leading Desert Orchid three fences from home, he fell and broke a hind fetlock.

Desert Orchid was in front to half-way, but then Sherwood allowed Ten Plus to go ahead. Sherwood was still biding his time when Ten Plus fell, and reckons the favourite would have won anyway.

Ten Plus's departure still did not leave matters easy, because the almost unconsidered Yahoo then took command, and had a slight lead over the final two fences.

Tackling the uphill run-in, Desert Orchid inched ahead. The lead steadily increased to one-and-a-half lengths. Desert Orchid edged left towards Yahoo in his fatigue, but Sherwood straightened him in time to prevent any interference.

'Desert Orchid gave every ounce; I am honoured to be associated with such a horse,' said the winning jockey.

Charter Party, successful in last year's Gold Cup, finished eight lengths behind Yahoo in third place. Bonanza Boy was a distant fourth.

The grey was mobbed by his admirers when returning to unsaddle. 'He took it all in good part, and knew he had accomplished something special,' said Sherwood.

Tom Morgan, who rode Yahoo, was hopeful of scoring an upset until his mount began to 'tie up' towards the finish. 'They were two tired horses,' said Morgan.

Desert Orchid characteristically running from the front in the Cheltenham Gold Cup. His bravery and obvious enjoyment of racing endeared him to the public.

Faldo fights back in US Masters

By Michael Williams in Augusta, Georgia
PUBLISHED MONDAY 10 APRIL

Nick Faldo yesterday played the greatest last round of his life and the gods were kind enough to smile on him when, having tied the Masters at Augusta National with Scott Hoch after a last round of 65, he won the play-off at the second extra hole.

It was here that Faldo, 31, holed a putt of some five yards for a birdie three and to that Hoch had no answer, for he had already played three, missing the green with his second shot, chipping short of the flag and not having

to putt since he could do no better than take four.

Faldo follows Sandy Lyle as Masters champion just as he also followed in his great rival's footsteps by winning the Open championship two years ago. Appropriately it was Lyle who had to help Faldo into his green jacket, which is the custom of the immediate past champion.

Richly as his victory was deserved after his magnificent final round, luck was nevertheless on Faldo's side, for it had looked to all the world as if he was to be beaten at the first extra hole.

Faldo did not hit the best of drives down the 10th fairway and he was bunkered in two, whereas Hoch was safely on the green with his second shot.

Faldo came out none too well and took five, leaving Hoch with a putt of less than two feet for the title. It was the shortest putt ever to have been missed for the Masters.

Having had his reprieve, Faldo made no mistake at the second extra hole, the 11th. In the deepening gloom that would surely not have allowed a third extra hole, he hit the front of the green and a few minutes later he was throwing his arms to the sky in exultant victory.

Faldo takes a first prize of $200,000, having come good in his eighth tournament in America this year, his best previous finish having been 22nd in the Los Angeles Open. In two other tournaments he failed to qualify.

It was only justice for Faldo to have taken this great prize in golf, for last year he had suffered the bitterness of defeat when losing the United States Open to Curtis Strange in a play-off at Brookline in June.

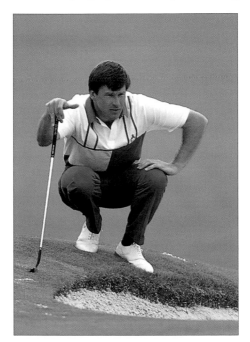

Bunkered: Nick Faldo faces a tricky shot on the way to his first Masters win. Faldo dominated world golf over the following three years.

SPORT IN BRIEF

BOXING
On 25 February British boxer Frank Bruno challenges American Mike Tyson for the undisputed world heavyweight championship. Although Tyson has not been in the ring for eight months, Bruno is still the underdog. He does get one good right hook in before succumbing to Tyson's superior power in the fifth round. It is Tyson's seventh successful defence of his title.

EQUESTRIANISM
Ginny Leng wins her second Badminton on Beneficial **(right)**. She also wins gold in the individual and team three-day events in the European championships this year, on Master Craftsman.

FOOTBALL
Luton Town reach the final of the League Cup for the second year running, but are defeated 3–1 by Nottingham Forest.

Scudamore reaches historic score of 201 winners

PUBLISHED FRIDAY 28 APRIL

Peter Scudamore reached a historic score of 201 winners in a National Hunt season when completing a four-timer on Old Kilpatrick, Canford Palm, Gay Moore and Market Forces at Towcester last night.

He had earlier drawn a blank from four rides at Hereford's afternoon meeting.

Scudamore, who in February established a record score for a National Hunt campaign, becomes the first jockey to ride 200 winners in a season since Gordon Richards rode 231 on the flat in 1952.

Gay Moore, the horse on whom Scudamore reached the double century, was picked up as a spare ride by the champion jockey and he started at 10–1.

The eight-year-old looked reluctant and jumped slowly in the early stages, but Scudamore persevered and the pair drew clear at the second-last.

Scudamore's association with Martin Pipe's West Country stable has helped him shatter countless records this season, and many believe his, and Pipe's, may never be broken.

Scudamore, 30, joined Stan Mellor and John Francome as the only National Hunt jockeys to ride 1,000 winners when completing a hat trick at Newton Abbot on 14 February.

That milestone followed the fastest 50 winners in a season, achieved on 24 October; a remarkable 100 before Christmas (15 December) and the breaking of Jonjo O'Neill's record of 149 winners in a season (7 February).

Scudamore's unique achievement in one season's jump racing is underlined by the fact that John Francome reached four figures in the twilight of his career. His final total of 1,136 should be beaten by Scudamore next season.

Riding winners is Scudamore's job, one he does so successfully that records he does not chase fall to him too. He recently told a Sunday magazine, 'I feel I am beginning to fulfil my potential a bit now.'

Peter Scudamore riding Antimatter. The horse was his 150th winning mount of the 1988–9 season.

1989

1989

By Colin Gibson

PUBLISHED MONDAY 17 APRIL

By 2.30 on Saturday afternoon, with half an hour to go before the kick-off, most of the Nottingham Forest supporters, with only a short M1 drive to negotiate, were in place at the Penistone Road end of the Sheffield Wednesday ground.

There was the usual mounting excitement inside the ground, but in the calm of the press box there was no clue to the growing drama outside the ground at the Leppings Lane end. This was where the Liverpool supporters had been allocated their tickets. There, too, the excitement was rising. But so was the tension.

A few minutes before the game started, although none of us inside the ground knew it, a senior police officer made a fateful decision to open one of the huge metal doors at the Leppings Lane end.

Fellow spectators try desperately to reach those being crushed inside the fencing at the Leppings Lane end (left). People continue to be lifted to safety in the background (below) as survivors spill on to the pitch. The dead and injured are carried on makeshift stretchers to waiting ambulances.

Unaware of the impending disaster, the referee, Ray Lewis, started the match on time. As the crowd roared, more and more Liverpool fans poured through the narrow, dark tunnel in the centre of the Leppings Lane stand which offered them their first glimpse of the pitch.

They careered into the central pens, crushing those at the front, although there was room to accommodate the latecomers in pens to the right and the left.

As the police watched from their control box perched under a Hillsborough floodlight pylon to the right of the chaos, they were helpless.

Those unaware of people dying in the front of the stand pushed forward for a better view of the action. As they did so, more were trampled under foot and crushed into the pitch fencing.

Finally, after six minutes of the match, with fans spilling through a narrow escape gate on to the pitch, a policeman ordered the referee to halt the game.

Even then the sheer magnitude of the disaster was not apparent. Within seconds it was all too clear. By the time I had made my way to the pitch there was devastation.

Fencing had been ripped away to relieve the pressure, the mesh peeled back in the hope of dragging the injured to safety. Ambulancemen were working to save a middle-aged man.

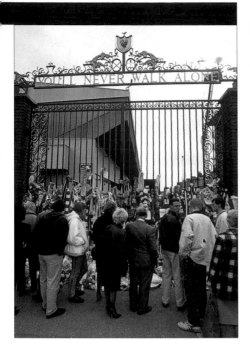

The gates at Anfield are draped with scarves and flowers, tributes to the 95 who died at Hillsborough.

Police officers, tears streaming down their faces, had suddenly been faced with a safety operation when they seemed more prepared to handle hooliganism.

Fans clambered into the seating areas behind and above the terraced area. Bodies were lifted forward. Most were children, who usually stand at the front of terraces so that they can have a better view.

Firemen and St John ambulancemen tried mouth-to-mouth resuscitation, often in vain. Nurses volunteered to rush ventilation equipment to the ground.

Medical facilities at football grounds are primitive. The dead were covered with their own clothes. Jumpers were pulled hastily over their faces.

Through the gymnasium door, left ajar, the bodies could be seen lined up, row after row. Fleets of ambulances waited to ferry survivors to the hospitals.

The air was filled with animosity. Forest fans, frustrated and bewildered, taunted the Liverpool supporters tending their dead. They were not to blame. No one had the sense to tell anyone what was happening.

It was 55 minutes before any useful announcement was made. When the Nottingham Forest fans discovered the magnitude of the disaster they behaved in an exemplary fashion.

By 4.50, the scheduled end of the game, the ground was empty. Clothes and individual shoes littered the terracing. A pile of broken advertising hoardings used as makeshift stretchers was left in front of the Leppings Lane end. Scarves were still tied to the crush barriers.

A floral arrangement had been brought from the boardroom and laid as a small, heartfelt, but totally inadequate memorial to the dead.

Soccer must end ritual of standing on terraces

By Colin Gibson

PUBLISHED MONDAY 17 APRIL

For the third time in four years the football authorities are left with the onerous task of restoring confidence in the fortunes of Britain's national sport.

In those 48 months football has staggered from the wounds inflicted by the Bradford fire disaster and the horrors of the Heysel Stadium in Brussels. Until Saturday it appeared narrowly to have survived.

Not only was it surviving, but there were signs of an encouraging, though gradual, revival. Attendances were climbing slowly after the dark, post-Heysel days.

In these circumstances it would be too easy to offer crass and simplistic solutions to prevent a repeat of this tragedy. What is clear is that something must be done.

In the next few years football must change its priorities and break away from what Graham Kelly, the Football Association's chief executive, describes as the 'ritual of standing on the terraces'. In simple terms that means a move towards all-seat stadiums – and quickly. There is no doubt that the Hillsborough tragedy would have been averted had it been an all-seat venue.

In the past the game has resisted, and even obstructed, attempts to convert the country's antiquated stadiums. Now the clubs must switch from terracing to seats – or face grounds being closed.

Mr Kelly, who has enhanced his reputation in the most difficult of situations, said yesterday: 'That must now be in the forefront of everyone's minds. Some way or another we must move the fans' preference away from the ritual of standing on the terraces.

'The sooner the predominance of our stadiums are all-seat, and the fans' preference is moved from standing, then the better it will be for our game.

'If anything is to be gained from this terrible situation then, from a selfish football point of view, we might be able to make the grounds more comfortable and amenable.'

Clubs will obviously plead poverty as an excuse for not taking that type of action. Of the Football Trust's £9 million, taken from revenue from the football pools companies, £1.5 million goes to police charges and that would leave more than £7 million to be ploughed into all-seat stadiums.

In England the only ground moving rapidly towards all seats is Wembley. It costs Wembley £75 for each seat installed, but Brian Wolfson, chairman of the Wembley Group, believes it is a small price to pay for safety at the ground. Maybe now football will see sense.

SPORT IN BRIEF

FOOTBALL

On 5 May Barcelona win the European Cup Winners' Cup, beating Sampdoria 2–0 in the final in Berne. Barcelona's Gary Lineker does not score; the goals come from Salinas and the substitute Recarte.

LAWN TENNIS

Eighteen-year-old Michael Chang wins the French Open in Paris. In a dramatic final he beats Stefan Edberg 6–1, 3–6, 4–6, 6–4, 6–2. Chang becomes the first American to win the title for 34 years.

FOOTBALL

On 30 April, Liverpool play their first match since the Hillsborough tragedy: a friendly against Celtic, which they win 4–0. After much agonising, Liverpool have decided to continue to play in the FA Cup, and will meet Nottingham Forest in the semi-final, to be held at Old Trafford.

Dalglish sets example for city

By Colin Gibson

PUBLISHED SATURDAY 6 MAY

Few football clubs, managers or players can understand what Liverpool, Mr Dalglish and his team have been through in the last three weeks.

For a city, for football and for Liverpool in particular it has been a time of grieving. They needed someone with dignity and direction. That someone was Mr Dalglish.

He has never sought public praise or publicity. In fact he has shied away from both. He was concerned only with the need for everyone to conduct themselves in a decent manner. Mr Dalglish, and his family, have offered a lead. When there was a time for mourning he was attending funerals and memorial services. He did not have to but he wanted to.

When the time came to resume playing, Mr Dalglish was leading from the front again. At Celtic, last Saturday, he pulled on the famous red No. 7 shirt in a meaningful gesture.

It would have been easy not to get involved, but anyone who knows Liverpool will recognise that the city focuses its sporting aspirations on the club. The two are eternally linked.

1989

1989

Liverpool pass test of character

By Colin Gibson
PUBLISHED MONDAY 22 MAY
Everton 2; Liverpool 3, after extra time

Deep in Wembley's sea of jubilation, oblivious to the confusion around him, Kenny Dalglish was sharing the most satisfying moment of his footballing career.

Joe Worrall's whistle had ended a crusade that began among the tears of Hillsborough 35 days before. Liverpool had won the FA Cup.

If more tears were shed in Mr Dalglish's clinch with coaches Ronnie Moran and Roy Evans – and no one was admitting it – they were through relief and joy.

Since that tragic afternoon in Sheffield, Liverpool have been carried along by an overwhelming desire to provide a final tribute to the 95 who had died following their team.

Winning the Cup had become an obsession at Anfield. The sense of achievement that Mr Dalglish felt was clear for everyone to see.

In the dark corridors of Wembley, Mr Dalglish summed up the emotions which had tormented and then delighted him in 120 minutes of high drama.

'How does it compare with everything else? This is the best one for me. It was an emotional day but it has given me a great deal of happiness,' he said.

It is a revealing insight into the depth that the Hillsborough tragedy touched Mr Dalglish, especially when you consider his footballing record.

As a player he won every domestic honour that Scottish and English football had to offer – as well as three European Cup Winners' medals – and in his first year of management he became the third manager this century to win the League and FA Cup double.

But, at a scorching Wembley on Saturday, a special chapter in English football was unfolding from the moment that the strains of 'Abide with Me' drifted away. Saturday was a fulfilment of promises Liverpool had made to the relatives of those who died at Hillsborough.

MILESTONES

The first all-weather horse-racing track in Britain was introduced at Lingfield Park in southeast England. The first winner on the new surface was Niklas Angel, owned by Conrad Allen and ridden by Richard Quinn.

Smith and Thomas win the title for Arsenal

By Colin Gibson
PUBLISHED SATURDAY 27 MAY
Liverpool 0; Arsenal 2

Michael Thomas won the First Division championship for Arsenal last night, his goal, 86 seconds into injury time, earning London its first title in 18 years. It was a memorable performance.

Thomas broke the hearts of the Liverpool team and their fans when he burst through after Alan Smith had fed him. Thomas put the ball beyond the diving Bruce Grobbelaar to give Arsenal the two-goal victory they needed. They are worthy champions.

Arsenal arrived on Merseyside giving the appearance of a team on a benefit tour. They presented Liverpool with a cheque for £30,000 as a contribution to the Hillsborough Disaster Appeal, and then offered bouquets to the Anfield supporters.

Arsenal took a deserved but controversial lead in the 52nd minute through Smith. Steve Nicol was punished for a foul on the edge of the Liverpool area, and Nigel Winterburn floated the ball towards the far post where Smith drifted in to head past Grobbelaar. While Arsenal celebrated, Liverpool players tried to bring to the referee's attention his linesman, who they claimed had flagged for a foul by David O'Leary. After a brief consultation the referee, much to Arsenal's delight, allowed the goal to stand.

Thomas might have won the championship for Arsenal after 73 minutes, but he shot straight at Grobbelaar. Seventeen minutes later he made no mistake, and North London celebrated.

Michael Thomas (on left, above) and Martin Hayes show off the victor's spoils. Liverpool and Arsenal were level in the First Division championship on goal difference; Arsenal won the title on goals scored.

Neath win Schweppes Welsh Cup

By John Mason
PUBLISHED MONDAY 8 MAY
Llanelli 13 pts; Neath 14

Neath, with one dishonourable exception, played with all the acceptable fire and fury that distinguishes rugby football to win the Schweppes Welsh Cup in Cardiff on Saturday.

Llanelli, the holders, led three times and got back to within a point in the last quarter before retiring with immense and lasting credit after a tempestuous match.

Yet a great occasion was more than spoiled. It was soiled, a word I have never used before in an account of a rugby match.

The disgrace was two-fold. Mark Jones, Neath's No. 8, ground his boot into the face of Laurance Delaney, the Llanelli tight-head and Wales international colleague, in the 28th minute.

Les Peard, the referee, was on the spot and instantly pointed to the touchline. Good riddance one thought. Astonishingly that was not the end of the matter. Jones's suspension, as a law dispensation in Wales permits, was temporary. Mr Peard, a police sergeant, had taken the soft option of dispatching Jones to the sin-bin.

All of this detracted hugely from Neath's first victory in the Cup final for 17 years. In scoring three tries to one, they demonstrated palpably why they are the best club in Wales.

Prost's title under threat by McLaren

By Richard Bright in Suzuka
PUBLISHED MONDAY 23 OCTOBER

Alain Prost was a sad and puzzled figure yesterday after being provisionally installed as Formula One world champion and then facing the prospect of his own team taking the title away from him.

The Frenchman, assuming he had won the title outright after Ayrton Senna, his McLaren-Honda teammate and rival, had been disqualified from the Japanese Grand Prix, shook hands with every mechanic in their garage before another unexpected postscript suspended the celebration.

The news that Ron Dennis, McLaren's managing director, had appealed against Senna's disqualification – for cutting across the chicane after the 47th-lap collision with Prost – left the Frenchman awaiting the outcome of a hearing in Paris on Thursday.

An International Automobile Federation (FIA) court of appeal, similar to that which recently heard Nigel Mansell's case in the 'black flag controversy', will decide the outcome of the race and with it the likely destiny of this year's world championship.

Senna issued a statement which showed he was determined to retain the title he won in Japan a year ago.

Senna said: 'The results as they stand provisionally do not reflect the truth of the race in either the sporting sense or in the sense of the regulations. I see this result as temporary.... It was obvious that I won the race on the track...as to the incident, that was the only place where I could overtake and somebody who should not have been there just closed the door and that was that.'

Prost had appeared to be heading for a narrow but well-merited victory when he led Senna towards the chicane with only six laps to go.

When Prost approached the first bend wide he had no idea that the defending champion would attempt to force his way through on the inside. Inevitably they collided and ran off. Prost abandoned his car but Senna, with the help of a marshall, restarted and cut across the chicane as he rejoined the race.

Prost (left, in the Brazilian Grand Prix) was eventually confirmed as world champion. It was his third title.

1989

315

1990

Macari and Hillier found guilty of betting breach

By John Ley

PUBLISHED TUESDAY 13 FEBRUARY

Lou Macari, the former Swindon Town manager, and Brian Hillier, the club chairman, were yesterday found guilty by the Football Association of breaching the rule regarding betting on matches. Mr Macari, now manager of West Ham, was fined £1,000 and censured while Mr Hillier was suspended from taking an active role in the game for six months.

Swindon were also found guilty and fined £7,500. All three parties will share the adjusted costs of the hearing. West Ham, represented at the hearing by secretary Tom Finn, issued a statement confirming that Mr Macari's future at the club was secure.

The rule in question, Rule 26a (iv) states that a member shall be found guilty of misconduct if they are found guilty of '…betting on any football match other than on authorised and registered Football Pools.'

The match concerned was an FA Cup tie at Newcastle in January 1988, which Swindon lost 5–0. There has been no suggestion that the result was in any way affected, although Mr Hillier admitted he placed a bet.

Graham Kelly, the FA chief executive, answered questions over the apparent leniency of the verdict, when he said: 'I haven't seen any evidence of widespread abuse of this rule. We regarded the charges as serious and imposed the appropriate penalties.'

It appears likely that, by fining Mr Macari only £1,000, the FA have accepted that he was not directly involved in the bet but, perhaps, had knowledge of it. Mr Finn said: 'It's apparent from the punishments imposed on Mr Macari that this minimal involvement in respect of these matters was accepted by the FA.

'During the last six weeks, Mr Macari and his family have been subjected to intense pressure.'

MILESTONES

New Zealand fast bowler Richard Hadlee became the first bowler in cricket history to take 400 Test wickets when he dismissed Indian batsman Sanjar Manjrekar on his home ground of Christchurch on 4 February. Hadlee would take another 31 wickets before announcing his retirement later this year.

Gatting's rebel cricket tour cut short

By Stephen Robinson in Johannesburg

PUBLISHED WEDNESDAY 14 FEBRUARY

The South African cricket authorities yesterday cut short the troubled tour of Mike Gatting's official English team, largely as a result of the release of Mr Nelson Mandela from prison last weekend.

The violence which marred Mr Mandela's first day of freedom, combined with a limpet-mine explosion the same night at the cricket ground in Cape Town where the second 'Test' was due to begin on Friday, convinced the South African Cricket Union (SACU) that the risk to the players and protesters had become too great.

South African cabinet ministers have let it be known that they were deeply concerned at the prospect of serious civil unrest escalating during the final weeks of the tour. Officials of the SACU have been in almost daily contact with ministers to discuss the security implications of the tour continuing.

After several days of speculation that the tour was in deep trouble, Mr Geoff Dakin, president of the SACU, confirmed yesterday that 'in view of the recent dramatic political developments

Gatting (above, right) appears at the toss-up before the first 'Test', while a protester (below) makes clear his view of the 'rebel' tour. Many people felt that to stage the tour at a time of such great political change in South Africa was highly insensitive.

in South Africa' the tour programme had been curtailed and the Cape Town test cancelled.

Mr Ali Bacher, SACU's managing director, later confirmed that Mr Mandela's release was the biggest single factor in their decision. He said that in view of the changing political climate in South Africa, 'a gesture of conciliation and compromise is appropriate'.

The English tourists will now play only four one-day games against the Springboks before flying home two weeks earlier than originally planned. Mike Gatting, the tour captain, said all his players were 'deeply disappointed' not to be able to continue with the cricket.

'We were invited out here to play cricket and earn a living, as do many other people who come to this country. But I have no regrets about coming. I now understand a lot more about South Africa.'

Douglas must wait for championship confirmation

By Richard Bright

TOKYO, MONDAY 12 FEBRUARY

James 'Buster' Douglas, one of the biggest underdogs in the history of boxing, yesterday reigned for a mere six hours as the undisputed heavyweight champion of the world after knocking out Mike Tyson in the tenth round at the Tokyo Dome.

The 'impossible' happened when the undefeated Tyson, 23, his left eye closed and already groggy from many left- and right-hand jabs and hooks to the head, went down for the full count following a four-punch combination after 1 minute 23 seconds of the round.

'All four punches were lethal,' said the delighted Douglas, 29, who was so underrated that Las Vegas bookmakers would not offer odds on the fight. But his elation was short-lived.

The Tyson camp, led by the flamboyant Don King, promoter and guiding hand behind the former champion, lodged an official complaint against the decision, maintaining that the referee, Octavio Meyrian, had made a mistake while counting a knock-down against Douglas in the eighth round — when Tyson had taken brief control of the fight.

Officials of the three governing bodies controlling the fight — the World Boxing Council, World Boxing Association and International Boxing Federation — went into session — and six hours later the WBC and WBA combined to produce the second 'impossible' happening of an astonishing day.

Although the IBF will recognise Douglas as their world champion, José Sulaiman, the WBC president, announced: 'As of today, no one is heavyweight champion until 20 February when I meet with the WBC executive committee.'

WBA officials said that they expected a decision around the same time. They claimed that, in the controversial count in the eighth round, the referee had ignored the usual practice of taking over the official timekeepers' count which starts the moment a boxer hits the canvas. The timekeepers claim the referee should have begun his count at 'four' on their signal. According to these officials, Douglas was on the canvas for 12 or 13 seconds — and he should have been counted out at ten.

Naturally, Douglas did not agree. 'The WBA and WBC and Don King can all go to hell as far as I'm concerned.'

Ironically, all the anguish and frustration Douglas was forced to accept yesterday was a continuation of other personal upsets and tragedies in his life. His mother died last month and the mother of his 11-year-old son is terminally ill.

But no one can take away from him the glory of giving the so-called invincible Tyson something of a boxing lesson.

The boxer from Columbus, Ohio, is used to not being rated highly. He fought Tony Tucker for the International Boxing Federation title in May 1987, again as the underdog. But despite using his brilliant jab to lead on points late in the fight, he lost.

Always a top athlete, winning a two-year basketball scholarship to a college in Kansas, he used his height — 6 ft 4 in — and his powerful jab to knock out opponents.

He was determined not to lose to Tyson. But fate, which has hardly treated him kindly, has decreed that beating the champion does not automatically mean being crowned himself.

Despite the objections, James 'Buster' Douglas was awarded the world heavyweight title. He surrendered it on 26 October to Evander Holyfield.

SPORT IN BRIEF

FOOTBALL

Following the inquiry into the 1989 Hillsborough disaster, Lord Justice Taylor's report recommends that all-seat stadiums be established in the First and Second Divisions by 1994, and at other grounds by 1999.

HORSE RACING

Trained by Sirrel Griffiths and ridden by Graham McCourt, the 100–1 outsider Norton's Coin wins the Cheltenham Gold Cup. Desert Orchid, the previous year's winner and odds-on favourite, finishes third.

FOOTBALL

Italian teams dominate European club competition. AC Milan beat Benfica to take the European Cup; Sampdoria, with two goals from Gianluca Vialli, beat Anderlecht to take the Cup Winners' Cup; and Juventus defeat another Italian team, Fiorentina, to claim the UEFA Cup.

AMERICAN FOOTBALL

The San Francisco 49-ers win the Super Bowl for the second year running when they beat the Denver Broncos 55–10 in the Louisiana Superdome in New Orleans.

MARTINA NAVRATILOVA (1956–)

ONE OF THE MOST FORMIDABLE CHAMPIONS in the women's game, Martina Navratilova was born in Prague on 18 October 1956. Her father's surname was Subertov, but her parents separated when she was three, and Martina took her stepfather's name.

Navratilova devoted herself to tennis from an early age, inspired by a performance by Rod Laver in the Prague sports arena. By the age of nine, she was receiving state coaching, and in 1972 she won the national championships. A year later, she gained the junior title at Wimbledon and was allowed to compete in the professional circuit. As she climbed up the rankings, the friction between Navratilova and the Czech federation increased. They accused her of becoming too Americanised and tried to limit the competitions she could enter. So, in 1975, she defected to the United States.

Navratilova rapidly became one of the top earners on the circuit. She was strong, fast around the court and, as Virginia Wade put it: 'She has every shot in the book and is working on the sequel.' After beating Chris Evert in the final of Wimbledon in 1978, Navratilova dominated the 1980s.

To add to her nine victories in other majors and her 31 doubles titles, Navratilova won Wimbledon for a record ninth time in 1990. She took professionalism to the limits, using a retinue of fitness trainers, coaches and nutritionists. She finally retired in 1994, having captured a record-breaking 167 singles titles.

1990

Even All Blacks will respect these triple champions

By John Mason

PUBLISHED MONDAY 19 MARCH

Scotland, whose forthright and prickly challenge was hugely underestimated by those with English sympathies, go to New Zealand in May as worthy winners of the Grand Slam, the Triple Crown and the Calcutta Cup after beating England 13–7. The All Blacks will pay them every respect.

The tour party, which will be announced tomorrow, will travel secure in the knowledge that their single-minded endeavours in the Five Nations season have justly earned themselves a place of honour in Scottish sporting history.

As an example of how tight matches should be played, Saturday's victory, by a try and three penalty goals to a try and penalty goal, would have been difficult to improve upon. England were challenged constantly at the source of their strength and, harried into error, lofty calm deserted them.

The poise and control that brought England 23 points against Ireland, 26 against France and 34 against Wales surfaced only occasionally. Not even the sweetest of tries by Jeremy Guscott could save previously unbeaten England from the defeat that hurt the most.

As English promise faltered and faded in the face of aggressive defence, the Scots, mostly unsung elsewhere in Britain, savoured the joys that accompanied the sound of English bodies continually slipping up on a host of banana skins. It was not the slightest consolation to England's players to know that they were not alone.

While mindful that Scotland would have attended to their homework earnestly, I did not think England's forwards, the power base of the side, would be overcome.

From the moment that David Sole, already a leader of imposing stature after a handful of matches, led out Scotland, doubts began to invade English hearts. The team did not run on to the pitch, they did not march – they walked, a stately, dignified stride more eloquent than a thousand words.

The ability of the Scots to get a man between the ball and an England player was masterly. The sustained, hard, bruising work of John Jeffrey, the match's outstanding player, was extraordinary.

Without too much control, a minimum of quality possession and some repetitious schemes that did not work, England struggled. The Scottish forwards took England on, Gary Armstrong sniped and snarled at their heels – his best match by far for Scotland – and Craig Chalmers did everything asked of him. Not even the excellent Rob Andrew could disturb his composure.

Hungry Scotland did the job they had set their hearts on. There can be no grumbles.

Scotland scrum half Gary Armstrong prepares to feed the ball out during their Calcutta Cup victory at Murrayfield. It was Scotland's third Grand Slam: they also won the title in 1925 and in 1984.

England revellers wary of Viv Richards' warning

By Peter Deeley

KINGSTON, FRIDAY 2 MARCH

England took only two hours yesterday to round off their first Test victory against the West Indies for 16 years. After losing the fourth day's play because of rain when the home side were on the verge of defeat, the 20–1 underdogs completed a nine-wicket win in brilliant sunny conditions at Sabina Park, Jamaica.

England's euphoric mood once they had completed their victory here yesterday did not disguise the awareness in the dressing room that there is still a lot of sting in this wounded West Indies side. The champagne was flowing and the Union Jacks were waving, as they should have been, for this historic moment. But as Viv Richards warned above the hubbub from the visitors' dressing room: 'We needed a kick up the backside and we got it. That is what great teams need. We are not like other sides and other selectors. If we start losing we don't panic. We shall return.'

After the years of humiliation at the hands of Caribbean sides under first Clive Lloyd – now the West Indies manager – and then Richards, revenge was never sweeter for an England side universally written off as 'no-chancers' when they left home in January.

No man could have relished the moment more than Graham Gooch, who has been here twice before and on the losing end both times.

He admitted that he was particularly disappointed not to have been out in the middle at the moment the winning run was scored by Wayne Larkins.

You might think that climbing the cricket mountain, as his side had just done, would have made up for everything. But Gooch is a very competitive and single-minded person who wants to do everything right: he does not take kindly to losing his wicket.

Gooch was in the dressing room – which has no view of the pitch – packing his belongings when he heard the shout go up for Larkins's straight-driven four off Bishop which brought the scores level. 'So I stood on a bench looking through the window for the one that gave us the game.'

Celebrations among the England party and their 200–300 supporters who had flown out for this game began the moment that opening batsman Larkins struck the winning run.

The final moments were watched with elation by several former England cricketers, among them Sir Leonard Hutton, Alec Bedser and David Gower.

Gooch described the win as 'one of the great moments of my international career'.

Faldo's double first earns place in the history books

By Michael Williams

Augusta, Georgia, Monday 9 April

Nick Faldo (**right**) yesterday carved a special place in sporting, as well as golfing history when he became only the second man successfully to defend the Masters as, after a final round of 69 to tie with Raymond Floyd at Augusta National, he snatched an heroic victory in the play-off.

He therefore equals Jack Nicklaus's two consecutive victories in 1965–66. Faldo came from four behind with six to play, making three birdies, although he was further helped by three putts from Floyd, who won the Masters in 1976, at the 17th. They therefore finished level on 278, ten under par, and five strokes clear of Lanny Wadkins and John Huston, who tied third on 283.

It was yet another absolutely gripping afternoon, very much in the tradition of the Masters, and one can only take one's hat off to Faldo for the manner in which he came back. His self-control and ability to forget the odd mistake and keep plugging on was wonderfully rewarded, though one has sympathy, too, for Floyd who – had he won – would have become the oldest champion. He is 47, whereas Nicklaus was 46 when he gained his record sixth victory in 1986.

On a lovely, sunny and warm day, these two were throughout the central figures. There were four strokes between them with only six holes to play. It was then that Faldo began to make his glorious move: he was on the green in two at the long 13th and with two putts he had another birdie under his belt.

Then, at the 15th, though over the back in two, he chipped well and sank a telling putt for another birdie four. When Faldo hit a fine tee shot for the short 16th and sank a putt of 20 foot for a two, the margin between them was only a single stroke.

At the same hole, Floyd applauded himself with a beautifully judged downhill putt close to the hole for his three; but it was his putter that betrayed him at the 17th, the penultimate hole.

Up and ahead, Faldo must have seen the news on the big scoreboards and, when he made his four at last, Floyd had to match it for a tie. He did so, and what a very brave four it was, too.

Yet again, Faldo was in that right-hand bunker going down the tenth, the first extra hole; but this time he got up and down in two, and a few minutes later he was raising his arms on the 11th green, just as he had a year ago, as the champion. It was a sad end for Floyd but another great day for European golf.

Palace destroy Liverpool to reach their first Cup final

By Colin Gibson

Published Monday 9 April

Crystal Palace 4; Liverpool 3, after extra time

No one had doubted, after their 9–0 victory over Crystal Palace in the League in September, that Liverpool would score three goals in yesterday's FA Cup semi-final at Villa Park.

Yet no one dreamed that Palace would score four, end the Merseysiders' ambitions of a League and Cup Double, and become the bookmakers' 6–5 favourites to win the trophy.

Alan Pardew became the unlikely hero as Crystal Palace brought off one of the biggest shocks in the history of the competition, to reach the Wembley final for the first time in their unremarkable 85-year history.

Pardew, recruited from the old FA Cup fighters of Yeovil Town, suddenly popped up in Liverpool's penalty area, after 109 minutes of enthralling football, to head the winning goal.

At 2–2, Pemberton made an unnecessary challenge on Steve Staunton, and the referee pointed to the penalty spot. John Barnes scored and Liverpool appeared safe. But with only two minutes remaining, they made another hash of clearing a free kick, and Andy Gray bundled the ball into the net.

At 3–3, it was Palace's game again. Andy Thorn should have scored a minute later, but he headed Gray's free kick against the bar. When extra time offered Liverpool a chance to regain their composure, Palace produced the final twist.

Liverpool were unhinged by another high cross, this time a Gray corner, which was flicked on by Thorn – and Pardew scored his historic goal.

Liverpool sank to their knees. Palace owe much to Mark Bright's determination, Nigel Martyn's bravery and Pardew's opportunism.

Palace drew 3–3 after extra time with Manchester United in the FA Cup final, but lost 1–0 in the replay.

1990

319

1990

Gooch joins the all-time greats

By Peter Deeley and Richard Savill
PUBLISHED SATURDAY 28 JULY

Graham Gooch (below) relaxed with a bottle of champagne last night after his 333-run innings, the third highest score by an England Test batsman.

Only five players from any country have scored more runs in one Test innings. Gooch was 33 runs short of beating Sir Garfield Sobers' world record of 365 not out when he was bowled after ten and a half hours.

He said: 'Once I got past 300 and then 330, I was going to go on. I wasn't batting to get the record but I knew it was possible. Then I got bowled.

'Initially when I was out, I felt a bit disappointed. But not really now. I am happy with what I got.'

But Gooch's moment of triumph when he reached 300 was missed by his wife, Brenda, who returned home from taking their daughter Hannah to a birthday party, only to find that the BBC was showing racing instead of the Test match against India.

'That's marvellous,' she said, when the news was broken to her by a journalist. 'I am very proud of him and just wish that I'd been there to see it happen. I'm going to Lord's tomorrow but that's a bit late, isn't it?'

The BBC's decision to switch to the racing when Gooch was on 299 infuriated viewers, who complained. A BBC spokesman said: 'It was sheer bad luck that our coverage coincided with the moment Graham Gooch's innings reached 300. Every ball of his innings was recorded and we were able to show the moment he scored his 300th run very shortly afterwards.'

But infuriated cricket fans pointed out that, long after the winner passed the post, the BBC was lingering over scenes in the enclosure, the measured views of experts – and even the result of the 3.45 at Carlisle.

DID YOU KNOW?

Roger Milla, star of the Cameroon team, whose goal-celebration wiggles were the sensation of the tournament, became the oldest player to score a goal in a World Cup, aged 38. He scored two against Romania and two against Colombia.

Senna clinches title but Prost is disgusted

By Timothy Collings
SUZUKA, MONDAY 22 OCTOBER

Ayrton Senna clinched the second drivers' world championship of his career in the most dramatic and controversial circumstances yesterday when he collided with Alain Prost on the first corner of the Japanese Grand Prix and, in the process, revived the most acrimonious feud in motor sport.

Senna's McLaren-Honda and Prost's Ferrari disappeared in a cloud of dust, sand and debris only seconds after the start of a stirring race, won in commanding style by Nelson Piquet, who led his Benetton-Ford teammate and fellow Brazilian, Roberto Moreno, home in front of a record crowd at Suzuka.

The incident revived memories of their infamous collision at Suzuka last year. On that occasion, Senna recovered his car and went on to finish first before being disqualified when Prost was crowned champion.

This time, it was Prost who was to lose out as Senna's kamikaze-style attack prompted their abrupt removal from the race and wrecked the Frenchman's last hopes of retaining the title. Senna's 'success' and the subsequent retirements of both Nigel Mansell, in the second Ferrari, and Gerhard Berger, in the McLaren, also ensured McLaren of the constructors' title.

Prost, aware that he and Senna had shaken hands on a new *entente cordiale* only last month at Monza, could

Ayrton Senna tests his McLaren-Honda at Imola; he won six of the 16 grands prix in 1990.

not suppress his sense of injustice afterwards. 'He did it on purpose,' said Prost. 'He knew that if I made a good start my car was better than his and he would have no chance to win the race. So he pushed me out.

'I have no problems with losing the world championship. I have lost many. But not this way...the outcome is no good from the sporting point of view.'

Sadly, neither the euphoria of Benetton's win nor the champagne celebration in the McLaren offices could erase a deep sense of disappointment at the way in which the championship was settled.

Robson's men pay price of this cruel Russian roulette

By Michael Calvin
PUBLISHED THURSDAY 5 JULY
West Germany 1; England 1, after extra time
West Germany win 4–3 on penalties

The world shared England's sense of desolation when they played Russian roulette in the Delle Alpi Stadium and discovered a deadly bullet in the chamber.

It was no time for rational analysis. There was nothing remotely consoling in England gaining more respect from artificial defeat than a string of victories which attracted persistent criticism.

There was an eerie feeling of *déjà vu* as Chris Waddle had to be helped to his feet and teammates threw protective arms around the distraught Stuart Pearce; but it was not until England's players reached their dressing room that they realised the enormity of what they had let slip.

The contrivance of a penalty shoot-out provides dramatic,

enduring images of human distress and delight. This morning it is appropriate to reflect upon the fairness of placing such inordinate pressure on individuals.

The scenes are becoming all too familiar, and tend to devalue a tournament which has as its primary objective the natural selection of the world's best football team. Who, on the evidence of a breezy evening in Turin, can decide the relative merits of England and West Germany?

Who, using Tuesday night's penalty shoot-out as a guide, can claim without the merest hint of unease that Argentina are a better balanced side than Italy?

Individual images – the delayed shock on Waddle's face, for instance – are difficult to forget. Each successful conversion is greeted by a skip of relief. The man who misses must walk back, head bowed. As Terry Butcher summed up: 'This is a cruel, cruel way to go out of the World Cup.'

'Gazza' (Paul Gascoigne) cries after being booked in the semi-final. The offence would have meant him missing the World Cup final – but the issue proved academic when West Germany beat England on penalties.

Germans' triumph is sullied as Argentina are disgraced

By Colin Gibson

ROME, MONDAY 9 JULY

Argentina 0; West Germany 1

Argentina were shamed as West Germany last night became the world champions for the third time. Argentina, who have neither behaved nor played like defending champions in the last month, had two players sent off in the Stadio Olympico last night.

This was Diego Maradona's last World Cup and his last international appearance. Everyone in Rome held their breath in the expectation of something special.

But instead of conjuring a piece of magic, Maradona could only stand and watch as Argentina produced one of the poorest performances to blot a World Cup final.

There may have been worse finals in the previous 13 competitions, but nobody in Rome could remember one. It took a dubious penalty six minutes from time, when Rudi Völler was fouled, to separate the sides. Andreas

West Germany's Jürgen Klinsmann flying high; his team beat Argentina with a penalty six minutes before time.

Brehme struck his shot low to Goycochea's right, and the West Germans were champions once more.

Argentina have been a shadow of the side that performed in Mexico four years ago. This time there seemed no doubt that the Germans would exact their revenge. The only argument was when they would break down this most negative of Argentinian sides.

Argentina have collected 21 yellow cards and have now had three players sent off. They have relied entirely on the inspiration of Maradona, but he has been a fading star during the last four years. Argentina's reputation for being one of the most skilful teams in World Cup history is now completely and utterly destroyed.

Maradona cried for himself. There were those who felt like crying for the spectacle that had been ruined by Argentina's antics. At least they did not prosper.

1990

1992

Guilty Tyson faces 11-year jail sentence

By Charles Laurence
PUBLISHED WEDNESDAY 12 FEBRUARY

Grey-faced and scowling as the weight of his rape conviction the night before sank in, former boxing champion Mike Tyson returned to court yesterday to prepare a plea for mercy. He faces up to 60 years in jail for the rape of an 18-year-old beauty queen and two counts of forced deviate sexual conduct when he is sentenced on 6 March. Whatever the outcome, the years in jail seem certain to end his career at the age of 25.

The conviction stripped Tyson of his habitual threatening swagger. As he returned to court yesterday in a sober dark blue suit, he kept his head bowed and trotted quickly up the steps. He had been called to register at the probation office; probation officers will assess his character and likely danger to fellow inmates, and recommend both the level of security he should endure and the length of his sentence.

Tyson entered the court late on Monday night to face the jurors, knowing a quick verdict could mean conviction. He sat slumped in his chair, struggling to control his fears. The colour drained from his face, leaving his nose and lips the colour of khaki. He wrung his huge fists, staring fixedly at the table, and his chest heaved as he struggled to control his breathing.

Suddenly he looked like an overweight schoolboy called to punishment rather than the 'thug in the dark alley' the prosecution had successfully labelled him. He rose unsteadily as the judge called the jury.

The jury avoided Tyson's eyes, the old signal of a conviction due. The foreman handed a slip of paper to the judge. She pursed her thin lips, and read out three guilty verdicts. The man described as the world's most powerful athlete slumped again.

Mr Garrison, a colourful local lawyer whose folksy style did much to persuade the jury in a case where hard evidence was thin, stood on the court steps to hail the case a 'victory for women'.

DID YOU KNOW?

In an effort to combat time-wasting in football matches, the International Football Association board barred goalkeepers from handling deliberate back passes by defenders. From now on, goalkeepers must kick these balls.

Referee's bravery during anarchic match

By John Mason
PUBLISHED MONDAY 17 FEBRUARY

Stephen Hilditch applied the laws of the game. French front-row forwards Gregoire Lascube and Vincent Moscato applied the law of the jungle and paid the price as England won 31–13 in the Five Nations championship at Parc des Princes.

The grateful thanks of all who wish to present rugby football, of necessity a sport of violent physical contact, as a reasonable, worthwhile pastime, are due to the Irish referee, Mr Hilditch.

He could have taken the easy options when requiring the assistance of Owen Doyle, a touch judge, before dismissing Lascube for stamping on Martin Bayfield and, four minutes later, when Moscato head-butted Jeff Probyn. For the first time in the history of the championship, two players from the same team had been sent off.

The French pair have been banned until 1 September, a sharply salutary punishment which, if nothing else, indicates that rugby's authorities are mindful of the need to uphold the word of the referee.

Quite where all of this leaves France is a fearful conundrum. Strictures on discipline have a nasty habit of rebounding, and while England were blameless, that was not the case in the match against Scotland.

England's David Pears gets the ball away during a match that at times verged on anarchy.

Germans share Krabbe's guilt

By Iain Macleod
PUBLISHED MONDAY 17 FEBRUARY

They will never erect a statue to the memory of Katerina Krabbe, or to her two colleagues, Grit Breuer and Silke Moeller, who were suspended for four years on Saturday by the German Athletic Federation (DLV), for attempting to manipulate the result of a urine test.

But the athletes may still have a part to play, notably to serve as a monument to human avarice, and the self-delusion of high-ranking sports officials who, uneasy at the thought of their sport being tainted, propagate the one fallacy that doping is on the wane.

Urine tests taken from the three athletes on 24 January, during a spell of warm-weather training in South Africa, showed irregularities which the DLV said clearly amounted to the equivalent of a doping offence. In a statement issued by the DLV, it was claimed that the manipulation 'could have been done only by the athletes or with their agreement, with the intention of falsifying urine tests made to establish if illegal performance-enhancing means had been used'.

The mere fact that three German athletes, who displayed astonishing ignorance of the realities of doping control, attempted a major cover-up, speaks volumes for the shabby state of modern sport, now sadly weighted down by commercial considerations. It also highlights the complicity of coaches and possibly officials, too, in an evil business which has dragged sport into an abyss.

Krabbe, triumphant after her 100- and 200-m victories in Tokyo in 1991, was in 1992 found guilty of falsifying urine tests.

Kevin Keegan returns to the fold as manager

By Colin Malam and Ian Whittell
PUBLISHED THURSDAY 6 FEBRUARY

Kevin Keegan bustled back into the life of Newcastle United yesterday as the struggling Second Divison club sacked Ossie Ardiles and took the astonishing gamble of appointing the glamorous former England international as their 15th manager since the war.

Presented with the formidable challenge of saving the northeastern giants from the indignity of relegation to the Third Division for the first time, Mr Keegan struck a positive attitude that will be familiar to all who saw him play: 'I would not have gone back to Liverpool or Southampton or any other club. This is the only job in the world that I would ever have taken,' he said after being presented by Newcastle chairman Sir John Hall as the club's new manager to a stunned media gathering.

'The supporters are this club's greatest asset,' he added. 'They're going to help us turn this club around…. I'm not used to failure and I don't intend to be a failure here.'

While listening to Mr Keegan's rallying cry, the media were trying to work out how Mr Ardiles had been sacked only three days after director, Douglas Hall, Sir John's son, had said that the former Argentinian international's £120,000-a-year job was 'safe as houses'. Only three days, too, after Sir John himself had said in a newspaper interview: 'I have had long talks with Ossie Ardiles about what is needed, and let's kill off once and for all the rumours that his job as manager is on the line. If he leaves this club, it will be of his own volition.'

Yesterday, the Newcastle chairman did his best to sound contrite. 'This was the hardest decision I have ever had to make,' he said. 'I had a lot of time for Ossie. He has tried but the results haven't been there.'

Predictably, Sir John took the view that Mr Keegan could become one of the game's great managers. 'Graeme Souness and Kenny Dalglish didn't have any managerial experience when they started,' he said, 'and look what they have done.'

Mr Keegan, 41 a week tomorrow, has not yet signed a contract and his salary has not been revealed.

1992

Underwood feels anti-climax

By Michael Calvin

PUBLISHED MONDAY 9 MARCH

Rory Underwood stood on the balcony in Twickenham's West Stand and savoured a scene he had imagined the instant he woke that morning. A mass jostled beneath him, bawling farewell to men who had embellished rugby legend. Remember this, he told himself. This is the last time. Yet such were the conflicting emotions after England secured a second successive Grand Slam that he was consumed by a sense of anti-climax back in the dressing room.

There was, to use Rob Andrew's telling phrase, 'no ecstasy in people's eyes' after the 24–0 defeat of Wales. Players who have shared so much could manage only a brief chorus of Jerusalem and Rule Britannia before immersing themselves in private thoughts.

Only Underwood and Simon Halliday committed themselves to immediate retirement. 'I've pushed my luck long enough,' said Halliday. 'I've stood up to it for ten years, but I've been struggling with injuries. I feel them more and more.'

Andrew, who has feared the burn-out factor for the last three of his eight seasons, traces the problem to a fundamental change of attitude on the watershed tour of Australia in 1988. 'In a sense we have created our own pressure,' he said. 'In Australia we knew it was not worth carrying on as we were. We could either make the effort or be no-hopers, and end our careers with nothing.

'There's no doubt careers are going to be shorter in the future. The demands are virtually non-stop, international matches come at you one after the other. Bang, bang, bang.'

Underwood, a notably level-headed character, made the startling admission that he had not enjoyed the game for the past year. He has been increasingly unable to justify the toll international rugby has taken on his family and professional life. 'It just became clear in my mind that this was the right time to go.'

MILESTONES

Sachin Tendulkar became the first cricketer to be given out by the 'third umpire', who sits in the pavilion and gives his judgement based on television replays. Tendulkar is adjudged run out in the first Test between South Africa and India.

Ugly scenes as cricket board refuse Test refunds

By Peter Deeley

PUBLISHED SATURDAY 6 JUNE

There were ugly scenes outside the Edgbaston pavilion last night when the day's 15,000 Test ticket-holders were told they would not be getting a refund because two balls were bowled.

Officials were jostled by angry spectators, and when police reinforcements were called in, players, their friends and members of the Test and County Cricket Board were ushered out of a side door.

Almost £300,000 had been taken in advance sales for yesterday's second day, but as there were three minutes of play, the TCCB stood by the reimbursement clause on the back of tickets, which says: 'If due to adverse weather conditions no play whatsoever takes place . . .'

Yesterday's announcement that the second-day tickets would be valid on the last day was greeted with jeers and boos. A crowd of about 100 vented their wrath on anyone leaving the pavilion. One man grabbed me, waving his ticket and shouting, 'Apart from the ticket it cost me £40 to get here and I can't come back on Monday.'

A board spokesman explained: 'We feel sympathy for the people who have suffered so patiently, but under the refund scheme there is no proviso for giving money back. We recognise that there is a moral problem here, but if money was refunded when some play had taken place – even just two balls bowled – it would set a precedent for the future. Just where do you draw the line?'

The Test and County Cricket Board have taken almost £5 million in advance ticket sales for the Test series and the one-day internationals. The first two Texaco games alone produced gross takings of more than £1 million.

The board refused to talk about the insurance they have taken out against bad weather, on the grounds that it is a 'commercial secret'.

Denmark complete fairy tale

By Colin Gibson in Gothenburg

PUBLISHED SATURDAY 27 JUNE

Denmark 2, Germany 0

Denmark last night wrote a romantic chapter in the history of European football when they overcame all odds to win the European championship in Gothenburg. In the 32 years of this tournament there has never been a performance to equal that of the Danes, who were only in Sweden after the United Nations decided to cut sporting links with Yugoslavia. The Danes proceeded to bring the championship to life.

They limped, still battered and bruised after their semi-final success, into last night's final in the Ullevi

332

Imran's class of '92 pass biggest test

By Christopher Martin-Jenkins
PUBLISHED THURSDAY 26 MARCH

Sheer exuberant talent, leavened with a little shrewd experience from the two oldest heads in the team, Imran Khan and Javed Miandad, won the World Cup for Pakistan at Melbourne yesterday

Their 22-run defeat of England was their fifth win in succession in a tournament which had begun most unpromisingly with the loss of Waqar Younis before a ball was bowled .

Imran's assessment before the game that 'England have more experience but I believe we have more talent', was undeniably true, but often the sum of Pakistan teams has not been as great as its individual parts. To win against England's strong batting yesterday Pakistan needed good performances from their three best bowlers, Wasim Akram, Aqib Javed and Mushtaq Ahmed.

Each rose admirably to the occasion after Imran and Javed had paved the way for a late innings assault by Akram and Inzamam-ul-Haq with a third-wicket stand of 139. In a nutshell, Pakistan won because their bowling was more positive and penetrative than England's.

Imran Khan and Inzamam-ul-Haq savour the taste of success after defeating England in the World Cup.

Stadium as the confirmed underdogs. However, after a performance of courage and character, they left clutching the European championship trophy. No team can have deserved success more.

If one man has personified the bravery and determination that flows through this Danish team, then it has to be Kim Vilfort. He scored the second goal, which

confirmed Denmark's first triumph in a major championship, 12 minutes from the final whistle.

Vilfort has been missing from the Danish team's hotel this week. He has been at the bedside of his daughter in a Copenhagen hospital where she has been fighting leukaemia. He flew home when her condition worsened last week, but a family meeting insisted he should return.

He did, and played an influential part in the defeat of Holland in the semi-final. Then last night he won Denmark the European championship.

The Danes, physically shattered, were clinging to the single-goal lead set by John Jensen, under surveillance by Nottingham Forest, when Vilfort broke through to score. The cynical and often spiteful tackling of the disappointing Germans had been punished again on the edge of their area. Although Nielsen's initial shot was blocked, substitute Christiansen headed the ball into the path of Vilfort, who minutes earlier had squandered an equally inviting opportunity. This time the tall midfielder cut inside the two German defenders and, though his left-footed shot hit the foot of the post, it rolled into the net.

The celebrations in Gothenburg were mirrored across the Baltic in Copenhagen, where 100,000 fans had packed into the town centre.

Although this Danish side may not be as talented as the teams they sent to the European championship in France in 1984 and the World Cup in 1986, they do possess a mental toughness. Their refusal to crack, even under the most intense pressure, caused the Germans to lose their cool.

An explosive finish: Denmark celebrate a great victory in the European championship.

SPORT IN BRIEF

FOOTBALL
Leeds United, managed by Howard Wilkinson and with Eric Cantona in the team, win the League championship when Manchester United falter towards the end of the season. Leeds finish on 82 points, four ahead of Manchester United and seven ahead of Sheffield Wednesday, who finish in third place.

CRICKET
Hampshire beat Kent by 41 runs to win the Benson and Hedges Cup. Robin Smith gets the Man-of-the-Match award for his innings of 90. It is the second year running that Hampshire have won a one-day trophy; they won the NatWest Trophy in 1991, when Robin Smith again won Man of the Match for his innings of 78.

FOOTBALL
Gary Lineker's illustrious international career is ended abruptly by the England manager, Graham Taylor, in the European championship. One goal behind Bobby Charlton's record 49 international goals, Lineker has a chance to equal the achievement in England's match against Sweden. but 29 minutes from the end, with England needing to score a goal, the striker is taken off. England lose the match 2–1 – and one of the game's great role models.

CRICKET
Pakistan are the tourists in England. Opener Ramiz Raja and bowler Waqar Younis **(right, with umpire Palmer)** are among the World Cup stars who appear in the series. Pakistan take the series 2–1, defeating England by ten wickets in the final Test at the Oval. Waqar Younis and Wasim Akram take 22 and 21 wickets respectively.

1992

1992

By Michael Williams
PUBLISHED MONDAY 20 JULY

Nick Faldo (**below**) came home on a wing and a prayer in the Open championship at Muirfield yesterday, at one moment throwing away what had long seemed a certain victory, but then retrieving it when, amid the breathless excitement of this final afternoon, all had seemed lost.

Seldom have fortunes changed so dramatically as Faldo, three strokes clear with eight holes to play, found himself two behind with only four to play but then completed those holes in par, birdie, par to beat John Cook of the United States by a stroke.

His final round of 73, after the first three had all been in the 60s, told much of the inner torment he had to endure, and when he holed his final putt from not much more than a foot for the title, he was overwhelmed with a mixture of emotion and relief.

Faldo's whole body sagged, his head dropped and the tears welled as he struggled to recompose himself for the formality of the checking and signing of his card before he emerged again to the warm embrace of his wife, Jill, who had somehow gained custody of the 18th-hole flagstick as a memento.

So Faldo becomes the first British golfer to win the Open championship three times since Henry Cotton in 1948, the neat coincidence being that both completed this trinity of titles at Muirfield, the home of the Honourable Company of Edinburgh Golfers.

Faldo's total was 272, 12 under par, as compared with his 279 in 1987, and this time he took home with him a cheque for £95,000 as well as the knowledge that he has now restored himself to the top of the world rankings where he surely belongs.

His five major championships, three Opens and two Masters, brings him level with Severiano Ballesteros, whose distribution is exactly the same and who, at the age of 35, is far from finished yet.

By Michael Calvin
PUBLISHED MONDAY 3 AUGUST

Linford Christie's face, as he made the 40 most important strides of his life, revealed the man. It was a portrait of aggression, the mask of a champion. His eyes bulged, his cheeks were as taut as a snare drum and his veins stood out on his forehead. Every sinew strained to breaking point in the 100-m final.

'That was Linford, right there,' Frank Dick, the British coach, reflected yesterday. 'Total commitment, the "no second chance" mentality. He was making a statement about himself.'

Christie has never succumbed easily to self-analysis. His natural shyness, given a harsh edge of suspicion by his subjection to racial prejudice, makes him aloof.

His personality is suited to sprinting. He is utterly self-absorbed, so dismissive of distractions that the drug scandal involving Jason Livingston, his protégé, was reduced to an inconvenience.

'I can't afford to be emotional,' he explained. 'What happened in the British camp last week was an Olympic problem. Life has got to go on. You have to put such things behind you and get on with what you want to do.'

Such statements encourage simplistic conclusions about a complex character whose fundamental influences are his paternal grandmother, who brought him up in Jamaica, and the gentle, grey-haired Ron Roddan, his coach since 1979.

Christie can be cold, intolerant, and resentful. Yet, when the mood is right, he can be warm, attentive and gracious. He craves respect, but then alienates athletes who accept his excellence without reservation.

Derek Redmond retaliated against Christie's criticism of the world championship 400-m relay team by branding him 'Britain's best balanced athlete, because he has a chip on both shoulders'.

A performance as inspirational as Christie's in the Montjuic Stadium has a profound influence on team morale. His gold medal was being passed around the athletes' village yesterday morning with the respect afforded to a holy relic.

Christie places great store by loyalty and values the normality that will be difficult to retain after a victory that, conservatively, will be worth £1 million before he retires. The world's fastest human being is a marketable commodity.

Nine of the last 14 Olympic 100-m champions have been black, and it was predictable that all eight of Saturday's finalists should be of West African descent. Research by British scientists suggests that black sprinters are best suited to the event. They have a narrower pelvis, thinner calf muscles and longer legs and arms.

Christie's height is a problem at the start, where he has a habit of losing fractions of a second by swaying in

Linford Christie wins the 100 m in 9.96 seconds.

his first three strides, but it is compensated by strength of will. One glimpse at Leroy Burrell, who looked like a rabbit trapped in the headlights of a car on Saturday evening, proved that medals are won in the mind.

Even someone with such a well-defined sense of himself as Christie is not immune from the strains. 'I always expect to be in the mix,' he said, 'but there are times no one doubts me more than I doubt myself.'

Christie had 25 minutes to kill after the semi-final. He received a massage and never allowed himself to be diverted by the scale of his opportunity. 'No one can help you on the line,' he reminded himself.

Dennis Mitchell, the bronze medallist, visualised himself as a bullet, about to be projected down the barrel of a gun. Christie was rather more practical. 'I was running scared,' he admitted. 'I run with a controlled fear of losing. When you are frightened in that way it's amazing what you can achieve.'

DID YOU KNOW?

On his way to this year's drivers' championship, British motor-racing driver Nigel Mansell won nine out of 16 grands prix in the season, which was a record. He also achieved pole position a record 14 times.

Mansell wins British Grand Prix

By Robert Hardman

PUBLISHED MONDAY 13 JULY

The British Grand Prix trophy went to the new British Grand Prix record-holder yesterday as extraordinary scenes of chaotic jubilation came within a few feet of tragedy at Silverstone.

Nigel Mansell won comfortably on the track he calls his favourite and extended his lead in the drivers' championship to 36 points. His Canon Williams teammate, Riccardo Patrese, came second and Britain's Martin Brundle, equalling his best, came third.

Afterwards, Mansell dedicated what he called 'the most incredible experience of my life' to 'the fans out there'. But the emotions of the 150,000 fans out there, rewarded with the result they wanted, meant that the hero of the day returned to the podium in a rescue van.

No sooner was Mansell over the finish and on his victory lap than thousands of ecstatic supporters started to spill on to the grass verge of the track where several cars were still racing. Despite commentators' pleas for restraint, the crowd continued to invade the perimeters. The remaining cars slowed down and no one was hurt, but Silverstone spokeswoman, Corinna Phillips, last night confirmed that a full inquiry would be made.

Mansell's celebratory circuit was cut short a mile from home, where he ground to a halt, mobbed by Union Jack-shrouded supporters. Once on the podium, he rewarded the chanting sea of red, white and blue with one of his most energetic champagne-spurting displays.

Afterwards, he had nothing but praise for the fans. 'I've never seen anything like it. I've never seen a British crowd so enthusiastic.'

Nigel Mansell winning at San Marino. He secured the Formula One championship with four races remaining.

SPORT IN BRIEF

HORSE RACING
Lester Piggott, aged 56, rides his 30th British Classic winner when he wins the 2,000 Guineas at Newmarket on Rodrigo de Triano. It is a record that will probably stand for all time.

FOOTBALL
The Premier League is introduced in England. The three lower divisions will still be affiliated to the Football League. The satellite television company BSkyB has promised £304 million over five years for the new League.

BOXING
In October Duke McKenzie defeats Jess Benavides on points to take the WBO super-bantamweight world championship. He becomes the first British fighter to claim world titles in three different divisions, having won the IBF flyweight championship in 1988 and the WBO bantamweight championship in 1991.

RUGBY UNION
The South Africans return to the world stage, playing Australia and New Zealand at home. It is New Zealand's first match against South Africa since the 1981 tour, which was disrupted by angry protests about South Africa's attitude towards Maori and Polynesian players. In the post-apartheid era, South Africa lose 27–24 against New Zealand and 26–3 against Australia. In November the South Africans visit Twickenham for the first time since 1969. They lose 33–16 to England, their worst Test defeat to date.

CRICKET
India take a winter tour to Zimbabwe, which becomes the ninth country to take part in Test matches. The Zimbabwean captain, David Houghton, scores 121 in the first Test, and is the first player to score a century in a country's first Test match since Charles Bannerman in 1876.

1992

335

1993

Grand National turns into farce

By J. A. McGrath

PUBLISHED MONDAY 5 APRIL

The 1993 Martell Grand National, the 150th to be run, will be remembered as one of the greatest ever sporting disasters.

The alleged failure of a casually employed flag man, paid £28 for a day's work, to signal a second false start – and the subsequent failure of seven jockeys to pull-up their mounts before a second circuit of the course was completed – reduced the event to farce.

The race was declared void, and yesterday at a press conference at Aintree, Peter Greenall, the chairman of the racecourse company said the race would not be re-run.

Trainers who have been consulted overwhelmingly say that it would not be practical, from the horse point of view, to run the Grand National again this season, Greenall explained.

The fiasco, which was televised live to millions of viewers worldwide, has cost racing, the betting industry and the Treasury dearly. Yesterday they were still counting the cost, with bookmakers William Hill threatening to sue Aintree racecourse for losses they claim amount to in excess of £150,000 in their marketing of the race.

Their lawyers and directors were meeting late yesterday to decide whether to take action.

The no-race has also cost those involved in the racing fraternity much time and effort, and the heartbreak of the episode was yesterday being realised. The outspoken John Upson, trainer of Zeta's Lad, said the atmosphere in his yard was as if there had been a funeral.

Racegoers will be offered free admission at Aintree's November meeting. Owners and trainers can look forward to being reimbursed their travelling expenses, while owners will also be reimbursed the jockeys' riding fees. All entry fees on the race will be automatically returned.

The prestigious name and reputation of the Grand National have taken an almighty battering this weekend, but Peter Greenall remained convinced that its reputation had not been irreparably damaged. Mr Greenall also said there will be a full enquiry.

An official waves a red flag (below) in a vain attempt to stop racers after a second false start. Animal rights protesters had delayed the race, then several riders became caught up in the starting tape. On the second restart the tape entangled horses and riders again, but other jockeys, unaware another false start had been called, continued round the course. John White rode Esha Ness to what he believed was a National victory.

Senna shows genius at Donington

By Timothy Collings

PUBLISHED MONDAY 12 APRIL.

Ayrton Senna can have won few greater victories in his extraordinary career than that in the cloudbursts which turned the European Grand Prix at Donington Park yesterday into a lottery.

Starting fourth on the grid in a downpour, he mixed inspired tactics with sheer good fortune to steer his Marlboro McLaren-Honda to the 38th win of his career.

It was a victory to savour not only for the 33-year-old Brazilian, still driving on a race-by-race agreement with the team, but also for the drenched 50,000 crowd – a disappointing attendance for Tom Wheatcroft's first grand prix at his Leicestershire track.

Where others slid and spun in ever-changing track conditions, Senna was steady all the way from green lights to chequered flag. Showing uncanny car control on slick tyres, he finished a lap ahead of his rivals, except Damon Hill, who brought his Canon Williams-Renault home 1 min 23.1999 sec behind the McLaren.

Ayrton Senna beats Damon Hill into second place in the European Grand Prix at Donington Park.

Alain Prost, who had challenged strongly early in the race before suffering a catastrophic pit-stop, was third in the second Williams, one lap down, ahead of Johnny Herbert's Castrol Lotus-Ford. Italians Riccardo Patrese, in the new Camel Benetton-Ford, and Fabrizio Barbazza, in a Minardi-Ford, were fifth and sixth respectively. It was Barbazza's first championship point.

Senna's victory lifted him 12 points clear of Prost in the early stages of the drivers' championship and left McLaren and Williams level on 26 points in the constructors' title race.

'It was fantastic,' said Senna, who had been hoping for a wet race to negate the power advantage of the Williams cars. 'The conditions were unpredictable and, of course, unknown too. On a circuit like this you have to commit yourself to a corner before you have any feeling for it. If you try too hard, you are off and if you try too easy, they come and get you.'

Monica Seles stabbed by spectator

By Barry Martin and John Parsons in Hamburg
PUBLISHED SATURDAY 7 MAY

Monica Seles is comforted by her brother Zoltan and a tournament official after being stabbed.

Monica Seles, the world No. 1 woman tennis player, was stabbed by a spectator as she rested between games during a tournament in Hamburg yesterday.

The 19-year-old Yugoslav was sitting on her chair when a middle-aged man lunged at her from the crowd with a large knife. She screamed and ran to the middle of the court where she collapsed. The assailant was wrestled to the ground by security staff.

Seles, who is an ethnic Hungarian from Serbia and lists her country as Yugoslavia, has been on the receiving end of death threats for years. There was immediate speculation that the attack might have been in protest over Bosnia, but last night all police would say was that her attacker was a 38-year-old eastern German and his motive was unclear.

Seles received a single stab wound about one to two centimetres deep between the shoulders. Her lungs were not thought to have been hit. A tournament spokesman said: 'It seems that Monica heard someone shout a warning to her just before the man struck, and she turned away. That probably saved her from a much more serius injury.'

Eyewitnesses said a man, carrying a bundle and walking as though drunk, shuffled past spectators in the front-row seats of the stand and lunged at the player's back. Seles stood up with a shriek and walked a few steps on to the court with her arm behind her back. She looked woozy as she reached for a spot on her upper-back. Then she was helped to a sitting position. Although Seles remained conscious, her face was twisted in pain.

Seles, who has lived in America since 1986, has been the target of abuse because of the actions of Serbia in the last two years. At last year's Wimbledon she attributed her defeat in the women's singles final in part to the fact that she had been unable to sleep the night before the match because of bomb threats received at the London house where she was staying.

Seles has ruled the world of tennis for the last two years. At just 17 and four months, she became the No. 1 on the women's world ranking list.

In 1991 and last year, she won three of the four Grand Slam events. She won the French, Australian and US Opens in both years, and in 1992 also reached the final of Wimbledon.

In just 13 attempts, she has won seven Grand Slam tournaments. But she has been widely criticised for loud grunting after shots, and many opponents claimed they could not concentrate because of the noise.

SPORT IN BRIEF

CRICKET

Australia are hosts to the West Indies in the winter tour. In the fourth Test Australia need 186 to win, but crash to 74 for seven. Australia's last-wicket pair manage to add 40 runs, though, and need just one run to bring the scores level. West Indies bowler Courtney Walsh smashes their hopes when he gets the wicket of Craig McDermott, ensuring a victory by one run for the tourists. West Indies also take the series 2–1.

BOXING

WBO super-middleweight title-holder Chris Eubank faces WBC title-holder Nigel Benn in Manchester. The judges cannot separate the two. In 1990 Benn was beaten for the first time in his professional career by Eubank.

FOOTBALL

On 27 April, 18 members of the Zambian football team are killed when their plane crashes off the coast of Gabon. In spite of the tragedy, Zambia come close to reaching the 1994 World Cup finals. They lose their last qualifying game 1–0 to Morocco; a draw would have seen them through.

MOTOR RACING

In April Nigel Mansell is involved in a crash in practice for the Phoenix Indy Grand Prix **(below)**. Despite this setback, Mansell has a great season, winning the IndyCar championship driving for Newman-Haas, the team part-owned by the actor Paul Newman.

1993

The bright new world of cricket

By Richard Savill

PUBLISHED MONDAY 10 MAY

Spectators at county grounds across England were welcomed yesterday to what the match programme at Chelmsford described as 'the bright new world of Sunday cricket'.

But the brightness of coloured kit in place of traditional white brought mixed reactions as Essex turned out in yellow and Yorkshire in royal blue.

As for the umpires in pale blue coats, one Chelmsford spectator suggested that they looked as though they should be working in a garage. The same thought struck the Kent players at Lord's. They regaled Merv Kitchen, one of the umpires there, with a chorus of 'You can't get better than a KwikFit fitter'.

At Leicester the umpire, Don Oslear, walked on to the cricket pitch carrying a crate of empty milk bottles and shouting 'Milko'.

'I find it difficult to take this seriously,' said Mr Donald Scott, 46, an Essex member. 'It is as if they are trying to turn cricketers into athletes.'

But the designer clothes, introduced with white balls and black sight screens for Sunday League matches in an effort to broaden the appeal of the game and attract younger spectators, were welcomed by other enthusiasts. Business was brisk at the Essex club shop, where 45 replica county shirts were sold, at a price of £24.99, during the day.

Among those in favour of the new clothes was Mrs Carol Proctor, manager of the shop, who said: 'I think they look beautiful.' However, she does not want coloured kit for championship or Test matches.

Back in the Lord's museum, the curator, Mr Stephen Green, pulled out a book on the history of the game. It showed that when the present Lord's ground was first used in 1814, the average cricketer would be wearing breeches, a black beaver hat, a brightly coloured shirt and bow tie, wide braces and a belt with metal clasps.

DID YOU KNOW?

Zimbabwe-born Graeme Hick became the youngest batsman to score more than 20,000 runs in first-class cricket at the age of 27 years and 20 days, beating the record set by Englishman Walter Hammond in 1931.

Lewis earns right to be called champion

Lennox Lewis (left) fights Tony Tucker at Las Vegas. Although Lewis won, many were unimpressed by his performance, and predicted defeat against Frank Bruno later in the year. They were wrong.

By Steve Bunce

PUBLISHED MONDAY 10 MAY

Lennox Lewis, who did not have to throw a punch in anger when he was given the World Boxing Council's heavyweight title in January, won the right to call himself champion in Las Vegas on Saturday night.

He comfortably out-pointed American Tony Tucker over 12 rounds at the Thomas & Mack Center, all three judges returning wide scores in favour of Lewis, 27, born in London, raised in Canada but Jamaican at heart.

His tactics were somewhat erratic, however, and some of the doubts, which have persisted since Lewis was awarded Riddick Bowe's belt by default, remain.

There is also a doubt about whether Lewis's much-debated £18 million fight with Frank Bruno will come off in the autumn despite his victory here. Frank Maloney, Lewis's manager, will consider in the next five weeks a counter-offer of £5.5million from Las Vegas for Lewis's second defence.

Evander Holyfield's name came into the equation last night, and Bruno will have to wait until mid-June to learn whether he has a third shot at the world title. Lewis's camp believe Bruno is asking too much money for a fight which will generate little interest outside Britain.

'We are not going to fall over ourselves for the Bruno fight,' said Mr Maloney. 'He wants more than the 25 per cent a challenger is entitled to. It's been said before and I'm saying it again – Bruno mustn't be too greedy in his demands.'

Saturday's contest started tentatively, and was even dull enough to prompt the crowd to boo as early as the second round. But Lewis noticeably increased the pace in the third and followed a stiff jab with a powerful right cross that connected perfectly. For the first time in 51 fights, Tucker was sent crashing heavily to the canvas.

Tucker, 34, beat the count and survived the final 30 seconds before collapsing into the desperate hands of his trainers. The punch had the reverse effect on the crowd and close to 13,000 people stood up as Tucker went down. At the end of the fight Lewis said to Tucker: 'Respect.' But it appears that, from some quarter at least, it is respect that Lewis still lacks. Winning's not enough. In Las Vegas on Saturday we settled for a British world heavyweight champion but, funnily enough, we expected more.

By Christopher Davies

PUBLISHED FRIDAY 14 MAY

Terry Venables, chief executive and 22 per cent shareholder of Tottenham Hotspur, will be asked to resign from the board today.

Alan Sugar, chairman and majority shareholder with 43 per cent, has called an emergency board meeting for this morning and wants Venables to quit the club.

Venables said last night that he would fight Sugar – head of the Amstrad computer company – and the board all the way.

As former Spurs player Chris Waddle was being presented with the Footballer-of-the-Year award at a London hotel, Venables said: 'He [Alan Sugar] wants to run the whole thing himself. It looks like I'm going to be removed from the club for reasons I don't know.

'I'm waiting until tomorrow but I won't let it die. I'm going to fight. It's not unexpected, even though we've had our differences of opinion. When you invest money you realise that you can lose it if things go wrong. But profits are up so something must have been going right. I think I've succeeded.'

Venables took out big loans to finance his investment when he and Sugar bought the club two years

ago and his holding at yesterday's stock market price of 89p would be worth about £3.3 million. The City expects Tottenham to return profits of about £5 million this year.

Venables said: 'I've invested my life in Spurs. I've put in everything and more. We have the beginning of something big and I am looking forward to next season.'

Neil Ruddock summed up the feeling of his teammates when he said: 'When I heard the news I felt like crying. If Terry Venables goes, most of the players will want to go, too.'

Venables was seen as a club saviour, not least because he fought off the challenge from the late Robert Maxwell to buy Spurs, and it was Venables who encouraged Sugar to invest in the club.

Few thought he would be able to mastermind the saving of Tottenham but he did – partly by the sale of Paul Gascoigne to Lazio for £5.5 million and by winning the FA Cup in 1991.

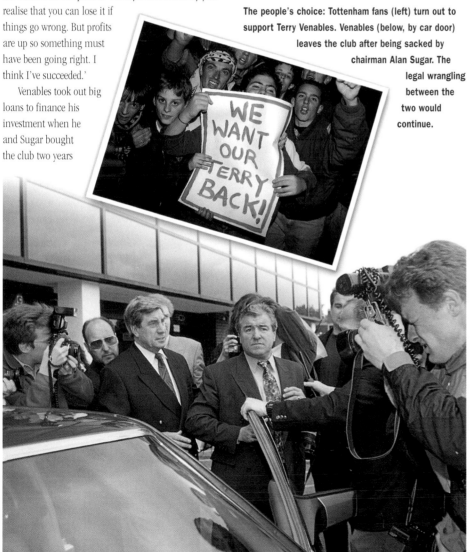

The people's choice: Tottenham fans (left) turn out to support Terry Venables. Venables (below, by car door) leaves the club after being sacked by chairman Alan Sugar. The legal wrangling between the two would continue.

SPORT IN BRIEF

FOOTBALL

Arsenal and Sheffield Wednesday feature in both the FA Cup and League Cup finals. Arsenal win the League Cup 2–1. In the FA Cup the final finishes in a 1–1 draw. In the replay Arsenal again beat Sheffield Wednesday 2–1. Defender Andy Linighan scores the winner in the last minute of a disappointing match.

CRICKET

In July, in the middle of the Ashes series, 25-year-old Michael Atherton is appointed England captain. He succeeds Graham Gooch, who presided over a terrible winter tour in which England lost all three Tests against India, and who has now seen his team lose three out of four matches against Australia. The man who appoints Atherton, Ted Dexter, then resigns his position as chairman of selectors during the Edgbaston Test, the fifth, and Atherton's first as captain. As England's seven previous captains have done, Atherton loses his first match in charge, in this case by eight wickets, but England manage to draw the final Test.

CHESS

After a dispute with the world chess organisation, the Fédération Internationale des Échecs (FIDE), the hitherto undisputed world champion, Gary Kasparov, forms a breakaway group, the Professional Chess Association (PCA), in order to play against England's Nigel Short. Kasparov wins the series comfortably, 12.5 to 7.5.

LAWN TENNIS

A dramatic Wimbledon ladies' final ends in tears as Steffi Graf comes back from 1–4 down in the final set against Jana Novotna to take the title 7–6, 1–6, 6–4. The Duchess of Kent has to comfort a tearful Novotna at the presentation ceremony.

1993

Senna wins Australian Grand Prix

By Timothy Connings in Adelaide
PUBLISHED MONDAY 8 NOVEMBER

Ayrton Senna made history and ended an era yesterday when he drove to his second successive victory and fifth win of the year with a flawless, emotion-charged performance in front of more than 97,000 spectators at the Australian Grand Prix.

The Brazilian's 41st triumph, in his 158th race, was the perfect ending to his six-year roller-coaster career with McLaren. It established the Woking-based team as the most successful in Formula One history, with 104 wins.

It also denied Senna's great rival Alain Prost the victory he so wanted in his 199th and final grand prix. Prost, who finished second in his Williams-Renault, now heads into retirement with his family in Switzerland. His British teammate Damon Hill was third, but never threatened in a race which delivered little of the drama and melodrama which both preceded and followed it.

The race concluded one of the sport's most intense and acrimonious rivalries. Senna admitted afterwards: 'Awards don't count very much to us. We both love motor racing. We both are world champions and despite the difficult times we've had in the past, today is the end of an era – for him and for me.'

The post-race words from the two drivers who have dominated Formula One for a decade hardly amounted to a reconciliation, though their half-embrace in the pit-lane and on the podium at least indicated a deep mutual respect.

Senna's performance – he dominated both qualifying and the 79-lap race – in his final drive for McLaren, before replacing Prost at Williams, was one of his best of the year. Prost, who made a dignified exit after claiming four world titles in 13 years at the top admitted as much.

McLaren managing director Ron Dennis seemed to greet his team's win with mixed feelings. 'It's a great way to finish the season,' he said. 'I hope Ayrton will enjoy his holiday in Didcot, though I also hope it's not too much of a success.'

The 38-year-old Prost was more generous to his old rival than might have been expected. 'I think we had good times,' he said. 'Very good times. Especially in 1988, when he won the championship and I finished second.'

Asked about his own future, Prost said: 'I think it will change very much. I hope I don't get fat and lazy, that's for sure. I will feel a little bit more free and my life should be a little bit better. It's not easy to say what is going to be my life in the future.

'But I am quite happy to change and maybe I will be much, much happier. For sure my life will be different.'

Fond farewell: Ayrton Senna is congratulated by his old rival Alain Prost (on left, above), after winning the Australian Grand Prix. It was Prost's last race.

MILESTONES

The first rugby union World Cup Sevens tournament was held at Murrayfield in Edinburgh. Underdogs England took the Melrose Cup after beating Australia in the final. The seven-a-side game originated in Melrose, Scotland, in 1883.

Holyfield regains his world heavyweight title

By Paul Hayward
PUBLISHED MONDAY 8 NOVEMBER

So the giant was Holyfield **(right)**, not Bowe. After a night that exhausted the possibilities of drama at Casears Palace, the older, smaller, less-fancied fighter regained his world heavyweight title. Desire prevailed.

If celebrity is a mask that eats into the face, then Riddick Bowe will be counting the cost of fame's disfigurement today. Bowe lost his WBA and IBF belts on a majority points decision after failing to reproduce the passion he had shown in winning the titles from Evander Holyfield 12 months ago. The challenger was a vengeful colossus here, Bowe a victim of his own spectacular ascent over the last year.

It was bizarre and bracing in equal measure. By the end of the seventh round Bowe had lost both his wife, Judy, and trainer, Eddie Futch, to the local hospital after a lunatic by the name of James Miller parachuted into the arena and crashed into the side of the ring amid scenes of mayhem.

Judy Bowe, who is three months pregnant, fainted, while Futch was affected by the heart palpitations that have troubled him through most of his long and distinguished career as a cornerman. Neither was seriously endangered.

Though it split the contest into two phases, Miller's intrusion was not a decisive factor in the result. If anything the 20-minute delay favoured Bowe, who had looked listless and wounded at the end of the fifth after a succession of quick combinations from Holyfield.

'He [Bowe] was not mentally or physically prepared for this fight,' Holyfield's trainer, Emanuel Steward, said. Even the Bowe camp admitted it was true.

When Holyfield said he could take revenge on Bowe, most observers looked at their feet and mumbled with embarrassment. Now they will hail one of the more heroic comebacks in heavyweight boxing while holding up Bowe as an example of what can happen to over-indulgent champions. If Holyfield decides to fight on it is he, and not Bowe, whom Britain's Lennox Lewis will face in a unifying contest.

Gunnell takes gold and record

By Iain Macleod, Stuttgart

PUBLISHED FRIDAY 20 AUGUST

Sally Gunnell ran the finest race of her life in Stuttgart last night to win the world 400-m hurdles title in a world record time of 52.74 sec.

This shaved 0.2 seconds off the record previously held by Marina Stepanova of Russia and set seven years ago.

It was a stunning performance by the 27-year-old from Essex, who overcame the effects of a cold to add the title to her Olympic and Commonwealth crowns.

Her gold medal is Britain's second this week – Linford Christie won the world 100-m title.

Gunnell has been in outstanding form this season and before the world championships had been unbeaten in six races. But nothing she has done in her career compares with her achievement last night.

She did not dominate from start to finish as she often tends to do and, coming into the home straight, the American Sandra Farmer-Patrick, second to Gunnell in

On top of the world: Sally Gunnell celebrates her record-breaking feat. She also won the European Cup 400-m hurdles this year.

last year's Olympic final, was putting on a better technical display than of late.

The strength and grit of Gunnell finally won the day, though Farmer-Patrick must take credit for providing the opposition to enable the Olympic champion to dig deep and find new reserves of determination.

Gunnell said: 'It is a dream come true. Already in the semis I knew it was going to be a fast race. But all I wanted to do was win. Sandra ran a great race, but I kept saying to myself, "You can run that fast, too." At the start I was having a hard time trying to concentrate – the crowd was so overwhelming. I couldn't be sure that I had won, so I didn't start celebrating in case I looked a fool.'

She is the first British woman to break a world record in an Olympic event since the javelin thrower Fatima Whitbread did so in the same stadium in 1986.

SPORT IN BRIEF

CYCLING

In July Chris Boardman breaks the world hour record, which has stood for just six days, recording a distance of 52.27 km in the time. The record will stand for nine months. It is a further success for Boardman, who won Olympic gold in 1992 in the 4,000-m pursuit event. Later in the year Boardman will turn professional, and in 1994 has a successful first Tour de France, winning the prologue time trial and, as race leader, wearing the yellow jersey for the first three days.

RUGBY UNION

The British Lions, captained by Gavin Hastings of Scotland, lose to New Zealand by two Tests to one. In a close battle they lose the first match 20–18 and win the second 20–7. In the third Test they are 10–0 up at half-time, but go on to lose the match 30–13.

FOOTBALL

England, under the management of Graham Taylor, fail to qualify for the 1994 World Cup. The final humiliation for Taylor and his men comes in the final round of qualifying games when San Marino's Davide Gualtieri scores against them after just nine seconds of the match – the fastest goal scored in the World Cup competition. Due to previous woeful performances, England need to win by a seven-goal margin against San Marino and need Poland to beat Holland. England win 7–1 and Holland beat Poland.

GOLF

The Americans retain the Ryder Cup when Tom Watson's men triumph over Bernard Gallacher's squad by two strokes at the Belfry. Europe lead by one stroke going into the final day's singles, but the Americans prove too strong for them.

1993

341

1994

By Sandra Stevenson in Lillehammer
PUBLISHED FRIDAY 25 FEBRUARY

Ice-dance officials are likely to defend their controversial marking system at a press conference tomorrow. The meeting has been called in the wake of an outcry over the judging of the free-dance section which placed Jayne Torvill and Christopher Dean third, despite the fact that the Britons were winners with the crowd.

The sport is under threat. Juan Antonio Samaranch, president of the International Olympic Committee, has said it should be pulled out of the Games if it cannot justify its subjective judging procedures.

However, television executives are strongly opposed to expulsion and it is their money which pays for the Games. They were responsible for getting ice dance included in the 1976 Games.

The 23 million viewers in Britain, and the billions worldwide who tuned in on Monday night, were certainly entertained by the ice dancing, even if they disagreed with the result.

Torvill and Dean undoubtedly won gold in the estimation of the audience and in the eyes of the British judge. Two of the other eight judges thought them worthy of silver, but the rest relegated them to third.

Ice-dance referee Hans Kutschera said Torvill and Dean's routine contained illegalities, although the version presented in Copenhagen, when they won the European title in January, did not. They had made significant changes to their 'Let's Face the Music and Dance' routine between the European and Olympic events.

The British champions countered Kutschera's criticism by explaining in detail how their moves were legal. They have called a press conference for when they return to Britain on Tuesday.

Kutschera is also the head of the ISU's ice-dance technical committee. He is familiar with both sides of the skating barrier, having finished last in three world championships, placings with which he might disagree.

MILESTONES

The winter Olympics were held in a different year from the summer Olympics for the first time. In an effort to raise more advertising revenue, from now on the winter and summer Games would be held alternately every two years.

Fairy-tale start for Kerrigan

By Michael Calvin in Lillehammer
PUBLISHED THURSDAY 24 FEBRUARY

The conventions of the fairy tale were duly observed in the winter Olympics last night when American Nancy Kerrigan won the short programme in the women's figure-skating competition in Hamar.

Tonya Harding, implicated in the assault on her American teammate seven weeks ago, could finish only tenth. Her medal chances are gone but Kerrigan is in contention for gold. 'It will be great to leave here with a gold medal,' she said last night, 'but most of all I want to leave here feeling good about myself.'

The heavily-made-up Harding, wearing a stark tasselled red costume, fell during her warm-up. The crowd mostly treated her with indifference, though a smattering of boos marked her arrival. She was seized by an asthma attack soon after finishing a disappointing programme.

The medals will be decided on Friday evening when the skaters perform their long programme. But Hollywood awaits. A Walt Disney film on Kerrigan's life will help swell her post-Olympic earnings to £15 million.

Nancy Kerrigan wins the silver medal at the winter Olympics. Associates of teammate Tonya Harding had assaulted Kerrigan; Kerrigan became the heroine of the ice rink and centre of media attention.

Genius Lara tops 300 as champion of a new era

By Christopher Martin-Jenkins
PUBLISHED MONDAY 18 APRIL

There are many good Test batsmen; a few great ones. Perhaps once in a cricketing generation there are also champions, players so superior to the rest that their contemporaries can only marvel. This winter season, and especially this last weekend in Antigua, Brian Lara, 24, the Trinidadian, has assumed the mantle first worn by George Headley, and passed on through the 'three Ws' [Worrell, Weekes and Walcott] to Garfield Sobers and Vivian Richards.

Despite having his innings interrupted four times and a total of 23 overs being lost to rain on the second day, Lara reached only the 13th Test triple hundred a little before five pm yesterday on the second day of the fifth and final Test. He had hit 38 fours across an outfield of thick grass: the other batsmen between them had managed a total of 11 boundaries.

Lara, 320 not out, is the 12th man to score a Test triple hundred, and the third West Indian after Sir Gary and Lawrence Rowe. Sobers' record 365 not out against Pakistan at Kingston in 1957–8 is clearly in jeopardy. So garlanded of late that his shoulders must be aching, Sir Gary is in Antigua and would not be sorry to relinquish the honour.

Lara is a genius making the most of his gift. What is more, he expresses it with charm and modesty.

In the fifth Test against England, Trinidadian Brian Lara (right) reaches a record Test score of 375, a total confirmed (below) by the scoreboard.

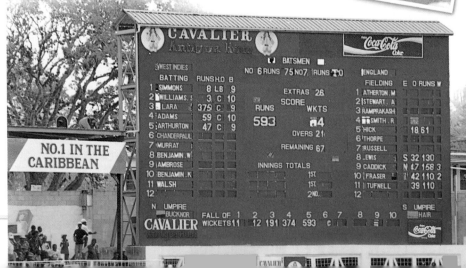

Manchester United win the Double

By Paul Hayward
Published Monday 16 May

Manchester United take their second successive League title, and the League and FA Cup Double.

Fear will be the last thing in the thoughts of United as they reflect on their League and FA Cup Double after another seemingly endless winter. But still the highest accomplishment of the Busby era – victory in the European Cup – pokes beguilingly through the smoke of Saturday's unsatisfactory encounter, and the harder minds are turning already to the question of what Alex Ferguson should do to perfect his expeditionary force before autumn.

Those hearing the 4–0 scoreline on crackly radios deep in Africa will assume it was a pageant. Instead, United's ordination as only the fourth side this century to complete the Double simply encouraged the curmudgeons who, by a strange British reflex, automatically hiss venom at such consistently dominant clubs. In typical stubborn-kid style, United produced one of their worst performances against Chelsea to complicate the business of assessing just how good they are.

They won the Premiership – comfortably in the end – after playing much the best football of any British team. They won the FA Cup with the handbrake on. They reached the final of the Coca-Cola Cup in the middle of a downswing, and were outwitted by Aston Villa. But now the real scar line: Galatasaray, who felled United early in the European Cup and were then used for shooting practice by the other big powers.

Dominance at home, dominance abroad. Two different things, as the ghost of Sir Matt Busby may yet whisper to Ferguson as he scans the horizon for new signings. With so many non-Englishmen at Old Trafford,

Ferguson has to pick up his poaching hat and chequebook to make United the equals of Milan, Barcelona and Bayern. With Ferguson, Arsenal, Newcastle and Blackburn on the prowl this summer, lock-up-your-sons will be the watchword among smaller clubs.

Seldom has an FA Cup result looked so bizarre on the page. This was a meal of thin air, an empty gallery which the gush of second-half goals did nothing to fill. It was just one of those days. Even the scoreboard got it all wrong, flashing up Tony Cascarino, of Chelsea, as the scorer after Brian McClair had tapped in United's fourth.

In one paragraph you would reflect that United, travelling with a whole convoy of good luck, underperformed for the third successive time at Wembley, but were still good enough to dispose of improving but still average Premiership opponents.

One image played in the mind as the match became a victory lap for United, and Liverpool, Arsenal and Tottenham made room in the élite club of Double winners. After Andrei Kanchelskis was substituted, he sat acknowledging the cheers and waves of the crowd. Then he spotted a line of United supporters in wheelchairs and walked along the row, bending to talk to them and shaking hands and patting backs as he went. In a year in which United were often accused of being graceless, arrogant, violent even, the most noble of impulses were borne throughout by Kanchelskis, who has agreed to stay at Old Trafford to help Ferguson's empire grow. For that, and most of what United gave through ten exacting months, we ought to be thankful.

1994

343

1994

Brian Lara: genius at work in phenomenal feat

By Christopher Martin-Jenkins
PUBLISHED TUESDAY 7 JUNE

Word had seeped through the Trent Bridge press box long before England had completed their innings victory against New Zealand. Brian Lara was breaking records again, and this time it might be something really special.

In the time that it took me to get from Nottingham to Birmingham, Lara's score moved from 315 to 429. On the way, Radio Five Live was transmitting, movingly, the events commemorating D-Day from the beaches of Normandy. They put the significance of what was happening at Edgbaston into perspective, but 6 June, nonetheless, will be a never-to-be-forgotten date in cricket's history, too.

It was not as hot as it had been in Antigua, seven weeks before, when Lara passed Sir Gary Sobers' Test record; nor were the circumstances as demanding – the game was destined to be drawn from the moment he resumed this innings at 111 not out – as they had been in the early stages of the fifth Test against England when he had begun by rescuing the West Indies from a start of 12 for two. Nevertheless, this was phenomenal batting by an imperishable genius.

I was in time to see him go past Bill Ponsford (437), B. B. Nimbalkar (443) and Don Bradman, whose 452 not out, along with Len Hutton's 364, were the best-known records of my schooldays.

By now the premier Durham bowlers had retired to the shadows of the outfield, though the fielding remained, surprisingly, admirably keen. They must all have been tired, but none more so, surely, than Lara. Yet when he was on 459, a drive to extra cover off Phil Bainbridge failed for once to reach the extra-cover boundary, and Lara ran four instead.

Finally, at half-past five, a ball after he had been hit on the head, changing his mind about hooking at a 'bouncer' from John Morris, he crashed his 62nd four, between mid-off and extra cover, to claim the record that has pride of place as the first in Wisden.

One of the first to pay tribute was Hanif Mohammad, whose world record he broke. Denis Compton said: 'I don't know how he does it. He's obviously a very great young player who is going to keep on breaking records. But why talk about records? He's quite simply a great young player, one of the best ever.'

British rider leads in the Tour de France

By Phil Liggett in Rennes
PUBLISHED SATURDAY 9 JULY

The French (not to mention the British) were unprepared for another surprise turn of events yesterday when Sean Yates, one of two British riders in the Tour de France, became the new leader by a single second. Never, since 1962, has a British rider led the event until this year, and Yates emulated his team rival, Chris Boardman, when he finished sixth on the longest stage of 170 miles from Cherbourg to Rennes to become the second home leader in the race's opening week.

Ironically, the only time a British rider has not led the Tour, which began last Saturday in Lille, has been during the two days spent in Britain. Italian Flavio Vanzella was the leader then, and yesterday he slipped back to fifth, but only six seconds behind the leader.

Yates, 34, said: 'The day had to come when the Italian GB-MG team would crack, so we just waited and watched, and when we attacked we went flat out.' His move came about 12 miles from the end after almost seven hours' riding, and the group of seven riders,

DID YOU KNOW?

France became the first national rugby union team since the South Africans in 1937 to win a series against the All Blacks in New Zealand. Having drawn against the Wallabies in Australia, the French team met their 1987 World Cup conquerors, and won the series 2–0.

including Motorola teammate Frankie Andreu, quickly gained over a minute. 'When the lead went up to one minute and 20 seconds, I realised I had a chance of the jersey, but I really didn't want to think about it,' added Yates, as he waited to be presented with his first *maillot jaune* in his 11th tour. After crossing the line yesterday it was only a short wait before realising the enormity of his achievement.

Throughout the day, the French organisers had continued to pay tribute to the way the two British stages had been run, and a British leader seemed fitting again, especially after the race had started by touring the D-Day beaches.

The long haul south from Normandy to Rennes proved too much for the former world champion and triple Tour winner, Greg LeMond, who almost certainly said *au revoir* to the race which has made him a pedalling millionaire. LeMond gave up after 110 miles with no excuses other than to say he was feeling terrible and could not explain it. 'This isn't the way I wanted to go,' he said. 'I gave it everything in the time trial [to help British rider Chris Boardman, on whose team he rides] and perhaps I did too much.'

LeMond's decision to go home has weakened Boardman's Gan team further, as injury has caused Didier Rous to limp along in last place. While newcomer Boardman is the best member of the team, he cannot expect to progress alone.

Tour cyclists race through the Hampshire village of Wherwell. The Tour first passed over British soil in 1974; this was its second visit.

344

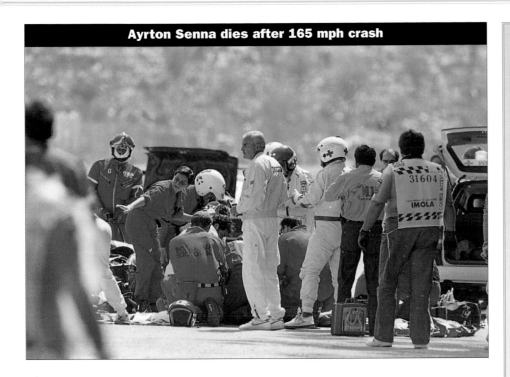

Ayrton Senna dies after 165 mph crash

By Tim King and Timothy Collings

PUBLISHED MONDAY 2 MAY

Ayrton Senna, three times world champion of Formula One motor racing, died yesterday after crashing at 165 mph during the San Marino Grand Prix at Imola, Italy.

The 34-year-old Brazilian was leading on the seventh lap when he careered into a concrete crash barrier. He was dragged unconscious from the wreckage of his Williams car and at one point the medical team had to restart his heart.

Senna was taken by helicopter to a hospital in Bologna with severe head injuries. He never regained consciousness and was pronounced brain dead four hours after he was admitted. Dr Maria Teresa Fiandri, head of intensive care at the Maggiore Hospital said: 'With the first aid at the track, during transport here, and in the hospital, we did all we could.'

Last night it was announced that there would be three days of national mourning in Brazil.

The German, Michael Schumacher, who was following Senna when the accident happened, said, 'Ayrton looked nervous from the very first lap. The lap before I saw he was a little unstable and skittish in that corner. The next time he went sideways and then lost it.'

Senna had written in a German newspaper that he was having handling problems with his Williams-Renault on the Imola track.

Senna was the second Formula One driver to be killed in little more than 24 hours. The Austrian Roland Ratzenberger died after crashing during a qualifying

Senna's funeral was held in São Paolo; his crash helmet was placed on his coffin (right).

The medical team surround Senna after the crash at Imola that would prove fatal. During his racing career, Senna won 41 Formula One races, starting in pole-position an unparalleled 64 times.

round on Saturday. On Friday Rubens Barrichello crashed his Jordan Hart car but escaped with a broken nose and concussion.

The deaths were the first in Formula One since Italy's Ricardo Paletti died in the Canadian Grand Prix of 1982.

The veteran British racer Stirling Moss described Senna as the benchmark for driving skill. 'He was the greatest driver ever seen,' he said. 'The person to compare him with was [Juan Manuel] Fangio.' He added that it was too soon to speculate on causes but, while mechanical failure was most likely, there was also a chance that Senna had passed out in the cockpit. 'He made no attempt to corner, and that isn't Senna at all.'

SPORT IN BRIEF

GOLF

South African Ernie Els wins his first major title when he triumphs at Oakmont to take the US Open. Els finishes the four rounds in a three-way tie with Loren Roberts and Colin Montgomerie, The three players go into an 18-hole play-off, which Roberts and Els complete in 74, four fewer than Montgomerie. Els and Roberts then enter a sudden-death play-off, which Els wins on the second hole.

FOOTBALL

Arsenal, under the management of George Graham, defeat Parma 1–0 to take the European Cup Winners' Cup. Alan Smith scores the only goal in the final.

GOLF

Nick Price of Zimbabwe wins the British Open at Turnberry. Although both he and Swede Jesper Parnevik are one behind the leaders going into the final day, it soon becomes clear that they will be competing for the trophy. Parnevik bogeys the 18th hole for a final round of 67; Price gets round in 66 for a total of 268, clinching the title by one shot.

AYRTON SENNA (1960–94)

AYRTON SENNA WAS REGARDED as the finest racing-driver of his generation and perhaps one of the greatest of all time. His full name was Ayrton Senna da Silva and he was born in São Paolo, Brazil, on 21 March 1960, into a wealthy family that had made its money in business.

In 1981 Senna moved to England, embarking on his Formula One career three years later. In 1985, he joined the Lotus Renault team, winning two races in his first season with them. Then, in 1988, he switched to McLaren, a key

decision which helped to bring him his three world championship titles.

Senna felt that Formula One was in danger of becoming a contest between computerised motor systems, rather than the racing skills of individual drivers. 'I want to be challenged by someone made of skin and bone...not by someone else's computer,' he once said.

Although Senna could appear aloof and curt he engaged in very public rows with arch-rival Alain Prost – he was a driver of enormous talent.

1994

345

1994

Diane Modahl banned for drug-taking

By Caroline Davies

PUBLISHED THURSDAY 15 DECEMBER

Diane Modahl, the former 800-m Commonwealth gold medallist, was found guilty of taking a performance-enhancing drug yesterday and banned from competing for four years. The unanimous verdict of the five-strong British Athletic Federation disciplinary panel was announced after a one-day hearing on Tuesday. The panel dismissed claims that the high level of testosterone – 42 times greater than normal – could have been caused by mishandling in the Portuguese laboratory where her urine sample was analysed.

Modahl, 28, who is married to her coach Vicente, is the first British woman to have tested positive for drugs. She has protested her innocence since being told of the test result as she was about to compete in the Commonwealth Games in Victoria on 24 August.

Dr Martin Lucking, panel chairman, said: 'Having heard all the evidence and considered all the documents, the committee was satisfied, unanimously, that a doping offence had been committed by Mrs Modahl.'

Modahl said she was horrified at the BAF decision, and will fight to clear her name.

DID YOU KNOW?

Forty-five-year-old George Foreman became the oldest man to win a version of the world heavyweight title when he defeated Michael Moorer, who had in turn conquered Evander Holyfield for the WBA and IBF titles.

By Paul Hayward

PUBLISHED MONDAY 18 JULY

For Brazil, the long wait is over: for the first time since 1970 the World Cup will be borne aloft in football's spiritual homeland. Justice was done in the US.

The player to seal Brazil's victory was, ironically enough, Italy's Roberto Baggio, who missed the fifth of his country's penalties in the first World Cup final penalty shoot-out.

It was a poor game, but a just outcome. Brazil reached this final having scored more goals and conceded fewer than any side up to the semi-final stage. They thrilled and beguiled us like no other team.

For more than two decades, Brazil have possessed a tortured footballing soul. When the jinga gave way to the jingle of European money, many Brazilian players returned bearing coarse new methods, but a compromise has been found – skill, allied with hardness – and a new path laid down to the highest of honours and glories.

It was a painfully unsatisfactory end to a fine tournament. After 90 mostly sterile minutes, the game staggered into extra time. The tempo increased significantly, but the story of this game was a faltering Brazilian attack failing to break down a resolute Italian defence. That forced the teams into the bingo game of a five-penalty climax, in which Franco Baresi, Daniele Massaro and, finally, Roberto Baggio all failed to score.

After the draining sequence of penalties, the Brazilians formed a circle of solidarity and defiance of the sort which enabled them finally to overcome the Italian side. Brazil had rediscovered its birthright.

A dejected Roberto Baggio ponders his penalty miss (left), which gave Brazil the World Cup trophy (below).

Schumacher crash ends Hill's title chase

By Timothy Collings

PUBLISHED MONDAY 14 NOVEMBER

Damon Hill's hopes of winning the Formula One drivers' championship ended in controversy yesterday when he was in a collision with Michael Schumacher in the Australian Grand Prix. Both drivers were forced out of the race.

The crash confirmed Schumacher as champion with 92 points, one point ahead of Hill. Many observers felt the German deliberately caused the accident to prevent Hill from passing him to win the race and take the title.

The crash came on the 36th lap of the 81-lap race in Adelaide. Hill had been running a close second to Schumacher, and putting him under pressure when, quite unexpectedly, the German made a mistake, went off the circuit and hit a wall.

When he bounced back on to the track, he tried to retake control of the racing line but succeeded only in colliding with Hill as the Englishman moved inside to pass him at the next corner.

'I am not making any comment on the accident,' said Hill. 'These things happen in motor racing sometimes. I saw a gap and went for it.'

Michael Schumacher acknowledges the crowd's cheers as he is crowned world champion, taking the title by one point from Damon Hill after the controversial clash in the Australian Grand Prix. Hill's teammate, Nigel Mansell, won the race, his first victory in Australia in eight attempts.

Mike Atherton fined £2,000 for two 'crimes'

By Christopher Martin-Jenkins

PUBLISHED MONDAY 25 JULY

Ray Illingworth's decision to fine Michael Atherton £2,000 after his team had been beaten in four days by South Africa at Lord's yesterday sadly raises more questions than it answers.

One thousand pounds is the maximum amount the chairman of selectors is permitted to impose on any count, but he found Atherton guilty of two 'crimes', as England's hitherto unblemished captain called them.

England lost the Test by the humbling margin of 356 runs, but Atherton will remain captain for the last two matches of the series. It was a sad end to a disastrous day for English cricket and an undeserved diversion from the singular triumph of Kepler Wessels and his team.

Having been exonerated by the match referee, the former Australian Test batsman, Peter Burge, Atherton was punished firstly for using dirt inside his trouser pocket – earth picked up from the rough areas at the end of the pitch – to dry his fingers; secondly for failing to tell Mr Burge, when he investigated television recordings on Saturday evening, that he had earth in his pocket.

The second decision is entirely understandable. Atherton's explanation was that if he had mentioned having dirt in his pocket it might be misconstrued

by Burge as using an artificial substance to alter the ball's condition. That is understandable, but he should have known that to tell only half the truth is always unwise. He has paid heavily for not trusting the referee to make up his own mind on the facts.

If this is reason for regret, the second fine, for using dirt in the first place, might be one for indignation. Provided that the ball's condition was not altered, as the referee, chairman and umpires have all accepted, there was nothing illegal in Atherton's drying of his fingers on the dirt.

It was, however, highly unusual. Indeed, no one to my knowledge has ever put earth in his pocket before to dry his fingers.

Atherton accepts that he would have been better advised to rub the palm of his hand into the ground, as Ian Salisbury for one often does, to remove the sweat. Unfortunately, by fining him for the use of dirt, the chairman seems to have signalled that he does not share the captain's view of his innocence.

Speaking with confidence and candour to a crowded press gathering after the match, and declaring that his conscience was clear, Atherton sought to explain that his sole purpose was to use the dirt to dry his fingers 'in order not to dampen the ball. I did it to dry my fingers on a very hot and humid day in order to dry the ball and help my bowlers obtain reverse swing.'

SPORT IN BRIEF

CRICKET
Playing at the Oval in the third Test match against South Africa, Devon Malcolm completes the sixth best bowling analysis in cricket history when he takes nine wickets for 57 runs in South Africa's second innings. Malcolm had been hit on the head by a bouncer the day before, and had determined to wreak his revenge on the South Africans. England win by eight wickets.

FOOTBALL
Colombian Andres Escobar scores an own goal as his team lose 2–1 to the United States in the World Cup and fail to qualify for the second round. On his return home Escobar is waylaid in Medellin and shot dead. After a huge public outcry, Colombian Humberto Munoz Castro is arrested and sentenced to 43 years in jail for the crime.

GOLF
Britain's Laura Davies achieves a remarkable tally when she wins on five different tours in the course of the year. She wins three tournaments in the United States, two in Europe, one in Thailand, one in Japan and one in Australia. This year she tops the US tour earnings list, with $687,201. Davies has played for the European team in the Solheim Cup for the third time this year. Her three wins in the competition in 1992 helped Europe break the United States' domination and take the trophy for the first time.

BASEBALL
The World Series is cancelled for the first time in its 90-year history when major-league players go on strike. Team owners have capped their salaries. The case goes to court and will be settled next year as the players' claim of unfair labour practices is upheld.

1994

347

1995

European Super League planned

By John Whalley

PUBLISHED THURSDAY 6 APRIL

Rugby league could become part of a £50 m European Super League following reports last night that representatives of media magnate Rupert Murdoch were on their way to Britain.

It is understood that Murdoch's News Limited plan to put £300 million into the worldwide operation, with £250 million of it already being injected into an Australian Super League, currently in the process of being set up amid chaotic scenes down under.

The European set-up, which could be in operation by summer 1996, would have British bases in London, Cardiff and Manchester, while the Continental teams would be based in Paris and Toulouse.

The champions of both the Australian and European Leagues would meet in an end of season play-off. The move follows a meeting at British clubs in Leeds yesterday whereby the idea of summer rugby was reported to be favoured by the majority of clubs.

Initial details of the scheme were put to the Rugby League Council yesterday afternoon, and RL chief executive Maurice Lindsay said last night: 'News Corporation executives have flown in. The English Rugby League has followed the developments in Australia and is excited by them. We need to talk to Mr Murdoch and his representatives because they share our vision of taking rugby league to the world.' A major announcement revealing the full plans is expected to be made today.

The Australian RL and New Zealand RU were unlikely allies yesterday in their opposition to the new Super League as worried officials from both codes pondered the possible effects of the bitter dispute in Australasia.

With over 100 professional players indicating they would play in the new League, including several established internationals, the search for talent is widening to cover British internationals and leading rugby union players.

DID YOU KNOW?

Wigan added their eighth successive rugby league Challenge Cup to their trophy haul this year. Wigan captain Shaun Edwards had now played in and won 41 consecutive games in the Challenge Cup competition.

Cantona attacks fan after being sent off

By Toby Harnden and Henry Winter

PUBLISHED THURSDAY 26 JANUARY

The footballing future of Manchester United's Eric Cantona was in doubt last night after he attacked a spectator. The incident, which is certain to earn Cantona a lengthy ban from the game, arose after 52 minutes of an FA Carling Premiership match at Crystal Palace. The Frenchman was sent off for kicking an opponent. On his way to the dressing room, Cantona reacted violently to barracking from the home fans. He lunged with both feet at a supporter standing behind a touchline barrier before exchanging punches.

The fracas was broken up by police and stewards before Cantona was led away. Police said that there had been allegations of assault against both Cantona and

Eric Cantona is led away after launching his 'kung-fu' attack on a spectator. He was banned from football for the rest of the season and fined. A prison sentence was commuted to 120 hours' community service on appeal.

another United player, Paul Ince, from two spectators. A spokesman at the ground said both players would be interviewed over the next few days.

One Crystal Palace fan, Mr Mark Coote, 37, said, 'This guy came down from behind me and started hurling abuse at Cantona…the two started trading punches before everyone intervened.'

The Football Association promised rapid action against Cantona. A statement said, 'Charges of improper conduct and of bringing the game into disrepute will inevitably and swiftly follow.'

Australians hope for League peace

By John Whalley

PUBLISHED SATURDAY 29 APRIL

Officials of the Australian Rugby League have held talks with Rupert Murdoch's News Limited in what could be a breakthrough in the impasse between the two organisations over the setting up of a Super League.

John Quayle and Ken Arthurson, chief executive and chairman of the ARL, which is sponsored by Murdoch's media rival Kerry Packer, were involved in negotiations, after which Quayle said he was hopeful of a compromise.

News Limited plan a ten- or 12-strong competition featuring teams from Australia and New Zealand in opposition to the Australian Rugby League's 88-year-old Winfield Cup competition.

'There has been some behind-the-scenes discussion through our chairman Mr Arthurson,' said Quayle. 'The main thing is there is always hope as long as we talk.'

Keighley have postponed a move to sue the Rugby Football League until the position of the controversial new European Super League becomes clearer.

The Second Division champions were due to begin legal proceedings at Leeds High Court yesterday against the RFL for money already claimed to have been lost because of their omission from the revolutionary competition. But the club's barrister Jonathan Crystal asked for an adjournment of the hearing following reports that Murdoch, who has already pledged £77 million to the new Super League, is prepared to raise the stakes still further.

Wigan take title, Widnes celebrate

By John Whalley

PUBLISHED SATURDAY 15 APRIL

Wigan won the Stones Bitter championship for the sixth successive season yesterday with a 34–18 victory over St Helens as Widnes celebrated a Super League reprieve.

It was announced that France will field only one side, instead of two, in the new £75 million, 14-club competition which will kick off next March, and so Widnes, who had refused to merge with Warrington to form a Cheshire club, will step in.

Jim Mills, the Widnes chairman, said: 'We're delighted because we always believed we deserved a place in our own right. We've been the second most successful club in the rugby League behind Wigan during the last 20 years.

'We've had our problems but our finances are now on an even keel and Halton Borough Council are rebuilding a £6 million ground at Naughton Park this summer.

'We could have been guaranteed a Super League place by merging with Warrington, but that was never going to be realistic with so much rivalry between the two clubs.'

Meanwhile Oldham's shareholders have rejected the idea of a merger with Salford to form a club from Manchester and the two will be locked in battle for one Super League place.

The losers will play in a newly formed First Division. Jim Quinn, the Oldham chairman, said: 'It seems a shame when Oldham and Salford are already in the top flight and Humberside are granted a place in the Super League even though Hull and Hull KR would have been in the Second Division next season. But we are 13 miles apart and it's illogical to merge.'

A number of clubs are still unhappy about the Super League and Rochdale want sides involved in the competition excluded from the Silk Cut Challenge Cup.

Denis Betts, a member of all Wigan's successful sides over the last six years, conceded the Super League will eventually make Wigan's job much harder, but added that he did not expect matters to change quickly. Betts leaves to join Auckland next month and explained why Wigan's appetite to keep winning remains insatiable: 'The way things are, there will be more notoriety for players involved with a losing Wigan side than the one which has kept winning,' said Betts.

'The Super League will even things out and I would have liked to have been part of it, but nothing will change overnight and I expect it to take two or three years for most sides to catch Wigan.'

Captain Shaun Edwards (far left) and delighted Wigan teammates lift the Stones Bitter Cup – for the sixth time in succession.

SPORT IN BRIEF

SNOOKER

Steve Davis **(below)** wins his 70th professional tournament. He has appeared in 93 finals. Davis dominated snooker in the 1980s, winning three world championships and 85 out of 96 matches between 1980 and 1985.

MOTOR RACING

Nigel Mansell makes his return to Formula One racing when McLaren invite him to drive for them. His relationship with the team does not last long; he cannot start in the first two grands prix because he is too big for the car, and after two disappointing races – a tenth place in San Marino and a retirement in Spain – he leaves the team.

CRICKET

Australia's tour of the West Indies ends with a fantastic series victory for Australia captained by Mark Taylor. It is the first time in 15 years that the West Indies have been defeated, and the first time they have lost at home since 1973. After a win each and a draw, the result hinges on the final Test in Kingston, Jamaica. The Waugh twins have an astonishing match: Steve Waugh scores 200 runs and Mark 126.

1995

Blackburn win League

By Paul Hayward

PUBLISHED TUESDAY 16 MAY

The cotton kings who dominated Blackburn in the 19th century did little but take. Jack Walker **(above on right, with Alan Shearer)**, man of steel, has repaid the debts of his ancestors by forging a modern championship-winning club where once there were cobbles and a tramline. They were hanging out streamers yesterday in football's new Jerusalem.

By the entrance to the club shop, a steeplejack had returned excitedly from Anfield and shimmied up a chimney stack to hang out a Union Jack. In the morning, he had returned to paint the word 'champions' in white letters down one side.

'When I sold Walkersteel I saw the possibility of doing something sensible,' Walker told the fans in a written address. It was an unlikely choice of words for a £60 million gamble in this volatile futures market. In the faces of the town's children yesterday, he would have seen the glowing effects of such philanthrophy.

Blackburn are English football's new superpower. If Walker's munificence continues and Kenny Dalglish maintains his prowling presence on the touchline, then the club should remain a force into the next century.

The trophy has travelled just 30 miles from Manchester, but it has taken the 81 years since Blackburn last won the League to get there.

DID YOU KNOW?

Steve Elkington and Colin Montgomerie finished the US PGA championship at Riviera, Los Angeles, level on 267. The score for the 72 holes was the lowest total ever achieved in the competition. Elkington won the play-off.

By John Mason

JOHANNESBURG, SATURDAY 24 JUNE
South Africa 15 pts; New Zealand 12

South Africa, who will play England in November as world champions, did rugby union a huge favour by beating New Zealand on Saturday. In greatly reducing the rugby league value of several All Blacks, François Pienaar and company added considerably to their own potential earning capacity in rugby union's new world.

Principal beneficiaries, besides Peinaar, will include Joost van der Westhuizen, André Joubert, Ruben Kruger and Chester Williams. On the list, too, will be Joel Stransky, whose expert goal-kicking ensured that South Africa, deservedly, won the William Webb Ellis trophy in extra time. At the end of the rainbow there is, truly, a crock of gold.

On another famous day in the history of the new South Africa, they also unearthed another trim, eager No. 6 to rival the potency of Pienaar, albeit an old favourite in a new guise. President Mandela's supreme sense of public relations made his inspired decision to wear a replica Springbok No. 6 jersey in no way cosmetic or embarrassing.

Many things made South Africa's winning of the World Cup possible: a fervent tide of national emotion personified by President Mandela, deep pride and sheer bloody-mindedness in demonstrating to the rest of the world that being South African was nothing of which to be ashamed. Those, though, were ingredients only. The driving force on the pitch was Pienaar. Off it, too.

For a long time it appeared that South Africa might falter on the last agonising lap. Churlish as it will sound, New Zealand let the big one get away. Handling was suspect long before South Africa applied the defensive brakes, passing slapdash. At times the besetting desire to get Jonah Lomu, the giant on the left, into the action was counterproductive. Flanker Josh Kronfeld battled well but was ultimately seen off by Kruger. When the All Blacks suddenly appreciated that they had a match on their hands, the boys among the All Blacks looked vulnerable: Jeff Wilson, Glen Osborne, Andrew Mehrtens. Poor Mehrtens, brave as his penalty goal from 55 yards in the opening minutes of extra time, his dropped goal miss from in front two minutes from full time will haunt him for ever.

New Zealand, the World Cup within tantalising reach half-a-dozen times in a spellbinding contest, were finally undone by Stransky, the outside half. New Zealand led 3–0, 6–3 and, in the second minute of extra time, 12–9. South Africa, having drawn level three times, got back to 12 points each in the 12th of the 20 minutes of extra time. Renewed pleas from Pienaar plus superb policing of Lomu did the trick.

There were six minutes 26 seconds remaining when Stransky made an indelible entry in the record books: a dropped goal which will earn him many a crust in future.

Driving force: Springbok captain François Pienaar shields the ball against an All Black onslaught. Pienaar said afterwards: 'We did not have 63,000 fans behind us today, we had 43 million South Africans.'

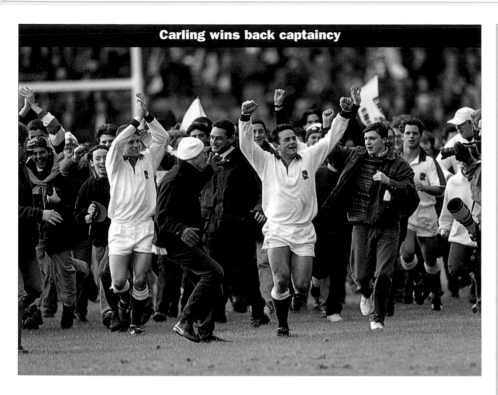

Carling wins back captaincy

By John Mason

PUBLISHED TUESDAY 9 MAY

Will Carling will, after all, lead England in the World Cup. After the tournament, which begins in South Africa on 25 May, his future as captain will be further reviewed by the RFU.

The contemptuous anger of the England squad and the massive public support for Carling forced Dennis Easby, the Rugby Football Union's beleaguered president, to reverse swiftly last Friday's decision by the six senior officers to sack the most successful captain England have had.

After protracted discussions and further apologies all round, RFU officials ratified Carling's reinstatement last night.

Easby said: 'Perhaps the RFU have shown after all that we are aware of the strength of public opinion. It has been a wearing few days for everyone.'

Carling was 'flattered' by the public support for him and said: 'My sole aim is to help England win the Cup.'

The RFU statement said: 'Will Carling wishes to apologise to every member of the committee of the Rugby Football Union for his offensive comment.

'All 25 members of England's World Cup squad have indicated their support for Will Carling as captain and have respectfully requested the RFU officers to reconsider their decision to terminate his appointment.

'In the light of these circumstances, the RFU are agreeable to reinstate Will Carling as England's captain for the period of the World Cup.'

Carling leads England in a lap of honour (above) after beating Scotland 24–12 to take the Grand Slam. In more reflective mood, Carling attends a press conference with Dennis Easby (left) to offer a fulsome apology for his remarks about members of the RFU.

Thus, salvaging as much self-respect as possible from a wreckage not entirely of their own making, the RFU managed a spectacular about-turn yesterday, the smartness and swiftness of which would have delighted a drill sergeant. What the past three days have done for the RFU's overall image is open to debate.

Of the senior players in England's squad, neither Dean Richards (Leicester) nor Rob Andrew (Wasps) would have accepted the captaincy if offered. The squad requested the officers to reconsider their decision.

Ostensibly Carling was given the elbow because of a juvenile remark in a documentary on Channel Four last Thursday. His fade-out words were that the RFU was being run by a bunch of '57 old farts'.

Will Carling's more obvious failings are a lack of manners and an inability to count; the punishment decreed in the name of the 56, not 57, members of the RFU was out of all proportion to the offence.

In the be-blazered corridors of rugby power, Carling has been seen as the unacceptable face of advancing professionalism – money – in a sport which prides itself on its amateur ethic.

SPORT IN BRIEF

CRICKET

Yorkshire's Darren Gough **(with arm raised, above)** is forced to return home early from England's tour of Australia because of injury. In what has been a dismal tour for England, Gough has performed exceptionally. He has taken 20 wickets in the first three Tests, and leads an England comeback in the third with a flamboyant batting display, hitting 51 off 56 balls. He then takes six Australian wickets for 49 runs. Australia retain the Ashes 3–1.

BOXING

Irishman Steve Collins ends Chris Eubank's 43-fight unbeaten record and becomes the WBO super-middleweight champion on a points decision.

HORSE RACING

Trainer Jenny Pitman has a second Grand National success when Royal Athlete, a 40–1 long-shot ridden by Jason Titley in his first National, crosses the line first.

CYCLING

Thirty-one-year-old Spanish cyclist Miguel Indurain wins the Tour de France for a record fifth consecutive time. It is also the fifth consecutive win for his team, Banesto.

1995

1995

Cardiff ready to pull off Davies transfer coup

By John Kennedy and John Whalley

PUBLISHED THURSDAY 5 OCTOBER

Cardiff are hopeful of pulling off rugby's biggest transfer coup, bringing Jonathan Davies back from rugby league to Welsh rugby union. After protracted talks yesterday with Warrington, Davies's club, they expect to hear confirmation of the move next week. It means Davies could play in the rugby league World Cup, in which Wales kick off against France in Cardiff on Monday, and then switch codes to play in the Five Nations championship in the New Year.

Gareth Davies, chief executive at the Arms Park, headed up the M6 yesterday afternoon after a two-hour session with his namesake. While his rugby league teammates were all claiming that Davies, 32, has signed a contract with Cardiff, the Welsh champions were playing down the talks.

Jonathan Davies has made no secret of the fact he wants to finish his playing days in his native country. 'If everything is sorted out I'll be coming home and playing for Cardiff or some other club. I'd like to return. There's been a lot of interest.'

The final obstacle to his return to the union code was removed by the International Rugby Board last weekend when they sanctioned a free gangway between union and league. If he signs, the mercurial outside half will become the first Welsh player to take advantage of the new situation.

Davies, who has captained Wales at union and league, played for Neath and Llanelli before signing for Widnes almost seven years ago. His loss was felt in union as he has been the most outstanding and charismatic Welsh rugby player since the 1970s.

If the deal – believed to be a package worth £100,000 a year – is struck, Davies will immediately be vying for a place in the Welsh team for the Five Nations, his first championship campaign since 1988.

DID YOU KNOW?

Juventus were Italian champions for the 23rd time and winners of the Italian Cup for the ninth time this year. The famous black-and-white stripes of Juve were copied from the oldest surviving football club in the world, Notts County.

By Iain Macleod

PUBLISHED WEDNESDAY 19 JULY

Jonathan Edwards last night achieved what he has been threatening to do for the last month when he broke the world triple-jump record in Salamanca, northern Spain. Edwards jumped 17.98 m on his second attempt, to eclipse by one centimetre the ten-year-old mark of the American, Willie Banks.

Edwards, 29, has been in outstanding form this summer and has on three occasions jumped beyond Banks's record, only to be denied the record as each jump was assisted by a following wind in excess of the legal limit of two metres per second.

This time Edwards – now clear favourite for the world championship title in Gothenburg next month – was aided by a following wind of 1.8 metres per second.

Edwards first gave notice that he was within sight of the record at the European Cup in Lille last month. His

Jonathan Edwards savours a sweet moment after breaking the world triple-jump record. 'Technically the jump was not good,' he admitted afterwards. 'I started the run too far forward.'

jump of 18.43 m was the first 60-foot jump in history, but was assisted by a following wind of 2.4 metres per second; he jumped 18.39 m in the same competition but, again, that did not make the record books because of the wind.

A week later, in his home town of Gateshead, Edwards tried again, only to be foiled by a wind reading of 2.9 metres per second, which denied him the record after he had jumped 18.03 m.

He missed the later stages of last night's competition with an apparent muscle strain.

Afterwards he said; 'The first thing I did was look at the wind speed. The day was perfect and the Salamanca track is very fast. Under these conditions I knew I could beat the record again.'

FA release details about George Graham

By Henry Winter

PUBLISHED FRIDAY 10 NOVEMBER

The Football Association yesterday released details of their inquiry into George Graham **(below)**. Angered by the sacked Arsenal manager's comments about the bung inquiry in his autobiography, Lancaster Gate released the three-man disciplinary commission's report to 'set the record straight'.

Graham's greed dominates the nine-page judgement. Graham admitted receiving £140,500 in £50 notes at the Park Lane hotel and a banker's draft for £285,000 from the Norwegian agent Rune Hauge, but insists they were 'unsolicited gifts'. Both sums were paid within weeks of Graham negotiating with Hauge to purchase Paal Lydersen and John Jensen for inflated fees.

The commission reported: 'Mr Graham gave evidence about the payments being unsolicited. However, even if this is right, as a respected manager...we find that he must have known how serious a matter it was for him to be receiving this amount from an agent.

'Mr Graham did not tell anyone connected with Arsenal about the payments until a meeting with Messrs Friar and Hill-Wood [managing director Ken Friar and chairman Peter Hill-Wood] on 19 September 1994.' He repaid the money, plus interest, on 1 December 1994 and was dismissed on 21 February 1995.

One question is why Arsenal's board waited so long before dismissing Graham.

The FA acted yesterday because they were unable to charge Graham with bringing the game into disrepute following his book serialisation. The Scot was out of the FA's jurisdiction, having been banned until 30 June 1996. 'As a private citizen outside football he had a right [to re-open public debate on his case],' the FA said. 'Equally, the Football Association has a right, and now a responsibility, to set the record straight.'

Hall to fund Newcastle rugby union club

By Graham Tait

PUBLISHED WEDNESDAY 6 SEPTEMBER

Sir John Hall, the man behind the resurgence of Newcastle United Football Club, declared yesterday that he was going to turn the city's senior rugby union club into a major force. Hall, who has already funded Kevin Keegan's revolution at St James's Park and snapped up ice-hockey club Durham Wasps, has set his sights on guiding the Courage League Two side to the heights of English rugby.

'It's great for rugby in the area and I'm delighted for Tyneside,' said Hall. 'Over the last few years we have turned Newcastle United into a formidable force nationally, now we want to do the same with rugby.'

Just what Hall's role will be is still uncertain, but there seems little doubt that his cash injection has been prompted by the recent relaxation of regulations regarding professionalism.

Many club members were astounded at the announcement yesterday, few being aware of any negotiations having taken place. The statement covering the agreement stated simply that eventually Newcastle Gosforth will be known as Newcastle Rugby Football Club Limited.

Rob Andrew joins Newcastle in £750,000 deal

By John Mason

PUBLISHED FRIDAY 22 SEPTEMBER

Rob Andrew became rugby union's best-paid professional yesterday when he was appointed Newcastle United Sporting Club's first rugby development director. Andrew, 32, who has played 70 times for England, has signed a five-year contract believed to be worth £750,000.

The announcement, which follows the recent decision to end restrictions on players' pay, was made at a news conference at St James's Park, home of Newcastle Utd, which took Newcastle Gosforth Rugby Football Club under its wing 17 days ago. Andrew's appointment could spark off more high-profile signings. His brief is to turn Newcastle into 'one of the foremost clubs in Europe'.

'We've got the Kevin Keegan of rugby,' said Sir John Hall, chairman of Newcastle United. 'Rob will do for the club what Kevin has done for football. We're delighted he has decided his future lies in the northeast. He is an inspirational appointment for a club that is going places. His appointment shows Newcastle means business.'

Andrew, England's record points-scorer with 396, said, 'I am thrilled to be joining Newcastle at such an exciting time for rugby union.'

1995

1996

Gareth Southgate's penalty miss costs England Euro 96 semi-final

PUBLISHED THURSDAY 27 JUNE

The hopes and prayers of a nation were shattered last night when England were beaten by Germany in a thrilling semi-final of Euro 96 at Wembley. In a dramatic repeat of the World Cup match six years ago, the Germans won on penalties after a 1–1 draw. Gareth Southgate was the player unfortunate enough to feel the weight of expectation too much to bear, missing the decisive penalty.

After both sides had successfully converted their first five kicks, Southgate's penalty was saved and Andreas Möller stepped up to win the shoot-out 6–5 for his side.

It was the fourth successive victory for Germany over England in major soccer tournaments since 1966. England's World Cup final win that year remains their only triumph in world or European championships. Few of the 69,000 distressed England fans appreciated the irony that it was now Germany's turn to win in a Wembley extra-time showdown.

Terry Venables, the England coach, was quick to console Southgate. 'I feel very sad for Gareth and he is very down at the moment, but he's a top man and he's relatively inexperienced,' he said. 'He wanted to take the penalty when I asked him about it earlier. He's been absolutely first class throughout the tournament. It can be a wonderful game but it can also be a cruel one as well. They players' morale is on the floor at the moment and I really believe they deserve better.'

Southgate choked back the tears as he relived the awful moment. 'It's bitterly disappointing to know it is my miss that has stopped the whole country from cheering us in the final. I know that I'll just be remembered for that miss.'

The result came as a terrible anti-climax to the hordes of fans at Wembley and to the nation as a whole. Days of burgeoning hope were cast into darkest night at the end of a game of incredible excitement and then almost unbearable tension.

After the match fans went on the rampage in Trafalgar Square. Youths hurled hundreds of bottles during confrontations with riot police, who mounted two baton charges. Several people were treated for cuts.

John Major, speaking moments after the match ended, mirrored the nation's disappointment but was also quick to pay tribute. He said: 'Congratulations to both teams on a fine match.'

Klinsmann fulfils dream at Wembley

By Henry Winter
PUBLISHED MONDAY 1 JULY
Czech Republic 1; Germany 2

If Tony Adams could not lift the European championship, who better than Jürgen Klinsmann? It did not matter that Klinsmann had just played possibly his worst game of football in England.

A life-long admirer of Wembley, a man almost in tears when Tottenham Hotspur failed to reach the 1995 FA Cup final, Klinsmann realised his dream last night when he led Germany up those 39 stairs to receive the Henri Delaunay Trophy from the Queen.

The German masses danced in celebration. The Czechs were too stunned to move because the end of Euro 96 had come so suddenly, sneaking up on them like a thief in the night.

A controversial penalty from Patrik Berger had given the Czechs not only a second-half lead but also hope that they could upset bookmakers' odds that had stood at 80–1 a month before. Germany, though, muscled their way back, equalising through Olivier Bierhoff, who then

> ### DID YOU KNOW?
>
> Peter Shilton, the most capped England player with 125 appearances in goal, became the first player to compete in an amazing 1,000 football League games when his latest club, Leyton Orient, beat Brighton 2–0 in December.

struck four minutes into extra time with a goal that will always be golden for Germany.

For all the local talk of 66, this Euro 96 final contained echoes only of 76. West Germany had lost that European championship climax, on penalties, to the Czechs, then with Slovakia in tow. Long-held German hopes of settling this old score were lifted when Klinsmann was declared fit following his calf injury. Although he contributed little, his presence clearly inspired his colleagues.

The sight of Klinsmann warming up, however gingerly initially, was greeted with rapture by the massed German fans, receiving their second surprise of the night. The first had been the mass distribution of free plastic bowler hats, in Germany's colours, by one of the major newspapers, which last week had hailed them as 'Fritz'.

How odd. Klinsmann, the athletic embodiment of German football, had given England a beautiful season, his smile and sporting excellence doing much to eradicate the 'Fritz' mentality in English grounds. It was a marvellous sight to see Klinsmann leading out his country at the home of English football.

Poignant for him, too. During his sojourn at Tottenham Hotspur, the thoughtful striker often spoke of his wonderment of Wembley, which he had experienced only once before, and that as a substitute. Yesterday his wish was granted.

Jürgen Klinsmann (left) and Stefan Kuntz celebrate Germany's victory over the Czech Republic in Euro 96.

Golden triumph of Pinsent and Redgrave

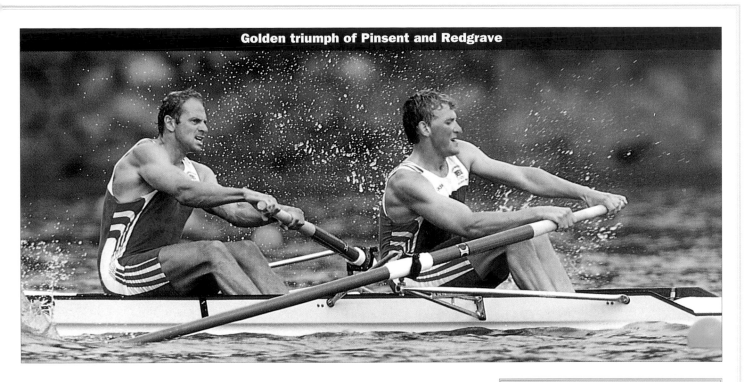

By Michael Calvin in Atlanta

PUBLISHED MONDAY 29 JULY

Steve Redgrave began to sob when he reached out to hug his children, his future. The gold medal around his neck represented Olympic history, his past.

The two strands in his life had come together, at the moment of supreme self-fulfilment. It will take months for him to discover whether it is possible to exist without the addictive torture of rowing. Only then will his promises of retirement, reaffirmed on the day he became Britain's greatest Olympian by retaining his coxless pairs title with Matthew Pinsent on Lake Lanier, have validity.

Pinsent is, understandably enough, too preoccupied by his own internal struggle to come to any rational conclusions about their future.

Redgrave and Pinsent, partners for six years, faced an uncertain future after their Olympic gold win. 'In some ways continuing will be a cop-out,' said Pinsent. 'There are more challenges to life than winning gold medals.'

Redgrave's wife, Ann, admits she will not be surprised if the lure of a fifth consecutive gold, in the Millennium Games in Sydney, proves irresistible. Jürgen Grobler, his coach, is to advise him to reassess his priorities after a six-month sabbatical from the sport.

'It frightens me to think what I'm going to do with my life,' Redgrave acknowledged. 'It's an empty feeling. I've been doing this for 20 years, and I'm walking away from it. You put so much effort into trying to achieve something, and, suddenly, you do it. There's a big hole in your life.'

Rampant commercialism of the Olympic Games

By Iain Macleod

PUBLISHED TUESDAY 6 AUGUST

The normally cheery farewell wave from Juan Antonio Samaranch, the president of the International Olympic Committee, seemed to contain a veiled thumbs-down for Atlanta as the 26th Olympiad ended here on Sunday night.

Amid the customary pomp and ceremony, Samaranch unusually refused to give an unqualified endorsement that these Games were the greatest. 'Most exceptional,' was as far as he would go. In IOC-speak that can be considered a rebuke to Billy Payne, president of the Atlanta Committee for the Olympic Games, all the more so as the ceremony was shown live around the world, and

Samaranch had earlier stated that 'commercialism must not run the Games'.

Samaranch added: 'We need commercialisation, but this must be controlled by the organising committee or the IOC. Without commercialisation, it's impossible to organise the Games.'

The private entrepreneurial exercise that cluttered the streets of Atlanta and became one of the major derogatory images from Atlanta will not be allowed to happen again.

The 17 days were characterised in the first week by seemingly never-ending transportation problems and systems failures and the bomb in Centennial Park; and in the second by a magnificent track and field meeting that helped to salvage some of Atlanta's reputation.

1996

359

1996

England make peace to save Five Nations tournament

PUBLISHED FRIDAY 6 SEPTMEBER

Sanity and goodwill have finally prevailed. The Five Nations tournament, the bedrock of British and French rugby for over 100 years and much beloved by players and spectators alike, has been saved after a wounding row that intensified alarmingly throughout an acrimonious summer.

England's insistence on negotiating their own television deal with Sky resulted in their expulsion from the competition in July, and peace only broke out in Bristol in the early hours of yesterday morning, when an agreement was concluded after a meeting lasting eight hours and ten minutes.

Perhaps exhaustion and the need for sleep resulted in a weakening of entrenched positions. More likely, though, it was the overwhelming public pressure that has been brought to bear in all the participant nations.

Full details will be announced at a press conference in Dublin on Monday, after the respective unions have given their final go-ahead. For once that should be a formality – it is unthinkable that anybody should contemplate prolonging the argument further.

Wales were meeting last night, England have a full committee meeting planned for today, as do the Scots and Irish. France, who only reluctantly became involved in the dispute, will also happily fall into line.

The RFU's treasurer, Colin Herridge, confirmed that the RFU's controversial £87.5 million contract with Sky remains in place, as does the £4.5 million per season, earmarked for the top clubs from the proceeds of that TV contract. He explained that the meeting in Bristol 'had resulted in an accord which has saved the Five Nations championship for the coming season and for the foreseeable future'.

'Resolving the Five Nations issue must help in the jigsaw of problems that we face,' said RFU secretary Tony Hallett. 'It's a weight off our shoulders.'

DID YOU KNOW?

When jockey Frankie Dettori won all seven races on the card it was a costly day for the bookmakers. The cumulative odds against the achievement reached more than 25,000–1, and the bookies lost up to £30 million.

Damon Hill emulates the success of his father

PUBLISHED THURSDAY 21 NOVEMBER

It was such a marvellous story, such a fabulous day, that even the veteran race commentator Murray Walker wept into his microphone. As the world watched, Damon Hill **(opposite right)** coasted to victory at the Japanese Grand Prix last month, winning the 1996 Formula One world championship and driving straight into the history books as the only man in the history of motor sport to emulate the success of his father.

'I can't go on; I'm too emotional,' screeched Murray Walker, perhaps overwhelmed by memories of Graham Hill winning the championship way back in 1962 and 1968. Out on the track, Damon savoured his lap of honour, letting the tears pour down his cheeks behind the privacy of his visor. Thoughts of his father – he used to race his pedal car against his dad's Jaguar – must have been powerful.

'In all honesty, I didn't think about him at all,' says Hill bluntly. When I express surprise, he explains: 'Look, my father died when I was 15 and I got to this point in my career entirely without his help. In motor sport, being my father's son was a dead story after I won my first race in 1993. Yeah, I used his memory to help me concentrate then, because that is what he used to say to me – concentrate, Damon.'

Sentimentality, one feels, is not his strong suit.

In fact, Damon Hill is so intense, it's scary. Deep in the bowels of a Chelsea Harbour hotel, the 1996 Formula One world champion sits behind an oak table, his face impassive, his gaze locked somewhere on the glossy panelling above the door.

Sometimes we have seen his eyes closed in grim meditation as he prepares to hurtle around the track at speeds of more than 200 mph, but mostly they are pinpoints of remote concentration. Even in this small room, you have to step right into his vision before he acknowledges your presence with a start. It is the first, but not the last time, that you feel Hill may inhabit a parallel universe. You could trot around the Silverstone circuit in a pair of stilettos during the pauses between asking him a question and receiving an answer.

Frankie Dettori rides to seven victories in one day

By Hotspur (J. A. McGrath)
PUBLISHED MONDAY 30 SEPTEMBER

Frankie Dettori was unable to give a repeat performance at Ascot yesterday, registering only one win from seven rides. Hopes that he would emulate Sir Gordon Richards' 1933 record by riding another five successive winners were extinguished the moment Sunbeam Dance, his mount in the opening Sunday Conditions Stakes, came under pressure approaching the

final furlong before fading into fourth. His sole winner, Altamura, was in the final contest.

But it would have been asking too much to expect the dream to continue. When Dettori, 25, went through the card, riding all seven winners at Ascot's Festival on Saturday, he treated the public to the most exhilarating sporting experience most could have imagined.

What set this feat apart – after all, Pat Eddery rode seven winners in a day (at two meetings) in June 1992, and Willie Carson six winners at Newcastle on June 30 1990 – was that Dettori set up an extraordinary occasion through a series of superlative efforts in the saddle, which allowed the tension to mount until breaking point was reached a few minutes before the final race, the Gordon Carter Handicap, over two miles.

With the finale set to commence from stalls in front of the stands, it was as if the occasion had been stage-managed. The crowd cheered and clapped Dettori as he cantered Fujiyama Crest up the straight to the starting point. The applause was as warm and spontaneous as any I have heard on a racecourse anywhere.

In a magnificent display of judging pace from the front, the Italian-born champion took the race by the scruff of the neck after 100 yards. He crossed sharply to the inside, and quickly set off into the lead. The dream was starting to unfold before our eyes.

On a high: jockey Frankie Dettori performs his traditional leap after enjoying an extraordinary day at Ascot. He won all seven races on the card.

360

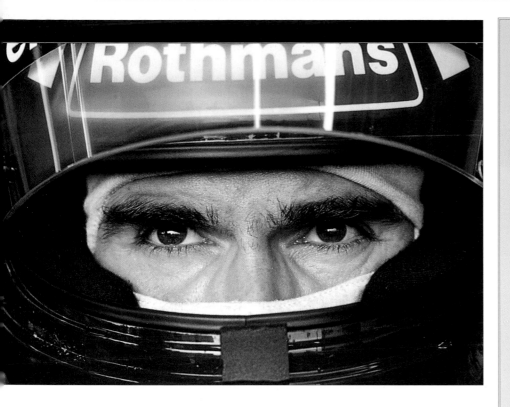

Test between New Zealand and South Africa

By Stuart Barnes

PUBLISHED MONDAY 2 SEPTEMBER

The city of Johannesburg is nearly 5,000 feet above sea level. Watching the final Test in a real Ben Hur of a series between South Africa and New Zealand at Ellis Park, it might as well have been 5,000 miles in rugby terms. It was that remote from any of the action we are likely to see in the northern hemisphere this season. But we should not be despondent about a gulf that is wider than a pair of Bay City Roller's flares.

Rugby union has probably never been played at such a rarefied intensity. In my rugby lifetime, nothing has come within light years. The 1995 World Cup final appears a Sunday stroll in comparison. If you wanted to sell the sport of rugby union to the Martians, it's the latest, greatest Test series fought out in South Africa that will clinch the deal. New Zealand may have lost on Saturday, but that should not conceal the fact that they rank among the finest rugby teams in history.

The raw pace of the team, combined with the visionary skills of Zinzan Brooke, Justin Marshall and Andrew Mehrtens forged entertainment fit for an emperor. Despite appearing to take half a dozen steps backwards into less enlightened ways, the sheer bravery and power of South Africa's showing on the pitch would deservedly spare them from the death-dealing thumb verdict.

It was not rugby from heaven, it was too hard for that, but for fire, brimstone and sheer bravura, it will be almost impossible to match. South Africa's final winning stand was played out live on television. The hors d'oeuvre was Orrell against England's unparalleled achievers, Bath. It was some contrast.

British rugby has long been hindered by an excess of caution and stifled ambition. So extreme has been the conservative grip, it is inevitable that when teams adopt a positive approach they will err on the side of excess. We need to swing too far to the wide of the game before we establish the balance that is the wonderful mix-and-match game of New Zealand.

It is to New Zealand that we must look for reassurance. As recently as 1994, Laurie Mains, then the New Zealand coach, nearly lost his job for transforming the All Blacks from efficient machine to romantic dream. New Zealand lost their way but the experiment had started. It was left to John Hart to tighten the parts and complete the experiment that leaves them the world's finest.

Zinzan Brooke (on left) holds the Tri-Nations and Winfield cups. He won his 47th cap against South Africa.

1996

1997

Ibrox giants make it nine Scottish League titles

By Glenn Gibbons
PUBLISHED THURSDAY 8 MAY
Rangers 1; Dundee United 0

Rangers' seemingly interminable wait for their ninth successive championship ironically lasted only another 11 minutes, the time it took Brian Laudrup to score the goal which gave them the title with a match to spare, while Old Firm rivals Celtic could only draw 0–0 at home to Kilmarnock.

Paul Gascoigne, playing his first full match in 14 weeks, was the star, however, deservedly accorded an ovation as he left the field, replaced by Derek McInnes.

The kind of match in which quarter was never likely to be asked or given produced plenty of goalmouth activity and man-to-man collisions. There was an eight-minute spell during the first half in which five players were booked – Rangers' Laudrup, Alan McLaren, Craig Moore and Gordan Petric, and United's Lars Zetterlund – but before then, Laudrup had given Rangers the lead.

Only 11 minutes had been played when the Dane struck, allowing the travelling fans to believe that, on this occasion, there would be no slips.

There was certainly a hint of no-more-Mr-Nice-Guy about the way Rangers went about asserting themselves. Miller gathered the ball on the left and delivered a cross of such precision that Laudrup had only to step forward and make contact with his forehead to bullet the ball away to the right of Dykstra from ten yards.

In the 23rd minute, Miller once again was the provider, releasing Laudrup through the middle and leaving the winger with only Dykstra to beat. He did this easily, then he drove the ball against the legs of the frantically retreating Erik Pedersen. The ball broke straight to Gascoigne, who then repeated Laudrup's error by knocking the ball off the legs of Pedersen and away for a corner kick. It was an extraordinary double miss.

Then Gascoigne had one of those little moments which are peculiar to the great talents. The ball was handled by Pressley, but the referee played advantage as the ball ran to the England midfielder. A little shimmy took him to the edge of the penalty area and his low, right-foot shot snaked past Dykstra before thudding off the foot of the post. Later Miller, who made a huge contribution, rattled the crossbar with another shot that had the goalkeeper helpless. By then United must have been looking for a white flag.

By Henry Winter
PUBLISHED THURSDAY 9 JANUARY

Kevin Keegan **(below)** resigned as manager of Newcastle United yesterday, shocking a city that draws such comfort and joy from the club.

The moment the whispers were confirmed, supporters converged in their hundreds on St James's Park, the club's stadium. A banner was raised stating, 'Please stay Kevin, we all believe in you.' But the fans' hopes crashed when a club official read out a statement from Keegan.

'It was my decision and my decision alone to resign,' Keegan said. 'I offered my resignation at the end of last season but was persuaded by the board to stay. I feel that I have taken the club as far as I can and that it would be in the best interests of all concerned if I resigned now. I wish the club and everyone concerned with it the very best for the future.'

While the timing is surprising, with the team well placed in three major competitions, there is no doubt that Keegan, 45, has been ill-at-ease recently. Like Newcastle's colours, his hair has become a mixture of black and white, a reflection of the unremitting pressure that comes with managing a club as large as Newcastle.

Keegan, an emotional individual, has also become tetchy with the increasingly ravenous media, often despatching Terry McDermott, his assistant, to conduct press conferences. The crushing weight of expectation that tumbles from the club's terraces appears to have taken its toll.

Anyone who has attended a match at St James's will appreciate the burden Keegan lived with. Anyone who has watched Newcastle train before 1,000 autograph-seeking fans will understand that this pressure is relentless.

Part of Keegan's problem is that he cares for the people of Tyneside. Born in the pit village of Armthorpe, his father and grandfather were Newcastle miners. Having also played for Newcastle, Keegan was considered a true Geordie. On each match day, as a crescendo of noise signals the imminent kick-off, the final song is always the same: the theme tune of *Local Hero*. It is for Keegan.

The adulation is little short of phenomenal. Keegan's name is tattooed on many a forearm. Across the region, baby boys rise from fonts christened 'Kevin'.

He is a man of deep generosity, and no one should begrudge him a desire to think of himself for once. What no one expected was the timing. Despite inconsistent form and an erratic defence, Newcastle are lying fourth in an open championship race, having reached the quarter-finals of the UEFA Cup, and are still in the FA Cup.

Pressure from fans, media and, however subtly, the board, must have made this millionaire wonder whether it was all worth it.

Kenny Dalglish, now installed as the bookies' favourite to replace Keegan, resigned from Liverpool because he said he felt his 'head was going to explode', such was the pressure, much of it rooted in Hillsborough.

'There are now heightened expectations at all the top clubs,' said John Williams of the Sir Norman Chester football research centre. 'Both fans and directors want accelerated success and that puts almost unbearable pressures on managers.'

DID YOU KNOW?

Chelsea's Roberto di Matteo recorded the fastest goal in FA Cup final history when he scored against Middlesbrough after 43 seconds of the game. The previous record of 45 seconds was set by Newcastle's Jackie Milburn in 1955.

Tiger Woods wins the Masters

By Lewine Mair
PUBLISHED MONDAY 14 APRIL

Tiger Woods last night changed the face of what has always been seen as a white man's game. As the 21-year-old prodigy set out for his final round in the US Masters with a nine-shot lead, the crowd knew that history was unfurling before their eyes. No black golfer had ever won the Masters. Not only that, but Woods was going to be the youngest-ever champion, eclipsing Severiano Ballesteros, who was 23 when he won in 1980.

The son of Earl Woods, a retired lieutenant-colonel in the US Army and Kultida, a native of Thailand, Eldrick Woods was born on 30 December 1975.

The child's fighting qualities soon put his father in mind of a South Vietnamese soldier called Tiger, with whom he had fought in Indochina. He nicknamed his son Tiger and it stuck.

Earl Woods remembers how, aged six months, his son would watch him hitting practice shots. At the age of two, the boy was putting alongside Bob Hope on television. At three, he shot 48 for nine holes.

In a thrilling US Masters, 21-year-old Tiger Woods stormed home with a record 12-stroke lead to become the first black golfer to win the tournament.

Few players have arrived on the tour amid such fanfare and expectations, and Woods, who has already won four tournaments, does not look like disappointing. 'It means a lot,' he said of his potential victory. 'It's going to open up a lot of doors, and draw a lot of people into golf who never thought of playing.'

His control of self is maybe the most extraordinary thing of all. Woods started off with $60 million in contracts, including $40 million from Nike. Phil Knight, the founder of Nike, was told he had paid too much but people are now agreeing it was a smart investment. 'We expected Tiger to be good, but we didn't expect he would be showing this kind of dominance this early.'

The money would not seem to have affected Woods. He is out to make history and to do the best for his people, and not least for black golfers such as Charlie Sifford and Lee Elder, who, because of the era in which they played, suffered as he has never had to suffer. He said he wanted nothing so much as for golf programmes for inner-city children to be a success.

Colin Montgomerie, who played alongside Woods on Saturday was, by his own admission, left dazed. 'I knew that he hit the ball for miles and was magic with his irons. What I didn't appreciate was how well he putted.' Having said his piece, a patently humbled Montgomerie departed. 'I'd better go, Tiger is waiting.'

1997

1997

By Robert Philip
PUBLISHED FRIDAY 11 JULY

Some of the nicest and most honourable sportsmen I have ever met are ex-boxers: Ken Buchanan, Glen McCrory and Jimmy Ellis immediately spring to mind. Just how they – and the thousands of other honest, decent and proud fighters who use their fists to earn a living – came to inhabit the same world as Mike Tyson **(above, in background)** and his entourage remains an abiding mystery. Like Tyson, McCrory, the former world cruiserweight champion turned Sky commentator, was a hard man who used his fists to survive in a hard, violent trade. Unlike Tyson, McCrory would have considered using his teeth to take a chunk out of an opponent's ear as an obscenity.

If I cannot actively condone boxing, the knowledge that it is heavily populated by people like McCrory means I cannot join in the increasing calls for its abolition.

But if boxing is to survive into the third millennium, then the life ban imposed on Tyson would have to be exactly that. He should never be allowed into the ring again. However, despite Nevada State Athletic Commission's stern pronouncements, Tyson will be back in the ring in 12 months' time when his appeal succeeds.

And that is when the circus macabre will start all over again. You can almost hear the ringmaster Don King exercising his tonsils in preparation: 'Roll up, roll up, come and see Cannibal Mike; the only man Hannibal Lecter is frightened to invite round for lunch.' Etc, etc.

The day Tyson is welcomed back is the day boxing loses any right it had to describe itself as a sport.

Lions relish thought of clean sweep

By Brendan Gallagher in Durban
PUBLISHED MONDAY 30 JUNE

No, you were not dreaming. The British Lions did beat South Africa 18–15 at King's Park on Saturday, a remarkable, nigh-on miraculous victory that clinched the series and put a spring in the step of every rugby follower in Britain and Ireland.

Even now it almost defies belief that the Lions were able to absorb the unrelenting pressure of a super-charged Springboks side to win at the death. Rarely can a side have won a major international while so remorselessly under the cosh. Analytically there was absolutely no way the Lions should have won, but this squad have rejoiced in making the impossible possible. As the final whistle blew the Lions' joy was unconfined. Tim Rodber hugged replacement Eric Miller, his great rival for the No. 8 shirt; an exhausted Keith Wood gave a clenched fist of triumph before being helped off by Jason Leonard.

Jeremy Guscott, whose 76th-minute dropped goal clinched the issue, stole away from the lap of honour to shake hands with Ian McGeechan, his coach on three strenuous but rewarding Lions tours.

Captain Martin Johnson called all the non-playing reserves on to the field to share the moment while John Bentley wheeled away to a corner of the massive East Stand to applaud the noisiest section of the Barmy Army. The Springboks, meanwhile, sloped off in a state of shock – bemused and beaten.

Matt Dawson dives over to score the Lions' only try in their nail-biting match against South Africa.

So how did the Lions win? In simple terms they defended with such ferocity and courage that a rampant Springbok side were restricted to three tries. Joost van der Westhuizen burrowed his way over after 34 minutes and debutant Percy Montgomery struck a minute into the second half when Alan Tait threw an ill-advised back-hand pass inside his own 22 for Henry Honiball to pounce and feed the young centre. It really did look all over in the 54th minute when André Joubert rounded Bentley to score a fine try, but the Lions refused to concede any further ground. Scott Gibbs was again an inspiration. A storming run midway through the second half also fired the Lions at an important stage, the sight of 20-stone prop Os du Randt rebounding off the Swansea tank lifting their morale.

A special vote of thanks must also go to Austin Healey who, though only on the field for five minutes as a replacement wing for Tait, rescued the Lions in the 80th minute. Showing his marvellous anticipation in defence, he raced back to retrieve the situation after Neil Jenkins had spilled a high ball. 'That was international sport at its best,' enthused Rob Andrew, whose winning drop goal against Australia in the World Cup quarter-final is now joined in the Hall of Fame by Guscott's effort. 'The Lions clung on by their fingertips and then played it just right when their time came.'

DID YOU KNOW?

Sri Lankan batsmen Sashan Jayasuriya and Roshan Mahanama established a record for the second wicket when they put on an incredible 576 runs against India. The Sri Lankans made 952 for six, the highest ever Test score.

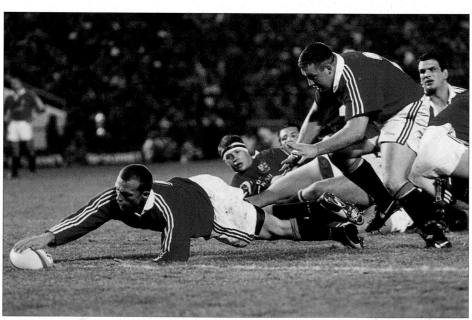

England lose Ashes

By Christopher Martin-Jenkins

Published Tuesday 12 August

Two questions gnawed at the mind like hungry mice on the day after Australia's unexpectedly sudden seizure of the last great prize of the international season: why did England bat in the way that they did, and will Mike Atherton continue as captain after the final Test at the Oval, which will be played before full houses from next Thursday even though the Ashes have been lost?

There is more than one answer to the first question. The glib one is that it was a Sunday afternoon and England batted accordingly. They were bowled out for 186, an average score in the AXA League, in only eight overs and five balls more than they would have received had they been wearing the coloured clothes. Less glib is the observation that if they are to play 25 matches of 50 overs from 1998, the instincts towards betting like gamblers – not to mention the unfamiliarity with bowling first and foremost to take wickets, will be even more ingrained in the psyche of the English professional.

The way we are going, England may win the World Cup in 1999, but will never have the patience with bat or ball to win Test series against really top-class sides.

Australian vice-captain, Steve Waugh, batting at the Oval; he made two centuries there and won the Man-of-the-Match award. Australia won the series 3–2.

Atherton said after a night's reflection that he had no qualms about the way the top-order batsmen played. 'We were probably never going to save the game, and a draw was no good to us as far as the Ashes were concerned,' he told me. 'What happened was a mixture of trying to get on top of the bowling and simpy taking the opportunities presented by attacking fields.... Lower down the order there were some disappointing shots played, but I suppose by then it was a lost cause.'

Indeed it was, and Robert Croft, a talented cricketer who bowled well without luck but who has had a rude lesson in what it is like to play against a really tough cricket team, will and probably should pay, only temporarily I hope, for the way that he was prepared to sacrifice himself at Trent Bridge.

David Graveney said yesterday that he still felt Atherton was the best man to captain England in the West Indies. Atherton wants time to consider all the implications, but will have made up his mind before the Oval Test.

SPORT IN BRIEF

LAWN TENNIS

British players Greg Rusedski and Tim Henman both reach the quarter-finals at Wimbledon. In a gripping match, Rusedski is beaten 6–4, 4–6, 6–4, 6–3 by eventual finalist Cedric Pioline, while Henman loses to Michael Stich of Germany 6–3, 6–2, 6–4. American Pete Sampras wins the final.

CRICKET

Glamorgan, captained by Matthew Maynard, win the county championship. In an exciting race for the title between the Welsh team and Kent, Glamorgan clinch victory in the last round of matches when they complete a ten-wicket victory over Somerset.

GOLF

American Justin Leonard wins the British Open at Troon with a phenomenal display of putting to finish 12 under par. He is three shots ahead of his nearest challengers, Darren Clark of Northern Ireland and Jesper Parnevik of Sweden.

SQUASH

Jansher Khan **(below)** wins his sixth successive British Open title when he defeats the 24-year-old Scot Peter Nichol 17–15, 9–15, 15–12, 8–15, 15–8 in Cardiff. Of the six finals he has contested, it is the closest Jansher has come to losing.

1997

British Athletic Federation goes bankrupt

By Tom Knight
PUBLISHED WEDNESDAY 15 OCTOBER

The British Athletic Federation called in the administrators yesterday after being forced to declare itself insolvent and then listed top athletes such as Linford Christie, Roger Black and Colin Jackson among its creditors. The surprise announcement that the British governing body of the most successful Olympic sport had finally admitted defeat, after a long running battle against what was thought to be merely a cash-flow problem, came from David Moorcroft, the former athlete who took over as its chief executive less than a fortnight ago.

Fighting hard to maintain his composure, Moorcroft said that the federation – a limited company – called in administrators after realising the stark reality of its precarious financial situation at a management board meeting last Friday.

'After seeing the figures there was no option,' he said. 'The company is insolvent and cannot pay off its current debts. The future of the BAF is uncertain and that has massive implications for the organisation of sport in this country. But the future of athletics itself is not in doubt.'

Among the debts outstanding are payments to British athletes for appearances on the track during the summer. Roger Black said: 'I haven't been paid yet so I am concerned about the immediate future. But what is more important is the future of youngsters like Mark Richardson and Iwan Thomas. They deserve support which can keep them on the world stage.'

Moorcroft added: 'I am devastated by what has happened. If I'd known the extent of the problem I certainly wouldn't have taken the job. But I don't think I was misled.'

It now seems inevitable that a sport which has resisted change with a passion, since the Amateur Athletic Association was set up as its first governing body in 1880, will undergo a radical and painful facelift. The roots of the crisis can be traced to the mid-1980s, when athletics began to enjoy a golden era. Then ITV was willing to pay £10.8 million over four years to screen the sport and blue-chip companies queued up to sponsor domestic meetings. Athletics reached a new peak of popularity in 1993 when Christie, Jackson and Sally Gunnell won gold at the world championships.

But in 1995 the bubble burst. John Lister, its treasurer, admitted athletics was living off its savings. ITV lost interest when Christie and Jackson, through their company Nuff Respect, fell out with the BAF over appearance fees. Sponsors drifted away and, in the next three seasons, only Jonathan Edwards won gold at a major championship. At the beginning of this year Channel Four paid just £1.3 million for a four-year contract with the sport, and sponsorship income over the last nine months has fallen by 45 per cent.

British athletes failed to win gold at the world championships in Athens and most domestic meetings play to half-empty stadiums.

The sport has continued to pay its athletes well, however. In 1995, for instance, Christie was paid £35,000 a race and the sums spent on the élite have often been a source of concern to those at grass-roots level. But yesterday Jackson countered, 'We are worth our market value to perform in this country. You can't blame us. Maybe the BAF took on too many events.'

Grobbelaar and Segers have FA bans suspended

By a Daily Telegraph *correspondent*
PUBLISHED SATURDAY 13 DECEMBER

The goalkeepers Bruce Grobbelaar and Hans Segers were given suspended bans and £10,000 fines yesterday after they admitted a betting misconduct charge. An FA committee said the two players, cleared of match-fixing charges earlier this year, had received thousands of pounds for helping a Far East betting syndicate to predict the outcome of matches in which they were not involved.

Steve Double, an FA spokesman, said both punishments of a six-month ban and a fine would be suspended for two years, considering the 'severe financial hardship and three-year blight on their careers' that they had already suffered.

Earlier this year Grobbelaar and Segers, along with John Fashanu, the former Wimbledon striker, and a Malaysian businessman, were found not guilty at Winchester Crown Court of criminal charges of match-fixing. But in their evidence, Grobbelaar, the former Liverpool and Southampton goalkeeper, and Segers, who used to play for Wimbledon, both admitted taking money from a betting syndicate.

Grobbelaar had received over £8,000 for his services while Segers had picked up between £45,000 and £48,000.

After the FA announced the punishment, Grobbelaar vowed to continue his career and to pursue a libel action against the newspaper which published the original match-fixing allegations. Grobbelaar insisted: 'I've not been effectively let off. It's a serious matter. Had I known the penalties before I would never have entered into the agreement with certain people.'

Grobbelaar said he had been 'devastated' by the original match-fixing allegations three years ago. 'I have now been exonerated and I'm happy to resume my career. Whether that is in this country or not, I do not know. I shall wait for offers,' he added.

Flanked by policemen, Grobbelaar attends court on charges of match-fixing. He and Hans Segers admitted breaching FA rules, but were cleared of match-fixing. 'I was naive,' admitted Grobbelaar afterwards.

Seve Ballesteros captains Europe to Ryder Cup victory

By Lewine Mair at Valderrama

PUBLISHED WEDNESDAY 29 OCTOBER

Seve Ballesteros skippered Europe to victory over the Americans in the Ryder Cup at Valderrama, in Spain, yesterday, then announced that he would be standing down.

'I'm not going to be captain again in 1999. It's for the simple reason that I would like to recover my game. I would really like to play in the 1999 match.

'As for being captain, maybe I'll do it again at some other time in the future – maybe in 2005 in Ireland.'

Europe retained the cup, but only just. Ahead 10½ to 5½ going into the afternoon singles, they should have won by the proverbial mile. Instead they captured only three of the 12 singles and halved two more to squeeze home by the odd point. The score was 14½ to 13½.

No one was more relieved than Ballesteros when Scotland's Colin Montgomerie came in with the half point his team needed from the last match to finish.

Ballesteros had been criticised earlier in the week on several counts, not least for the way he did not tell his men who would be playing on Friday and who would not. Of the singles points Europe won, the best belonged to Constantino Rocca – a four and two win over Tiger Woods, the 21-year-old American who won the Masters earlier this year.

When he won on the 16th green, Ballesteros gave him a hug and a kiss before Rocca took off round the green with his wife, Antonella, in his arms.

Per-Ulrik Johansson, from Sweden, and Bernhard Langer pinned down full points, while Montgomerie's half was matched by one from Denmark's Thomas Bjorn.

'Europe did everything they had to do,' said Tom Kite at the end of the contest. The American captain said of his own men: 'They had the heart of a lion and the eye of a tiger…. I'm proud to stand next to them.'

Ryder Cup captain Seve Ballesteros celebrates a great European victory in the Ryder Cup.

SPORT IN BRIEF

LAWN TENNIS

Victories over David Wheaton, Marcos Ondruska, Jens Knippschild, Daniel Vacek, Richard Krajicek and Jonas Bjorkman take Greg Rusedski into the US Open final. Australian Patrick Rafter, seeded 13, beats Rusedski in four sets, 6–3, 6–2, 4–6, 7–5 to take the title.

FOOTBALL

In October England win through to the 1998 World Cup finals when they hold Italy to a draw in Rome in the final qualifying game. In a tense match Ian Wright hits the post for England in the closing stages, and at the other end Christian Vieri puts a header just wide.

LAWN TENNIS

A new star arrives in the world of women's tennis. Martina Hingis of Switzerland beats Mary Pierce 6–2, 6–2 to win the Australian Open, Jana Novotna 2–6, 6–3, 6–3 to win Wimbledon and Venus Williams 6–0, 6–4 to take the US Open title. She is denied the Grand Slam by Iva Majoli, who beats her in the final of the French Open, 6–4, 6–2.

MOTOR RACING

In a closely fought championship contest, Michael Schumacher and Jacques Villeneuve head the points table, with the lead changing hands several times during the season. The title rests on the final race. Schumacher, driving a Ferrari, collides with Villeneuve's Williams-Renault in an incident reminiscent of his clash with Damon Hill in 1994. This time, however, Schumacher crashes out while Villeneuve is able to continue, finishing third and taking the drivers' championship with 81 points. Schumacher is second with 78 points, but is later disqualified by the FIA.

1997

1998

Racing mourns the loss of One Man

by Hotspur (J. A. McGrath)
PUBLISHED SATURDAY 4 APRIL

The death of One Man, the most popular steeplechaser since Desert Orchid, cast a shadow over the Martell Grand National meeting at Aintree yesterday. The dashing grey jumper broke a leg after crashing through the ninth fence in the Mumm Melling Chase and had to be put down. Tears were flowing freely when it became obvious that the Gordon Richards-trained gelding was not going to get up after ploughing through the fence.

When the green screens were erected to shield the badly injured horse, it brought to a close a spectacularly successful career, which included triumphs in the Hennessy Cognac Gold Cup, two King George VI chases, and more recently the Queen Mother Champion Chase at Cheltenham.

Jockey Brian Harding walked back in tears when it was confirmed that One Man was dead. Regular jockey Tony Dobbin missed the ride through injury. 'It's terrible, the public loved this horse,' he said.

Pitch fires knockout blow

by Christopher Martin-Jenkins
PUBLISHED FRIDAY 30 JANUARY

The first Test between the West Indies and England was abandoned in Kingston, Jamaica, after an hour's play when the pitch was deemed dangerous.

After 10.1 overs, England, who chose to bat first, had crumbled to 17 for three as fast bowlers Curtly Ambrose and Courtney Walsh took advantage of a newly laid pitch which provided plenty of pace but hugely variable bounce. One full-length delivery to Alec Stewart leapt high over wicketkeeper David Williams's head for four byes. The next, off a similar length, barely got above ankle height.

The difficult conditions were eventually deemed dangerous after England physiotherapist Wayne Morton had been forced to go on to the field six times to treat injuries, mainly to the batsmen's fingers.

'There was a bit of war out there and you always fear for a batsman's safety,' he said. 'You don't often see too many apologies from West Indian fast bowlers but they seemed pretty embarrassed by it.'

As early as the third over, one of the umpires, Srin Venkataraghavan, got in touch with match referee Barry Jarman to alert him to the dangers.

England captain Mike Atherton, who had already been dismissed, went out to join his opposite number Brian Lara and the umpires at a drinks break. Jarman, who later described the pitch as 'horrific', joined them in the middle before everyone left the field and the International Cricket Council in London were contacted.

'The pitch is unfit and dangerous to the players,' said Pat Rousseau, president of the West Indies Cricket Board, at a hastily arranged Press conference. It was the first time that such action has been taken in the 121-year history of Test cricket.

England opener Alec Stewart put a brave face on events. 'A couple of pieces came out of the wicket and we took a few blows, but that's part of cricket. We just had to cope as best we could,' he said.

England and West Indies captains Mike Atherton and Brian Lara discuss the state of the Sabina Park pitch with the umpires and match referee. The series resumed in Trinidad; the West Indies won it 3–1.

Celtic end Rangers' decade of dominance

by Roddy Forsyth
PUBLISHED MONDAY 11 MAY
Celtic 2; St Johnstone 0

The weather forecast on BBC's News 24 TV Channel on Friday night was devoted to the prospects for the weekend's sporting events. The barometer, we learned, was set fair for Saracens' date with Wasps at Twickenham, and Glamorgan v Middlesex at Cardiff. Of Celtic's home meeting with St Johnstone, there was nary a mention, although it was guaranteed to produce the second biggest crowd in Britain for an occasion of stomach-churning tension as

Wim Jansen and his players attempted to bring Rangers' domination of Scottish football to an overdue conclusion.

This habitual myopia generates understandable irritation north of the border and is almost certainly a contributory factor to the stunning surge in popularity of the Scottish National Party. There was no shortage of politicians at Celtic Park on Saturday for the visit of St Johnstone, whose defeat was necessary for Celtic to win their first championship in ten years.

At 3.02 pm, it appeared that the speculation had been brought to an abrupt end. Henrik Larsson, gathering possession from Paul Lambert on the left, wheeled along the edge of the St Johnstone penalty area and curled a dazzling strike around Alan Main, the Perth goalkeeper. Now Celtic, it appeared, had the destiny of the championship precisely where they wanted it. By half-time, though, the score was unchanged. By the hour mark, the anxiety around the ground was ominously

palpable. Wim Jansen, a man who hoards substitutes like gold doubloons, sent on Harald Brattbakk.

Brattbakk knows how to run into space and he did so to decisive effect when Tom Boyd lobbed the ball to Jackie McNamara. The Scotland wing played the ball behind the St Johnstone defenders and Brattbakk clipped it first time behind Main. At last, the pent-up frustrations of the decade exploded in volcanic fervour. When full-time sounded fireworks exploded over the stadium; an hour later the pitch was still crowded with cavorting spectators.

The weather, incidentally, was balmy. Whether the climate at Celtic Park or, for that matter, Scottish football, is about to change for the longer term is a matter which has so far confounded all forecasters.

Celtic head coach Wim Jansen and assistant Murdo MacLeod celebrate winning the Scottish Premier League. Jansen resigned the following week.

MILESTONES

Switzerland's Martina Hingis became the youngest player to retain a Grand Slam tennis title when she beat Conchita Martinez 6–3, 6–3 in the final of the Australian Open. She was 17 years old.

England's backs to the wall as disaster follows disaster

by Mick Cleary

PUBLISHED MONDAY 6 JULY

The England squad flew out of Cape Town last night with not a backward glance. What remained behind them was not nice at all. The last five weeks have been a salutary experience: in turn traumatic, soul-destroying, tedious, frustrating, irritating and utterly predictable. What was true when the tour hitched its wagons back at the end of May was still true when the trimmed-down squad unbuckled its cargo at Heathrow this morning.

England never had the personnel to compete. Their forwards were always going to give an account of themselves, but the back line were so callow that they ought to have been sponsored by Farley's Rusks. No matter how resilient, how crafty the pack managed to be, they knew, and the opposition knew, that there was nothing threatening beyond Matt Dawson. So are England a shambolic ruin? The team, no. The infrastructure with its political in-fighting, yes. That sour, chaotic backdrop brought about this tour in the first place.

There is no doubt that a full-strength England would be highly competitive. They showed that last autumn. The southern hemisphere has got its nose in front at the moment but then it was always so in amateur days of old.

In shock: exhausted England players absorb their 76–0 defeat by Australia. They lost all their matches, conceding 328 points, on a disastrous tour of New Zealand, Australia and South Africa.

Professionalism, Super 12, the slick marketing approach of the game down there has not fundamentally altered that balance as far as England are concerned.

So, was it all worth it? Was it worth the humiliation, the constant ridicule, the morale-sapping accumulation of defeats? And for what? So that a learning curve could be plotted to a point somewhere in the stratosphere?

Clive Woodward will argue that this is precisely why it was worth it. At least he should now know who can cut it and who can't. But does he? There were seven matches, four of them Tests. The schedule was so fierce and unrelenting that seasoned internationals would have been scalded by the experience.

The tour was badly planned and poorly realised. Let's hope the experience really has been chastening for everyone. Let's hope that a tour like this will never be allowed to happen again. Let's hope that political differences will be buried once and for all. Any more time wasted bickering will only bring about this same sorry state of affairs. And that is a truly awful thought.

SPORT IN BRIEF

CRICKET
In the second Test against South Africa in Sydney, Australian wrist-spinner Shane Warne turns in another exceptional performance, taking six for 34 in the second innings for match figures of 11 for 109. Warne has now become the second Australian to take 300 Test wickets. Australia win the match by an innings and 21 runs, having drawn the first Test. The final Test in Adelaide is also drawn; Australia take the series 1–0.

BASEBALL
In January the Denver Broncos win the 32nd Super Bowl, defeating the Green Bay Packers 31–24.

RUGBY UNION
The English Rugby Football Union become the last of the 'five nations' to agree Italy's entry into the tournament. From the year 2000 Italy will join the home nations and France in a new Six Nations competition. It is the first alteration to the championship since 1910, when France gained admission.

FOOTBALL
Newcastle United directors Freddy Shepherd and Douglas Hall face calls for their resignation after newspaper allegations that they have insulted the club's fans, the women of Newcastle, and the Newcastle striker and England captain, Alan Shearer. A sustained protest from furious club supporters eventually results in their resignations, but within four months they return to the board with apologies and promises of more money for players.

ATHLETICS
Irish athlete Sonia O'Sullivan wins the 4-km and 8-km world cross-country titles. She has enjoyed great success on the track over the past few years; in 1994 she set the world 2,000-m record, won European gold at 3,000 m, and won her third grand prix title in succession.

1998

1998

Tour de France in crisis

by Paul Hayward

PUBLISHED SATURDAY 25 JULY

Around four o'clock this afternoon, France's most sacred sporting institution is scheduled to honk and swish its way into the Provence town of Carpentras at the end of another 121-mile pageant. Most summers they would rest a night before making the gruelling climb to the summit of Mont Ventoux, 'the Giant of Provence', past the roadside memorial to Britain's Tommy Simpson, whose amphetamine-fuelled heart gave up on him on 13 July 1967 as he made his own frantic ascent to sport's dark peak. Like mourners with a guilty secret, the riders of the 1998 Tour de France will pass another way.

They will pass that way in turmoil: a vast convoy of rage and recrimination that may not make it to the Champs-Elysées at the end of the race tomorrow week. Yesterday TVM were threatened with expulsion after drugs were found in the hotel where they were staying, and three Festina riders admitted to police that they had used banned substances to help them race.

The world's greatest cycle race is supposed to be the ultimate sporting test of human endurance. But if the current prognosis is right, we are seeing a 20th-century lunacy exposed. Is the Tour de France an event that cannot be done, never mind won, without performance-enhancing drugs? At the end of the century, a reckoning may be upon us, started by a Customs check that shone a light not just on a narcotic stockpile but on the moral legitimacy of a sport.

Riders protest before the 12th stage of the Tour de France. They said they would not be 'treated like cattle' following doping allegations.

France on top of the world

by Henry Winter

PUBLISHED MONDAY 13 JULY
Brazil 0; France 3

Like a bolt from the blue, France dethroned the world champions last night with two exceptional headed goals from Zinedine Zidane. France's first World Cup triumph was founded on the goals of Zidane and a late strike from Emmanuel Petit, and the masterful way these midfielders shook Brazil out of their measured stride.

This was a marvellous moment for the hosts, a trigger for the party which will run into and through

England's penalty heartbreak

by Henry Winter

PUBLISHED WEDNESDAY 1 JULY
Argentina 2; England 2, after extra time
Argentina win 4–3 on penalties

Never outplayed, never outfought, never outsung, England are nevertheless out of the World Cup. Resisting calls to restore the old guard, England's coach had unleashed his young guns again. Michael Owen, spring-heeled as he tore forward, precipitated England's first-half revival, a magnificent show of defiance after the shock of Gabriel Batistuta's fifth-minute penalty.

Having not conceded a goal for eight matches, Argentina let in a second after 15 minutes. If there were doubts about the way Owen earned England's first, his own strike was beyond dispute, a sensational run and

finish that encapsulated everything that so excites the nation about the Liverpool forward.

Argentina attempted to revive their tattered ambitions. On the cusp of half-time, Juan Veron slid the ball forward to Javier Zanetti, whose first touch created a chance which he took confidently, the ball racing past Seaman.

Just after the break, David Beckham was dismissed. Diego Simeone went into the back of him and the Manchester United midfielder flicked a leg at Simeone, who went down as if hit by the 3.40 from Buenos Aires.

England could not quite manage the Great Escape, despite the unbelievable response of the players, for whom Paul Ince was a king among lions. Sadly, Ince became one of two players to miss penalties for England. The other was David Batty, whose final kick, saved by Carlos Roa, brought England's campaign to a shattering end.

France celebrate their first World Cup triumph. They were the seventh country to win the trophy, and the first new champions since Argentina 20 years before.

There was an optimistic note for the Blues with news that Ronaldo was out. According to the changing team-sheets, Ronaldo was in and out like a can-can dancer. Ronaldo, though, was anonymous, his lack of training showing as the French midfield took the firmest of grips.

Just before the half-hour, the flaws in Brazil's defence were exposed. Their concentration slipped. Their organisation crumbled. It was left to Leonardo, not the most imposing presence, to challenge Zidane, who comfortably placed his header past Taffarel. Confidence coursed through Aimé Jacquet's players. Zidane added a second with another header, this time following a left-wing corner.

The crown was slipping. Mario Zagallo had to gamble. Denilson arrived for the ineffectual Leonardo. France were living on the counter, welcome breaks from the yellow waves crashing towards them. France were standing firm but after 66 minutes they lost a mainstay of their defence, Desailly, dismissed for a second bookable offence. Patrick Vieira arrived as France continued to frustrate the Brazilians. Petit then completed the triumph by finishing off Dugarry's through ball.

tomorrow's Bastille celebrations. Stirred by a crowd who came to cheer throughout, the most precious 90 minutes in the history of French football showed the team at their best, capable of great creativity but allied to real guts. And strong hearts and legs were needed when Marcel Desailly was dismissed midway through the second half.

Sampras douses Henmania

by Martin Johnson

PUBLISHED SATURDAY 4 JULY

There were moments on the Centre Court yesterday when it seemed as though Tim Henman (**below right**) might well make England's World Cup exit a distant memory. But in the end Pete Sampras came through in four sets to thwart Henman's dream of becoming the first Briton to reach the men's final since Bunny Austin in 1938. It did, however, require some sublime tennis from Sampras to stop him, and Henman now knows that he has the ammunition and the temperament to become Wimbledon champion.

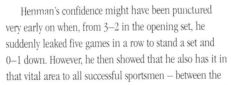

Henman's confidence might have been punctured very early on when, from 3–2 in the opening set, he suddenly leaked five games in a row to stand a set and 0–1 down. However, he then showed that he also has it in that vital area to all successful sportsmen – between the ears – by breaking Sampras twice and taking the set 6–4.

Henman continued to draw deeply on his reserves of courage, not least when saving three set points in the third set, but when he finally lost it, Sampras killed him off with clinical efficiency.

P. Sampras (US) bt T. Henman (GB), 6–3, 4–6, 7–5, 6–3

SPORT IN BRIEF

FOOTBALL

Hearts win the Scottish Cup for the first time in 42 years, with a surprise 2–1 victory over Rangers.

ATHLETICS

In June Ethiopian runner Haile Gebrselassie takes an astonishing five seconds off the 10,000-m world record. Later in the month he also breaks the 5,000-m world record, clocking 12 min 39.36 sec.

LAWN TENNIS

The men's final of the All-England championships at Wimbledon pits Pete Sampras against Croatian Goran Ivanisevic. In a hard-fought match, Sampras finally triumphs 6–7, 7–6, 6–4, 3–6, 6–2. In the women's final Jana Novotna beats Nathalie Tauziat 6–4, 7–6 to win her first Wimbledon title. It is compensation for Novotna's devastating defeat in 1993, when Steffi Graf recovered from 1–4 down in the third set to take the title and reduce Novotna to tears.

GOLF

Mark O'Meara picks up his second major title of the year when he beats fellow-American Brian Watts in a four-hole play-off to win the British Open at Royal Birkdale. Making his debut at the tournament is 17-year-old British amateur Justin Rose, who holes an astonishing 45-metre putt at the 18th hole to finish in joint fourth place. It is the best finish by an amateur in the Open for 45 years.

SWIMMING

Irish swimmer Michelle de Bruin, who won three gold medals in the 1996 Olympics, is banned from the sport for four years for allegedly tampering with her urine sample.

FOOTBALL

The satellite broadcasting company BSkyB, headed by Australian media tycoon Rupert Murdoch, makes a bid of £575 m for Manchester United.

1998

Murali completes England rout

by Christopher Martin-Jenkins
PUBLISHED TUESDAY 1 SEPTEMBER

A phenomenal individual performance by Muttiah Muralitharan **(below)** was more than a match for England, and Sri Lanka won an extraordinary Test by ten wickets with only nine overs of the final day left.

Had Alec Stewart not been run out in the morning, Muralitharan would surely have become only the second bowler in the history of the game to take all ten wickets in a Test innings. As it is, his 16 for 220 from 113.5 overs is the fifth-best Test analysis recorded.

It was Sri Lanka's second successive win over England, five years after the last game in Colombo in March 1993. That was their first home win against England, but to have repeated it overseas, albeit in conditions which suited their talents so well, was a triumph which deserves no qualification.

They won the World Cup with batting of unprecedented imagination and flair and now they are winning Tests by classical attacking batting and a bowler who can destroy sides by himself. On a true, dry pitch like this they could beat anyone, in any five-day game, anywhere. And no wonder Lancashire want Muralitharan as their overseas successor to Wasim Akram.

It has been one of the oddities of history that Tony Lock took only one wicket at Old Trafford in 1956 when Jim Laker, whose haul of 193 Test wickets Murali has now surpassed, dismissed 19 Australians. In this Sri Lankan team, the 26-year-old off-spinner with the double-jointed wrist was a one-man attack.

Muralitharan's figures were his best in 42 Tests in which he has now taken 203 wickets. He has claimed five wickets in an innings 16 times, and ten or more in a match twice, first against Zimbabwe last winter in his home town, up in the green hills at Kandy.

He was only 20 when he took five wickets in the 1993 Test between these two countries. What was striking then was his flight as much as his curious, wristy action. He has got better and better, and if he bowls for another ten years in Test cricket he could become the biggest wicket-taker of them all.

Mantle passes to new generation

by Tom Knight in Budapest
PUBLISHED MONDAY 24 AUGUST

The 17th European athletics championships ended with British athletes almost colliding as they completed their laps of honour yesterday evening. Three times in the space of half an hour, the capacity crowd heard 'God Save the Queen'.

It took one triple jump from Jonathan Edwards, one javelin throw by Steve Backley, and a textbook 400-m relay, courtesy of Mark Hylton, Jamie Baulch, Iwan Thomas and Mark Richardson, and Britain's athletes ended their most successful week in history sitting proudly on top of the medals table. Given the problems the sport has had to endure over the 11 months since the British Athletic Federation's financial crash, the success achieved by a team comprising a host of new names and youngsters takes on an even greater significance. It is the first time Britain have topped the medals table.

Iwan Thomas (above), in the 400 m, and Denise Lewis (left), in the heptathlon, were two of nine British athletes who won gold in Hungary.

A mighty blow for the world's other half

by Paul Hayward
PUBLISHED MONDAY 7 DECEMBER
England 13; South Africa 7

So, Gulliver's travels ended with the Lilliputians roping him down at Twickenham. It took the non-South African rugby world 18 Tests to wrestle the giant to the ground. Valiantly they revived the belief that north can beat south in what was becoming an alarmingly polarised sport.

'The plan,' said Dan Luger, a revelation on England's wing, 'was to take them on, play attractive rugby, play faster than them.'

Luger created one try for Jeremy Guscott and stopped one for South Africa at the end. His was a panic-free zone. He had never played at Twickenham before. The thought – yet thankfully not the reality – was all too much for him as he pulled into the stadium. Now he has his own store of memories that will never be denuded by time.

The Springboks, in contrast, traipsed out of the casino having seen the last grand gamble go down. For 1,360 minutes they played winning rugby. But here the relentless scoring finally ceased. They had their fingertips on a record, but then Luger got his fingertips on a Springbok pass which, had it reached the intended recipient, would have led to a spectacular last-gasp breakaway try. After more than 23 hours of South African invincibility, wounded, derided England stretched out their fingers and took it all away.

MILESTONES

In September the Football Association announced that in future the FA Cup final would be decided by penalties if there was no winner after extra time had been played.

England's bolt from the blue

by Christopher Martin-Jenkins

PUBLISHED WEDNESDAY 30 DECEMBER

Of all the belated English victories against the trend of a series; of all the heroic fourth-innings efforts in their recent, apparently interminable years of struggle, this was the most astounding and the most emotional. At the last, it was sheer character and inspired fielding, the two ingredients which seemed to have prevented this enigmatic touring team from making the most of their abilities and opportunities, which carried them to a 12-run defeat of Australia.

Australia, needing only 175, failed on a very good batting pitch. At one stage, they were 130 for three and coasting, but wins can come from the blue in cricket and this Australian side have demonstrated several times that they are vulnerable when chasing runs in the fourth innings. In an atmosphere of frenzied excitement – no longer the breathless hush of poetry – England took their last seven wickets for 32.

There was only minimal movement and some bounce yesterday to encourage England's hero Dean Headley, but five of his six wickets for 60 were taken for only 26 runs in a marvellously well-sustained second spell from the southern end.

This was all the more remarkable for the fact that Mark Waugh had cut two long hops for four in an over costing ten when Alec Stewart brought Headley back.

Ramprakash runs to congratulate a triumphant Dean Headley. The England bowler took six wickets for 60 to turn around the fourth Test match against Australia.

Headley responded with a maiden over and then with four wickets for four in his next 14 balls.

Waugh made two misjudgements as the game reached its thrilling climax. With advice from Taylor, Waugh opted to stay in the middle despite the lengthening shadows which made the light difficult for batsmen. Stewart was only too keen to get England off. Waugh's second error was to run a single off the first ball of what turned out to be the final over. Stuart MacGill was castled by a ball fired towards his blockhole, and two balls later Glenn McGrath was leg-before.

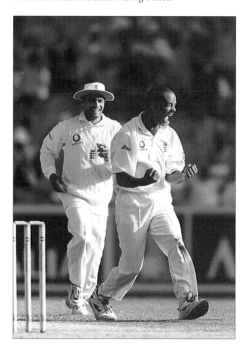

Records go tumbling as Kiwis polish off Britain

by John Whalley

PUBLISHED MONDAY 9 NOVEMBER
Great Britain 16; New Zealand 36

There have been many occasions when Great Britain have flopped over the last decade after raising hopes that they are ready to take on the world's best, but it is hard to remember a time when supporters could have been so depressed as after the appalling second-half display which saw New Zealand take the Lincoln series at Bolton on Saturday.

Though there was no shortage of lows against the Kiwis in 1996 when suffering a 3–0 thrashing, there were genuine excuses that many leading players were absent. There are no mitigating circumstances this time. The withdrawals of Adrian Morley and Paul Newlove through injury were major blows, but that was not apparent for the first 40 minutes when Britain lifted the highest expectations from the near 28,000 crowd.

It makes this result so hard to bear. Britain were so much in charge at half-time, there was no hint of the debacle to come as the records tumbled, virtually unchallenged, with 28 unanswered points. The biggest defeat by the Kiwis and the fifth successive loss against New Zealand were recorded, leaving the Lions with only one victory over Australia or New Zealand in the last ten attempts.

Andy Goodway, the Great Britain coach, said he wanted to study a video of the game before reaching conclusions, but the facts are stark enough. The captain, Andy Farrell, described it as the worst 40 minutes he had been involved in.

It is churlish to take anything away from New Zealand. They were almost faultless and highly entertaining. They set up their first series win in England for 27 years having won the first game at Huddersfield.

The third match in the series was tied 23–23.

1999

Australia triumph at brink of defeat

by Michael Henderson

PUBLISHED FRIDAY 18 JUNE

Australia (213) tied with South Africa

We've seen just about everything now. After far and away the best game of the current competition, Australia reached the World Cup final by the squeakiest means available. By virtue of finishing second in the Super Sixes, ahead of South Africa on run rate, they will play Pakistan at Lord's on Sunday.

This was a magnificent game, which, quite literally, had something for everybody. There was doughty batting by Steve Waugh and Jonty Rhodes; a display of immense courage from Jacques Kallis; overwhelming fast bowling by Allan Donald and Shaun Pollock; and superb out cricket by the finest fielding teams in the world.

Above it all, and let's shout it from the rooftops, there was a performance by Shane Warne that people will talk about when they are old and grey and nodding by the fire. Combining the brilliance and bravery that is granted only to the great, he took hold of this match when it was drifting away from Australia and enabled them to win it.

The closing passage of play was almost too intense to take in. South Africa, who needed 18 from the last two overs, with three wickets in hand, lost two of them when Glenn McGrath ripped out Mark Boucher's middle stump and Paul Reiffel's return was deemed to have beaten Steve Elworthy. South Africa needed 16, and Klusener immediately belted six, and then pinched the strike. It was now nine from the last over.

Klusener smote the first ball through cover for four. He found a withering drive for the next ball: four more through extra cover. The scores were level. The third ball almost brought a run-out. Klusener drove the next ball to mid-off, where Michael Bevan fielded. He relayed it to Fleming, who rolled it to Adam Gilchrist. Donald, hopelessly short of safety, was out.

This was a great game of cricket, and it was won by a great player. Warne is back on the big stage, and Sunday can't come quickly enough.

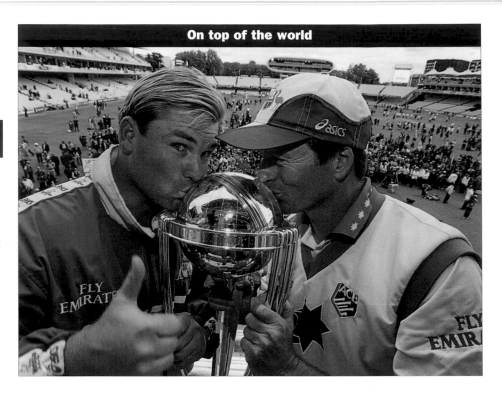

by Michael Henderson at Lord's

PUBLISHED MONDAY 21 JUNE

In their own minds, Pakistan were running away with this World Cup. Yesterday, faced with the intransigence all good Australians imbibe with their mother's milk, they saw it run away from them. Steve Waugh held the trophy aloft to confirm what everybody knows: Australia are the best team in the world.

Three years ago, in Lahore, Australia lost the final to Sri Lanka after playing the best cricket in the competition. This time, they did things differently. They lost two of their first three group matches and won the other, unconvincingly, against Scotland.

Waugh said after Pakistan had beaten them by ten runs at Headingley on 23 May that his players would have to win their next seven games, and that, give or take the jaw-dropping tie with South Africa, is exactly what they achieved. Pakistan were dismissed for 132, the lowest total in any World Cup final, and so masterly was the batting of Adam Gilchrist and Mark Waugh that Australia needed only 20 overs to find the runs.

Their dominance was total from the moment Mark Waugh caught a superb two-handed slip catch to dismiss Wajahatullah Wasti in Glenn McGrath's third over. No Pakistan batsman made more than 22, except the valiant last man, extras, who contributed 25. Pakistan batted badly and, later, when all hope had evaporated, they fielded badly. It was a shame for Wasim Akram, who had led them wonderfully through the competition, but he has known such days before.

Australia are worthy winners, though it was Lance Klusener who was named Player of the Tournament for his 17 wickets and 281 runs. It won't comfort him to recall that if he had made one run more, South Africa would have contested a final that proved so disappointingly one-sided.

Shane Warne and Steve Waugh kiss the cricket World Cup after Australia's easy victory in the final.

World Cup Super Six

	P	W	L	T	NR	NRR	Pts
Pakistan	5	3	2	0	0	0.65	6
Australia	5	3	2	0	0	0.36	6
S. Africa	5	3	2	0	0	0.17	6
N. Z.	5	2	2	0	1	-0.52	5
Zimb.	5	2	2	0	1	-0.79	5
India	5	1	4	0	0	-0.15	2

Includes points carried through from group stage

Semi-finals

Pakistan v New Zealand at Old Trafford. New Zealand 241–7 in 50 overs *(S. P. Fleming 41, R. G. Twose 46, C. L. Cairns 44; Shoaib 3–55)*; Pakistan 242–1 in 47.3 overs *(Anwar 113*, Wajahatullah Wasti 84)*. **Pakistan won by nine wickets.**

Australia v South Africa at Edgbaston. Australia 213 all out in 49.2 overs *(S. R. Waugh 56, M. G. Bevan 65; S. M. Pollock 5–36, A. Donald 4–32)*; South Africa 213 all out in 49.4 overs *(J. H. Kallis 53, J. N. Rhodes 43, L. Klusener 30*; S. K. Warne 4–29)*. **Australia tied with South Africa.**

Final

Pakistan v Australia at Lord's. Pakistan 132 all out in 39 overs *(S. K. Warne 4–33; G. D. McGrath 2–13)*; Australia 133 for 2 in 20.1 overs *(A. C. Gilchrist 54, M. E. Waugh 37*)*. **Australia won by eight wickets.**

United land the Treble

by Henry Winter

PUBLISHED THURSDAY 27 MAY

Bayern Munich 1; Manchester United 2

This magnificent Manchester United side simply refuse to give up. Yesterday, when all seemed lost, when the German jinx again appeared to hold sway over an English side, United score twice in the final seconds through Teddy Sheringham and Ole Gunnar Solskjaer to lift the European Cup on the day that marked Sir Matt Busby's 90th birthday. Amazing.

United have this alarming habit of making life difficult for themselves in Europe. Scarcely five minutes had elapsed when the champions of England conceded the sloppiest of goals. Peter Schmeichel, captain on his last appearance for United, stood helpless as the ball swerved in to his left, sending the Germans into paroxysms of delight. A brutal lesson unlearned, United still struggled defensively, although Bayern failed to press home an unexpected advantage.

Lacking Roy Keane's midfield drive and leadership, United desperately sought for one of their rank to stand up and lift them from this mess of their own making. David Beckham picked up the gauntlet. As United's faithful ran through their songbook, Beckham ran through his passing repertoire. This was his stage, his hour, but the Germans refused to buckle.

The strivings of England's finest midfielder were watched and assessed by the great and the good of the global game, Pelé even taking time out to describe Beckham as one of the world's great players just behind Rivaldo and Zinedine Zidane.

Of Alex Ferguson's decision to hand Beckham the central play-making role, Brazil's most famous son said: 'With a player like David Beckham, you must give him his freedom.' Now it was United who needed liberating from Bayern's cold clutch.

Beckham's first-half promise foundered on the rock of German determination and organisation. The second half beat to the same rhythm. United pressurising and Bayern parrying. Carsten Jancker sent Schmeichel into a slithering save, then Marcus Babbel misjudged a header with United's goal gaping. Ryan Giggs fashioned chances for Dwight Yorke, whose header was blocked, and Jesper Blomqvist, who could not keep his shot down. As the clock ticked ever louder, urgent action became essential.

Sheringham came off the bench for Blomqvist, yet it was Bayern that threatened. But then a miracle. Beckham's corner swung over and there was Schmeichel, up from the back, pressurising Bayern's proud defence. Yorke headed back, Giggs shot in, and there was Sheringham playing the poacher. In added time, Beckham swung in another corner, Sheringham headed on, and there was Solskjaer to hook the ball in. The Treble was complete. Amazing.

Treble triumph: David Beckham lifts the European Cup – Manchester United's third trophy of the season – after their last-minute victory over Bayern Munich.

Five for 2000

In February Sir Peter 'Blakey' Blake's Team New Zealand will attempt to defend the America's Cup. New Zealand were only the second country in 144 years to take the cup from the United States when they won it in 1995.

The new Six Nations rugby union tournament reaches its climax in April. For the first time Italy will join France, England, Scotland, Ireland and Wales in competing for the championship.

The finals of Euro 2000 take place in Holland and Belgium. Germany will be looking to repeat their Euro 96 success, when they beat the Czech Republic in the final, 2–1.

England host the rugby league World Cup, with a minimum of ten teams taking part. Australia will be aiming for their sixth consecutive world title. The next World Cup will be in 2002 in Australia, and will then revert to being held every four years.

In September the 27th Olympiad opens in Sydney, Australia. More than 10,000 athletes from 198 countries will take part in 28 sports.

SPORT IN BRIEF

BOXING

America's Evander Holyfield and Britain's Lennox Lewis meet in New York for their world heavyweight unification fight. Although Lewis appears to have clearly outfought Holyfield, registering over 600 punches to Holyfield's 385, only one judge scores in his favour, the other giving Holyfield the judgement and the third scoring the fight as a tie.

LAWN TENNIS

In a thrilling Davis Cup encounter in Birmingham, Great Britain come from 2–0 down against the United States to level the scores at 2–2, with Tim Henman recording a brilliant five-set victory over American Todd Martin. Britain's Greg Rusedski meets Jim Courier in the final rubber, but is beaten in the fifth set.

GOLF

In the US Masters José-Maria Olazabal has a last round of 71 to give him an aggregate of 280, eight under par. It is his second Masters win; Olazabal last put on the green jacket in 1994.

MOTOR RACING

In June Britain's Damon Hill announces that he will retire from Formula One racing. Although only beginning in Formula One at the age of 32, he has won 22 grands prix, as well as the world championship, in his seven seasons at the top.

LAWN TENNIS

In the All-England championships at Wimbledon, the winners of the 1999 French Open tournament – Steffi Graf and André Agassi – are both defeated in the finals. American Lindsay Davenport records a 6–4, 7–5 victory over Graf to win her first Wimbledon singles title, and deny the German her eighth. In the men's final Pete Sampras beats Agassi, also in straight sets, 6–3, 6–4, 7–5. The win gives Sampras a sixth men's championship title, a record this century.

1900–1909

ATHLETICS

British and Irish Olympic gold medals
1900 800 m Alfred Tysoe; 1,500 m Charles Bennett; 4,000-m steeplechase John Rimmer
1904 Combined events (later decathlon) Thomas Kiely (Ire)
1906 10,000 m Henry Hawtrey; high jump Con Leahy (Ire); triple jump Peter O'Connor (Ire)
1908 400 m Wyndham Halswelle; 5 miles Emil Voigt; 3,200-m steeplechase Arthur Russel; triple jump Tim Ahearne (Ire); 3-miles team race; 3,500-m walk George Larner; 10-mile walk George Larner; tug-of-war team

BASEBALL

World Series
1903 Boston Red Sox
1904 Not held
1905 New York Giants
1906 Chicago White Sox
1907 Chicago Cubs
1908 Chicago Cubs
1909 Pittsburgh Pirates

BOXING

British and Irish world champions
1903 Light-heavyweight, George Gardner (Ire); light-heavyweight, Bob Fitzsimmons
1904 Bantamweight, Joe Bowker
1907 Bantamweight, Owen Moran
1908 Welterweight, Jimmy Gardner (Ire)

CRICKET

County cricket champions
1900 Yorkshire
1901 Yorkshire
1902 Yorkshire
1903 Middlesex
1904 Lancashire
1905 Yorkshire
1906 Kent
1907 Nottinghamshire
1908 Yorkshire
1909 Kent

CYCLING

Tour de France
1903 Maurice Garin (Fr)
1904 Henri Cornet (Fr)
1905 Louis Trousselier (Fr)
1906 René Pottier (Fr)
1907 Lucien Petit-Breton (Fr)
1908 Lucien Petit-Breton (Fr)
1909 Francois Faber (Lux)

FOOTBALL

Football League
1900 Aston Villa
1901 Liverpool
1902 Sunderland
1903 Sheffield Wednesday
1904 Sheffield Wednesday
1905 Newcastle United
1906 Liverpool
1907 Newcastle United
1908 Manchester United
1909 Newcastle United

FA Cup
1900 Bury 4; Southampton 0
1901 Tottenham Hotspur 3; Sheffield United 1 (in replay after 2–2 draw)
1902 Sheffield United 2; Southampton 1 (in replay after 1–1 draw)
1903 Bury 6; Derby County 0
1904 Manchester City 1; Bolton Wanderers 0
1905 Aston Villa 2; Newcastle United 0
1906 Everton 1; Newcastle United 0
1907 Sheffield Wednesday 2; Everton 1
1908 Wolverhampton Wanderers 3; Newcastle United 1
1909 Manchester United 1; Bristol City 0

Scottish League
1900 Rangers
1901 Rangers
1902 Rangers
1903 Hibernian
1904 Third Lanark
1905 Celtic
1906 Celtic
1907 Celtic
1908 Celtic
1909 Celtic

Scottish Cup
1900 Celtic 4; Queens Park 3
1901 Hearts 4; Celtic 3
1902 Hibernian 1; Celtic 0
1903 Rangers 2; Hearts 0 (in replay after 1–1 and 0–0 draws)
1904 Celtic 3; Rangers 2
1905 Third Lanark 3; Rangers 1 (in replay after 0–0 draw)
1906 Hearts 1; Third Lanark 0
1907 Celtic 3; Hearts 0
1908 Celtic 5; St Mirren 1
1909 Cup withheld after crowd riot at Rangers–Celtic replay

GOLF

British Open *(winners from Britain except as indicated)*
1900 J. H. Taylor
1901 James Braid
1902 Alex Herd
1903 Harry Vardon
1904 Jack White
1905 James Braid
1906 James Braid
1907 Arnaud Massy (Fr)
1908 James Braid
1909 J. H. Taylor

US Open *(winners from US except as indicated)*
1900 Harry Vardon (GB)
1901 Willie Anderson
1902 Laurie Auchterlonie
1903 Willie Anderson
1904 Willie Anderson
1905 Willie Anderson
1906 Alex Smith
1907 Aleck Ross
1908 Fred McLeod
1909 George Sargent

HORSE RACING

2,000 Guineas
1900 Diamond Jubilee
1901 Handicapper
1902 Sceptre
1903 Rock Sand
1904 St Amant
1905 Vedas
1906 Gorgos
1907 Slieve Gallion
1908 Norman III
1909 Minoru

Derby
1900 Diamond Jubilee
1901 Volodyovski
1902 Ard Patrick
1903 Rock Sand
1904 St Amant
1905 Cicero
1906 Spearmint
1907 Orby
1908 Signorinetta
1909 Minoru

St Leger
1900 Diamond Jubilee
1901 Doricles
1902 Sceptre
1903 Rock Sand
1904 Pretty Polly
1905 Challacombe
1906 Trout Beck
1907 Wool Winder
1908 Your Majesty
1909 Bayardo

Grand National
1900 Ambush II
1901 Grudon
1902 Shannon Lass
1903 Drumcree
1904 Moifaa
1905 Kirkland
1906 Ascetic's Silver
1907 Eremon
1908 Rubio
1909 Lutteur III

ICE SKATING

British and Irish Olympic gold medals
1908 Figure skating Madge Syers

LAWN TENNIS

Australian Open
1905 Rodney Heath (Aus)
1906 Tony Wilding (NZ)
1907 Horace Rice (Aus)
1908 Fred Alexander (US)
1909 Tony Wilding (NZ)

French Open *(open only to French players until 1925)*
1900 P. Aymé; C. Masson
1901 A. Vacherot; P. Girod
1902 A. Vacherot; C. Masson
1903 M. Decugis; C. Masson
1904 M. Decugis; K. Gillou
1905 M. Germot; K. Gillou
1906 M. Germot; K. Fenwick
1907 M. Decugis; M. de Kermel
1908 M. Decugis; K. Fenwick
1909 M. Decugis; J. Mattey

All-England (Wimbledon) championships *(winners from Britain except as indicated)*
1900 Reginald Doherty; Blanche Hillyard
1901 Arthur Gore; Charlotte Cooper Sterry
1902 Lawrence Doherty ; Muriel Robb
1903 Lawrence Doherty; Dorothea Douglass
1904 Lawrence Doherty; Dorothea Douglass
1905 Lawrence Doherty; May Sutton
1906 Lawrence Doherty; Dorothea Douglass
1907 Norman Brookes (Aus); May Sutton (US)
1908 Arthur Gore; Charlotte Cooper Sterry
1909 Arthur Gore; Dora Boothby

US Open *(winners from US except as indicated)*
1900 Malcolm Whitman; Myrtle McAteer
1901 William Larned; Elisabeth Moore
1902 William Larned; Marion Jones
1903 Lawrence Doherty (GB); Elisabeth Moore
1904 Holcombe Ward; May Sutton
1905 Beals Wright; Elisabeth Moore
1906 William Clothier; Helen Homans
1907 William Larned; Evelyn Sears
1908 William Larned; Maud Barger-Wallach
1909 William Larned; Hazel Hotchkiss

ROWING

British and Irish Olympic gold medals
1908 Single sculls, Harry Blackstaffe; coxless pairs; coxless fours; eights

RUGBY LEAGUE

Challenge Cup
1900 Swinton 16; Salford 8
1901 Batley 6; Warrington 0
1902 Broughton Rangers 25; Salford 0
1903 Halifax 7; Salford 0
1904 Halifax 8; Warrington 3
1905 Warrington 6; Hull Kingston Rovers 0
1906 Bradford 5; Salford 0
1907 Warrington 17; Oldham 3
1908 Hunslet 14; Hull 0
1909 Wakefield Trinity 17; Hull 0

RUGBY UNION

Four/Five Nations championship
1900 Wales
1901 Scotland
1902 Wales
1903 Scotland
1904 Scotland
1905 Wales
(France joins championship)
1906 Ireland & Wales
1907 Scotland
1908 Wales (and Grand Slam)
1909 Wales (and Grand Slam)

SWIMMING

British and Irish Olympic gold medals
1900 1,000-m freestyle John Jarvis; 4,000-m freestyle John Jarvis; water polo
1906 1,500-m freestyle Henry Taylor
1908 400-m freestyle Henry Taylor; 1,500-m freestyle Henry Taylor; 200-m breaststroke Frederick Holman; 4 x 200-m men's freestyle relay; water polo

YACHTING

America's Cup
1901 *Columbia* (US, skipper Charlie Barr)
1903 *Reliance* (US, skipper Charlie Barr)

1910–1919

ATHLETICS

British and Irish Olympic gold medals
1912 1,500 m Arnold Jackson; 4 x 100-m men's relay

BASEBALL

World Series
1910 Philadelphia Athletics
1911 Philadelphia Athletics
1912 Boston Red Sox
1913 Philadelphia Athletics
1914 Boston Braves
1915 Boston Red Sox
1916 Boston Red Sox
1917 Chicago White Sox
1918 Boston Red Sox
1919 Cincinnati Reds

BOXING

British and Irish world champions
1913 Flyweight, Sid Smith; flyweight, Bill Ladbury
1914 Welterweight, Matt Wells; lightweight, Freddie Welsh; flyweight, Percy Jones; flyweight, Joe Symonds
1915 Welterweight, Ted 'Kid' Lewis
1916 Flyweight, Jimmy Wilde
1917 Welterweight, Ted 'Kid' Lewis

CRICKET

County cricket champions
1910 Kent
1911 Warwickshire
1912 Yorkshire
1913 Kent
1914 Surrey
1915–18 Not held
1919 Yorkshire

CYCLING

Tour de France
1910 Octave Lapize (Fr)
1911 Gustavo Garrigou (Fr)
1912 Odile Defraye (Bel)
1913 Philippe Thijs (Bel)
1914 Philippe Thijs (Bel)
1915–18 Not held
1919 Firmin Lambot (Bel)

FOOTBALL

Football League
1910 Aston Villa
1911 Manchester United
1912 Blackburn Rovers
1913 Sunderland
1914 Blackburn Rovers
1915 Everton
1916–19 Not held

FA Cup
1910 Newcastle United 2; Barnsley 0 (in replay after 1–1 draw)
1911 Bradford City 1; Newcastle United 0 (in replay after 0–0 draw)
1912 Barnsley 1; West Bromwich Albion 0, after extra time (in replay after 0–0 draw)
1913 Aston Villa 1; Sunderland 0
1914 Burnley 1; Liverpool 0
1915 Sheffield United 3; Chelsea 0
1916–19 Not held

Scottish League
1910 Celtic
1911 Rangers
1912 Rangers
1913 Rangers
1914 Celtic
1915 Celtic
1916 Celtic
1917 Celtic
1918 Rangers
1919 Celtic

Scottish Cup
1910 Dundee 2; Clyde 1 (in replay after 2–2, 0–0 draws)
1911 Celtic 2; Hamilton Academicals 0 (in replay after 0–0 draw)
1912 Celtic 2; Clyde 0
1913 Falkirk 2; Raith Rovers 0
1914 Celtic 4; HIbernian 1 (in replay after 0–0 draw)
1915–19 Not held

GOLF

British Open (winners from Britain except as indicated)
1910 James Braid
1911 Harry Vardon
1912 Ted Ray
1913 J. H. Taylor
1914 Harry Vardon
1915–9 Not held

US Open (winners from US except as indicated)
1910 Alex Smith (GB)
1911 John McDermott
1912 John McDermott
1913 Francis Ouimet
1914 Walter Hagen
1915 Jerome Travers
1916 Charles Evans Jr
1917–18 Not held
1919 Walter Hagen

US PGA
1916 Jim Barnes (US)
1917–18 Not held
1919 Jim Barnes (US)

HORSE RACING

2,000 Guineas
1910 Neil Gow
1911 Sunstar
1912 Sweeper II
1913 Louvois
1914 Kennymore
1915 Pommern
1916 Clarissimus
1917 Gay Crusader
1918 Gainsborough
1919 The Panther

Derby
1910 Lemberg
1911 Sunstar
1912 Tagalie
1913 Aboyeur
1914 Durbar II
1915 Pommern
1916 Fifinella
1917 Gay Crusader
1918 Gainsborough
1919 Grand Parade

St Leger
1910 Swynford
1911 Prince Palatine
1912 Tracery
1913 Night Hawk
1914 Black Jester
1915 Pommern
1916 Hurry On
1917 Gay Crusader
1918 Gainsborough
1919 Keysoe

Grand National
1910 Jenkinstown
1911 Glenside
1912 Jerry M
1913 Covetcoat
1914 Sunlock
1915 Ally Sloper
1916 Vermouth
1917 Ballymacad
1918 Poethlyn
1919 Poethlyn

LAWN TENNIS

Australian Open
1910 Rodney Heath (Aus)
1911 Norman Brookes (Aus)
1912 Cecil Parke (GB)
1913 E. F. Parker (Aus)
1914 Pat O'Hara Wood (Aus)
1915 Francis Lowe (GB)
1916–18 Not held
1919 A. R. F. Kingscote (GB)

French Open (open only to French players until 1925)
1910 M. Germot; J. Mattey
1911 A. Gobert; J. Mattey
1912 M. Decugis; J. Mattey
1913 M. Decugis; M. Broquedis
1914 M. Decugis; M. Broquedis
1915–19 not held

All-England (Wimbledon) championships
1910 Tony Wilding (NZ); Dorothea Douglass Lambert Chambers (GB)
1911 Tony Wilding (NZ); Dorothea Lambert Chambers (GB)
1912 Tony Wilding (NZ); Ethel Larcombe (GB)
1913 Tony Wilding (NZ); Dorothea Lambert Chambers (GB)
1914 Norman Brookes (Aus); Dorothea Lambert Chambers (GB)
1915–18 Not held
1919 Gerald Patterson (Aus); Suzanne Lenglen (Fr)

US Open (winners from US except as indicated)
1910 William Larned; Hazel Hotchkiss
1911 William Larned; Hazel Hotchkiss
1912 Maurice McLoughlin; Mary Browne
1913 Maurice McLoughlin; Mary Browne
1914 Richard Williams; Mary Browne
1915 William Johnston; Molla Bjurstedt (Nor)
1916 Richard Williams; Molla Bjurstedt (Nor)
1917 R. L. Murray; Molla Bjurstedt (Nor)
1918 R. L. Murray; Molla Bjurstedt (Nor)
1919 William Johnston; Hazel Hotchkiss Wightman

MOTOR RACING

Indianapolis 500
1911 R. Harroun
1912 J. Dawson
1913 J. Goux
1914 R. Thomas
1915 R. DePalma
1916 D. Resta
1917–8 no competition
1919 H. Wilcox

ROWING

British and Irish Olympic gold medals
1912 Single sculls, William Kinnear; eights

RUGBY LEAGUE

Challenge Cup
1910 Leeds 26; Hull 12 (in replay after 7–7 draw)
1911 Broughton Rangers 4; Wigan 0
1912 Dewsbury 8; Oldham 5
1913 Huddersfield 9; Warrington 5
1914 Hull 6; Wakefield 0
1915 Huddersfield 37; St Helens 3
1916–19 not held

RUGBY UNION

Five Nations championship
1910 England
1911 Wales (and Grand Slam)
1912 England & Ireland
1913 England (and Grand Slam)
1914 England (and Grand Slam)
1915–19 not held

SWIMMING

British and Irish Olympic gold medals
1912 Women's 4 x 100-m freestyle relay

YACHTING

America's Cup
Not held

1920–1929

ATHLETICS

British and Irish Olympic gold medals
1920 800 m Albert Hill;
1,500 m Albert Hill; 3,000-m
steeplechase, Percy Hodge; 4 x
400-m men's relay; tug-of-war
1924 100 m Harold Abrahams;
400 m Eric Liddell; 800 m
Douglas Lowe
1928 800 m Douglas Lowe;
400-m hurdles Lord Burghley;
hammer Patrick O'Callaghan
(Ire)

BASEBALL

World Series
1920 Cleveland Indians
1921 New York Giants
1922 New York Giants
1923 New York Yankees
1924 Washington Senators
1925 Pittsburgh Pirates
1926 St Louis Cardinals
1927 New York Yankees
1928 New York Yankees
1929 Philadelphia Athletics

BOXING

British and Irish world champions
1923 Light-heavyweight, Mike
McTigue (Ire)

CRICKET

County cricket champions
1920 Middlesex
1921 Middlesex
1922 Yorkshire
1923 Yorkshire
1924 Yorkshire
1925 Yorkshire
1926 Lancashire
1927 Lancashire
1928 Lancashire
1929 Nottinghamshire

CYCLING

Tour de France
1920 Philippe Thijs (Bel)
1921 Leon Scieu (Bel)
1922 Firmin Lambot (Bel)
1923 Henri Peussier (Fr)
1924 Ottavio Bottecchia (It)
1925 Ottavio Bottecchia (It)
1926 Lucien Buysse (Bel)
1927 Nicolas Frantz (Lux)
1928 Nicolas Frantz (Lux)
1929 Maurice Dewaele (Bel)

FOOTBALL

Football League
1920 West Bromwich Albion
1921 Burnley
1922 Liverpool
1923 Liverpool
1924 Huddersfield Town
1925 Huddersfield Town
1926 Huddersfield Town
1927 Newcastle United
1928 Everton
1929 Sheffield Wednesday

FA Cup
1920 Aston Villa 1; Huddersfield
Town 0, after extra time
1921 Tottenham Hotspur 1;
Wolverhampton Wanderers 0
1922 Huddersfield Town 1;
Preston North End 0
1923 Bolton Wanderers 2; West
Ham United 0
1924 Newcastle United 2; Aston
Villa 0
1925 Sheffield United 1; Cardiff
City 0
1926 Bolton Wanderers 1;
Manchester City 0
1927 Cardiff City 1; Arsenal 0
1928 Blackburn Rovers 3;
Huddersfield Town 1
1929 Bolton Wanderers 2;
Portsmouth 0

Scottish League
1920 Rangers
1921 Rangers
1922 Celtic
1923 Rangers
1924 Rangers
1925 Rangers
1926 Celtic
1927 Rangers
1928 Rangers
1929 Rangers

Scottish Cup
1920 Kilmarnock 3; Albion
Rovers 2
1921 Partick Thistle 1;
Rangers 0
1922 Morton 1; Rangers 0
1923 Celtic 1; Hibernian 0
1924 Airdrieonians 2;
Hibernian 0
1925 Celtic 2; Dundee 1
1926 St Mirren 2; Celtic 0
1927 Celtic 3; East Fife 1
1928 Rangers 4; Celtic 0
1929 Kilmarnock 2; Rangers 0

GOLF

Ryder Cup
1927 United States 9½, Great
Britain & Ireland 2½
1929 Great Britain & Ireland 7,
United States 5

US Open *(winners from US
except as indicated)*
1920 Ted Ray (GB)
1921 Jim Barnes
1922 Gene Sarazen
1923 Bobby Jones
1924 Cyril Walker
1925 Willie Macfarlane Jr
1926 Bobby Jones
1927 Tommy Armour
1928 Johnny Farrell
1929 Bobby Jones

US PGA *(winners from US
except as indicated)*
1920 Jock Hutchison
1921 Walter Hagen
1922 Gene Sarazen
1923 Gene Sarazen
1924 Walter Hagen
1925 Walter Hagen
1926 Walter Hagen
1927 Walter Hagen
1928 Leo Diegel
1929 Leo Diegel

Walker Cup
1922 United States 8, Great
Britain & Ireland 4
1923 United States 6, Great
Britain & Ireland 5
1924 United States 9, Great
Britain & Ireland 3
1926 United States 6, Great
Britain & Ireland 5
1928 United States 11, Great
Britain & Ireland 1

British Open *(winners from
US as indicated)*
1920 George Duncan (GB)
1921 Jock Hutchison
1922 Walter Hagen
1923 Arthur Havers (GB)
1924 Walter Hagen
1925 Jim Barnes
1926 Bobby Jones
1927 Bobby Jones
1928 Walter Hagen
1929 Walter Hagen

HORSE RACING

2,000 Guineas
1920 Tetratema
1921 Craig An Eran
1922 St Louis
1923 Ellangowan
1924 Diophon
1925 Manna
1926 Colorado
1927 Adam's Apple
1928 Flamingo
1929 Mr Jinks

Derby
1920 Spion Kop
1921 Humorist
1922 Captain Cuttle
1923 Papyrus
1924 Sansovino
1925 Manna
1926 Coronach
1927 Call Boy
1928 Fellstead
1929 Trigo

St Leger
1920 Caligula
1921 Polemarch
1922 Royal Lancer
1923 Tranquil
1924 Salmon-Trout
1925 Solario
1926 Coronach
1927 Book Law
1928 Fairway
1929 Trigo

Grand National
1920 Troytown
1921 Shaun Spadah
1922 Music Hall
1923 Sergeant Murphy
1924 Master Robert
1925 Double Chance
1926 Jack Horner
1927 Sprig
1928 Tipperary Tim
1929 Gregalach

Prix de l'Arc de Triomphe
1920 Comrade
1921 Ksar
1922 Ksar
1923 Parth
1924 Massine
1925 Priori
1926 Biribi
1927 Mon Talisman
1928 Kantar
1929 Ortello

LAWN TENNIS

Australian Open *(open only to men until 1922; winners from Australia except as indicated)*
1920 Pat O'Hara Wood
1921 Rhys Gemmell
1922 Pat O'Hara Wood; Margaret Molesworth
1923 Pat O'Hara Wood; Margaret Molesworth
1924 James Anderson; Sylvia Lance
1925 James Anderson; Daphne Akhurst
1926 John Hawkes; Daphne Akhurst
1927 Gerald Patterson; Esna Boyd
1928 Jean Borota (Fr); Daphne Akhurst
1929 John Gregory (GB); Daphne Akhurst

French Open *(open only to French players until 1925; winners from France except as indicated)*
1920 A. Gobert; Suzanne Lenglen
1921 J. Samazeuilh; Suzanne Lenglen
1922 Henri Cochet; Suzanne Lenglen
1923 P. Blanchy; Suzanne Lenglen
1924 Jean Borotra; Suzanne Lenglen
1925 René Lacoste; Suzanne Lenglen
1926 Henri Cochet; Suzanne Lenglen
1927 René Lacoste; Kea Bouman (Neth)
1928 Henri Cochet; Helen Wills (US)
1929 René Lacoste; Helen Wills (US)

All-England (Wimbledon) championships
1920 Bill Tilden (US); Suzanne Lenglen (Fr)
1921 Bill Tilden (US); Suzanne Lenglen (Fr)
1922 Gerald Patterson (Aus); Suzanne Lenglen (Fr)
1923 Bill Johnston (US); Suzanne Lenglen (Fr)
1924 Jean Borotra (Fr); Kathleen McKane (GB)
1925 Réne Lacoste (Fr); Suzanne Lenglen (Fr)
1926 Jean Borotra (Fr); Kathleen McKane Godfree (GB)
1927 Henri Cochet (Fr); Helen Wills (US)
1928 Réne Lacoste (Fr); Helen Wills (US)
1929 Henri Cochet (Fr); Helen Wills (US)

US Open *(winners from US except as indicated)*
1920 Bill Tilden; Molla Bjurstedt Mallory
1922 Bill Tilden; Molla Mallory
1923 Bill Tilden; Helen Wills
1924 Bill Tilden; Helen Wills
1925 Bill Tilden; Helen Wills
1926 René Lacoste (Fr); Molla Mallory
1927 René Lacoste (Fr); Helen Wills
1928 Henri Cochet (Fr); Helen Wills
1929 Bill Tilden; Helen Wills

MOTOR RACING

Indianapolis 500
1920 G. Chevrolet
1921 T. Milton
1922 J. Murphy
1923 T. Milton
1924 L. L. Corum, J. Boyer
1925 P. DePaolo
1926 F. Lockhart
1927 G. Souders
1928 L. Meyer
1929 R. Keech

Le Mans
1923 A. Lagache/R. Léonard (Chenard-Walcker)
1924 J. Duff/F. C. Clément (Bentley)
1925 H. de Courcelles/A. Rossignol (Lorraine-Dietrich)
1926 R. Bloch/A. Rossignol (Lorraine Dietrich)
1927 J. D. Benjafield/S. C. H. Davis (Bentley)
1928 W. Barnato/B. Rubin (Bentley)
1929 W. Barnato/H. R. S. Birkin (Bentley)

ROWING

British and Irish Olympic gold medals
1924 Single sculls, Jack Beresford; men's coxless fours
1928 Men's coxless fours

RUGBY LEAGUE

Challenge Cup
1920 Huddersfield 21; Wigan 10
1921 Leigh 13; Halifax 0
1922 Rochdale Hornets 10; Hull 9
1923 Leeds 28; Hull 3
1924 Wigan 21; Oldham 4
1925 Oldham 16; Hull Kingston Rovers 3
1926 Swinton 9; Oldham 3
1927 Oldham 26; Swinton 7
1928 Swinton 5; Warrington 3
1929 Wigan 13; Dewsbury 2

RUGBY UNION

Five Nations championship
1920 England, Scotland and Wales
1921 England (and Grand Slam)
1922 Wales
1923 England (and Grand Slam)
1924 England
1925 Scotland (and Grand Slam)
1926 Ireland and Scotland
1927 Ireland and Scotland
1928 England (and Grand Slam)
1929 Scotland

SNOOKER

World championship
(finalists from Britain except as indicated)
1927 Joe Davis 20; Tom Dennis 11
1928 Joe Davis 16; Fred Lawrence 13
1929 Joe Davis 19; Tom Dennis 14

SQUASH

British women's Open championship *(winners from Britain except as indicated)*
1922 Joyce Cave
1923 Sylvia Huntsman
1924 Joyce Cave
1925 Cecily Fenwick
1926 Cecily Fenwick
1928 Joyce Cave
1929 Nancy Cave

SWIMMING

British and Irish Olympic gold medals
1924 Women's 200-m breaststroke Lucy Morton

YACHTING

America's Cup
1920 *Resolute* (US, skipper Harold Vanderbilt)

1930-39

British and Irish Olympic gold medals
1932 800 m Thomas Hampson; 400-m hurdles Robert Tisdall (Ire); 50-km road walk Thomas Green; hammer Patrick O'Callaghan (Ire)
1936 4 x 400-m men's relay; 50-km road walk Harold Whitlock

BASEBALL

World Series
1930 Philadelphia Athletics
1931 St Louis Cardinals
1932 New York Yankees
1933 New York Giants
1934 St Louis Cardinals
1935 Detroit Tigers
1936 New York Yankees
1937 New York Yankees
1938 New York Yankees
1939 New York Yankees

BOXING

British and Irish world champions
1930 Junior welterweight, Jackie 'Kid' Berg
1932 Flyweight (NBA), Jackie Brown
1933 Welterweight, Jimmy McLarnin (Ire)
1934 Welterweight, Jimmy McLarnin (Ire)
1935 Flyweight (NBA), Benny Lynch
1937 Flyweight, Benny Lynch
1938 Flyweight, Peter Kane

CRICKET

County cricket champions
1930 Lancashire
1931 Yorkshire
1932 Yorkshire
1933 Yorkshire
1934 Lancashire
1935 Yorkshire
1936 Derbyshire
1937 Yorkshire
1938 Yorkshire
1939 Yorkshire

CYCLING

Tour de France
1930 André Leducq (Fr)
1931 Antonin Magne (Fr)
1932 André Leducq (Fr)
1933 Georges Speicher (Fr)
1934 Antonin Magne (Fr)
1935 Romain Maes (Bel)
1936 Sylvère Maes (Bel)
1937 Roger Lapebie (Fr)
1938 Gino Bartali (It)
1939 Sylvère Maes (Bel)

FOOTBALL

World Cup
1930 Uruguay 4; Argentina 2
1934 Italy 2; Czechoslovakia 1, after extra time
1938 Italy 4; Hungary 2

Football League
1930 Sheffield Wednesday
1931 Arsenal
1932 Everton
1933 Arsenal
1934 Arsenal
1935 Arsenal
1936 Sunderland
1937 Manchester City
1938 Arsenal
1939 Everton

FA Cup
1930 Arsenal 2; Huddersfield Town 0
1931 West Bromwich Albion 2; Birmingham City 1
1932 Newcastle United 2; Arsenal 1
1933 Everton 3; Manchester City 0
1934 Manchester City 2; Portsmouth 1
1935 Sheffield Wednesday 4; West Bromwich Albion 2
1936 Arsenal 1; Sheffield United 0
1937 Sunderland 3; Preston North End 1
1938 Preston North End 1; Huddersfield Town 0, after extra time
1939 Portsmouth 4; Wolverhampton Wanderers 1

Scottish League
1930 Rangers
1931 Rangers
1932 Motherwell
1933 Rangers
1934 Rangers
1935 Rangers
1936 Celtic
1937 Rangers
1938 Celtic
1939 Rangers

Scottish Cup
1930 Rangers 2; Partick Thistle 1 (in replay after 0–0 draw)
1931 Celtic 4; Motherwell 2 (in replay after 2–2 draw)
1932 Rangers 3; Kilmarnock 0 (in replay after 1–1 draw)
1933 Celtic 1; Motherwell 0
1934 Rangers 5; St Mirren 0
1935 Rangers 2; Hamilton Academicals 1
1936 Rangers 1; Third Lanark 0
1937 Celtic 2; Aberdeen 1
1938 East Fife 4; Kilmarnock 2 (in replay after 1–1 draw)
1939 Clyde 4; Motherwell 0

GOLF

Ryder Cup
1931 United States 9; Great Britain & Ireland 3
1933 Great Britain & Ireland 6½; United States 5½
1935 United States 9; Great Britain & Ireland 3
1937 United States 8; Great Britain & Ireland 4

US Masters (winners from US except as indicated)
1934 Horton Smith
1935 Gene Sarazen
1936 Horton Smith
1937 Byron Nelson
1938 Henry Picard
1939 Ralph Guldahl

US Open (winners from US except as indicated)
1930 Bobby Jones
1931 Billy Burke
1932 Gene Sarazen
1933 Johnny Goodman
1934 Olin Dutra
1935 Sam Parks Jr
1936 Tony Manero
1937 Ralph Guldahl
1938 Ralph Guldahl
1939 Byron Nelson

US PGA (winners from US except as indicated)
1930 Tommy Armour
1931 Tom Creavy
1932 Olin Dutra
1933 Gene Sarazen
1934 Paul Runyan
1935 Johnny Revolta
1936 Densmore Shute
1937 Densmore Shute
1938 Paul Runyan
1939 Henry Picard

Walker Cup
1930 United States 10; Great Britain & Ireland 2
1932 United States 8; Great Britain & Ireland 1
1934 United States 9; Great Britain & Ireland 2
1936 United States 9; Great Britain & Ireland 0
1938 Great Britain & Ireland 7; United States 4

British Open (winners from US except as indicated)
1930 Bobby Jones
1931 Tommy Armour
1932 Gene Sarazen
1933 Densmore Shute
1934 Henry Cotton (GB)
1935 Alfred Perry (GB)
1936 Alfred Padgham (GB)
1937 Henry Cotton (GB)
1938 R.A. Whitcombe (GB)
1939 Richard Burton (GB)

HORSE RACING

2,000 Guineas
1930 Diolite
1931 Cameronian
1932 Orwell
1933 Rodosto
1934 Colombo
1935 Bahram
1936 Pay Up
1937 Le Ksar
1938 Pasch
1939 Blue Peter

Derby
1930 Blenheim
1931 Cameronian
1932 April the Fifth
1933 Hyperion
1934 Windsor Lad
1935 Bahram
1936 Mahmoud
1937 Mid-day Sun
1938 Bois Roussel
1939 Blue Peter

St Leger
1930 Singapore
1931 Sandwich
1932 Firdaussi
1933 Hyperion
1934 Windsor Lad
1935 Bahram
1936 Boswell
1937 Chulmleigh
1938 Scottish Union
1939 Not run

Grand National
1930 Shaun Goilin
1931 Grakle
1932 Forbra
1933 Kellsboro' Jack
1934 Golden Miller
1935 Reynoldstown
1936 Reynoldstown
1937 Royal Mail
1938 Battleship
1939 Workman

Prix de l'Arc de Triomphe
1930 Motrico
1931 Pearl Cap
1932 Motrico
1933 Crapom
1934 Brantome
1935 Samos
1936 Corrida
1937 Corrida
1938 Eclair au Chocolait
1939 Not run

LAWN TENNIS

Australian Open *(winners from Australia except as indicated)*
1930 Gar Moon; Daphne Akhurst
1931 Jack Crawford; Coral Buttsworth
1932 Jack Crawford; Coral Buttsworth
1933 Jack Crawford; Joan Hartigan
1934 Fred Perry (GB); Joan Hartigan
1935 Jack Crawford; Dorothy Round (GB)
1936 Adrian Quist; Joan Hartigan
1937 Vivian McGrath; Nancye Wynne
1938 Don Budge (US); Dorothy Bundy (US)
1939 John Bromwich; Emily Westacott

French Open
1930 Henri Cochet (Fr); Helen Wills Moody (US)
1931 Jean Borotra (Fr); Cilly Ausem (Ger)
1932 Henri Cochet (Fr); Helen Wills Moody (US)
1933 John Crawford (Aus); Margaret Scriven (GB)
1934 Gottfried von Cramm (Ger); Margaret Scriven (GB)
1935 Fred Perry (GB); Hilde Sperling (Den)
1936 Gottfried von Cramm (Ger); Hilde Sperling (Den)
1937 Henner Henkel (Ger); Hilde Sperling (Den)
1938 Don Budge (US); Simone Mathieu (Fr)
1939 Don McNeill (US); Simone Mathieu (Fr)

All-England (Wimbledon) championships
1930 Bill Tilden (US); Helen Wills Moody (US)
1931 Sidney Wood (US); Cilly Aussem (Ger)
1932 Ellsworth Vines (US); Helen Wills Moody (US)
1933 Jack Crawford (Aus); Helen Wills Moody (US)
1934 Fred Perry (GB); Dorothy Round (GB)
1935 Fred Perry (GB); Helen Wills Moody (US)
1936 Fred Perry (GB); Helen Jacobs (US)
1937 Donald Budge (US); Dorothy Round (GB)
1938 Donald Budge (US); Helen Wills Moody (US)
1939 Bobby Riggs (US); Alice Marble (US)

US Open *(winners from US except as indicated)*
1930 John Doeg; Betty Nuthall (GB)
1931 Ellsworth Vines; Helen Wills Moody
1932 Ellsworth Vines; Helen Jacobs
1933 Fred Perry (GB); Helen Jacobs
1934 Fred Perry (GB); Helen Jacobs
1935 Wilmer Allison; Helen Jacobs
1936 Fred Perry (GB); Alice Marble
1937 Don Budge; Anita Lizana (Chile)
1938 Don Budge; Alice Marble
1939 Bobby Riggs; Alice Marble

MOTOR RACING

Le Mans
1930 W. Barnato/G. Kidston (Bentley)
1931 E. Howe/H. R. S. Birkin (Alfa Romeo)
1932 R. Sommer/L. Chinetti (Alfa Romeo)
1933 R. Sommer/T. Nuvolari (Alfa Romeo)
1934 L. Chinetti/P. Etancelin (Alfa Romeo)
1935 J. S. Hindmarsh/L. Fontés (Lagonda)
1936 no competition
1937 J. P. Wimille, R. Benoist (Bugatti)
1938 E. Chaboud, J. Tremoulet (Delahaye)
1939 J. P. Wimille, P. Veyron (Bugatti)

Indianapolis 500
1930 W. Arnold
1931 L. Schneider
1932 F. Frame
1933 L. Meyer
1934 W. Cummings
1935 K. Petillo
1936 L. Meyer
1937 W. Shaw
1938 F. Roberts
1939 W. Shaw

ROWING

British and Irish Olympic gold medals
1932 Coxless pairs; coxless fours
1936 Double sculls

RUGBY LEAGUE

Challenge Cup
1930 Widnes 10; St Helens 3
1931 Halifax 22; York 8
1932 Leeds 11; Swinton 8
1933 Huddersfield 21; Warrington 17
1934 Hunslet 11; Widnes 5
1935 Castleford 11; Huddersfield 8
1936 Leeds 18; Warrington 2
1937 Widnes 18; Keighley 5
1938 Salford 7; Barrow 4
1939 Halifax 20; Salford 3

RUGBY UNION

Five/Four Nations championship
1930 England
1931 Wales
(France expelled for paying players)
1932 England, Ireland and Wales
1933 Scotland
1934 England
1935 Ireland
1936 Wales
1937 England
1938 Scotland
1939 England, Ireland and Wales

SNOOKER

World championship
(finalists from Britain except as indicated)
1930 Joe Davis 25; Tom Dennis 12
1931 Joe Davis 25; Tom Dennis 21
1932 Joe Davis 30; Clark McConachy 19
1933 Joe Davis 25; Willie Smith 18
1934 Joe Davis 25; Tom Newman 23
1935 Joe Davis 25; Willie Smith 20
1936 Joe Davis 34; Horace Lindrum 27
1937 Joe Davis 32 ;Horace Lindrum 29
1938 Joe Davis 37; Sidney Smith 24
1939 Joe Davis 43; Sidney Smith 30

SQUASH

British Open *(winners from Britain except as indicated)*
1930 Don Butcher; Nancy Cave
1931 Don Butcher; Cecily Fenwick
1932 Don Butcher; Susan Noel
1933 Abdelfattah Amr Bey (Egypt); Susan Noel
1934 no challenge; Susan Noel
1935 Abdelfattah Amr Bey (Egypt); Margot Lumb
1936 Abdelfattah Amr Bey (Egypt); Margot Lumb
1937 Abdelfattah Amr Bey (Egypt); Margot Lumb
1938 Abdelfattah Amr Bey (Egypt); Margot Lumb
1939 James Dear; Margot Lumb

YACHTING

America's Cup
1930 *Enterprise* (US, skipper Harold Vanderbilt)
1934 *Rainbow* (US, skipper Harold Vanderbilt)
1937 *Ranger* (US, skipper Harold Vanderbilt)

1940–1949

BASEBALL

World Series
1940 Cincinnati Reds
1941 New York Yankees
1942 St Louis Cardinals
1943 New York Yankees
1944 St Louis Cardinals
1945 Detroit Tigers
1946 St Louis Cardinals
1947 New York Yankees
1948 Cleveland Indians
1949 New York Yankees

BOXING

British and Irish world champions
1943 Flyweight, Jackie Paterson
1947 Flyweight (NBA), Rinty Monaghan
1948 Flyweight, Rinty Monaghan; light-heavyweight, Freddie Mills

CRICKET

County cricket champions
1940–5 Not held
1946 Yorkshire
1947 Middlesex
1948 Glamorgan
1949 Middlesex/Yorkshire

CYCLING

Tour de France
1940–6 Not held
1947 Jean Robic (Fr)
1948 Gino Bartali (It)
1949 Fausto Coppi (It)

EQUESTRIANISM

Badminton Horse Trials
1949 John Shedden

FOOTBALL

Football League
1940–6 Not held
1947 Liverpool
1948 Arsenal
1949 Portsmouth

FA Cup
1940–5 Not held
1946 Derby County 4; Charlton Athletic 1, after extra time
1947 Charlton Athletic 1; Burnley 0, after extra time
1948 Manchester United 4; Blackpool 2
1949 Wolverhampton Wanderers 3; Leicester City 1

Scottish League
1940–6 Not held
1947 Rangers
1948 Hibernian
1949 Rangers

Scottish Cup
1940–6 Not held
1947 Aberdeen 2; Hibernian 1
1948 Rangers 1; Morton 0 (in replay after 1–1 draw)
1949 Rangers 4; Clyde 1

Scottish League Cup
1947 Rangers 4; Aberdeen 0
1948 East Fife 4; Falkirk 1 (in replay after 0–0 draw)
1949 Rangers 2; Raith Rovers 0

GOLF

Ryder Cup
1947 United States 11; Great Britain & Ireland 1
1949 United States 7; Great Britain & Ireland 5

US Masters (*winners from US except as indicated*)
1940 Jimmy Demaret
1941 Craig Wood
1942 Byron Nelson
1943–5 Not held
1946 Herman Keiser
1947 Jimmy Demaret
1948 Claude Harmon
1949 Sam Snead

US Open (*winners from US except as indicated*)
1940 Lawson Little Jr
1941 Craig Wood
1942–5 Not held
1946 Lloyd Mangrum
1947 Lew Worsham
1948 Ben Hogan
1949 Cary Middlecoff

US PGA (*winners from US except as indicated*)
1940 Byron Nelson
1941 Vic Ghezzi
1942 Sam Snead
1943 Not held
1944 Bob Hamilton
1945 Byron Nelson
1946 Ben Hogan
1947 Jim Ferrier
1948 Ben Hogan
1949 Sam Snead

Walker Cup
1947 United States 8, Great Britain & Ireland 4
1949 United States 10, Great Britain & Ireland 2

British Open
1940–5 Not held
1946 Sam Snead (US)
1947 Fred Daly (Ire)
1948 Henry Cotton (GB)
1949 Bobby Locke (SA)

HORSE RACING

2,000 Guineas
1940 Djebel
1941 Lambert Simnel
1942 Big Game
1943 Kingsway
1944 Garden Path
1945 Court Martial
1946 Happy Knight
1947 Tudor Minstrel
1948 My Babu
1949 Nimbus

Derby
1940 Pont l'Eveque
1941 Owen Tudor
1942 Watling Street
1943 Straight Deal
1944 Ocean Swell
1945 Dante
1946 Airborne
1947 Pearl Diver
1948 My Love
1949 Nimbus

St Leger
1940 Turkham
1941 Sun Castle
1942 Sun Chariot
1943 Herringbone
1944 Tehran
1945 Chamossaire
1946 Airborne
1947 Sayajirao
1948 Black Tarquin
1949 Ridge Wood

Grand National
1940 Bogskar
1941–5 Not run
1946 Lovely Cottage
1947 Caughoo
1948 Sheila's Cottage
1949 Russian Hero

Prix de l'Arc de Triomphe
1940 Not run
1941 La Pacha
1942 Djebel
1943 Verso II
1944 Ardan
1945 Nikellora
1946 Caracella
1947 Le Paillon
1948 Migoli
1949 Coronation

LAWN TENNIS

Australian Open (*winners from Australia except as indicated*)
1940 Adrian Quist; Nancye Wynne
1941–5 Not held
1946 John Bromwich; Nancye Wynne Bolton
1947 Dinny Pails; Nancye Wynne Bolton
1948 Adrian Quist; Nancye Wynne Bolton
1949 Frank Sedgman; Doris Hart (US)

French Open
1940–5 Not held
1946 Marcel Bernard (Fr); Margaret Osborne (US)
1947 Josef Asboth (Hung); Patricia Todd (US)
1948 Frank Parker (US); Nelly Landry (Belg)
1949 Frank Parker (US); Margaret Osborne Du Pont (US)

All-England (Wimbledon) championships
1940–5 Not held
1946 Yvon Petra (Fr); Pauline Betz (US)
1947 Jack Kramer (US); Margaret Osborne (US)
1948 Bob Falkenburg (US); Louise Brough (US)
1949 Ted Schroeder (US); Louise Brough (US)

US Open (*winners from US except as indicated*)
1940 Don McNeill; Alice Marble
1941 Bobby Riggs; Sarah Palfrey Cooke
1942 Ted Schroeder; Pauline Betz
1943 Joseph Hunt; Pauline Betz
1944 Frank Parker; Pauline Betz
1945 Frank Parker; Sarah Palfrey Cooke
1946 Jack Kramer; Pauline Betz
1947 Jack Kramer; Louise Brough
1948 Ricardo (Pancho) Gonzales; Margaret Du Pont
1949 Ricardo (Pancho) Gonzales; Margaret Du Pont

MOTOR RACING

Le Mans
1940–8 No competition
1949 L. Chinetti/Lord Selsdon (Ferrari)

Indianapolis 500
1940 W. Shaw
1941 F. Davis, M. Rose

1942–5 No competition
1946 G. Robson
1947 M. Rose
1948 M. Rose
1949 W. Holland

ROWING

UK and Irish Olympic gold medals
1948 Men's coxless pairs; men's double sculls

RUGBY LEAGUE

Challenge Cup
1940 Not held
1941 Leeds 19; Halifax 2
1942 Leeds 15; Halifax 10
1943 Dewsbury bt Leeds 16–9, 0–6
1944 Bradford Northern bt Wigan 0–3, 8–0
1945 Huddersfield bt Bradford 7–4, 6–5
1946 Wakefield Trinity 13; Wigan 12
1947 Bradford Northern 8; Leeds 4
1948 Wigan 8; Bradford 3
1949 Bradford Northern 12; Halifax 0

RUGBY UNION

Four/Five Nations Championship
1940–6 Not held
(*France readmitted after the war*)
1947 England and Wales
1948 Ireland (and Grand Slam)
1949 Ireland

SNOOKER

World championship
(*finalists from Britain except as indicated*)
1940 Joe Davis 37; Fred Davis 36
1946 Joe Davis 78; Horace Lindrum 67
1947 Walter Donaldson 82; Fred Davis 63
1948 Fred Davis 84; Walter Donaldson 61
1949 Fred Davis 80 ;Walter Donaldson 65

SQUASH

British Open
1940–6 Not held
1947 Mahmoud Karim (Egypt); Joan Curry (GB)
1948 Mahmoud Karim (Egypt); Joan Curry (GB)
1949 Mahmoud Karim (Egypt); Joan Curry (GB)

1950–1959

ATHLETICS

British and Irish Olympic gold medals
1956 3,000-m steeplechase Chris Brasher

BASEBALL

World Series
1950 New York Yankees
1951 New York Yankees
1952 New York Yankees
1953 New York Yankees
1954 New York Giants
1955 Brooklyn Dodgers
1956 New York Yankees
1957 Milwaukee Braves
1958 New York Yankees
1959 Los Angeles Dodgers

BOXING

British and Irish world champions
1950 Flyweight, Terry Allen
1951 Middleweight, Randolph Turpin

CRICKET

County cricket champions
1950 Lancashire and Surrey (shared)
1951 Warwickshire
1952 Surrey
1953 Surrey
1954 Surrey
1955 Surrey
1956 Surrey
1957 Surrey
1958 Surrey
1959 Yorkshire

CYCLING

Tour de France
1950 Ferdi Kubler (Swi)
1951 Hugo Koblet (Swi)
1952 Fausto Coppi (It)
1953 Louison Bobet (Fr)
1954 Louison Bobet (Fr)
1955 Louison Bobet (Fr)
1956 Roger Walkowiak (Fr)
1957 Jacques Anquetil (Fr)
1958 Charly Gaul (Lux)
1959 Federico Bahamontes (Sp)

EQUESTRIANISM

World showjumping championship (men)
1953 Francisco Goyoago (Sp)
1954 Hans Gunter Winkler (Ger)
1955 Hans Gunter Winkler (Ger)
1956 Raimondo d'Inzeo (It)

Badminton Horse Trials
(winners from Britain except as indicated)
1950 Tony Collings
1951 Hans Schwarzenbach (Swi)
1952 Mark Darley (Ire)
1953 Lawrence Rook
1954 Margaret Hough
1955 Frank Weldon
1956 Frank Weldon
1957 Sheila Wilcox
1958 Sheila Wilcox
1959 Sheila Wilcox Waddington

FOOTBALL

World Cup
1950 Uruguay 2; Brazil 1
1954 West Germany 3; Hungary 2
1958 Brazil 5; Sweden 2

European Champions Cup
1956 Real Madrid 4; Reims 3
1957 Real Madrid 2; Fiorentina 0
1958 Real Madrid 3; AC Milan 2, after extra time
1959 Real Madrid 2; Reims 0

Inter-Cities Fairs Cup
1958 Barcelona bt London 2–2, 6–0

Football League
1950 Portsmouth
1951 Tottenham Hotspur
1952 Manchester United
1953 Arsenal
1954 Wolverhampton Wanderers
1955 Chelsea
1956 Manchester United
1957 Manchester United
1958 Wolverhampton Wanderers
1959 Wolverhampton Wanderers

FA Cup
1950 Arsenal 2; Liverpool 0
1951 Newcastle United 2; Blackpool 0
1952 Newcastle United 1; Arsenal 0
1953 Blackpool 4; Bolton Wanderers 3
1954 West Bromwich Albion 3; Preston North End 2
1955 Newcastle United 3; Manchester City 1
1956 Manchester City 3; Birmingham City 1
1957 Aston Villa 2; Manchester United 1
1958 Bolton Wanderers 2; Manchester United 0
1959 Nottingham Forest 2; Luton Town 1

Scottish League
1950 Rangers
1951 Hibernian
1952 Hibernian
1953 Rangers
1954 Celtic
1955 Aberdeen
1956 Rangers
1957 Rangers
1958 Hearts
1959 Rangers

Scottish Cup
1950 Rangers 3; East Fife 0
1951 Celtic 1; Motherwell 0
1952 Motherwell 4; Dundee 0
1953 Rangers 1; Aberdeen 0 (After 1–1 draw)
1954 Celtic 2; Aberdeen 1
1955 Clyde 1; Celtic 0 (After 1–1 draw)
1956 Hearts 3; Celtic 1
1957 Falkirk 2; Kilmarnock 1 (After 1–1 draw)
1958 Clyde 1; Hibernian 0
1959 St Mirren 3; Aberdeen 1

Scottish League Cup
1950 East Fife 3; Dunfermline Athletic 0
1951 Motherwell 3; Hibernian 0
1952 Dundee 3; Rangers 2
1953 Dundee 2; Kilmarnock 0
1954 East Fife 3; Partick Thistle 2
1955 Hearts 4; Motherwell 2
1956 Aberdeen 2; St Mirren 1
1957 Celtic 3; Partick Thistle 0 (After 0–0 draw)
1958 Celtic 7; Rangers 1
1959 Hearts 5; Partick Thistle 1

GOLF

Ryder Cup
1951 United States 9½; Great Britain & Ireland 2½
1953 United States 6½; Great Britain & Ireland 5½
1955 United States 8; Great Britain & Ireland 4
1957 Great Britain & Ireland 7½; United States 4½
1959 United States 8½; Great Britain & Ireland 3½

US Masters *(winners from US except as indicated)*
1950 Jimmy Demaret
1951 Ben Hogan
1952 Sam Snead
1953 Ben Hogan
1954 Sam Snead
1955 Cary Middlecoff
1956 Jack Burke Jr
1957 Doug Ford
1958 Arnold Palmer
1959 Art Wall Jr

US Open *(winners from US except as indicated)*
1950 Ben Hogan
1951 Ben Hogan
1952 Julius Boros
1953 Ben Hogan
1954 Ed Furgol
1955 Jack Fleck
1956 Cary Middlecoff
1957 Dick Mayer
1958 Tommy Bolt
1959 Billy Casper

US PGA *(winners from US except as indicated)*
1950 Chandler Harper
1951 Sam Snead
1952 Jim Turnesa
1953 Walter Burkemo
1954 Chick Harbert
1955 Doug Ford
1956 Jack Burke
1957 Lionel Hebert
1958 Dow Finsterwald
1959 Bob Rosburg

Walker Cup
1951 United States 6; Great Britain & Ireland 3
1953 United States 9; Great Britain & Ireland 3
1955 United States 10; Great Britain & Ireland 2
1957 United States 8; Great Britain & Ireland 3
1959 United States 9; Great Britain & Ireland 3

British Open
1950 Bobby Locke (SA)
1951 Max Faulkner (GB)
1952 Bobby Locke (SA)
1953 Ben Hogan (US)
1954 Peter Thomson (Aus)
1955 Peter Thomson (Aus)
1956 Peter Thomson (Aus)
1957 Bobby Locke (SA)
1958 Peter Thomson (Aus)
1959 Gary Player (SA)

HORSE RACING

2,000 Guineas
1950 Palestine
1951 Ki Ming
1952 Thunderhead II
1953 Nearula
1954 Darius
1955 Our Babu
1956 Gilles de Retz
1957 Crepello
1958 Pall Mall
1959 Taboun

Derby
1950 Galcador
1951 Arctic Prince
1952 Tulyar
1953 Pinza
1954 Never Say Die
1955 Phil Drake
1956 Lavandin
1957 Crepello
1958 Hard Ridden
1959 Parthia

St Leger
1950 Scratch II
1951 Talma II
1952 Tulyar
1953 Premonition
1954 Never Say Die
1955 Meld
1956 Cambremer
1957 Ballymoss
1958 Alcide
1959 Cantelo

Grand National
1950 Freebooter
1951 Nickel Coin
1952 Teal
1953 Early Mist
1954 Royal Tan
1955 Quare Times
1956 ESB
1957 Sundew
1958 Mr What
1959 Oxo

Prix de l'Arc de Triomphe
1950 Tantieme
1951 Tantieme
1952 Nuccio
1953 La Sorellina
1954 Sica Boy
1955 Ribot
1956 Ribot
1957 Oreso
1958 Ballymoss
1959 Saint Crespin

ICE SKATING

British and Irish Olympic gold medals
1952 Figure skating Jeanette Altwegg

LAWN TENNIS

Australian Open (winners from Australia except as indicated)
1950 Frank Sedgman; Louise Brough (US)
1951 Dick Savitt (US); Nancye Wynne Bolton
1952 Ken McGregor; Thelma Long
1953 Ken Rosewall; Maureen Connolly (US)
1954 Mervyn Rose; Thelma Long
1955 Ken Rosewall; Beryl Penrose
1956 Lew Hoad; Mary Carter
1957 Ashley Cooper; Shirley Fry (US)
1958 Ashley Cooper; Angela Mortimer (GB)
1959 Alex Olmedo (Peru); Mary Carter-Reitano

French Open
1950 Budge Patty (US); Doris Hart (US)
1951 Jaroslav Drobny (Czech); Shirley Fry (US)
1952 Jaroslav Drobny (Czech); Doris Hart (US)
1953 Ken Rosewall (Aus); Maureen Connolly (US)
1954 Tony Trabert (GB); Maureen Connolly (US)
1955 Tony Trabert (GB); Angela Mortimer (GB)
1956 Lew Hoad (Aus); Althea Gibson (US)
1957 Sven Davidson (Swed); Shirley Bloomer (GB)
1958 Mervyn Rose (Aus); Zsuzsi Kormoczy (Hung)
1959 Nicola Pietrangeli (Ita); Christine Truman (GB)

All-England (Wimbledon) championships (winners from US except as indicated)
1950 Budge Patty; Louise Brough
1951 Dick Savitt ; Doris Hart
1952 Frank Sedgman (Aus); Maureen Connolly
1953 Vic Seixas; Maureen Connolly
1954 Jaroslav Drobny (Czech); Maureen Connolly
1955 Tony Trabert; Louise Brough
1956 Lew Hoad (Aus); Shirley Fry
1957 Lew Hoad (Aus); Althea Gibson
1958 Ashley Cooper (Aus); Althea Gibson
1959 Alex Olmedo (Peru); Maria Bueno (Braz)

US Open (winners from US except as indicated)
1950 Arthur Larsen; Margaret Du Pont
1951 Frank Sedgman (Aus); Maureen Connolly
1952 Frank Sedgman (Aus); Maureen Connolly
1953 Tony Trabert; Maureen Connolly
1954 Vic Seixas; Doris Hart
1955 Tony Trabert; Doris Hart
1956 Ken Rosewall (Aus); Shirley Fry
1957 Malcolm Anderson (Aus); Althea Gibson
1958 Ashley Cooper (Aus); Althea Gibson
1959 Neale Fraser (Aus); Maria Bueno (Braz)

MOTOR RACING

World championship
1950 Giuseppe Farina (Alfa Romeo)
1951 Juan Manuel Fangio (Alfa Romeo)
1952 Alberto Ascari (Ferrari)
1953 Alberto Ascari (Ferrari)
1954 Juan Manuel Fangio (Maserati/Mercedes)
1955 Juan Manuel Fangio (Mercedes-Benz)
1956 Juan Manuel Fangio (Lancia-Ferrari)
1957 Juan Manuel Fangio (Maserati)
1958 Mike Hawthorn (Ferrari)
1959 Jack Brabham (Cooper-Climax)

Constructors' championship
1958 Vanwall
1959 Cooper-Climax

Le Mans
1950 L. Rosier/C. Rosier (Talbot-Lago)
1951 P. D. Walker/P. N. Whitehead (Jaguar)
1952 H. Lang/F. Reiss (Mercedes-Benz)
1953 A. P. R. Rolt/J. D. Hamilton (Jaguar)
1954 J. F. Gonzalez/M. Trintignant (Ferrari)
1955 J. M. Hawthorn/I. Bueb (Jaguar)
1956 R. Flockhart/N. Sanderson (Jaguar)
1957 R. Flockhart/I. Bueb (Jaguar)
1958 P. Hill/O. Gendebien (Ferrari)
1959 R. Salvadori/C. Shelby (Aston Martin)

Indianapolis 500
1950 Johnnie Parsons
1951 Lee Wallard
1952 Troy Ruttman
1953 Bill Vukovich
1954 Bill Vukovich
1955 Bob Sweikert
1956 Pat Flaherty
1957 Sam Hanks
1958 Jimmy Bryan
1959 Rodger Ward

RUGBY LEAGUE

World Cup
1954 Great Britain
1957 Australia

Challenge Cup
1950 Warrington 19; Widnes 0
1951 Wigan 10; Barrow 0
1952 Workington Town 18; Featherstone 10
1953 Huddersfield 15; St Helens 10
1954 Warrington 8; Halifax 4 (in replay after 4–4 draw)
1955 Barrow 21; Workington 12
1956 St Helens 13; Halifax 2
1957 Leeds 9; Barrow 7
1958 Wigan 13; Workington 9
1959 Wigan 30; Hull 13

RUGBY UNION

Five Nations championship
1950 Wales (and Grand Slam)
1951 Ireland
1952 Wales (and Grand Slam)
1953 England
1954 England, France and Wales
1955 France and Wales
1956 Wales
1957 England (and Grand Slam)
1958 England
1959 France

SNOOKER

World championship (finalists from Britain except as indicated)
1950 Walter Donaldson 51; Fred Davis 46
1951 Fred Davis 58; Walter Donaldson 39
1952 Horace Lindrum (Aus) 94; Clark McConachy (NZ) 49

(Due to a disagreement, world snooker championship was suspended until 1964; in the interim players organised their own tournament, the Professional Match-Play.)

Professional Match-Play championship (finalists from Britain except as indicated)
1952 Fred Davis 38; Walter Donaldson 35
1953 Fred Davis 37; Walter Donaldson 34
1954 Fred Davis 39; Walter Donaldson 21
1955 Fred Davis 37; John Pulman 34
1956 Fred Davis 38; John Pulman 35
1957 John Pulman 39; Jackie Rea 34
(tournament ended)

SQUASH

British Open
1950 Hashim Khan (Pak); Janet Morgan (GB)
1951 Hashim Khan (Pak); Janet Morgan (GB)
1952 Hashim Khan (Pak); Janet Morgan (GB)
1953 Hashim Khan (Pak); Janet Morgan (GB)
1954 Hashim Khan (Pak); Janet Morgan (GB)
1955 Hashim Khan (Pak); Janet Morgan (GB)
1956 Roshan Khan (Pak); Janet Morgan (GB)
1957 Hashim Khan (Pak); Janet Morgan (GB)
1958 Azam Khan (Pak); Janet Morgan (GB)
1959 Azam Khan (Pak); Janet Morgan (GB)

SWIMMING

British and Irish Olympic gold medals
1956 100-m breaststroke Judy Grinham

YACHTING

America's Cup
1958 Columbia (US, skipper Briggs Cunningham)

Admiral's Cup
1957 Team: Great Britain
1959 Team: Great Britain

1960–1969

AMERICAN FOOTBALL

Super Bowl
1967 Green Bay Packers
1968 Green Bay Packers
1969 New York Jets

ATHLETICS

British and Irish Olympic gold medals
1960 50,000-m road walk Don Thompson
1964 800 m Ann Packer; long jump Mary Rand; 20,000-m road walk Ken Matthews; long jump Lynn Davies
1968 400-m hurdles David Hemery

BASEBALL

World Series
1960 Pittsburgh Pirates
1961 New York Yankees
1962 New York Yankees
1963 Los Angeles Dodgers
1964 St Louis Cardinals
1965 Los Angeles Dodgers
1966 Baltimore Orioles
1967 St Louis Cardinals
1968 Detroit Tigers
1969 New York Mets

BOXING

British and Irish world champions
1961 Middleweight, Terry Downes
1966 Flyweight (WBC), Walter McGowan
1968 Featherweight (WBC), Howard Winstone

CRICKET

County cricket champions
1960 Yorkshire
1961 Hampshire
1962 Yorkshire
1963 Yorkshire
1964 Worcestershire
1965 Worcestershire
1966 Yorkshire
1967 Yorkshire
1968 Yorkshire
1969 Glamorgan

Sunday League champions
1969 Lancashire

Gillette Cup
1963 Sussex bt Worcestershire by 14 runs
1964 Sussex bt Warwickshire by 8 wickets
1965 Yorkshire bt Surrey by 175 runs
1966 Warwickshire bt Worcestershire by 5 wickets
1967 Kent bt Somerset by 32 runs
1968 Warwickshire bt Sussex by 4 wickets
1969 Yorkshire bt Derbyshire by 69 runs

CYCLING

Tour de France
1960 Gastone Nencini (Ita)
1961 Jacques Anquetil (Fr)
1962 Jacques Anquetil (Fr)
1963 Jacques Anquetil (Fr)
1964 Jacques Anquetil (Fr)
1965 Felice Gimondi (Ita)
1966 Lucien Aimar (Fr)
1967 Roger Pingeon (Fr)
1968 Jan Janssen (NL)
1969 Eddy Merckx (Bel)

EQUESTRIANISM

World showjumping championship (men)
1960 Raimondo d'Inzeo (Ita)
1966 Pierre Jonqueres d'Oriola (Fr)

World showjumping championship (women)
1965 Marion Coakes (GB)

Badminton Horse Trials
1960 Bill Roycroft (Aus)
1961 Lawrence Morgan (Aus)
1962 Anneli Drummond-Hay (GB)
1963 Susan Fleet (GB)
1964 James Templer (GB)
1965 Eddie Boylan (Ire)
1966 Not held
1967 Celia Ross-Taylor (GB)
1968 Jane Bullen (GB)
1969 Richard Walker (GB)

FOOTBALL

World Cup
1962 Brazil 3; Czechoslovakia 1
1966 England 4; West Germany 2, after extra time

European championship
1960 USSR 2; Yugoslavia 1, after extra time
1964 Spain 2; USSR 1
1968 Italy 2; Yugoslavia 0 (After 1–1 draw)

European Champions Cup
1960 Real Madrid 7; Eintracht Frankfurt 3
1961 Benfica 3; Barcelona 2
1962 Benfica 5; Real Madrid 3
1963 AC Milan 2; Benfica 1
1964 Inter-Milan 3; Real Madrid 1
1965 Inter-Milan 1; Benfica 0
1966 Real Madrid 2; Partizan Belgrade 1
1967 Celtic 2; Inter-Milan 1
1968 Manchester United 4; Benfica 1, after extra time
1969 AC Milan 4; Ajax 1

European Cup Winners' Cup
1961 Fiorentina bt Glasgow Rangers 2–0, 2–1
1962 Atletico Madrid 3; Fiorentina 0 (After 1–1 draw)
1963 Tottenham Hotspur 5; Atletico Madrid 1
1964 Sporting Lisbon 1; MTK Budapest 0 (After 3–3 draw)
1965 West Ham United 2; Munich 1860 0
1966 Borussia Dortmund 2; Liverpool 1, after extra time
1967 Bayern Munich 1; Glasgow Rangers 0, after extra time
1968 AC Milan 2; SV Hamburg 0
1969 Slovan Bratislava 3; Barcelona 2

Inter-Cities Fairs Cup
1960 Barcelona bt Birmingham City 0–0, 4–1
1961 AS Roma bt Birmingham City 2–2, 2–0
1962 Valencia bt Barcelona 6–2, 1–1
1963 Valencia bt Dynamo Zagreb 2–1, 2–0
1964 Real Zaragoza 2; Valencia 1
1965 Ferencvaros 1; Juventus 0
1966 Barcelona bt Real Zaragoza 0–1, 4–2
1967 Dynamo Zagreb bt Leeds United 2–0, 0–0
1968 Leeds United bt Ferencvaros 1–0, 0–0
1969 Newcastle United bt Ujpest Dozsa 3–0, 3–2

Football League
1960 Burnley
1961 Tottenham Hotspur
1962 Ipswich Town
1963 Everton
1964 Liverpool
1965 Manchester United
1966 Liverpool
1967 Manchester United
1968 Manchester City
1969 Leeds United

FA Cup
1960 Wolverhampton Wanderers 3; Blackburn Rovers 0
1961 Tottenham Hotspur 2; Leicester City 0
1962 Tottenham Hotspur 3; Burnley 1
1963 Manchester United 3; Leicester City 1

1964 West Ham United 3; Preston North End 2
1965 Liverpool 2; Leeds United 1, after extra time
1966 Everton 3; Sheffield Wednesday 2
1967 Tottenham Hotspur 2; Chelsea 1
1968 West Bromwich Albion 1; Everton 0, after extra time
1969 Manchester City 1; Leicester City 0

League Cup
1961 Aston Villa bt Rotherham United 0–2, 3–0
1962 Norwich City bt Rochdale 3–0, 1–0
1963 Birmingham City bt Aston Villa 3–1, 0–0
1964 Leicester City bt Stoke City 1–1, 3–2
1965 Chelsea bt Leicester City 3–2, 0–0
1966 West Bromwich Albion bt West Ham United 1–2, 4–1
1967 Queens Park Rangers 3; West Bromwich Albion 2
1968 Leeds United 1; Arsenal 0
1969 Swindon Town 3; Arsenal 1, after extra time

Scottish League
1960 Hearts
1961 Rangers
1962 Dundee
1963 Rangers
1964 Rangers
1965 Kilmarnock
1966 Celtic
1967 Celtic
1968 Celtic
1969 Celtic

Scottish Cup
1960 Rangers 2; Kilmarnock 0
1961 Dunfermline Athletic 2; Celtic 0 (After 0–0 draw)
1962 Rangers 2; St Mirren 0
1963 Rangers 3; Celtic 0 (After 1–1 draw)
1964 Rangers 3; Dundee 1
1965 Celtic 3; Dunfermline Athletic 2
1966 Rangers 1; Celtic 0 (After 0–0 draw)
1967 Celtic 2; Aberdeen 0
1968 Dunfermline Athletic 3; Hearts 1
1969 Celtic 4; Rangers 0

Scottish League Cup
1960 Hearts 2; Third Lanark 1
1961 Rangers 2; Kilmarnock 0
1962 Rangers 3; Hearts 1 (in replay after 1–1 draw)
1963 Hearts 1; Kilmarnock 0

1964 Rangers 5; Morton 0
1965 Rangers 2; Celtic 1
1966 Celtic 2; Rangers 1
1967 Celtic 1; Rangers 0
1968 Celtic 5; Dundee 3
1969 Celtic 6; Hibernian 2

GOLF

Ryder Cup
1961 United States 14½; Great Britain & Ireland 9½
1963 United States 23; Great Britain & Ireland 9
1965 United States 19½; Great Britain & Ireland 12½
1967 United States 23½; Great Britain & Ireland 8½
1969 Drawn 16–16

US Masters (winners from US except as indicated)
1960 Arnold Palmer
1961 Gary Player (SA)
1962 Arnold Palmer
1963 Jack Nicklaus
1964 Arnold Palmer
1965 Jack Nicklaus
1966 Jack Nicklaus
1967 Gay Brewer
1968 Bob Goalby
1969 George Archer

US Open (winners from US except as indicated)
1960 Arnold Palmer
1961 Gene Littler
1962 Jack Nicklaus
1963 Julius Boros
1964 Ken Venturi
1965 Gary Player (SA)
1966 Billy Casper
1967 Jack Nicklaus
1968 Lee Travino
1969 Orville Moody

US PGA (winners from US except as indicated)
1960 Jay Hebert
1961 Jerry Barber
1962 Gary Player (SA)
1963 Jack Nicklaus
1964 Bobby Nichols
1965 Dave Marr
1966 Al Geiberger
1967 Don January
1968 Julius Boros
1969 Ray Floyd

Walker Cup
1961 United States 11; Great Britain & Ireland 1
1963 United States 14; Great Britain & Ireland 8
1965 Drawn 12–12
1967 United States 15; Great Britain & Ireland 9
1969 United States 13; Great Britain & Ireland 11

British Open
1960 Kel Nagle (Aus)
1961 Arnold Palmer (US)
1962 Arnold Palmer (US)
1963 Bob Charles (NZ)
1964 Tony Lema (US)
1965 Peter Thomson (Aus)
1966 Jack Nicklaus(US)
1967 Roberto de Vicenzo (Arg)
1968 Gary Player (SA)
1969 Tony Jacklin (GB)

SNOOKER

World professional championship (*finalists from Britain except as indicated*) *Challenge matches*
1964 John Pulman 19; Fred Davis 16
1964 John Pulman 40; Rex Williams 33
1965 John Pulman 37; Fred Davis 36
1965 John Pulman 25; Rex Williams 22
1965 John Pulman 39; Freddie van Rensburg (SA) 12
1966 John Pulman 5; Fred Davis 2
1968 John Pulman 39; Eddie Charlton (Aus) 34
Knock-out
1969 John Spencer 37; Gary Owen 34

HORSE RACING

2,000 Guineas
1960 Martial
1961 Rockavon
1962 Privy Councillor
1963 Only for Life
1964 Baldric II
1965 Niksar
1966 Kashmir II
1967 Royal Palace
1968 Sir Ivor
1969 Right Tack

Derby
1960 St Paddy
1961 Psidium
1962 Larkspur
1963 Relko
1964 Santa Claus
1965 Sea Bird II
1966 Charlottown
1967 Royal Palace
1968 Sir Ivor
1969 Blakeney

St Leger
1960 St Paddy
1961 Aurelius
1962 Hethersett
1963 Ragusa
1964 Indiana
1965 Provoke
1966 Sodium
1967 Ribocco
1968 Ribero
1969 Intermezzo

Grand National
1960 Merryman II
1961 Nicolaus Silver
1962 Kilmore
1963 Ayala
1964 Team Spirit
1965 Jay Trump
1966 Anglo
1967 Foinavon
1968 Red Alligator
1969 Highland Wedding

Prix de l'Arc de Triomphe
1960 Pussaint Chef
1961 Molvedo
1962 Soltikoff
1963 Exbury
1964 Prince Royal II
1965 Sea Bird II

1966 Bon Mot
1967 Topyo
1968 Vaguely Noble
1969 Levmoss

LAWN TENNIS

Australian Open (*winners from Australia except as indicated*)
1960 Rod Laver; Margaret Smith
1961 Roy Emerson; Margaret Smith
1962 Rod Laver; Margaret Smith
1963 Roy Emerson; Margaret Smith
1964 Roy Emerson; Margaret Smith
1965 Roy Emerson; Margaret Smith
1966 Roy Emerson; Margaret Smith
1967 Roy Emerson; Nancy Richey (US)
1968 Bill Bowrey; Billie Jean King (US)
1969 Rod Laver; Margaret Smith Court

French Open
1960 Nicola Pietrangeli (Ita); Darlene Hard (US)
1961 Manuel Santana (Sp); Ann Haydon (GB)
1962 Rod Laver (Aus); Margaret Smith (Aus)
1963 Roy Emerson (Aus); Lesley Turner (Aus)
1964 Manuel Santana (Sp); Margaret Smith (Aus)
1965 Fred Stolle (Aus); Lesley Turner (Aus)
1966 Tony Roche (Aus); Ann Haydon Jones (GB)
1967 Roy Emerson (Aus); Francois Durr (Fr)
1968 Ken Rosewall (Aus); Nancy Richey (US)
1969 Rod Laver (Aus); Margaret Smith Court (Aus)

All-England (Wimbledon) championships
1960 Neale Fraser (Aus); Maria Bueno (Braz)
1961 Rod Laver (Aus); Angela Mortimer (GB)
1962 Rod Laver (Aus); Karen Susman (US)
1963 Chuck McKinley (US); Margaret Smith (Aus)
1964 Roy Emerson (Aus); Maria Bueno (Braz)
1965 Roy Emerson (Aus); Margaret Smith (Aus)
1966 Manuel Santana (Sp); Billie Jean King (US)

1967 John Newcombe (Aus); Billie Jean King (US)
1968 Rod Laver (Aus); Billie Jean King (US)
1969 Rod Laver (Aus); Ann Jones (GB)

US Open
1960 Neale Fraser (Aus); Darlene Hard (US)
1961 Roy Emerson (Aus); Darlene Hard (US)
1962 Rod Laver (Aus); Margaret Smith (Aus)
1963 Raphael Osuna (Mex); Maria Bueno (Braz)
1964 Roy Emerson (Aus); Maria Bueno (Braz)
1965 Manuel Santana (Sp); Margaret Smith (Aus)
1966 Fred Stolle (Aus); Maria Bueno (Braz)
1967 John Newcombe (Aus); Billie Jean King (US)
1968 (*Amateur*) Arthur Ashe (US); Margaret Smith Court (Aus)
1968 (*Open*) Arthur Ashe (US); Virginia Wade (GB)
1969 (*Amateur*) Stan Smith (US); Margaret Court (Aus)
1969 (*Open*) Rod Laver (Aus); Margaret Court (Aus)

MOTOR RACING

World championship
1960 Jack Brabham (Cooper-Climax)
1961 Phil Hill (Ferrari)
1962 Graham Hill (BRM)
1963 Jim Clark (Lotus-Climax)
1964 John Surtees (Ferrari)
1965 Jim Clark (Lotus-Climax)
1966 Jack Brabham (Brabham-Repco)
1967 Denny Hulme (Brabham-Repco)
1968 Graham Hill (Lotus-Ford)
1969 Jackie Stewart (Matra-Ford)

Constructors' championship
1960 Cooper-Climax
1961 Ferrari
1962 BRM
1963 Lotus-Climax
1964 Ferrari
1965 Lotus-Climax
1966 Brabham-Repco
1967 Brabham-Repco
1968 Lotus-Ford
1969 Matra-Ford

Le Mans
1960 P. Frère/O. Gendebien (Ferrari)
1961 P. Hill/O. Gendebien (Ferrari)
1962 P. Hill/O. Gendebien (Ferrari)
1963 L. Scarfiotti/L. Bandini (Ferrari)
1964 J. Guichet/N. Vaccarella (Ferrari)
1965 M. Gregory/J. Rindt (Ferrari)
1966 B. McLaren/C. Amon (Ford Mk II)
1967 A. J. Foyt/D. Gurney (Ford Mk IV)
1968 P. Rodriguez/L. Bianchi (Ford GT 40)
1969 J. Ickx/J. Oliver (Ford GT 40)

Indianapolis 500
1960 Jim Rathmann
1961 A. J. Foyt Jr
1962 Rodger Ward
1963 Parnelli Jones
1964 A. J. Foyt Jr
1965 Jim Clark
1966 Graham Hill
1967 A. J. Foyt Jr
1968 Bobby Unser
1969 Mario Andretti

RUGBY LEAGUE

World Cup
1960 Great Britain
1968 Australia

Challenge Cup
1960 Wakefield Trinity 38; Hull 5
1961 St Helens 12; Wigan 6
1962 Wakefield Trinity 12; Huddersfield 6
1963 Wakefield Trintiy 25; Wigan 10
1964 Widnes 13; Hull Kingston Rovers 5
1965 Wigan 20; Hunslet 16
1966 St Helens 21; Wigan 2
1967 Featherstone Rovers 17; Barrow 12
1968 Leeds 11; Wakefield 10
1969 Castleford 11; Salford 6

RUGBY UNION

Five Nations championship
1960 England and France
1961 France
1962 France
1963 England
1964 Scotland and Wales
1965 Wales
1966 Wales
1967 France
1968 France (and Grand Slam)
1969 Wales

SQUASH

British Open
1960 Azam Khan (Pak); Sheila Macintosh (GB)
1961 Azam Khan (Pak); Fran Marshall (GB)
1962 Mohibullah Khan (Pak); Heather Blundell (Aus)
1963 Abdelfattah Abou Taleb (Egypt); Heather Blundell (Aus)
1964 Abdelfattah Abou Taleb (Egypt); Heather Blundell (Aus)
1965 Abdelfattah Abou Taleb (Egypt); Heather Blundell (Aus)
1966 Abdelfattah Abou Taleb (Egypt); Heather Blundell McKay (Aus)
1967 Jonah Barrington (GB); Heather McKay (Aus)
1968 Jonah Barrington (GB); Heather McKay (Aus)
1969 Geoff Hunt (Aus); Heather McKay (Aus)

SWIMMING

British and Irish Olympic gold medals
1960 200-m Breaststroke Anita Lonsborough

YACHTING

America's Cup
1962 *Weatherly* (US, skipper Emil Mosbacher Jr)
1964 *Constellation* (US, skipper Bob Bavier Jr)
1967 *Intrepid* (US, skipper Emil Mosbacher Jr)

Admiral's Cup
1961 Team: United States
1963 Team: Great Britain
1965 Team: Great Britain
1967 Team: Australia
1969 Team: United States

1970–1979

AMERICAN FOOTBALL

Super Bowl
1970 Kansas City Chiefs
1971 Baltimore Colts
1972 Dallas Cowboys
1973 Miami Dolphins
1974 Miami Dolphins
1975 Pittsburgh Steelers
1976 Pittsburgh Steelers
1977 Oakland Raiders
1978 Dallas Cowboys
1979 Pittsburgh Steelers

ATHLETICS

British and Irish Olympic gold medals
1972 Pentathlon Mary Peters

BASEBALL

World Series
1970 Baltimore Orioles
1971 Pittsburgh Pirates
1972 Oakland Athletics
1973 Oakland Athletics
1974 Oakland Athletics
1975 Cincinnati Reds
1976 Cincinnati Reds
1977 New York Yankees
1978 New York Yankees
1979 Pittsburgh Pirates

BOXING

British and Irish world champions
1970 Lightweight (WBA), Ken Buchanan
1974 Light-heavyweight (WBC), John Conteh
1975 Welterweight (WBC), John H Stracey
1979 Junior middleweight (WBC), Maurice Hope
1979 Lightweight (WBC), Jim Watt

CRICKET

World Cup
1975 West Indies bt Australia by 17 runs
1979 West Indies bt England by 92 runs

County cricket champions
1970 Kent
1971 Surrey
1972 Warwickshire
1973 Hampshire
1974 Worcestershire
1975 Leicestershire
1976 Middlesex
1977 Kent and Middlesex
1978 Kent
1979 Essex

Sunday League champions
1970 Lancashire
1971 Worcestershire
1972 Kent
1973 Kent
1974 Leicestershire
1975 Hampshire
1976 Kent
1977 Leicestershire
1978 Hampshire
1979 Somerset

Gillette Cup
1970 Lancashire bt Sussex by 6 wickets
1971 Lancashire bt Kent by 24 runs
1972 Lancashire bt Warwickshire by 4 wickets
1973 Gloucestershire bt Sussex by 40 runs
1974 Kent bt Lancashire by 4 wickets
1975 Lancashire bt Middlesex by 7 wickets
1976 Northamptonshire bt Lancashire by 4 wickets
1977 Middlesex bt Glamorgan by 5 wickets
1978 Sussex bt Somerset by 5 wickets
1979 Somerset bt Northamptonshire by 45 runs

Benson & Hedges Cup
1972 Leicestershire bt Yorkshire by 5 wickets
1973 Kent bt Worcestershire by 39 runs
1974 Surrey bt Leicestershire by 27 runs
1975 Leicestershire bt Middlesex by 5 wickets
1976 Kent bt Worcestershire by 43 runs
1977 Gloucestershire bt Kent by 64 runs
1978 Kent bt Derbyshire by 6 wickets
1979 Essex bt Surrey by 35 runs

CYCLING

Tour de France
1970 Eddy Merckx (Bel)
1971 Eddy Merckx (Bel)
1972 Eddy Merckx (Bel)
1973 Luis Ocaña (Sp)
1974 Eddy Merckx (Bel)
1975 Bernard Thévenet (Fr)
1976 Lucian Van Impe (Bel)
1977 Bernard Thévenet (Fr)
1978 Bernard Hinault (Fr)
1979 Bernard Hinault (Fr)

EQUESTRIANISM

World showjumping championship (men)
1970 David Broome (GB)
1974 Hartwig Steenken (W. Ger)
1978 Gerd Wilffang (W. Ger)

World showjumping championship (women)
1970 Janou Lefebvre (Fr)
1974 Janou Lefebvre Tissot (Fr)

World three-day event championship
1970 Mary Gordon-Watson (GB)
1974 Bruce Davidson (US)
1978 Bruce Davidson (US)

Badminton Horse Trials
1970 Richard Meade (GB)
1971 Mark Phillips (GB)
1972 Mark Phillips (GB)
1973 Lucinda Prior-Palmer (GB)
1974 Mark Phillips (GB)
1975 Abandoned
1976 Lucinda Prior-Palmer (GB)
1977 Lucinda Prior-Palmer (GB)
1978 Jane Bullen Holderness-Roddam (GB)
1979 Lucinda Prior-Palmer (GB)

FOOTBALL

World Cup
1970 Brazil 4; Italy 1
1974 West Germany 2; Holland 1
1978 Argentina 3; Holland 1, after extra time

European championship
1972 West Germany 3; USSR 0
1976 Czechoslovakia 2; West Germany 2 (Czechoslovakia won 5–3 on penalties)

European Champions Cup
1970 Feyenoord 2; Celtic 1, after extra time
1971 Ajax 2; Panathinaikos 0
1972 Ajax 2; Inter-Milan 0
1973 Ajax 1; Juventus 0
1974 Bayern Munich 4; Atletico Madrid 0 (in replay after 1–1 draw)
1975 Bayern Munich 2; Leeds United 0
1976 Bayern Munich 1; St Etienne 0
1977 Liverpool 3; Borussia Moenchengladbach 1
1978 Liverpool 1; FC Bruges 0
1979 Nottingham Forest 1; Malmo 0

European Cup Winners' Cup
1970 Manchester City 2; Gornik Zabrze 1
1971 Chelsea 2 ;Real Madrid 1, after extra time (in replay after 1–1 draw)
1972 Glasgow Rangers 3; Moscow Dynamo 2
1973 AC Milan 1; Leeds United 0
1974 Magdeburg 2; AC Milan 0
1975 Dynamo Kiev 3; Ferencvaros 0
1976 Anderlecht 4; West Ham United 2
1977 SV Hamburg 2; Anderlecht 0
1978 Anderlecht 4; Austria/WAC 0
1979 Barcelona 4; Fortuna Dusseldorf 3, after extra time

Inter-Cities Fairs Cup
1970 Arsenal bt Anderlecht 1–3, 3–0
1971 Leeds United bt Juventus 2–2, 1–1 (Leeds won on away goals)

UEFA Cup
1972 Tottenham Hotspur bt Wolverhampton Wanderers 2–1, 1–1
1973 Liverpool bt Borussia Moenchengladbach 3–0, 0–2
1974 Feyenoord bt Tottenham Hotspur 2–2, 2–0
1975 Borussia Moenchengladbach bt Twente Enschede 0–0, 5–1
1976 Liverpool bt FC Bruges 3–2, 1–1
1977 Juventus bt Athletic Bilbao 1–0, 1–2 (Juventus won on away goals)
1978 PSV Eindhoven bt Bastia 0–0, 3–0
1979 Borussia Moenchengladbach bt Red Star Belgrade 1–1, 1–0

Football League
1970 Everton
1971 Arsenal
1972 Derby County
1973 Liverpool
1974 Leeds United
1975 Derby County
1976 Liverpool
1977 LIverpool
1978 Nottingham Forest
1979 Liverpool

FA Cup
1970 Chelsea 2; Leeds United 1, after extra time (in replay after 2–2 draw)
1971 Arsenal 2; Liverpool 1, after extra time
1972 Leeds United 1; Arsenal 0
1973 Sunderland 1; Leeds United 0
1974 Liverpool 3; Newcastle United 0
1975 West Ham United 2; Fulham 0
1976 Southampton 1; Manchester United 0
1977 Manchester United 2; Liverpool 1
1978 Ipswich Town 1; Arsenal 0
1979 Arsenal 3; Manchester United 2

League Cup

1970 Manchester City 2; West Bromwich Albion 1, after extra time
1971 Tottenham Hotspur 2; Aston Villa 0
1972 Stoke City 2; Chelsea 1
1973 Tottenham Hotspur 1; Norwich City 0
1974 Wolverhampton Wanderers 2; Manchester City 1
1975 Aston Villa 1; Norwich City 0
1976 Manchester City 2; Newcastle United 1
1977 Aston Villa 3; Everton 2, after extra time (in replay after 0–0, 1–1 draws)
1978 Nottingham Forest 1; Liverpool 0 (in replay after 0–0 draw)
1979 Nottingham Forest 3; Southampton 2

Scottish League

1970 Celtic
1971 Celtic
1972 Celtic
1973 Celtic
1974 Celtic
1975 Rangers

Scottish Premier League
1976 Rangers
1977 Celtic
1978 Rangers
1979 Celtic

Scottish Cup

1970 Aberdeen 3; Celtic 1
1971 Celtic 2; Rangers 1 (in replay after 1–1 draw)
1972 Celtic 6; Hibernian 1
1973 Rangers 3; Celtic 2
1974 Celtic 3; Dundee United 0
1975 Celtic 3; Airdrieonians 1
1976 Rangers 3; Hearts 1
1977 Celtic 1; Rangers 0
1978 Rangers 2; Aberdeen 1
1979 Rangers 3; Hibernian 2 (in replay after 0–0, 0–0 draws)

Scottish League Cup

1970 Celtic 1; St Johnstone 0
1971 Rangers 1; Celtic 0
1972 Partick Thistle 4; Celtic 1
1973 Hibernian 2; Celtic 1
1974 Dundee United 1; Celtic 0
1975 Celtic 6; Hibernian 3
1976 Rangers 1; Celtic 0
1977 Aberdeen 2; Celtic 1
1978 Rangers 2; Celtic 1
1979 Rangers 2; Aberdeen 1

GOLF

Ryder Cup
1971 United States 18½; Great Britain & Ireland 13½
1973 United States 19; Great Britain & Ireland 13
1975 United States 21; Great Britain & Ireland 11
1977 United States 12½; Great Britain & Ireland 7½
(contested between United States and Europe from 1979)
1979 United States 17; Europe 11

US Masters *(winners from US except as indicated)*
1970 Billy Casper
1971 Charles Coody
1972 Jack Nicklaus
1973 Tommy Aaron
1974 Gary Player (SA)
1975 Jack Nicklaus
1976 Ray Floyd
1977 Tom Watson
1978 Gary Player (SA)
1979 Fuzzy Zoeller

US Open *(winners from US except as indicated)*
1970 Tony Jacklin (GB)
1971 Lee Trevino
1972 Jack Nicklaus
1973 Johnny Miller
1974 Hale Irwin
1975 Lou Graham
1976 Jerry Pate
1977 Hubert Green
1978 Andy North
1979 Hale Irwin

US PGA *(winners from US except as indicated)*
1970 Dave Stockton
1971 Jack Nicklaus
1972 Gary Player (SA)
1973 Jack Nicklaus
1974 Lee Trevino
1975 Jack Nicklaus
1976 Dave Stockton
1977 Lanny Wadkins
1978 John Mahaffey
1979 David Graham (Aus)

Walker Cup
1971 Great Britain & Ireland 13; United States 11
1973 United States 14; Great Britain & Ireland 10
1975 United States 15½; Great Britain & Ireland 8½
1977 United States 16; Great Britain & Ireland 8
1979 United States 15½; Great Britain & Ireland 8½

British Open *(winners from US except as indicated)*

1970 Jack Nicklaus
1971 Lee Trevino
1972 Lee Trevino
1973 Tom Weiskopf
1974 Gary Player (SA)
1975 Tom Watson
1976 Johnny Miller
1977 Tom Watson
1978 Jack Nicklaus
1979 Seve Ballesteros (Sp)

HORSE RACING

2,000 Guineas
1970 Nijinsky
1971 Brigadier Gerard
1972 High Top
1973 Mon Fils
1974 Nonoalco
1975 Bolkonski
1976 Wollow
1977 Nebbiolo
1978 Roland Gardens
1979 Tap On Wood

Derby
1970 Nijinsky
1971 Mill Reef
1972 Roberto
1973 Morston
1974 Snow Knight
1975 Grundy
1976 Empery
1977 The Minstrel
1978 Shirley Heights
1979 Troy

St Leger
1970 Nijinsky
1971 Athens Wood
1972 Boucher
1973 Peleid
1974 Bustino
1975 Bruni
1976 Crow
1977 Dunfermline
1978 Julio Mariner
1979 Son of Love

Grand National
1970 Gay Trip
1971 Specify
1972 Well To Do
1973 Red Rum
1974 Red Rum
1975 L'Escargot
1976 Rag Trade
1977 Red Rum
1978 Lucius
1979 Rubstic

Prix de l'Arc de Triomphe

1970 Sassafras
1971 Mill Reef
1972 San San
1973 Rheingold
1974 Allez France
1975 Star Appeal
1976 Ivanjica
1977 Alleged
1978 Alleged
1979 Three Troikas

ICE SKATING

British and Irish Olympic gold medals
1976 Figure skating, John Curry

LAWN TENNIS

Australian Open
1970 Arthur Ashe (US); Margaret Court (Aus)
1971 Ken Rosewall (Aus); Margaret Court (Aus)
1972 Ken Rosewall (Aus); Virginia Wade (GB)
1973 John Newcombe (Aus); Margaret Court (Aus)
1974 Jimmy Connors (US); Evonne Goolagong (Aus)
1975 John Newcombe (Aus); Evonne Goolagong (Aus)
1976 Mark Edmondson (Aus); Evonne Goolagong Cawley (Aus)
1977 (January) Roscoe Tanner (US); Kerry Reid (Aus)
(tournament moved to December from January)
1977 (December) Vitas Gerulaitis (US); Evonne Cawley (Aus)
1978 Guillermo Vilas (Arg); Chris O'Neill (Aus)
1979 Guillermo Vilas (Arg); Barbara Jordan (US)

French Open
1970 Jan Kodes (Czech); Margaret Court (Aus)
1971 Jan Kodes (Czech); Evonne Goolagong (Aus)
1972 Andres Gimeno (Sp); Billie Jean King (US)
1973 Ilie Nastase (Rom); Margaret Court (Aus)
1974 Björn Borg (Swe); Chris Evert (US)
1975 Björn Borg (Swe); Chris Evert (US)
1976 Adriano Panatta (Ita); Sue Barker (GB)
1977 Guillermo Vilas (Arg); Mima Jausovec (Yug)
1978 Björn Borg (Swe); Virginia Ruzici (Rom)
1979 Björn Borg (Swe); Chris Evert Lloyd (US)

All-England (Wimbledon) championships

1970 John Newcombe (Aus); Margaret Court (Aus)
1971 John Newcombe (Aus); Evonne Goolagong (Aus)
1972 Stan Smith (US); Billie Jean King (US)
1973 Jan Kodes (Czech); Billie Jean King (US)
1974 Jimmy Connors (US); Chris Evert (US)
1975 Arthur Ashe (US); Billie Jean King (US)
1976 Björn Borg (Swe); Chris Evert (US)
1977 Björn Borg (Swe); Virginia Wade (GB)
1978 Björn Borg (Swe); Martina Navratilova (Czech)
1979 Björn Borg (Swe); Martina Navratilova (US)

US Open

1970 Ken Rosewall (Aus); Margaret Court (Aus)
1971 Stan Smith (US); Billie Jean King (US)
1972 Ilie Nastase (Rom); Billie Jean King (US)
1973 John Newcombe (Aus); Margaret Court (Aus)
1974 Jimmy Connors (US); Billie Jean King (US)
1975 Manuel Orantes (Sp); Chris Evert (US)
1976 Jimmy Connors (US); Chris Evert (US)
1977 Guillermo Vilas (Arg); Chris Evert (US)
1978 Jimmy Connors (US); Chris Evert (US)
1979 John McEnroe (US); Tracy Austin (US)

MOTOR RACING

World championship
1970 Jochen Rindt (Lotus-Ford)
1971 Jackie Stewart (Tyrrell-Ford)
1972 Emerson Fittipaldi (Lotus-Ford)
1973 Jackie Stewart (Tyrrell-Ford)
1974 Emerson Fittipaldi (McLaren-Ford)
1975 Niki Lauda (Ferrari)
1976 James Hunt (McLaren-Ford)
1977 Niki Lauda (Ferrari)
1978 Mario Andretti (Lotus-Ford)
1979 Jody Scheckter (Ferrari)

Constructors' championship
1970 Lotus-Ford
1971 Tyrrell-Ford
1972 Lotus-Ford
1973 Lotus-Ford
1974 McLaren-Ford
1975 Ferrari
1976 Ferrari
1977 Ferrari
1978 Lotus-Ford
1979 Ferrari

Le Mans
1970 R. Attwood/H. Hermann (Porsche)
1971 G. van Lennep/H. Marko (Porsche)
1972 G. Hill/H. Pescarolo (Matra-Simca)
1973 G. Larrousse/H. Pescarolo (Matra-Simca)
1974 G. Larrousse/H. Pescarolo (Matra-Simca)
1975 D. Bell/J. Ickx (Gulf Mirage-Ford)
1976 J. Ickx/G. van Lennep (Porsche)
1977 J. Ickx/J. Barth/H. Haywood (Porsche)
1978 J-P. Jaussaud/D. Pironi (Renault-Alpine)
1979 K. Ludwig/D. Whittington/B. Whittington (Porsche)

Indianapolis 500
1970 Al Unser
1971 Al Unser
1972 Mark Donohue
1973 Gordon Johncock
1974 Johnny Rutherford
1975 Bobby Unser
1976 Johnny Rutherford
1977 A. J. Foyt Jr.
1978 Al Unser
1979 Rick Mears

RUGBY LEAGUE

League champions
1974 Salford
1975 St Helens
1976 Salford
1977 Featherstone Rovers
1978 Widnes
1979 Hull Kingston Rovers

Premiership Trophy
1975 Leeds
1976 St Helens
1977 St Helens
1978 Bradford Northern
1979 Leeds

Challenge Cup
1970 Castleford 7; Wigan 2
1971 Leigh 24; Leeds 7
1972 St Helens 16; Leeds 13
1973 Featherstone Rovers 33; Bradford 14
1974 Warrington 24; Featherstone 9
1975 Widnes 14; Warrington 7
1976 St Helens 20; Widnes 5
1977 Leeds 16; Widnes 7
1978 Leeds 14; St Helens 12
1979 Widnes 12; Wakefield 3

RUGBY UNION

Five Nations championship
1970 Wales and France
1971 Wales (and Grand Slam)
1972 Tournament not completed
1973 Five-way tie
1974 Ireland
1975 Wales
1976 Wales (and Grand Slam)
1977 France (and Grand Slam)
1978 Wales (and Grand Slam)
1979 Wales

Scottish League champions
1974 Hawick
1975 Hawick
1976 Hawick
1977 Hawick
1978 Hawick
1979 Heriots FP

Pilkington Cup
1972 Gloucester 17; Moseley 6
1973 Coventry 27; Bristol 15
1974 Coventry 26; London Scottish 6
1975 Bedford 28; Rosslyn Park 12
1976 Gosforth 23; Rosslyn Park 14
1977 Gosforth 27 ;Waterloo 11
1978 Gloucester 6; Leicester 3
1979 Leicester 15; Moseley 12

SWALEC Cup
1972 Neath 15; Llanelli 9
1973 Llanelli 30; Cardiff 7
1974 Llanelli 12; Aberavon 10
1975 Llanelli 15; Aberavon 6
1976 Llanelli 15; Swansea 4
1977 Newport 16; Cardiff 15
1978 Swansea 13; Newport 9
1979 Bridgend 18; Pontypridd 12

SNOOKER

World professional championships *(finalists from Britain except as indicated)*
Challenge matches
1970 Ray Reardon 37; John Pulman 33
1971 John Spencer 37; Warren Simpson (Aus) 29
1972 Alex Higgins 37; John Spencer 32
1973 Ray Reardon 38; Eddie Charlton (Aus) 32
1974 Ray Reardon 22; Graham Miles 12
1975 Ray Reardon 31; Eddie Charlton (Aus) 30
1976 Ray Reardon 27; Alex Higgins 16
1977 John Spencer 25; Cliff Thorburn (Can) 21
1978 Ray Reardon 25; Perrie Mans (SA) 18
1979 Terry Griffiths 24; Dennis Taylor 16

Women's world championship
1976 Vera Selby

SQUASH

World Open
1975 Geoff Hunt (Aus)
1976 Geoff Hunt (Aus); Heather McKay (Aus)
1977 Geoff Hunt (Aus)
1979 Geoff Hunt (Aus); Heather McKay (Aus)

British Open
1970 Jonah Barrington (GB); Heather McKay (Aus)
1971 Jonah Barrington (GB); Heather McKay (Aus)
1972 Jonah Barrington (GB); Heather McKay (Aus)
1973 Jonah Barrington (GB); Heather McKay (Aus)
1974 Geoff Hunt (Aus); Heather McKay (Aus)
1975 Qamar Zaman (Pak); Heather McKay (Aus)
1976 Geoff Hunt (Aus); Heather McKay (Aus)
1977 Geoff Hunt (Aus); Heather McKay (Aus)
1978 Geoff Hunt (Aus); Susan Newman (Aus)
1979 Geoff Hunt (Aus); Barbara Wall (Aus)

SWIMMING

British and Irish Olympic gold medals
1976 200-m Breaststroke David Wilkie

YACHTING

America's Cup
1970 *Intrepid* (US, skipper Bill Ficker)
1974 *Courageous* (US, skipper Ted Hood)
1977 *Courageous* (US, skipper Ted Turner)

Admiral's Cup
1971 Team: Britain
1973 Team: West Germany
1975 Team: Britain
1977 Team: Britain
1979 Team: Australia

AMERICAN FOOTBALL

Super Bowl
1980 Pittsburgh Steelers
1981 Oakland Raiders
1982 San Francisco 49-ers
1983 Washington Redskins
1984 LA Raiders
1985 San Francisco 49-ers
1986 Chicago Bears
1987 New York Giants
1988 Washington Redskins
1989 San Francisco 49-ers

ATHLETICS

British and Irish Olympic gold medals
1980 100 m Allan Wells; 800 m Steve Ovett; 1500 m Sebastian Coe; decathlon Daley Thompson
1984 Javelin Tessa Sanderson; 1500 m Sebastian Coe; decathlon Daley Thompson

BASEBALL

World Series
1980 Philadelphia Phillies
1981 Los Angeles Dodgers
1982 St Louis Cardinals
1983 Baltimore Orioles
1984 Detroit Tigers
1985 Kansas City Royals
1986 New York Mets
1987 Minnesota Twins
1988 Los Angeles Dodgers
1989 Oakland Athletics

BOXING

British and Irish world champions
1980 Middleweight, Alan Minter
1983 Flyweight (WBC), Charlie Magri
1985 Featherweight (WBA), Barry McGuigan (N. Ire)
1986 Welterweight, Lloyd Honeyghan; light-heavyweight (WBC), Dennis Andries
1987 Welterweight (WBC & IBF), Lloyd Honeyghan; light-welterweight (IBF), Terry Marsh
1988 Welterweight (WBC), Lloyd Honeyghan; flyweight (IBF), Duke McKenzie
1989 Cruiserweight (IBF), Glenn McCrory; light-heavyweight (WBC), Dennis Andries; flyweight (IBF), Dave McAuley

CRICKET

World Cup
1983 India bt West Indies by 43 runs
1987 Australia bt England by 7 runs

County cricket champions
1980 Middlesex
1981 Nottinghamshire
1982 Middlesex
1983 Essex
1984 Essex
1985 Middlesex
1986 Essex
1987 Nottinghamshire
1988 Worcestershire
1989 Worcestershire

Sunday League
1980 Warwickshire
1981 Essex
1982 Sussex
1983 Yorkshire
1984 Essex
1985 Essex
1986 Hampshire
1987 Worcestershire
1988 Worcestershire
1989 Lancashire

Gillette Cup
1980 Middlesex bt Surrey by 7 wickets
NatWest Trophy
1981 Derbyshire bt Northamptonshire (fewer wickets lost)
1982 Surrey bt Warwickshire by 9 wickets
1983 Somerset bt Kent by 24 runs
1984 Middlesex bt Kent by 4 wickets
1985 Essex bt Nottinghamshire by 1 run
1986 Sussex bt Lancashire by 7 wickets
1987 Nottinghamshire bt Northamptonshire by 3 wickets
1988 Middlesex bt Worcestershire by 3 wickets
1989 Warwickshire bt Middlesex by 4 wickets

Benson & Hedges Cup
1980 Northamptonshire bt Essex by 6 runs
1981 Somerset bt Surrey by 7 wickets
1982 Somerset bt Nottinghamshire by 9 wickets
1983 Middlesex bt Essex by 4 runs
1984 Lancashire bt Warwickshire by 6 wickets
1985 Leicestershire bt Essex by 5 wickets

1986 Middlesex bt Kent by 2 runs
1987 Yorkshire bt Northamptonshire (fewer wickets lost)
1988 Hampshire bt Derbyshire by 7 wickets
1989 Nottinghamshire bt Essex by 3 wickets

CYCLING

Tour de France (*winners from France except as indicated*)
1980 Joop Zoetemelk (NL)
1981 Bernard Hinault
1982 Bernard Hinault
1983 Laurent Fignon
1984 Laurent Fignon
1985 Bernard Hinault
1986 Greg LeMond (US)
1987 Stephen Roche (Ire)
1988 Pedro Delgado (Sp)
1989 Greg LeMond (US)

EQUESTRIANISM

World showjumping championship
1982 Norbert Koof (W. Ger)
1986 Gail Greenhough (Can)

World three-day event championship
1982 Lucinda Green (GB)
1986 Virginia Leng (GB)

Badminton Horse Trials
1980 Mark Todd (NZ)
1981 Mark Phillips (GB)
1982 Richard Meade (GB)
1983 Lucinda Prior-Palmer Green (GB)
1984 Lucinda Green (GB)
1985 Virginia Holgate (GB)
1986 Ian Stark (GB)
1987 Not held
1988 Ian Stark (GB)
1989 Virginia Holgate Leng (GB)

FOOTBALL

World Cup
1982 Italy 3; West Germany 1
1986 Argentina 2; West Germany 2

European championship
1980 West Germany 2; Belgium 1
1984 France 2; Spain 0
1988 Holland 2; USSR 0

European Champions Cup
1980 Nottingham Forest 1; SV Hamburg 0
1981 Liverpool 1; Real Madrid 0
1982 Aston Villa 1; Bayern Munich 0
1983 SV Hamburg 1; Juventus 0
1984 Liverpool 1; AS Roma 1, after extra time (Liverpool won 4–2 on penalties)
1985 Juventus 1; Liverpool 0
1986 Steaua Bucharest 0; Barcelona 0, after extra time (Steaua won 2–0 on penalties)
1987 FC Porto 2; Bayern Munich 0
1988 PSV Eindhoven 0; Benfica 0, after extra time (PSV Eindhoven won 6–5 on penalties)
1989 AC Milan 4; Steaua Bucharest 0

European Cup Winners' Cup
1980 Valencia 0; Arsenal 0, after extra time (Valencia won 5–4 on penalties)
1981 Dynamo Tbilisi 2; Carl Zeiss Jena 1
1982 Barcelona 2; Standard Liège 1
1983 Aberdeen 2; Real Madrid 1, after extra time
1984 Juventus 2; FC Porto 1
1985 Everton 3; Rapid Vienna 1
1986 Dynamo Kiev 3; Atletico Madrid 0
1987 Ajax 1; Locomotiv Leipzig 0
1988 Mechelen 1; Ajax 0
1989 Barcelona 2; Sampdoria 0

UEFA Cup
1980 Eintracht Frankfurt bt Borussia Moenchengladbach 2–3, 1–0 (Eintracht Frankfurt won on away goals)
1981 Ipswich Town bt AZ 67 Alkmaar 3–0, 2–4
1982 IFK Gothenburg bt SV Hamburg 1–0, 3–0
1983 Anderlecht bt Benfica 1–0, 1–1
1984 Tottenham Hotspur bt Anderlecht 1–1, 1–1 (Tottenham won 4–3 on penalties)
1985 Real Madrid bt Videoton 3–0, 0–1
1986 Real Madrid bt Cologne 5–1, 0–2
1987 IFK Gothenburg bt Dundee United 1–0, 1–1
1988 Bayer Leverkusen bt Espanol 0–3, 3–0 (Leverkusen won 3–2 on penalties)
1989 Napoli bt VFB Stuttgart 2–1 3–3

Football League
1980 Liverpool
1981 Aston Villa
1982 Liverpool
1983 Liverpool
1984 Liverpool
1985 Everton
1986 Liverpool
1987 Everton
1988 Liverpool
1989 Arsenal

FA Cup
1980 West Ham United 1; Arsenal 0
1981 Tottenham Hotspur 3; Manchester City 2 (in replay after 1–1 draw)
1982 Tottenham Hotspur 1; Queens Park Rangers 0 (in replay after 1–1 draw)
1983 Manchester United 4; Brighton & Hove Albion 0 (in replay after 2–2 draw)
1984 Everton 2; Watford 0
1985 Manchester United 1; Everton 0, after extra time
1986 Liverpool 3; Everton 1
1987 Coventry City 3; Tottenham Hotspur 2, after extra time
1988 Wimbledon 1; Liverpool 0
1989 Liverpool 3; Everton 2, after extra time

League Cup
1980 Wolverhampton Wanderers 1; Nottingham Forest 0
1981 Liverpool 2; West Ham United 1 (in replay after 1–1 draw)
1982 Liverpool 3; Tottenham Hotspur 1, after extra time
1983 Liverpool 2; Manchester United 1, after extra time
1984 Liverpool 1; Everton 0 (in replay after 0–0 draw)
1985 Norwich City 1; Sunderland 0
1986 Oxford United 3; Queens Park Rangers 0
1987 Arsenal 2; Liverpool 1
1988 Luton Town 3; Arsenal 2
1989 Nottingham Forest 3; Luton Town 1

Scottish League
1980 Aberdeen
1981 Celtic
1982 Celtic
1983 Dundee United
1984 Aberdeen
1985 Aberdeen
1986 Celtic
1987 Rangers
1988 Celtic
1989 Rangers

Scottish Cup
1980 Celtic 1; Rangers 0
1981 Rangers 4; Dundee United 1 (in replay after 0–0 draw)
1982 Aberdeen 4; Rangers 1, after extra time
1983 Aberdeen 1; Rangers 0, after extra time
1984 Aberdeen 2; Celtic 1, after extra time
1985 Celtic 2; Dundee United 1
1986 Aberdeen 3; Hearts 0
1987 St Mirren 1; Dundee United 0, after extra time
1988 Celtic 2; Dundee United 0
1989 Celtic 1; Rangers 0

Scottish League Cup
1980 Dundee United 3; Aberdeen 0 (in replay after 0–0 draw)
1981 Dundee United 3; Dundee 0
1982 Rangers 2; Dundee United 1
1983 Celtic 2; Rangers 1
1984 Rangers 3; Celtic 2
1985 Rangers 1; Dundee United 0
1986 Aberdeen 3; Hibernian 0
1987 Rangers 2; Celtic 1
1988 Rangers 3; Aberdeen 3 (Rangers won 5–3 on penalties)
1989 Rangers 3; Aberdeen 2

Ryder Cup
1981 United States 18½; Europe 9½
1983 United States 14½; Europe 13½
1985 Europe 16½; United States 11½
1987 Europe 15; United States 13
1989 Drawn 14–14

US Masters (winners from US except as indicated)
1980 Seve Ballesteros (Sp)
1981 Tom Watson
1982 Craig Stadler
1983 Seve Ballesteros (Sp)
1984 Ben Crenshaw
1985 Bernhard Langer (W. Ger)
1986 Jack Nicklaus

1987 Larry Mize
1988 Sandy Lyle (GB)
1989 Nick Faldo (GB)

US Open (winners from US except as indicated)
1980 Jack Nicklaus
1981 David Graham
1982 Tom Watson
1983 Larry Nelson
1984 Fuzzy Zoeller
1985 Andy North
1986 Ray Floyd
1987 Scott Simpson
1988 Curtis Strange
1989 Curtis Strange

US PGA (winners from US except as indicated)
1980 Jack Nicklaus
1981 Larry Nelson
1982 Ray Floyd
1983 Hal Sutton
1984 Lee Trevino
1985 Hubert Green
1986 Bob Tway
1987 Larry Nelson
1988 Jeff Sluman
1989 Payne Stewart

Walker Cup
1981 United States 15; Great Britain & Ireland 9
1983 United States 13½; Great Britain & Ireland 10½
1985 United States 13; Great Britain & Ireland 11
1987 United States 16½; Great Britain & Ireland 7½
1989 Great Britain & Ireland 12½; United States 11½

British Open (winners from US except as indicated)
1980 Tom Watson
1981 Bill Rogers
1982 Tom Watson
1983 Tom Watson
1984 Seve Ballesteros (Sp)
1985 Sandy Lyle (GB)
1986 Greg Norman
1987 Nick Faldo (GB)
1988 Seve Ballesteros (Sp)
1989 Mark Calcavecchia

2,000 Guineas
1980 Known Fact
1981 To-Agori-Mou
1982 Zino
1983 Lomond
1984 El Gran Señor
1985 Shadeed
1986 Dancing Brave
1987 Don't Forget Me
1988 Doyoun
1989 Nashwan

Derby
1980 Henbit
1981 Shergar
1982 Golden Fleece
1983 Teenoso
1984 Secreto
1985 Slip Anchor
1986 Shahrastani
1987 Reference Point
1988 Kahyasi
1989 Nashwan

St Leger
1980 Light Cavalry
1981 Cut Above
1982 Touching Wood
1983 Sun Princess
1984 Commanche Run
1985 Oh So Sharp
1986 Moon Madness
1987 Reference Point
1988 Minster Son
1989 Michelozzo

Grand National
1980 Ben Nevis
1981 Aldaniti
1982 Grittar
1983 Corbiere
1984 Hallo Dandy
1985 Last Suspect
1986 West Tip
1987 Maori Venture
1988 Rhyme 'N Reason
1989 Little Polveir

Prix l'Arc de Triomphe
1980 Detroit
1981 Gold River
1982 Akiyda
1983 All Along
1984 Sagace
1985 Rainbow Quest
1986 Dancing Brave
1987 Trempolino
1988 Tony Bin
1989 Carroll House

British and Irish Olympic gold medals
1980 Men's figure skating, Robin Cousins
1984 Ice dance, Jayne Torvill and Christopher Dean

Australian Open
1980 Brian Teacher (US); Hana Mandlikova (Czech)
1981 Johan Kriek (SA); Martina Navratilova (US)
1982 Johan Kriek (SA); Chris Evert Lloyd (US)
1983 Mats Wilander (Swe); Martina Navratilova (US)
1984 Mats Wilander (Swe); Chris Evert Lloyd (US)
1985 Stefan Edberg (Swe); Martina Navratilova (US)
1986 No tournament
1987 Stefan Edberg (Swe); Hana Mandlikova (Czech)
1988 Mats Wilander (Swe); Steffi Graf (W. Ger)
1989 Ivan Lendl (Czech); Steffi Graf (W. Ger)

French Open
1980 Björn Borg (Swe); Chris Evert Lloyd (US)
1981 Björn Borg (Swe); Hana Mandlikova (Czech)
1982 Mats Wilander (Swe); Martina Navratilova (US)
1983 Yannick Noah (Fr); Chris Evert Lloyd (US)
1984 Ivan Lendl (Czech); Martina Navratilova (US)
1985 Mats Wilander (Swe); Chris Evert Lloyd (US)
1986 Ivan Lendl (Czech); Chris Evert Lloyd (US)
1987 Ivan Lendl (Czech); Steffi Graf (W. Ger)
1988 Mats Wilander (Swe); Steffi Graf (W. Ger)
1989 Michael Chang (US); Arantxa Sanchez Vicario (Sp)

All-England (Wimbledon) championships
1980 Björn Borg (Swe); Evonne Cawley (Aus)
1981 John McEnroe (US); Chris Evert Lloyd (US)
1982 Jimmy Connors (US); Martina Navratilova (US)
1983 John McEnroe (US); Martina Navratilova (US)
1984 John McEnroe (US); Martina Navratilova (US)
1985 Boris Becker (W. Ger); Martina Navratilova (US)
1986 Boris Becker (W. Ger); Martina Navratilova (US)

1987 Pat Cash (Aus); Martina Navratilova (US)
1988 Stefan Edberg (Swe); Steffi Graf (W. Ger)
1989 Boris Becker (W. Ger); Steffi Graf (W. Ger)

US Open (winners from US except as indicated)
1980 John McEnroe; Chris Evert Lloyd
1981 John McEnroe; Tracy Austin
1982 Jimmy Connors; Chris Evert Lloyd
1983 Jimmy Connors; Martina Navratilova
1984 John McEnroe; Martina Navratilova
1985 Ivan Lendl (Czech); Hana Mandlikova (Czech)
1986 Ivan Lendl (Czech); Martina Navratilova
1987 Ivan Lendl (Czech); Martina Navratilova
1988 Mats Wilander (Swe); Steffi Graf (W. Ger)
1989 Boris Becker (W. Ger); Steffi Graf (W. Ger)

World championship
1980 Alan Jones (Williams-Ford)
1981 Nelson Piquet (Brabham-Ford)
1982 Keke Rosberg (Williams-Ford)
1983 Nelson Piquet (Brabham-BMW)
1984 Niki Lauda (McLaren-TAG)
1985 Alain Prost (McLaren-TAG)
1986 Alain Prost (McLaren-TAG)
1987 Nelson Piquet (Williams-Honda)
1988 Ayrton Senna (McLaren-Honda)
1989 Alain Prost (McLaren-Honda)

Constructors' championship
1980 Williams-Ford
1981 Williams-Ford
1982 Ferrari
1983 Ferrari
1984 McLaren-TAG
1985 McLaren-TAG
1986 Williams-Honda
1987 Williams-Honda
1988 McLaren-Honda
1989 McLaren-Honda

Le Mans
1980 J. Rondeau/J-P. Jaussaud (Rondeau-Ford)
1981 D. Bell/J. Ickx (Porsche)
1982 D. Bell/J. Ickx (Porsche)
1983 A. Holbert/H. Hayward/V. Schuppan (Porsche)
1984 H. Pescarolo/K. Ludwig (Porsche)
1985 K. Ludwig/J. Winter/P. Barillo (Porsche)
1986 D. Bell/H. Stuck/A. Holbert (Porsche)
1987 D. Bell/H. Stuck/A. Holbert (Porsche)
1988 J. Lammers/J. Dumfries/A. Wallace (Jaguar)
1989 J. Mass/Reuter/Dickens (Mercedes)

Indianapolis 500
1980 Johnny Rutherford
1981 Bobby Unser
1982 Gordon Johncock
1983 Tom Sneva
1984 Rick Mears
1985 Danny Sullivan
1986 Bobby Rahal
1987 Al Unser
1988 Rick Mears
1989 Emerson Fittipaldi

ROWING
British and Irish Olympic gold medals
1984 Men's coxed fours
1988 Men's coxless pairs

RUGBY LEAGUE
World Cup
1988 Australia

League champions
1980 Bradford Northern
1981 Bradford Northern
1982 Leigh
1983 Hull
1984 Hull Kingston Rovers
1985 Hull Kingston Rovers
1986 Halifax
1987 Wigan
1988 Widnes
1989 Widnes

Premiership Trophy
1980 Widnes
1981 Hull Kingston Rovers
1982 Widnes
1983 Widnes
1984 Hull Kingston Rovers
1985 St Helens
1986 Warrington
1987 Wigan
1988 Widnes
1989 Widnes

Challenge Cup
1980 Hull Kingston Rovers 10; Hull 5
1981 Widnes 18; Hull Kingston Rovers 9
1982 Hull 18; Widnes 9 (in replay after 14–14 draw)
1983 Featherstone Rovers 14; Hull 12
1984 Widnes 19; Wigan 6
1985 Wigan 28; Hull 24
1986 Castleford 15; Hull Kingston Rovers 14
1987 Halifax 19; St Helens 18
1988 Wigan 32; Halifax 12
1989 Wigan 27; St Helens 0

Regal Trophy
1989 Wigan

RUGBY UNION
World Cup
1987 New Zealand 29; France 9

Five Nations championship
1980 England (and Grand Slam)
1981 France (and Grand Slam)
1982 Ireland
1983 France and Ireland
1984 Scotland (and Grand Slam)
1985 Ireland
1986 France and Scotland
1987 France (and Grand Slam)
1988 France and Wales
1989 France

Scottish League champions
1980 Gala
1981 Hawick
1982 Hawick
1983 Gala
1984 Hawick
1985 Hawick
1986 Hawick
1987 Hawick
1988 Kelso
1989 Kelso

Pilkington Cup
1980 Leicester 21; London Irish 9
1981 Leicester 22; Gosforth 15
1982 Gloucester 12; Moseley 12, after extra time (title shared)
1983 Bristol 28; Leicester 22
1984 Bath 10; Bristol 9
1985 Bath 24; London Welsh 15
1986 Bath 25; Wasps 17
1987 Bath 19; Wasps 12
1988 Harlequins 28; Bristol 22
1989 Bath 10; Leicester 6

SWALEC Cup
1980 Bridgend 15; Swansea 9
1981 Cardiff 14; Bridgend 6
1982 Cardiff 12; Bridgend 12 (Cardiff won on most tries scored)
1983 Pontypool 18; Swansea 6
1984 Cardiff 24; Neath 19
1985 Llanelli 15; Cardiff 14
1986 Cardiff 28; Newport 21
1987 Cardiff 16; Swansea 15, after extra time
1988 Llanelli 28; Neath 13
1989 Neath 14; Llanelli 13

SNOOKER
World championship
(finalists from Britain except as indicated)
Knock-out
1980 Cliff Thorburn (Can) 18; Alex Higgins 16
1981 Steve Davis 18; Doug Mountjoy 12
1982 Alex Higgins 18; Ray Reardon 15
1983 Steve Davis 18; Cliff Thorburn (Can) 6
1984 Steve Davis 18; Jimmy White 16
1985 Dennis Taylor 18; Steve Davis 17
1986 Joe Johnson 18; Steve Davis 12
1987 Steve Davis 18; Joe Johnson 14
1988 Steve Davis 18; Terry Griffiths 11
1989 Steve Davis 18; John Parrott 3

Women's world championship
1980 Lesley McIlraith
1981 Vera Selby
1982 (not held)
1983 Sue Foster
1984 Stacey Hillyard
1985 Allison Fisher
1986 Allison Fisher
1987 Anne-Marie Farren
1988 Allison Fisher
1989 Allison Fisher

SQUASH
World Open
(women's tournament held every other year)
1980 Geoff Hunt (Aus)
1981 Jahangir Khan (Pak); Rhonda Thorne (Aus)
1982 Jahangir Khan (Pak)
1983 Jahangir Khan (Pak); Vicki Cardwell (Aus)
1984 Jahangir Khan (Pak)
1985 Jahangir Khan (Pak); Susan Devoy (NZ)
1986 Ross Norman (NZ)
1987 Jansher Khan (Pak); Susan Devoy (NZ)
1988 Jahangir Khan (Pak)
1989 Jansher Khan (Pak); Martine Le Moignan (GB)

British Open
1980 Geoff Hunt (Aus); Vicki Hoffman (Aus)
1981 Geoff Hunt (Aus); Vicki Hoffman (Aus)
1982 Jahangir Khan (Pak); Vicki Cardwell (Aus)
1983 Jahangir Khan (Pak); Vicki Cardwell (Aus)
1984 Jahangir Khan (Pak); Susan Devoy (NZ)
1985 Jahangir Khan (Pak); Susan Devoy (NZ)
1986 Jahangir Khan (Pak); Susan Devoy (NZ)
1987 Jahangir Khan (Pak); Susan Devoy (NZ)
1988 Jahangir Khan (Pak); Susan Devoy (NZ)
1989 Jahangir Khan (Pak); Susan Devoy (NZ)

SWIMMING
British and Irish Olympic gold medals
1980 100-m breaststroke, Duncan Goodhew
1988 100-m breaststroke, Adrian Moorhouse

YACHTING
America's Cup
1980 *Freedom* (US, skipper Dennis Conner)
1983 *Australia II* (Aus, skipper John Bertrand)
1987 *Stars & Stripes* (US, skipper Dennis Conner)
1988 *Stars & Stripes* (US, skipper Dennis Conner)

Admiral's Cup
1981 Team: Great Britain
1983 Team: West Germany
1985 Team: West Germany
1987 Team: New Zealand
1989 Team: Great Britain

1990–1999

AMERICAN FOOTBALL

Super Bowl
1990 San Francisco 49-ers
1991 New York Giants
1992 Washington Redskins
1993 Dallas Cowboys
1994 Dallas Cowboys
1995 San Francisco 49-ers
1996 Dallas Cowboys
1997 Green Bay Packers
1998 Denver Broncos
1999 Denver Broncos

ATHLETICS

British and Irish Olympic gold medals
1992 100 m Linford Christie; 400-m hurdles Sally Gunnell

BASEBALL

World Series
1990 Cincinnati Reds
1991 Minnesota Twins
1992 Toronto Blue Jays
1993 Toronto Blue Jays
1994 Not held
1995 Atlanta Braves
1996 New York Yankees
1997 Florida Marlins
1998 New York Yankees

BOXING

British and Irish world champions
1990 Light-heavyweight (WBC), Dennis Andries; middleweight (WBO), Nigel Benn; middleweight(WBO), Chris Eubank
1991 Super-middleweight (WBO), Chris Eubank; featherweight(WBC), Paul Hodkinson; bantamweight (WBO), Duke McKenzie
1992 Heavyweight (WBC), Lennox Lewis; super-middleweight (WBC), Nigel Benn; featherweight (WBO), Colin McMillan; super-bantamweight (WBO), Duke McKenzie; super-flyweight (WBA), Katsuya Onizuka; flyweight (WBO), Pat Clinton
1993 Middleweight (WBO), Chris Pyatt; welterweight (WBO), Eamonn Loughran (Ire); featherweight (WBO), Steve Robinson; strawweight (WBO), Paul Weir
1994 Heavyweight (WBO), Herbie Hide; middleweight (WBO), Steve Collins (Ire); light-flyweight (WBO), Paul Weir
1995 Heavyweight (WBC), Frank Bruno; super-middleweight (WBO), Steve Collins (Ire); featherweight (WBO), Naseem Hamed; bantamweight (WBC), Wayne McCullough (Ire)
1996 Heavyweight (WBO), Henry Akinwande; super-middleweight (WBC), Robin Reid; bantamweight (WBO), Robbie Regan
1997 Heavyweight (WBC), Lennox Lewis; heavyweight (WBO), Herbie Hide; cruiserweight (WBO), Carl Thompson; super-middleweight (WBO), Jo Calzaghe; featherweight (WBC & IBF), Naseem Hamed
1998 Heavyweight (WBC), Lennox Lewis; heavyweight (WBO), Herbie Hide; cruiserweight (WBO), Carl Thompson; super-middleweight (WBC), Richie Woodhall; super-middleweight (WBO), Jo Calzaghe; featherweight (WBO), Naseem Hamed

CRICKET

World Cup
1992 Pakistan bt England by 22 runs
1996 Sri Lanka bt Australia by 7 wickets
1999 Australia bt Pakistan by 8 wickets

County cricket champions
1990 Middlesex
1991 Essex
1992 Essex
1993 Middlesex
1994 Warwickshire
1995 Warwickshire
1996 Leicestershire
1997 Glamorgan
1998 Leicestershire

Sunday League champions
1990 Derbyshire
1991 Nottinghamshire
1992 Middlesex
1993 Glamorgan
1994 Warwickshire
1995 Kent
1996 Surrey
1997 Warwickshire
1998 Lancashire

NatWest Trophy
1990 Lancashire bt Northamptonshire by 7 wickets
1991 Hampshire bt Surrey by 4 wickets
1992 Northamptonshire bt Leicestershire by 8 wickets
1993 Warwickshire bt Sussex by 5 wickets
1994 Worcestershire bt Warwickshire by 8 wickets
1995 Warwickshire bt Northamptonshire by 4 wickets
1996 Lancashire bt Essex by 129 runs
1997 Essex bt Warwickshire by 9 wickets
1998 Lancashire bt Derbyshire by 9 wickets

Benson & Hedges Cup
1990 Lancashire bt Worcestershire by 69 runs
1991 Worcestershire bt Lancashire by 65 runs
1992 Hampshire bt Kent by 41 runs
1993 Derbyshire bt Lancashire by 6 runs
1994 Warwickshire bt Worcestershire by 6 wickets
1995 Lancashire bt Kent by 35 runs
1996 Lancashire bt Northamptonshire by 31 runs
1997 Surrey bt Kent by 8 wickets
1998 Essex bt Leicestershire by 192 runs

CYCLING

Tour de France
1990 Greg LeMond (US)
1991 Miguel Indurain (Sp)
1992 Miguel Indurain (Sp)
1993 Miguel Indurain (Sp)
1994 Miguel Indurain (Sp)
1995 Miguel Indurain (Sp)
1996 Bjarne Riis (Den)
1997 Jan Ullrich (Ger)
1998 Marco Pantini (It)

EQUESTRIANISM

World showjumping championship
1990 Eric Navet (Fra)
1994 Franke Sloothaak (Ger)
1998 Rodrigo Pessoa (Bra)

World three-day event championship
1990 Blyth Tait (NZ)
1994 Vaughan Jefferis (NZ)
1998 Blyth Tait (NZ)

Badminton Horse Trials
1990 Nicola McIrvine (GB)
1991 Rodney Powell (GB)
1992 Mary Thompson (GB)
1993 Virginia Leng (GB)
1994 Mark Todd (NZ)
1995 Bruce Davidson (US)
1996 Mark Todd (NZ)
1997 David O'Connor (US)
1998 Chris Bartle (GB)
1999 Ian Stark (GB)

FOOTBALL

World Cup
1990 West Germany 1; Argentina 0
1994 Brazil 0; Italy 0, after extra time (Brazil won 3–2 on penalties)
1998 France 3; Brazil 0

European championship
1992 Denmark 2; Germany 0
1996 Germany 2; Czech Republic 1, won by 'golden goal' after sudden death extra time

European Champions Cup
1990 AC Milan 1; Benfica 0
1991 Red Star Belgrade 0; Marseille 0, after extra time (Red Star won 5–3 on penalties)
1992 Barcelona 1; Sampdoria 0, after extra time
1993 Marseille 1; AC Milan 0 (Marseille were later stripped of title)
1994 AC Milan 4; Barcelona 0
1995 Ajax 1; AC Milan 0
1996 Juventus 1; Ajax 1, after extra time (Juventus won 4–2 on penalties)
1997 Borussia Dortmund 3; Juventus 1
1998 Real Madrid 1; Juventus 0
1999 Manchester United 2; Bayern Munich 1

European Cup Winners' Cup
1990 Sampdoria 2; Anderlecht 0
1991 Manchester United 2; Barcelona 1
1992 Werder Bremen 2; Monaco 0
1993 Parma 3; Antwerp 1
1994 Arsenal 1; Parma 0
1995 Real Zaragoza 2; Arsenal 1, after extra time
1996 Paris St Germain 1; Rapid Vienna 0
1997 Barcelona 1; Paris St Germain 0
1998 Chelsea 1; Vfb Stuttgart 0
1999 Lazio 2; Real Mallorca 1

UEFA Cup
1990 Juventus bt Fiorentina 3–1, 0–0
1991 Inter Milan bt AS Roma 2–0, 0–1
1992 Ajax bt Torino 2–2, 0–0 (Ajax won on away goals)
1993 Juventus bt Borussia Dortmund 3–1, 3–0
1994 Inter Milan bt Salzburg 1–0, 1–0
1995 Parma bt Juventus 1–0, 1–1
1996 Bayern Munich bt Bordeaux 2–0, 3–1
1997 Schalke 04 bt Inter Milan 1–0, 0–1 (Schalke won 4–1 on penalties)
1998 Internazionale 3; Lazio 0
1999 Parma 3; Marseilles 0

Football League
1990 Liverpool
1991 Arsenal
1992 Leeds United

FA Premier League
1993 Manchester United
1994 Manchester United
1995 Blackburn Rovers
1996 Manchester United
1997 Manchester United
1998 Arsenal
1999 Manchester United

FA Cup
1990 Manchester United 1; Crystal Palace 0 (in replay after 3–3 draw)
1991 Tottenham Hotspur 2; Nottingham Forest 1, after extra time
1992 Liverpool 2; Sunderland 0
1993 Arsenal 2; Sheffield Wednesday 1, after extra time (in replay after 1–1 draw)
1994 Manchester United 4; Chelsea 0
1995 Everton 1; Manchester United 0
1996 Manchester United 1; Liverpool 0
1997 Chelsea 2; Middlesbrough 0
1998 Arsenal 2; Newcastle 0
1999 Manchester United 2; Newcastle 0

League Cup
1990 Nottingham Forest 1; Oldham Athletic 0
1991 Sheffield Wednesday 1; Manchester United 0
1992 Manchester United 1; Nottingham Forest 0
1993 Arsenal 2; Sheffield Wednesday 1
1994 Aston Villa 3; Manchester United 1
1995 Liverpool 2; Bolton Wanderers 1
1996 Aston Villa 3; Leeds United 0
1997 Leicester City 1; Middlesbrough 0, after extra time (in replay after 1–1 draw)
1998 Chelsea 2; Middlesbrough 0
1999 Tottenham Hotspur 1; Leicester City 0

Scottish League
1990 Rangers
1991 Rangers
1992 Rangers
1993 Rangers
1994 Rangers
1995 Rangers
1996 Rangers
1997 Rangers
1998 Celtic
1999 Rangers

Scottish Cup
1990 Aberdeen 0; Celtic 0 (Aberdeen won 9–8 on penalties)
1991 Motherwell 4; Dundee United 3
1992 Rangers 2; Airdrieonians 1
1993 Rangers 2; Aberdeen 1
1994 Dundee United 1; Rangers 0
1995 Celtic 1; Airdrieonians 0
1996 Rangers 5; Hearts 1
1997 Kilmarnock 1; Falkirk 0
1998 Hearts 2; Rangers 1
1999 Rangers 1; Celtic 0

Scottish League Cup
1990 Aberdeen 2; Rangers 1, after extra time
1991 Rangers 2; Celtic 1, after extra time
1992 Hibernian 2; Dunfermline Athletic 0
1993 Rangers 2; Aberdeen 1, after extra time
1994 Rangers 2; Hibernian 1
1995 Raith Rovers 2; Celtic 2 (Raith won 6–5 on penalties)
1996 Aberdeen 2; Dundee 0
1997 Stranraer 1; St Johnstone 0
1998 Celtic 3; Dundee 0

National League
1993 Arsenal
1994 Doncaster Belles
1995 Arsenal
1996 Croydon
1997 Arsenal
1998 Everton

Women's FA Cup
1993 Arsenal
1994 Doncaster Belles
1995 Arsenal
1996 Croydon
1997 Millwall Lionesses
1998 Arsenal
1999 Arsenal

League Cup
1993 Arsenal
1994 Arsenal
1995 Wimbledon
1996 Wembley
1997 Millwall Lionesses
1998 Arsenal

GOLF

Ryder Cup
1991 United States 14½; Europe 13½
1993 United States 15; Europe 13
1995 Europe 14½; United States 13½
1997 Europe 14½; United States 13½

US Masters
1990 Nick Faldo (GB)
1991 Ian Woosnam (GB)
1992 Fred Couples (US)
1993 Bernhard Langer (Ger)
1994 José-Maria Olazábal (Sp)
1995 Ben Crenshaw (US)
1996 Nick Faldo (GB)
1997 Tiger Woods (US)
1998 Mark O'Meara
1999 José-Maria Olazábal (Sp)

US Open (winners from US except as indicated)
1990 Hale Irwin
1991 Payne Stewart
1992 Tom Kite
1993 Lee Janzen
1994 Ernie Els (SA)
1995 Corey Pavin
1996 Steve Jones
1997 Ernie Els (SA)
1998 Lee Janzen

US PGA (winners from US except as indicated)
1990 Wayne Grady (Aus)
1991 John Daly
1992 Nick Price (Zimb)
1993 Paul Azinger
1994 Nick Price (Zimb)
1995 Steve Elkington
1996 Mark Brooks
1997 Davis Love III
1998 Vijay Singh (Fiji)

Walker Cup
1991 United States 14; Great Britain & Ireland 10
1993 United States 19; Great Britain & Ireland 5
1995 Great Britain & Ireland 14; United States 10
1997 United States 18; Great Britain & Ireland 6

Solheim Cup
1990 United States 11½; Europe 4½
1992 Europe 11½;, United States 6½
1994 United States 13; Europe 7
1996 United States 16; Europe 11
1998 United States 16; Europe 12

British Open
1990 Nick Faldo (GB)
1991 Ian Baker-Finch (Aus)
1992 Nick Faldo (GB)
1993 Greg Norman (Aus)
1994 Nick Price (Zimb)
1995 John Daly (US)
1996 Tom Lehman (US)
1997 Justin Leonard (US)
1998 Mark O'Meara (US)

HORSE RACING

2,000 Guineas
1990 Tirol
1991 Mystiko
1992 Rodrigo de Triano
1993 Zafonic
1994 Mister Baileys
1995 Pennekamp
1996 Mark of Esteem
1997 Entrepreneur
1998 King of Kings
1999 Island Sands

Derby
1990 Quest for Fame
1991 Generous
1992 Dr Devious
1993 Commander in Chief
1994 Erhaab
1995 Lammtarra
1996 Shaamit
1997 Benny the Dip
1998 High-Rise
1999 Oath

St Leger
1990 Snurge
1991 Toulon
1992 User Friendly
1993 Bob's Return
1994 Moonax
1995 Classic Cliché
1996 Shantou
1997 Silver Patriarch
1998 Nedawi

Grand National
1990 Mr Frisk
1991 Seagram
1992 Party Politics
1993 Not run
1994 Minnehoma
1995 Royal Athlete
1996 Rough Quest
1997 Lord Gyllene
1998 Earth Summit
1999 Bobbyjo

Prix de L'Arc de Triomphe
1990 Saumarez
1991 Suave Dancer
1992 Subotico
1993 Urban Sea
1994 Carnegie
1995 Lammtarra
1996 Helissio
1997 Peintre Celebre
1998 Sagamix

LAWN TENNIS

Australian Open
1990 Ivan Lendl (Czech); Steffi Graf (Ger)
1991 Boris Becker (Ger); Monica Seles (Yug)
1992 Jim Courier (US); Monica Seles (Yug)
1993 Jim Courier (US); Monica Seles (Yug)
1994 Pete Sampras (US); Steffi Graf (Ger)
1995 Andre Agassi (US); Mary Pierce (Fr)
1996 Boris Becker (Ger); Monica Seles (US)
1997 Pete Sampras (US); Martina Hingis (Swi)
1998 Petr Korda (Cze); Martina Hingis (Swi)
1999 Yevgeny Kafelnikov (Rus); Martina Hingis (Swi)

French Open
1990 Andres Gomez (Ecu); Monica Seles (Yug)
1991 Jim Courier (US); Monica Seles (Yug)
1992 Jim Courier (US); Monica Seles (Yug)
1993 Sergi Bruguera (Sp); Steffi Graf (Ger)
1994 Sergi Bruguera (Sp); Arantxa Sanchez Vicario (Sp)
1995 Thomas Muster (Aut); Steffi Graf (Ger)
1996 Yevgeny Kafelnikov (Rus); Steffi Graf (Ger)
1997 Gustavo Kuerten (Braz); Iva Majoli (Croatia)
1998 Carlos Moya ((Sp); Arantxa Sanchez-Vicario (Sp)
1999 André Agassi (US); Steffi Graf (Ger)

All-England (Wimbledon) championships
1990 Stefan Edberg (Swe); Martina Navratilova (US)
1991 Michael Stich (Ger); Steffi Graf (Ger)
1992 Andre Agassi (US); Steffi Graf (Ger)
1993 Pete Sampras (US); Steffi Graf (Ger)
1994 Pete Sampras (US); Conchita Martinez (Sp)

1995 Pete Sampras (US); Steffi Graf (Ger)
1996 Richard Krajicek (NL); Steffi Graf (Ger)
1997 Pete Sampras (US); Martina Hingis (Swi)
1998 Pete Sampras (US); Jana Novotna (Cze)
1999 Pete Sampras (US); Lindsay Davenport (US)

US Open
1990 Pete Sampras (US); Gabriela Sabatini (Arg)
1991 Stefan Edberg (Swe); Monica Seles (Yug)
1992 Stefan Edberg (Swe); Monica Seles (Yug)
1993 Pete Sampras (US); Steffi Graf (Ger)
1994 Andre Agassi (US); Arantxa Sanchez Vicario (Sp)
1995 Pete Sampras (US); Steffi Graf (Ger)
1996 Pete Sampras (US); Steffi Graf (Ger)
1997 Patrick Rafter (Aus); Martina Hingis (Swi)
1998 Patrick Rafter (Aus); Lindsay Davenport (US)

MOTOR RACING

World championship
1990 Ayrton Senna (McLaren-Honda)
1991 Ayrton Senna (McLaren-Honda)
1992 Nigel Mansell (Williams-Renault)
1993 Alain Prost (Williams-Renault)
1994 Michael Schumacher (Benetton-Ford)
1995 Michael Schumacher (Benetton-Renault)
1996 Damon Hill (Williams-Renault)
1997 Jacques Villeneuve (Williams-Renault)
1998 Mika Hakkinen (McLaren Mercedes)

Constructors' championship
1990 McLaren-Honda
1991 McLaren-Honda
1992 Williams-Renault
1993 Williams-Renault
1994 Williams-Renault
1995 Benetton-Renault
1996 Williams-Renault
1997 Williams-Renault
1998 McLaren-Mercedes

Le Mans
1990 Nielsen/Brundle/Cobb (Jaguar)
1991 Herbert/Gachot/Wendler (Mazda)
1992 Warwick/Blundell/Dalmas (Peugeot)
1993 Bouchot/Helary (Peugeot)
1994 Dalmas/Haywood/Baldi (Porsche)
1995 Dalmas/Lehto (McLaren)
1996 Jones/Reuter/Wurtz (Porsche)
1997 Alboreto/Johansson/Kristensen (Joest)
1998 McNish/Ortelli/Aiello (Porsche AG)
1999 Dalmas/Martini/Winkelhock (BMW)

Indianapolis 500
1990 Arie Luyendyk
1991 Rick Mears
1992 Al Unser Jr
1993 Emerson Fittipaldi
1994 Al Unser Jr
1995 Jacques Villeneuve
1996 Buddy Lazier
1997 Arie Luyendyk
1998 Eddie Cheever
1999 Kenny Brack

ROWING
British and Irish Olympic gold medals
1992 Men's coxless pairs; men's coxed pairs
1996 Coxless pairs

RUGBY LEAGUE
World Cup
1992 Australia
1995 Australia

League champions
1990 Wigan
1991 Wigan
1992 Wigan
1993 Wigan
1994 Wigan
1995 Wigan
Super League
1996 St Helens
1997 St Helens
1998 Wigan

Premiership trophy
1990 Widnes
1991 Hull
1992 Wigan
1993 St Helens
1994 Wigan
1995 Wigan
1996 Wigan
1997 Wigan
1998 Wigan

Challenge Cup
1990 Wigan 36; Warrington 14
1991 Wigan 13; St Helens 8
1992 Wigan 28; Castleford 12
1993 Wigan 20; Widnes 14
1994 Wigan 26; Leeds 16
1995 Wigan 30; Leeds 10
1996 St Helens 40; Bradford 32
1997 St Helens 32; Bradford 22
1998 Sheffield 17; Wigan 8
1999 Leeds 52; London 16

Regal Trophy
1990 Wigan
1991 Warrington
1992 Widnes
1993 Wigan
1994 Wigan
1995 Wigan
1996 Wigan
(Discontinued 1996)

RUGBY UNION
World Cup
1991 Australia 12; England 6
1995 South Africa 15; New Zealand 12, after extra time

Five Nations championship
1990 Scotland (and Grand Slam)
1991 England (and Grand Slam)
1992 England (and Grand Slam)
1993 France
1994 Wales
1995 England (and Grand Slam)
1996 England
1997 France (and Grand Slam)
1998 France (and Grand Slam)
1999 Scotland

English League champions
1990 Wasps
1991 Bath
1992 Bath
1993 Bath
1994 Bath
1995 Leicester
1996 Bath
1997 Wasps
1998 Newcastle
1999 Leicester

Welsh League champions
1991 Neath
1992 Swansea
1993 Llanelli
1994 Swansea
1995 Cardiff
1996 Neath
1997 Pontypridd
1998 Swansea
1999 Llanelli

Scottish League champions
1990 Melrose
1991 Boroughmuir
1992 Melrose
1993 Melrose
1994 Melrose
1995 Stirling County
1996 Melrose
1997 Melrose
1998 Watsonians
1999 Heriots FP

All-Ireland League champions
1991 Cork Constitution
1992 Garryowen
1993 Young Munster
1994 Garryowen
1995 Shannon
1996 Shannon
1997 Shannon
1998 Shannon
1999 Cork Constitution

Pilkington Cup
1990 Bath 48; Gloucester 6
1991 Harlequins 25; Northampton 13, after extra time
1992 Bath 15; Harlequins 12, after extra time
1993 Leicester 23; Harlequins 16
1994 Bath 21; Leicester 9
1995 Bath 36; Wasps 16
1996 Bath 16; Leicester 15
1997 Leicester 9; Sale 3
1998 Saracens 48; Wasps 18
Tetley's Bitter Cup
1999 Wasps 29; Newcastle 19

SWALEC Cup
1990 Neath 16; Bridgend 10
1991 Llanelli 24; Pontypool 9
1992 Llanelli 16; Swansea 7
1993 Llanelli 21; Neath 18
1994 Cardiff 15; Llanelli 8
1995 Swansea 17; Pontypridd 12
1996 Pontypridd 29; Neath 22
1997 Cardiff 33; Swansea 26
1998 Llanelli 19; Ebbw Vale 12
1999 Swansea 37; Llanelli 10

SNOOKER
World championship
(players from Britain except as indicated)
Knock-out
1990 Stephen Hendry 18; Jimmy White 12
1991 John Parrott 18; Jimmy White 11
1992 Stephen Hendry 18; Jimmy White 14
1993 Stephen Hendry 18; Jimmy White 5

1994 Stephen Hendry 18; Jimmy White 17
1995 Stephen Hendry 18; Nigel Bond 9
1996 Stephen Hendry 18; Peter Ebdon 12
1997 Ken Doherty 18; Stephen Hendry 12
1998 John Higgins 18; Ken Doherty 12
1999 Stephen Hendry 18; Mark Williams 11

Women's world championship *(winners from Britain except as indicated)*
1990 Karen Corr
1991 Allison Fisher
1992 (not held)
1993 Allison Fisher
1994 Allison Fisher
1995 Karen Corr
1996 Karen Corr
1997 Karen Corr
1998 Kelly Fisher

SQUASH
World Open championship
1990 Jansher Khan (Pak); Susan Devoy (NZ)
1991 Rodney Martin (Aus); Susan Devoy (NZ)
1992 Jansher Khan (Pak); Susan Devoy (NZ)
1993 Jansher Khan (Pak); Michelle Martin (Aus)
1994 Jansher Khan (Pak); Michelle Martin (Aus)
1995 Jansher Khan (Pak); Michelle Martin (Aus)
1996 Jansher Khan (Pak); Sarah Fitz-Gerald (Aus)
1997 Rodney Eyles (Aus); Sarah Fitz-Gerald (Aus)
1998 Jonathon Power (Can); Sarah Fitz-Gerald (Aus)

British Open *(winners from Pakistan except as indicated)*
1990 Jahangir Khan; Susan Devoy (NZ)
1991 Jahangir Khan; Lisa Opie (GB)
1992 Jansher Khan; Susan Devoy (NZ)
1993 Jansher Khan; Michelle Martin (Aus)
1994 Jansher Khan; Michelle Martin (Aus)

1995 Jansher Khan; Michelle Martin (Aus)
1996 Jansher Khan; Michelle Martin (Aus)
1997 Jansher Khan; Michelle Martin (Aus)
1998 Peter Nicol (Sco); Michelle Martin (Aus)

SWIMMING
British and Irish Olympic gold medals
1996 200-m individual medley, Michelle Smith (Ire); 400-m individual medley, Michelle Smith (Ire); 400-m freestyle, Michelle Smith (Ire)

YACHTING
America's Cup
1992 *America 3* (US, skipper Bill Koch)
1995 *Black Magic 1* (US, skipper Russell Coutts)

Admiral's Cup
1991 Team: France
1995 Team: Italy
1997 Team: United States

Fredericks, Roy 293
Freeman, Bertram 38
Freyberg, General 94
Friar, Ken 353
Froggatt, Jack 114
Froitzheim, Otto 38
Fry, C. B. 10–11, *11*, 13, 32
Fry, Shirley 110
Fujiyama Crest (horse) 360
Fulham FC 47, 98, 113, 214
Fullmer, Gary 137
Furniss, (footballer) 108
Futch, Eddie 340
future of sport 322–3

G

Gabe, Rhys 17
Gadsby, Peter 327
Gaetjens, (footballer) 109
Gainsborough (horse) 43
Galatasaray 343
Galica, Divina 175
Gallacher, Bernard 276, 327, 341
Gallacher, Hughie *64, 67*
Gallaher, Dave 19, 47
Gandhi, Indira 283
Garbacz, Lori 302
Gardner, E. 54
Gardner, Maureen 103, 290
Gardner, Robert 55
Garin, Maurice 14
Garmisch-Partenkirchen: winter Olympics 85
Garner, Joel *248*, 280
Garrett, Robert 9
Garrincha 142, 241, 277
Garvey, Philomena 132
Gascoigne, Paul *320*, 324, 327, 339, 357
Gasnier, (rugby league player) 163
Gatting, Mike 226, 264, 298, 303, *303*, 307, 316, *316*, 355
Gaul, Charles 158
Gault, Willie 275
Gavaskar, Sunil 197
Gay Crusader (horse) 42
Gay Moore (horse) 311
Gebrselassie, Haile 371
Gehrig, Lou 91, 93
Geldard, Albert 76, 80
Gemmell, Archie 241
Gemmell, Tommy 178
Gentle Moya 132
Gento, Francisco 148
George V, King 51, 55
George, Charlie 198
George, Ricky 203
Germany (football):
    v Czech Republic 358
    v Denmark 332–3
    v England 89, 177, 193, 358
    v Hungary 124
Germany (West) (football):
    v Argentina 295, 321, *321*

    v Czechoslovakia 230
    v England 320
    v France 227
    v Holland 214
    v Italy 269
    v Russia 202
    World Cup 142, 214, 267, 269, 295, 320–1
Germany (West) (hockey) 223, 309
Gerson 192, 241
Gerulaitis, Vitas 230, 237
Gethin, Peter 207
Giacomelli, Bruno 268
Giardello, Joey 171
Gib (horse) 71
Gibb, P. A. 99
Gibbs, Harry 196
Gibbs, Lance 139, 187, 195
Gibbs, Scott 364
Gibson, Althea 136, 224
Gibson, C. 183
Gibson, Mike 212
Gifford, Josh 260
Giggs, Ryan 375
Gilchrist, Adam 374
Giles, Johnny 220
Gilkes, James 244
Gilks, Gillian 273
Gill, Henderson 297
Gillette Cup 61
Gilman, Frank 266
Gilmour, Gary *222*, 228
Gilzean, Alan 169
Ginther, Richie 162
Gipsy Moth IV (yacht) *176*
Glamorgan CCC 321, 365
Glasgow Rangers FC *see* Rangers FC
Glint of Gold (horse) 261
Gloucestershire CCC 32
Goalby, Bob 183
Goculdas, M. 54
Godard, J. D. 136
Goddard, John 109
Going, Sid 208
Gold, Sir Arthur 308
Golden, Johnny 64
Golden King (horse) 76
Golden Miller (horse) 81, *81*, 210, 221
Golden Willow (horse) 104
golf balls 13, 19
golf clubs 9
Gomez, G. 109
Gonzales, Froilan 113, 117, *117*, 121, 144
Gonzales, Ricardo 186, *186*
Gonzalez, Jaime 280
Gonzalez, Pancho 182, 198
Gooch, Graham 223, 240, 248, 266, 289, 303, 318, 320, *320*, 321, 339
Good Brandy (horse) 118
Goodall, F. R. *67*
Goodway, Andy 310, 373
Goodyear, (footballer) 306

Goolagong (Cawley), Evonne 200, *200*, 224, *224*, 255
Gordino, Amedée 95
Gordon, Jacqueline 100
Gore, A. Wentworth 24, 28, 29
Gorman, Susan 249
Gornik Zabrze 191
Gosden, Christine 142
Gothenburg (IFK) 301
Gough, Darren 351, *351*
Gough, Richard 298
Gould, Bobby 306
Goulding, Bobby 325
Goux, Jules 33, 36, 39
Gower, David 21, 243, 251, 271, 289, *289*, 318
Goycochea, (footballer) 321
Grace, W. G. 26, *26*, 27, 40, 44, 59, 60, 82, 100
Graf, Steffi 131, 309, *309*, 339, 361, 371, 375
Graham, David 262, *262*
Graham, George 345, 353, *353*
Graham, Herol 328
Graham, Miss M. A. 17
Grakle (horse) 71
Gran Señor (horse) 283
Grand National 45, 336, 363
Grant, Chris 319
Grant, Mick 240
Gratton, Mike 268
Graveney, David 365
Graveney, Tom 126, 137
Gray, Andy 237, 287, 319
Graziani, (footballer) 269
Greasepaint (horse) 273, 281
Great Britain (football) 101
Great Britain (golf) 50, 64, 69, 72
Great Britain (hockey) 281, 309
Great Britain (ice hockey) 85
Great Britain (rugby league) 123
    v Australia 39, 71, 141, 157, 270, 297
    v France 127, 157
    v New Zealand 141, 155, 203, 238, 373
    World Cup 203
Great Britain (rugby union):
    v Australia 17, 106, 147, 163, *163*, 315
    v Australian states 198
    v New Zealand 17, 106, 147, 201, *201*, 277, 341
    v S. Africa 127, 129, 183, 216, 257, 364, *364*
Great Britain (tennis) 57, 190, 375
Great Britain (3-day eventing) 116
Great Britain (women's golf) 115, *115*, 132
Great Britain & Ireland (golf) 199, *199*, 225
Greaves, Jimmy 152, *152, 153*, 155, 157, 162, 169
Green Bay Packers 179, 369

Green, Lucinda *see* Prior-Palmer, Lucinda
Green, Stephen 338
Greenall, Peter 336
Greenhoff, Brian 229
Greenwood, J. T. 129
Greenwood, Ron 168, 219, 236, 237
Gregory, Jack 51, 61, 293
Gregory, S. E. 16
Greig, Tony (A. W.) 61, 214, 232, 239
Grenoble: winter Olympics 183
Grey Sombrero (horse) 210
Greyling, Piet 188
Griffin, Geoff 149
Griffith, Charlie 163
Griffith, Emile 165
Griffith-Joyner, Florence 308, *308*, 373
Griffiths, Sirrel 317
Grima, (rugby league player) 310
Grimsby Town FC 49
Grinham, Judy 135, *135*, 142
Grittar (horse) 266
Grobbelaar, Bruce 294, *306*, 314, 366, *366*
Grobler, Jürgen 359
Grodotzki, Hans *151*
Grout, A. T. W. 152, 250
Groves, (footballer) 162
Grundy (horse) 223
Gualtieri, Davide 341
Gudjohnsen, (footballer) 283
Guess, Cadet *42*
Guest, Raymond 156, 221
Guilford, Jesse 50
Gullit, Ruud 305
Gunn, George 68
Gunnell, Sally 341, *341*, 366
Gurney, Bobby 86
Gurney, Dan 162, 166, 180
Gurusinha, Asantha 356
Guscott, Jeremy 318, 329, 364, 372
Guy, Dickie 220
Gyulai, Istvan 356

H

Haagenson, Nils 250
Haan, (footballer) 199
Haarlem FC: disaster 271
Hadlee, Richard 275, 289, 316
Haegg, Gundar 123
Hafeez, Abdul *see* Kardar, A. H.
Haffey, Frank 152, 160
Hagen, Walter 47, 52, *52*, 64, 66, 69, 72, 121, 204
Haggas, William 359
Hagler, Marvin 251, 256, *256*, 299, *299*
Hahn, Archie *23*
Hailwood, Mike 153, 171, *171*, 207, 211, 246, *246*

Hain, Peter 188, 190
Haiti (football) 215
Hakkinen, Mika 373
Halberg, Murray 135, *151*
Halifax Rugby League Club 93
Hall, Caroline 353
Hall, Douglas 331, 369
Hall, Harry 181
Hall, John 283
Hall, Nim 118
Hall, Sir John 331, 353
Hall, Wes 163, 182
Haller, H. 177
Hallett, Tony 360
Hallez (horse) 201
Halliday, Simon 332
Hallo Dandy (horse) 281
Halswelle, Lieut. Wyndham 23
Hamburg (SV) 255
Hamed, Prince Naseem 353, 373
Hamilton, (footballer) 53
Hamlyn, Peter 328
Hammond, Frank 251
Hammond, (golfer) 292
Hammond, Walter R. 70, 90, 94, 101, 137, 338
Hampshire CCC 32, 153, 333
Hampson, Steve 310
Hanif Mohammad 344
Hanley, Ellery 310, 325, *325*
Hannah, George 127
Hansen, Alan 294, *294*
Hapgood, Eddie 78
Harada, Mashiko 'Fighting' 189
Hard, Darlene 146
Hardaker, Alan 168
Hardie, Brian 287
Hardin, Glen 75
Harding, Brian 368
Harding, Jeff 319
Harding, Tonya 342
Hardstaff, J. 99
Hardy, (rugby union player) 110
Harkness, (footballer) 67
Hart, J. G. M. 112
Hart, John 361
Hart, Miss 110, *110*
Hartlepool United FC 300
Harvey, Joe *111*
Harvey, Neil 105, 125, 127, 237
Hashim Khan 114
Haskell, Coburn 13
Haslam, Ron 240
Hassett, A. Lindsay 89, 94, 120
Hastings, Gavin 293, 315, 341
Hastings, Scott 293
Hathorn, Gina 175
Hauge, Rune 353
Havelange, Joao 173
Havers, Arthur 64, 72
Havlicek, John 241
Hawke, Lord 35
Hawthorn, Mike 119, 121, 138, 142, *142*, 144, *144*
Hayes, J. J. 26, *26*, 27
Hayes, Joe 133
Hayes, John 206

Picture credits

All pictures © Allsport UK Limited, except for the following: **42–43** *Illustrated London News*, **94** (*top*) Popperfoto, **95** *Illustrated London News*, **190–1** Popperfoto, **208–9** *Western Daily News*, **251** Popperfoto, **303** Popperfoto, **336** (*bottom*) Popperfoto, **337** (*top*) Rex Features, **352** Popperfoto.

All journalists' portraits © *The Daily Telegraph*

While every effort has been made to trace the copyright holders of illustrations reproduced in this book, this has not always been possible in every case. The publishers will be pleased to rectify any omissions or inaccuracies in the next printing.